THE
Macmillan
Small Business
Handbook

THE
Macmillan
Small Business
Handbook

Mark Stevens

Macmillan Publishing Company
New York

Macmillan Publishing Company
866 Third Avenue, New York, N.Y. 10022
Collier Macmillan Canada, Inc.

Library of Congress Cataloging-in-Publication Data
Stevens, Mark, 1947–
   The Macmillan small business handbook / Mark Stevens.
      p.   cm.
   Includes index.
   ISBN 0-02-614490-5
   1. Small business—Management.   I. Title.
HD62.7.S819   1988
658′.022—dc19   88-13329   CIP

Macmillan books are available at special discounts for bulk purchases
for sales promotions, premiums, fund-raising, or educational use.
For details, contact:

Special Sales Director
Macmillan Publishing Company
866 Third Avenue
New York, N.Y. 10022

10 9 8 7 6 5 4 3 2 1

Printed in the United States of America

For Justin Ari, Better Known As JB

Contents

Contents

Foreword

You own your own business or you plan to. Congratulations. You are living the American dream. Self-employed, responsible to no one but yourself, you run your company and your life as you see fit. No boss, no peers, no corporate rules to complicate (or interfere with) the management process. Your word is the law: no one can counter your decision.

But wait. Is independence just another word for isolation? Does the "self" in self-employed imply an unhealthy reliance on the owner/proprietor/president? It may. Are decisions made in a vacuum as reliable and effective as those tempered by the experience and insights of a corporate staff? They may not be. Does the small company's dearth of in-house expertise pose a competitive disadvantage vis-à-vis big corporations? It can.

Rewarding as self-reliance can be—and as efficiently as the streamlined venture can operate—what's missing is the small business owner's ability to tap a comprehensive and convenient source of information. Without an extensive staff, without specialized departments in law, accounting, taxation, marketing, personnel, and benefits, the president finds himself grappling with complex issues singlehandedly. His independence—his isolation—proves to be a critical handicap.

This book fills the gap, providing the business owner-manager with a desktop network of information sources. Think of it as a round-the-clock management team. No longer isolated, you have expertise in every conceivable management problem, every field, every subject, at your disposal.

Need to borrow money but can't qualify for bank financing? Check the section on SBICs—Small Business Investment Companies. Looking to buy accounting software without hiring a computer consultant? Turn to the section on computerized accounting.

The Macmillan Small Business Handbook anticipates your problems and your questions and provides the answers and the insights in an easy-to-read, simple-to-use format.

The table of contents gives the broad picture. Find your subject, then browse through the section. You'll probably find more than one subtopic that meets your needs. Assume, for example, that you want to merge with another small business, but only if the merger will not be treated as a taxable event. Need to hire an accountant or tax attorney to find the answer? Not necessarily. With your desktop management resource, you can turn to the section on Tax Cutting Strategies (beginning on page 347), and then find the listings for "Private Rulings." Here, you'll learn how to petition the Internal Revenue Service for free binding opinions on the tax consequences of business transactions.

If you're starting out as an entrepreneur and want help getting the venture going, you can use the pinpoint approach to your ques-

1

tions using the extensive index beginning on page 399. Here you'll find entries on accounts receivable management, brokers of used equipment, cash parking lots, diversification, exports, family business, inventory control, loss-leader pricing, patents, regulations, shotgun strategies, telemarketing, turnkey systems houses, warmware, and hundreds of other topics.

With glossaries, charts, graphs, addresses, telephone numbers, recommendations, checklists, surveys, management advice, and professional opinions, *The Macmillan Small Business Handbook* ends the isolation of the self-employed. Now when you face a business problem, when you need information, or when you are just curious, you know exactly whom to ask. Think of this book as your closest adviser. It is always there when you need it.

I. Getting Started

◇══════════════════════════════════════◇

How to Be a Start-up Entrepreneur

For many would-be entrepreneurs, launching a business from scratch appears to be an impossible challenge. But that need not be the case. By breaking down the start-up process into its component parts—and by tackling each step in a systematic fashion—even those with little or no business experience can find themselves successfully self-employed.

Step one, according to those who have launched profitable ventures, is to look for the obvious.

"Every day, the best business opportunities stare you in the face," says James R. Cook, founder and president of Investment Rarities, Inc., a precious metals and securities firm. "Think of those shops or services that are currently serving the public poorly. Say they have nasty employees or dirty facilities. These deficiencies make them vulnerable to competitive assault.

"When I started my company, I did little things no one else was doing, like telephoning investors to tell them their orders were received and the metals were being shipped. They responded enthusiastically by investing with us repeatedly. It goes to show that by running your business better than the others, you can win substantial customers from the start."

Equally promising is to fill so-called market gaps, providing a product or service currently unavailable in the marketplace.

"Before McDonald's was founded, traveling Americans in search of a light meal didn't know if the restaurant they stopped at would be fabulous or fatal," says Cook, who has written a book, *The Start-Up Entrepreneur.* "By bringing uniform quality and cleanliness to the fast-food business, McDonald's filled a need the public was quick to respond to. Think of products you yourself would like to see in the marketplace and use that as a starting point for your business ideas."

Once the opportunity is identified, entrepreneurs are advised to start small, launching a business they can properly finance and manage in the formative stages. A prospective franchisor, for example, should test one to three operating units before actively selling franchises to the public. Because the start-up entrepreneur gains much of his knowledge through trial and error, working on a small scale makes it easier to spot initial mistakes and to correct them before the business takes on major proportions.

Consider these additional guidelines for successful start-ups:

- Raise money by selling equity (up to 25 percent of the stock) in your fledgling enterprise. Rather than seeking loans—which are rarely available to start-ups—or looking for a Daddy Warbucks with deep pockets (who'll likely want more than half the company in return) sell modest equity

3

positions to investors willing to risk as little as $5,000 each.

"In working with small investors, one contact can lead to another," Cook says. "When I went out looking for seed financing, one of my first investors was a doctor who put up his own money and referred me to nine of his colleagues, four of whom also invested. In short order, I had the $64,000 I needed."

- Find a unique way to promote your business. When the founders of a fast growing company in the office furnishings business first started up, they positioned their company as more than vendors of merchandise.

"We went directly to the Fortune 500, promoting ourselves not as office furniture salesmen but as project managers—specialists in planning and installing open office systems," says the company's chairman. "Because this concept was unique, and because it matched a real need in the marketplace, our company was successful from the start."

- Be generous with employees. Pay top scale wages to everyone from telephone operator to sales staff. This helps the company to assure excellence, giving it an edge over established competitors.
- Once the company is functioning smoothly, expand beyond the initial product or service. This can fuel growth and balance out cyclical sales patterns.

"Make certain the diversification is in a related business or in a field you know well," Cook advises. "When I attempted to break into the paint and varnish business—one I knew little about—I lost a lot of money quickly. On the other hand, my diversification within the investment field, from precious metals to securities, has proven highly successful."

You need some luck to build and run a company of your own, that's for sure, but you also need to know your strengths and your limitations. That's a key component of success.

Checklist for Going into Business

Summary

Thinking of owning and managing your own business? It's a good idea—provided you know what it takes and have what it takes.

Starting a business is risky at best; but your chances of making it go will be better if you understand the problems you'll meet and work out as many of them as you can before you start.

Here are some questions and worksheets to help you think through what you need to know and do. Check each question if the answer is YES. Where the answer is NO, you have some work to do.

Before You Start

How about you?

Are you the kind of person who can get a business started and make it go? (Before you answer this question, use worksheet number 1.) ____

Think about *why* you want to own your own business. Do you want to badly enough to keep you working long hours without knowing how much money you'll end up with? ____

Have you worked in a business like the one you want to start? ____

Have you worked for someone else as a foreman or manager? ____

Have you had any business training in school? _____

Have you saved any money? _____

How about the money?

Do you know how much money you will need to get your business started? (Use worksheets 2 and 3 to figure this out.) _____

Have you counted up how much money of your own you can put into the business? _____

Do you know how much credit you can get from your suppliers—the people you will buy from? _____

Do you know where you can borrow the rest of the money you need to start your business? _____

Have you figured out what net income per year you expect to get from the business? _____

Count your salary and your profit on the money you put into the business. Can you live on less than this so that you can use some of it to help your business grow? _____

Have you talked to a banker about your plans? _____

How about a partner?

If you need a partner with money or know-how that you don't have, do you know someone who will fit; someone you can get along with? _____

Do you know the good and bad points about going it alone, having a partner, and incorporating your business? _____

Have you talked to a lawyer about it? _____

How about your customers?

Do most businesses in your community seem to be doing well? _____

Have you tried to find out whether stores like the one you want to open are doing well in your community and in the rest of the country? _____

Do you know what kind of people will want to buy what you plan to sell? _____

Do people like to live in the area where you want to open your store? _____

Do they need a store like yours? _____

If not, have you thought about opening a different kind of store or going to another neighborhood? _____

(Questions continue after Worksheets No. 1 and 2.)

Worksheet No. 1

Under each question, check the answer that says what you feel or comes closest to it. Be honest with yourself.

Are you a self-starter?

☐ I do things on my own. Nobody has to tell me to get going.

☐ If someone gets me started, I keep going all right.

☐ Easy does it. I don't put myself out until I have to.

How do you feel about other people?

☐ I like people. I can get along with just about anybody.

☐ I have plenty of friends—I don't need anyone else.

☐ Most people irritate me.

Can you lead others?

☐ I can get most people to go along when I start something.

□ I can give the orders if someone tells me what we should do.

□ I let someone else get things moving. Then I go along if I feel like it.

Can you take responsibility?

□ I like to take charge of things and see them through.

□ I'll take over if I have to, but I'd rather let someone else be responsible.

□ There's always some eager beaver around wanting to show how smart he is. I say let him.

How good an organizer are you?

□ I like to have a plan before I start. I'm usually the one to get things lined up when the group wants to do something.

□ I do all right unless things get too confused. Then I quit.

□ You get all set and then something comes along and presents too many problems. So I just take things as they come.

How good a worker are you?

□ I can keep going as long as I need to. I don't mind working hard for something I want.

□ I'll work hard for a while, but when I've had enough, that's it.

□ I can't see that hard work gets you anywhere.

Can you make decisions?

□ I can make up my mind in a hurry if I have to. It usually turns out O.K., too.

□ I can if I have plenty of time. If I have to make up my mind fast, I think later I should have decided the other way.

□ I don't like to be the one who has to decide things.

Can people trust what you say?

□ You bet they can. I don't say things I don't mean.

□ I try to be on the level most of the time, but sometimes I just say what's easiest.

□ Why bother if the other fellow doesn't know the difference?

Can you stick with it?

□ If I make up my mind to do something, I don't let anything stop me.

□ I usually finish what I start—if it goes well.

□ If it doesn't go right away, I quit. Why beat your brains out?

How good is your health?

□ I never run down!

□ I have enough energy for most things I want to do.

□ I run out of energy sooner than most of my friends seem to.

Now count the checks you made.
How many checks are there beside   ____
the first answer to each question?
How many checks are there beside   ____
the second answer to each question?
How many checks are there beside   ____
the third answer to each question?

If most of your checks are beside the first answers, you probably have what it takes to run a business. If not, you're likely to have more trouble than you can handle by yourself. Better find a partner who is strong on the points you're weak on. If many checks are beside the third answer, not even a good partner will be able to shore you up.

Now go back and answer the first question.

Worksheet No. 2

Estimated Monthly Expenses Item	Your estimate of monthly expenses based on sales of $_____ per year	Your estimate of how much cash you need to start your business (See column 3.)	What to put in column 2 (These figures are typical for one kind of business. You will have to decide how many months to allow for in your business.)
	Column 1 $	Column 2 $	Column 3
Salary of owner-manager			2 times column 1
All other salaries and wages			3 times column 1
Rent			3 times column 1
Advertising			3 times column 1
Delivery expense			3 times column 1
Supplies			3 times column 1
Telephone			3 times column 1
Other utilities			3 times column 1
Insurance			Payment required by insurance company
Taxes, including Social Security			4 times column 1
Interest			3 times column 1
Maintenance			3 times column 1
Legal and other professional fees			3 times column 1
Miscellaneous			3 times column 1
Starting Costs You Have to Pay Only Once			Leave column 2 blank
Fixtures and equipment			Fill in worksheet 3 and put the total here
Decorating and remodeling			Talk it over with a contractor
Installation of fixtures and equipment			Talk to suppliers from whom you buy these

Worksheet No. 2 (Continued)

Estimated Monthly Expenses Item	Your estimate of monthly expenses based on sales of $_____ per year	Your estimate of how much cash you need to start your business (See column 3.)	What to put in column 2 (These figures are typical for one kind of business. You will have to decide how many months to allow for in your business.)
Starting inventory			Suppliers will probably help you estimate this
Deposits with public utilities			Find out from utilities companies
Legal and other professional fees			Lawyer, accountant, and so on
Licenses and permits			Find out from city offices what you have to have
Advertising and promotion for opening			Estimate what you'll use
Accounts receivable			What you need to buy more stock until credit customers pay
Cash			For unexpected expenses or losses, special purchases, etc.
Other			Make a separate list and enter total
Total Estimated Cash You Need to Start		$	Add up all the numbers in column 2

Getting Started

Your building
Have you found a good building for your store? ____
Will you have enough room when your business gets bigger? ____
Can you fix the building the way you want it without spending too much money? ____

Can people get to it easily from parking spaces, bus stops, or their homes? ____
Have you had a lawyer check the lease and zoning? ____

Equipment and supplies
Do you know just what equipment and supplies you need and how ____

much they will cost?
(Worksheet 3 and the lists you
made for it should show this.)
Can you save some money by   _____
buying secondhand equipment?

Your merchandise
Have you decided what things you   _____
will sell?
Do you know how much or how   _____
many of each you will buy to open
your store with?
Have you found suppliers who will   _____
sell you what you need at a good
price?
Have you compared the prices and   _____
credit terms of different suppliers?

Your records
Have you planned a system of   _____
records that will keep track of your
income and expenses, what you owe
other people, and what other people
owe you?
Have you worked out a way to keep   _____
track of your inventory so that you
will always have enough on hand
for your customers but not more
than you can sell?
Have you figured out how to keep   _____
your payroll records and take care
of tax reports and payments?
Do you know what financial   _____
statements you should prepare?
Do you know an accountant who   _____
will help you with your records and
financial statements?

Your store and the law
Do you know what licenses and   _____
permits you need?
Do you know what business laws   _____
you have to obey?
Do you know a lawyer you can go   _____
to for help with legal papers?

Protecting your store
Have you made plans for protecting   _____
your store against thefts of all
kinds—shoplifting, robbery,
burglary, employee stealing?
Have you talked with an insurance   _____
agent about what kinds of insurance
you need?

Buying a business someone else has started
Have you made a list of what you   _____
like and don't like about buying a
business someone else has started?
Are you sure you know the real   _____
reason why the owner wants to sell
this business?
Have you compared the cost of   _____
buying the business with the cost of
starting a new business?
Is the stock up to date and in good _____
condition?
Is the building in good condition?   _____
Will the owner of the building   _____
transfer the lease to you?
Have you talked with other business _____
owners in the area to see what they
think of the business?
Have you talked with the company's   _____
suppliers?
Have you talked with a lawyer   _____
about it?

Making It Go
Advertising
Have you decided how you will
advertise?
(Newspapers—posters—handbills—   _____
radio—mail?)
Do you know where to get help   _____
with your ads?
Have you watched what other stores   _____
do to get people to buy?

The prices you charge

Do you know how to figure what you should charge for each item you sell? _____

Do you know what other stores like yours charge? _____

Buying

Do you have a plan for finding out what your customers want? _____

Will your plan for keeping track of your inventory tell you when it is time to order more and how much to order? _____

Do you plan to buy most of your stock from a few suppliers rather than a little from many, so that those you buy from will want to help you succeed? _____

Selling

Have you decided whether you will have salesclerks or self-service? _____

Do you know how to get customers to buy? _____

Have you thought about why you like to buy from some salesclerks while others turn you off? _____

Your employees

If you need to hire someone to help you, do you know where to look? _____

Worksheet No. 3
List of Furniture, Fixtures, and Equipment

Leave out or add items to suit your business. Use separate sheets to list exactly what you need for each of the items below.	If you plan to pay cash in full, enter the full amount below and in the last column.	If you are going to pay by installments, fill out the columns below. Enter in the last column your down payment plus at least one installment.			Estimate of the cash you need for furniture, fixtures, and equipment
		Price	Down payment	Amount of each installment	
Counters	$	$	$	$	$
Storage shelves, cabinets					
Display stands, shelves, tables					
Cash register					
Safe					
Window display fixtures					
Special lighting					
Outside sign					
Delivery equipment if needed					

Total Furniture, Fixtures, and Equipment $

(Enter this figure also in Worksheet 2 under "Starting Costs You Have to Pay Only Once.")

Do you know what kind of person ____
you need?

Do you have a plan for training ____
your employees?

Credit for your customers

Have you decided whether or not to ____
let your customers buy on credit?

Do you know the good and bad ____
points about joining a credit-card
plan?

Can you tell a deadbeat from a ____
good credit customer?

A Few Extra Questions ____

Have you figured out whether or
not you could make more money
working for someone else?

Does your family go along with ____
your plan to start a business of your
own?

Do you know where to find out ____
about new ideas and new products?

Do you have a work plan for ____
yourself and your employees?

Have you gone to the nearest Small ____
Business Administration office for
help with your plans?

If you have answered all these questions
carefully, you've done some hard work and
serious thinking. That's good. But you have
probably found some things you still need to
know more about or do something about.

Do all you can for yourself, but don't hesitate to ask for help from people who can tell
you what you need to know. Remember, running a business takes guts! You've got to be
able to decide what you need and then go
after it.

Good luck!

Credit: U.S. Small Business Administration

Entrepreneurship: Starting a New Business

In America, every person is free to start a
business, and a surprising number take advantage of that opportunity. This is reflected
in the great number of new firms started
every year. As many as 8,400 new corporations are started in a typical week.

For the person starting a business, the decision can represent a major commitment. It
may involve quitting a job, working long
hours, investing savings, and borrowing
from relatives or banks. Whether the business is successful or not, the person's life may
be different from that time onward.

For society, this flow of new businesses
can provide many benefits. New businesses
can offer additional choices to consumers.
For instance, a new restaurant might offer a
different menu, or lower prices, or a more
convenient location. New businesses can
also provide jobs. These job opportunities
may be particularly attractive to those people who are most happy and effective in a
small business environment. New businesses can also be centers of innovation.
They are not tied to existing ways of doing
things. Available evidence suggests that a
high percentage of the most significant inventions have originated in small firms.[1]
New firms challenge older established businesses in many ways, causing them to become more efficient and more responsive to
consumer needs.

However, at the same time that all these
new firms are being created, many others are
going out of business. It appears that about
two out of three new firms close their doors

[1]*Advisory Committee on Industrial Innovation: Final Report* (Washington, D.C.: U.S. Government Printing Office, 1979).

within four years of their founding.[2] In every community there are some store fronts on which a new sign goes up every six months, as a new entrepreneur tries to get a business started. Some of these stores seem to need revolving doors—not for customers, because there aren't many, but for the company founders as they come and go.

Many of the businesses that close down have been failures from the start. Others have been successful in the past, possibly supporting the owner and family for many years. However, conditions can change. The owner may choose to retire. The industry or the neighborhood may become less attractive, so that the owner decides to enter a different kind of business.

For the businesses that are founded and survive, there are different degrees of success. Many new firms have very few employees and primarily provide a living for the founder and members of the family. These small businesses may have founders who have technical skills such as being able to style hair, repair automobiles, or do electrical contracting. The business may be started to permit the founder to practice his or her trade. As such, it is unlikely to experience much growth.

Other new businesses grow to become what might be called "stable, high-payoff" firms. They may be set up to serve a local market, as with the local Chevrolet dealership or McDonald's franchise. These businesses are often large enough so that additional managers can be hired. They are usually much more profitable than the businesses built around the owner's trade. However, they also require more capital to start and more management skills to run successfully.

A few new businesses become "high-

[2]*Patterns for Success in Managing a Business* (New York: Dun and Bradstreet, 1967).

growth firms." Almost every large company in the United States was once a new firm. Companies such as Polaroid or Xerox or Texas Instruments were once young and small. These high-growth companies usually are located in industries that are growing rapidly. Their growth requires that the owners take risks in introducing new products, in borrowing money to build new factories or stores, and in adding new people to their organizations. When successfully managed, these businesses can make their founders wealthy.

There are about 14 million businesses in this country. Most are small and many are new. However, the individual businesses that make up this sea of firms are constantly changing. They are starting, closing, and being acquired. Many are succeeding modestly, and some are achieving outstanding success. We shall now consider how these companies get started.

Entrepreneurs

There are some who think that people who start businesses—entrepreneurs—are "born, not made." Yet the study of company founders suggests that a variety of experiences may make people more or less likely to start their own businesses. These experiences may involve their families, or take place in school or on the job.

One major influence is the family. People who start companies are more likely to come from families in which their parents or close relatives were in business for themselves. These older people were examples or "models" for the children. Whether they were successful or not probably didn't matter. However, for the children growing up in such a family, the action of starting a new business seems possible—something they can do.

In the same way, many cultural groups,

such as Jews in America, Cuban immigrants in Miami, or the Chinese in Southeast Asia have a tradition of members starting new businesses. Sometimes, they have been prevented from working for others because of prejudice. Children growing up in such groups are surrounded by examples of entrepreneurship. They learn what is involved in working in businesses. It becomes easy for them to think of themselves as people who can start businesses also.

People who start companies seem to have certain psychological characteristics. They believe that they can control their own destinies. They are less likely to think that forces beyond their control, such as luck or fate, will determine their success. They believe that through their efforts, determination, and hard work they can make their businesses succeed.

Many entrepreneurs also tend to be goal-setters. They gain satisfaction from setting goals that are moderately challenging (but not impossibly difficult) and then achieving those goals. They see themselves as taking moderate risks in achieving their goals. To an outside observer, the process of starting a firm may seem to involve enormous risks. However, to the entrepreneur, who believes that he or she can make that business successful, the risks seem more moderate.

The age of the founder at the time he or she is interested in starting a business is also a factor. People of all ages start businesses, but many are in the age range of about twenty-five to forty. Younger people might have strong desires to start businesses, but often do not have the money or experience needed. Older people may have money and experience, but they also often have obligations to support families and may be reluctant to risk what they have achieved.

So we see that some backgrounds are most typical for entrepreneurs. However,

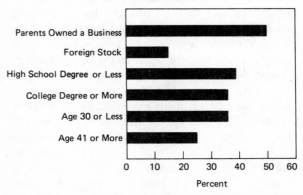

Personal Characteristics of New Business Starters

Source: Cooper and Dunkleberg, *A New Look at Business Entry: Experiences of 1805 Entrepreneurs*

this does not mean that people with other backgrounds cannot or do not start businesses. It is just that a certain background may make a person more prepared—more likely to take the step if the right opportunity arises.

All this suggests that some people are more likely to start new businesses than others. Whether they actually do depends upon other factors which we shall now consider.

Motivation

Many people have the background and psychological makeup which could lead them to start new firms. Yet only some of these people ever take the step of giving up a job and investing their time and money in a new business.

One factor at work here involves what might be called dislocations or pushes. These are forces which cause a person to move out of a comfortable "rut." Why should anyone give up the security of a job for the uncertainties of trying to get a business started? It helps if the person is at a time of change—if the decision has already been made to give up a previous job or an existing lifestyle. Thus, immigrants such as the Cubans who have come to Miami are at a point of change in their lives. Workers who lose their jobs because of layoffs must decide what to do next. Managers who are frustrated because their companies turn down their ideas or because they don't get a promotion may decide to make a change. Often, a specific event will "trigger" the change. A person may foresee an approaching birthday and think, "I'll soon be forty. It's now or never." Or a fight with the boss may move a person to a stage in which he or she begins to think, "What will I do next?"

Of course, most people who make changes in their lives don't start new businesses. Those who do take this step often have the characteristics listed earlier. They may also be influenced by what they know of others who have started businesses. If these are people they can identify with—relatives, fellow employees, or friends—they are more likely to see this as something that they can do. Some families have a history of entrepreneurship; some industries, such as advertising, construction, or the manufacture of electronic components, are noted for a high birth rate of new firms; some organizations have many employees leaving to start new firms. People who are involved in such families, industries, or organizations are surrounded by examples of what is involved in starting a company. Not only can they learn from others, they can see what is involved. For them, it is psychologically easier to take this step.

Preparation

Many people may wish to start businesses, but they are unable to do so. They lack the experience, contacts, or resources which are needed. A new company is very much built around the entrepreneur. The owner-manager must be able to perform those key activities which are required for success. If it is a clothing store, the manager must be good at buying the right merchandise, as well as displaying, advertising, and pricing it. The manager must also be able to do the selling (or train others to do it) and handle the record-keeping, paying of suppliers, etc. An alert employee of a clothing store can learn many of these needed skills and become capable of starting a successful clothing store. People often start businesses in fields they already know in order to draw upon their previous backgrounds.

Thus, we might think of established organizations as "incubators," giving their employees experiences which make them more or less prepared to become entrepreneurs. However, industries vary widely in the extent to which they provide promising environments for new firms. If large organizations and heavy capital investments are required, then it is difficult for an entrepreneur to assemble the needed resources. Thus, we see few new automobile manufacturers being planned. An employee of a steel mill, no matter how motivated, would find it difficult to start a similar business because of the capital requirements. If industry sales are not growing, it is difficult for a new firm to get established because to do so it must take sales away from established businesses. Accordingly, we do not see new railroads being organized to participate in the declining railroad industry.

By contrast, in growing industries with low capital requirements, we observe many new firms being organized. Examples are companies producing computer software and solar power equipment. For the same reasons, an experienced real estate salesman in a growing metropolitan area might find it relatively easy to spin off and start a new firm.

We should also note that, even within the same organization, employees develop different kinds of experience. Some stay in the same job and never achieve much breadth in experience or contacts. Others become specialists, good in their jobs, but narrow and lacking in the basic skills needed to produce or sell a product and get a company started. Some employees are in better positions to develop external contacts and to learn about market opportunities. Thus, an industrial salesman may learn that customers would buy a particular product if only it were available. The salesman may conclude that a new company could get started by offering that product.

All this is not to suggest that an entrepreneur cannot start a firm in a field in which he or she has no experience. It happens every day. If the founder gets started by buying an existing business or by entering into an agreement with a franchisor (such as McDonald's or Baskin-Robbins), then previous experience is less important. However, available evidence suggests that more than 50 percent of all entrepreneurs start businesses in industries in which they already have experience. The previous educational and job choices that a person makes help to determine what kind of business, if any, he or she might someday be in a position to start.

Educational background also influences whether a person might be prepared to start particular kinds of businesses. The person who does not understand computers is not prepared to start a computer software company. The person who cannot analyze financial statements would find it difficult to raise capital from investors or banks for a large venture. Formal education can help to prepare the entrepreneur. Thus, the decisions a person makes about education help to determine those future opportunities which may be open.

Motivation and preparation are not enough. Most new businesses require capital—sometimes lots of it. In 1980, a McDonald's franchise required several hundred thousand dollars. Examples of other capital-intensive ventures include racquetball clubs, motel complexes, automobile dealerships, and many manufacturing companies. The capital requirements depend upon the nature of the industry and upon the initial plans of the founder.

Industries vary in their capital requirements. For instance, utilities require big investments in generating equipment and power lines. By contrast, advertising agencies require only a desk, telephone, and some money for working capital to get started.

Even within a given industry, a founder can make plans that minimize capital requirements. For instance, a person starting a business to repair automobiles may rent a building rather than buy one and may postpone investment in repair equipment which is expensive and rarely used. Many manufacturing firms have started with used equipment in garages or lofts.

Where do company founders usually get the money to get started? Personal savings appear to be the most important source of funds. Loans from relatives and friends are also a common source. (It has sometimes been suggested that one of the best ways to secure venture capital is to choose your parents carefully.) Bank loans, which are so important for established small businesses, play a smaller role. One reason is that the new company has no record of accomplishment by which a banker might judge the ability to repay. Loans may be easier to obtain when there is collateral, such as real estate, which can be sold to repay the loan if the venture is unsuccessful. Other sources of financing include credit from suppliers, who may ship goods but be willing to accept payment at a later date.

Promising new companies with prospects for high growth may be able to raise venture capital from outside investors. This is more likely if the new business is in an industry experiencing rapid growth or current popularity in the stock market. Investors may then anticipate that they will make a later profit when the growing company sells stock to the public or is acquired by a larger firm.

An entrepreneur's ability to raise capital is by no means assured. Many new businesses have been dreamed up but never brought into existence because the founder could not raise the needed capital. If the entrepreneur has a good "track record"—if he or she has the kind of record of success which inspires confidence—then chances for successful financing are improved. If the business plans are carefully investigated, then investors have more reason for confidence in the proposed business.

Many factors make a particular geo-

Age Starting Business

People in all age groups become entrepreneurs. Most people start their businesses between the ages of 25 and 40.

Source: National Federation of Independent Business Research and Education Foundation

graphic region more or less favorable for starting new businesses. Regions vary in the extent to which there is local wealth which might be invested in new ventures. Local banks differ in the extent to which they might make loans for particular kinds of ventures. If, within a given region, investors and banks have successfully backed agricultural ventures in the past, then they may look with favor upon proposed new businesses related to agriculture. However, they might be uncomfortable evaluating a proposed business to develop computer software.

Other factors also affect the regional climate for entrepreneurship. Easy access to suppliers and customers may be important. Thus, many tool-and-die shops have started around Detroit, where they can work closely with their customers in the automobile industry. A prosperous area experiencing population growth needs new stores, restaurants, apartments, etc. By contrast, the entrepreneur trying to start a retail store in a community with declining population must undertake the difficult task of taking sales away from established competitors.

Most people start businesses where they are already living and working. They can thereby use their local contacts and "feel" for the local market. It is then possible to start the business part time, or at least to avoid all the problems of moving a family and opening shop in another area. One implication is the regional environment may or may not be supportive for starting a particular business. Some would-be entrepreneurs are more favorably located than others.

The process of starting a firm begins with developing an idea or learning of an opportunity. The entrepreneur must then try to evaluate the proposed business, anticipating the investment needed, operating costs, competition, sales, and profits. Careful evaluation may involve a great deal of data gathering, including talking to suppliers, prospective customers, and people who are knowledgeable about the industry. If the entrepreneur is already in contact with such people, investigation is simplified. Sometimes some aspects may be clearly determined, such as the rental cost of a store, while other aspects, such as expected sales, may remain highly uncertain. Some businesses can be started on a part-time basis or with a low investment; the founder can then get feedback from the marketplace in deciding whether to make a greater commitment. Other businesses require substantial investments before the first dollar of sales can be generated. Often, the entrepreneur will discover that the plans should be modified. Thus, a new restaurant offering ice cream and sandwiches may be changed to a steak house if initial sales are disappointing.

Despite these comments about careful investigation, we should recognize that many entrepreneurs push ahead impulsively, with little understanding of what they are getting into. Often, they lack the managerial skills to evaluate or run their new businesses. The result is that many new firms are unsuccessful.

Credit: National Federation of Independent Business and Arnold Cooper

Alternative Business Organizations

If you are in business for yourself or are contemplating going into business, your business will likely be organized in one of the following forms:

- Sole proprietorship;
- Partnership (general, limited, joint venture);
- Corporation; or
- S corporation

No one form is best for everyone. Advantages and disadvantages hinge on the type of business you are in, number of people involved, and size of operations.

Below are a number of factors to consider in determining which organization best suits your needs.

	Sole Proprietorship	Partnership	Corporation	S Corporation
Ownership	By a single individual. Simplest form of business, usually best suited for small-scale organizations.	Similar to sole proprietorship, except two or more persons involved.	By unlimited number of shareholders.	By shareholders; number of shareholders limited to 35.
Management	Left entirely in hands of owner or owner's agent.	By general partners.	Centralized in corporation's board of directors.	Same as regular corporation.
Life	Will terminate with death or disability of owner.	Generally for a specific agreed-upon term. Partnership may be terminated by death, withdrawal, insolvency, or legal disability of a general partner.	Unlimited, unless by state law or charter.	Same as regular corporation.

continues on next page

	Sole Proprietorship	Partnership	Corporation	S Corporation
Liability	Owner liability unlimited. Owner's personal property can be attached by creditors to settle business debts.	Unlimited for general partners. General partners are jointly and severally liable for obligations of partnership. Limited partner's liability limited to amount invested.	Shareholders' liability limited to their investment in corporation stock.	Same as regular corporation.
Availability of outside financing	Principally dependent on personal wealth of owner.	Principally dependent on credit of individual partners and contributions of new partners.	Can sell stocks or bonds to public or secure debt from outside lenders.	Limited. Only one class of stock can be outstanding. Outstanding shares must be identical to rights of holders in profits and assets of corporation, but differences in voting rights among shares are permitted. "Straight debt" not considered second class of stock.
Taxation	Owner taxed on business profits whether or not distributed.	Partners taxed on share of partnership income whether or not distributed.	Corporation taxed on taxable income, whether or not distributed to shareholders.	Shareholders taxed on taxable income of corporation, whether or not distributed.
Earnings distribution	No effect.	No effect.	Considered ordinary dividends to the extent of earnings and profits; taxed to shareholders as such.	No effect.
Accumulated earnings	Unlimited because earnings taxed to owner on individual return whether distributed or not.	Unlimited because earnings taxed to partners on individual returns whether distributed or not.	Subject to penalty tax if accumulated earnings are unreasonable.	Unlimited because earnings taxed to shareholders whether distributed or not.
Net operating loss	Owner may deduct, but only to extent of prior and succeeding years' income.	Partner may deduct, but only to extent of partnership basis.	Deductible within prescribed carryback and carryover period.	Deductible by shareholders, but only to extent of shareholder's basis.
Charitable contributions	Deductible by owner on individual return, subject to limitations.	Deductible by partners on their individual returns, subject to limitations applicable to individuals.	Deductible by corporation, limited to 10 percent of taxable income. Excess carried over.	Same as partnership.

	Sole Proprietorship	Partnership	Corporation	S Corporation
Owner's salary	Amounts paid considered partial distribution of earnings; not deductible by sole proprietorship or taxable to owner.	Amounts paid considered partial distributions of earnings; not deductible by partnership or taxable to partner. However, if distribution is guaranteed payment of salary, amounts deductible by partnership and ordinary income to partner.	Taxable to owners and deductible by corporation. Salaries must be reasonable relative to services rendered.	Same as regular corporation. Reasonableness of salaries is not important unless salaries are used as a device for shifting income among stockholders within a family group.
Retirement plan	Sole proprietor may participate in qualified plan; however, plans determined to be "top heavy" must meet special, more stringent qualification requirements. Employees and sole proprietor may set up IRAs, even if covered by qualified plans.	Partners may participate in qualified plan; however, plans determined to be "top heavy" must meet special, more stringent qualification requirements. Employees and partners may set up IRAs, even if covered by qualified plans.	Owners who are employees may participate in qualified plan; however, plans determined to be "top heavy" must meet special, more stringent qualification requirements. Employees may set up IRAs, even if covered by qualified plans.	Owners with compensation income may participate in a qualified plan; however, plans determined to be "top heavy" must meet special, more stringent qualification requirements. Employees and owners may set up IRAs, even if covered by qualified plans.
Ownership transfer	Existing entity is terminated and new entity is created.	May require approval of other partners.	Stock easily transferred with no effect on corporation.	Same as regular corporation, except effect of transfer on S corporation election should be considered to ensure that unintended termination does not occur.
Adjustments to basis of business assets upon death or sale	At death, basis adjusted to fair market value when transferred to heirs. No basis adjustment needed when sold.	Basis of partnership assets applicable to transfer or partner's interest may be adjusted if proper election is made.	None.	None.

Credit: Peat Marwick, "Tax Planning for the Owner-Managed Business"

Forming a New Business

Guidelines from the law firm of Jones, Day, Reavis & Pogue

A new business venture can be organized in several ways.

A sole proprietorship is simply an individual doing business for himself, perhaps with some employees working for him, and perhaps using a properly filed "fictitious business name" such as "The Acme Company" (not including the word "corporation" or "incorporated"). This is not a separate taxable entity, and the individual simply files tax reports of his business activity on Form 1040, in a special section.

Where there is more than one owner of the business, a sole proprietorship becomes a partnership, which again can operate under a "fictitious business name" and can have employees. A partnership is not a separate taxable entity, but it does file a separate tax return, allocating its items of income and deduction to its partners and reporting those allocations to each of its partners on a Form K-1 which it mails to them annually, so that each partner can report on his individual Form 1040 each year his share of the income and deductions of the partnership. Certain tax choices can also be made at the partnership level, affecting the individual partners.

In both the sole proprietorship and the general partnership, each of the owners of the business is personally liable for all the obligations of the business, including the results of any lawsuits which might be filed against the business. Particular loans to the business can, by written agreement with the lenders, be made "nonrecourse" (that is, without obligation of the individual partners). This protection cannot be obtained against lawsuits in a sole proprietorship or general-partnership format, although some protection can be obtained by means of insurance.

Where there are passive investors in the business who do not wish to be subject to these potential liabilities, a limited partnership can be formed, if a certificate of limited partnership is timely and properly filed in the appropriate governmental offices. A limited partnership functions in the same manner as the general partnership described above, except that in addition to the general partners operating the business, there are limited partners who have no part in the day-to-day operations of the business (although they can be consulted and vote upon such major matters as selling all of the business). These limited partners, so long as they do not involve themselves directly or indirectly in the business, are protected against liability for debts or lawsuits against the business except, of course, to the extent of such capital as they may have invested in the business.

In theory a general partnership can be created orally, but it is generally preferable to have a written agreement spelling out the rights and obligations of the partners with respect to one another. A limited partnership can only be created by a written document filed in the appropriate governmental offices.

Where the owners of the business wish to have both limited liability and an active role in controlling the operations of the business, they may form a corporation. So long as the corporation is not too thinly capitalized, and so long as its corporate form is respected, and its finances and operations not commingled with that of its owners, its shareholder-owners will have no personal liability as such for its debts or for lawsuits against the corporation. Of course, if a shareholder signs a personal guaranty of a loan to the corporation or of a lease to the corporation, or if a shareholder participates personally in some claimed wrong, he may have some exposure individually. The corporation, however, is a widely used vehicle to limit personal liability and create a separate legal entity in which to do business.

A corporation is a taxable entity. It is possible that its income can be taxed once at the corporate level and a second time at the shareholder level, when it is distributed in dividends to the shareholders. However, if corporate earnings are paid out in reasonable compensation they are deductible to the corporation and income to the shareholders, so that in effect they are taxed only once. Also, an "S corporation election" timely filed with the IRS can cause the corporation to be taxed like a partnership, although this is not effective for the taxes of certain states. There is much more that could be said on the subject of corporate taxation, or indeed on any of these subjects.

If a corporate form is chosen, a state of incorporation must be selected, which is ordinarily the state where the corporation will do its principal business, or a state with favorable corporate laws, such as Delaware. The corporation, like an individual, may use a fictitious business name, and it must be qualified to do business, and pay state taxes, in each state where it actually does business. If there is some flexibility in selecting a corporate headquarters, a state such as Nevada, which has no state income tax, should be considered.

A joint venture is essentially a partnership formed for a limited business purpose. Like a general or limited partnership, it can include corporations or other partnerships among its venturers.

Business Plans: How to Raise Money

Imagine this: on the same day, in the same town, two entrepreneurs of equal drive and talent have the same brainstorm for an innovative software package. Both design prototypes, launch companies, and prepare to enter the ranks of computer millionaires. But a year later, while one is booking orders as fast as his salesmen can write, the other finds himself with little more than an empty dream.

The difference, not surprisingly, is a matter of money. Not in making it (although that's certainly the ultimate objective) but in raising enough to take the brainstorm from drawing board to marketplace. It is in this crucial transition—this critical financial bridge—that the vast bulk of better ideas go to their final resting place, most without ever having seen the light of day.

Which brings up a critical and widely overlooked distinction between consistently successful entrepreneurs and those whose business careers are mired hopelessly in dreams: the ability to raise money. While some call it a "gift," success in this endeavor is not so much in the genes as in the knowledge of the capital markets—mostly, who to contact and how to structure your appeal.

"Those seeking to raise money from lenders or investors have to recognize that they are dealing with individuals and institutions," says Herbert Speiser, a partner with Phillips, Gold CPAs. "The key prerequisite then is to learn what makes them tick—the kinds of projects that excite them, the kinds of returns they look for, and the fields or industries they're most active in. Without this information—which serves as a road map for the capital search—entrepreneurs are just shooting in the dark."

While all agree that raising money is part art, part science, and a healthy dose of luck, the following tactics (recommended for fledgling entrepreneurs and those seeking expansion capital) can help to tip the odds in your favor:

1. Before approaching a single source, prepare a comprehensive, well-documented business plan describing your product (with emphasis on its unique features) and its market, your management team, how much money will be required, how it will be put to use, when and how much it will pay off. Reveal the venture's opportunities, as well as its obstacles (competition, government regulations, legal barriers) and how you plan to surmount them. Be thorough and candid.

"From time to time, I'll take a flyer on a company that, based on its numbers alone, doesn't really qualify for the loan it wants," says a vice-president with Manufacturers Hanover. "But I'll go ahead because I can tell from the business plan that there's nothing down the road that management hasn't considered. They've thought of all the contingencies, revealed them in the business plan, and spelled out just how they'll deal with them. This gives me an all-important feeling of confidence in making a loan.

"Prospective borrowers have to understand that you can't tell a banker enough. We thrive on information. With this in mind, I'd be highly impressed with a borrower who attached a separate sheet to his business plan listing 20 questions informed observers might have about his business and intelligent answers to those questions. After reading a business plan, I like to be left with the distinct impression that management has its act together. I'd take this Q and A approach as a sign that they do."

The banker makes this additional point: "Sprinkle the business plan with reasonableness. Bankers prefer to see sound, realistic projections rather than those based on the entrepreneur's pie-in-the-sky dreams. Back up your numbers with a detailed analysis on how you propose to achieve them."

2. Design the business plan from two perspectives: the company's and the investor's. Indicate not only how you'll make the business grow but equally important, how it will reward the money men.

"When deciding which ventures to fund, every lender and investor asks himself a critical question: 'What's in it for me?'" says a consultant specializing in small business financing. "This is especially true for small, private company deals. Because the investments start off as highly illiquid—the stock rarely has a ready market—the investor wants to know when he can convert his holdings into cash.

"Entrepreneurs seeking capital can respond to this concern—and thus vastly improve their chances of hitting paydirt—by including in their business plans or related documents a projected date for the company's public offering, its sale to another company, or some other means of rewarding the investor. One of my clients, an entrepreneur in the software business, listed in his business plan the names of four potential suitors who would likely buy the company once it proved itself in the marketplace. This appealed to investors, and as it turned out, with good reason. The company was sold to one of the corporations named in the plan."

3. Find a prominent sponsor willing to introduce your proposal to the investment community. Well-connected lawyers, accountants, business consultants, and corporate executives can open doors that may be closed to entrepreneurs acting alone.

"Gaining attention for your idea, your loan proposal, is half the battle," says a vice-president of Providence, Rhode Island–based Fleet National Bank. "With so many applications coming over the transom, loan officers may not give each one as much attention as the entrepreneur would like. But when the proposal comes to us through a prominent intermediary—one we have worked with over the years and whose business judgment we respect—it carries more weight. Not that we'll necessarily approve the loan but it will be considered very carefully."

Finding prominent sponsors is not as difficult as it may seem. Simply ask your bank to refer you to a reputable accountant or attorney in the community. Chances are they'll recommend three or four practitioners—all close to the bank and wired into its lending officers.

"We recently funded a leveraged buyout for a small steel company that was being cast off by its parent corporation because it was too small," says the Fleet Bank vice-president. "The borrowers got the money for the deal, in part, because they came to us by way of a high official in the local development agency. His participation helped to make the deal happen."

4. Pitch your proposal to a carefully screened group of banks and investors.

"Look for those cash sources with a proven history of funding ventures in your chosen field," says a partner with the accounting/consulting firm of Laventhol & Horwath (L & H). "Because they're familiar with your industry's finances, they may accept risks others reject out of hand.

"The construction industry is a good example. As a high-risk, high-reward field prone to cyclical earnings, it makes a lot of lenders nervous. But those accustomed to dealing with construction outfits know that the good ones can ride out the doldrums and come back with a vengeance when conditions improve. So they may be willing to make a new loan, or stretch the terms on an existing one, in order to properly finance the business."

5. Maintain good banking relationships by touching bases with loan officers even when the company doesn't need money.

"The banker who has lent you money in the past is the one most likely to lend you money again—providing you maintain your ties with him," the L & H partner says. "That means informing him of the company's performance, good and bad. Keeping depressed earnings a secret only to have the banker find out when the business deteriorates and can't pay its bills is a sure way to close off that lender as a source of additional funds. Instead, call the banker as often when you don't need money as when you do. You'll find that builds trust and confidence—two components crucial to the bank's decision making."

6. Whenever possible, demonstrate your ability to guarantee business loans personally. Prepare financial statements listing all personal assets, including stocks, bonds, and cash. Bear in mind that the banker wants evidence of net worth beyond your home and business.

"This can be a swing factor," says a vice-president specializing in small business for Chemical Bank. "Sometimes the company's finances are marginal but the owner's personal resources are strong enough to make the deal fly."

7. Attend a meeting of a venture-capital club in your community (see Venture-capital Clubs, page 87). These nonprofit organizations bring together entrepreneurs and investors to share information and make deals. At many clubs, so-called five-minute forums give entrepreneurs the opportunity to present their business ideas to the group, explaining what they hope to accomplish and how much capital they require. Interested investors attending the session may request additional information, a business plan, or a subsequent meeting.

Last but not least, try to pay back your loans and investments in advance. Making the last payment ahead of schedule always builds goodwill and can lead to more substantial financing the next time around.

"To use a familiar term, nothing succeeds like success," Speiser says. "Prove that you can make money work for others—that you are a responsible and productive borrower—and the tables will turn: capital sources will come to you. That's the position every small business, every entrepreneur, wants to be in."

Outline for a New Venture Business Plan

I. Executive Summary

This section should not be a mere listing of topics but should emphasize the high points of your proposal, including: a) the purpose of the plan (e.g., to attract investment by professional venture capitalists); b) a characterization of the market potential; c) significant product features; d) product development milestones; e) financial results such as "achieving $1 million in sales in 1989, breaking even in second quarter 1990, and growing to $35 million in sales and $3.5 million in after-tax profits by 1991." The major technical, operational, and financial milestones represent "risk step-down" points. Achieving these milestones lends substantial credibility that the company will succeed. The executive summary should be a succinct overview of the entire new venture business plan.

II. Table of Contents

This section of a business plan should be designed to assist readers in locating specific sections and points in the plan. Excessive detail should be avoided here, however.

III. Company Description

A. What business are you in?

B. What are your principal:

1. Products or services?
2. Markets?
3. Applications?

C. What is your **distinctive competence**? (What are the chief factors that will account for your success?)

This section should provide potential investors a specific picture of your objectives and give them good reasons for believing you will succeed. Since all professional investors have excellent alternative opportunities, you must show that your chances for success are better than these alternatives. If you are entering a competitive field (and most entrepreneurs are), the distinctive competence description is very important. It is important that the distinctive competence be related to a need. Examples (stated informally) include the following:

— "Our software technology makes it easy for a customer to convert from his existing obsolete system to new hardware. This will meet an important need because conversion has been one of the industry's major problems."
— "Due to a technological and manufacturing breakthrough, we will be the lowest-cost entry in a market that is very price-sensitive."
— "We have very strong business relationships with design engineers for customers that order $50 million a year, and our product (or service) solves numerous problems inherent in developing their new product lines."

IV. Market Analysis and Marketing

A. Industry description and outlook
   1. What industry are you in?
   2. How big is it now? How big will it be in five years? Ten years?

3. What are its chief characteristics?
4. Who are or will be the major customers? Specifically, are they Fortune 100 or 500 companies, or are they small proprietorships?
5. What are or will be the major applications of your product or service?
6. What are the major trends in the industry?

B. Target markets
1. What are the major segments you will penetrate?

   Analysis of market segmentation may be one of the most critical parts of the plan. Major mistakes have been made in this area. Some common ones include:

   a. Assuming the size of customers is normally distributed and that the median equals the mean. If the distribution is not normal, 50 percent of the customers may not be above the average. If an "average-sized" customer can afford the product, this may only be 10 percent of the total customer base.

   b. In many markets, 20 percent of the customers may represent 80 percent of the demand. Ignoring factors that prevent penetration of this 20 percent may cripple the entire marketing effort.

   c. Even very successful companies often have surprisingly low market shares. Consequently, market-share assumptions should be realistic. Even a realistic market-share assumption of 10 percent could really represent 50 percent if careful market definition and segmentation showed that only 20 percent of the assumed market "qualified" as potential customers. For instance, given that any business above the average size was a prime target, this situation could occur if careful analysis showed that only 10 percent, not 50 percent, of customers were above the mean.

   d. Lack of clear definition of the products or services to be sold.

   e. No accurate estimate of the profitability of each product or service.

2. For each major application, what are the following:

   a. Requirements by the customer or regulatory agencies?

   b. Current ways of filling these requirements?

   c. Buying habits of the customer?

   d. Impact on the customer of using your product or service?
   —User economics. (How much will it save him per year? What return on investment will he get?)
   —Other impacts. (Will he have to change his way of doing things? Buy other equipment? Change work habits? Modify organizational structure?)

   e. How will these segments and applications change over the next three to five years?

C. Competition
1. What companies will you compete with (including those like you who are not yet in the market)?
2. How do you compare with other competitive companies?
3. What competition will you meet in each product or service line?
4. How does your product or service compare with others (especially

through the eyes of the customer)?

5. What is the market share of each existing competitor?

6. Do you threaten the major strategic objectives or self-image of competition or just financial results (e.g., will competition seek to destroy you at any cost)?

7. Do you interface with important, noncompetitive equipment whose manufacturer might still be reluctant to support your product due to warranty, liability, or image considerations?

D. Reaction from specific prospective customers

1. What prospective customers have you talked to?

2. What was their reaction?

3. Have they seen or tested a realistic prototype of the product or service?

4. If so, what was their reaction?

E. Marketing activities

1. What are your plans for:
   a. Marketing strategy ("one-stop shopping," specialization, market-share objectives, image)?
   b. Distribution (direct, retail)?
   c. Promotion (advertising, conventions, etc.)?
   d. Pricing (demand pricing or cost-based pricing, volume discounts—how will pricing change over time)?
   e. Sales appeals?
   f. Geographical penetration (domestic, Europe, Far East, etc.)?
   g. Field service or product support?
   h. Setting priorities among segments, applications, marketing activities? The limited human resources in a new venture cannot be all things to all people, regardless of the opportunities.

F. Selling activities

1. How will you identify prospective customers? Consider not just the companies, but the relevant decision-makers who can spend money on your product, either from discretionary or budgeted funds.

2. How will you decide whom to contact and in what order?

3. What level of selling effort will you have (for example, the number of salespeople)?

4. What efficiency will you have (for example, how many calls per salesperson)?

5. What conversion rates will you be able to obtain (for example, how many calls per demonstration; how many demonstrations per sale)?

6. How long will each of the above activities take in person-days? In elapsed time?

7. What will your initial order size be? What is the likelihood and size of repeat orders?

8. Based on the above assumptions, what is the sales productivity of each salesperson?

9. What is the commission structure for the salespeople? Does it have increasing or decreasing rates for exceeding quota? What will the average salesperson earn per year and how long will he/she have to wait to receive commissions (e.g., sales cycle milestones)?

10. What evidence do you have to back up your answers to the estimates above?

This section on marketing and marketing analysis is often of critical importance. Probably the most common single error is to assume you can validly predict what you can sell by gathering some general numbers on the size of the market, then project a market share for yourself. The argument usually goes like this: "We will be selling a new microcomputer. The total market for these computers is about $100 million a year and growing 10 percent a year. Of this, 25 percent is automatic typewriters. Thus, the portion available to us is $25 million the first year, $27.5 million the second year, $30.3 million the third, $33.3 million the fourth, and $36.6 million the fifth year. We project capturing ½ of 1 percent the first year, or $125,000; and growing to 10 percent of the market, or $3.67 million, by the fifth year." Unless this kind of reasoning is backed up with detailed answers to the kinds of questions asked above, it is unconvincing and probably wrong.

V. Technology: Research and Development

A. What is the essence and status of your current technology (idea, prototype, small production runs, etc.)?
B. What is your patent or copyright position?
   1. How much is patented or copyrighted?
   2. How much can be patented or copyrighted?
   3. How comprehensive and how effective will the patents or copyrights be?
   4. Which companies have technology that is superior or equal to yours?
   5. Are there additional means of protecting your technology (such as secrecy or speed in putting out the product or service)?
C. What new technologies or scientific approaches exist that may become practical in the next five years? What factors limit their development or acceptance?

One common pitfall here is to compare the technology you are working on now and will have on the market in a year or two with that which competition has now. Instead, you should compare what you will have by the time you are in the market with what others will have then.

D. What are key research and development activities and related milestones and risks?
E. What new products, hopefully derived directly from first-generation products, do you plan to develop to meet changing market needs?
F. Are there any regulatory or approval requirements (U/L, EPA, FCC, etc.)?

VI. Manufacturing/Operations

A. How will you accomplish production or conduct service operations?
   1. How much will you do internally and by what methods?
   2. How much through subcontracts, both initially and after one or two years?
B. What production or operating advantages do you have?
C. What is your present capacity for level of production or operations? How can this be expanded?
D. What are critical parts? Are any of these parts "single- or sole-sourced" or do you have backup vendors? What are the lead times of these parts?
E. What are the standard costs for production at different volume levels?

VII. Management and Ownership

A. Who are your key managers?
B. How do you intend to attract and com-

pensate key people (i.e., stock, incentive bonus, etc.)?

C. What are their skills and, particularly, their experience, and how does this relate to the success requirement of your venture?

You should think carefully about these issues for two reasons. First, it is extremely important to differentiate between ownership and management roles, even when assumed by the same individuals. Second, it may be better to defer hiring an individual rather than have the job outgrow him/her in a year.

D. What has their track record been, and how does this relate to your requirements?

The most common problem here is failing to relate your team's capability to the success requirement of your business. As an example, the chief engineer might be described as having a fine MIT education and important-sounding job titles with sophisticated companies, but with no mention of work he has actually done. This information does not directly substantiate that he really could design the complex product necessary for the company.

E. What staff additions do you plan, when, and with what required qualifications?

For example, you may not now have a candidate for the vice-president of finance position—or even need one immediately—but it is important to state your plans to support this function when required.

F. Do any managers have outstanding "noncompete" agreements with previous employers? If so, get opinion of counsel regarding the validity or applicability of these agreements.

G. Who is on your board of directors?

It is important to think ahead about the role of your board when you become operational. It may be inappropriate to have certain early investors serve on the board if their potential for nonmonetary contributions is not substantial.

H. Who are your current stockholders, and how many shares does each own? (Include comments about options and related prices.)

While it may be necessary or expedient to permit investment by many small and/or unsophisticated investors, their presence may cause concern among professional investors or headaches or diversion of management effort during the evolution of the company.

I. What is the amount of stock currently authorized and issued?

VIII. Organization and Personnel

A. How many people will you need by type?

B. What compensation method will be used by type: salary, stock, profit-sharing, etc.?

C. Show sample organizational structures for formative years and thereafter.

IX. Funds Required and Their Uses

A. How much money do you require now?

B. How much will you require over the next five years, and when will it be required?

C. How will these funds be used?

D. What portion of the funds are expected to be raised from debt rather than equity? Use two debt assumptions for your capital requirements after the break-even point.

E. What terms?

If this is a first request for outside investment, you should prepare a scenario for the attraction of required capital, approximate price per share and timing, and show the dilution or percentage ownership of the initial and subsequent investors.

F. When do you plan to "go public"?

A major concern of professional investors is both the future value and liquidity of their investments. A company that is not profitable enough or large enough (e.g., less than $20+ million sales) within five years might not be of interest. This is also true if management indicates an unwillingness to go public for fear of losing control.

X. Financial Data

A. Present historical financial statements and projections for the next three to five years, including:
  1. Profit-and-loss or income statements by month or quarter, at least until break-even, and then annually to cover a five-year period. (It is common to present monthly statements for the first year, quarterly statements for the next two years, and then for two or three annual periods.) This analysis should show the results based on two different debt vs. equity assumptions with resultant interest expense. The break-even point should be clearly identified. Show market value of the company based on a P/E ratio of similar companies.
  2. Balance sheets at the end of each year.
  3. Cash budgets.
  4. Capital budgets for equipment, etc.
  5. Manufacturing/shipping plan.

B. What key assumptions have been made in your pro formas, and how good are these assumptions?

This section is especially important. These assumptions should most often reflect industry performance and, if not, specific justification should be given. Key considerations are whether these are "best-case" numbers, "worst-case," or something in the middle, which is preferred. The data should be based on several different assumptions to determine the reasonableness of the information. It is important to note, however, that too much financial information can be worse than too little. Each company must project those points it believes are most appropriate.

XI. Administrative Considerations

A. Careful thought should be given to naming the new business. The name, especially for a new business, should reflect the major thrust of the business or be distinctive in some way, such as the Apple computer. In addition, possible trademarks and service marks should be identified.

A subsequent search by an attorney to see if the name or trademarks are available for use should be undertaken early and, if available, they should be reserved.

B. The plan should be printed and bound.

C. Copies of the plan should be controlled and distribution recorded.

D. Private placement disclaimers should be included, if the plan is being used to raise capital.

XII. Appendices or Exhibits (as required)

A. Resumes of key managers.

B. Pictures of the product/prototype.

C. Professional references.

D. Market studies, articles from trade journals.

E. Patents.

Credit: Arthur Young

Business Plans

One important purpose of the business plan is to indicate the expected financial results of operations. It also depicts the financial potential of your venture and its capital needs. For anyone investing or lending money to your business, it tells them why they should provide funds, when they can expect a return, and how large that return is expected to be. It is a plan for the future. Therefore, any presentation of financial information about your business or your product must be future-oriented.

In the case of an existing business seeking expansion capital, balance sheets and income statements for the current year and prior two years should be included. Other historical financial information necessary to understanding the plan should be attached in an appendix.

In making your forecasts and projections, assumptions must be made. These include but are certainly not limited to:

- Revenue
- Growth rates
- Time periods required
- Taxes/rates
- Production facilities
- Operating expenses
- Capital expenditures
- Environmental conditions
- General economic conditions
- Contracts to be negotiated
- Competitors' actions
- Turnovers
- Interdependencies

You should list your assumptions for the user(s) of the plan and to allow verification.

Items to be included in the financial section are:

- Projected income statements:
  Monthly for planning year
  Annually or quarterly for the second and third years
- Projected cash flow analyses:
  Monthly for planning year
  Annually or quarterly for the second and third years
- Projected balance sheets.
- Projected statements of changes in financial position.
- Cost-volume-profit analysis where appropriate.

Your financial projections should be realistic, with reasonable margins that conform to experience and industry standards. Don't forget to include assumptions in the rest of your plan concerning necessary or possible capital requirements such as increased personnel, expanded manufacturing facilities, or equipment needs. Otherwise your plan will create an overly "optimistic" picture for management, which will create difficulties in the budgeting process and plan evaluation. It can also create skepticism in the potential investor.

Financial projection matrices, available for use with microcomputers, can greatly facilitate the preparation of projections.

Remember that the budgetary process is the money portion of your business plan. It is integral to the plan, not separate from it. The budget should be the last step in the planning process. Only after gathering the information, setting objectives, and assessing your needs can the budget be realistically formulated. It can then serve to steer any necessary changes in your objectives, action steps, or timetable.

Credit: Peat Marwick, "Business Planning"

Budgeting in a Small Service Firm

A budget is a plan that enables you to set a goal and list the steps which are necessary to reach that goal. Thus, a budget helps you think about what you want your business to do in the future. By planning, you are in a better position to act to prevent crises.

In its simplest form a budget is a detailed plan of future receipts and expenditures—a projected profit-and-loss statement. Thus once the period for which you have budgeted is completed, you can compare actual results with anticipated goals. If some of your expenses, for example, are higher than you expected, you can start looking for ways to cut them. Conversely, if you have fallen short of your goal, you may want to look for ways to increase your income.

Budget makers can start either with a forecast of sales and work down or with a forecast of profits and work up. Most small service businesses use the latter method. In other words, you decide what profit you want to make and then list the expenses that you will incur in order to make that predetermined profit.

A Plan for Increased Profit

Before you can use a budget as a plan for increased profit, you have to be sure that your present profit is what it should be. In a service business, the year-end profit should be large enough to make a return on your investment and a return on your own work—pay you a salary.

Value of owner's service. Skilled crafts people who own service businesses are kidding themselves if their firms' profits are less than they can earn working for someone else.

Your net profit after taxes should be at least as much as you can earn if you worked at your trade for a weekly paycheck.

Return on investment. The year-end profit is too low if it does not also include a return on the owner-manager's investment. That investment includes the money you put into the firm when you started it and the profit of prior years which you left in the firm—retained earnings. You should check to be sure that the rate of return on your investment is what it should be. Your trade association should be able to provide guidelines about the rate of return on investment in your line of business. Your accountant and banker are also sources of help.

Your targeted income. After you know what you made last year, you can set a profit goal for next year. Be sure that your goal includes a return on your services and a return on your investment. Your goal should also include an amount for state and federal taxes. Keep in mind that the larger your goal, the larger the amount that will have to be added to account for taxes. Your accountant can help you determine that amount.

Can You Reach the Goal?

Once you have decided on your profit target, the next step in preparing a budget is to determine whether you can achieve it. To do this, you must project your fixed costs and your variable costs. From these three figures—profit, fixed expenses, and variable expenses—you can determine your "hoped-for" total income.

In gathering figures, keep in mind that without accurate information planning becomes guessing. The owner-manager who has never budgeted should talk with an accountant about a record-keeping system.

Changes may be needed to provide the necessary budget information. It may be that your present system does not break costs down into fixed and variable expenses, or it may be that you need to have a profit and loss (or income) statement at more frequent intervals to determine the seasonal fluctuations of your revenues and expenses.

Fixed expenses. Regardless of sales, fixed expenses stay the same. Several examples of fixed expenses are insurance, rent, taxes on property, wages paid to salaried employees, depreciation of equipment, interest on borrowed money, building maintenance costs, officer salaries, and office expenses.

Variable expenses. This type of expense varies with sales. In some service businesses, the cost of labor is the biggest factor. Sales commissions, payroll taxes, insurance, advertising, and delivery expenses are other examples of variable expenses.

Determine your expected service income. Your expected service income contribution is the difference between sales and the variable expenses that are necessary to produce these sales. When this difference equals fixed expenses and the desired profit, you have a workable budget.

Lucy's Beauty Shop

Lucy's Beauty Shop (all names are fictitious) illustrates the principles of budgeting in a small service business. The owner-manager is Mrs. Lucy Doe. The shop's income is from two sources: (1) from beauty services which are performed by three operators and (2) from cosmetics and perfumes which are sold by the receptionist. The receptionist also answers the telephone, keeps the shop's daily records, and prepares the checks for Mrs. Doe to sign.

Targeted income. In making a budget, Mrs. Doe decided that she wanted to increase her net profit after taxes. She set the goals at $10,000 for net profit after taxes. This figure meant that the shop's profit before taxes had to be about $13,333 because she figured that her taxes would amount to about $3,333.

This goal was an ambitious one because her previous year's net profit before taxes was $8,390. For details on that year see "Lucy's Beauty Shop—Profit-and-Loss Statement."

Determining fixed expenses. As shown in "Lucy's Beauty Shop—Profit-and-Loss Statement," the shop's fixed expense items are: depreciation of equipment, receptionist's salary, insurance, rent, interest on equipment obligations, and utilities (heat and air conditioning). In addition, about half the laundry and shop maintenance expense is fixed. In budgeting her fixed expenses for next year, Mrs. Doe took into account: (1) the raise she intended to give the receptionist, (2) a change in amount of interest, and (3) a change in her insurance expense.

She estimated that her fixed expenses for next year would be $11,000.

Determining variable expenses. In Mrs. Doe's beauty shop, the variable expenses— those that vary with sales—are cost of cosmetics sold, shop supplies, payroll taxes and costs, utilities (water and electricity), about half of laundry and shop maintenance, and operators' salaries. These salaries are variable because each operator receives half the total price charged the customer.

When determining variable expenses, Mrs. Doe uses her trade journals for information on budgeted percentages. For budgeting purposes, all costs are expressed as a percentage of the sales dollar. In her case, the percentages are: beauty shop supplies, 10;

laundry, including uniforms, 3; water and variable utilities, 1; and payroll costs, 5.

She estimates her total payroll costs at 5 percent of gross revenue from service or 10 percent of salaries. Payroll taxes, both state and federal, account for 7.9 percent of the 10 percent, and payments for workers' compensation and other employee insurance account for 2.1 percent.

Determining expected service income. The next step in preparing a budget for Lucy's Beauty Shop is to determine the expected service income contribution. The basis for estimating this income for next year is the average revenue for each operator's appointment with one customer. This figure is $4. See the following table, "Service Income Contribution."

One half of the $4 belongs to the operator. Other variable expenses take 76 cents. Thus, from each $4 unit of services that is sold, $1.24 is left for service income contribution. The service revenue for 12 months is shown in the table, "Determination of Total Service Contribution." Mrs. Doe arrived at these estimates as follows:

1. From the appointment book, she learned that each operator averages 15 appointments a day.
2. The shop's income from each operator is $30 a day (15 times $2).
3. Each operator works 5 days a week.
4. Each operator contributes $630 a month to the shop's income (21 days times $30).

On this $630, the shop clears $390.60

LUCY'S BEAUTY SHOP
PROFIT-AND-LOSS STATEMENT
FOR THE YEAR ENDED DECEMBER 31, 19____

	Variable	Fixed	Total		
Revenue:					
Merchandise				$12,000	
Beauty Shop Service				42,000	
Total Revenue				$54,000	
Cost of Merchandise Sold				6,000	
					$48,000
Gross Margin					
Expenses					
Depreciation		$ 300	$ 300		
Salaries and wages	$21,000	2,700	23,700		
Supplies	4,200		4,200		
Insurance		110	110		
Rent		4,800	4,800		
Payroll taxes and costs	2,370		2,370		
Interest		250	250		
Utilities	420	1,000	1,420		
Laundry and shop maintenance	1,260	1,200	2,460		
	$29,250	$10,360			$39,610
Net Income Before Taxes					$8,390

SERVICE INCOME CONTRIBUTION
EXPRESSED AS A PERCENT OF SALES DOLLAR

Average Service Revenue	*$4.00*	*100%*
Variable Expenses		
Operator salaries	$ 2.00	50%
Beauty supplies	.40	10%
Laundry and uniforms	.12	3%
Water	.04	1%
Payroll costs	.20	5%
Total Variable Expenses	2.76	69%
Income Contribution from Services	$1.24	31%

because 76 cents of each $2 that the shop receives from an operator's work goes for variable expenses (see the table, "Service Income Contribution").

The shop's cosmetic sales contribute a net revenue of 50 cents on the sales dollar. Mrs. Doe estimated, based on past experience, that she could get a 50 percent increase in the sales of cosmetics without additional advertising.

Determination of Total Service Contribution

Revenue per Operator for the Year ($1,260 per month × 12 months)	$15,120
Service Income Contribution per Operator ($390.60 × 12 months)	4,687*
Total Service Contribution from Beauty Shop (3 operators × $4,687)	14,061
From Cosmetic Sales ($18,000 × 50%)	9,000
Total Service Contribution Based on Present Outlook	$23,061

*Figures are rounded to the nearest dollar.

Comparing revenue and cost. After Mrs. Doe determines her variable expenses, fixed expenses, and the service income contribution, she is ready to test her budget. She does this by adding her total fixed expenses of $11,000 and the desired gross profit of $13,333. This total comes to $24,333.

But her estimated service revenue (see the table, "Determination of Total Service Contribution") is only $23,061. It will not cover her fixed expenses and desired profit. Resources will be about $1,300 short of the desired goal.

Where Can She Go?

Because resources are not enough to cover fixed expenses and the desired profit, Mrs. Doe has to adjust her budget. She can go in at least three directions. One possibility is to add another operator. Another is to try to increase cosmetic sales. A third solution is to reduce her expected profit. In order to decide what to do, Mrs. Doe needs answers to several questions about each possibility. She may have to work up several tentative budgets to determine what to do.

Add another operator. This possibility

poses the following questions: Is the relationship between fixed expenses and revenue in line with industry trends? Is there space for an additional booth? What additional fixed expenses will be incurred? Can another operator be kept busy? If so, the additional revenue can help to offset Mrs. Doe's rent, which is slightly higher than the average for her line of business. That average is 10 percent of gross beauty service income. The shop has sufficient space for another booth. However, if a booth is added, fixed expenses will increase because equipment for the new booth will mean additional financing costs.

Increase cosmetic sales. This possibility seems to be a logical way to increase income because each dollar of sales will increase the revenue by 50 cents. The first question is how much of an increase in cosmetic sales will be needed? Mrs. Doe calculated that these sales must be increased by about 95 percent rather than by 50 percent, as she originally planned. Other questions to answer here are: By what method will sales be increased? By what additional advertising? By offering the receptionist and operators a commission on cosmetic sales? By reducing prices? What effect will these methods have on revenue? How much additional inventory will be needed? How will it be financed? Is storage and display space sufficient to accommodate increased sales?

Reduce expectations. Sometimes the only practical solution is to reduce the expected profit. Mrs. Doe decided that $10,000 net profit after taxes was not in the picture next year. Based on her knowledge of the beauty shop business, she felt that her shop was not quite ready to add another operator. For one thing, she foresaw the possibility of personnel trouble if a new operator was not kept busy.

She also felt that trying to push cosmetic sales up by more than 50 percent could cause customer dissatisfaction. She reminded herself that customers regarded the shop's beauty service highly and decided that any major growth in sales must come from that end of the business. Another operator and $10,000 or more net profit after taxes might be feasible the year after next. She would keep the possibility in mind as she moved into next year.

Periodic Feedback and Control

A budget provides a tool for control. You start building this facility when your budget for 12 months is completed. Break it down into quarters. Such a breakdown allows you to check for any discrepancies that may not show up readily in a 12-month budget. When many items are added together, it is easy for an error to creep into the totals.

During the year, this quarterly division provides a handle for getting a hold on expenses and other activities.

For example, by looking at next quarter's budget you can anticipate peak periods and schedule stock and labor to handle peak sales volume. You can plan vacations, special promotions, and inventory taking for the slow periods.

A monthly or quarterly profit-and-loss statement allows you to keep the items in your budget in line with operations. Ask your accountant to show the actual and the planned revenues and expenses on the income statement so you can compare them. Thus, you can pinpoint and work on the problems that have occurred during the month or the quarter. Your objective is to guide your activities toward the most profitable type of operations.

Credit: U.S. Small Business Administration and Professor Phyllis A. Barker

Buying a Business: A Checklist

Like used-car buyers, those in the market for small companies may be in for a rude awakening: what they see may not be what they get. Unless prospective buyers do their homework, a "profitable cream puff" can turn out to be a money-losing clunker.

"When business buyers wind up regretting their purchases, nine times out of ten the cause of dissatisfaction can be traced to incomplete research before the deal is concluded," says a partner in the New York-based law firm of Parker Chapin Flattau & Kimpl. "Because the buyer fails to probe behind the exterior, he really doesn't know what he's bought until the once-hidden problems are his responsibility."

Attorneys active in small business practice advise would-be buyers to review a checklist of critical factors that can detract from a company's appeal and its market value.

"The discovery of significant problems may not rule out a pending purchase," the lawyer says. "After all, every business has an element of risk. But it can prompt the buyer to reduce his bid. Learning of an undisclosed liability, for example, can be valid reason to cut the purchase offer by an equivalent sum."

First-time buyers and seasoned entrepreneurs making new investments should review this prepurchase checklist:

1. Explore the terms of the company's outstanding loans. Two problems may be buried in the financing agreements: The negative covenants may be unacceptable to the buyer or worse yet, the bank may be entitled to call demand notes when the business changes hands. An unexpected liability could cripple new management soon after it takes over.

"You want to maintain continuity of financing," says Herbert C. Speiser, a partner with Phillips, Gold CPAs. "In most cases, this means keeping the existing bank relationships. Certainly, the new owners don't want to find themselves in the market for new loans on top of the debt they incurred to buy the business. So the rule is to negotiate with the bankers before committing to the purchase."

2. Study lease provisions to determine if the landlord can evict the new owners or substantially increase their rents. If this is not clear from the lease terms, prospective buyers are advised to meet with the landlords to determine where they stand or to negotiate new agreements.

3. Order a Uniform Commercial Code search to identify unreported liens against the business. Assets pledged to secure outstanding loans may be subject to seizure by financial institutions. This puts the buyer in the unacceptable position of paying for property for which he cannot claim clear title. Attorneys can conduct UCC searches on the state and local levels.

4. Check for ongoing audits or unsettled tax liabilities. Even audits dormant for a year or more can lead to sudden claims for back taxes. Make provision for this in the sales contract by placing part of the purchase price in an escrow account.

5. Make certain that trade secrets vital to the company's success have not been revealed to outsiders. Proprietary recipes, formulas, or manufacturing processes that enter the public domain cannot always be protected from competitive use.

6. Insist on audited financial statements. Books prepared by in-house staff are often lacking in detail and accuracy.

7. Whenever possible, review the corporate minutes as well as general correspondence. This may reveal previously undisclosed sales contracts, noncompetition

clauses, restrictions on the transfer of corporate stock, and costly retirement plans.

"Above all else, don't be stampeded into signing a contract until all the relevant facts can be studied," the Parker Chapin partner warns. "Sellers who pressure buyers into instant decisions often have something to hide."

Buying a Business: The Choice of a Stock or Asset Purchase: A Comparison

Advice from the national law firm of Jones, Day, Reavis & Pogue

Generally, in a stock purchase, the acquired business continues to be operated in the same corporate entity. Only the ownership of the entity changes, and the historical attributes of the entity remain unchanged. In an asset purchase, the business generally is transferred to a new entity, often one formed specifically to receive the assets. The sellers continue to own the old entity which, instead of being an operating business, will now consist primarily of the sale proceeds. Sometimes the sellers will liquidate the old entity; other times they will continue its corporate existence as an investment company or as the owner of another operating business.

Stock purchases have a number of different characteristics from asset purchases. Whether these characteristics are advantages or disadvantages to a buyer or seller often will depend upon the specific circumstances of a particular transaction. The major differences between stock and asset transactions are found in four critical categories: flexibility, complexity, contingent liabilities, and tax considerations.

Flexibility

Generally, an asset transaction is considered to be more flexible than a stock transaction. When stock of a corporation is sold, the buyer is in essence acquiring all the assets which the corporation owns. Often this is not intended. For example, the corporation may own assets which the selling shareholders wish to retain (e.g., company cars, an airplane, a receivable from a shareholder, or, most frequently, cash). Getting these assets out of the corporation and into the hands of the shareholders can have unintended tax consequences and, without careful planning, can result in dividend income to the selling shareholders and taxable gain to the corporation. In an asset transaction, however, only the assets that the buyer wishes to buy and the seller wishes to sell need be the subject of the transaction. Similarly, a buyer of stock acquires all the corporation's liabilities while a buyer of assets may assume only specifically identified liabilities.

An asset transaction also provides greater flexibility if the assets of the business are not to be acquired by the same entity. For example, a corporation may acquire the operating business assets while the individual shareholders may acquire the corporate real estate. A stock transaction makes this difficult to accomplish, but an asset transaction provides this flexibility.

Whether the increased flexibility of an asset transaction is an advantage to the buyer or seller will depend on the specific circumstances. If the seller wishes to retain certain assets, an asset transaction may be an advantage to him. On the other hand, if the buyer wishes to take advantage of the tax benefits associated with individual ownership of the real estate, the asset transaction may be more advantageous to him. But there is a price tag associated with each of these considerations.

A buyer who has based his purchase price on the ability to take advantage of the tax benefits associated with individual ownership of real estate (i.e., an asset transaction) generally should be willing to accept a stock transaction if the loss of these tax benefits were reflected in a reduced purchase price. Similarly, a seller who has based his selling price on the retention of certain corporate assets might be willing to part with those assets in a stock transaction if the price were increased accordingly.

Complexity

Generally, asset transactions are considered more complex than stock transactions. An asset transaction requires the conveyance of each specific asset of the business. Conveyance of real estate may pose special problems, as may patents, trademarks, and the name and goodwill of the business. Another complexity associated with an asset transaction can be the necessity of sending notices and obtaining consents from third parties. A bulk transfer of inventory may require compliance with local bulk-sales laws. Consents from lenders and landlords may be required. Some items such as permits and licenses may not be assignable at all, and the buyer may have to obtain his own. Special attention also is required for insurance policies, prepaid items, and employee benefit plans.

Stock transfers also can be complex. Many leases and mortgage documents will provide that a transfer of stock will be deemed to constitute a transfer of the underlying asset for purposes of consent and notice requirements. Also, if there are a large number of shareholders, some of whom may not be in favor of the transaction, an asset transaction will not require unanimity while a stock transaction generally will.

Contingent Liabilities

One of the major differences between stock transactions and asset transactions is in the area of contingent liabilities. A buyer of stock acquires the corporation, "warts and all." Thus, without appropriate contractual provisions, the buyer would bear the economic brunt of any undisclosed liabilities. For example, if the IRS audits a preacquisition year and assesses a tax deficiency against the corporation, the buyer would bear the burden of that deficiency since the corporation would remain in existence and owe the additional tax. The same is true for pending or threatened litigation.

For this reason, it is customary in stock transactions for the buyer to obtain very strict representations, warranties, and indemnities from the sellers concerning various aspects of the business. A major purpose of these is to shift the burden of preacquisition liabilities back to the sellers, where they belong. Often, sellers of stock are uncomfortable making these representations and warranties personally. This is particularly true where some of the shareholders have not been actively involved with the business. Disputes often arise among the selling shareholders as to who will stand behind the representations and warranties if some of the shareholders have been active in the business while others are merely passive investors. The negotiation of these provisions can materially increase the cost of a stock transaction and the length of time it takes to agree on a purchase agreement.

In an asset transaction, the selling corporation would make any representations and warranties, and thus the selling shareholders would limit their personal exposure. In addition, the representations and warranties demanded by an asset purchaser generally are less onerous than those required in a stock transaction because it is easier to identify specifically the assets being acquired and the liabilities being assumed.

An asset transaction does not completely eliminate the need for representations and warranties, however, because there is an emerging judicial doctrine known as "successor liability" which imposes upon an asset buyer certain continuing responsibilities for preacquisition actions of the business enterprise if the selling corporation has been liquidated. An example of this would be product-liability claims.

Another aspect of this issue is continuing liability for personal guaranties of corporate obligations which the selling shareholders may have entered into. It is quite common for third parties dealing with closely held corporations such as banks, landlords, and important suppliers to require personal guaranties from the corporation's shareholders. It is often difficult to secure the release of these guaranties even though the stock of the corporation is being sold. Thus, a stock sale often puts the selling shareholders in a position of remaining contingently liable on corporate obligations while at the same time losing control over the corporation's payment of these obligations. In an asset transaction, it is possible to leave with the selling corporation the responsibility for satisfying certain corporate obligations. Of course, this generally is taken into account in establishing the purchase price so that the sellers are not economically harmed. The advantage to the sellers, however, is that they retain control over payment of these liabilities.

Thus, an asset transaction may be preferable to a stock transaction from both the standpoint of the seller and the buyer in connection with contingent liabilities. The buyer can feel more comfortable that he is acquiring only those specific liabilities identified in the contract, and the seller can avoid making onerous representations and warranties and can retain control over the payment of certain corporate obligations.

Asset Sales under Tax Reform Act of 1986

When it comes to selling your business, the tax benefits of an asset sale are no longer the attractive shelter they once were.

Blame it on a key provision of the Tax Reform Act of 1986 that repeals the so-called general utilities doctrine. With this step, Congress has effectively closed down a popular strategy commonly used to reduce the tax bite on business sales.

"In the past, the owner of a business could adopt a plan of liquidation, sell the company's assets and in the process avoid corporate taxes on the sale," says a tax partner with Kenneth Leventhal, CPAs. "The only tax on the gain would be paid by the owner when he received the cash. But the new law puts an end to this technique. Effective January 1, 1987, these transactions are now subject to a dual tax, first at the corporate level and then to the shareholders. While the very smallest closely-held companies have full or partial exemptions through 1988, the new rule applies in full to companies worth in excess of $10 million.

"What's more, the repeal of the capital gain tax means that the shareholders will find their tax bite from business sales rising from 20 percent in 1986 to 28 percent in 1987."

The numbers speak for themselves. Assume Jones started his business 20 years ago for $100,000. Today Jones Inc. is worth $15 million, with most of that value reflected in the company's appreciated assets. If the company had liquidated in 1986, Mr. Jones would have paid a 20-percent capital gains tax, or $2,980,000, on the $14,900,000 built-in gain. Including the original $100,000 investment, he'd be left with $12,020,000.

But with the same sale consummated in 1987, the corporation would first be hit with a 40-percent tax on the $14,900,000 gain, with the balance taxed at the 28-percent shareholder rate, leaving a net of $6,536,800 including the original $100,000 investment.

Want to have your cake and eat it too? To hold on to your company for several years while avoiding both a current capital gain tax and a dual tax at the time of sale? Then the "one month liquidation" may be for you. With this tax planning technique, the assets pass to the shareholders without a step up in value and therefore without an immediate tax. In the case of Jones Inc., the $14,900,000 gain would not be recognized at the time of liquidation. The tax would be due only when the company is sold. The caveat with the "one month" option is that taxes on retained earnings, cash or securities may be due at the time of liquidation.

A third option—one that also avoids the dual tax on business sales—calls for making the election to become an S corporation. Assets sold ten years or more after the election is made are not subject to a corporate tax on the built-in gain.

Review all options with a tax professional.

WHERE TO FIND IT

National Association of Women Business Owners
600 South Federal Street
Chicago, IL 60605
(312) 346-2330

NFIB (National Federation of Independent Business)
Administrative Offices
150 W. 20th Avenue
San Mateo, CA 94403
(415) 341-7441

Government Relations and Research Offices
600 Maryland Avenue SW, Suite 700
Washington, DC 20024
(202) 554-9000

Department of Commerce

District Offices:

ALABAMA
908 South 20th Street, Suite 200–201

Birmingham, AL 35205
(205) 254-1331

ALASKA
701 C Street, P.O. Box 32
Anchorage, AK 99513
(907) 271-5041

ARKANSAS
Suite 635, Savers Federal Building
320 W. Capitol Avenue
Little Rock, AR 72201
(501) 378-5794

CALIFORNIA
Room 800
11777 San Vicente Blvd.
Los Angeles, CA 90049
(213) 824-7591

110 West C Street
San Diego, CA 92101
(714) 293-5395

Federal Building, Box 36013
450 Golden Gate Avenue
San Francisco, CA 94102

COLORADO
Room 177, U.S. Customhouse
721 19th Street
Denver, CO 80202
(303) 837-3246

CONNECTICUT
Room 610-B, Federal Office Building
450 Main Street
Hartford, CT 06103
(203) 244-3530

DELAWARE
(see Pennsylvania)

DISTRICT OF COLUMBIA
(see Maryland)

FLORIDA
City National Bank Building, Room 821
25 West Flagler Street
Miami, FL 33130
(305) 350-5267

128 North Oseceola Avenue
Clearwater, FL 33515

3 Independent Drive
Jacksonville, FL 32202
(904) 791-2796

Collins Building, Room G-20
Tallahassee, FL 32304
(904) 488-6469

GEORGIA
Room 222, U.S. Courthouse
P.O. Box 9746
125-29 Bull Street
Savannah, GA 31412
(912) 944-4204

Suite 600, 1365 Peachtree
Street, N.E.
Atlanta, GA 30309
(404) 881-7000

HAWAII
Room 4106, Federal Building
P.O. Box 50026
300 Ala Moana Blvd.
Honolulu, HI 96850
(808) 546-8694

IDAHO
(See Oregon)

ILLINOIS
Room 1046, Mid-Continental
Plaza Building
55 East Monroe Street
Chicago, IL 60603
(312) 353-4450

Commerce Business Daily
Room 1304, 433 West Van
Buren Street
Chicago, IL 60607
(312) 353-2950

INDIANA
Room 357
U.S. Courthouse and Federal
Office Building
46 East Ohio Street
Indianapolis, IN 46204
(317) 269-6214

IOWA
Room 817 Federal Building
210 Walnut Street
Des Moines, IA 50309
(515) 284-4222

KANSAS
(see Missouri)

KENTUCKY
Room 636-B
U.S. Post Office and Court
House Building
Louisville, KY 40202
(502) 582-5066

LOUISIANA
Int'l Trade Mart Building
No. 2 Canal Street, Room 432
New Orleans, LA 70130
(504) 589-6546

MAINE
1 Memorial Circle
Casco Bank Building
Augusta, ME 04330
(207) 623-2239

MARYLAND
Room 415, U.S. Custom House
Gay and Lombard Streets
Baltimore, MD 21202
(301) 962-3560

MASSACHUSETTS
441 Stuart Street, 10th Floor
Boston, MA 02116

MICHIGAN
Room 445, Federal Building
231 West Lafayette
Detroit, MI 48226
(313) 226-3650

300 Monroe Avenue, NW,
Room 409
Grand Rapids, MI 49503
(616) 456-2411, 2433

MINNESOTA
Room 218, Federal Building
110 South Fourth Street
Minneapolis, MN 55401

MISSISSIPPI
Jackson Mall Office Center,
Suite 3230
300 Woodrow Wilson Blvd.
Jackson, MS 39213
(601) 960-4388

MISSOURI
120 South Central Avenue
St. Louis, MO 63105
(314) 425-3302

Room 1840
601 East 14th Street
Kansas City, MO 64106
(816) 374-3142

MONTANA (see Wyoming)

NEBRASKA
300 S. 19th Street
Empire State Building, First
Floor
Omaha, NE 68102
(402) 221-3664

NEVADA
777 W. 2nd Street, Room 120
Reno, NV 89503
(702) 784-5203

NEW HAMPSHIRE
(see Massachusetts)

NEW JERSEY
Capital Plaza, 8th Floor
240 West State Street
Trenton, NJ 08608
(609) 989-2100

NEW MEXICO
505 Marquette Avenue NW,
Suite 1015
Albuquerque, NM 87102
(505) 766-2386

NEW YORK
Room 1312, Federal Building
111 West Huron Street
Buffalo, NY 14202
(716) 846-4191

Federal Office Building, Room 3718
26 Federal Plaza, Foley Square
New York, NY 10278
(212) 264-0634

NORTH CAROLINA
Room 203, West Market Street
Federal Building
P.O. Box 1950
Greensboro, NC 27402
(919) 378-5345

NORTH DAKOTA
(see Nebraska)

OHIO
Federal Office Building
Room 10504
550 Main Street
Cincinnati, OH 45202
(513) 684-2944

Room 600, 666 Euclid Avenue
Cleveland, OH 44114

OKLAHOMA
4024 Lincoln Blvd.
Oklahoma City, OK 73105
(405) 231-5302

OREGON
Room 618, 1220 S.W. 3rd Avenue
Portland, OR 97204
(503) 221-3001

PENNSYLVANIA
Room 2002, Federal Building
1000 Liberty Avenue
Pittsburgh, PA 15222
(412) 644-2850

Room 9448 Federal Building
600 Arch Street

Philadelphia, PA 19106
(215) 597-2866

PUERTO RICO
(Hato Rey)
Room 659, Federal Building
San Juan, PR 00918
(809) 753-4555, Ext. 555

RHODE ISLAND
7 Jackson Walkway
Providence, RI 02903
(401) 277-2605, Ext. 22

SOUTH CAROLINA
Strom Thurmond Federal Building
1835 Assembly Street
Suite 172
Columbia, SC 29201
(803) 765-5345

Room 505, Federal Building
334 Meeting Street
Charleston, SC 29403
(803) 677-4361

P.O. Box 5823, Station B
Greenville, SC 29603
(803) 235-5919

SOUTH DAKOTA
(see Nebraska)

TENNESSEE
Room 710, 147 Jefferson Avenue
Memphis, TN 38103
(901) 521-3213

Andrew Jackson Office Building
Room 1020
Nashville, TN 37219
(615) 251-5161

TEXAS
Federal Building, Courthouse
Room 2625
515 Rusk Street
Houston, TX 77002
(713) 226-4231

C. Carmon Stiles, Director
Room 7A5, 1100 Commerce Street
Dallas, TX 75242
(214) 767-0542

UTAH
U.S. Courthouse
350 S. Main Street
Salt Lake City, UT 84101
(801) 524-5116

VERMONT (see Massachusetts)

VIRGINIA
8010 Federal Building
400 North Eight Street
Richmond, VA 23240
(804) 771-2246

8550 Arlington Blvd.
Fairfax, VA 22031
(703) 560-6460

WASHINGTON
Room 706, Lake Union Building
1700 Westlake Avenue, North
Seattle, WA 98109
(206) 442-5615

WEST VIRGINIA
New Federal Building, Room 3000
500 Quarrier Street
Charleston, WV 25301
(304) 343-6181, Ext. 375

WISCONSIN
Federal Building, U.S. Courthouse
517 East Wisconsin Avenue
Milwaukee, WI 53202
(414) 291-3473

WYOMING
8007 O'Mahoney Federal Center
2120 Capital Avenue
Cheyenne, WY 82001
(307) 772-2151

Federal Emergency Management Agency (FEMA)

Regional Offices:

Region I (Boston)
Regional Director
442 J.W. McCormack
Courthouse
Boston, MA 02109
(617) 223-4741 or 4271

Region II (New York)
Regional Director
26 Federal Plaza, Room 1349
New York, NY 10278
(212) 264-8980

Region III (Philadelphia)
Regional Director
Curtis Building, 7th Floor
6th and Walnut Streets
Philadelphia, PA 19106
(212) 597-9416

Region IV (Atlanta)
Regional Director
Gulf Oil Building, Suite 664
1375 Peachtree Street, N.E.
Atlanta, GA 30309
(404) 881-2400

Region V (Chicago)
Regional Director
300 S. Wacker Drive, 24th
Floor
Chicago, IL 60602
(312) 353-1500

Region VI (Dallas)
Regional Director
Federal Regional Center, Room
206
Denton, TX 76201
(817) 387-5811

Region VII (Kansas City)
Regional Director
Old Federal Office Building,

Room 300
911 Walnut Street
Kansas City, MO 64106
(816) 374-5912

Region VIII (Denver)
Regional Director
Federal Regional Center,
Building 710
Denver, CO 80225
(303) 234-2553

Region IX (San Francisco)
Regional Director
Building 105
Presidio of San Francisco
San Francisco, CA 94129

Region X (Seattle)
Regional Director
130-228th Street, S.W.
Bothell, WA 98011
(206) 481-8800

Bureau of Labor Statistics

Regional Offices:

Region I
(Connecticut, Maine,
Massachusetts, New
Hampshire, Rhode Island,
Vermont)
JFK Government Center, Room
1603-B
Boston, MA 02203
(617) 223-6727

Region II
(New Jersey, New York, Puerto
Rico, Virgin Islands,
Canal Zone)
1515 Broadway
New York, NY 10036
(212) 944-3121

Region III
(Delaware, District of
Columbia, Maryland,

Pennsylvania, Virginia,
West Virginia)
For letter mail: P.O. Box 13309
Philadelphia, PA 19101
3535 Market Street
Philadelphia, PA 19104
Public Information: (215)
596-1154

Region IV
(Alabama, Florida, Georgia,
Kentucky, Mississippi,
North Carolina, South
Carolina, Tennessee)
1371 Peachtree Street, NE,
Room 540
Atlanta, GA 30309
(404) 881-4416

Region V
(Illinois, Indiana, Michigan,
Minnesota,
Ohio, Wisconsin)
Federal Office Building, 9th
Floor
230 South Dearborn Street
Chicago, IL 60604
(312) 353-7226

Region VI
(Arkansas, Louisiana, New
Mexico, Oklahoma, Texas)
555 Griffin Square Building,
2nd Floor
Dallas, TX 75202
(214) 767-6971

Regions VII and VIII
(Colorado, Iowa, Kansas,
Missouri, Montana,
Nebraska, North Dakota, South
Dakota, Utah, Wyoming)
Federal Office Building
911 Walnut Street, Room 1500
Kansas City, MO 64106
(816) 374-2378

Regions IX and X
(Alaska, Arizona, California,

Hawaii, Idaho,
Nevada, Oregon, Washington)
450 Golden Gate Avenue
P.O. Box 36017
San Francisco, CA 94102
(415) 556-3178
(415) 556-4678

Federal Mediation and Conciliation Services (FMCS)

Regional Offices:

Southern Region
Virginia, Maryland (except two western counties) Tennessee; North Carolina; South Carolina; Georgia; Alabama; Florida; Mississippi, Louisiana; Arkansas; Kentucky; Texas (except for two western counties); Oklahoma; south and central Missouri; southern Illinois; southern Indiana; southern Ohio; southeast Kansas; West Virginia; and the Canal Zone)
1422 Peachtree Street, NW,
Suite 400
Atlanta, GA 30309

Western Region
(California; Nevada; Arizona; New Mexico; westernmost Texas; Hawaii, Guam; Alaska; Washington; Oregon; Colorado; Utah; Wyoming; Montana; Idaho; Nebraska; Kansas; Iowa; northern Missouri; American Samoa, and Wake Island)
Francisco Street
San Francisco, CA 94133
(415) 556-4670

Central Region
(Northern and central Illinois; Wisconsin; Minnesota; North Dakota; South Dakota; Michigan; and northern and central Ohio)
Insurance Exchange Building,
Room 1659
175 W. Jackson Blvd.
Chicago, IL 60604
(312) 353-7350

Eastern Region
(Maine, New Hampshire; Vermont; Connecticut; Rhode Island; Massachusetts; New York; Puerto Rico; the Virgin Islands; Pennsylvania; Delaware; New Jersey; westernmost Maryland; and two northern counties in West Virginia)
Jacob K. Javits Federal Building
26 Federal Plaza, Room 2937
New York, NY 10278
(212) 264-1000

Small Business Innovation Research (SBIR)

Program Representatives:

Department of Agriculture
Office of Grant and Program Systems
Department of Agriculture
West Auditors Bldg., Room 112
15th & Independence Avenue,
SW
Washington, DC 20251
(202) 475-5022

Department of Defense
Director, Small Business and Economic Utilization
Office of Secretary of Defense
Room 2A340-Pentagon
Washington, DC 20301
(202) 697-9383

Department of Education
SBIR Program Coordinator
Office of Educational Research and Improvement
Department of Education
Mail Stop 40
Washington, DC 20208
(202) 254-8247

Department of Energy
c/o SBIR Program Manager
U.S. Department of Energy
Washington, DC 20545
(301) 353-5867

Department of Health and Human Services
Director, Office of Small and Disadvantaged Business Utilization
Department of Health and Human Services
200 Independence Avenue, SW,
Room 513D
Washington, DC 20201
(202) 245-7300

Department of Interior
Chief Scientist
Bureau of Mines
U.S. Department of the Interior
2401 E Street, NW
Washington, DC 20241
(202) 634-1305

Department of Transportation
Director, Transportation System Center
Department of Transportation
Kendall Square
Cambridge, MA 02142
(614) 494-2222

Environmental Protection Agency
Office of Research and Development
Environmental Protection Agency

401 M Street, SW
Washington, DC 20460
(202) 382-5744

**National Aeronautics and
Space Administration**
National Aeronautics and
Space Administration
SBIR Office—Code RB-8
600 Independence Avenue, SW
Washington, DC 20546
(202) 755-2306

National Science Foundation
Mr. Ritchie Coryell
SBIR Program Managers
National Science Foundation
1800 G Street, NW
Washington, DC 20550
(202) 357-7527

**Nuclear Regulatory
Commission**
Office of Nuclear Regulatory
Research
Nuclear Regulatory
Commission
Washington, DC 20460
(301) 427-4301

**General Services
Administration**
Business Service Centers:

California
300 North Los Angeles Street
Los Angeles, CA 90012
(213) 688-3210
525 Market Street
San Francisco, CA 94105
(415) 454-9144

Colorado
Denver Federal Center
Building 41
Denver, CO 80225
(303) 234-2216

District of Columbia
Seventh and D Streets SW
Washington, DC 20407
(202) 472-1804

Georgia
75 Spring Street
Atlanta, GA 30303
(404) 221-5103

Illinois
230 South Dearborn Street
Chicago, IL 60604
(312) 353-5383

Massachusetts
John W. McCormack Post
Office and Courthouse
Boston, MA 02109
(617) 223-2868

Missouri
1500 East Bannister Road
Kansas City, MO 64131
(816) 926-7203

New York
26 Federal Plaza
New York, NY 10278
(212) 264-1234

Pennsylvania
9th and Market Streets
Philadelphia, PA 19107
(215) 597-9613

Texas
819 Taylor Street
Fort Worth, TX 76102
(817) 334-3284

Washington
440 Federal Building
915 Second Avenue
Seattle, WA 98174
(206) 442-5556

**Federal Trade Commission
(FTC)**
Regional Offices:
Room 13209, Federal Bldg.,
11000 Wilshire Blvd.
Los Angeles, CA 90024
(213) 209-7575

450 Golden Gate Avenue
Box 36005
San Francisco, CA 94102
(415) 556-1270

Room 1000, 1718 Peachtree
Street, NW, Atlanta, GA 30367
(404) 881-4836

Suite 1437, 55 E. Monroe Street
Chicago, IL 60603
(312) 353-4423.

Room 1301, 150 Causeway
Street Boston, MA 02114
(617) 223-6621

Room 2243-EB, Federal Bldg.,
26 Federal Plaza
New York, NY 10278
(212) 264-1207

Suite 500, The Mall Bldg.
118 St. Clair Avenue
Cleveland, OH 44114
(216) 522-4207

8303 Elmbrook Drive
Dallas, TX 75247
(214) 767-7050

28th Floor, Federal Bldg.
915 Second Avenue
Seattle, WA 98174
(206) 442-4655

1405 Curtis Street, Suite 2900
Denver, CO 80202
(303) 837-2271

Room 6324, 300 Ala Moana
Honolulu, HI 96850
546-5685

Offices of Small and Disadvantaged Business Utilization (OSDBU)

Directors:

Department of Agriculture
14th & Independence Avenue
SW, Room 127-W
Washington, DC 20520

Department of Commerce
14th & Constitution Avenue,
NW, Room 6411
Washington, DC 20230
(202) 377-1472

Department of Defense
The Pentagon, Room 2A330
Washington, DC 20307
(202) 697-1151

Department of the Air Force
The Pentagon, Room 4C255
Washington, DC 20330
(202) 697-4126

Department of the Army
The Pentagon, Room 2A712
Washington, DC 20301
(202) 697-2868

Department of Energy
1000 Independence Avenue, SW
Room 1E061
Washington, DC 20585
(202) 252-8201

Department of Health and Human Services
200 Independence Ave., SW
Room 513D
Washington, DC 20201
Telephone: (202) 245-7300

Department of Housing and Urban Development
7th and D Street, SW,
Room 10226
Washington, DC 20410
(202) 755-1428

Department of the Navy
Building 5, Crystal Plaza
Room 604
Washington, DC 20360
(202) 692-7122

Defense Logistics Agency
Cameron Station
Alexandria, VA 22314
(703) 274-6471

Department of Education
400 Maryland Avenue,
Room 3021
Washington, DC 20202
(202) 245-9582

Department of Interior
18th & C Streets, NW,
Room 2527
Washington, DC 20240
(202) 343-8493

Department of Justice
10th & Pennsylvania Avenue,
NW
Washington, DC 20530
(202) 724-6271

Department of Labor
200 Constitution Avenue, NW,
Room S-1004
Washington, DC 20210
(202) 523-9148

Department of State
2201 C Street, NW,
Room 513 (SA-6)
Washington, DC 20520
Telephone: (202) 235-9579

Department of Transportation
400 7th Street, SW,
Room 9412
Washington, DC 20590
(202) 426-1930

Department of the Treasury
15th & Pennsylvania Ave., NW
Room 1320, Main Treasury
Washington, DC 20220
(202) 566-9616

Agency for International Development
320 21st Street, NW
Washington, DC 20523
(202) 632-8244

Federal Maritime Commission
1100 L Street, NW, Room
10101
Washington, DC 20573
(202) 523-5900

Federal Emergency Management Agency
Federal Center Plaza
500 C Street, SW, Room 728
Washington, DC 20472
(202) 287-3826

General Services Administration
18th and F Streets, NW,
Room 6002
Washington, DC 20405
(202) 566-1021

International Communication Agency
1717 H Street, NW,
Room 613
Washington, DC 20547
(202) 653-5570

National Aeronautics and Space Administration
FB-10B-Code K

600 Independence Avenue, SW,
Room 116
Washington, DC 20456
(202) 453-2088

National Science Foundation
1800 G Street, NW,
Room 511-A
Washington, DC 20550
(202) 357-7464

**Nuclear Regulatory
Commission**
Mail Stop 7217 MNBB
Washington, DC 20550
(202) 492-4665

**U.S. Government Printing
Office**
North Capitol & H Streets, NW,
Room A 332
Washington, DC 20401
(202) 275-2470

Tennessee Valley Authority
1000 Commerce Union Bank
Building
Chattanooga, TN 37401
(615) 751-2624

Veterans Administration
811 Vermont Avenue, NW,
Room 310
Washington, DC 20420
(202) 389-3515

Franchise Rip-offs: Look Before You Leap: How to Avoid Franchise Rip-offs

Take this quiz. Franchising is (a) the surest route to the American dream, (b) a shortcut to financial disaster, (c) all of the above, (d) none of the above.

Need a hint? Consider this: For every franchisee who turns a modest investment into a fried chicken chain, another would-be entrepreneur dead-ends at his local burger haven. So the correct answer is (c): franchising is at once the safest of all business ventures and the one most fraught with risk.

The difference between success and failure is determined not by how the burgers are broiled or the chicken is fried—criteria used by inexperienced investors to judge franchise opportunities—but by the strength and track record of the franchisor and the terms of its franchise agreement. These critical indicators are spelled out in a document that is must reading for everyone thinking of buying a franchise.

"The best way to avoid franchise rip-offs—and to make an intelligent appraisal of franchise opportunities—is to carefully read the so-called disclosure document that franchisors must give to investors at least 10 business days before they take your money or ask you to sign a contract," says an attorney specializing in franchise practice with the law firm of Kaufmann, Caffey, Gildin, Rosenblum & Schaeffer. "The document provides a revealing glimpse of the franchisor's financial status and its operating procedures. There's no better indicator of precisely what the prospective franchisee will be getting, and not getting, in return for his investment."

With disclosure statements running 100 pages or more—and looking to the untutored eye like a document only a lawyer could love—where do you begin? What key passages offer revealing insights into the investment's true potential? How can you determine your rights and obligations?

Consider the following:

1. Review the franchisor's audited financial statements (at least three years must be given), paying particular attention to sales and earnings trends. Regardless of what the sales representative says, a franchise showing progressively weaker numbers hardly qualifies as a growth business.

"Because you'll be committing to a relationship that can continue for 20 years or more, you'll want to be convinced that the franchisor has the financial resources to provide critical support services over the long term," the attorney says. "For this reason, I'd be wary of a franchisor with a negative net worth as opposed to one with a net worth of, say, $20 million. Not that the former should necessarily be ruled out. Some of the best franchise opportunities are with newer, less established companies. But you have to understand that investing with them carries a greater level of risk."

2. Check for a history of litigation and bankruptcy proceedings against the company and its top management. A clear pattern of failed business, of fraud convictions, or of law suits with existing franchisees should be a red flag to potential investors. Ask your lawyer to seek additional information and call franchisees directly to see how they have fared with the company. Don't act unless you can be satisfied that the legal problems don't reflect poorly on the franchisor's offering.

3. Scrutinize the franchise contract (a copy of which must be attached to the disclosure document). This agreement, which establishes the ground rules for your relationship with the franchisor, can have the greatest impact on your profit potential.

With fair and reasonable contracts, both parties can prosper; not so with one-sided deals and outright rip-offs, where only the franchisor gains.

"The franchise concept, like how the burgers are cooked and marketed in a fast-food operation, may determine if the franchise is a good business," says attorney David C. Hjelmfelt, author of *Understanding Franchise Contracts*, "but the contract determines if the person running the business can make any money at it."

For example, the contract specifies the percentage of monthly gross sales that must be paid as royalties to the franchisor. Depending on the deal, this can range from 3 to 9 percent. While investors prefer the lowest percentages, anything from 3 to 7 percent is generally considered reasonable. But at the higher reaches—8 percent or more—the franchisee may find the royalty poses a severe hardship that threatens his ability to stay in business.

Is a high royalty an attempt to enrich the franchisor at the investor's expense? Perhaps. But does it rule out the franchise as a potential investment? Not necessarily. In many cases, franchise contracts are negotiable, allowing you and your attorney to hammer out a better deal than the stock agreement provides. This can be the best way to nip potential rip-offs in the bud and to shape a deal that gives you the best shot at financial success.

"Just how flexible the franchisor will be is often a function of how badly he wants to sell franchises," says a partner with the law firm of Jones, Day, Reavis & Pogue. "Generally, the most successful and established franchisors are the least flexible. But it never hurts to try and win concessions."

The following are key points for contract negotiations:

1. The sale of the franchise interests should be allowed with minimum interference by the franchisor. Once you've built a successful business, you'll want the right to sell it to others (and thus to cash in on your success). The franchisor, on the other hand, will want to limit ownership to qualified individuals who reflect well on the company and are capable of generating maximum earnings. The contract should reconcile these goals by identifying the reasons that a transfer of interests can be denied. This reduces the likelihood of arbitrary and unreasonable decisions.

2. When the franchise contract requires you to manage your unit according to the franchisor's operating manual—which generally covers store hours, employee dress codes, and service policies—revisions in the manual may force major changes in the business. Seek to make major changes subject to

mutual agreement. This provides a critical check against the franchisor's power to reach in and alter the course of your business.

3. Check for clauses protecting against the sale of competitive franchise outlets in the same trading area. You'll want to make certain that your exclusive territory is large enough to sustain a profitable business. In a classic rip-off, the franchisor is more concerned with selling units than in supporting them and helping them succeed. Unless the company is willing to provide for reasonable competitive protection, investors may find themselves competing in a hopelessly saturated market.

"The prospective franchisee must ask himself, am I looking to buy something with exclusive rights or just the authority to use a franchise concept along with others in the community," says the Jones, Day partner. "In most cases, the small business person investing money in a venture will want the former. Just how much exclusivity he gets may be negotiated."

4. Make certain all of your rights, including staff and management training, are written into the contract. Do not rely on verbal agreements.

"And never," warns the attorney with Kaufmann, Caffey, "accept a salesman's *guarantee* as to how much money you'll earn. Legitimate franchisors don't make that kind of promise. They can't. They know there are too many variables in any franchise venture."

Incorporating a Small Business

Choosing the Location

The majority of small and medium-sized businesses, especially those whose trade is local in nature, find it advisable to obtain their charter from the state in which the greatest part of their business is conducted.

Out-of-state, or "foreign," incorporation often results in the additional payments of taxes and fees in another jurisdiction. Moreover, under the laws of many states the property of a foreign corporation is subject to less favorable treatment, especially in the area of attachment of corporate assets. This legal difference could prove especially hazardous to a small business.

On the other hand, you should look into possible benefits to be gained from incorporation in another state. Such factors as state taxes, restrictions on corporate powers and lines of business in which a company may engage, capital requirements, restrictions upon foreign corporations in your state, and so forth, should be taken into consideration in selecting the state of incorporation. For example, you should be aware that some states require a foreign corporation to obtain a certificate to do business in their state. Without such certification the corporation may be deprived of the right to sue in those states.

The fee or organization tax charged for incorporation varies greatly from state to state.

Certificate of Incorporation

Generally, the first step in the required procedure is preparation, by the incorporators, of a "certificate of incorporation." Most states used to require that the certificate be prepared by three or more legally qualified persons, but the modern trend is to require only one incorporator. An incorporator may, but not necessarily must, be an individual who will ultimately own stock in the corporation.

For purposes of expediting the filing of

organizers. They typically elect their successors and resign at the meeting of the incorporators.

Many states have a standard certificate of incorporation form which may be used by small businesses. Copies of this form may be obtained from the designated state official who grants charters and, in some states, from local stationers as well. The following information is usually required:

1. The corporate name of the company. Legal requirements generally are (a) that the name chosen must not be so similar to the name of any other corporation authorized to do business in the state and (b) that the name chosen must not be deceptive so as to mislead the public. In order to be sure that the name you select is suitable, check out the availability of the name through the designated state official in each state in which you intend to do business before drawing up a certificate of incorporation. This check can be made through a service company. In some states, there is a procedure for reserving a name.

2. Purposes for which the corporation is formed. Several states permit very broad language, such as "the purpose of the corporation is to engage in any lawful act or activity for which corporations may be organized." However, most states require more specific language in setting forth the purposes of the corporation. Even where state law does not require it, the better practice is to employ a "specific object" clause which spells out in broad descriptive terms the projected business enterprise. At the same time take care to allow for the possibility of territorial, market, or product expansion. In other words, the language should be broad enough to allow for expansion and yet specific enough to convey a clear idea of the projected enterprise.

The use of a specific object clause, even where not required by state law, is advisable for several reasons. It will convey to financial institutions a clearer picture of the corporate enterprise and will prevent problems in qualifying the corporation to do business in other jurisdictions. Reference books or certificates of existing corporations can provide examples of such clauses.

3. Length of time for which the corporation is being formed. This may be a period of years or may be perpetual.

4. Names and addresses of incorporators. In certain states one or more of the incorporators is required to be a resident of the state within which the corporation is being organized.

5. Location of the registered office of the corporation in the state of incorporation. If you decide to obtain your charter from another state, you will be required to have an office there. However, instead of establishing an office, you may appoint an agent in that state to act for you. The agent will be required only to represent the corporation, to maintain a duplicate list of stockholders, and to receive or reply to suits brought against the corporation in the state of incorporation.

6. Maximum amount and type of capital stock which the corporation wishes authorization to issue. The proposed capital structure of the corporation should be set forth, including the number and classification of shares and the rights, preferences, and limitations of each class of stock.

7. Capital required at time of incorporation. Some states require that a specified percentage of the par value of the capital stock be paid in cash and

banked to the credit of the corporation before the certificate of incorporation is submitted to the designated state official for approval.

8. Provisions for preemptive rights, if any, to be granted to the stockholders and restrictions, if any, on the transfer of shares.
9. Provisions for regulation of the internal affairs of the corporation.
10. Names and addresses of persons who will serve as directors until the first meeting of stockholders or until their successors are elected and qualify.
11. The right to amend, alter, or repeal any provisions contained in the certificate of incorporation. This right is generally statutory, reserved to a majority or two-thirds of the stockholders. Still, it is customary to make it clear in the certificate.

If the designated state official determines that the name of the proposed corporation is satisfactory, that the certificate contains the necessary information and has been properly executed, and that there is nothing in the certificate or the corporation's proposed activities that violates state law or public policy, the charter will be issued.

Officers and Stockholders

Next, the stockholders must meet to complete the incorporation process. This meeting is extremely important. It is usually conducted by an attorney or someone familiar with corporate organizational procedure.

In the meeting the corporate bylaws are adopted and a board of directors is elected. This board of directors in turn will elect the officers who actually will have charge of the operations of the corporation—for example, the president, secretary, and treasurer. In small corporations, members of the board of directors frequently are elected as officers of the corporation.

Bylaws

The bylaws of the corporation may repeat some of the provisions of the charter and state statute but usually cover such items as the following:

1. Location of the principal office and other offices of the corporation.
2. Time, place, and required notice of annual and special meetings of stockholders. Also, the necessary quorum and voting privileges of the stockholders.
3. Number of directors, their compensation, their term of office, the method of electing them, and the method of creating or filling vacancies on the board of directors.
4. Time and place of the regular and special directors' meetings, as well as the notice and quorum requirements.
5. Method of selecting officers, their titles, duties, terms of office, and salaries.
6. Issuance and form of stock certificates, their transfers, and their control in the company books.
7. Dividends, when and by whom they may be declared.
8. The fiscal year, the corporate seal, the authority to sign checks, and the preparation of the annual statement.
9. Procedure for amending the bylaws.

Credit: U.S. Small Business Administration

More on Corporations: Corporate Formation, Capitalization, and Control

Here are some of the factors and alternatives you will want to consider in organizing a new corporation.

Formation

Once a state of incorporation has been selected, based on the principal place of business of the new corporation, corporate laws, and tax considerations, the incorporator signs the articles of incorporation, which are filed in the office of the secretary of state. To draft the articles, one needs the name of the corporation, its address, the name of the agent for service of process and his address, the number of shares of corporate stock authorized to be issued, and the terms of any special classes of shares. Often, a large number of shares, say 100,000, is authorized in the articles so as to provide flexibility in later activities.

The corporate name should be checked before filing, to assure that it is not already in use by another party, and it may be advisable to conduct a name search among fictitious business name filings, in the phone directory or elsewhere, in the locale where the corporation is to do business to assure it is not confusingly similar to that of a business already being done, either as a corporation, a partnership, or otherwise.

Once the articles of incorporation have been filed, the corporation is in existence. The incorporator may then elect a board of directors, who in turn adopt bylaws and corporate minutes authorizing the opening of bank accounts and electing officers of the corporation.

Under many state laws, there must be at least three directors, or if there are fewer shareholders there may be as many directors as shareholders. There will be a president, treasurer, and secretary of the corporation, which in many states can be the same person, and there may be a chairman, one or more vice-presidents, or other officers you may wish to designate. A federal tax identification number should be applied for, and there may be local business licenses to be obtained.

The bylaws will specify a time and place for the annual meeting, but corporate activities can be authorized by telephone conference meetings in many states, or by written actions of the directors, signed by all directors, rather than by actual meetings. The bylaws may also contain a provision requiring any compensation or expenses found unreasonable by the IRS to be repaid to the corporation. If included in the initial bylaws, this can be an inconspicuous provision of later importance in attempting to avoid undesirable tax consequences.

The officers run the corporation day to day and are elected by the directors, who make policy decisions and are elected by the shareholders, who own the corporation. The officers can be removed and replaced by the directors, who in turn can be removed and replaced by the shareholders.

Capitalization and Control

Once formed, the corporation can issue stock. Corporate securities filings must ordinarily be made upon issuance of stock in the corporation; these may be very simple state filings where stock is being sold to a few people within one state for cash at the same price per share, or they can be very complex if a public offering is involved.

Often, there is only one class of stock, which is sold to the owners of the corporation in exchange for, and in proportion to, their initial cash investment. Sometimes this initial cash investment is relatively small, and in addition one or more of the shareholders make loans to the corporation, or guarantee bank loans, to provide its initial operating capital. Such loans should be represented by promissory notes bearing interest, in order to demonstrate to the Internal Revenue Service that they are genuine loans. These loans can later be repaid by the corporation without being taxed as dividends or compensation.

However, the IRS may argue that such repayments should be treated as taxable dividends rather than true repayments of loans, on the ground that the loans were not made on terms on which a third party would lend money to a corporation. This is particularly likely if the loans are made in proportion to the shareholdings of the corporation. You will need to decide how much each shareholder will invest in the corporation for stock, and how much if any will be lent to the corporation.

There is often only one class of stock issued in a corporation, but it is sometimes desirable to provide in the articles of incorporation for a second class of stock with specified rights. For example, a preferred stock can provide that its investors are repaid on redemption (mandatory or at either party's option at specified times) before repayment of the common stockholders' investment, but only dollar for dollar rather than sharing in any growth in value of the corporation. They may have specified dividend rights, cumulative or not. This can be used by investors wanting a limited but preferred return or by parents who are only interested in receiving a small return of their investment, leaving the greater increase in the value of the business for their children who own the common stock.

The voting power of the shareholders is specified in the articles of incorporation. For example, all the voting power could be given to the preferred shareholders, with the common shareholders having no vote. Or the reverse could be done. Or two classes of common stock, A and B, could be created, which are exactly alike in their economic interests in the company, but one of which has all the voting power and the other none, or only the power to vote on specified matters, such as sale of all of the assets of the corporation. A great variety in mechanisms for corporate control can be devised in this way.

Other types of stock rights, such as warrants or options, can also be issued, and can be made convertible into stock on certain terms and conditions and for specified prices. One class of stock may also be made convertible into another class at a specified price or time and on specified terms.

Irrevocable proxies or voting trusts can also be used to confer upon some shareholders the right to vote the shares of others, but these are subject to particular limitations and requirements which differ in the various states.

The shareholders, directors, and officers of the corporation have fiduciary duties to one another such that if the power of control is used to improperly disadvantage one group of shareholders versus another, that group may have a basis to seek damages from the others or even to dissolve the corporation.

Credit: Jones, Day, Reavis & Pogue

Proprietorship, Partnership, Corporation: Which Should You Be?

SEE ALSO *Corporation, Partnership*

The three basic forms of business organization—proprietorship, partnership, corporation—offer a mixed bag of tax, legal, and operating features. Deciding which one to choose should be based not on a single factor but on the total of the benefits and drawbacks.

"All too often, small business owners consider only one criterion, be it protection against personal liability or the ability to claim income tax deductions," says a partner with accountants Deloitte, Haskins & Sells. "While these may be genuine concerns, focusing on a narrow range of issues blinds the entrepreneur to the widest range of options.

"For example, it is often said that if you want to shield personal assets from business losses, you must form a standard corporation. But that may be simplistic. If the venture throws off substantial losses in the first years of operation, the entrepreneur may want to capture some of this red ink on his personal tax return, thus offsetting income from other sources. A hybrid entity, the S corporation, may be the ideal choice because it combines limited liability with profit-and-loss flow-through. The point is that by examining all of the issues, the owner is likely to select the most appropriate type of business organization."

Accountants and attorneys offer the following guidelines:

1. Stability: While the loss of a principal may cause an unincorporated business to terminate or dissolve, the corporation survives both deaths and retirements. As a separate legal entity, it has a life of its own. This continuity can help to cement strong relationships with customers, suppliers, and distributors.

"But those who prefer the partnership form may be able to achieve similar results," a CPA notes. "Although the partnership may terminate from a tax standpoint at the death of a partner, it may continue to do business under the same name if this is so provided in the partnership agreement."

2. Fringe Benefits: Once shunned by many for their relatively low limits on contributions to tax-deductible retirement plans, proprietorships and partnerships have gained virtual parity with corporations. All forms now allow for personal contributions of up to $30,000 annually in defined contribution plans.

"All those who in the past automatically

incorporated to take advantage of the more liberal retirement plans—as did many professionals—must now base their decision on other factors," says a partner with the law firm of Ballon, Stoll, Itzler. "The corporation is no longer superior in this regard."

3. Tax on Profits: Corporate profits are subject to double taxation, first in the form of income tax on the company's earnings and subsequently on the dividends paid to the shareholders. Proprietorships, partnerships, and S corporations avoid this by allocating profits directly to the owners or shareholders. The tax at the corporate level is eliminated.

4. Availability of Capital: As a general rule, investors and lending institutions prefer to work with corporations.

"Banks think of corporations—as compared to unincorporated firms—as more disciplined, more responsible, and generally better managed operations," explains the Ballon, Stoll partner. "This can have a strong positive influence on the decision to finance a small business."

5. Transfer of Interests: Selling or gifting business interests for estate planning, tax purposes, or capital gain is easier with the corporate form. To accomplish this, the entrepreneur need only transfer shares of stock. But with unincorporated forms, personal interests may be hard to subdivide or may require the approval of the partnership.

"As a business matures, the features that first attracted it to one of the legal forms may become less and less important," says the Deloitte, Haskins & Sells partner. "Management may want to make a change somewhere down the road. One wise tax-planning strategy, for example, is to start out on an unincorporated basis—in order to claim early losses on personal returns—and then incorporate once the business moves into the black. But as always, the tax benefits must be viewed in the context of the other advantages and disadvantages of proprietorships, partnerships, and corporations."

Seek professional assistance in selecting and structuring the company's legal entity.

Business Organization— Comparing the Options

Advantages of the Sole Proprietorship

Ease of formation. There is less formality and fewer legal restrictions associated with establishing a sole proprietorship. It needs little or no governmental approval and is usually less expensive than a partnership or corporation.

Sole ownership of profits. The proprietor is not required to share profits with anyone.

Control and decision making vested in one owner. There are no co-owners or partners to consult. (Except possibly your spouse.)

Flexibility. Management is able to respond quickly to business needs in the form of day-to-day management decisions as governed by various laws and good sense.

Relative freedom from government control and special taxation.

Disadvantages of the Sole Proprietor

Unlimited liability. The individual proprietor is responsible for the full amount of business debts, which may exceed the proprietor's total investment. This liability extends to all the proprietor's assets, such as house and car. Additional problems of liability, such as physical loss or personal injury, may be lessened by obtaining proper insurance coverage.

Unstable business life. The enterprise may be crippled or terminated upon illness or death of the owner.

Less available capital, ordinarily, than in other types of business organizations.

Relative difficulty in obtaining long-term financing.

Relatively limited viewpoint and experience. This is more often the case with one owner than with several.

Advantages of the Corporation

Limitations of the stockholder's liability to a fixed amount of investment. However, do not confuse corporate liability with appropriate liability insurance considerations.

Ownership is readily transferable.

Separate legal existence.

Stability and relative permanence of existence. For example, in the case of illness, death, or other cause for loss of a principal (officer or owner), the corporation continues to exist and do business.

Relative ease of securing capital in large amounts and from many investors. Capital may be acquired through the issuance of various stocks and long-term bonds. There is relative ease in securing long-term financing from lending institutions by taking advantage of corporate assets and often personal assets of stockholders and principals of guarantors. (Personal guarantees are very often required by lenders.)

Delegated authority. Centralized control is secured when owners delegate authority to hired managers, although they are often one and the same.

The ability of the corporation to draw on the expertise and skills of more than one individual.

Disadvantages of the Corporation

Activities limited by the charter and by various laws. However, some states do allow very broad charters.

Manipulation. Minority stockholders are sometimes exploited.

Extensive government regulations and required local, state, and federal reports.

Less incentive if manager does not share in profits.

Expense of forming a corporation.

Double tax—income tax on corporate net income (profit) and on individual salary and dividends.

Advantages of the Partnership

Ease of formation. Legal formalities and expenses are few compared with the requirements for creation of a corporation.

Direct rewards. Partners are motivated to apply their best abilities by direct sharing of the profits.

Growth and performance facilitated. It is possible to obtain more capital and a better range of skills than in a sole proprietorship.

Flexibility. A partnership may be relatively more flexible in the decision-making process than a corporation. But it may be less so than a sole proprietorship.

Relative freedom from government control and special taxation.

Disadvantages of the Partnership

Unlimited liability of at least one partner. Insurance considerations such as those mentioned in the proprietorship section apply here also.

Unstable life. Elimination of any partner constitutes automatic dissolution of partnership. However, operation of the business can continue based on the right of survivorship and possible creation of a new partnership. Partnership insurance might be considered.

Relative difficulty in obtaining large sums of capital. This is particularly true of long-term financing when compared to a corporation. However, by using individual partners' assets, opportunities are probably greater than in a proprietorship.

Firm bound by the acts of just one partner as agent.

Difficulty of disposing of partnership interest. The buying out of a partner may be difficult unless specifically arranged for in the written agreement.

Credit: U.S. Small Business Administration and Antonio M. Olmi, Business Management Specialist

Partnerships: For Better or for Worse

Most partnerships get started for the wrong reasons. Two guys just out of college flirt with taking jobs in the corporate arena, and then decide to start up a company of their own. And why not? One of them knows engineering and production, and the other is strong in marketing and finance. Their skills are a perfect match. And what's more, they're best friends—the chemistry is right. How can they go wrong?

Let me count the ways. First of all, sure,

chemistry is crucial in a business partnership. But the chemistry between these two guys is based on friendship, not on business. And friendship and business are not one and the same. In fact, the criteria for picking a business partner are vastly different from the criteria for picking friends. You pick friends, whether you know it or not, because they're like you—they think like you, they act like you.

That's exactly what you want to avoid in a business partner. But before I tell you what to look for in a business partner, let's look at why most people choose a partner in the first place. The obvious reasons apply: you want someone who'll complement your skills, or you want someone who can bring cash into the deal, or you want someone to share the risk. However, the main reason two or more people team up to start a business is much more basic and much less discussed. You see, there's a great deal of anxiety involved at the front end of a business. And more than wanting someone to share the risks with, people bring in a partner to alleviate that anxiety.

And let me share another little secret I've learned: at the outset of any partnership, you always think the other partner is smarter than you are—that he's bringing more than 50 percent into the deal. After all, he knows something that you don't. Right? All those things, like sales and marketing and distribution—he knows about them. You just know engineering. You'd be lost without him.

Of course, later this dynamic changes. But in the beginning, the anxiety is often just too great for most people to go it alone. So they bring in a partner that they think is half Einstein and half Iacocca.

But if alleviating anxiety isn't the ideal reason for bringing in a partner, what is? Since most people aren't Superman, they need one or more people to round out a business plan. And partnerships find it easier to find financing than individuals. Venture capi-

talists definitely prefer partnerships over go-it-alone entrepreneurs, because they don't like putting all their eggs into one basket. If something happens to the main entrepreneur, they want someone in the deal they can fall back on. It's safer.

In looking for a partner, you want to find someone who fills in the rest of the puzzle—someone you can work with, but not necessarily someone who'll become your best friend. So to avoid getting the wrong partner, I recommend you follow these guidelines (before I close, I'll tell you how to find the right partner):

- *Look into Past Partnerships.* Does the person have a history of business partnerships? Do former partners recommend him? And remember, it's always helpful to speak to one or two people who don't necessarily like your potential partner. While you should take what they say with a grain of salt, their candidness can be very telling.
- *Check the Track Record.* What is this person's actual experience and training? Does he or she really know the business? Keep in mind that a past business failure shouldn't automatically eliminate a potential partner. (One entrepreneur I know actually prefers partners who've experienced a business failure. One bankruptcy, he feels, is more valuable than two years at the Harvard Business School.) But avoid anyone who makes up excuses for failure or puts the blame on someone else.
- *Examine a Potential Partner's Life-style.* Meet a potential partner's family. The way he or she acts with a spouse is an indicator of how he or she will act in a partnership. Further, it helps (but is not absolutely necessary) if you get along with his or her spouse. Also, avoid a partner who's obviously living above his means. When their

bills come due, you don't want a young business to be the place they look for cash.

- *Talk About the Business.* At the outset, it's essential that your goals for the business match. While these goals will doubtless grow apart over time, in the beginning, you want to make sure that you're both going into the same business.
- *Look for More than Just a Complement in Talents.* While you want someone whose talents complement your own, you also want someone whose background, personality, and business philosophy complement yours. The most successful companies are formed by two partners whose combined abilities give depth to the enterprise and differing backgrounds serve as a buffer against excesses of any kind.

Now that the basic guidelines are established, how do you structure the deal? Most partnerships start out as fifty-fifty arrangements, which in my opinion is the worst of all choices. Someone has to be in charge, and that someone has to have enough clout to make the decisions. But since fifty-fifty is the way most partnerships begin, let's play it out a little. As soon as a business starts making money, it's almost invariable that one dominant partner will emerge. Partnerships, by their nature, are stressful relationships. Two people never see things the same way, especially when money is involved. And the bigger the money, the bigger the disagreements. In a fifty-fifty partnership, this can become downright bloody.

One alternative I like to recommend is to bring in a "godfather." That's a forty-nine-forty-nine partnership, with 2 percent held (in stock or in exercisable options) by an outside person who serves as a referee and has the power to step in to make the decisions if

he has to. I've been godfather to several companies, and I've never had to exercise the options. The very fact that someone from the outside might step in to make key decisions helped the partners resolve their problems.

Another alternative, and I recommend this to all entrepreneurs, whether they're in partnerships or not, is to establish a strong board of directors in the very beginning. An outside group of involved peers can often spot and head off problems before they begin.

While many consultants swear by elaborate partnership agreements, I believe quite the opposite. The meat of what goes into partnership agreements—who's responsible for what—should already be down in a business plan. Beyond that, all that's really necessary is a basic buy/sell agreement. From the very start, it should be agreed that if one partner ever wants to buy the other one out, the other has the option to buy the first out *at the same price!* It's funny how this one little piece of paper does more for clarifying a business arrangement than some twenty- and thirty- page partnership agreements that don't include it.

Further, before entering into a business partnership, make sure the opportunity is a strong one, because even the greatest partnership will have a hard time succeeding in a marginal situation. It's much better to bring a marginal partner into a great opportunity than to bring a great partner into a marginal opportunity.

Of course the optimal situation is to have a great partner in a can't-miss deal. But while every deal is going to be different, let me share a constant about partnerships. It's well documented that the perfect partnership pairs Mr. Inside with Mr. Outside—an engineering and production man (Mr. Inside) who stays behind the scenes, and a sales and marketing man (Mr. Outside) who gets all of the attention. One example of this is the partnership that began Apple Computer. Steve Wozniak was Mr. Inside, while Steven Jobs remains the quintessential Mr. Outside. (You'll remember that once Apple took off, Jobs emerged as the dominant partner, and Wozniak eventually severed ties with the company. Then Jobs completed the entrepreneurial cycle by being forced out by professional management.)

But while America has no shortage of Mr. Outsides, it's the Mr. Insides that are hard to find. The main reason for this is that entrepreneurs simply don't know where to look. Given the following matrix for potential partners, entrepreneurs will make the wrong pick every time:

	Lazy	Energetic
Dumb		
Bright	X	

The natural choice is "Bright" and "Energetic." But the right choice is "Bright" and "Lazy." Let me explain. By picking a bright and energetic partner, an entrepreneur is picking someone who is too much like him or herself. Put two entrepreneurs together in one business and sparks are guaranteed to fly, because the hardest thing in the world for an entrepreneur to do is to give up control. And, except in the rarest of situations, control has to rest with one person.

That's why a bright and lazy partner makes the perfect Mr. Inside. He or she can quickly assimilate information and can delegate jobs and authority well. Further, he or she will serve as a buffer between the entrepreneur and the organization.

That doesn't necessarily mean that Mr. Inside enjoys the role. Partnerships always involve competition. And competition brings stress. An electronics company I worked with several years ago fit this situation exactly. Mr. Outside would bring in orders that were impossible to ship. Mr. Inside would be furious, but he'd get it into his head that he was going to "ship the damn orders and show that s.o.b." And he'd do it. And the business thrived on account of it.

Of course, this kind of situation can only go on for so long. These two guys, who'd once been close friends, really came to despise one another. But while the partnership, and the friendship, were eventually casualties, the synergy and competition between them built a $100,000,000 company in a matter of years.

And that's my final point. While partnerships in general have a poor track record (I've heard that as many as 70 percent fail within the first two years), the companies they build very often survive and prosper. And more often than not, these companies would have never existed if they didn't begin with the complement of talents that only a partnership can provide.

Credit: *Entrepreneurial Manager's Newsletter*, February 1986, Vol. 7, Issue 5, from Center for Entrepreneurial Management, New York

Incubators Nurture New Businesses

Growing businesses from infancy to independence—that's the idea behind the network of "business incubators" now springing up across the nation. Designed to give new ventures their first lease on life, incubators bring together under one roof all the elements crucial to successful business start-ups.

"We draw fledgling entrepreneurs out of their basements and garages and into controlled environments structured for the care and feeding of new businesses," says the executive director of the National Business Incubation Association (NBIA). "Typically, the entrepreneurs work together in facilities that provide them with inexpensive space, shared support services, and consulting expertise that can guide them through the most treacherous years of business formation."

Sponsored by private investors, universities, or government agencies, incubators vary widely in their objectives and fee structures. Those operated on a venture-capital basis may limit admission to promising growth companies, in which the sponsors take an equity stake (generally 20 to 50 percent of the stock) in exchange for the space, services, and management assistance. The aim here is to profit handsomely as the business expands, increases in value, and ultimately goes public.

Nonprofit incubators take a more charitable approach, operating to provide consulting opportunities for the academic community or to attract and stimulate local industry. Most have liberal entry requirements—insisting only that tenants be new businesses—and charge rents or fees rather than taking equity positions.

"We thought that the best way to get new business in this area was to grow our own," says the manager of the Maple City Business and Technology Center, a business incubator. "That meant creating a facility that would give new ventures a head start on the road to success. To do this, our incubator offers entrepreneurs a full-service business facility at below-market rents as well as one-stop shopping for business information. Located on the premises is a service core including the chamber of commerce, the small business development corporation, a SCORE chapter, and the local zoning administrator. Tenants can walk across the hall for all the advice they need."

Pooled on-site services distinguish incubators from traditional office buildings. Rather than each tenant procuring its own secretarial staff, computers, and photocopying equipment, the incubator provides these facilities on a joint basis, allowing the tenants to pay for these services as they are used.

"This is critical because it reduces the need for working capital, one of the major reasons for business failure," says the NBIA director. "Cash—always a precious commodity in new businesses—can be put to work in building the business rather than supporting costly overhead.

"Equally important, incubators make management assistance available to the tenants. This can be business-school professors, a consulting firm, or experienced entrepreneurs. They'll provide advice on everything from business organization to production techniques to the preparation of business plans. With this support, it is hoped that the business will eventually outgrow the incubator's limited space and will graduate to a facility of its own."

The president of a company that makes mobile pet shelters appears to be on his way.

"I chose to start my business in an incubator for two reasons. First, I was not well versed in business operations so I welcomed the opportunity to get advice and recommendations on how to make my company successful. Second, the costs of space and services here are at least 60 percent below that of general market rates. I've only been in this facility for four months, but sales are already going quite well. It's safe to say I wouldn't be this far along without the incubator."

Entrepreneurs seeking the location of the nearest business incubator (there are more than 140) may write to the National Business Incubation Association, 114 North Hanover Street, Carlisle, Pennsylvania 17013. Be sure to compare several facilities, checking that rents and other forms of payment are commensurate with the services provided.

"Perhaps the greatest benefit of incubators is that they enable entrepreneurs to share their experiences and to encourage one another," says an executive with the Economic Development Council of Richmond, Virginia. "It takes entrepreneurs out of isolation and into a cooperative environment."

WHERE TO FIND IT

Inventors' Associations

Inventors' Associations provide advice on a new product development, idea evaluation, etc. They frequently publish newsletters so inventors can keep in touch with one another and with the new trends in engineering design. They also advertise inventions. Listed below are some of these associations. You can use these associations to talk with people "who have gone through it all before" and can give advice on other sources of help.

American Society of Inventors
134 Narberth Avenue
Room 101
Narberth, PA 19072

California Inventors' Council
Box 2096
Sunnyvale, CA 94087

Central Florida Inventors' Club
2511 Edgewater Drive
Orlando, FL 32804

Inventors' Assistance League
345 West Cypress
Glendale, CA 91204

Inventors of California/
National Innovation Workshop
P.O. Box 158
Rheem Valley, CA 94570

Inventors' Workshop
International
Box 251,
Tarzana, CA 91356
 and
32–22 92nd Street
Queens, NY 11369

Minnesota Inventors' Congress
Box 71
Redwood Falls, MN 56283

Mississippi Society of Scientists
& Inventors
Box 2244
Jackson, MS 39205

Oklahoma Inventors' Congress
Box 53043
Oklahoma City, OK 73162

Technology Transfer Society
11720 W. Pico Boulevard
Los Angeles, CA 90064

Credit: U.S. Small Business Administration

Life-Cycle Financing: Where to Find the Money to Start and Grow Your Own Business

"If only I had the money."

With that wistful statement, millions of frustrated entrepeneurs dream of starting a business of their own. Blessed with a bright idea and the will to make it succeed, all that stands in their way is the lack of capital.

They're not alone. Others get into business only to find that they don't have enough cash to make it expand. No money for inventory, equipment, or staff. The problem is universal: at every stage of a company's life cycle, from start-up to maturity, money is both the obstacle to growth and the fuel to propel it.

Whether you find capital readily available or a scarce commodity depends in large measure on when and where you look for it. Although the picture may at times look bleak, various sources of capital are available through the key stages of a company's life cycle. Providing you know whom to contact and how to base your appeal, you may never find yourself saying "If I only had the money."

Consider this life-cycle financing scenario:

1. Start-up

The business, now in its infancy, has little more than a prototype product or service, no sales, and no customers. Capital is required to move from conceptual to market-oriented operations and will be used for market research, product samples, and staffing.

Because this is a high-risk stage from which many companies never emerge, commercial bankers are rarely willing to put their money on the line. They are, by tradition, a conservative lot accustomed to lending only after the business has established a track record. Instead, you'll have to turn to venture capitalists. These specialists in high-risk financing provide seed capital in return for a hefty chunk of the company's equity— from 20 to 60 percent of the stock.

Although you may chafe at surrendering so much of your fledgling business, this may be the only way to secure the necessary funding. Conventional wisdom holds that it is preferable to have part ownership in a successful venture than to retain all the stock in a business that never leaves the drawing board. A hard point to argue with.

Venture capitalists range from individual investors to investment groups and subsidiaries of commercial banks.

"Although your bank's local lending officer is likely to reject a request for start-up funding, you should inquire if the bank has a venture-capital arm," says a partner with the financial-institutions group of Jones, Day, Reavis & Pogue, a major law firm. "If the answer is 'yes'—and most of the big banks now have venture-capital operations—you may find that while one banking door is closed, another is wide open."

(A comprehensive list of more than 600 venture capitalists, including names, addresses, telephone numbers, and investment criteria, is published in *The Guide to Venture Capital Sources*, available from Venture Economics, P.O. Box 348, Wellesley, Massachusetts 02181.)

Should professional venture capitalists prove uninterested in your business concept, you may hit paydirt with so-called informal capitalists, including friends, relatives, and local business owners looking to invest in start-up companies. With the entrepreneurial boom now sweeping the nation, many affluent individuals are moving away from the stock market to real estate and venture-capital investments. This may be the ideal source for the first $50,000 to $250,000 of capital, enough to open the company's doors and bring its first offerings to market.

2. First Stage

But you're not out of the woods yet. If it's at all typical, your company is still losing money and needs additional capital for inventory, facilities, and promotion. Here again, venture capitalists are the most likely source (the company is still in a high-risk embryonic stage) for the next $1 million or more of equity capital. But now your position is somewhat stronger. With the business generating modest sales and indicating that it can succeed in the marketplace, you may be able to interest previously reluctant financing sources while at the same time negotiating for a better equity split (giving away substantially less than 50 percent of the stock). While the informal capitalists may have claimed some equity, they generally settle for less than professional investors.

3. Second Stage

This signals the all-important shift from equity to debt capital. You can now raise money without giving up stock or other ownership interests.

At this stage, the company is profitable, boasts a significant customer base, and needs capital for expansion rather than survival.

Cash sources include banks and commercial finance companies. Although your firm may not yet be a prime-rate borrower, it should be able to secure financing for limited expansion geared to clearly identified objectives. With increasing competition in today's banking marketplace, institutions that once shied away from companies with limited track records or marginal lending ratios (the most common ratio measures debt to worth, with 3:1 generally considered favorable) are now finding ways to finance these ventures.

In another second-stage option, asset-based lending, the loan is secured by the company's existing assets, including real estate, equipment, and accounts receivable. A pledge against the owner's personal assets may also be required.

4. Third Stage

By now the company has strengthened its operations and proven itself as a worthy borrower. The key transition in this stage is from piecemeal financing to the initiation of a comprehensive banking relationship. In exchange for assigning your account to the bank, you can demand creative solutions to your financial needs.

"For a company concerned with fluctuating interest rates, we might structure a fixed-rate match-funded loan," a Fleet National Bank vice-president explains. "With this type of financing the bank actually goes out and acquires funds from depositors specifically for that loan. It pays the investor a fixed rate and passes that on, plus a markup, to the borrower. For a match-funded loan of $1 million, the interest rate would be prime plus several points and the term would be from five to eight years. During this period the borrower is protected from rising interest rates."

Regardless of the company's age or its stage in the financing cycle, it is always a good idea to shop for the best terms, whether they be from bankers, finance companies, or venture capitalists. Use whatever strength your company has—be it a promising idea or several years of sharply rising profits—to negotiate a favorable deal.

Management by Objectives: Planning and Goal Setting for Small Business

Traditionally, people have worked according to job descriptions that list the *activities* of the job. The Management by Objectives (MBO) approach, on the other hand, stresses *results*.

Let's look at an example. Suppose that you have a credit manager and that his or her job description simply says that the credit manager supervises the credit operations of the company. The activities of the credit manager are then listed. Under MBO, the credit manager could have five or six goals covering important aspects of the work. One goal might be to increase credit sales enough to support a 15-percent increase in sales.

The traditional job description for a personnel specialist might include language about conducting the recruiting program for your company. Under MBO, the specialist's work might be covered in five or six goals—one which could be "recruit five new employees in specified categories by July 1."

Thus, MBO looks for results, not activities. With MBO, you view the job in terms of what it should achieve. Activity is never the essential element. It is merely an intermediate step leading to the desired result.

What Business Am I In?

In making long-range plans, the first question you ought to think about is "what business am I in?" Is the definition you have of your business right for today's market? Are there emerging customer needs that will require a changed definition of your business next year?

For example, one owner-manager's business was making metal trash cans. When sales began to fall off, the owner was forced to re-examine the business. To regain lost sales and continue to grow, the owner redefined the product as metal containers and developed a marketing plan for that product.

How you view your business will provide the framework for your planning with respect to markets, product development, buildings and equipment, financial needs, and staff size.

Your long-range objectives for your business will be the cornerstone in the MBO program for your company. At a minimum, they must be clearly communicated to your managers; however, for a truly vital program your managers should have a part in formulating these long-range goals. Your managers will base their short-range goals on these objectives. If they have had a role in establishing the long-range objectives, they will be more committed to achieving them.

The Complete MBO Program

Management by Objectives may be used in all kinds of organizations. But not everyone has had the same degree of success in using this concept. From examining those MBO programs that failed, it is clear that the programs were incomplete.

The minimum requirements for an MBO program are:

1. Each manager's job includes five to ten goals expressed in specific, measurable terms.
2. Each manager reporting to you proposes his or her goals to you in writing. When you both agree on each goal, a final written statement of the goal is prepared.
3. Each goal consists of the statement of the goal, how it will be measured, and the work steps necessary to complete it.
4. Results are systematically determined at regular intervals (at least quarterly) and compared with the goals.
5. When progress toward goals is not in accordance with your plans, problems are identified and corrective action is taken.
6. Goals at each level of management are related to the level above and the level below.

Goal Setting

Goals for each of your managers are the crucial element in any MBO system. Goals at middle levels of management must be consistent with those at top levels. Goals of first-line supervisors must relate to those at middle levels. Goals prepared by the manager responsible for certain steps in a large processing operation must tie in with those of managers responsible for other steps in the processing. And all goals must relate to and support your long-range objectives for the company.

When all these goals are consistent, then an MBO system will be developed. Until then, there will be many like the middle manager of a research and development company who exclaimed in a seminar, "How can I set my goals when I don't know where top management wants to go?"

Each manager will probably find between five and eight goals enough to cover those aspects of the job crucial to successful performance. These are the elements that you will use to judge his or her performance. Of course, other duties that do not fall into the above goals should not be neglected. But they are of secondary importance.

When you first start your MBO program, your managers will undergo a learning period. They must learn how to prepare a goal that will make them stretch but is not beyond their capabilities. They must learn to develop ways to effectively measure their performance. They must learn to anticipate real problems that threaten the achievement of the goals and then take steps to cope with the problems.

During this learning period, your managers should first set a few goals. Then as they learn how to develop and achieve goals, the coverage and number of goals can be extended.

The Miniature Work Plan

Your managers may find the miniature work plan useful. On this work plan the manager can show each of the major work steps (subgoals) necessary to reach the goal. Then, if each work step is performed by the indicated date, the goal will be reached when the last work step is completed.

You may also use this form to discuss goals with your manager. By looking at this form, you can see not only the goal but also the plan for reaching that goal. This will allow you to ask questions about the work steps and anticipated problems, as well as to question how the goal will be measured. By pointing out the relationship between the manager's goal and your goal, you'll be helping each of your managers to understand how his/her goals relate to those of the company.

A Manager's Goal: Instructions for Completing Form

Management by Objectives provides for the establishment of four to ten goals by each manager. You should set up goals in each of several important areas in your job. You might try to establish at least one in each of these categories: Regular, Problem Solving, Innovative, and Development. By following this approach you will be more likely to see the full range of possibilities open to you through goal setting.

Develop each goal as a miniature work plan. The steps that follow will result in goals which are complete and useful to both you and your boss.

Goal. (Be specific and concise)

_____

_____

_____

Measurement. (The bench mark that tells you that you have achieved the goal should be expressed in quantitative terms)

_____

_____

_____

Major problems anticipated.

_____

_____

_____

Work steps. (List three or four most essential steps; give completion dates for each)

_____

_____

_____

Superior's goal. (Give goal at next higher level to which your goal relates)

_____

_____

_____

Whenever a problem is listed on the work plan, the manager should include a work step to deal with it. For example, suppose the head of your supply department set a goal to deliver all packages within one day of receipt. He thought he might have difficulty in getting his people to follow the new procedures. So he included a work step to teach these procedures before the new program went into effect.

Kinds of Goals

When your managers begin to set their goals, they may want to know what areas are suitable for goal setting. What are the really important aspects of their jobs rather than that part which is most visible to them? How can they be sure that their program is balanced for the long haul, rather than just reacting to immediate, pressing problems? How can they set goals that are most likely to help them control their jobs?

It might be useful for them to have a classification of goals that suggests areas of opportunity. Generally, each manager should have between five and eight goals. One or two goals in each of these areas should be helpful:

1. Regular work goals.
2. Problem-solving goals.
3. Innovative goals.
4. Development goals.

Regular work refers to those activities that make up the major part of the manager's responsibilities. The head of production would be primarily concerned with the amount, quality, and efficiency of production. The head of marketing would be primarily concerned with developing and conducting the market research and sales programs. Each manager should be able to find opportunities to operate more efficiently, to improve the quality of the product or service, and to expand the total amount produced or marketed.

Problem-solving goals will give your managers an opportunity to define their major problems. Then they may set a goal to eliminate each one. There is no danger of anyone ever running out of problems. New problems or new versions of old problems always seem to replace those overcome.

Innovative goals may be viewed the same way. A goal for innovation may apply to an actual problem, but some innovation may not deal with a problem. For example, the head of building management sets a goal to invigorate the employee suggestion program by putting five suggestions into effect during the next four months. There was no specific problem to be solved; the manager was just trying to do the best job possible. The development goal recognizes how important the development of your employees is to your business. Your managers can be encouraged to develop their people just as they are to produce more effectively. Every manager must be to some extent a teacher and coach; each manager must plan for the employees' continued growth in both technical areas and in working together effectively.

By asking your managers to set at least one goal in the four areas listed above, you may open their eyes to possibilities they had not seen before. The goal-setting process can be a useful educational step, even for those who are primarily specialists.

Progress Reports

An MBO program without provision for regular reports on progress is worthless. That is why some articles and books on MBO call the concept MBO/R. The "R" refers to results. Nothing is accomplished by setting goals or objectives unless the program calls for a regular review of progress toward results.

A large organization issued nearly 100 pages of goals prepared by many of its managers. Most of the goals were well developed. The document was very impressive. But there was absolutely no provision for a reporting system of any kind. It is easy to imagine the reaction of those who set goals for the first year when they were asked the following year to draw up new goals.

A monthly or quarterly review of progress toward goals will help you determine where progress is below expectations. For example, suppose that one of your goals calls for a reduction of overtime by 50 percent this year, and the first quarter reduction is only 15 percent. A special effort must be made in the succeeding quarters to regain the lost ground or the goal will not be achieved by the end of the year. When progress is below expectations, the problem or problems holding back progress should be identified and assigned to someone, usually the manager, for resolution. Make these assignments part of the company MBO files so that responsibility for correcting the problem areas cannot be evaded.

Performance Evaluation

You will have to evaluate the performance of every person working for you in some way, either formally or informally. When your managers are working to achieve a full set of five to eight goals, their ability to get results on each goal can be a good, objective measure of performance.

Traditional performance evaluation systems have been strongly criticized because they deal with subjective matters such as leadership qualities rather than the more objective measure of results. Evaluating performance by MBO, while objective, is a complex task, which must be undertaken with care by someone who fully understands

MBO. Failure to reach goals can be a result of setting the wrong objectives in the first place, the existence of organizational restrictions not taken into account, inadequate or improper measures of goal achievement, personal failure, or a combination of factors.

Installing MBO

When installing an MBO program, many owner-managers have found it best to start by asking their managers to define their jobs. What are their major responsibilities? Then, for each responsibility, the manager and the boss decide how they will measure performance in terms of results.

The result of this exercise may surprise you. Often managers and their bosses do not even agree on the manager's major responsibilities. Also, you may find that no one is performing some of the functions that you consider important.

As the owner-manager, you must appreciate what the system will do. You have to show interest in the concept from the beginning. You have to set the example for your subordinate managers, if the MBO system is to be a success.

The education of your managers may be a formidable task. They have probably thought in terms of specific functions—managing a sales department, directing a credit office—rather than in terms of goals that contribute to the organization.

It might be best to start with a seminar of six to nine hours in a classroom. This ought to be enough to introduce MBO to the managers who will be setting goals. Either you or a consultant might conduct the seminar. (If you choose a consultant, be sure that you are there for the entire seminar.)

Provide enough time so that your managers can express their doubts, reservations, or opposition to MBO. It is best to get their feelings out into the open as soon as possible. Other participants can help them deal with their concerns.

A useful part of such a seminar is the preparation of an actual goal by each participant. In small group sessions, your managers can help one another by reviewing work plans and offering suggestions to improve one another's plans.

Working with goal setting, periodic review of goals, and other aspects of MBO will be a learning experience for most managers. If they set annual goals, it may take three to four years before good results from this new system of managing appear. MBO may look simple on the surface, but it requires experience and skill to make it work effectively.

Threats to the MBO System

Not all MBO programs are successful. Some of the leading reasons why past programs failed to reach their potential are:

1. Top management did not get involved.
2. Corporate objectives were inadequate.
3. MBO was installed as a crash program.
4. It was difficult to learn the system because the nature of MBO was not taught.

It is hard to get people to think in terms of results rather than activities relating to their work. However, it can be done. The sequence of steps one owner-manager uses may not work for another. It is often an individual matter. Results are what count.

If you feel that you are ready to introduce MBO to your company, why not set this as a goal for yourself. Turn back and follow through with the work plan. List your goal, measurement, anticipated problems, and the work steps necessary to get your company managing by objectives.

Credit: U.S. Small Business Administration and Raymond F. Pelissier, Management Consultant

Market Research

One of the greatest needs of small business managers is having adequate, accurate, and current information on which to base decisions concerning the marketing of their products and/or services. These managers need to have answers to such questions as: Who is apt to buy my products or services? Where are these customers located? How often will they buy? In what amounts? What styles and colors do they prefer? What sizes are needed? Only after they have answers to these questions and other data can they decide how to chart the course of their products (and services) from the factory (or office) to consumers.

Marketing research provides this information about consumer buying habits. Good research is costly, but poor research is even more costly when wrong information produces wrong decisions. And because of limited financial resources, a small business has only a small margin for error.

While good marketing research is essential, in-house marketing research is not practical for many small firms. This is because research depends on:

- A complete understanding of the marketing and economic environment of the problem being researched; and
- The use of proper research procedures.

These two requirements often demand a

quality of talent smaller firms usually cannot afford to employ on a full-time basis. As alternatives, they should use consultants who are trained in marketing research or advertising agencies with a market research capability.

Whether marketing research procedures yield useful information depends on the person using them. A good marketing researcher should know techniques from many disciplines, including economics, psychology, sociology, statistics, accounting, industrial engineering, and mathematics. He uses these techniques when working through the steps of marketing research procedures. Moreover, the experienced researcher completes each step before going on to the next one.

As a small business owner or manager interested either in doing your own research or in hiring a consultant, there are six steps to follow:

1. Defining the Problem
In this step, the problem is clearly and accurately stated in order to determine what issues are involved in the research, what questions to ask, and what types of solutions are needed. It is a crucial step and should not be rushed to get on with the research. Time and money spent on determining the exact nature of the problem frequently saves time and money on the overall project.

2. Making a Preliminary Investigation
The objective of preliminary investigation is to develop a sharper definition of the problem and a set of tentative answers. These tentative answers are developed by examining the internal facts and the published data and by talking with persons who have some experience with the problem. These answers are tested by further research to determine the ones that appear to be the solution to the problem.

3. Planning the Research
At this stage, the researcher knows what facts are needed to resolve the identified problem and what facts are available. He compares the two sets of facts and makes plans on how to gather the data. Some of the techniques he may use are questionnaire surveys, sales forecasting, market measurements, motivation research, operations research, and specialized quantitative techniques, such as factor analysis and probability models.

4. Gathering Factual Information
Once the basic research plan has been completed, the information can be collected—by mail, telephone, or personal interview. The choice depends on the plan and the available sources of information.

5. Interpreting the Information
Facts by themselves do not always provide a sound solution to the market research problem. They must be interpreted so as to determine the choices that are available to the business manager. In addition to weighing facts, the researcher must consider the intangibles that may be part of the situation. Then, by searching for the meaning of objective facts, he can come to a reasonable solution to the problem.

6. Reaching a Conclusion
Sometimes the conclusion is obvious when the facts are interpreted. According to the facts, the logical thing to do is such and such. However, in some cases, reaching a conclusion may not be so easy because of gaps in the information or intangible factors that are difficult to evaluate. If and when the evidence is insufficient, it is important to say so when drawing a conclusion.

Credit: U.S. Small Business Administration and Lloyd M. De Boer

Free-of-charge consulting services for small business

Service Corps of Retired Executives (SCORE)
National Office:
1129 20th Street, NW,
Suite 410
Washington, DC 20036
(202) 653-6279

What Is a Patent?

A patent is an exclusive property right to an invention and is issued by the Commissioner of Patents and Trademarks, U.S. Department of Commerce. It gives an inventor the right to exclude others from making, using, or selling an invention for a period of 17 years in the United States, its territories, and possessions. A patent cannot be renewed except by act of Congress. Design patents for ornamental devices now are granted for 14 years. You will find many useful facts in the booklet *General Information Concerning Patents,* available from the Government Printing Office, Washington, D.C. 20402. You may also want to request a leaflet entitled *Publications Obtainable from the United States Patent and Trademark Office.*

Trademarks are also registered by the Commissioner of Patents and Trademarks on application by individuals or companies who distinguish, by name or symbol, a product used in commerce subject to regulation by Congress. They can be registered for a period of 20 years.

Copyrights, administered by the Copyright Office (Library of Congress, Washington, D.C.), protect authors, composers, and artists from the "pirating" of their literary and artistic work.

First Steps

When you get an idea for a product or process that you think is mechanically sound and likely to be profitable, write down your idea. Consider specifically what about your new device is original or patentable and superior to similar devices already on the market (and patented). Your idea should be written in a way that provides legal evidence of its origin because your claim could be challenged later. Next you need help to determine your device's **novelty** and to make a proper application for a patent.

Professional assistance. Professional assistance is strongly recommended because patent procedures are quite detailed. Also, you may not know how to make use of all the technical advantages available. For instance, you may not claim broad enough protection for your device. As a rule, therefore, it is best to have your application filed by a patent lawyer or agent.

Only attorneys and agents who are registered with the Patent Office may prosecute an application. That office has geographical and alphabetical listings of more than 11,000 such people. It will not, however, recommend any particular attorney or agent, nor will it assume responsibility for your selection.

Establishing novelty. This is one of the most crucial and difficult determinations to make, involving two things: (1) analyzing the device according to specified standards and (2) seeing whether or not anyone else has patented it first. The only sure way of accomplishing this is to make a search of Patent Office files.

Analyzing your device. This should be done according to the following standards of what is patentable:

1. Any new, useful, and unobvious process

(primarily industrial or technical); machine; manufacture or composition of matter (generally chemical compounds, formulas, and the like); or any new, useful, and unobvious improvement thereof;

2. Any new and unobvious original and ornamental design for an article of manufacture, such as a new auto body design (note that a design patent may not always turn out to be valuable because a commercially similar design can easily be made without infringing the patent);

3. Any distinct and new variety of plant, other than tubes-propagated, which is asexually reproduced.

Another way of analyzing your product is to consider it in relation to what is **not** patentable, as follows:

1. An idea (as opposed to a mechanical device);

2. A method of doing business (such as the assembly-line system); however, any structural or mechanical innovations employed might constitute patentable subject matter;

3. Printed matter (covered by copyright law);

4. An inoperable device;

5. An improvement in a device which is obvious or the result of mere mechanical skill (a new assembly of old parts or an adaptation of an old principle—aluminum window frames instead of the conventional wood).

Applications for patents on machines or processes for producing fissionable material can be filed with the Patent and Trademark Office. In most instances, however, such applications might be withheld if the subject matter affects national security and for that reason should not be made public.

The invention should also be tested for novelty by the following criteria:

1. Whether or not known or used by others in this country before the invention by the applicant;

2. Whether or not patented or described in a printed publication in this or a foreign country before the invention by the applicant;

3. Whether or not described in a printed publication more than one year prior to the date of application for patent in the United States.

4. Whether or not in public use or on sale in the country more than one year prior to the date of application for patent in the United States.

These points are important. For example, if you describe a new device in a printed publication or use it publicly or place it on sale, you must apply for a patent before one year has gone by; otherwise you lose any right to a patent.

Although marking your product "patent pending" after you have applied affords no legal protection, it often tends to ward off potential infringers.

Search of existing patents and technical literature. It is not necessary for you or your attorney to travel personally to Arlington, Virginia, to make a search of Patent and Trademark Office files. Arrangements can be made with associates in Arlington, Virginia, to have this done. Only the files of patents granted are open to the public. Pending applications are kept in strictest secrecy and no access is given to them except on written authority of the applicants or their duly authorized representatives. Existing patents may be consulted in the Search Room of the Patent and Trademark Office, where records of over 4 million patents issued since 1836 are maintained. In addition, over 9 million copies of foreign patents may also be seen in the Patent Library. That library contains a quantity of scientific books and periodicals that may carry a description of your idea and thus affect its patentability.

A search of patents, besides indicating whether or not your device is patentable, may also prove informative. It may disclose patents superior to your device but not already in production that might profitably be manufactured and sold by your company. A valuable business association may result.

Points of Caution

While the advantages of obtaining a patent are fairly obvious, it must be recognized that a number of pitfalls and obstacles lurk in the path of every applicant. For example, a patent by no means guarantees immunity from law suits, but rather sometimes seems to attract challenges to its legality. As one patent lawyer has said, "A patent is merely a fighting interest in a lawsuit."

Interference. One of these snags is interference (occurring in about only 1 percent of the cases), when two or more applicants have applications pending for substantially the same invention. Because a patent should be granted to only one applicant, the parties in such a case must give proof of the date the invention was made. Ordinarily, the applicant who proves that he or she was the first to conceive the invention and produce a working device will be held to be the prior inventor. If no other evidence is submitted, the date of filing the applications is used to settle the controversy. Priority questions are determined on evidence submitted to a board of examiners.

Infringement. Unauthorized manufacture, use, or sale of subject matter embraced by the claims of a patent constitutes infringement. The patent owner may file suit in a federal court for damages and/or an injunction prohibiting the continued use or manufacture of the patented article. If an item is not marked "patented," the holder of the patent may sue for damages on account of infringement but no damages can be received covering the period before the infringer is so notified. Moreover, no recovery of damages is possible for any infringement occurring more than six years before the filing of the complaint. There is no established method of learning of any infringement. A clipping service and a sharp eye for references in trade literature may be helpful, but the responsibility lies entirely with the patentee (patent holder).

Foreign patents. If you wish to market your patented product in a foreign country, you should apply for patent protection in the particular country to prevent infringement. Consult a patent attorney or agent, who can assist in getting you foreign patents.

Selling part interest. Once you get a patent, consider how to make the best use of it. You have several choices of action. If you have the facilities and money, you can manufacture and sell the article. Alternatively, you can sell all or part of the patent or you can license or assign it to someone else.

Probably the trickiest operation of all is selling part interest in a patent. Remember that joint ownership holds many pitfalls unless restricted by a contract. A joint owner, no matter how small his or her interest, may use the patent just like the original owner. He may make use of or sell the item for his own profit, without regard to any other owner, and he may also sell his interest in it to someone else. A new part owner is responsible for making sure that any such transfer is recorded within three months at the Patent and Trademark Office.

This is what could happen. An inventor offers to sell a patent for $100,000, but the prospective buyer, claiming this is too expensive, proposes to buy part interest of, say, $10,000, or 10-percent interest in it. If the sale were concluded, the new part owner—unless specifically restrained from doing so by contract—could go ahead and manufacture and sell the item as if he owned it 100 percent, without accounting to the other part owner (who is the original investor and patent holder).

Assignments and licenses. A patent is personal property and can be sold or even mortgaged. You can sell or transfer a patent or patent application. Such a transfer of interest is an assignment; the assignee then has the rights to the patent that the original patentee had. A whole or part interest can be assigned.

Like an assignment, a grant conveys an interest in a patent but only for a specified area of the United States.

A mortgage of patent property gives ownership to the lender for the duration of the loan.

You can license your patent, which means someone pays you for the right to your patent according to the conditions of the license.

All assignments, grants, licenses, or conveyances of any patent or application for a patent should be notarized and must be recorded with the Patent and Trademark Office within three months of the transfer of rights. If not, it is void against a subsequent buyer unless it is recorded prior to the subsequent purchase.

All references and documents relating to a patent or a patent application should be identified by the number, date, inventor's name, and the title of the invention. Adequate identification will lessen the difficulties of determining ownership rights and what patents and applications are in issue.

Other problems you confront as an inventor. Even though your invention passes the expert, impartial judgment of a patent examiner as to novelty and workability, it still must be commercially acceptable if you are to make money from it. In this respect you should expect no help from the Patent and Trademark Office, since it can offer no advice on this point.

Also, you should realize that, in modern technology, the vast majority of patents granted are merely improvements or refinements on a basic invention. The claims allowed on an improvement patent are narrow, as compared with those of a basic invention. Because of this, the inventor therefore runs a proportionately greater risk of infringement if a basic patent is in force.

Here is an example: Inventor George Westinghouse patented an entirely new device—the air brake. For this he was granted broad protection by the Patent and Trademark Office. Suppose that later, inventor "B" devised a structural improvement, such as a new type of valve for the compressed air. Inventor "B" would have received relatively narrow protection on the valve and would not have been able to manufacture the complete air brake without infringing Westinghouse's patent. Nor could anyone else to whom "B" licensed the patent make the whole brake.

Also, be aware that United States patent laws make no discrimination with respect to the citizenship of an inventor. Regardless of citizenship, any inventor may apply for a patent on the same basis as an American citizen.

Finally, purchasing is an important aspect of all business and touches upon patents. Purchase orders can have clauses dealing with patent infringement. Practice, type of goods, and many factors affect the clause, but such a clause could be as follows:

Seller shall indemnify and save harmless

the buyer and/or its vendees from and against all cost, expenses, and damages arising out of any infringement or claim of infringement of any patent or patents in the use of articles or equipment furnished hereunder.

Application for a Patent

If you find, after preliminary search, that your invention appears to be patentable, the next step is the preparation of a patent application. File it with the Commissioner of Patents and Trademarks, Washington, D.C. 20231. All subsequent correspondence should also be addressed to the Commissioner.

The patent application. With few exceptions the patent application must be filed in the name of the inventor. Even the application for a patent on an invention by a company's researcher must be filed in the inventor's name. If there is more than one inventor, a joint application is made. The patent application can be assigned, however, to an individual or a corporation, and then the patent will be granted to the assignee, although filed in the inventor's name.

Often employment agreements require an employee to assign to the employer any invention relating to the employer's business. Even without such an agreement, the employer may have a "shop right" to use (free) an invention developed on the job by an employee.

Application for a patent is made to the Commissioner of Patents and Trademarks and includes:

1. A written document that comprises a petition, a specification (descriptions and claims), and an oath;
2. A drawing in those cases in which a drawing is possible; and

3. The filing fee.

The exacting requirements of the Patent and Trademarks Office for a patent application are described in Title 37, Code of Federal Regulation, which may be purchased from the Superintendent of Documents, Government Printing Office, Washington, D.C. 20402. The construction of the invention, its operation, and its advantages should be accurately described. From the "disclosure" of the application, any person skilled in the field of the invention should be able to understand the intended construction and use of the invention. Commercial advantages, which would be attractive to a prospective manufacturer, need not be discussed.

The claims at the end of the specification point out the patentably new features of the invention. Drawings must be submitted according to rigid Patent and Trademark Office regulations.

What happens to your application in the patent office. When your application is received in the Patent and Trademark Office, it is given a preliminary examination to determine whether or not all requirements are met. If the application is in order, you will be notified of that fact and your application assigned a serial number and filing date. These govern its position on the docket. If there is some very minor deficiency, such as some irregularity in the drawings, the date and number will be assigned and the necessary revision requested later. If the application is incomplete, you will be notified and your application will be held up until you supply the required information to correct the deficiency.

After your application is filed, it is examined by an examiner trained and experienced in the field of your invention. Frequently, the examiner finds existing patents showing inventions enough like yours that revision of the application claims will have to be made. Sometimes several revisions and arguments by your patent attorney (or agent) are necessary to overcome successive objections raised by the examiner. Each objection constitutes an action by the Patent and Trademark Office; if no response is made to an action within a prescribed period, the application is considered abandoned. An abandoned application is dropped from further consideration. Because each application must ordinarily await its turn to be considered or reconsidered, it generally takes an average of 19 months to get a patent.

If the examiner finally refuses to grant a patent on the basis of the claims requested, the application may be appealed to the Board of Appeals of the Patent Office. When all the examiner's objections are satisfied, a patent may be obtained by payment of a final fee. A brief description of each patent issued is published weekly in the *Official Gazette of the U.S. Patent Office*. At the same time, specifications and drawings of current issuances are published separately, and copies are generally available to the public for a slight charge.

Making applications special. Only under limited conditions may a petition be filed requesting that an application be given special treatment; that is, taken up for examination before its normal turn is reached. These requirements are of particular importance to small business owners who are eager to obtain a patent before starting a manufacturing program. If you ask for special treatment for that reason, you must state under oath:

1. That you have sufficient capital available and facilities to manufacture the invention in quantity. If you are acting as an individual, there must also be a corroborating affidavit from an officer of a bank, showing that you have obtained sufficient capital to manufacture the invention.
2. That you will not manufacture unless it is certain that the patent will be granted.
3. That you will obligate yourself or your company to produce the invention in quantity as soon as patent protection has been established. A corporation must have this commitment agreed to in writing by its board of directors.
4. That if the application is allowed, you will furnish a statement under oath within three months of such allowance, showing (a) how much money has been expended, (b) the number of devices manufactured, and (c) labor employed.

Your attorney must file an affidavit to show that he or she has made a careful and thorough search of the prior art and believes all the claims in the application are allowable. The attorney will also be expected to make sure that the last sworn statement described above is properly filed.

Credit: U.S. Small Business Administration

Starting Your New Store: Keep the Customer in Mind

Retail Buying

Beginning with the turn of the century and continuing for many years, small retailers and buyers for retail stores concentrated all their buying efforts on the selection of merchandise they thought their customers would like and would purchase. These buyers were product-oriented. It was called subjective retailing because the buyer based the buying decision on a personal view of the likes and dislikes of customers.

Within recent years the consumer movement (consumerism) has forced a change in the retailer's buying efforts from a subjective attitude to an objective one. The retailer now has to measure the likes and dislikes of the customers before a buying decision can be made. The buyer has to be consumer-oriented. Retailing has entered into the new era of the marketing of merchandise.

The Marketing Approach

It was now necessary to obtain the answers, through research and study, to the where, who, what, when, and why of the consumer's buying habits and choices. The "where" refers to the trading area from which the retailer attracts its customers. The "who" refers to the demographic descriptions of these customers, which provide a profile of the potential customers. The "what" refers to the types of merchandise these potential customers want to buy and, therefore, want the retailer to stock. The "when" refers to the time of year when the customers make their purchases. The "why" refers to the psychographics of the customers, which reflect their varied life-styles and the projection of these life-styles into purchasing habits.

As a result of this consumerism, the small retailer and the buyer for the larger store has had to learn the significance of a new vocabulary to successfully effect this marketing of the merchandise approach. The new vocabulary includes such phrases as: *target group*, an understanding of the wants and needs of the consumers the retailer has selected to serve; *marketing positioning*, the merchandising policies the retailer has established upon which to develop a reputation as a price, value, quality, assortment, and fashion leader; *market penetration*, the extent to which the retailer has succeeded in interpreting and satisfying the merchandise wants and needs of the target group; *the new tools*, the new approach of marketing the merchandise that requires a knowledge and understanding of the tools necessary to effectively buy for retail stores; and *the merchandise plan* (see below), which is a timetable of merchandising objectives to be achieved within a stated time frame to ensure that your planned market positioning and market penetration are realized.

The Merchandise Plan

The plan is applicable to all forms of retailing at all sales levels. It is most often a six-month merchandise plan but there can be variations depending upon the merchandise.

The first six-month plan includes February-March-April (spring) and May-June-July (summer). This plan is prepared and finalized in the previous August to permit early buying of imports and other merchandise. The second six-month plan includes August-September-October (fall) and November-December-January (winter). This plan is prepared and finalized in the previous February for the same reasons.

The important items to be considered monthly when developing your six-month merchandise plan are:

Net sales. This figure represents a realistic dollar estimate of your monthly merchandise sales. These sales estimates are based on past experiences and on future considerations including: business conditions, competition, inflation, promotional plans, merchandising opportunities, and merchandise availability.

Stock. In order to achieve your estimated

(planned) sales figure you must provide sufficient stock to permit a satisfactory selection for your customers. This stock figure can be determined by calculating your inventory turnover rate or your sales-stock ratio, or by estimating the maximum quantity for each item or the stock requirements based on expected weekly sales.

Reductions. Reductions refer to the lowering of retail value of your inventory and is caused by planned markdowns, shrinkage (stock shortage), and discounts to employees or other special groups. Since these are the only three things that can cause the retail value of the inventory at the end of a period to have a lower valuation than it had at the beginning of the period, they are to be included in the plan.

Purchases. This figure represents the dollar value of merchandise the buyer must purchase to replenish the stock likely to be sold to your retail customers. It is calculated by subtracting the dollar value of the stock on hand at the beginning of the month from the total dollar value of the planned net sales, shrinkage, and reductions for the month. The result is the planned purchases for the month.

Open-to-buy. To arrive at the open-to-buy figure for the month, it is necessary to subtract (from the above planned purchases figure) the dollar value of the commitments already placed for delivery during the same month. Since each month is an entity by itself, it is not possible to carry any unspent open-to-buy commitments over to the next month. Knowledgeable buyers generally commit about 50 percent of the planned purchase figure in order to allow funds for reorders, fill-ins, and to take advantage of unexpected marketing opportunities.

In addition to the above items and depending upon the retail operation, the following elements may also be included in your six-month plan: turnover, markdown, payroll, advertising, gross margin, number of transactions, and average sale. It should be noted that the six-month plan is flexible and can be adjusted at any time to meet changing business conditions.

The Stock Plan

After determining the broad categories of merchandise the store is to stock (men's clothing, stationery, costume jewelry, etc.), the retailer divides the broad categories into smaller categories called classifications (men's suits, tuxedoes, raincoats, etc.). In turn, the classifications are divided into subclassifications (single-breasted, double-breasted, etc.). A unit stock plan of the number of items to be stocked in each by price, style, color, and size is then prepared. The purpose of this approach is to ensure that the stock will present an assortment that will satisfy the wants and needs of the broad section of targeted consumers. One element of the stock plan approach is the model stock or basic stock list. This list will contain those items that the customer expects to find in stock at all times. These are the *musts* or *never-out* items, sometimes referred to as the bread-and-butter items.

The number of items in all stock plans is multiplied by the price line to arrive at the dollar value of the planned inventory. Adjustments in the stock plan may be necessary if the financial constraints preclude an ambitious stock assortment.

The Buying Plan

One of the important aspects of market penetration is to have the items in stock when the customers want to buy them. This implies going into the market to buy the goods early enough to ensure delivery to the store at the proper time. For example, to ensure on-time delivery of children's Easter clothes, you must place the orders and commit the resources in the previous September. So buying for a retail store requires advance planning to determine the merchandise needs for each month and then placing the commitments without procrastination. Since retailers offer the new items for sale months before the actual beginning of the new season, it is imperative that buying plans be formulated early enough to allow for intelligent buying without last-minute panic purchases. The main reason for this early offering for sale of new items is that the retailer regards the calendar date for the beginning of the new season as the merchandise date for the end of the old season. For example, March 21, from a merchandising viewpoint, is the end of spring while June 21 is the end of summer and December 21 the end of winter.

The period following the calendar date for the beginning of the season is used by the retailer to sell closeouts, job lots, imperfects, irregulars, seconds, distress merchandise, off-price purchases, and markdowns from regular stock.

In summary the buying plan should detail:

1. When the market should be visited to see, examine, and study the new offerings for the coming season;
2. When commitments should be placed; and
3. When the first delivery should be received at the store.

The Selling Plan

The selling plan is closely allied to the buying plan. Once the merchandise has been purchased, plans must be formulated to ensure the sale of the greatest number of units during the period of customer acceptance. The selling plan should detail:

a. When the items should be promoted through advertising, window and interior displays, etc.;
b. When the inventory should be peaked;
c. When reorders should no longer be placed;
d. When markdowns from regular stock should be taken; and
e. When the item should no longer be in stock.

The buyer for the retail store must determine at the time the merchandise is purchased when the item should be introduced, when it should be reordered, when it should be marked down, and when it should be removed from stock. This procedure can be compared to the tides—low and high. In merchandising terms it is referred to as the ebb and flow of merchandise. The old must go and the new must take its place.

The Unit Control Plan

To maintain an in-stock position of wanted items and to dispose of unwanted items, it is necessary to establish an adequate form of control over the merchandise on order and the merchandise in stock. For the small retailer there are many simple, inexpensive forms of unit control. They are:

1. Visual or eyeball control, enabling the retailer to examine the inventory visually to determine if additional inventory is required;
2. Tickler control, enabling the retailer to count a small portion of the inventory each day so that each segment of the inventory is counted every so many days on a regular basis;

3. Stub control, enabling the retailer to retain a portion of the price ticket when the item is sold. The retailer can then use the stub to record the items that were sold; and finally, a

4. Click sheet control, enabling the retailer to record the item sold (at the cash register) on a sheet of paper. Such information is then used for reorder purposes.

For the large retailer more technical and sophisticated forms of unit control are used. They include:

1. Point-of-sale terminals that relay to the computer the information of the item sold. The buyer receives information printouts at regular intervals for review and action;

2. Off-line point-of-sale terminals that relay information directly to the supplier's computer, which uses the information to ship additional merchandise automatically to the retailer; and

3. A manufacturer's representative who visits the large retailer on a scheduled basis and takes the stock count and writes the reorder. Unwanted merchandise is removed from stock and returned to the manufacturer through the procedure of an authorized level.

A sound unit control must include control over open orders so that delivery dates are adhered to and to ensure that stores do not receive goods they did not order.

Conclusion

Finally, buying for a retail store requires the buyer to be an aware person, aware of the changing tones, the changing consumer, and the changing products. To remain *au courant* with these changes, an aware buyer: (1) reads trade journals and newspapers, consumer and business publications; (2) talks to customers, salespeople, and vendors; (3) sees all manufacturers, salespersons, and vendors; (3) sees all manufacturers, salespersons, and their merchandise lines; (4) visits museums, art shows, lively arts performances, and sporting events; and (5) visits off-beat fashion areas. In short, the buyer for a retail store keeps an alert ear to new consumer rumblings and a sharp eye to look out for new merchandising horizons and selling opportunities.

WHERE TO FIND IT

Small Business Administration
1441 L Street, NW
Washington, DC 20416

SBA issues a wide range of management and technical publications designed to help owner-managers and prospective owners of small business.

Where availability of an individual listing is indicated by GPO (Government Printing Office), the material may be ordered from the Superintendent of Documents, U.S. Government Printing Office, Washington, DC 20402.

Small Business Stock: Want to Start Your Own Business? Three Tax Strategies Can Cut the Risks

Admit it. You've always dreamed of going into business for yourself but a nagging fear has kept you from taking the plunge. You wake in the night wondering, "What if I lose all that money?" The risk is unthinkable.

Needless to say, entrepreneurship is never a sure thing but there are ways to cushion the risk. You can thank Uncle Sam for that. In an effort to encourage small business start-ups, Congress has enacted a handful of tax provisions enabling fledgling entrepreneurs to recover their risk capital. Dollars lost to star-crossed ventures may be reclaimed as tax savings.

Let's review the options:

1. Small Business Stock: You can begin protecting your investment as soon as the company is launched by issuing stock in accordance with Section 1244 of the Internal Revenue Code. This so-called small business stock entitles investors to the best of both worlds: limited liability of the corporate structure plus the personal benefit of current tax write-offs should the stock become worthless.

"Assume an individual invests $25,000 in a business that proves unsuccessful," explains a partner with Price Waterhouse, accountants. "Providing the taxpayer is in the 33 percent bracket, the Section 1244 loss would yield a current-year tax benefit of $8,250. This effectively cuts the business loss in half. Had the owner held regular corporate stock, his write-off would have been limited to as little as $3,000 that year, saving only $990."

Section 1244 stock is subject to the following rules:

- Losses can be taken only if the stock becomes worthless or is sold for a loss.
- The stock must have been issued to the individual claiming the loss. Shares transferred will not carry with them section 1244 benefits.
- Money or property must be paid for the stock; shares may not be issued solely for services rendered.
- The corporation issuing 1244 stock must qualify as an "operating company" for the five most recent taxable years preceding the date of the stockholder's loss. (If the

company is less than five years old, it must qualify as an operating company for all the taxable years of its existence.) Corporations earning 50 percent or more of their gross receipts from passive sources—such as rents, royalties, and dividends—generally do not qualify as operating companies.

- Only "small business corporations"—those receiving a maximum of $1 million for their shares—can issue 1244 stock.
- Although an existing corporation cannot convert outstanding shares to 1244 status, a new corporation can be formed to raise money for additional ventures. You may want to go this route when diversifying into new markets or expanding operations.
- Companies seeking to issue 1244 stock must make this election when the stock is issued.
- The ordinary loss on 1244 stock is subject to a $50,000 annual limit, or $100,000 for a joint return. Investors in losing ventures can allocate the additional $50,000 loss to a spouse even if the spouse is not a shareholder in the corporation.

2. S Corporations: 1244 stock is limited in that losses cannot be written off until the shares are sold or deemed worthless. But a related strategy provides for immediate relief should the company fall on hard times. By organizing your business as an S corporation, you can claim personal tax deductions for operating losses as they are incurred. Because S corporations are not taxed at the corporate level, all income and losses flow through to the shareholders.

It works this way: Say you earn $60,000 a year working for a major corporation. Your spouse starts a small business that loses $20,000 in the first year of operation. With an S corporation that loss can be claimed on your joint tax return, thus reducing your taxable income to $40,000. The tax saving substantially reduces the business loss. Once the company moves into the black, the owner can elect to move out of the S form, thus subjecting the income to a maximum 46 percent corporate tax, as opposed to the personal rate of up to 50 percent.

3. Amortize Start-up Costs: Another tax-saving safety net for new ventures covers expenses incurred before the business is launched. Section 195 of the tax code allows many of the costs associated with business start-ups to be amortized over a period of at least 60 months. Before 195 became law, most of these expenses were nondeductible, and as such had to be carried on the books until the company was liquidated.

Two categories of expenditures are eligible for amortization under Section 195:

- Investigatory expenses, such as market research, incurred in deciding whether to enter a line of business. The write-off can be claimed only if the business is actually launched.
- Preopening expenses incurred after a decision has been made to start a business but before the company begins to operate. Include here the cost of setting up supply and distribution networks, hiring workers, and conducting initial advertising campaigns.

To make a Section 195 election, the taxpayer attaches a statement to the return for the year in which the amortization period begins. This document lists each expenditure, giving its date and dollar amount, the month in which the taxpayer began the business, and the number of months in the amortization schedule.

Just how the amortization can help a fledgling venture is illustrated in the case of hypothetical company ABC, which opened its

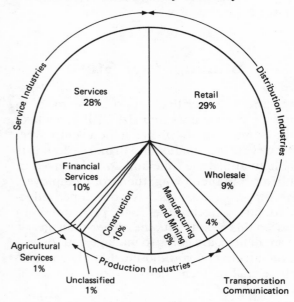

Small Business by Industry

Most small businesses are in the retail and service sectors.

Source: National Federation of Independent Business Research and Education Foundation

doors in April. In the preceding three months, start-up costs for market research, training, and advertising totaled $82,000.

"By amortizing these expenses over 60 months," the Price Waterhouse partner explains, "the taxpayer can deduct $16,400 for each full year of operations. Assuming the company earns $100,000 annually, the yearly tax savings comes to $6,560."

Work with an accountant or a tax attorney in selecting and claiming start-up and business loss deductions. Professionals can steer you through the maze of rules and regulations. Making the right decisions can cushion the impact of losses, speed capital recovery, and generally reduce the risks of entrepreneurship.

With that comforting thought, go out and make a success of it.

Staffing Your Store

Staffing is of critical importance to businesses of all shapes and sizes. All firms take the same risk in hiring a new employee. However, the smaller the firm, the less it is able to afford the time and costs involved in hiring, and then firing, the wrong employee.

Bigger companies have developed effective hiring techniques and procedures to lessen this risk. If you, the owner-manager of a small firm, are going to manage your operation effectively, you too must apply some of these staffing techniques.

Setting Personnel Policies

First of all, know yourself. Know what business you are in. Know your own personal abilities and weaknesses, and try to anticipate how you will deal with the situations that you expect to arise in the daily operation of your business.

Then formulate your policies in writing. Include all matters that would affect employees, such as wages, promotions, vacations, time off, grievances, fringe benefits, and even retirement policies, which are now available for the small retailer.

Employment and training procedures must be established so that you have a better chance of getting the job done the way you want it done. You might want to consider written policy decisions for the following areas.

Hours. Consider here the number of hours to be worked per week, the number of days per week, evening and holiday work, and the time and method of payment for both regular and overtime work. Unnecessary payment of overtime at premium rates is a source of needless expense. By planning ahead, you may be able to organize your employees' work to keep overtime to a minimum. When peak periods do occur, you can often handle them by using part-time help paid at regular rates.

Compensation. The bulk of the retail salesperson's earnings should come from a base salary competitive with the pay offered by other similar local firms. It may be possible to supplement the base salary with some form of incentive, such as a small commission or quota bonus plan. Try to relate the incentive to both your goals and the goals of your employees. Whatever plan you use, be sure each employee understands it completely.

Fringe benefits. You may consider offering your employees discounts on merchandise, free life insurance, health insurance, pension plan, and tuition payments at schools and colleges. You might also look into joining with other merchants in a group disability plan and a group workers' compensation plan. Such a plan could mean a considerable savings in your premium costs.

Vacations. How long will vacations be? Will you specify the time of the year they may be taken? With or without pay?

Time off. Will you allow employees time off for personal needs, emergencies in the family, holidays, special days such as Election Day, Saturday or Sunday holidays?

Training. You must make sure that each employee is given adequate training for the job. In a small store, the training responsibility normally falls to the owner-manager. If you have supervisors, each one should recognize the importance of being a good teacher and should schedule time to teach new people.

Retirement. What are your plans for retirement age benefits such as Social Security, pension plans, and annuity plan insurance?

Grievances. You may expect conflicts with your employees without regard for the quality of the employment you offer. The best course of action is to plan for them and establish a procedure for handling grievances. Consider the employee's rights to demand review, and establish provisions for third-party arbitration.

Promotion. You will want to consider such promotion matters as normal increases of wages and salaries, changes of job titles, and the effect your store's growth will have on this area.

Personnel review. Will you periodically review your employees' performance? If so, what factors will you consider? Will you make salary adjustments, training recommendations?

Termination. Even though this is a distasteful matter to many retailers, it would be wise to have a written policy on such matters as layoffs, seniority rights, severance pay, and the conditions warranting summary discharge.

When you have developed your personnel policies, write down the policy on all matters that affect your employees and give each one a copy. For the small store, this statement may consist of only one or two typed pages. Matters such as the following should be standardized and not left to the whim of a supervisor: hours of work, time recordkeeping, paid holidays, vacations, deportment and dress regulations, wage payment system, overtime, separation procedure, severance pay, pension and retirement plan, hospitalization and medical care benefits, and grievance procedure.

Determining Needed Skills and Abilities

The trick to getting the right person for the job is in deciding what kind of skill is needed to perform the job. Once you know what it takes to do the job, you can match the applicant's skills and experience to the job's requirements.

The first step in analyzing a job is to describe it. Suppose, as a busy owner-manager, you decide to hire someone to relieve you of some of your duties. Look at the many functions you perform and decide what your stronger and weaker areas are.

Further suppose that you have decided you will need help in the office. The phone is always ringing. Letters that need answering are piling up. Merchandise must be ordered.

Once you have a job description on paper, decide what skills the person must have to fill the job. What is the lowest level of skill you will accept? In this example, let us assume that you decide initially to hire a secretary, but discover that secretaries are scarce and expensive. Moreover, in your area, stenographers are almost as hard to find and nearly as expensive as secretaries.

Perhaps you could get by with a typist. Hiring a typist may be both easier and cheaper than hiring a secretary or stenographer. Many high school students are well qualified as typists, and many are seeking part-time work.

One additional point: When you start to look for someone to fill your job, make sure you spell out just what you want. Imagine that an owner-manager advertised for a "sales clerk." What should the applicant be able to do? Tally sales receipts accurately? Keep a customer list and occasionally promote your products to these people? Run the store while you are away? The job of "sales clerk" means different things to different people. Make sure that you know what skills you need and what skills you can get by with, as determined by what kind of training you can give the employee.

Finding Applicants

When you know the kind of skills you need in your new employee, you are ready to contact sources that can help you recruit job applicants.

Each state has an employment service (sometimes called Public Employment, Unemployment Bureau, or Employment Security Agency). All are affiliated with the U.S. Employment Service, and local offices are ready to help businesses with their hiring problems.

The employment service will screen applicants for you by giving aptitude tests (if any are available for the skills you need). Passing scores indicate the applicant's ability to learn the work. So be as specific as you can about the skills you want.

Private employment agencies will also help in recruitment. However, the employee or the employer must pay a fee to the private agency for its services.

Another source of applicants is a "Help Wanted" sign in your own front window. Of course, a lot of unqualified applicants may inquire about the job, and you cannot interview an applicant and wait on a customer at the same time.

Newspaper advertisements are another source of applicants. You reach a large group of job seekers and you can screen them at your convenience. If you list a phone number at the store, you may end up on the phone instead of dealing with a customer.

Job applicants are readily available from local schools. The local high school may have a distributive education department where the students work in your store part time while learning about selling and merchandising along with their school courses. Many part-time students stay with the store after they finish school.

You may also find job applicants by contacting friends, neighbors, customers, suppliers, present employees, local associations such as the Junior Chamber of Commerce, service clubs to which you belong, or even a nearby armed forces base where people are leaving the service. However, do not overlook the problems of such recruiting. What happens to the goodwill of these sources if they recommend a friend whom you do not hire, or if you have to fire the person they recommend?

Your choice of recruitment method depends on your type of business, your location, and you. You have many sources available to you. A combination may serve your needs best. The important thing is to find the right applicant with the correct skills for the job you want to fill, whatever the source.

Developing Application Forms

The hardest part of your work, if you did a good job listing the skills needed, is in finding and hiring the one right employee. You need some method of screening the applicants and selecting the best one for the position.

The application form is a tool that you can use to make your tasks of interviewing and selection easier. The form should have blank spaces for all the facts you need as a basis for judging the applicants.

You will want a fairly complete application so you can get sufficient information. However, keep the form as simple as you can.

Have the applicants fill out the application before you talk to them. It makes an excellent starting point for the interview. It is also a written record of experience and former employers' names and addresses.

Remember, the Civil Rights Act of 1964 prohibits discrimination in employment practices because of race, religion, sex, or national origin. Public Law 90–202 prohibits discrimination on the basis of age with respect to individuals who are at least 40 but less than 70. Federal laws also prohibit discrimination against the physically handicapped.

When an applicant has had work experience, other references are not very important. However, if the level of work experience is limited, additional references may be obtained from other individuals, such as school counselors, who can give objective information. Personal references are almost useless, since an applicant would only list people who have a kind word for them.

Interviewing Job Applicants

The objective of the job interview is to find out as much information as you can about the job applicant's work background, especially work habits and skills. Your major task is to get the applicants to talk about themselves and about their work habits. The best way to go about this is to ask each applicant specific questions: What did you do on your last job? How did you do it? Why was it done?

As you go along, evaluate the applicants' replies. Do they know what they are talking about? Are they evasive or unskilled in the job tasks? Can they account for discrepancies?

When the interview is over, ask the applicant to check back with you later, if you think you may be interested in that applicant. Never commit yourself until you have interviewed all likely applicants. You want to be sure that you select the right applicant for the job.

Next, verify the information you have obtained. A previous employer is usually the best source. Sometimes a previous employer will give out information over the telephone. But it is usually best to request your information in writing and get a written reply.

To help ensure a prompt reply, you should ask previous employers a few specific questions about the applicant that can be answered yes or no, or with a very short answer. For example: How long did the employee work for you? _____ Was his or her work poor _____, average _____, or excellent _____? Why did the employee leave your employment?

After you have verified the information on all your applicants, you are ready to make your selection. The right employee can help you make money. The wrong employee will cost you much wasted time and materials, and may even drive away customers.

Credit: U.S. Small Business Administration and Professor Walter Green

Start-up Strategies: Starting a Business the Right Way

To millions of Americans, self-employment is the proverbial pot of gold at the end of the rainbow. Owning a business, they believe, brings power, control, and personal wealth.

While this dream does sometimes come true, for every Cinderella story scores of failures slip quietly from view. The trick is not simply to start a business but to start it right.

By taking a series of calculated steps at the earliest stages of entrepreneurship, prospective business owners can shift the odds in their favor, turning more dreams into profitable ventures.

"Quite often, the entrepreneur's fate is determined by his choice of businesses," says Joseph Mancuso, president of the Center for Entrepreneurial Management, a nonprofit organization active in business formation. "Should he start the wrong type of venture, his efforts may be doomed regardless of the energy and talent he devotes to it. This happens all too frequently when the person chooses a mature, slow-growth business—such as a shoemaking factory or a local pharmacy—for his first venture. Surrounded by entrenched competition and faced with severe price pressure, the owner is hard pressed to make a go of it. All his customers must be drawn away from established companies.

"A much wiser choice is to get started in an emerging field just beginning to take off. Video film shops were in that position about five years ago. Those who got in on the ground floor profited from the market's explosive growth and had time to build a loyal following before swarms of competitors got in on the act. They proved a key point: when starting a business, it's best to look for a developing industry with little competition and low capital requirements."

Some say the best route to business is through a salaried job.

"Time and again, employees see problems or opportunities in a business that management overlooks," says a partner specializing in emerging companies for Price Waterhouse, accountants. "Like how to correct a product deficiency, cut operating expenses, or sell more effectively. When employees bring their ideas to the top, they're often dismissed out of hand. If it wasn't the boss's idea, the thinking goes, it can't be good.

"Rather than licking their wounded pride, employees in this position should consider taking the idea to market themselves. Sometimes a niche that's too small for their employer to fill is ideal for the entrepreneur. In a typical case, a salesman for a restaurant equipment firm found he often lost potential sales when interested prospects didn't have enough cash to make a deal. With this in mind, he left his employer and started a successful venture that leases rather than sells equipment."

Raising money—one of the traditional barriers to entrepreneurship—is more complex than just landing a loan or attracting investment capital. To start the business right, the entrepreneur must first determine how much money will be required to support the venture through the early, often money-losing years.

"The saddest thing to behold is a business with excellent products or services that fails before it has the chance to achieve its potential," says a partner with the national accounting firm of Seidman & Seidman. "When that happens, poor capitalization is often the cause. The owner simply opened his doors without adequate financing.

"You can't just pick a number out of the air—say, $500,000—and decide that's what you'll need. The entrepreneur must create a detailed business plan projecting the venture's sales, expenses, and break-even point. And this must be revised to reflect changes in the business. Assume a new company starts out manufacturing five products, four of which perform according to projections but one, although promising, needs further development and testing. Unless the business plan is flexible, funds for this product may not be available in time to save it."

Perhaps the hardest pill for entrepreneurs to swallow is the advice that they respond to success by relinquishing management control.

"Like every other mortal, entrepreneurs must recognize their limitations," the Seidman partner warns. "Most have brilliant minds that are nevertheless incapable of focusing on the minutiae that go hand in hand with daily business management. They have what it takes to create a business, but not to manage it once it's up and running. That job should be passed on to a professional manager—one who is brought in to relieve the entrepreneur and to protect his company while he goes off in pursuit of more creative endeavors. A blow to the ego, perhaps, but far better than losing the venture he worked so hard to create."

Venture-capital Clubs Help Launch New Businesses

When the chief executive of a small lighting manufacturer sought capital to take his fledgling business from drawing board to marketplace, he paid a timely visit to a local venture-capital club. Meeting with a group of like-minded entrepreneurs—all experienced in applying for or attracting venture capital—he picked up valuable pointers in the capital search process. Within six months, he raised enough money to make his dream a reality.

The entrepreneur's experience—virtually unheard of only a few years ago—is now increasingly common as venture capital clubs spring up across the nation. Designed to support the entrepreneurial process, the clubs provide a forum for venture capitalists, en-

trepreneurs, investment bankers, lawyers, and accountants experienced in business formation.

"Before the clubs were formed, entrepreneurs were an isolated species," says Thomas Murphy, founder of the Association of Venture Capital Clubs, a nonprofit trade group representing 40 clubs across the nation. "They had no way of connecting with others who shared similar interests and objectives. An entrepreneur starting a software company, for example, would not have known that an investor in the same town was looking to invest in that kind of venture. Venture-capital clubs bridge this gap by keeping potential business partners in touch with one another and by encouraging their joint ventures."

Entrepreneurs say the clubs teach them how to succeed.

"When I went to my first club meeting, I was overwhelmed by the problems and the obstacles an entrepreneur faces in raising money," says the lighting manufacturer. "There are so many closed doors, so many empty corridors. But it doesn't have to be that way. The club taught me how to approach the investment community—how to develop a formula for raising capital. Armed with this information, I structured a limited partnership that brought in more than $800,000 in risk capital—enough to take my product, an innovative lighting device, from the developmental stage to full-scale operations."

Clubs vary slightly by rules and procedures but generally follow these guidelines:

1. Membership is open to all segments of the business community.
2. Annual dues of $200 to $300 a year cover meeting fees and a subscription to a club newsletter.
3. Meetings, held on a monthly basis, are divided into three segments.

"First a speaker addresses the group on an issue relevant to the entrepreneurial process," Murphy explains. "This might be 'How the Reagan tax law will affect high-tech businesses' or 'How to hire a skilled manager.' Then the 'five-minute forums' give members the opportunity to present thumbnail sketches of their business ideas. The hope is to arouse the interest of others in attendance, specifically those in a position to make investments. In the 'postmeeting period' the real deal making occurs. Here members get together to discuss their mutual interests. An investment banker excited by a five-minute forum will use this opportunity to touch bases with the appropriate entrepreneur."

At some clubs, additional meeting segments are devoted to the design and presentation of business plans.

"We give entrepreneurs 20 minutes to present their business plans to a panel of experts," says a director of the Long Island Venture Group. "They describe their products, market strategy, and financing objectives. The panel then critiques the presentations, telling where they are weak and how they can be improved."

Club activities extend beyond capital raising.

"At our first club meeting, we were introduced to a businessman with contacts at Computerland," says an executive with a small company marketing computer systems to the retail industry. "Soon after the introduction, we negotiated a major sale that brought our company a welcome infusion of cash and market exposure."

Adds Tom Murphy: "One entrepreneur who is buying small companies and assembling them into a tiny conglomerate has used his venture-capital club contacts to develop relationships with lawyers and accountants willing to accept stock in lieu of cash fees. Because entrepreneurs typically need every penny of capital to get their businesses off the ground, this arrangement can be an enormous advantage."

For the name and address of the venture-capital club nearest you—and for guidelines on forming a club in your community—write The Association of Venture Capital Clubs, 538 Camino Del Monte Sol, Santa Fe, New Mexico 87501.

WHERE TO FIND IT

SBA Field Offices: Addresses and Commercial Telephone Numbers

City	State	Zip Code	Address	Phone Number
Agana	GU	96910	Pacific Daily News Bldg., Room 508	(671) 477-8420
Albuquerque	NM	87110	5000 Marble Avenue, NE, Room 320	(505) 766-3430
Anchorage	AK	99513	701 C Street	(907) 271-4022
Atlanta	GA	30309	1720 Peachtree Street, NW, 6th Floor	(404) 881-4749
Augusta	ME	04330	40 Western Avenue, Room 512	(207) 622-8378
Bala Cynwyd	PA	19004	231 St. Asaphs Road, Suite 400 East Lobby	(215) 596-5889
Biloxi	MS	39530	111 Fred Haise Blvd., 2nd Floor	(601) 435-3676
Birmingham	AL	35205	908 South 20th Street, Room 202	(205) 254-1344
Boise	ID	83701	1005 Main Street, 2nd Floor	(208) 334-1696
Boston	MA	02114	150 Causeway Street, 10th Floor	(617) 223-3224
Buffalo	NY	14202	111 West Huron Street, Room 1311	(716) 846-4301
Casper	WY	82602	100 East B Street, Room 4001, P.O. Box 2839	(307) 261-5761

Cedar Rapids	IA	52402	373 Collins Road NE	(319) 399-2571
Charleston	WV	25301	Charleston National Plaza, Suite 628	(304) 343-6181
Charlotte	NC	28202	230 S. Tryon Street, Suite 700	(704) 371-6563
Chicago	IL	60604	219 South Dearborn Street, Room 437	(312) 353-4528
Cincinnati	OH	45202	550 Main Street, Room 5028	(513) 684-2814
Clarksburg	WV	26301	109 North 3rd Street, Room 302	(304) 623-5631
Cleveland	OH	44199	1240 East 9th Street, Room 317	(216) 552-4170
Columbia	SC	29202	1835 Assembly, 3rd Floor P.O. Box 2786	(803) 765-5376
Columbus	OH	43215	85 Marconi Blvd.	(614) 469-6860
Concord	NH	03301	55 Pleasant Street, Room 211	(603) 224-4041
Coral Gables	FL	33134	2222 Ponce De Leon Blvd., 5th Floor	(305) 350-5521
Corpus Christi	TX	78408	3105 Leopard Street, P.O. Box 9253	(512) 888-3331
Dallas	TX	75242	1100 Commerce Street, Room 3C36	(214) 767-0605
Denver	CO	80202	721 19th Street	(303) 837-2607
Des Moines	IA	50309	210 Walnut Street, Room 749	(515) 284-4422
Detroit	MI	48226	477 Michigan Avenue	(313) 226-7241
Elmira	NY	14901	180 Clemens Center Parkway, Room 412	(607) 733-4686
El Paso	TX	79902	4100 Rio Bravo, Suite 300	(915) 543-7586
Fairbanks	AK	99701	101 12th Avenue	(907) 456-0211
Fargo	ND	58108	657 2nd Avenue, North, Room 218, P.O. Box	(701) 237-5771
Fresno	CA	93712	2202 Monterey Street	(209) 487-5189
Harlingen	TX	78550	222 East Van Buren Street, P.O. Box 2567	(512) 423-8934
Harrisburg	PA	17101	100 Chestnut Street, Suite 309	(717) 782-3840
Hartford	CT	06103	One Financial Plaza	(203) 244-3600
Hato Rey	PR & VI	00919	Carlos Chardon Ave, Fed. Bldg. Rm. 691	(809) 753-4572
Helena	MT	59601	301 S. Park Avenue, Room 528, Drawer 10054	(406) 449-5381
Honolulu	HI	96850	300 Ala Mona, Room 2213, P.O. Box 50207	(808) 546-8950
Houston	TX	77054	2525 Marworth, Room 43	(713) 660-4401
Indianapolis	IN	46204	575 North Pennsylvania Street, Room 578	(317) 269-7272
Jackson	MS	39269	100 West Capitol Street, Suite 322	(601) 960-4378
Jacksonville	FL	32202	400 West Bay Street, Room 261, Box 35067	(904) 791-3782
Kansas City	MO	64106	1150 Grande Avenue, 5th Floor	(816) 374-3416
Knoxville	TN	37902	502 South Gay Street, Room 307	(615) 637-9300
Las Vegas	NV	89101	301 E Stewart, P.O. Box 7525, Downtown Station	(702) 385-6611
Little Rock	AR	72201	320 West Capitol Avenue, P.O. Box 1401	(501) 378-5871
Los Angeles	CA	90071	350 S. Figueroa Street, 6th Floor	(213) 688-2956
Louisville	KY	40201	600 Federal Plaza, Room 188, P.O. Box 3517	(502) 582-5971
Lubbock	TX	79401	1205 Texas Avenue, Room 712	(806) 762-7466
Madison	WI	53703	212 East Washington Avenue, Room 213	(608) 264-5261
Marquette	MI	49855	220 West Washington Street, Room 310	(906) 225-1108
Melville	NY	11747	35 Pinelawn Road, Room 102E	(516) 454-0750
Memphis	TN	38103	167 North Main Street, Room 211	(901) 521-3588
Milwaukee	WI	53202	517 East Wisconsin Avenue, Room 246	(414) 291-3941

Minneapolis	MN	55403	100 North 6th Street	(612) 349-3550
Montpelier	VT	05602	87 State Street, Room 204, P.O. Box 605	(802) 229-0538
Nashville	TN	37219	404 James Robertson Parkway, Suite 1012	(615) 251-5881
New Orleans	LA	70113	1001 Howard Avenue, 17th Floor	(504) 589-6685
Newark	NJ	07102	970 Broad Street, Room 1635	(201) 645-2434
New York	NY	10278	26 Federal Plaza, Room 3100	(212) 264-4355
Oklahoma City	OK	73102	200 N.W. 5th Street, Suite 670	(405) 231-4301
Omaha	NB	68102	19th & Farnum Street, 2nd Floor	(402) 221-4691
Phoenix	AZ	85012	3030 North Central Avenue, Suite 1201	(602) 241-2200
Pittsburgh	PA	15222	960 Penn Avenue, 5th Floor	(412) 644-2780
Portland	OR	97204	1220 S.W. Third Avenue, Room 676	(503) 294-5221
Providence	RI	02903	40 Fountain Street	(401) 528-4580
Rapid City	SD	57701	515 9th Street, Room 246	(605) 343-5074
Richmond	VA	23240	400 North 8th Street, Room 3015, P.O. Box 10126	(804) 771-2617
St. Louis	MO	63101	One Mercantile Tower, Suite 2500	(314) 425-6600
Salt Lake City	UT	84138	125 South State Street, Room 2237	(314) 425-5800
San Antonio	TX	78206	727 East Durango Street, Room A-513	(512) 229-6250
San Diego	CA	92188	880 Front Street, Room 4-S-29	(714) 293-5440
San Francisco	CA	94105	211 Main Street, 4th Floor	(415) 974-0642
Santa Ana	CA	92701	2700 North Main Street	(714) 547-5089
Seattle	WA	98174	915 Second Avenue, Room 1744	(206) 442-5534
Sikeston	MO	63801	731A N Main Street	(314) 471-0223
Sioux Falls	SD	57102	101 South Main Avenue, Suite 101	(605) 336-2980
South Bend	IN	46601	501 E Monroe Street, Suite 120	(219) 232-8163
Spokane	WA	99210	West 920 Riverside Avenue, Room 651, P.O. Box 2167	(509) 456-5310
Springfield	IL	62701	Four North, Old State Capital Plaza	(217) 492-4416
Springfield	MO	65806	309 N. Jefferson	(417) 864-7670
Syracuse	NY	13260	100 South Clinton Street, Room 1073	(315) 423-5383
Towson	MD	21204	8600 LaSalle Road, Room 630	(301) 962-4392
Washington	DC	20417	1111 18th Street, NW, 6th Floor	(202) 634-4950
Wichita	KS	67202	110 East Waterman Street	(316) 267-6571
Wilkes-Barre	PA	18702	20 North Pennsylvania Avenue	(717) 826-6497
Wilmington	DE	19801	844 King Street, Room 5207	(302) 573-6294

II. Cash to Start and Grow

Financial Terms Glossary

Certificate of Deposit. Also CD, a certificate for a time deposit in a commercial bank, earning a specified rate of interest over a given time.

Common Stock. Securities that represent an ownership interest in a corporation.

Community Property. Property acquired during a marriage and held to be equally owned by husband and wife under the laws of a state providing for such ownership.

Credit Life Insurance. Term life insurance which pays off a loan if the borrower dies; sometimes required by lenders.

Cumulative Preferred Stock. A preferred stock with the provision that if one or more of its dividends are omitted, these arrears must be paid before dividends are paid on the common stock.

Dividend. The pro-rata proportion of net earnings paid to its stockholders by a corporation. In preferred stock, dividends are usually fixed; with common shares, dividends vary with the fortunes of the company.

Equity. The value of a person's ownership in real property or securities. For instance, the current market value of a home, less the principal remaining on its mortgage, is the equity of that property. Also, a person's total holdings, including real estate, stocks, vested interests in annuities or pensions, etc.

Estate Taxes. Taxes imposed by the federal government (and by some state governments) on the taxable estate of a person who has died.

Face Amount. The amount stated on the face of the policy, which is the amount paid at death or at contract maturity, less any policy loans or withdrawals made.

Gift Taxes. Taxes imposed by the federal government upon an individual's lifetime transfers of money or property by gift.

Government Obligations. Instruments of the U.S. government public debt. Examples are treasury bills, notes, bonds, savings bonds, and retirement plan bonds. These are fully backed by the U.S. government, as opposed to U.S. government agency securities.

Group Life Insurance. Employers or unions offer insurance to their employees or members on a group basis. This often results in lower cost premiums and no medical examination.

Inheritance Taxes. Taxes imposed by some

states on the passing of property of a deceased person's estate to the heirs. It is a tax upon the heir's right to receive his share of the estate.

Joint and Survivor. An arrangement under which the owner of the annuity elects to have payments continue to another person during the latter's lifetime, after the original annuitant's death.

Joint Tenancy. A form of co-ownership which provides that each joint tenant has an undivided interest in the whole property. When one joint tenant dies, his interest passes to the surviving joint tenant or tenants. The last surviving joint tenant obtains title to the entire property.

Level-Premium Insurance. This is a type of insurance where the yearly premium is the same over the life of the policy.

Limited Partnership Investment. A form of business between a general partner who supplies expertise and ability to operate in a certain industry (e.g., real estate and oil and gas) and a group of limited partners who invest in capital. The partnership itself pays no taxes; instead, as partners, the investors report their pro rata share of partnership profits, losses, and deductions on their own individual tax returns.

Margin. A partial payment on investment units, the remainder of which is lent by the trader. When an investor buys on margin he hopes the price will go up fast enough to cover his loan, and thereby increase his buying power. If prices drop, however, he will also increase his losses.

Money Markets. Markets where short-term securities are traded.

Money Market Fund. A mutual fund that specializes in investing in short-term securities.

Mortgage. A lien on property created by a pledge of that property as security for repayment of a loan. It provides for the transfer of the property to the lender if the borrower defaults.

Municipal Bonds. The obligations of states, cities, towns, school districts, and public authorities are known as municipal bonds. There are two principal types of municipal bonds: general obligation bonds and revenue bonds. In general, interest paid on municipal bonds is exempt from federal taxes.

Municipal Bond Fund. A mutual fund that specializes in investing in municipal bonds. Investors in municipal funds will also enjoy federal income tax exemptions on their dividends.

Mutual Fund. A mutual fund pools the dollars of many people and undertakes to invest those dollars more productively than individuals could for themselves.

Permanent or Whole Life Insurance. This is any type of life insurance, other than term, which has the following characteristics: a cash value that can be borrowed, used as collateral, or withdrawn by surrendering the policy; and a lump sum benefit payable at death.

Personal Property. Generally, any property other than real estate.

Portfolio. All assets held by a mutual fund at any specific time and, thus, held by the shareholders. Or total investments held by an individual.

Preferred Stock. A class of stock with a claim on the company's earnings before payment may be made on the common stock if the company liquidates or declares a dividend.

Principal. The amount of money that is financed, borrowed, or invested.

Probate of a Will. Literally, the process of proving that the written will of the deceased is valid.

Proceeds. The amount payable under a life insurance policy upon the death of the insured. The proceeds consist of the face amount of the contract, plus accumulated dividends (if any), plus whatever amounts may be payable on riders, less any money owed to the life insurance company on the policy in the form of loans and interest on those loans.

Retirement Plan. A tax-favored employer benefit plan, which defers taxation of contributions until retirement, can be established by any business, whether incorporated or not incorporated. Employees as well as business owners participate on a nondiscriminatory basis. Contributions are deductible as a business expense. Contribution and benefit limits may fluctuate from year to year.

Security. An investment of money in a common enterprise with the expectation of profit from the effort of others.

Stock Option. Companies often provide the opportunity for the employees or underwriters to buy stock in the company at favorable prices and terms.

Tax-Exempt. Certain kinds of income not subject to income tax. Included for American taxpayers are income from most state and municipal bonds, Social Security payments, dividends up to specified sums, and veterans' pensions.

Tax-Exempt Bonds. The securities of states, cities, and other public authorities specified under federal law, the interest on which is either wholly or partly exempt from federal income taxes. Municipal bonds are often called tax-exempts.

Tax-Exempt Interest. The interest earned on tax-exempt securities is not includable in a shareholder's gross income for federal income tax purposes. In most states, the income from municipal bonds issued within a state is tax-exempt to residents of the state.

Tax Shelter. In some instances, a device whereby a taxpayer may shelter income from tax. Examples: investments in oil drilling activities or certain real estate investments.

Tenancy in Common. A form of co-ownership. Upon the death of a co-owner, his interest passes to his estate and not the surviving owner or owners.

Term Life Insurance. This type of insurance covers a limited specific period of time. In the event of death, benefits will be paid only if death occurs during the period the policy is in force. There is a type of term insurance, called convertible term, which is guaranteed to be exchanged for other types of insurance even if the policyholder would not otherwise qualify.

Treasury Bond. A U.S. government long-term security sold to the public and having a maturity greater than five years.

Treasury Stock. A stock issued by a company

company's treasury indefinitely, reissued to the public, or retired. Treasury stock receives no dividends and has no vote while held by the company.

Trust. A legal arrangement by which title to property is given to one party, who manages it for the benefit of a beneficiary or beneficiaries.

Trustee. An individual or corporation appointed or required by law to administer or execute the trust for the beneficiaries of the trust.

Unit Investment Trust. A limited portfolio of bonds or other securities in which investors may purchase shares. It differs from a

mutual fund in that no new securities will be added to the portfolio.

Will. A declaration of a person's wishes concerning the disposition of his property after his death, the guardianship of his children, and the administration of his estate, executed in accordance with certain legal requirements.

Yield. Also known as return. The dividends or interest paid by a company expressed as a percentage of the current price or, if you own the security, its original price. The return on a stock is figured by dividing the total of dividends paid in the preceding 12 months by the current price or, if you are the owner, the original price.

AT A GLANCE

Debt-Funding Alternatives

	Commercial Banks	Savings & Loan Associations	Commercial Finance Companies (Asset-based Lenders)	Leasing Companies	Long-term Lenders	Government-assisted Sources	Industrial Revenue Bonds
Loan types:							
Demand	Frequent	Occasional	Rare			Rare	
Short term (5 yrs. or less)		Frequent	Occasional	Frequent	Operating and financing leases		Frequent
Intermediate (5–15 yrs.)	Occasionally up to 10 yrs.	Occasional	Occasional	Operating and financing leases	Occasional	Frequent	Frequent (sale-leasebacks)
Long term (over 15 yrs.)	Rare	Frequent	Occasional	Operating and financing leases	Frequent	Occasional	Frequent (sale-leasebacks)
Revolving credit	Occasional	Rare	Frequent			Occasional	
Uses:							
Working capital	Frequent	Occasional	Frequent		Occasional	Frequent	
Growth capital:							
Machinery and equipment	Frequent	Occasional	Frequent	Frequent	Frequent	Frequent	Frequent
Real estate	Occasional	Frequent	Occasional	Frequent	Frequent	Occasional	Frequent

Debt-Funding Alternatives (Continued)

	Commercial Banks	Savings & Loan Associations	Commercial Finance Companies (Asset-based Lenders)	Leasing Companies	Long-term Lenders	Government-assisted Sources	Industrial Revenue Bonds
Acquisitions or general expansion	Occasional	Rare	Frequent	Occasional	Frequent	Occasional	Occasional (expansion not acquisition)
Risk capital	Rare	Rare	Rare		Rare	Occasional to frequent (varies by provider)	
Amounts available	Varies by institution	Varies by institution	Varies by collateral provided	Varies by asset leased	Usually of substantial amounts over $1,000,000	Varies by provider (usually less than $1,000,000)	Varies by issuer and user
Interest-rate base	Prime rate plus 1–4 points	Long-term AAA or government bonds indices plus risk premiums varying in the circumstances	Prime plus 2–6 points	Prime plus 2–6 points	Various bond indices plus risk premiums varying in the circumstances	Varies by provider, SBA debentures or other government securities	Tax-free government bonds yields of issuer
Other terms, covenants:							
Affirmative	Occasional	Frequent	Frequent	Only as to leased asset	Always	Always	Always
Negative	Occasional	Frequent	Frequent	Only as to leased asset	Always	Always	Always
Guarantees	Frequent	Frequent	Frequent	Occasional	Frequent	Frequent	Generally
Security	Frequent	Frequent	Always	Title retained	Frequent	Frequent	Always
Other	Varies by loan type	Fees and other costs, extensive default provisions	Fees and other costs	Provisions on taxes, insurance, and maintenance	Can have extensive other terms and equity participation or conversion rights	Can have extensive public policy requirements	Very extensive tax and regulatory compliance provisions
Financial statements	Audited preferred	Audited preferred	Audited preferred	Audited preferred	Audited preferred	Audited preferred	Audited preferred
Request documents	Generally not complex; more detail required for longer terms; varies at times by security	Generally not complex, but requires extensive appraisals of securing assets	Generally not complex, but requires extensive supporting documents and appraisals of some securing assets; significant preparation aid furnished	Generally not complex; varies in circumstances	Complex and extensive; business plans and financial data required in detail	Complex and extensive; significant preparation aid may be provided	Complex and extensive, significant legal and tax compliance documentation

Debt-Funding Alternatives *(Continued)*

	Commercial Banks	Savings & Loan Associations	Commercial Finance Companies (Asset-based Lenders)	Leasing Companies	Long-term Lenders	Government-assisted Sources	Industrial Revenue Bonds
Borrower stage of development:							
Start-up	Occasionally with guarantees and security	Infrequent	Infrequent	Frequent	Rare	Frequent	Occasional
Growth	Frequent	Occasional	Preferred	Frequent	Occasional	Frequent	Frequent
Maturity	Preferred	Preferred	Frequent	Preferred	Preferred	Occasional	Frequent

Credit: Price Waterhouse, "Financing Your Business"

AT A GLANCE

Equity-Funding Alternatives*

	Wealthy Individuals	Venture Capitalist (Institutional Risk Takers)	Government-assisted Sources	Public Securities Markets	R & D Partnerships	Other Institutions (Long-term)
Frequent uses	Start-ups or early growth	Start-up (specialty sources) or growth (pre-public by 3–5 years)	Start-up, growth, or mature (especially for new locations or expansion)	Late growth or rapid growth, depending on market conditions or maturity	High-tech, usually involves a mature business contracting for R&D services	Mature
Devices/ structure preferred	Common stock and secured loans	Combination of equity (including preferred stock) and debt (with warrants, etc.)	Prefer loans with equity features	Common stock, preferred stock, and certain debt securities	Tax-shelter limited partnership providing services by contract with a sponsoring company	Loans with equity features and preferred stock
Amounts generally available	Varies by individual	Over $1,000,000	Usually under $1,000,000, varies significantly by provider	Amount varies but initial issues of $5–10,000,000 and 500,000 to a million shares preferred	Varies, can be a public issue	Over $1,000,000
Cost	Varies, criteria are not formal; current distributions of interest or dividends to the individual are commonly required	3 to 10 or more times investment over 5 or fewer years; requirements for current distributions of interest or dividends are minor, with capital gains potential preferred	Varies by source; could be based on tax-free yields obtainable by source or SBA debentures; current distribution frequent	15–20% of issue amount and additional continuing costs; current distribution and capital gains sought	Varies, less than debt and more than equity; continuous funding may be required	Varies, but comparable to public market indices; current distributions frequent; middleman fees of 1–4% of funds requested

Equity-Funding Alternatives *(Continued)*

	Wealthy Individuals	*Venture Capitalist (Institutional Risk Takers)*	*Government-assisted Sources*	*Public Securities Markets*	*R & D Partnerships*	*Other Institutions (Long-term)*
Ownership required	Significant minority position, 50/50 or 60/40 are common; criteria not formal	Minority positions 40% or less by direct ownership or future rights; pricing criteria are formal	Future rights to acquire minority positions, generally 25% or less	Varies, majority or very significant minority position preferred	Owned by limited partners; business contracting for services may or may not have ownership interest	Varies, future rights to minority position of 25% or less are common
Documentation	Informal	Formal and extensive business plans and implementing agreements	Formal and extensive business plans and implementing agreements; significant aid in preparation may be available	Varies by registration type or allowed exemption, usually complex and formal	Formal and extensive, terms for future use of technology developed are significant	Formal and extensive business plans and implementing agreements
Financial statements	Audited preferred	Audited preferred	Audited preferred	Audited required	Audited preferred	Audited preferred
Other	Active management involvement directly or on board; personal tax considerations are important	Passive or active management involvement varying by stage of growth; control, or influence through board of directors' seats; control of going public decision or "put" rights; can offer significant management assistance	Frequent public policy requirements; control influences are passive except in default	Significant continuing responsibilities and control influences, including state regulation	Very little management influence, may have financial statement impact on contracting business	Passive management influence through agreement provisions; potential sources include: insurance companies, pension funds, and savings banks
Preferred or principal method of contact	Direct or by referral	Referral	Direct through coordinating agencies such as SBA or state or local agencies; or other financial institutions	Investment bankers and underwriters	Direct; or investment bankers	Middlemen (mortgage and investment bankers)

*Various state and federal security laws will also apply. Consult your lawyer before any solicitation of equity funds is made.

Credit: Price Waterhouse, "Financing Your Business"

Capital Sources

Nonpublic Financing: Sources of Debt Capital

(1) Commercial Banks

Cost: Almost always a floating rate based on the prime rate plus up to 4 additional percentage points.

Maturity: Varies across the board from demand (or 90-day notes) to committed lines of credit (1 to 3 years) to intermediate-term loans (3 to 5 years) and long-term mortgages.

Collateral:
- Unsecured, general floating liens or specific liens on specific assets
- Personal guarantees

Generally used for:
- Working capital needs
- General expansion
- Purchase of machinery and equipment

Advantages:
- Universal source
- "Cradle-to-grave" relationships
- Usually low-cost provider of capital

Disadvantages:
- Preference given to stable, established businesses
- Start-up companies are avoided
- May require personal collateral or personal guarantees

(2) Commercial Finance Companies

Cost: Almost always a floating rate based upon the prime rate plus up to 6 additional percentage points.

Maturity: 1- to 8-year (usually depending upon loan size—the larger the loan, the longer the commitment) revolving credit agreements; term loans of up to 10 years.

Collateral: Always required; first liens on assets to be financed; personal guarantees usually required.

Generally used for:
- Financing increased working capital needs
- Acquisitions
- Purchase of machinery, equipment, and real estate

Advantages:
- Aggressive lenders against balance-sheet collateral
- Will lend to troubled situations
- Revolving credit arrangement allows availability to expand as asset base expands

Disadvantages:
- High-rate lenders
- If asset base contracts, borrower has to repay appropriate part of advance quickly
- Structured initially as demand obligations, will usually move quickly to liquidate if trouble occurs

(3) Leasing Companies

Cost: Usually a cost (implicit in the lease) equal to prime plus up to 6 percentage points; tax-advantaged leases (to the lessor) may be less expensive.

Maturity: Varies with type of asset leased; *operating* leases are short term (as short as a few months); *financing* leases approximate the useful life of the asset.

Collateral: Leasing is a form of secured lending since lessor retains title to the asset.

Generally used for:
- Machinery and equipment
- Real estate
- Acquisition financing

Advantages:
- Easy to deal with
- 100 percent of cost of asset can be financed
- Risk of ownership with lessor

Disadvantages:
- Usually high cost

- Benefits of ownership, such as appreciation, are generally retained by lessor.

(4) Savings and Loan Associations

Cost: Fixed or variable rate, usually tied to long-term market rates; on working capital loans, floating, tied to the prime rate, priced competitively with local commercial banks.

Maturity: Usually long term (15 years); occasionally lines of credit.

Collateral: Almost always secured.

Generally used for:
- Real estate
- Working capital and purchase of machinery and equipment

Advantages:
- Familiar, experienced lenders in real estate area
- Attractive rates
- Attractive loan to asset ratios

Disadvantages:
- Usually prefer strongly capitalized and established businesses
- Careful lenders to commercial businesses for working capital needs

(5) Life Insurance Companies/Pension Funds

Cost: Usually fixed rate tied to long-term market rates.

Maturity: Varying between 5 to 10 years and 25 years, depending on use of proceeds.

Collateral:
- Unsecured debentures for established, financially strong borrowers
- Secured for asset acquisition purposes

Generally used for:
- Machinery and equipment
- Real estate
- Long-term working capital support needs

Advantages:
- Provide long-term capital
- Market rates of interest

Disadvantages:
- Minimum loan amounts are usually high

(e.g., $1 million or more)
- Restrictive loan agreements usually required

(6) Small Business Administration

Cost: Can be floating or fixed, but subject to a government-imposed ceiling.

Maturity: 7 to 25 years, depending upon use of proceeds.

Collateral: Almost always secured by general floating liens on specific collateral; personal guarantees of owner required.

Generally used for:
- When business is ineligible for conventional financing
- Working capital
- Machinery and equipment
- Real estate

Advantages:
- "Lender of last resort"
- Cost not commensurate with risk
- Financing available for all types of assets

Disadvantages:
- All-inclusive liens usually required
- Guarantees of major stockholders required
- Financing available only to businesses that qualify

(7) Industrial Revenue Bonds

Cost: Can be floating or fixed, but at "tax-exempt" rate, which is usually 70 to 85 percent of prevailing prime rate.

Maturity: Usually 5 to 15 years.

Collateral: Almost always secured by fixed assets.

Generally used for:
- Machinery and equipment
- Real estate
- Rehabilitation of existing fixed assets
- Limited working capital financing
- Acquisition financing

Advantages:
- Low rate
- Acceptable maturities

- Usually funded by the company's commercial bank

Disadvantages:
- Can be hard to obtain, subject to market availability
- Government can change rules
- Higher closing costs, particularly higher legal fees

(8) Leveraged Buyouts (LBOs)

Definition: The acquisition of a business or a group of assets using a high level of debt and little equity.

Purpose: To increase the return of investors' committed capital by averaging a small equity infusion with a large amount of debt.

Generally used: To purchase an established business, where there is a strong asset base and existing cash flow. The existing cash flow is used to retire the purchase money debt, and the strong asset base is used to further cushion the lender.

Participating debt sources:
- Commercial banks, particularly where there is an existing strong cash flow
- Asset-based lenders, where cash flow may be weak but the asset (collateral) base is strong
- Industrial revenue bonds, to finance with an attractive rate and maturity basis the purchase of machinery and equipment and real property

Nonpublic Financing: Sources of Equity Capital

(1) Small Business Innovation Research (SBIR) Grants

Amount available: Initially $50,000, with later commitment of up to $500,000.

Deal structure: Grant by agency or department of federal government.

Cost: Well-researched, documented proposal must be constructed and offered for review.

Generally used for: Seed capital.

Advantages: Low cost, no equity give-up.

(2) R & D Partnerships

Amount available: Varying from quite small to hundreds of millions of dollars for publicly sponsored issues.

Deal structure: Tax-oriented limited partnership.

Cost: Varies depending on market conditions and success of project; structured, however, to be less expensive than debt, but more expensive than equity.

Generally used: When funds for new product research are needed, tax advantages cannot be immediately used by company, and company wishes to share risk with outside investors.

Advantages: High-risk funds come from outside the business.

Disadvantages: Can be very high cost if project is very successful.

(3) Professional Venture Capitalists

Amount available: Usually $500,000 and above.

Deal structure: Varies across the board; in many instances, convertible preferred stock.

Cost: Long-term capital gain sought in area of three to ten times money invested over 4- to 7-year investment horizon.

Generally used: When business has extremely high growth potential ($50 million to $100 million sales in 5 years) and company plans to go public rather than remain private.

Advantages: Large amounts of risk capital available, much more than in case of wealthy individuals; investors bring contacts and business experience.

Disadvantages: Company must follow planned high sales growth path expected by investors; company must become public, usually as soon as possible.

(4) Small Business Investment Companies (SBICs)

Amount available: Varies by SBIC, but usual range is from $100,000 to $1 million.

Deal structure: Varies from straight debt to straight equity; most common form of deal is hybrid security, either convertible debt or subordinated debt instrument with warrants to buy common stock attached.

Cost: Costs include both a rate of interest or dividend and equity participation in the business.

Generally used for: Expansion capital, working capital, acquisition financing, and leveraged buyouts.

Advantages: Provides subordinated capital, augmenting the equity base for borrowing purposes; by regulation, maturity on debt instruments must be at least 5 years; interest rates are usually fixed.

Disadvantages: Equity give-up required; investors may seek influence over business (e.g., board of directors' seat); usually must be fast-growth company with plans for going public within 3 to 5 years.

(5) Minority Enterprise Small Business Investment Companies (MESBICs)

Amount available: Varies by MESBIC, but usual range is from $100,000 to $1 million; MESBIC capital is available only to minority-owned businesses.

Deal structure: Similar to deals structured with SBICs.

Cost: Similar to costs of SBIC capital.

Generally used for: Start-up capital, working capital, expansion capital, acquisition financing, and leveraged buyouts.

Advantages: Source of risk/equity capital for minority-owned businesses; provides subordinated capital augmenting the equity base for borrowing purposes; interest rates are usually fixed.

Disadvantages: By law, can be used only to fund minority-owned businesses; equity give-up required; investors may seek influence over business; usually must be fast-growth company with plans for going public within 3 to 5 years.

Credit: Peat Marwick

Bankers

Advice from Joseph Mancuso, president, Center for Entrepreneurial Management

Know Thy Banker: How to Be Your Bank's Best Customer

I often hear small-business people complain that every time they go to the bank to talk about a loan they wind up talking to a different loan officer. Their previous loan officer has been promoted and is no longer handling their account, and that means starting all over again. It's a common problem, but it doesn't have to be that way.

If you're going to the bank only when you need to borrow, you're not doing your job. If you want the bank to take a genuine interest in what's best for your business, then you need to take an interest in theirs. Here are some tips on how to do just that:

Go to one of your bank's seminars on commercial lending

Most entrepreneurs never go to a seminar at their bank. They don't think they'll learn enough to make it worth their time. But by going there, you're demonstrating that you take a real interest in what your *bank* is doing. Being there also provides you with an easy opportunity to meet and make an impression on the loan committee.

Read the bank's annual report
It pays to have an idea of where your bank is headed and who's taking it there. Further, the annual report will tell you something about the bank's lines of authority. You should be on the bank's mailing list in any event, and if the bank is a public company, I recommend you buy a share of stock.

Attend the bank's annual stockholders' meetings
Make sure you sit up front and ask polite questions. Bankers are seldom congratulated for the work they're doing, and an innocuous question about the bank's accomplishments can bring big rewards. (Not only will you be noticed, but later, when the bank president asks who asked the question, your banker can say, "Oh, that was so-and-so. He's one of my customers.")

Cultivate your banker
Take a real interest in his career, and *ask* if he will hold on to your account as he climbs up the banking ladder. The key is to *ask*.

When you go to see your banker, have your business plan and financial papers ready. Make it easy for him to see what you need money for and why. When raising capital, it's your job to bring the element of risk to an acceptable level—which for bankers is zero.

Here are the five questions you need to be able to answer: (1) How much money do you need? (2) How long do you need it for? (3) What are you going to do with it? (4) When and how are you going to repay it? and (5)

What will you do if you don't get the loan?

It's in your interest to know what cards your banker is holding, so it pays to know your loan officer's lending limit, both for secured and unsecured loans. Don't be afraid to spend time investigating him. The amount of time you spend will be just a small fraction of the amount he will spend investigating you.

At the same time, you should never go over your banker's head. This will effectively end any relationship you've developed. If you think your banker isn't giving you a fair shake, change bankers *and* banks. If you only change bankers, there's a chance that he will sit on your loan committee. And bankers never forget a bad loan or a slight.

One of the most delicate issues between entrepreneurs and bankers is personal loan guarantees. No one likes signing personal guarantees, but not many people know that they don't always have to. Keep in mind that collateral never makes a bad loan good. What it does is bring the level of risk, for the bank, down to zero. But 99 percent of the loans a banker makes are paid back out of the cash flow the business generates. So a good loan shouldn't always require your personal guarantee.

Just ask if every commercial loan the bank has made has required that the business's president sign a personal guarantee. The honest answer is no. Then ask, "Well, what loans have you made that didn't require personal guarantees? And what do I have to do to get a loan without signing a personal guarantee?" Now you've got yourself a good bargaining chip.

Credit: *Success* magazine, June 1985, and Joseph Mancuso

Are You on Good Terms with Your Bank? Test Yourself—and Find Out

To be your bank's best customer, score 175 points or more on this quiz.

1. Can you draw an organizational chart of the bank, with your banker included? (25 points) You need to know where the decision-making power is and where your banker fits into it.

2. Did you give your banker a small Christmas present last year? (20 points; add 10 points if your banker came to your Christmas party) When I say a small gift, I mean something like a book (if you know he's got a hobby, like boating, give him a book that relates to that).

3. Do you know where your banker went to school? (10 points) One of the first things two people do when they get to know each other is to look for some common ground. Knowing what school your banker went to will not only tell you something about him, it can often provide an opener.

4. Do you know your banker's spouse's first name? (10 points) Again, people tend to trust familiarity (up to a point, of course), so it helps if you know your banker's spouse's name and ask after him or her once in a while.

5. Do you know your banker's boss's first and last name? (15 points) Bankers tend to move up quickly in their jobs—either changing banks or bouncing from one branch to another. If you know your banker's boss, then it's possible that when your banker moves, your account will be passed up to the boss rather than down to the new loan officer. And the higher the person you're dealing with, the better off you are.

6. Do you know the names and backgrounds of at least two members (not counting your banker) of the loan committee? (40 points) Ninety percent of the time, your loan officer makes the decision on your loan, but he has to get approval by the loan committee. If you know who's on the committee (and they know you), that will smooth the process.

7. Do you know your banker's home town? (10 points) Friendly interest is one key to a good relationship.

8. Do you know your banker's birthday? (15 points) When I mention that it's a good idea to give your banker a quick phone call on his birthday, the average person laughs and tells me that's corny. He laughs, but on *his* birthday he gets a kick out of the fact that someone remembers. (Also, calling your banker on his birthday tells him you have a good memory for dates and will remember when your loan payments come due.)

9. Have you taken your banker and/or his boss on a tour of your company in the last six months? (25 points) It's amazing how impressed a banker is when he actually sees a product being produced, sold, and shipped.

10. Have you been out socially (not as part of a loan request) with your banker in the last six months? (30 points) When I say you should take your banker out socially, I mean socially. No business. Don't make the mistake of asking an especially touchy question after a pleasant meal. And let your banker do 90 percent of the talking. The more you let him talk about his interests, the better impression you'll make.

Credit: *Success* magazine, June 1985, and Joseph Mancuso.

Banker's Acceptances Can Finance Trading Activities

An obscure financing instrument—the banker's acceptance—can help small companies raise money for trading activities in the U.S. and overseas. With acceptances, cash is available at fixed rates generally below that of standard short-term loans.

Put simply, a banker's acceptance is a time draft drawn on a bank that is payable at a future date. By accepting the draft, the bank promises to pay the face amount to any holder presenting it at maturity. In effect, the bank substitutes its credit standing for that of its customer. This is important because banks often sell the obligations to third parties as investment vehicles.

Banker's acceptances can be used to accomplish a number of objectives, including the accelerated receipt of funds on export sales.

"Assume U.S.-based company A is selling $10,000 worth of shirts to company B in France," says a vice-president with Manufacturers Hanover Trust. "Although B may have 90 days to pay, A will likely want the money immediately for working capital. Small, marginally capitalized businesses are especially hard pressed to wait for payments on trade transactions.

"To gain faster access to the funds, A goes to his bank, shows the shipping documentation, and draws a draft for the $10,000. Providing A has a good credit rating, the bank will accept the draft and pay him a discounted portion of the $10,000, say $9,650. The exact amount changes according to current rates and the maturity of the draft.

"The money advanced is actually a short-term financing to be repaid at the draft's maturity date by company A. By this time, B's payment will likely have been received."

Banker's acceptances are also useful for importers. Small companies importing goods for eventual resale in the U.S. may be required, through letters of credit, to pay the exporters as soon as the merchandise is shipped. Because it may be months before the importer earns revenues on the domestic sale of the goods, he may want to use the banker's acceptance as a financing bridge.

"By drawing a draft on the bank, the importer receives financing to pay for the imported merchandise," the banker says, "and he uses the revenue from the resale of the merchandise to retire the acceptance at maturity."

Because banks generally resell acceptances to investors in the money markets—and thus do not have to tie up their own funds—rates compare favorably to traditional loans.

"Charges for banker's acceptances are in two parts, the discount rate and the bank's commission," says a vice-president of New York-based European-American Bank. "Depending on the borrower's credit standing, the combined financing cost usually ranges from prime to slightly below prime."

Adds the president of a Houston-based trade consulting firm, "Banker's acceptances can provide small companies with infusions of short-term cash that can be highly beneficial for trading activities. In many cases, this method of financing compares very favorably, in terms of cost, to other options."

To be eligible for discounting by the banks, and in turn to provide the most attractive rates to borrowers, acceptances must comply with the following Federal Reserve Board provisions:

- The term of the draft cannot exceed six months.
- The acceptance must be created for a current shipment.

- The financing must be for import/export, movement of goods between foreign countries, the domestic shipment of goods, or the storage of "readily marketable staples" in the U.S. or abroad.

"One additional factor to consider is that there must not be any other financing extended on the same trade transaction," says a Manufacturers Hanover vice-president. "If an importer, for example, is already getting credit from his foreign source or from another financial institution, the acceptance may be deemed ineligible for discounting."

Contact a banker or independent financial adviser for details.

Cash Management Can Bolster the Bottom Line

When the president of ABC Stores, a small southeastern retailer, boasted that in 20 years of business his bank never charged him fees for checking services, his accountant shuddered.

"If your bank doesn't hit you with service charges, you're probably doing something wrong," says a partner with Phillips, Gold, CPAs. "Namely, enriching the bank at your own expense. Chances are there's a lot of money sitting idle in non-interest-bearing accounts. That's cash the bank's investing that the company should be putting to use for itself. Although the bank may take the investment gains in lieu of service charges, small business is better off reversing this by paying the bank fees and investing its own funds."

The name of the game is cash management. Companies must learn to husband cash resources by aggressively investing idle bank balances, gaining use of accounts receivable as quickly as possible, and playing the float on banking transactions.

"There are five critical areas of cash management," says a cash-management specialist with Peat Marwick, the national accounting firm. "Collection of receipts, concentration of receipts, disbursements, investing balances, and managing the flow of information. Unless these elements are carefully coordinated, the company will not be making the most efficient use of its cash. As such, it will lose out on income-producing opportunities and will be forced to engage in costly and unnecessary borrowing."

The following is a review of the major cash management components:

1. Collection of receipts: Typically, small business short-circuits the collection process by allowing incoming checks to accumulate at the company's offices.

"We find that checks are often addressed to the wrong people," explains the Peat Marwick specialist, "are lost in the office shuffle, or are simply held by the accounts receivable clerk until that person finds time to get to the bank. All these factors cost the company money. Receipts sitting on a desk when they could be earning money in an investment account is a prime example of poor cash management."

Consider these collection strategies:

- Instruct customers to send checks to the person or department responsible for processing them.
- Make certain that collections are deposited in the bank at least once a day.
- Explore the use of a lockbox. This speeds the collection process by having all receipts mailed directly to a post office box serviced by the company's bank. Couriers clear the box several times a day, bringing all receipts to the bank, where they are immediately credited to the company's account.
- Ask the bank to provide an "availability schedule," revealing its policy on clearing

out-of-state checks. This puts management in position to determine whether it is getting credit for available funds as quickly as possible.

"If the availability schedule says it takes two days for Connecticut checks to clear and a small business owner finds that his Hartford checks are taking a week to clear, he knows to argue for a faster turnaround," says the cash management specialist. "Having an availability schedule makes the company a more informed and effective bank customer. Management gets the benefit of a reduced bank float."

A partner with Touche Ross notes that the prompt clearance of funds can reduce financing costs.

"An interesting cash-management tactic is to negotiate for a faster clearance on receivables-based loans. Take the small business that gets bank cash advances for 80 percent of its receivables at 15 percent interest. If the company's average collection period is 30 days and the bank takes three days to credit the deposit of its receivables, the actual interest rate rises an additional 1.8 percent simply because of the bank's delay in crediting the funds. The formula: additional borrowing cost =

$$\frac{\text{number of bank clearing days}}{\text{receivable collection period}} \times$$

$$\frac{\text{stated interest rate}}{\text{percentage of receivables financed}}$$

"The goal is to get that clearance period down to one or two days, thus cutting the real interest rate."

2. Concentration: Banking activities should be conducted through a minimal number of accounts. This affords management greater control over its cash resources and allows for more effective use of its balances.

Small businesses tend to have too many bank accounts. Take a convenience store chain with 10 branch outlets and a separate bank account for each shop. The best approach here is to shift daily cash deposits to a central account at the company's lead bank. This way management can see at a glance early in the day how much it has to invest and can arrange for this investment with a single transaction.

Cash can be transferred to a central account in the following ways:

- Wire transfers allow for immediate accessibility of funds but produce significant service charges. Reserve this option for substantial sums of cash or when balances are needed immediately.
- Depository transfer checks are usually written by the central bank to draw money from the local banks. This costs less than wire transfers but may not provide immediate clearance.
- Automated clearinghouse transfers shift cash from one account to another electronically. The central bank simply debits the company's local account and credits the firm's central concentration account. This generally provides for one-day availability of funds and carries a relatively small service charge.

3. Disbursement: To hear cash-management experts tell it, bill paying is more than a business obligation—it's an art and a science.

"The way a company pays its bills can have a significant impact on its bottom line," says a partner with accountants Grant Thornton. "The objective is to time payments either to take advantage of cash discounts or to retain use of the money for as long as possible. If there are significant incentives for early payment, the company may want to make disbursements within 10 days of billing. On the other hand, in times of high interest rates, it may be preferable to stretch out disbursements beyond the ordinary payment date. During this time the company can invest its cash or use it for working capital. Management must compare the yield for both courses and take the most profitable route."

Another disbursement technique capitalizes on the concentration of funds in a single account. Take our hypothetical convenience chain with 10 bank accounts. In situations like this, each store would likely have a disbursement account with, say, $2,000 to cover routine expenditures. That means $20,000 is sitting idle. A better approach is to set up one central disbursement account, allowing each store to write checks on that account. This eliminates nine disbursement accounts and makes it less likely that balances would remain idle.

4. Investing balances: Many banks now offer sweep accounts which provide for automatic investment of balances above a specified level. Cash that is not needed to cover checks or to provide for compensating balances is invested in certificates of deposit or other money market instruments generally overnight or for the weekend. This way the company makes money with its money. While this type of account was once limited to the GMs of the world, competition has forced the banks to offer it to even the smallest companies. Entrepreneurs should shop around to find those banks with the best cash-management programs.

Adds the Touche Ross partner, "Banks may claim that keeping cash in the company's account—in so-called compensating balances—can reduce borrowing costs, but borrowers may actually be better off keeping little or no balances and paying higher financing rates. The trick is to calculate the real cost of capital."

Consider this: On a $250,000 five-year loan with interest at 17 percent and a compensating balance requirement of 15 percent of the outstanding loan, the real cost of the financing is 20 rather than 17 percent. Figure it this way:

$$\frac{\text{stated interest rate}}{\substack{\text{100\% minus the compensating} \\ \text{balance requirement}}} = \text{real cost}$$

By knowing the cost of the compensating balance—in this case 3 percent—the small business can determine whether to forgo this option and accept the higher interest rate.

While many companies used to accept compensating balance requirements without question, many are now getting more sophisticated about their cash-management practices. This means comparing the costs of alternatives.

5. Managing the flow of information: The familiar saying "garbage in, garbage out" is as true when applied to cash management as it is to computers. To manage cash effectively, small business owners must look beneath the surface to identify key trends and to determine the sum of their investable balances.

One source of critical information is the cash-flow projection. This estimates the company's cash position and borrowing needs over a specified period.

Here's how it can save money. Should projections indicate that the company will need to borrow $300,000 from the bank for the entire year, management may want to switch from a line of credit to a term loan. This can reduce the interest rate and in turn cut the financing costs.

Another vital source of information, the account analysis, provides data the standard bank statement omits. A key section of the analysis—the average daily investable balance—reveals the amount of funds available in the account for investing. Management can weigh this figure against banking fees and financing costs to determine if it is maintaining reasonable or excess balances. Ask the bank to provide a copy of the account analysis.

Work with an independent financial adviser to design and implement cash-management procedures.

AT A GLANCE

Cash Management

The primary goals of an efficient, integrated cash-management system are:

1. To reduce the operating costs of the cash-flow system so that cash benefits exceed costs.
2. To minimize investment in noncash assets to their most effective level in order to increase cash or reduce borrowing requirements.
3. To maximize non-interest-bearing or low-interest liabilities to increase cash or reduce borrowing requirements.
4. To "work" cash funds as hard as possible in order to gain the greatest interest benefits or reduce borrowing costs.
5. To reduce management's involvement in day-to-day cash-management operations.
6. To compensate banks fairly, but not excessively, for products used.
7. To pay bills on time and to take all discounts.
8. To create invoices and to ship goods as soon as reasonably possible.

Credit: Peat Marwick, "Cash Management"

Collections and Accounts-Receivable Management

The objectives of this area are to accelerate cash receipts, increase profits through increased sales, minimize the cost of carrying receivables, and minimize bad debts. Some of the questions that should be asked under each of the subsystems in this area are:

Order Entry

- How quickly are sales orders turned into invoices?
- Are there follow-up procedures for order mistakes/adjustments?
- Does the order entry system interface with billing, inventory, and accounts receivable?

Shipping/Freight

- How are products shipped?
- What are the average monthly freight charges as a percent of sales?

Billing

- How often are bills generated?
- Is billing a centralized function?
- How does the billing system interface with other related systems?

Remittance Patterns

- Who are your major customers?
- Are your sales seasonal?
- Are discounts taken by customers monitored to determine whether they have been earned?

Remittance Processing

- Are remittances received and posted on a centralized basis?

- Are payments received in your office?
- When and how are remittances deposited at your bank?
- Do you have a lockbox?
- Are any payments received electronically?
- Do you ever receive cash?

Accounts-Receivable Management

- What are your written credit policies?
- Do you age your receivables on a regular basis?
- What are your typical trade terms?

Bank Relationships: Understanding the Account Analysis

The delicate balance in business banking is to compensate the bank fairly for all of its services—and not a penny more. By keeping excess cash in their accounts, companies enrich the bank at their own expense.

Just where the midpoint occurs is revealed in a critical banking document that many small companies never see. Known as the "account analysis," it indicates the profit (or loss) the bank earns on each of its accounts.

"Typically, bank customers see only the monthly statement and think that's enough," says a principal with the accounting firm of Main Hurdman. "But this statement is only good for reconciling the account. It doesn't tell the small business how much the bank is earning from it and whether it is paying too much for banking services. The account analysis—which is generally available to any company that knows to ask for it—provides this information. It makes for interesting, and potentially profitable, reading."

Account analyses are typically divided into the following components:

1. Balance activity reports on the amount of money in the account on an average daily basis.

"It's a good idea to occasionally test the accuracy of this figure with data on the regular monthly statement," the CPA adds. "All you have to do is add up the total of each day's ending balances and divide by the number of days in the month. That's the average daily ledger balance."

From this figure the bank subtracts a "collection float," which is the amount of time it allots for checks to clear. This provides a yardstick for measuring the bank's handling of the account.

"You divide the average daily collection float by the average daily deposits," the accountant explains. "If the former is $120,000 and the latter is $100,000, that gives you a figure of 1.2 days for the funds to clear, which is good. Anything over 1.5 is suspect—the bank should explain it—and anything over 2.0 is generally unacceptable."

Also subtracted from the average daily balance is a "reserve requirement," generally ranging from 12 to 16 percent, which reflects that part of the balance the bank is prohibited by law from investing.

The net figure in this section of the analysis is the average daily investable balance available to the bank.

2. The cost of services section identifies the services provided by the bank and enumerates the charges for each, including item charges (per check or other transactions) and fixed charges (such as monthly maintenance and lockbox).

Fee data are most helpful as a means of making sure you're being charged for the right services and also as a yardstick for comparing your bank's fees with those charged by other banks. Once every year or two obtain a list of fees from competitor banks and see how they stack up against yours.

The bottom line of the account analysis converts services into balance requirements. By assigning an interest rate (earnings credit rate) to the investable balance, the bank comes up with a gross income figure for maintaining the account. This is applied to the total cost of services plus balance requirements for credit. If the figures are equal, the customer's compensating balance is sufficient to cover all bank fees; if the gross income is larger, the customer is probably maintaining excess balances.

"These are the balances that should be invested," the accountant says, "either by the business owner or through an automatic investment plan available at most banks. The goal is to develop a target balance—one that compensates the bank but does not leave excess idle funds—and to put the rest of the money to work earning more money for the company."

Adds a partner with the accounting firm of Phillips, Gold, "It's been my experience that if a business is not being asked by its bank to come up with additional fees now and then, it is probably keeping excess idle balances. Reviewing the account analysis on a regular basis can help management learn precisely how much cash it has to invest."

But there's another side to this issue. According to outspoken bankers, playing the float with business checking accounts may produce short-term profits at the expense of long-term bank relationships.

At a time when financial advisers are recommending aggressive cash-management practices—principally the investment of every dollar of available bank balances—the men in the pinstripe suits have another story to tell. By maintaining minimal or in some cases zero balances, they say, small compa-

nies deprive the bank of profit-making opportunities and in the process make themselves less attractive candidates for business loans.

"Those small companies that recognize the bank's legitimate need for profits as well as their own legitimate need for financing are the ones that stand the best chance of getting business loans when they need them," says an executive with Houston-based PetroBank. "Take a situation that arises in our bank almost daily. A small, marginal business—one that falls in the gray area of our credit standards—needs working capital. When the responsible bank officer goes before the loan committee, he's more likely to swing the deal if the company's been a profitable bank customer over the years. Most important, we look to see if management has kept significant balances. If so, there's more of an incentive on our part to come up with the loan."

By maintaining balances in excess of current cash requirements, companies provide a pool of funds the banks can invest for their own gain. Although this deprives the small business of incremental earnings, the trade-off—a more productive bank relationship—may make this worthwhile.

"If two companies make loan requests, the one that is the better bank customer—all other things being equal—gets preferential treatment," says an executive vice-president of New York's Sterling National Bank. "Although keeping adequate balances is not the only criterion for being judged a good customer, it is a key factor in the overall banking relationship. The business that just wants to write checks, and to come out ahead on the float, is not going to win favor with its bankers."

A cash-management specialist with Deloitte, Haskins & Sells, the national accounting firm, agrees—to a point.

"Marginal borrowers do have to provide their banks with some incentive for making loans. And there's no doubt that banks, like all other businesses, extend themselves for their most profitable customers.

"But that doesn't mean small companies should let all their money sit idle in checking accounts just to please the banks. There's a balance to be struck in keeping enough cash on hand to compensate the bank for its services and credit requirements and to assure the business a reasonable return on its idle funds. This sum can best be determined by the business owner in consultation with his bankers and financial advisers."

Consider these additional factors:

- Compensating balances may reduce interest charges. Companies keeping money with the bank should negotiate for lower loan rates.
- Excess balances may offset the cost of bank services such as checking account transactions and safety deposit boxes.
- The most credit-worthy businesses—with strong financial statements and solid track records—will likely attract bank financing regardless of cash balances.
- Companies keeping substantial balances should make certain that their banks provide superior service in return.

The Ten Commandments of Borrowing

So you need money to start or expand your business. Welcome to the club. At any given time, thousands of would-be borrowers are knocking on bankers' doors seeking loans and lines of credit. Some walk away with the cash, others walk away empty-handed. The difference is in how they approach the market.

"There's more to borrowing money than simply filling out forms and crossing your fingers," says Hauppauge, Long Island-based loan broker Leonard Primack. "It is an art and a science. You have to know which sources to contact, how to conduct yourself during the application process, and how to negotiate with prospective lenders."

Companies in the market for capital may fare well by heeding these ten commandments for successful borrowing:

1. Never rely on a single banker. By applying for loans at a number of institutions, and retaining relationships with these sources over the years, management improves the odds of keeping the flow of capital open at all times.

"Lending is often based on subjective factors," says a managing director of Hindin/Owen/Engelke Inc., investment bankers. "Where one loan officer sees marginal risk unworthy of bank credit, another may flash the green light. Reaching out to a number of banks boosts the chances of gaining a favorable decision."

2. Look to banks or finance companies specializing in your field or industry. Those institutions familiar with the risks and rewards in lending to your type of company are most likely to produce the needed cash. Ask colleagues or trade associations for the names of the most active lenders.

3. Plan ahead for financing needs, putting the wheels in motion before the money is needed. This gives you ample opportunity to shop the lending market and to act from a position of strength.

4. Avoid patchwork financing.

"Take the manufacturer in need of new equipment," says the investment banker. "Like many companies, it will lease the machine, obtain a working capital loan to support its implementation, and then seek a line of credit to finance the growth in business the equipment brings. This patchwork financing forces management to keep going back to the bank. Should it fail to get any of the loans, the expansion will fizzle out. That's why it's best to apply for the full loan up front."

5. Borrow more money than you think you need. In most cases, capital requirements exceed projections. Pad loan requests by 25 percent over the budgeted amount.

6. Treat borrowing as part of the management process.

"Big companies think of capital as a resource to be inventoried like coal or steel," says the investment banker. "Small companies should learn to do the same, building up reserves of capital and investing that portion that proves to be excessive in money market funds or certificates of deposit. The luxury of having the money at your disposal is worth the spread you'll have to cover between the cost of funds and the yield on your investments. In my opinion, paying $15,000 a year to know that you have a half million dollars on tap is a bargain."

7. When waiting for a bank's decision, never assume that no news is good news. While unseasoned borrowers take a banker's silence as an indication that a loan is being approved, the opposite is often true. Just when the borrower thinks that the deal is set, he learns to his dismay that the loan is denied. Protect yourself from this shock by asking the banker when his decision is expected and note to follow up on that date. Wise borrowers never leave anything to chance.

8. Time lending requests to favorable developments in your business. Propitious events include the signing of a major contract, the development of a promising product, or a substantial spurt in sales and profits. Remember, anything that builds the banker's confidence also loosens his purse strings.

9. Never equate tight money with no money. Even when the economy is weak, and loans are hard to come by, the capital markets do not dry up. Persistent borrowers unwilling to take "no" for an answer expand their sights beyond the banks to alternative financing sources including factors, finance companies, venture capitalists, government agencies, and private investors.

10. When comparing loan offers, look beyond the interest rate to the amount of available financing and the terms of the loan. Favor the lender offering the best mix of financing features.

ASSET-BASED FINANCING

How to Turn Your Assets into Loans

When a small manufacturer of hair and skin care products needed capital to fund its burgeoning growth, the president turned to an obscure cash source known as asset-based financing. More liberal and creative than unsecured bank lending, asset-based financing is pegged to a company's collateral rather than to its profitability. For this reason, prospective borrowers turned down by the banks can find a welcome mat at the asset-based lenders.

"Our members generally serve two kinds of companies," says an executive with the National Commercial Finance Association (NCFA), a New York City-based trade group representing asset-based lenders. "Those that are too young to qualify for bank borrowing and those that have been bank borrowers in the past but for one reason or another can no longer get money from the banks. Because we're not terribly concerned with the debt-to-worth ratios or profit levels that are so critical to bankers, we can make loans to those borrowers they reject."

From the asset-based lender's perspective, a borrower is as worthy as the assets it owns. Companies rich in receivables, inventory, real estate, or equipment can land substantial loans even if they are yet to earn a profit.

"We borrowed $800,000 on the strength of our receivables alone," says the president of the hair care company. "And that's the real advantage of working with asset-based lenders. They just aren't as fussy as the traditional lenders. While the banks demand that borrowers meet a series of broad financial tests, the asset-based people focus almost exclusively on the quality of the assets. If that checks out okay, you'll get the money."

Asset-based loans are open-ended lines of credit that expand and contract with the value of the assets. Just how the financing is applied in the real world is illustrated by the case of a family-owned distributor of Christmas ornaments.

"Every spring, the company orders its product line from manufacturers in the Far East," the NCFA executive explains. "Asset-based lenders—using existing assets as collateral—put up a letter of credit to make the purchase. When the merchandise arrives, the financing changes to an inventory loan collateralized by the goods themselves. Then, when the goods are shipped out to customers, the financing becomes a receivables loan that is paid down as collections are made. The process then begins anew the following spring.

"Asset-based loans are called 'evergreen' because they do not need to be paid off annually, as may be required with bank lines of credit."

The amount of money generally available to borrowers is based on the following percentages of asset values:

- 70 to 80 percent of accounts receivable (those less than 90 days old)
- 20 to 50 percent of inventory (staple goods such as toasters and tablecloths are at the high end of the spectrum while high-fashion or gadget items are at the low point)
- 70 percent of fixed assets (based on the price they would bring at liquidation)

Because they carry a greater level of risk—remember, credit is available to untested or in some cases unprofitable companies—asset-based loans also carry steeper financing charges. For loans in the $500,000 to $1.5 million range, figure interest rates of 2.5 to 5.5 points above the prime, or at least two points above unsecured bank borrowing. The gap closes for larger loans but is still generally more costly than traditional financing.

Also in the minus column, asset-based lenders require frequent financial reporting, including daily statements of receivables, sales, and cash receipts. Although the paperwork can be a burden to management, most borrowers consider it well worth the price of obtaining needed capital.

Who are the best candidates for asset-based financing? Lenders look most favorably at these applicants:

- Wholesalers, manufacturers, and distributors with assets that can be used as collateral
- Companies in stable industries rarely subject to extreme market fluctuations
- Businesses with good internal accounting systems and experienced management

Asset-based loans can be obtained from finance companies and the asset-based lending divisions of commercial banks.

NATIONAL COMMERCIAL FINANCE ASSOCIATION

225 West 34th Street, New York, NY 10001
(212) 594-3490

ROSTER OF MEMBERS

Abrams & Company, Inc.
250 West 57th Street
New York, NY 10019
(212) 315-2550

Accord Business Credit, Inc.
1440 St. Catherine Street W.
Montreal, Canada H3G 1R8
(514) 866-2711

Affiliated Asset-based Lending
Services, Inc.
8700 N. Waukegan Road,
Ste. 100, P.O. Box 98
Morton Grove, IL 60053
(312) 965-7810

Allegheny International Credit
Corporation
1 Allegheny Square,
Ste. 880
Pittsburgh, PA 15212
(412) 562-4086

Ambassador Factors
Corporation
1450 Broadway
New York, NY 10018
(212) 221-3000

American Acceptance Corp.
One Montgomery Plaza
Norristown, PA 19401
(215) 278-2600

American Commercial Capital
Corporation
310 Madison Avenue
New York, NY 10017
(212) 986-3305

American Factors of Texas, Inc.
2323 Bryan Street, LBJ 175
Dallas, TX 75201
(214) 969-9090

American National Bank &
Trust Company/Chicago
33 North LaSalle Street
Chicago, IL 60690
(312) 661-5000

Ameritrust Company National
Association
900 Euclid Avenue, Tower-6
Cleveland, OH 44115
(216) 687-5123

Amsave Credit Corporation
1370 Avenue of the Americas
New York, NY 10019
(212) 489-9111

Associates Business Loans
150 North Michigan Avenue
Chicago, IL 60601
(312) 781-2581

Associates Commercial Corp.
1040 Avenue of the Americas
New York, NY 10018
(212) 790-0110

AT Commercial Corporation
20 North Clark Street,
Ste. 3100
Chicago, IL 60602
(312) 750-6000

Atlantic Financial
50 Monument Road
Bala Cynwyd, PA 19004
(215) 668-6167

BancAmerica Commercial
Corporation
555 South Flower Street
Los Angeles, CA 90071
(213) 228-3485

BancBoston Financial
Two Pennsylvania Plaza
New York, NY 10001
(212) 613-3000

Bank Hapoalim B. M.
75 Rockefeller Plaza
New York, NY 10020
(212) 397-9650

Bank Leumi Trust Company of
New York
1430 Broadway, 8th Floor
New York, NY 10018
(212) 382-4560

Bank of Boston Canada
500 Dorchester Blvd. West,
Ste. 1400
Montreal, Quebec H2Z 1W7
(514) 397-9600

Bank of New England
28 State Street
Boston, MA 02106
(617) 742-4000

Bank of New York Commercial
Corporation
530 Fifth Avenue
New York, NY 10036
(212) 536-9050

Bank of Virginia
P. O. Box 25970
Richmond, VA 23260
(804) 771-7819

Bankers Trust Company
Asset-based Lending Group
1775 Broadway
New York, NY 10019
(212) 830-3210

Barclays American/Business
Credit, Inc.
111 Founders Plaza
East Hartford, CT 06106
(203) 528-4831

Barclays American/
Commercial Inc.
201 S. Tryon Street
Charlotte, NC 28231
(704) 372-8700

Barnett Bank of Jacksonville,
N.A.
100 Laura Street
Jacksonville, FL 32202
(904) 791-7450

Bay Area Financial
Corporation
606 Wilshire Blvd.,
Suite 604
Santa Monica, CA 90401
(213) 451-8445

Borg-Warner Commercial
Finance
1933 N. Meacham Road
Schaumburg, IL 60173
(312) 843-6859

Boston Financial & Equity
Corporation
P.O. Box 71
Kenmore Station
Boston, MA 02215
(617) 267-2900

BT Commercial Corporation
233 South Wacker Drive
Chicago, IL 60606
(212) 830-3213

Business Factors, Inc.
900 Lafayette Street
Santa Clara, CA 95050
(408) 984-7122

C P C Services, Inc.
141 South Central Avenue
Hartsdale, NY 10530
(914) 683-1144

Casco Northern Bank
1 Monument Square
Portland, ME 04111
(207) 774-8221

Celtic Capital Corporation
6310 San Vicente Blvd.,
Ste. 505
Los Angeles, CA 90048
(213) 934-8444

Centerre Bank of Kansas City,
N.A.
900 Walnut Street
Kansas City, MO 64141
(816) 474-6211

Centerre Bank, N.A.
One Centerre Plaza
St. Louis, MO 63101
(314) 554-6843

Century Business Credit Corp.
119 West 40th Street
New York, NY 10018
(212) 703-3500

CFC Capital Corporation
200 West Madison Street
Chicago, IL 60601
(312) 407-6440

Chase Federal Savings & Loan
Association
7300 North Kendall Drive
Miami, FL 33156
(305) 595-4200

Chase Manhattan Bank, N.A.
1411 Broadway
New York, NY 10018
(212) 391-6119

Chemical Bank
Factor & Finance Division
380 Madison Avenue
New York, NY 10017
(212) 309-4054

Chrysler Capital Corporation
Greenwich Office Park 1
Greenwich, CT 06830
(203) 629-3131

Citibank, N. A.
450 Mamaroneck Avenue
Harrison, NY 10528
(914) 899-7532

Citicorp Industrial Credit,
Inc.
450 Mamaroneck Avenue,
4th Fl.
Harrison, NY 10528
(914) 899-7540

Citizens & Southern National
Bank
33 North Avenue, N.E.
Atlanta, GA 30302
(404) 491-4610

Citizens Trust Company
870 Westminster Street
Providence, RI 02903
(401) 456-7316

Citytrust
961 Main Street
Bridgeport, CT 06602
(203) 384-5212

Coastfed Business Credit
Corporation
12121 Wilshire Blvd.
Los Angeles, CA 90025
(213) 820-6681

Comerica Bank-Detroit
211 W. Fort Street
Detroit, MI 48226
(313) 222-9260

Commerce Union Bank
One Commerce Place
Nashville, TN 37219
(615) 749-3441

Commercial Acceptance Corp.
411 W. 7th Street, Ste. 700
Los Angeles, CA 90014
(213) 626-1151

Commercial Finance (Division
Of International Factors
[Ireland])
Hume House, Ballsbridge
Dublin 4, Ireland
(01) 689-777

Commercial Trust Company of
New Jersey
15 Exchange Place
P.O. Box 307
Jersey City, NJ 07302
(201) 434-2422

Commonwealth Financial Corp.
2950 Buskirk Avenue
Walnut Creek, CA 94596
(415) 930-7550

Commonwealth National Bank
of Dallas
2964 LBJ Freeway
Dallas, TX 75234
(214) 247-3141

Compagnie Financière
Canadienne
400 Boul de Maisonneuve ouest
Bureau 1100
Montreal, Canada H3A 1L5
(514) 282-4550

Concord Leasing, Inc.
5 East 59th Street
New York, NY 10022
(212) 415-0684

Congress Financial Corp.
1133 Avenue of the Americas
New York, NY 10036
(212) 840-2000

Connecticut Bank & Trust
Company N.A.
100 Constitution Plaza
Hartford, CT 06115
(203) 244-5223

Connecticut Business Finance
Corporation
765 Asylum Avenue
Hartford, CT 06105
(203) 524-1800

Connecticut National Bank
777 Main Street
Hartford, CT 06115
(203) 728-2000

Continental Illinois National
Bank & Trust Co. of Chicago
231 LaSalle Street
Chicago, IL 60693
(312) 828-5740

Crocker National Bank
1350 Montego Blvd. (A-2)
Walnut Creek, CA 94598
(415) 947-2774

CSB Financial Corporation
65 LaSalle Street
West Hartford, CT 06107
(203) 233-1255

Deutsche Credit Corporation
2333 Waukegan Road
Deerfield, IL 60015
(312) 948-7272

DG Diskontbank AG
Wiesenhuttenstrasse 10
Postfach 160 247
6000 Frankfurt am Main 1
Frankfurt, Germany (D6500)

Dimmitt & Owens Financial,
Inc.
3250 West Big Beaver Road,
Suite 120
Troy, MI 48084
(313) 643-6084

Diversified Discount &
Acceptance Corporation
730 Hennepin Avenue,
Ste. 760
Minneapolis, MN 55403
(612) 339-8958

Dresser Finance Corporation
3201 N. Wolf Road
Franklin Park, IL 60131
(312) 451-3500

Eaton Financial Corporation
27 Hollis Street
P.O. Box 71, So. Station
Framingham, MA 01701
(617) 620-0099

Equitable Bank, N.A.
100 South Charles Street
Baltimore, MD 21201
(301) 547-4376

Essex Bank
One Essex Center Drive
Peabody, MA 01960
(617) 532-2500

European American Bank &
Trust Company
EAB Plaza
Uniondale, NY 11555
(516) 296-6345

Exchange National Bank of
Chicago
130 South LaSalle Street
Chicago, IL 60603
(312) 781-8484

FBS Business Finance Corp.
Peavey Bldg., Ste. 655,
P.O. Box 2902
Minneapolis, MN 55402
(612) 343-1400

Fidelcor Business Credit
Corporation
810 7th Avenue
New York, NY 10019
(212) 333-7445

Fifth Third Bank
38 Fountain Square Plaza
Cincinnati, OH 45263
(513) 579-4205

Finance Company of America
Munsey Building
Baltimore, MD 21202
(301) 752-8450

First American Bank of
New York
350 Park Avenue
New York, NY 10022
(212) 759-9898

First American Commercial
Finance, Inc.
First Amtenn Center
Nashville, TN 37237
(615) 748-2607

First Chicago Credit Corp.
20 So. Clark Street, Room 220
Chicago, IL 60670
(312) 732-5322

First Factors Corporation
P. O. Box 2730
High Point, NC 27261
(919) 889-2929

First Fidelity Bank, N.A.,
New Jersey
450 Broad Street
Newark, NJ 07192
(201) 565-5890

First Fidelity Bank, N.A.,
North Jersey
515 Union Blvd.
Totowa, NJ 07512
(201) 790-2051

First Interstate Commercial
Corporation
P.O. Box 7088
Pasadena, CA 91109
(818) 304-2886

First Jersey National Bank
2 Montgomery Street
Jersey City, NJ 07303
(201) 547-8005

First National Bank of
Louisville
101 South Fifth Street
Louisville, KY 40201
(502) 581-4200

First National Bank of
Maryland
P. O. Box 1596
Baltimore, MD 21201
(301) 244-3709

First Pennsylvania Bank N.A.
Commercial Finance
Department
1600 Market Street
Philadelphia, PA 19101
(215) 786-5000

First Tennessee Bank National
Association/Commercial
Finance
P. O. Box 84
Memphis, TN 38101
(901) 523-4633

First Union Commercial Corp.
First Union Plaza CORP-8
Charlotte, NC 28288
(704) 374-6337

First Wachovia Corporation
P. O. Box 3099
Winston-Salem, NC 27102
(919) 770-6201

First Wisconsin Financial
Corporation
622 North Cass Street,
Ste. 200
Milwaukee, WI 53202
(414) 765-4492

Fleet National Bank
Asset-Based Lending
111 Westminster Street
Providence, RI 02903
(401) 278-6393

Foothill Group, Inc.
2049 Century Park East,
Ste. 600
Los Angeles, CA 90067
(213) 556-1222

Franklin State Bank
P. O. Box 293
Somerset, NJ 08873
(201) 745-6323

General Electric Credit Corp.
East Territory
3003 Summer Street, 3rd Fl.
Stamford, CT 06905
(203) 357-6789

General Electric Credit Corp.
West Territory
8700 West Bryn Mawr Avenue,
Ste. 500S
Chicago, IL 60631
(203) 357-4703

GGS Company, Ltd.
2-20-15, Shinbashi,
Minato-Ku
Tokyo, Japan
(03) 572-5244

Gibraltar Corp. of America
350 Fifth Avenue
New York, NY 10118
(212) 868-4400

Gibraltar Savings
13401 North Freeway
Houston, TX 77060
(713) 872-3244

Glenfed Capital Corporation
330 North Brand Blvd.,
Ste. 250
Glendale, CA 91203
(818) 500-2784

Glenfed Financial Corporation
Commercial Finance Division
440 Sylvan Avenue
Englewood Cliffs, NJ 07632
(201) 569-9200

Glenfed Financial Corporation
104 Carnegie Center
Princeton, NJ 08540
(609) 452-0600

Goldome
745 Fifth Avenue,
34th Floor
New York, NY 10151
(212) 888-4780

Goldome FSB
One Fountain Plaza
Buffalo, NY 14203
(716) 847-5879

Goodman Factors, Inc.
3001 LBJ Freeway 3 230
Dallas, TX 75234
(214) 241-3297

Grand Pacific Finance
Corporation
One Penn Plaza,
Suite 3507
New York, NY 10119
(212) 564-0470

Great Western Bank & Trust
Commercial Finance
P.O. Box 33079
Phoenix, AZ 85067
(602) 241-6217

Hamilton Bank
P. O. Box 3959
Lancaster, PA 17604
(717) 569-8731

Heller Financial, Inc.
Central Commercial Finance
105 West Adams Street
Chicago, IL 60603
(312) 621-7402

Heritage Bank, N.A.
One Heritage Plaza
Jamesburg, NJ 08831
(609) 655-9373

Home Federal
Savings & Loan Association
625 Broadway,
Suite 225
San Diego, CA 92101
(619) 699-8609

Horizon Bank
National Association
225 South Street
Morristown, NJ 07960
(201) 285-2460

Huntington National Bank
41 South High Street
Columbus, OH 43215
(614) 463-4581

Intercontinental Credit Corp.
2 Park Avenue
New York, NY 10016
(212) 481-1800

Interfirst Bank Dallas, N.A.
P. O. Box 83732
Dallas, TX 75283
(214) 744-7237

Investors Lease Corporation
200 Park Avenue
New York, NY 10166
(212) 697-4590

Irving Trust Company
1290 Avenue of the Americas
New York, NY 10104
(212) 408-4990

William Iselin & Company, Inc.
357 Park Avenue South
New York, NY 10010
(212) 481-9400

Israel Discount Bank of N.Y.
511 Fifth Avenue
New York, NY 10017
(212) 551-8563

ITT Capital Resources Group
1400 N. Central Life Tower
P.O. Box 64777
Saint Paul, MN 55164
(612) 227-0011

J.L.B. Equities, Inc.
160 Summit Avenue
Montvale, NJ 07645
(201) 391-0400

KBK Financial Inc.
P. O. Box 61463
Houston, TX 77208
(713) 224-4791

Key Bank N.A.
60 State Street
Albany, NY 12207
(518) 447-3121

Key Bank of Central Maine
286 Water Street
Augusta, ME 04330
(207) 632-4721

Kredietbank N.V.
555 Madison Avenue
New York, NY 10022
(212) 832-7200

Landmark Commercial
Corporation
8866 Ladue Road
St. Louis, MO 63124
(314) 889-1608

Lazere Financial Corporation
60 East 42nd Street
New York, NY 10017
(212) 573-9700

Lion Financial Inc.
DBA Commercial Financing
17291 Irvine Blvd.,
Suite 104
Tustin, CA 92680
(714) 730-1313

Lloyds Bank California
612 South Flower Street
Los Angeles, CA 90017
(213) 613-2191

Lloyds Bank P L C
199 Water Street
New York, NY 10038
(212) 607-4353

Long Island Trust Company
1401 Franklin Avenue
Garden City, NY 11530
(516) 294-2242

Main Bank/Cole-Taylor
Financial Group
1965 Milwaukee Avenue
Chicago, IL 60647
(312) 278-6800

Manalis Finance Company
17141 Ventura Blvd.
Encino, CA 91316
(213) 872-0193

Manufacturers Hanover
Commercial Corporation
1211 Avenue of the Americas
New York, NY 10036
(212) 382-6805

Marine Midland Bank
Business Credit Group
One Marine Center
Buffalo, NY 14240
(716) 843-2424

Marine Midland Business
Loans, Inc.
824 Market Street Mall,
7th Floor
Wilmington, DE 19801
(302) 573-3539

Maryland National Industrial
Finance Corporation
Nottingham Centre
502 Washington Avenue,
Ste. 700
Towson, MD 21204
(301) 821-7666

Massachusetts Business
Development Corp.
1 Liberty Square
Boston, MA 02109
(617) 350-8877

John J. McDermott Co., Inc.
142 Riveredge Road
Tinton Falls, NJ 07724
(201) 750-0350

Mcredit Corporation
P.O. Box 660094
Dallas, TX 75266
(214) 698-5719

Meinhard-Commercial Corp.
135 West 50th Street
New York, NY 10020
(212) 408-6346

Mellon Bank (East), N.A.
Mellon Bank Center
Philadelphia, PA 19102
(215) 585-2160

Mellon Bank, N.A.
OMBC 4950
Pittsburgh, PA 15258
(412) 234-3097

Mellon Financial Services
Corporation
1415 West 22nd Street,
Ste. 700
Oak Brook, IL 60521
(312) 986-2000

Mercantile Business Credit,
Inc.
8000 Maryland Avenue,
Ste. 300
Clayton, MO 63105
(314) 862-7040

Mercantile Safe Deposit &
Trust Company
P. O. Box 1477
Baltimore, MD 21203
(301) 237-5781

Merchant Factors Corporation
108 West 39th Street
New York, NY 10018
(212) 840-7575

Meridian Commercial Credit
Corporation
650 Skippack Pike Blue
Bell West, Suite 122
Blue Bell, PA 19422
(215) 278-8901

Meritor Financial Group
1234 Market Street,
9th Fl.
Philadelphia, PA 19107
(215) 636-6304

Metro Factors, Inc.
10300 N. Central Expwy.
Bldg. 5-570
Dallas, TX 75231
(214) 363-4557

Midlantic Commercial Company
1455 Broad Street
Bloomfield, NJ 07003
(201) 266-8385

Midlantic National Bank
P. O. Box 1529
Bloomfield, NJ 07003
(201) 266-6395

Milberg Factors, Inc.
99 Park Avenue
New York, NY 10016
(212) 697-4200

Miller Martin & Company
750 Street Paul Street, Ste. 590
Dallas, TX 75201
(214) 922-0029

Mint Factors
215 Park Avenue South
New York, NY 10003
(212) 254-2377

Mitsui Manufacturers Bank
135 East Ninth Street
Los Angeles, CA 90015
(213) 688-8314

National Bank of Canada
535 Madison Avenue
New York, NY 10022
(212) 685-8803

National Westminster Bank
USA
592 Fifth Avenue
New York, NY 10036
(212) 602-2487

National Westminster USA
Credit Corporation
175 Water Street
New York, NY 10038
(212) 602-3515

Natwest Commercial Services,
Inc.
600 Madison Avenue
New York, NY 10022
(212) 980-3501

NBD Business Finance, Inc.
1190 First National Bldg.
Detroit, MI 48226
(313) 962-8600

NCNB Financial Services, Inc.
P.O. Box 30533
Charlotte, NC 28230
(704) 374-5087

Nelson Capital Corporation
591 Stewart Avenue
Garden City, NY 11530
(516) 222-2555

Norfac Credit Corporation
555 Chabanel Street W 1550
Montreal, Quebec,
Canada H2N 2J2
(514) 381-9151

Norwest Business Credit, Inc.
6600 France Avenue,
Suite 245
Edina, MN 55435
(612) 372-7988

Old Stone Bank
150 South Main Street
Providence, RI 02901
(401) 278-2000

Pacificorp Credit, Inc.
P.O. Box 1531
Portland, OR 97207
(503) 222-7920

Patriot Bancorporation
57 Franklin Street
Boston, MA 02110
(617) 451-9100

People's Bank
970 Lafayette Blvd.
Bridgeport, CT 06601
(203) 579-4980

Philadelphia National Bank
Broad & Chestnut Streets,
P.O. Box 7618
Philadelphia, PA 19101
(215) 629-3100

Phillips Factors Corporation
300 South Main Street
High Point, NC 27260
(919) 889-3355

Pittsburgh National Bank
P. O. Box 340700-P
Pittsburgh, PA 15265
(412) 355-4922

Presidential Financial Corp.
2200 Northlake Pkwy.,
Suite 280
Tucker, GA 30084
(404) 491-8345

Provident Bank
One East Fourth Street
Cincinnati, OH 45202
(513) 579-2666

Puritan Finance Corporation
55 West Monroe Street,
Ste. 3890
Chicago, IL 60603
(312) 372-8833

Republic Acceptance Corp.
P. O. Box 1329
Minneapolis, MN 55440
(612) 333-3121

Republic Factors Corporation
355 Lexington Avenue
New York, NY 10017
(212) 573-5500

Rhode Island Hospital Trust
National Bank
One Hospital Trust Plaza
Providence, RI 02903
(401) 278-8575

Riviera Capital Corporation
7400 Center Avenue,
Suite 102
Huntington Beach, CA 92647
(714) 898-4250

Rosenthal & Rosenthal
1451 Broadway
New York, NY 10036
(212) 790-1442

Sanwa Business Credit Corp.
One South Wacker Drive
Chicago, IL 60606
(312) 853-1322

Seattle First National Bank
701 Fifth Avenue
Seattle, WA 98104
(206) 442-3215

Security Pacific Business
Credit, Inc.
140 East 45th Street
New York, NY 10017
(212) 682-9290

Security Pacific Finance Group
228 East 45th Street
New York, NY 10017
(212) 309-9300

Shawmut Bank of Boston, N.A.
One Federal Street
Boston, MA 02211
(617) 292-3572

Shawmut Worcester County
Bank, N.A.
446 Main Street
Worcester, MA 01608
(617) 793-4225

Signal Capital Corporation
1111 Fannin Street
Houston, TX 77002
(713) 658-6724

Signal Capital Corporation
120 No. Robinson,
Ste. 880 C
Oklahoma City, OK 73102
(405) 272-4693

Slavenburg Corporation
One Penn Plaza
New York, NY 10001
(212) 564-8600

Society National Bank
800 Superior Avenue, N.E.
Cleveland, OH 44114
(216) 344-3000

South Shore Bank
1400 Hancock Street
Quincy, MA 02169
(617) 847-3100

Southeast Bank, N.A.
100 South Biscayne Blvd.
Miami, FL 33131
(305) 375-7151

Southern National Financial
Corporation
Southern National Ctr.,
200 S. College Street
Charlotte, NC 28202
(704) 377-5611

Southern States Financial Corp
6606 West Broad Street
Richmond, VA 23260
(804) 281-1647

Southtrust Bank of Alabama
National Association
112 20th North
P.O. Box 2554
Birmingham, AL 35290
(205) 254-5760

Sovran Bank/Maryland
6610 Rockledge Drive
Bethesda, MD 20817
(301) 493-7024

State Financial Corporation
1100 Glendon Avenue,
Suite 753
Los Angeles, CA 90024
(213) 208-2200

State Street Bank & Trust Co.
225 Franklin Street
Boston, MA 02101
(617) 786-3613

Sterling Bancorp
540 Madison Avenue
New York, NY 10022
(212) 826-8050

Summa Capital Corporation
350 Fifth Avenue
New York, NY 10118
(212) 244-1200

Sun Bank, N.A.
200 South Orange Avenue
Orlando, FL 32801
(305) 237-4709

James Talcott, Inc.
1633 Broadway
New York, NY 10019
(212) 484-0333

TCF Banking and Savings, F.A.
801 Marquette Avenue
Minneapolis, MN 55402
(612) 370-7164

Trade & Industry Corporation
(USA) Inc.
16 East 34th Street
New York, NY 10016
(212) 686-2420

Trust Company Bank
P. O. Box 4955
Atlanta, GA 30302
(404) 588-7711

Trust Company of New Jersey
35 Journal Square
Jersey City, NJ 07306
(201) 420-2810

Union Bank
225 So. Lake Avenue, 6th Fl.
Pasadena, CA 91101
(818) 304-1800

Union Trust Company
205 Church Street
New Haven, CT 06502
(203) 773-5632

Union Trust Company of
Maryland
P. O. Box 1077
Baltimore, MD 21203
(301) 332-5610

United Agri Products Financial
Services, Inc.
4687 18th Street, 2nd Fl. So.
Greeley, CO 80634
(303) 356-8893

United Credit Corporation
10 East 40th Street
New York, NY 10016
(212) 689-9480

United Jersey Bank
210 Main Street
Hackensack, NJ 07602
(201) 646-5103

United States Trust Company
30 Court Street
Boston, MA 02108
(617) 726-7102

United States Trust Company
of New York
45 Wall Street
New York, NY 10005
(212) 806-4500

United Virginia Bank
P. O. Box 26665
Richmond, VA 23261
(804) 782-5458

US Bancorp Financial
550 So. Hill Street, Ste. 1200
Los Angeles, CA 90013
(213) 622-3820

US Capital Corporation
525 Northern Blvd.
Great Neck, NY 11021
(516) 466-8550

US West Financial Services,
Inc.
6200 S. Quebec Street, #330
Denver, CO 80111
(303) 773-2363

Washington Square Financial
512 Nicollet Mall
P.O. Box 9402
Minneapolis, MN 55440
(612) 342-3100

Webster Factors, Inc.
11 Middle Neck Road
Great Neck, NY 11021
(516) 466-0200

Wells Fargo Bank
3130 Wilshire Blvd.
Los Angeles, CA 90010
(213) 683-7173

Wells Fargo Business Credit
12750 Merit Drive,
Suite 1300, Lock Box 9
Dallas, TX 75251
(214) 386-5997

Westinghouse Business Credit
2000 Oxford Drive
Bethel Park, PA 15102
(412) 854-7037

Winfield Capital Corporation
237 Mamaroneck Avenue
White Plains, NY 10605
(914) 949-2600

Zenith Financial Corporation
111 Great Neck Road
Great Neck, NY 11021
(516) 487-0320

Refinancing Can Boost Your Borrowing Power

Turning asset values into instant cash: that's the idea behind a financial strategy that gives growing companies the capital they need for real estate, equipment, and inventory. It's as simple as refinancing appreciated property.

"Quite often, the real value of a company's assets are not reflected on its balance sheet," says a tax partner with the accounting firm of Israeloff, Trattner. "Thank inflation for that. An office building purchased for $100,000 in 1970 and carried on the books at a partially depreciated value of $50,000 may in fact be worth $1 million.

"That value represents borrowing power—power that all too often goes underutilized. Rather than allowing the property's tenfold appreciation to sit idle until and if the building is sold, the owner can use it as collateral for a loan. The astronomical rise in the value of many business assets, including equipment and machinery as well as real estate, make this a propitious time to refinance."

But asset values are not the only factor favoring refinancing. With interest rates now at the lowest levels in years, small businesses are urged to scrap existing loans for those carrying a lighter debt service. Even if the principal amount remains unchanged—meaning the company does not assume additional debt—lower monthly payments boost cash flow, making more money available for working capital.

"Assume a company purchased a warehouse in 1981, taking out a $1 million, 15-percent mortgage to finance it," says a partner with Phillips, Gold, CPAs. "By refinancing that property today at 11 percent, the company will save about $40,000 a year—money that can help to support its growth."

Refinancings should be considered in the context of overall business planning. A merchant plotting a major diversification, for example, should consider paying for the expansion with operating income or, in what may be a wiser move, refinancing one of his stores to raise the cash. With the latter approach, asset utilization funds the company's growth, enabling management to pay for its costs over 25 years or more.

"Planning can also tell a company when it doesn't need money, no matter how much it can borrow at low interest rates," says the Israeloff, Trattner partner. "Should the retailer learn, through market research, that his target market has turned flat, he'd be advised to cancel or postpone the new borrowing. There's no reason to acquire a pool of money unless it can be put to productive use."

Financial experts make these additional points:

- As long as interest rates remain low, financing terms are a bargain. For this reason, even companies without refinancing options may want to borrow money now for needed equipment and real estate. Debt costs may not be that low again for many years.

- Consider paying off high-interest, short-term loans with the proceeds of mortgage refinancings. Reducing the interest rates and extending the payment terms benefits the company's finances.

  "By paying off a three-year, $250,000 loan at 15 percent with the cash it obtains from a 25-year, 12 percent refinancing, a company's monthly payments drop from $8,066 to $2,633," the Israeloff, Trattner partner explains. "The difference of $5,433 can have a very positive impact on cash flow."

- Factor in the "hidden expense" of proposed refinancings, including points, attorneys fees, and other closing costs.

  The business that pays closing costs of $60,000 just to save $1,000 a month in lower interest rates will have to wait five years just to break even. If the company doesn't plan to be in the facility for that long, refinancing doesn't make sense.

- When considering a refinancing, calculate how many months it will take to recover up-front costs by dividing total closing costs by monthly savings.

Armed with this figure, and with a good feel for how long you'll stay in the facility, you can make an intelligent decision on refinancing.

Factors Can Finance Your Business

Imagine a source of business financing that provides instant cash, assumes the risk of customer collections, and serves as a full-scale credit department. If it sounds too good to be true, you've never heard of "factors."

A little-known and often confused source of short-term business loans, factors base their lending on a company's receivables. Some say they function like credit card outfits.

"Just as MasterCard buys a retailer's receivables, paying the store as soon as a sale is made, factors do much the same on the wholesale level," says a vice-president with Manufacturers Hanover Commercial Corp. "Assume a manufacturer of wool hats ships a $50,000 order to one of its customers. Rather than waiting for the account to pay, the manufacturer can sell the receivables to a factor, receiving up to 85 percent of the total as soon as the goods leave the shipping dock. This speeds the collection process. The balance is paid when the factor collects from the customer."

Also like credit card companies, factors assume the risks of delinquent accounts, and ultimately of non-payment. Should a customer approved by the factor fail to pay, the factor absorbs the loss.

"Factoring can be a godsend for those companies that need their cash very quickly or that want to turn over responsibility for their receivables to a third-party guarantor," says a partner in the small business practice with Arthur Young. "Suppose the company's customers are scattered across a wide geographic area. Keeping credit data on these accounts, and collecting from them when they are slow to pay, can be a difficult and time-consuming process. With factoring, the business is spared all of this work and much of the risk that goes with it."

But factoring does not come free. Fees vary with the level of services provided. For those companies simply wanting the factor to serve as a credit department—checking customer credit and accepting the risk of non-payment—factors charge a commission of one-half to one and one-half percent of gross receivables. (The biggest clients, with the best-rated receivables, pay at the low end.) When the factor also advances money at the time of shipment, interest (generally two points above prime) is also charged until the money is collected from the customer.

In a typical example, ABC Manufacturing, which does $3 million a year in sales, gets cash advances of $400,000 annually. In return for the full range of factoring services, ABC pays $30,000 in commissions and $42,000 in interest.

Because factoring charges generally run several points above traditional bank lending, this form of financing should be used only when a company prefers to delegate credit and collections to others, or when it cannot qualify for standard loans. In many cases, financial institutions reluctant to make unsecured loans will approve requests for factoring because the latter is secured by the company's receivables.

Consider these additional points:

- When an order is received, the factor investigates the customer, either approving or rejecting the credit. If the findings are negative, the factor may try to collect from the customer but will not accept responsibility for non-payment.
- Factors demand 100 percent of a client's receivables. They will not limit their efforts to those receivables considered marginal or high risk.
- Generally, customers make payment directly to the factor. These instructions are noted on the invoice.
- The factor's responsibility is limited to poor credit risks. They will not cover non-payment attributed to defective merchandise or other vendor disputes.
- Although factoring has long been associated with the textile business, it can be used by companies in any field or industry.

Bank subsidiaries, finance companies, and specialized institutions offer factoring services. Ask your accountant for names and references.

Leveraged Buyouts Can Help You Buy Companies with Little Money of Your Own

Sometimes, the greatest rewards of entrepreneurship come with the sale of a business. Instantly, years of sweat equity are turned into personal wealth. That's why small business owners should be familiar with an innovative sales option: leveraged buyouts.

Put simply, LBOs (as the procedures are widely known) use a company's assets and cash flow to finance its sale. The assets collateralize the loan and the cash flow repays it. This built-in resource widens the ranks of prospective buyers, enabling those without sufficient capital of their own to bid for the company.

"Assume the entrepreneur who created a business from scratch finally wants to get liquid," says a managing director of corporate finance for Ladenburg, Thalmann, investment bankers. "He recognizes from the outset that his own general manager is the ideal candidate to buy the business. The man knows the company well and is eager to take an ownership position. But one problem looms: the manager lacks the financial resources to make the purchase."

In many cases, LBOs can help fill the gap. By using the company's assets (such as real estate, receivables, and equipment) for collateral—and by attracting lenders and investors who will take equity in the company in return for current income and appreciation—the buyer with little or no money of his own can claim 15 to 25 percent of the company.

"In a typical deal, the president of an apparel company agreed to buy the business from the chairman for $10 million," the investment banker explains. "Because he had only $500,000 to invest, he had to assemble an investment group with whom he would share equity in the business. Using this approach, he landed a $5.5 million bank loan collateralized by the company's assets, and attracted $4 million from investors who provided debt convertible into equity. All financing was made to the company, which would repay it with its own funds."

LBOs can also be used by entrepreneurs to buy out their co-owners. "Take the case of two brothers who owned a company," says a senior vice-president of Fleet National Bank. "When the older man decided to sell out, his younger brother—seeing a chance in a lifetime to control the business—was eager to buy the shares. But with a purchase price of $4 million (for his brother's stock), the deal seemed to be beyond his means. All of his equity was tied up in the business. He had no cash to invest."

The bankers solved the problem by finding an investor willing to put up $1 million of his own funds and by making a $3 million loan to the company. In a classic leveraged buyout, the proceeds were paid to the former owners and the bank debt was paid with the company's earnings.

"The bottom line," the Fleet banker says, "is that the investor wound up with 30 percent of the company—this for only $1 million of his own cash—and the younger brother increased his equity from 50 to 70 percent without investing a dollar of personal funds."

LBOs need not involve sales to insiders. When the owners of a valve manufacturing concern decided to sell their company for $8 million, they turned to an outside investor who put up $1 million of his own and arranged for a bank loan of $4 million to the company.

"In a leveraged buyout, a number of transactions occur more or less simultaneously," the Fleet banker adds. "In this case, the bank lent $4 million to the company and the investor provided his $1 million—all of which was immediately turned over to the former owners, along with $3 million in long-term notes, for their equity. Because the loans and notes were to be repaid by the company, the buyer was able to leverage his purchase of an $8 million company with a relatively small personal investment."

Who qualifies for leveraged buyouts? What kinds of companies are eligible for this financing? Successful candidates will have the following:

- Products or services in a clearly defined market niche.
- Sufficient operating margins to carry additional debt.
- The strength and flexibility to weather adverse economic conditions, such as rising interest rates.

As specialists in corporate finance, investment bankers can structure leveraged buyouts, doing everything from valuing the company to finding investors. Fees for this turnkey service range from 3 to 8 percent of the purchase price, with the larger deals qualifying for the lower rates. Look for bankers active in the small business market.

GOING PUBLIC

When to Take Your Company Public

To America's entrepreneurs, "going public" is synonymous with instant riches. Selling stock on the open market, they know, can raise millions for business expansion and personal wealth. The rewards are tantalizing.

But not every public offering succeeds. Some, launched before the companies are ready, fizzle with investors. Others achieve mixed results, selling out but at minimal share prices. How can entrepreneurs avoid these disappointments? When are their companies ready to go public? When do they have the right combination of products, management talent, and growth prospects to score big with investors? When can they claim the highest price per share?

"The market for initial public offerings is constantly changing, as investors favor one kind of company, and then another, and another," says a partner with a Big Eight accounting firm and a former Professional Accounting Fellow with the Securities and Exchange Commission. "In 1983, which was a record year for IPOs, some companies went public on the strength of an idea alone—no proven product, no assets, no sales. Investors were willing to take speculative flings. Today—in part because many of those same investors lost money—a company has to be in much stronger position to conduct a successful offering.

"Will it stay this way? Probably not. The IPO market has always been cyclical. A company that cannot consider going public today may find its shares are gobbled up six months from now. The idea is to time your offering to the appropriate market conditions. Invest-

ment bankers can help you decide when to proceed."

Market timing is more complicated than simply playing weak/strong, speculative/conservative trends. At any given time, investors may be turned on to companies in a specific field or industry when all others are in disfavor.

"In 1984, when the market for IPOs was relatively weak, investors took a shine to companies in so-called niche retailing," says an executive with Ladenburg, Thalmann, New York-based investment bankers. "These merchants focus on specialized markets such as discount fashion and appliances. A number of offerings for this type of retailer proved highly successful. At other times, technology and health care companies have bucked the trend. Small business owners who find they're in a hot group should consider going public at that time."

While membership in a glamorous industry is not a prerequisite for IPOs, companies seeking to go public must demonstrate above-average growth prospects. Investors look for products or services with a strong market niche and proven sales appeal in an emerging rather than a mature industry.

"Companies are ripe for a successful offering when it appears that their market success can translate into a return on equity of 20 to 25 percent," the investment banker says. "This kind of strong performance gives investors confidence to buy the company's shares. They know the business can do more than sell product—it can make money."

Want to take your company public? Does it meet these additional tests?

1. Size

In today's market, companies are advised to cross the threshold of $10 million in annual revenues before proceeding with a public offering.

"Investors favor going concerns with sufficient infrastructure to hold their own against competition, to weather economic downturns, and to achieve sustained growth," says a Big Eight CPA. "Sales of $10 million or more give them this comfort level. In speculative markets, however, companies with less than $1 million in sales could hold successful offerings. Again, the timing factor comes into play."

2. Management

It is often said that investors invest in management rather than in companies. Most want evidence that the principals have managerial skills as well as entrepreneurial genius. With this in mind, public offerings are best scheduled once the company has graduated from reliance on the founder as the sole executive to the formation of a management team. With officers in charge of marketing, finance, and production, the company is viewed as a more sophisticated enterprise—and one capable of carrying on after the founder departs.

3. Capital requirements

The company should have reached the point where it needs a substantial amount of capital for growth and expansion.

"If the company doesn't need at least $1 million that it can put to work earning a substantial return, it should postpone going public," says a financing specialist with accountants Arthur Young. "The costs and complexities of a public offering make it inappropriate before that time."

Just why going public works for some and not for others is not always clear. But one pivotal factor may be the company's contract with the investment bankers assigned to market its shares. The terms of the "underwriting agreement" can make the difference between a sellout and a washout.

"It's a mistake to assume that finding an underwriter to handle a company's public offering is a guarantee of raising the sought-after capital," says a Los Angeles-based partner with accountants Deloitte, Haskins & Sells. "This is very much a function of the company's deal with the underwriting firm. In some cases, there are guarantees; in others, the company may wind up with far less than it is seeking."

Consider the three basic types of underwriting contracts:

1. "Best efforts" is little more than an agreement by the underwriter to do its best to market the offering. Should sales fall short, the underwriter is under no obligation to make up the difference.

"This is the most treacherous type of offering because it exposes the company to the possibility of disappointing results," explains the Deloitte partner. "Assume management sought to raise $2 million but the underwriter, in a best-efforts deal, succeeded in selling only 25 percent of that, or $500,000 worth of stock. When you factor in the company's costs to conduct the offering, say $150,000, it has netted only $350,000. That's probably well below its capital requirements. The bottom line is that it has assumed the responsibilities of being a public company without the compensating benefits."

2. A variation on the best-efforts approach builds minimum/maximum parameters into the marketing agreement.

The offering may call for a floor of $3 million and a ceiling of $4 million. If the underwriter is unable to market enough securities to reach the minimum figure, the deal may be canceled without any of the stock being sold.

This way the company is spared having to go public for substantially less capital than it had sought. On the other hand, if the offering goes well, the underwriter is authorized to sell up to the maximum figure of $4 million.

3. "Firm commitment"—widely regarded as the ideal arrangement—requires the underwriter to purchase the entire offering and

remarket it to outside investors. A $3 million offering conducted on a firm-commitment basis assures the small company of this amount regardless of the underwriter's success—or lack of it—in selling the shares.

Strong, well-capitalized underwriters tend to operate on a firm-commitment basis only, believing that this offers greater protection for their clients and investors.

"If we don't think that a deal can be done on a firm-commitment basis, then we don't think it should be done at all," says an executive with Muller & Co., a New York–based underwriting firm that specializes in small company issues. "There's certainly a greater commitment to the offering when the underwriter stands squarely behind it."

But firm-commitment underwriters limit their support to the best-managed small firms with solid track records or bright prospects for future growth. Companies unable to meet these criteria may have to accept a best-efforts agreement or seek other forms of financing.

"I recommend to my clients that they negotiate for a minimum/maximum arrangement at the very least," says the Deloitte partner. "Failing that, they should consider other ways of raising money, such as gaining venture capital."

Accountants and attorneys experienced in securities transactions can help to match companies with reputable underwriters and can negotiate the terms of the offerings.

AT A GLANCE

Going Public

The Advantages

1. An Infusion of Capital. When a company issues and registers new shares for sale to the public, the money raised from the offering becomes permanent equity capital. It can then be used to expand production facilities, open new markets, diversify product lines, step up research, increase working capital, and retire existing debt—a major consideration during periods of high interest rates.

2. The Chance to Cash In. Founders of a company can cash in on an initial public offering and on subsequent offerings by registering a portion of their privately owned shares for sale. Usually an initial public offering includes a mix of new and existing shares.

3. Easier Credit. The proceeds of a public offering almost always improve a company's balance sheet and upgrade other criteria that are important to lenders. As a result, the company will be able to increase its bank lines of credit and to borrow or lease on more favorable terms. This is particularly true for new companies, which often boost their assets and net worth from a few thousand to several million dollars. Also, publicly traded shares are more acceptable collateral than privately held shares in securing loans for other investments.

4. Ease of Additional Equity Financing. If the newly issued stock continues to perform well in the all-important after-market, substantial additional equity capital can be raised from the public at terms more favorable than those of the initial offering.

5. Better Management. A company is better able to attract and retain top-quality management if it can include publicly traded stock in its compensation package. Candidates for key positions frequently lower salary requirements if stock options are added to their compensation package.

6. Expansion Possibilities. A company with publicly traded securities is in a position to trade stock, rather than cash, for a promising merger candidate. Acquiring other businesses thus becomes much easier. Computing the value of a privately held company is always difficult, as it includes a number of subjective elements.

7. Prestige and Goodwill. Public ownership is more than a source of pride and a sign of accomplishment for a company's founders; it is also good for public relations. Many of the company's customers and suppliers will become shareholders, acquiring a vested interest in purchasing its products or services.

The Drawbacks

1. Monetary Risk. After all the accounting, legal, and printing work is done and your company is ready to make its debut in the public market, the market's direction could turn abruptly. If the IPO market suddenly went sour, your offering would have to be postponed indefinitely. Your company could lose already incurred offering costs of $100,-000 or more.

2. Loss of Privacy. Publicly owned companies (and their directors, officers, and major stockholders) are subject to reporting, proxy, and trading regulations under the Securities Exchange Act of 1934.

Consequently, information that many owners of private companies are reluctant to disclose have to become public: salaries, sales, profits, competitive position, mode of operation, and materials contracts, among other things.

3. Loss of Flexibility. The owners of a private enterprise lose some flexibility in management after the company goes public. There may be practical, if not legal, limitations on salaries, fringe benefits, relatives on the payroll, etc. Many decisions that could be made informally and quickly in the past will now need the approval of shareholders and outside directors.

4. Long-range Costs. A public company commits itself to additional administrative expenses. Accounting and legal fees usually increase substantially. There are also the costs of preparing and distributing proxy material and annual reports to shareholders, filing reports with the SEC, and paying fees of transfer agents, registrar, public relations consultants, and investor-relations personnel.

5. Potential Loss of Control. If over half the company's shares are sold to the public, the original owners could technically lose control. The number of shares to be sold is determined through negotiation with the underwriters, who will try to make sure the initial public offering is large enough to leave a floating supply of the stock for sale in the after-market. An additional risk is that insiders' holdings are usually diluted by subsequent public offerings and acquisitions.

Keep in mind, however, that shares sold to the public are broadly distributed in small amounts. So, publicly owned companies can usually be controlled effectively by managements that hold a relatively small number of outstanding shares.

6. Management Headaches. Certain pressures on management amplify after a company enters the public market. Many corporations are able to sell a portion of stock to the public because they are thought to have "growth potential" or to be in a "growth industry."

The public may expect such a company to show substantial increases in sales and profits from year to year and quarter to quarter. Any reversal of the growth trend could cause shareholders to panic and dump their stock. Pressures to establish and maintain a solid dividend pattern are also strong.

Credit: KMG Main Hurdman, "Entrepreneur's Guide to Raising Capital"

Glossary of Terms for Going Public

Accredited Investors. Individual or institutional investors who meet the qualifying SEC criteria with respect to financial sophistication or financial assets.

All Hands Meeting. A meeting of all the parties involved in preparing the registration statement, including company management, the company's attorneys, accountants, underwriters, and the underwriters' attorneys.

Analyst. A specialist, often employed by an investment banking firm, who follows certain companies and analyzes their financial statements for the purpose of providing investment advice.

Bad Boy Provisions. Provisions that disqualify issuers from using certain registration exemptions if certain individuals involved in the offering have engaged in specified acts of misconduct with respect to the securities laws.

Best-efforts Underwriting. A type of underwriting agreement in which the underwriters agree only to use their best efforts to sell the shares on the issuer's behalf. The underwriters do not commit to purchase any unsold shares. (See, in contrast, "Firm-commitment Underwriting.")

Blue Sky Laws. A common term for state securities laws.

Blue Sky Memorandum. A memorandum, usually prepared by the underwriters' attorneys, which sets forth the various securities law provisions and restrictions applicable to each of the states in which the offering may be made.

Capitalization. The company's debt and equity structure.

Cheap Stock. Common stock issued to selected persons (e.g., company insiders and promoters) prior to a public offering at a price less than the public offering price. (Also applies to stock options, warrants, or other potentially dilutive instruments.)

Closing Meeting. The final meeting for the purpose of exchanging company securities for the proceeds of the offering.

Comfort Letter. A letter provided by a company's independent auditors detailing procedures performed at the request of the underwriters. The letter supplements the underwriters' due-diligence review.

Comment Letter. A letter from the staff of the SEC describing deficiencies noted in its review of a registration statement.

Dilution. The effect on prospective purchasers' equity interest caused by a disparity between the public offering price per share and the tangible book value per share immediately preceding the offering.

Due Diligence. The responsibility of those preparing and signing the registration statement to conduct a reasonable investigation so as to provide a reasonable basis for their belief that statements made in the registration statement are true and do not omit any material facts.

Effective Date. The date on which the registration statement becomes effective and actual sales of the securities can begin.

Financial Reporting Releases (FRRs). Releases from the SEC announcing new or revised rules (e.g., amendments to Regulation S-X or S-K, and to the various forms) and matters of general accounting and auditing interest.

Firm-commitment Underwriting. A type of underwriting agreement in which the underwriters agree to purchase all the shares in the offering and then resell them to the public. Any shares not sold to the public are paid for and held by the underwriters for their own account.

Foreign Corrupt Practices Act (FCPA). Enacted in 1977, the FCPA requires all public companies to maintain adequate accounting records and an adequate system of internal controls, and prohibits certain payments made to specified foreign officials and politicians.

Form 8-A. An abbreviated form for registration of a class of securities under the 1934 Act.

Form 8-K. A report required to be filed with the SEC when certain material events have occurred.

Form 10-K. The annual report required to be filed with the SEC.

Form 10-Q. The quarterly report required to be filed with the SEC.

Form S-1. The most comprehensive registration statement, used by issuers who are not eligible to use any of the abbreviated registration forms.

Form S-2. An abbreviated registration statement, used by certain seasoned companies, which relies on incorporation by reference of the annual report (and other periodic reports, as applicable) and requires delivery of the latest annual report to investors.

Form S-3. The most abbreviated registration statement used by certain seasoned companies, which relies on incorporation by reference of the annual report (and other periodic reports, as applicable), but does not require delivery of the latest annual report to investors.

Form S-18. A short-form registration statement for certain offerings of up to $7,500,-000.

Form SR. A report required to be filed periodically with the SEC describing, during and after an offering, the amount of proceeds from the offering to date and the use of the proceeds.

Insider Trading. Trading in a company's securities by company insiders or others with access to nonpublic information about the company.

Intrastate Offerings. An SEC-registration exempt offering made only to residents of the state in which the issuer resides and carries on its business.

Investment Bankers. Specialists who advise companies on available sources of financing, advise on the optimal time for a public offering of securities, and often also act as underwriters for a public offering.

Letter of Intent. A preliminary agreement between the underwriters and a company specifying the terms that will be contained in the actual underwriting agreement. This precludes a company from hiring another underwriter and authorizes the underwriters to incur expenses in connection with the proposed offering.

Limited Offering. Sales of securities exempt from registration pursuant to certain exemptions that limit the size of the offering and the number of purchasers.

Managing Underwriters. Also known as lead underwriters, they organize the underwriting syndicate and are the primary contact with the company.

Market Makers. The managing underwriters and some or all of the syndicated underwriters who offer to buy or sell shares at a firm price from the public, helping to sustain financial community interest and providing after-market support for a company's shares.

National Association of Securities Dealers (NASD). An association of U.S. securities brokers and dealers. Among other things, the NASD reviews underwriters' remuneration arrangements for all public offerings to ensure that they are fair and reasonable.

National Association of Securities Dealers Automated Quotations (NASDAQ). An automated information network that provides price quotations and volume information on securities traded over-the-counter.

Offering Circular. A disclosure document, similar in content to a registration statement, which is provided to investors for offerings exempt from SEC registration requirements.

Over-the-counter Market. The market for securities not listed on a stock exchange.

Price-earnings Ratio. The price of a share of common stock divided by earnings per share.

Pricing Amendment. The last amendment to the registration statement, which discloses the final offering price.

Primary Offering. An offering by a company of previously unissued securities.

Private Placement. Sales of securities not involving a public offering and exempt from registration pursuant to certain exemptions.

Prospectus. Part I of the registration statement, used as a selling document by the underwriting syndicate. The prospectus discloses information about the company and the offering, and is distributed as a separate document or booklet to prospective investors.

Proxy. A shareholder's written authorization for some other person to represent him and vote his shares at a shareholders' meeting.

Proxy Statement. The information required by the SEC to be given to shareholders by those soliciting shareholder proxies.

Red Herring. The preliminary prospectus that is distributed to the underwriting syndicate for further distribution to prospective investors. It includes a legend in red ink on the cover stating that the registration statement has not yet become effective.

Registrar and Transfer Agent. As an agent for the company, issues the securities sold to investors, maintains current records of all shareholders and their addresses, and maintains the records for subsequent transfers of securities upon resale.

Registration Statement. The disclosure document filed with the SEC pursuant to the registration requirements of federal securities laws. The registration statement includes the prospectus and other information required by the SEC.

Regulation A. SEC rules governing the exemption from registration of certain public offerings of up to $1,500,000.

Regulation C. Prescribes the procedures to be followed in preparing and filing a registration statement (e.g., paper size, numbers of copies).

Regulation D. SEC rules governing the exemptions from registration for private placements and limited offerings.

Regulation S-K. Regulations governing nonfinancial statement-related disclosures in both registration statements and periodic reports.

Regulation S-X. Regulations governing the form, content, and periods to be covered in financial statements included in registration statements and periodic reports.

Restricted Stock. Certain shares acquired in a private placement that are subject to resale limitations.

Road Show. A series of meetings in different cities to allow members of the underwriting syndicate and prospective investors to ask company management questions relating to the company and the offering.

Rule 144. The rule governing sales of shares by controlling shareholders and holders of restricted stock.

Safe Harbor Rule. Commonly used to describe SEC provisions that protect issuers from possible legal actions if they have made a good-faith effort to comply with certain specified requirements.

Securities Act of 1933 (1933 Act). Generally requires that public offerings of securities be registered with the SEC before they may be sold.

Securities and Exchange Commission (SEC). The government agency responsible for administration of U.S. federal securities laws, including the 1933 Act and the 1934 Act.

Securities Exchange Act of 1934 (1934 Act). Regulates securities exchanges and over-the-counter markets. Also, generally requires publicly held companies to file periodic reports with the SEC.

Short-swing Profits. Profits realized by specified company insiders on transactions in the company's securities completed within a six-month period, whether or not based on insider information.

Staff Accounting Bulletins (SABs). Published interpretations and practices followed by the staff of the SEC.

Tender Offer. An offer, usually in an attempt to gain control of another company, to purchase existing shareholders' securities.

Tombstone Ad. A published notice of an offering, generally disclosing only the amount of the offering, the name of the company, a description of the security, the offering price, and the names of the underwriters.

Transfer Agent. See "Registrar and Transfer Agent."

Underwriters. The underwriters include the managing underwriter and the underwriting syndicate. Their primary function is to sell securities to the investing public. See also "Investment Bankers."

Underwriting Agreement. The underwriting agreement contains the details of the company's arrangements with the underwriters, including the type of underwriting (i.e., best efforts or firm commitment), the underwriters' compensation, the offering price, and number of shares.

Typical Timetable for an Initial Public Offering

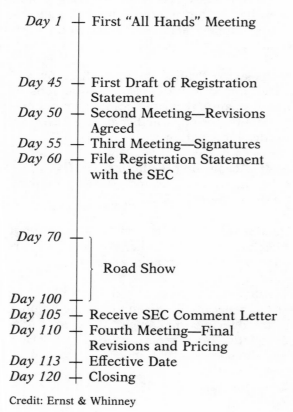

Day 1 — First "All Hands" Meeting

Day 45 — First Draft of Registration Statement
Day 50 — Second Meeting—Revisions Agreed
Day 55 — Third Meeting—Signatures
Day 60 — File Registration Statement with the SEC

Day 70 —

Road Show

Day 100 —
Day 105 — Receive SEC Comment Letter
Day 110 — Fourth Meeting—Final Revisions and Pricing
Day 113 — Effective Date
Day 120 — Closing

Credit: Ernst & Whinney

Typical Distribution of Gross Proceeds

($10 million offering)

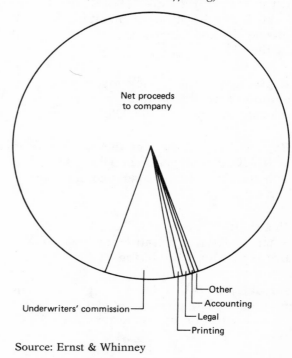

Net proceeds to company

Underwriters' commission

Other
Accounting
Legal
Printing

Source: Ernst & Whinney

Content of a Registration Statement

Most initial public offerings are filed on Form S-1. Although registration statements are referred to by form numbers, they are in fact prepared in a narrative and reasonably flexible format. The SEC requires certain minimum disclosures, and a standardized sequence and style has evolved over time. Nevertheless, a significant degree of subjectivity and judgment is required in drafting these disclosures.

Prospectus

The following is a summary of the major items generally required in Part I of the registration statement, the prospectus:

Outside front cover. Shows key facts about the offering, including the name of the company; the title, amount, and a brief description of the securities offered; a table showing the offering price, underwriting discounts and commissions, and proceeds to the company; and the date of the prospectus. If the offering is a secondary or partial secondary offering, a statement to that effect is included, and the proceeds to selling shareholders are shown. Generally, the managing underwriters' name is shown as well.

Inside front and outside back cover. Includes a table of contents, information about price stabilization, and a statement on dealers' delivery requirements for the prospectus.

Prospectus summary. May include an overview of the company and its business, a brief description of the security offered, estimated net proceeds and use of those proceeds, and selected financial data.

The company. Provides more detailed background information on the company, including where and when it was incorporated, location of its principal offices, and a brief description of its primary business activities.

Risk factors. Highlights any significant factors that make the offering a high risk or speculative. Examples would include dependence on a single supplier or a few customers, existing contractual restrictions on the company, an unproven market for its product, lack of business experience or earnings history, material dilution to public investors as a result of the offering, or potential dilution which may result from the exercise of any outstanding stock options or warrants. For particularly speculative offerings, this section must also be referenced on the prospectus cover.

Use of proceeds. Discloses the principal intended use of the net proceeds of the offering, including specified details if the offering is to reduce debt or acquire a new business. If there is no specific plan for the proceeds, the reason for the offering must be disclosed.

Dilution. Describes, generally in tabular form, any material dilution of the prospective purchasers' equity interest caused by a disparity between the public offering price and tangible book value of the shares immediately preceding the offering. As existing shareholders will often have acquired their shares at a significantly lower cost than the offering price (e.g., company founders, or through employee stock option or award plans), material dilution often does occur for new purchasers.

Dividend policy. Discloses the company's dividend history and present dividend policy. Any restrictions on the payment of dividends must also be disclosed. If a determination has been made to reinvest future earnings rather than pay dividends, as many newly public companies do, that fact is also disclosed.

Capitalization. Discloses the company's debt and equity capital structure, both before and after the offering. The "pro forma" capital structure after the offering is adjusted to reflect the securities issued and the intended use of the proceeds (e.g., to reduce long-term debt).

Selected financial data. Summarizes financial information for each of the last five years, and usually for the interim period since the last year end and the comparative interim period of the preceding year. This data generally includes net sales or operating revenues; income (or loss) from continuing operations, both in total and per-share amounts; total assets; long-term debt; capital leases and redeemable preferred stock; and cash dividends per share. Companies may include any additional data that would enhance an understanding of, and would highlight trends in, their financial condition and results of operations.

Management's discussion and analysis. Addresses the "why" for the financial condition and results of operations presented in the financial statements. Accordingly, it should cover the last three fiscal years, although reference may also be made to any trends in the five-year table of selected financial data. (Any interim periods presented must also be addressed.) The purpose of this section is to provide investors with information to assess your company by evaluating cash flows generated from both operations and outside sources of capital. The discussion should include information on liquidity and capital resources, including both short- and long-term commitments, plans, and expected sources of capital. The discussion must also address any significant facts in assessing results of operations, including unusual or infrequent items affecting prior years' income, and any uncertainties, trends, or changes that may affect future results.

Description of business. Provides investors with detailed insight into your company's business operations. Items addressed in this section include:

General development of the company and the business during the last five years.

Future operating plans if the company has not had revenue from operations in each of the last three years.

For each major geographic area: revenues, operating profit or loss, assets, and export sales for each of the last three years.

For each major industry segment: revenues, operating profit or loss, and assets for each of the last three years (certain of the information below is also presented by industry segment).

Principal products or services and their markets.

Status of any publicly announced new products or business segments.

Sources and availability of raw materials.

Any patents, trademarks, licenses, franchises, and concessions held.

Extent to which business is or may be seasonal.

Practices with respect to working capital items—for example, if required to carry significant amounts of inventory to meet rapid customer delivery requirements.

Any significant dependence on a single or a few customers.

Amount of any firm backlog of orders.

Government contracts potentially subject to termination or renegotiation.

Competitive conditions.

Expenditures for research and development in each of the last three years.

Effects of environmental laws.

Number of employees.

Properties. Discloses the location and a brief description of the major plants, mines, and other important physical properties owned or leased.

Legal proceedings. Describes any material

pending legal proceedings, other than ordinary routine litigation incidental to the business.

Management and certain security holders. Provides certain key information on the business experience and compensation of management, and on major shareholders. These disclosure requirements often give rise to objections from management because they now must publicly disclose the following information, much of which is generally considered strictly confidential by a private company:

The names, ages, and business experience (and any involvement in specified legal proceedings) of all current or nominated directors and executive officers, and other key employees.

The compensation, both direct and indirect (including stock options and other benefits), current and proposed, for directors and certain executives.

Loans to management and directors (and their immediate families) and certain transactions with management, directors, and major shareholders (and their immediate families).

Transactions with promoters, if the company has been in existence for less than five years.

Certain compensatory arrangements with officers and directors contingent on their resignation or termination or on a change in control of the company (known as "golden parachute" arrangements).

The shareholdings of all officers and directors, and of those shareholders who beneficially own more than 5 percent of any class of shares.

Description of securities to be registered. Describes the particular securities being offered, including the title of the security, dividend rights, conversion and voting rights, and liquidation rights. The terms of any warrants or rights offered are also described.

Underwriting. Describes the underwriting and plan of distribution for the securities offered, including the names of the principal underwriters in the syndicate, the number of shares underwritten by each underwriter, the method of underwriting (e.g., firm commitment), and any material relationships between the company and any of those underwriters. The underwriters' compensation, board representation, and indemnification are also disclosed.

Legal matters, experts, and additional information. Briefly identifies the attorneys and their opinion on the validity of the securities offered (and discloses any shareholdings in the company held by the attorneys), identifies any experts who have been relied on in the preparation of the registration statement (e.g., independent accountants), and refers to the availability of additional information in Part II of the registration statement filed with the SEC.

Financial statements. Contains the financial statements, including the accountants' report, for the following periods:

Audited balance sheets as of the end of each of the last two fiscal years.

Audited statements of income, changes in financial position, and shareholders' equity for each of the last three fiscal years.

If the anticipated effective date of the registration statement is more than 134 days after your fiscal year end, unaudited interim statements must be provided, with comparative unaudited interim statements for the preceding year.

Financial statements included in SEC filings generally must be consolidated, subject to certain narrowly defined exceptions relating, for example, to certain finance or insurance subsidiaries, and certain foreign subsidiaries operating under significant political, economic, or currency restrictions. Only if consolidation would not result in the most meaningful and useful disclosure should subsidiaries be excluded from consolidation.

The SEC requires that separate financial statements be presented for unconsolidated subsidiaries and investees that *individually* are greater than 20 percent of consolidated assets or income for the latest year. Also, if the 20-percent threshold is not met but unconsolidated subsidiaries and investees *aggregate* more than 10 percent of consolidated assets or income, summarized financial information or separate financial statements must be presented.

Separate audited financial statements also are required for certain businesses that have been acquired or that probably will be acquired. Depending on how significant the acquired business is to the consolidated statements, the periods required to be presented vary from one to three years. Separate financial statements are required only for those periods prior to the acquisition.

Pro forma financial information may also be required in certain circumstances. Pro forma financial information is historical information adjusted "as if" a given transaction had occurred at an earlier time. It generally includes a condensed income statement for the latest year and any subsequent interim period, and a condensed balance sheet as of the end of the latest period presented. Pro forma information generally must be provided for significant business acquisitions and dispositions, reorganizations, unusual asset exchanges, and debt restructurings.

In addition to the information specifically required, the SEC requires, and prudence dictates, the disclosure of any other information considered material. In this context, an omitted fact is material if there is a substantial likelihood that a reasonable investor would consider it important in deciding whether to buy the security at the price offered.

Credit: Ernst & Whinney, "Deciding to Go Public"

WHERE TO FIND IT

Write for free booklet:
Deciding to Go Public
Ernst & Whinney
2000 National City Center
Cleveland, OH 44114

HOT TIPS

Little-known Ways to Raise Money without Going Public

The SEC adopted Regulation D in 1982 in an effort to make the capital markets more easily accessible for small businesses. Regulation D served to reduce the burdensome and costly registration requirements applicable to small and private offerings of securities, and expanded the availability of the registration exemptions. Although limited and private offering exemptions were available prior to 1982, the rules were extremely technical and compliance was thus very burdensome and costly. Since the provisions of the exemptions were subject to varying interpretations, a significant risk often existed that a minor technical provision could be violated with the result that the entire offering could be subject to rescission by the purchasers of the securities. As noted below, some similar risks continue under Regulation D, but compliance is nevertheless significantly easier than it was in the past.

Certain portions of Regulation D represent a "nonexclusive safe harbor" under Section 4(2) of the 1933 Act. In other words, a company may be able to qualify for exemption under that Section of the 1933 Act, notwithstanding Regulation D.

However, most companies do claim exemptions from registration pursuant to Regulation D. Regulation D consists of the following six rules:

Rule 501 contains definitions of various terms used in the Rules.

Rule 502 deals with general conditions and limitations and informational requirements applicable to some or all of the exemptions contained in Rules 504 through 506.

Rule 503 deals with SEC notification requirements.

Rule 504 provides an exemption for certain offerings of up to $500,000.

Rule 505 provides an exemption for certain offerings of up to $5,000,000.

Rule 506 provides an exemption for certain offerings unlimited in amount.

Definitions

Rule 501 defines eight specific terms used in the Regulation. The most significant of these are:

Accredited investor. Accredited investors are defined as those who are, or who the issuer reasonably believes are: institutional investors, including banks, insurance companies, registered investment companies, business development companies, small business investment companies licensed by the Small Business Administration (SBA), and employee benefit plans subject to the Employee Retirement Income Security Act (ERISA) that have either a specified institutional fiduciary or total assets in excess of $5,000,000; certain tax-exempt organizations with total assets in excess of $5,000,000; any director, executive officer, or general partner of the issuer; any person who purchases at least $150,000 of the securities in exchange for cash, marketable securities, cancellation of debt, or an obligation to pay within five years, as long as the purchase does not exceed 20 percent of the investor's net worth, or joint net worth with spouse; any individual whose net worth or joint net worth with spouse exceeds $1,000,000; any individual who has had income in excess of $200,000 in each of the last two years and reasonably expects such income in the current year; and any entity owned entirely by accredited investors. Advice should be sought from your attorneys with respect to what steps should be taken to support a "reasonable belief" that a prospective investor qualifies as an accredited investor.

Number of purchasers. For the purposes of the specific exemptions in Rules 505 and 506, accredited investors need not be included in calculating the number of purchasers. In other words, an issuer may sell to an unlimited number of accredited investors in addition to the specified number of other purchasers. Also, certain loosely related parties may be counted as a single purchaser for this purpose.

General Conditions

The availability of Regulation D exemptions is not dependent on the size of the company, and the exemptions are available only to the issuer of securities and not to its affiliates or others for resale of the issuer's securities. They are also available for issuance of securities in connection with a business combination.

The rules provide that certain offerings of the same securities may be considered as a single offering (i.e., "integrated"), and thus combined in determining whether the amount and numbers of purchasers comply with the exemptive provisions if those offerings are made within six months of the start or termination of the Regulation D offering.

Other general conditions for the use of Regulation D exemptions are that there may be no general solicitation or general advertising in connection with the offering, and that certain procedures must be followed by the issuer to ensure the securities are not being acquired for public resale. These procedures include the exercise of reasonable care that a purchaser is not an underwriter or an agent for an underwriter, providing written disclosure of the resale limitations, and including a legend to that effect on the certificate itself. However, both of the foregoing conditions may be avoided for certain limited offerings up to $500,000 (pursuant to the Rule 504 exemption), as discussed below.

Finally, any company relying on a Regulation D exemption must file notices of sales of securities on a Form D. These notices must be filed with the SEC within 15 days of the first sale of securities; subsequent notices are then due every six months, with a final notice within 30 days after the last sale. Strict compliance with these notification requirements is absolutely critical, as failure to do so may result in the exemption no longer being available, thus leaving the entire offering open to rescission. Companies must also undertake to provide the SEC, upon written request, with copies of all information that was provided to certain purchasers of the securities. While that information would then become part of the public record, the SEC generally does not request such information.

Information Disclosure Requirements

The specific disclosure requirements under Regulation D vary according to whether the company is already an SEC registrant (i.e., a "reporting company") and according to the size of the offering and the particular exemption claimed. All companies using a Rule 505 or Rule 506 exemption are, however, subject to certain provisions dealing with the rights of nonaccredited investors to receive information furnished to accredited investors and the rights of all purchasers to ask questions of the issuer concerning the offering.

If the securities are sold only to accredited investors under any of the exemptions, or if the offering is less than $500,000 (and pursuant to Rule 504), then the SEC does not require any information to be furnished to investors. Of course, state laws and the investors themselves may nevertheless require certain information to be furnished.

Although the SEC does not impose information disclosure requirements in some registration-exempt circumstances (such as those noted above), companies often issue an offering circular or memorandum. This decision, which should be made in consultation with your attorneys, depends on a variety of factors including the number of offerees or purchasers, their existing relationship with the issuer, and their degree of investment sophistication. The SEC's antifraud provisions apply equally to registration-exempt offerings and lead many issuers voluntarily to make relevant disclosures as insurance against later charges by disgruntled investors that they were not informed of all material facts.

The information requirements for "reporting companies" are the same regardless of the size of the offering or the particular exemption claimed. These companies are permitted to provide copies of their latest annual report, proxy statement, and their most recent 10-K or registration statement.

Any other companies—including those going public for the first time, selling to one or more nonaccredited investors, and offering more than $500,000—are subject to specified information requirements.

Offerings Limited to $500,000—Rule 504

This exemption is the least restrictive of the exemptions with respect to everything but the amount, which is limited to $500,000. No restrictions are placed on the number or qualification of investors and no information requirements are imposed. The exemption is directed at and is well suited to a small business seeking to raise a reasonably small amount of capital. It may not be used by investment companies or "reporting companies."

Additionally, if the offering is made exclusively in, and in accordance with, the laws of states that provide for registration of the securities and require delivery of a disclosure document before sale, then the general Regulation D resale limitations and prohibitions on general solicitation and advertising do not apply. In such a situation, investors may be attracted in the same way as for a registered public offering and the shares purchased may be immediately resold by the purchasers, subject to any limitations imposed by state laws.

The $500,000 offering price limitation is reduced by the amount of any sales of securities sold concurrently, or within the last 12 months, which were in violation of the registration provisions of the Act, or were exempt from registration by this Rule, Rule 505, or Regulation A (discussed below).

Offerings Limited to $5,000,000—Rule 505

This exemption increases the amount that may be offered but also imposes some additional restrictions. The exemption is availa-ble to all issuers except investment companies and issuers disqualified because of specified acts of misconduct with respect to the securities laws. These so-called bad boy provisions apply not only to the issuer and its officers, directors, general partners, and major shareholders, but also to the underwriters and their partners, directors, and officers. Whether or not the issuer is aware of a disqualifying prior act of misconduct by one of the aforementioned, the exemption would be rendered unavailable. Accordingly, extreme care must be exercised, and your attorneys consulted, to take adequate precautions against such an event.

The exemption also limits the number of purchasers to 35 nonaccredited investors but places no limit on the number of accredited investors. As noted above, however, aggregation of certain related persons is allowed in calculating the "number of purchasers."

Unless the securities are sold exclusively to accredited investors, certain information requirements are specified as discussed earlier (see "Information Disclosure Requirements").

And, as with the Rule 504 exemption, the $5,000,000 offering price limitation for this exemption is reduced by the amount of any sales of securities sold concurrently, or within the last 12 months, that were in violation of the registration provisions of the Act or were exempt from registration by this Rule, Rule 504, or Regulation A (discussed below).

Unlimited Private Placements—Rule 506

This registration exemption is available to any issuer, including investment companies and "reporting companies," and is not subject to any "bad boy provisions." It may be used for offerings of any amount.

The number of purchasers is limited to 35 nonaccredited investors, but no limit is placed on the number of accredited investors. Certain "sophistication" requirements are imposed for nonaccredited investors, however (in contrast to Rules 504 and 505). Specifically, the issuer must reasonably believe that each nonaccredited investor, either alone or with his purchaser representative, has such knowledge and experience in financial and business matters that he is capable of evaluating the merits and risks of the prospective investment. Such "sophistication" relates to purchasers, not necessarily to offerees. Accredited investors are presumed to be "sophisticated."

Unless the securities are sold exclusively to accredited investors, certain information requirements are specified, as discussed earlier (see "Information Disclosure Requirements").

Accredited Investor Offering up to $5,000,000—Section 4(6)

Section 4(6), created in 1980, exempts from registration any offers and sales of up to $5,000,000 by an issuer if they are made exclusively to accredited investors. This exemption is very similar to the Regulation D, Rule 505 limited offering exemption, and generally compliance with Rule 505 would constitute compliance with Section 4(6).

There are some important differences, however, which may make a Section 4(6) accredited investor offering available to an issuer not able to use a Rule 505 limited offering exemption. Specifically, Section 4(6) does not contain the "bad boy provisions" which may block some issuers' use of Rule 505. And Section 4(6) is available to investment companies, while Rule 505 is not. Additionally, subject to the general integration rules discussed earlier, the $5,000,000 limit on Section 4(6) offerings is not reduced by sales in the previous 12 months under Rules 504 or 505, Regulation A, or in violation of the 1933 Act.

Apart from these differences, the provisions of Section 4(6) are very similar to those of Rule 505 with respect to accredited investor offerings. The definition of accredited investors is the same, no advertising or general solicitation is allowed, no information requirements are mandated, and similar SEC notification requirements are imposed.

Coordination with State Exemptions

When Regulation D was adopted by the SEC, it was hoped that state legislators would adopt parallel exemption provisions. The North American Securities Administrators Association (NASAA) has been directing an effort to develop a uniform limited offering exemption (ULOE) which could be adopted by all states. A number of states have already adopted an early version of this uniform exemption, with varying modifications. However, many consider the current version of the ULOE to be unworkable in some circumstances, and the NASAA is thus reconsidering those provisions. Your attorneys will advise you on the availability of these changing state exemptions.

Intrastate Offerings—Rule 147

The Securities Act exempts from registration any security that is offered and sold only to residents of a single state by an issuer that is resident and doing business in such state. Through the years, judicial and administrative interpretations of this section have resulted in various ambiguities and also some abuses of this exemption.

In response to the problems this created

for both issuers and the Commission, the SEC in 1974 adopted Rule 147, a nonexclusive "safe harbor" rule for intrastate offerings. This rule provides more objective, but also more restrictive, criteria for determining compliance with the exemption. Although Rule 147 is nonexclusive, meaning that an issuer may qualify for an intrastate offering exemption notwithstanding its noncompliance with the Rule, most companies do in fact rely on Rule 147 for intrastate exempt offerings.

The exemption is available to all issuers, regardless of size, and without limitations on the amount of the offering or the number or financial sophistication of purchasers. However, restrictions are imposed to ensure that the exemption is used only for genuinely local offerings.

The SEC notes that "the exemption was intended to apply only to issues genuinely local in character, which in reality represent local financing by the local industries, carried out through local investment." Accordingly, Rule 147 provides objective standards for determining whether an issuer is resident in and doing business within the state, and whether offerees and purchasers are resident in the state:

> An issuer is considered *resident* in a state if it is incorporated or organized in that state or, in the case of general partnerships and other such organizations not organized under any state law, if the principal office is located in that state.
>
> An issuer is deemed to be *doing business* in a state if it derives at least 80 percent of its consolidated gross revenues from that state, has at least 80 percent of its consolidated assets in the state, intends to use (and does use) 80 percent of the net proceeds of the offering in the state, and has its principal office in the state.
>
> A company or other business organization must have its principal office in a state, and individuals must have their principal residence in

a state, to be deemed to be a *resident* of that state. Note that these residence requirements apply not only to purchasers, but also to offerees.

In order to ensure that the securities "come to rest in the hands of resident investors," the Rule also imposes a limitation on resales of the securities. For nine months after the issuer's last sale of the securities, any resale may be only to other residents of the state. As a precaution against sales and resales to out-of-state investors, the issuer is required to disclose in writing the limitations on resale and must obtain written representation from each purchaser as to his residence. In addition, a legend must be printed on the securities stating that the securities have not been registered and noting the resale limitations.

One of the primary drawbacks of this exemption is the potential exposure to the issuer if even one share is sold, either initially or resold within nine months, to an investor nonresident in the state. This risk can be substantial, particularly if the offering is anticipated to be widely distributed. Although various precautions are prescribed, and other precautions can be taken, the rules of this exemption are absolute: a disqualifying sale can subject the entire offering to potential rescission, regardless of any precautions taken by the issuer.

Rule 147 does not prescribe any information disclosures. However, the offering is not exempt from the antifraud provisions or applicable state securities laws.

Unregistered Public Offerings up to $1,500,000—Regulation A

No longer widely used, Regulation A provides an exemption from registration for certain offerings of up to $1,500,000 in a 12-month period. The exemption is available to all issuers except investment companies and for the sale of oil or gas or other mineral rights. And the regulation's "bad boy provisions" (similar to those discussed earlier under Rule 505 of Regulation D) preclude use of the exemption if the issuer, its underwriters, or either of their directors, officers, or principals, have engaged in certain specified acts of misconduct. The exemption may also be used for sales of securities by affiliates, certain estates, and others, although lower limits (ranging from $100,000 to $500,000) are imposed for such sales.

Regulation A imposes no restrictions on the number or qualification of investors, or on resale of the securities, and certain advertising and general solicitation is allowed. Thus, in many respects it is very similar to going public with a registered public offering. But, as with the other registration exemptions, use of the Regulation A exemption does not in itself trigger the 1934 Act periodic reporting obligations.

But there are some significant drawbacks to the use of this exemption. The costs incurred are generally higher than for other exempt offerings, although still somewhat lower than for registered offerings of similar size. Regulation A requires that an offering circular be provided to investors, unless the offering is under $100,000. The circular is similar to a prospectus and must be filed with, and reviewed and cleared by, the SEC. Two years' financial statements must be included, although no audit requirements are imposed. However, many underwriters and state laws may nevertheless require audited financial statements and, if audited financial statements are otherwise required, they are included in the offering circular.

Because of the limitations on the amount of the offering, the risks introduced by the "bad boy provisions," the extensive disclo-sure requirements and the resultant costs, Regulation A is not frequently used.

Credit: Ernst & Whinney

Want to Raise Money? Try the Vancouver Stock Exchange

Small companies in search of equity capital may find a welcome mat at the stock exchange. Not the Big Board, but a little-known alternative located in British Columbia. In recent years, the Vancouver Stock Exchange has emerged as an attractive financing source for U.S. and Canadian businesses.

"It's one of the best kept secrets in the capital markets," says a partner in the Vancouver office of Peat Marwick Main. "Those who discover it find that for companies seeking to raise up to $5 million, the Vancouver Stock Exchange is a very attractive source of venture capital. The fees are low here and the entrepreneur winds up with a substantial share of the equity—60 percent or more in many deals. That's generally better than he'll do with a venture capital financing in the U.S."

Established shortly after the turn of the century as a financing medium for Canadian companies in the oil, gas, and minerals exploration fields, the Vancouver Exchange has only recently been discovered by emerging companies in a wide range of fields including financial services, high technology, and basic manufacturing. All are united by a common search for high-risk capital.

U.S. companies seeking to go public on the Vancouver Exchange must first win the support of a Canadian underwriter willing to sponsor the transaction. This means proving that the venture is worthy of financial backing. Securities firms look most favorably at candidates with the following credentials:

1. Experienced management with a proven track record in running small or mid-size companies. Balance is critical here. Underwriters will want to see expertise in each major operating function including finance, marketing, and production.

2. Entry into a dynamic industry with a projected annual growth rate of at least 50 percent over the next five years. This assures ample growing room without having to take market share from established competitors.

3. Emphasis on a market niche protected from wholesale competition. Best bets are those products or services designed for market segments too small to appeal to industry giants. A new software firm focusing on highly specialized engineering applications, for example, would likely be more attractive than one going head to head against the big producers of general accounting and spreadsheet programs. Immunity from competition makes investors optimistic about the company's long-term prospects.

4. Ability to meet the exchange's minimum listing requirements including distribution of stock to at least 150 shareholders and invested capital of $100,000 or more.

Once the company lines up a sponsor, the listing process can move quickly.

"The next step is to file a prospectus," says the Peat Marwick Main partner. "This detailed report on the company and its management is reviewed by the government and either approved or sent back for additional information. If all goes well, the prospectus is okayed and the company files a listing application with the exchange. Once that is cleared, the shares begin to trade."

It worked that way for a California-based company that produces a novel data entry system for computers.

"We raised $3.5 million through the Vancouver Exchange and found it to be an excellent source of capital," says the company's director of administration. "The market is stable, the underwriters are first rate, and the legal and accounting assistance available there is helpful and thoroughly professional. Although going public was a new experience for us, everything moved along without a hitch."

But there are caveats.

1. Entrepreneurs listing on any stock exchange must be prepared to assume the responsibilities of a public company. That means disclosing detailed financial information and being responsive to stockholders.

2. Unlike the over-the-counter market in the U.S., the Vancouver Exchange does not have market makers for each publicly traded issue. This means the companies must create a following for their own stock.

Entrepreneurs interested in exploring a listing can contact the Vancouver Stock Exchange, Manager of Listings, Stock Exchange Tower, P.O. Box 10333, 609 Granville Street, Vancouver, B.C., Canada V7Y1H1.

LOANS

How to Finance the Growing Business Through Its Life Cycles

As small business emerges from its cocoon, moving from start-up to established firm, the need for capital remains a constant challenge to management's skill and ingenuity. At each stage of the life cycle, there are new capital requirements and new options for fulfilling them.

But budding entrepreneurs as well as seasoned small business owners often view financing as an inflexible process that remains the same regardless of the company's financial status. In this way of thinking only the amounts of capital change, not the way it is raised or the objectives it is designed to serve. So simplistic an approach is bound to fail: the company obtains inadequate sums, often at prohibitive rates.

"Just as a growing company's income, operating procedures, and work force changes over the years, so too must its financing strategy," says a partner with Main Hurdman, the national accounting firm. "By knowing where to look for money at each stage of growth, management greatly improves the odds of satisfying its capital needs and thus graduating to the next life cycle. Crucial to this process is for management to know the company's strengths and weaknesses."

Consider the following life-cycle/financing scenario:

Start-up

The business, now in its infancy, has only a prototype product or service, no sales and little or no assets. Capital—required to move from conceptual to market-oriented operations—will be used for additional research and development, product samples, and staffing. Because this tends to be a very high-risk period—many companies never graduate from it—banks and other conservative sources of financing are rarely willing to provide money at this stage. For the most part, this is the preserve of the venture capitalists, who'll provide seed capital in return for a piece of the company's equity. They'll want anywhere from 20 to 60 percent of the ownership. A big price to pay, yes, but it may be the only way to raise money at this juncture.

Typically, venture capitalists demand common stock—with options for additional shares should the company prove successful—plus a management role, usually a seat on the board of directors.

First Stage

Management is making progress toward its objectives, with the first products or services now on the market. But the fledgling company is still losing money and needs additional capital for production, facilities, and promotion. Again, the venture capitalists are the most likely financiers. "If the company was launched with the founders' own capital, and the venture capitalists are first being brought in at this stage, management can negotiate for a better deal on the equity split than would have been possible at start-up," says the Main Hurdman partner. "Where the venture guys may have claimed 50 percent of the company for seed capital, they may be willing to settle for 35 percent at this somewhat less risky stage.

"On the other hand, if venture capitalists provided the start-up capital, the same firm will probably come up with the first-stage financing. At this juncture, the entrepreneur may negotiate for payment in convertible shares, rather than additional common stock, thus protecting against further equity dilution."

A Pittsburgh-based venture producing specialized software intentionally structured its financing in two stages for this purpose. "We wanted to keep more of the equity for ourselves," says the firm's chairman, "and we knew we'd have a better chance of accomplishing this if we didn't seek all the required funds at start-up. It's worked out well for us. We've raised about $2 million and we have a good relationship with the venture-capital firm that provided the funding."

Second Stage

This signals the all-important shift from equity to debt capital. The company has likely turned the corner on profitability, now boasts a significant customer base, and needs capital for expansion rather than pure survival. Preferred financing sources include growth-capital firms and banks.

Third Stage

Gains made in the second stage are consolidated as the company establishes a record, albeit a brief one, as a worthy borrower. "The financial ratios and other credit indicators that are so important to lenders start to gain strength at this point," the CPA notes. "The company may have an impressive track record, a backlog of orders, and may be able to secure the loan with inventory, equipment, or receivables."

The key transition in stage three is from piecemeal financing to the initiation of a comprehensive banking relationship. Because the company is a more attractive borrower, it can seek and obtain a wider range of banking services and can expect a deeper banking commitment. For assigning its account to the bank, the business can demand creative solutions to its financial needs.

"When a company's cash flow, current or projected, is sufficient to service debt, we like to work with it in establishing a complete and ongoing banking relationship," says a vice-president of Manufacturers Hanover Trust. "The sooner management and its bankers can develop an understanding of each other's requirements, the faster we can develop different types of financing to meet the company's changing needs. We prefer to work on the basis of a full-scale relationship rather than on the basis of isolated loans."

Providing the bank serves the company well, it may be its partner in financing for many years to come. But as the business grows, as it matures as an operating entity and as a borrower, it should continue to press for better terms, especially the most favorable interest rates.

Buyout Stage

At some point, the owner may seek to sell all or part of the business to investors. This may be accomplished through a public offering, a private sale, or an acquisition (see Going Public, page 126). "By going public, management may be able to generate very substantial sums of capital—more than may be available through borrowing—for a new round of business expansion," the Main Hurdman partner adds. "But because this means the company is once again giving up equity, it will want to make certain that it is getting a fair price for its shares."

Another type of financing, the leveraged buyout, can be used by small, publicly held companies to buy back shares management believes are undervalued. "They do it by going private again," says a vice-president with the New York investment banking firm of Drexel Burnham. "In a simplified example, to buy back a $1 million company, management could put up $100,000 and borrow $900,000, using the company's assets and cash flow to secure the debt. Years later, the owners may engineer a private sale. With the company now worth $2 million, they stand to profit substantially on their $100,000 investment. That's the power of leveraging."

Work with an independent financial adviser in setting a current and long-term financing strategy.

LOANS

How to Help Your Business Get a Loan

In the critical relationship between small business and its bankers, the latter clearly hold the upper hand. With access to the purse strings, they can approve or reject loans, determine the amount of the financing, and set the terms. But borrowers are not without influence. By understanding the banking process—and by taking steps to reassure and motivate bankers—they can help to shape their destiny in the capital markets.

The idea is to switch from the borrower's traditional passive role to that of a catalyst in the search for business loans. By taking a series of calculated steps designed to impress bankers and to win their confidence, savvy borrowers can stand out from the crowd, gaining an inside track on needed financing.

But what do bankers look for? How can you help your business get a loan? How can you build relationships that lead to long-term financing? Interviews with bankers across the nation indicate that the willingness to provide full information is of primary importance.

"I'm most impressed with prospective borrowers who volunteer comprehensive information about their businesses," says a vice-president and director of small business for New York's Chemical Bank. "On the other hand, those who fail to answer legitimate questions leave me feeling uncertain about their personal and professional capabilities. They're less likely to win my support."

Small business owners can satisfy the bankers' "need to know" by providing the following types of information:

- Financial statements for the past three years
- Three-year cash flow projections
- Inventory values, product mix, and turnover rate
- Receivables data, including total amount outstanding, concentration by customer, and aging analysis.

"But go beyond the numbers," advises a former chief executive of a small business and now a partner in the private companies practice for accountants Touche Ross. "You'll win even more points by inviting the banker to your place of business, letting him kick the tires, and allowing him to see what really makes your business tick. While many small business people fear that this will confuse the banker, it actually educates him and encourages him to be a more liberal lender."

Consider these additional steps for building productive banking relationships:

1. Protect the banker from unpleasant surprises. Inform him of business difficulties as soon as they emerge. Trying to cover up problems only erodes the banker's trust and makes him less agreeable to creative solutions.

"If the borrower alerts us to problems at the outset, we can look for ways to help him through them," the Chemical banker says. "Like searching for assets that can be used as collateral to extend the terms of the financing. But if we're kept in the dark until the bottom is ready to fall out, we may not have the time or the inclination to be so flexible."

2. Give the banker reason to share your enthusiasm for the company and its products.

"Sending along an occasional newspaper article that shows impressive growth projections for the borrower's product or service can spark our excitement," says a vice-president of Providence, Rhode Island's Fleet Bank. "The clipping will be placed in the borrower's credit file and will be a positive factor in the loan analysis."

3. Whenever possible, pay off loans in advance. Making the final payment ahead of time can build goodwill, leading to more substantial financing the next time around.

4. Demonstrate your ability to personally guarantee business loans. Prepare financial statements listing all personal assets including stocks, bonds, and cash. Bear in mind that bankers want evidence of net worth be-

yond the borrower's home and business.

"This can be a swing factor," the Chemical banker says. "Sometimes the company's finances are marginal but the owner's personal resources are strong enough to make the deal fly."

If your current bank proves intractable, shop around for a more cooperative lender. Use the competition among banks to serve your business needs.

Loan Brokers Can Help You Borrow Money

Small companies in the market for business financing find that the fastest route to loan approval is through a well-connected bank officer. Borrowers with access to these key decision makers stand the best chance of getting the green light. But those without contacts of their own can turn to loan brokers to fill the gap.

Loan brokers serve as intermediaries in the lending market, directing prospective borrowers to the most promising capital sources. Because they are familiar with the lending terms and criteria at a wide range of financial institutions, they can take some of the guesswork out of the search for business loans. Equally important, competent brokers can add substance to a loan application.

"Given two loan applications of absolutely equal merit, the fact that one is brought to us by a broker will not give it an advantage," says a vice-president with Union Savings Bank. "But where the broker does provide an advantage is in preparing his client's application so that it is superior to others. A good broker knows the kinds of things a lender wants to see in an application, such as detailed financial projections and compre-

hensive biographies of the principals. And he also knows which institution is most likely to approve a given loan. When a broker I respect presents an application to this bank, I know it's a deal we're probably interested in—that it deserves serious attention."

Adds a partner with the accounting firm of Phillips, Gold: "Experienced loan brokers know where the money is, who controls it, and how to get it. Because they can tap a network of cash sources, they can speed the loan-shopping process and give it better odds of succeeding. A small manufacturer producing high-tech, high-risk products may find that most banks are reluctant to lend to it. But the broker, with his invaluable network of contacts, may know of an institution that specializes in high-tech financing."

Typically, loan brokers offer a package service that includes:

- Meeting with the client to assess its borrowing needs
- Preparing the loan application and related documents
- Negotiating with lenders on rates and terms

"While anyone can fill out an application and present it to a bank, brokers provide services clients are hard pressed to duplicate on their own," says Leonard Primack, a loan broker based in Hauppauge, New York. "Like coming up with creative financing deals. To get a client purchasing a commercial property a bigger mortgage than he would otherwise qualify for, a broker might recommend that the lender take a second or third mortage on the borrower's home or other real assets. Small business owners—most of whom are only occasional borrowers—are rarely aware of all the options."

A partner with the accounting firm of Peat Marwick finds brokers most helpful in reaching lenders beyond the borrower's local market. "Sometimes a deal that's unacceptable to all the local lenders will be right for another institution in another city or state. I've seen brokers reach across geographic lines to get money."

But there are drawbacks:

1. Brokers charge for their services, usually claiming 1 to 5 percent of the loan amount payable at closing. Some require retainers or advance payments for out-of-pocket expenses.

2. Loan brokerage attracts charlatans as well as reputable practitioners. Some prey on clients' needs and aspirations, promising easy money at below-market rates. Be wary of those demanding large, nonrefundable fees up front.

"The fundamental rules for working with loan brokers," the Phillips, Gold partner says, "are to hire them only when your company needs special assistance in gaining loans—why else pay the fee?—and then to work only with those brokers referred by trusted sources."

Ask bankers, accountants, and business associates for the names of reputable brokers. Check references for evidence of a solid track record.

Loan brokers are not the only financial intermediaries. Lawyers and accountants—many with wide contacts among bankers, investors, and venture capitalists—can help to raise money for business start-ups and expansion.

Because professionals are generally hired for technical assignments, such as writing contracts and performing audits, their money-raising capabilities are often overlooked. But many perform this service well, tapping a network of sources throughout the financial community.

"When a client, or for that matter a prospective client, seeks to raise money, I'll use the sources within my practice to try and strike a deal," says a partner with the law firm of Parker Chapin Flattau & Klimpl. "In one case, an entrepreneur wanted to finance a new business through a public offering. Knowing that a good presentation is critical, I sent him to one of my clients who writes business plans. Later, I arranged an introduction with another client, an investment banker, who'd be in position to underwrite the offering. Not every deal works, but there's a clear advantage when the party seeking the money approaches financial sources with the imprimatur of a trusted professional."

A vice-president of Manufacturers Hanover Trust agrees: "Accountants and attorneys who've worked with us over the years are familiar with our lending criteria. So their loan requests have more credibility than those from unknown sources. In fact, we'll often ask professionals to give us leads on prospective borrowers. It's a two-way relationship that clients can benefit from."

"Relationship" is the key word. Parties active in business financing note that indiscriminate referrals do little more than raise expectations.

"If a lawyer's idea of raising money is simply taking a business plan from one envelope, putting it in another, and addressing it to the first source that comes to mind, the chances of hitting pay dirt are slim," says an attorney with Gaston Snow Beekman & Bogue. "To be successful, the lawyer must keep up-to-date records of who's currently in the market for investments, the amounts they want to invest, the industries they favor, and the terms they demand. Armed with this kind of data base, the professional can direct the proposal to those lenders and investors best suited for the deal."

Lawyers and accountants can help clients negotiate the amount and the terms of financing deals. "When an auto parts distributor needed a $150,000 line of credit to expand his

ETCETERA

Guidelines for Records Retention

	\multicolumn{5}{c}{Retention Period (Years)}				
	1	3	5	7	Permanent
I. Accounting Records					
Bank statements and deposit slips		X			
Cancelled checks: Normal				X	
Important payments (taxes, property purchases, etc.)					X
Payroll records and time cards				X	
Expense report from employees			X		
General ledger and books of original entry (journals)					X
Subsidiary ledgers				X	
Interim trial balances				X	
Petty cash vouchers		X			
Sales and purchase invoices			X		
Purchase orders	X				
Receiving reports	X				
Audit and accountant's reports					X
Copies of tax returns and closing workpapers					X
Fixed asset and depreciation records					X
II. Corporate Records					
Expired mortgage notes, leases, contracts				X	
Most other records, such as capital stock books, by-laws, minutes, etc.					X
III. Correspondence					
General	X				
Legal and tax					X
IV. Insurance					
Expired policies		X			
Accident reports			X		
Settled claims				X	
V. Personnel					
Expired contracts			X		
Personal files (terminated)			X		
Withholding tax statements				X	

Credit: Paneth, Haber & Zimmerman, *CPA Advisor* Newsletter, April 1986, and Andrew Glickman

facilities, we prepared a set of projections illustrating the company's good growth prospects and brought this to a local banker," says a partner with Touche Ross. "We not only got the loan but have since added to and improved it. The ceiling has been expanded to $300,000 and the interest rate dropped from 2.5 percent to 1.25 percent over prime. Our good relationship with the bank was the foot in the door. The client's performance took the ball from there."

Typically, professionals apply their standard hourly rate to money-raising activities. Introductions, business plans, and trips to the bank are billed on the same basis as other services.

"But there are exceptions," the Gaston Snow partner notes. "With start-ups, for example, the client may not have enough money to cover professional fees. In that case, creative compensation plans may be worked out. Some lawyers will take stock in the new venture or will postpone their fees until and if the deal goes through. If the professional is optimistic about the project and wants to serve the client, he may be willing to depart from his standard compensation."

Consider these additional points:

1. Professionals can tap a wide range of financing sources, including local development agencies, venture pools, and wealthy individuals. "Many affluent clients give us standing orders to call them if we hear of promising investment opportunities," says a partner with accountants Israeloff, Trattner. "Just recently, we paired a client who wanted to sell a division of his company with another who was in the market to buy a business."

2. The professional's success as a financial liaison depends in large measure on the quality of his client's project. Even the best contacts cannot fund a bad deal. Ask the banker or accountant for an honest appraisal of your prospects before approaching the capital markets.

Physical Disaster Business Loans

The U.S. Small Business Administration is authorized to make loans up to $500,000 to a business to repair or replace the business's property to its predisaster condition. Repair or replacement of real property, machinery, equipment, fixtures, inventory, and leasehold improvements may be included in a loan.

Any business located in a declared disaster area that has suffered damage as a result of a physical disaster is eligible to apply for a physical disaster loan to help repair or replace damaged property to its *predisaster condition.*

However, all physical disaster loans to businesses are limited to 85 percent of the verified damage to the business.

Any insurance that can be used in restoration, or other compensation, public or private, must be deducted from the sustained damage amount to determine the amount you are eligible to borrow from SBA.

The interest rate that the Agency charges on its disaster loans is determined by your ability to obtain "credit elsewhere" from nonfederal sources, taking into consideration the local financial situation in or near the community where your business is located.

Able to Obtain Credit Elsewhere

If SBA determines that your business does have the ability to obtain credit elsewhere, the agency can make a loan at an interest rate that will not exceed that being charged in the private market at the time of the physical disaster. The maturity of this loan *may not exceed three (3) years.*

Note: Charitable, religious, nonprofit, and similar organizations, although not classified by SBA as businesses, are eligible for physical disaster loans for 85 percent of the verified damage, for up to 30 years, at an interest rate based upon a different statutory formula. This rate can change annually. The nearest SBA Disaster Branch Office can supply you with the current interest rate.

Questions and Answers about Physical Disaster Loans to Businesses

Q. If I receive a disaster loan, may I spend the money any way I want?
A. No. The disaster loan is intended to help you return your property to the condition it was in before the disaster. Your loan will be made for specific and designated purposes. Remember that the penalty for misusing disaster funds is *immediate repayment of 1.5 times the original amount of the loan.* SBA insists that you obtain receipts and maintain good records of all loan expenditures as you restore your damaged property, and keep these receipts and records for three years.

Q. I already have a mortgage on my business. Can SBA refinance my mortgage?
A. In certain cases, yes. To be eligible for SBA refinancing, (1) the uninsured damage to your property must equal 30 percent or more of its predisaster value, (2) SBA must determine that you require mortgage refinancing to avoid undue financial hardship, (3) the amount of refinancing cannot exceed the actual amount of damage, and (4) the amount shall be reduced to the extent such mortgage or lien is satisfied by insurance or otherwise.

Q. Is collateral required for these loans?
A. Loans of $5,000 or less normally require the signature of the owner(s) of the property. Loans in excess of $5,000 require the pledging of collateral to the extent it is available.

Normally the collateral would consist of a first or second mortgage on the damaged real estate. No loan will be declined for lack of collateral, but you must pledge that collateral which is available.

Q. If my business is completely destroyed, can SBA lend me money to relocate my business?
A. If you are unable to obtain a building permit to rebuild your business at its original site, or for some other reason you are unable to restore or replace your property at that site, the cost of relocating your business might be included in the loan amount. But if you decide to relocate your business without being required to, an SBA loan can be obtained only for the exact amount of the damage.

Q. Must I use my own money or try to borrow from a bank before I come to SBA?
A. Not necessarily. It is not necessary to use your own resources before you apply to SBA for a disaster loan. However, your resources and ability to obtain credit elsewhere will be taken into consideration to determine the interest rate.

Q. How may I use the SBA disaster loan?
A. The loan is intended to help you restore your property as nearly as possible to its predisaster condition. Normally, SBA funds cannot be used to expand or upgrade a business. But in the event that city or county building codes require such upgrading, SBA loans may be used for that purpose.

Q. Should I wait for my flood insurance or other insurance settlement before I file my loan application?
A. Not necessarily. The application may be returned to SBA now, and insurance information added when a settlement is made. A

loan may be approved for the total replacement cost, but the insurance proceeds must be assigned to SBA. Don't miss the filing deadline by waiting for an insurance settlement.

Q. What information do I need to help me complete the loan application form?
A. Necessary information will include: (1) an itemized list of losses with your estimate of the repair or replacement cost of each item, (2) copies of your last three years' federal income tax returns, (3) a copy of your deed, mortgage, lease, or rental agreement, (4) a brief history of the business, and (5) personal and business financial statements. A contractor's estimate for repairing structural damage may be desirable, but you may make your own cost estimate, if you wish. Remember to sign each part of the application; it cannot be processed if you omit any form that requires your signature.

Q. I would like to get a contractor's estimate for the cost of repairing damage to my business, but I'm having difficulty in finding a contractor. Should I hold up my application until I get the estimate?
A. Not necessarily, because you might miss the deadline for filing your application by waiting for a contractor's estimate.

Q. I had to remove debris from my property after the disaster. Can this expense be included in my loan application?
A. Your own labor and that of family members cannot be included. But amounts paid to others and any equipment rental can be listed as part of repairs to real estate. Remember that the maximum loan limit on physical damage is 85 percent of the verified damage up to the maximum of $500,000, and debris removal is included in that limit.

Q. I am a farmer. Am I eligible to apply for SBA assistance?
A. Under recent legislative changes, you may apply to SBA *only* for a loan to cover the damage to your home and contents. Damage to all farm outbuildings and crops must be processed by the Farmers Home Administration, unless it is determined by the Farmers Home Administration that you are not eligible for assistance from them. In that case, you might be eligible for assistance from SBA. However, you must check first with Farmers Home Administration to determine your eligibility.

Q. Will SBA check the losses I claim?
A. Yes. Once you have returned your loan application, an SBA loss verifier will visit you to determine the extent of the damage and the reasonableness of the loan request.

Credit: U.S. Small Business Administration, Disaster Assistance Division

WHERE TO FIND IT

INDEPENDENT COMPUTER CONSULTANTS ASSOCIATION
Executive Director
443 North New Ballas
P.O. Box 27412
St. Louis, MO 63141
Toll-free number 800-GET-ICCA

From Seed Capital to Growth Financing

Entrepreneurs may optimistically believe that funding will be the easiest part of starting or running a business, but it usually turns out to be the hardest. For this reason, the business owner needs to do a substantial amount of work before even beginning to look for funds.

First, a realistic appraisal of the product or service must be made—the idea may in fact not be the greatest. Or possibly someone else already has the same product patented and selling, or is providing a comparable service at a competitive price.

Next, a critical question: "Do I really want to do this?" Starting a new business and making it grow can bring many frustrations, and an entrepreneur must be dedicated to seeing it through no matter what.

Third, in a large corporation many different people do things that the entrepreneur will have to do alone—buying supplies, dealing with regulatory agencies, hiring and evaluating employees, determining salaries, and so on. Starting a new company is more than just developing a product or service and finding financing; it is all the jobs in a corporate environment rolled into one—the job of the entrepreneur.

At this point it is useful to think about using outside advisers. Since hiring high-level executives is out of the question initially, the entrepreneur should seek out the best professionals available. It is extremely important to select carefully an accountant, an attorney, a banker, an insurance agent, and a public relations firm. These individuals must be competent, willing to take the time to understand the business, and experienced in the company's industry. These skills are necessary for the professional to provide a high level of executive expertise, both initially and as the company grows. Proper use of these professionals can be a cost-effective way to complete the myriad tasks necessary to launch a business and make it grow.

Initial Projections

Part of the initial legwork in starting a business is an estimate of the time it will take to get the product into production and onto the market, or the service available to customers. Along with the time estimate comes an estimate of the initial cost. Normally, getting a product or service to market takes much longer and costs much more than the initial estimates. It is simply impossible to anticipate all the little pitfalls that will be encountered.

During this phase, outside funding is virtually impossible to obtain, and the entrepreneur will need to have seed funds available to work with. Generally, additional sources of financing can be tapped only when the product or service is on the market. The key here is to be absolutely realistic and conservative—even overconservative. It would not be unwise to double any initial time frame and cost estimates. Many wonderful ideas have died because the entrepreneur underestimated the time and cost of getting to market.

Sowing the Seed

The seed capital, or initial funding, for a business is the most difficult to obtain. It is hard to find someone to invest in a company that has no track record or history. There is no one source for this seed capital, but the entrepreneur might want to start by attending family reunions—because family and close friends are a common source. Other initial financing sources include savings and a second mortgage on the house. Whichever source or combination of sources is used, this will be the most difficult time in the history of the business.

As the entrepreneur organizes the business and takes the product or service to market, the available sources of funding will increase. The sources will vary with the situation, but the following options should be considered.

Banks. Most people in need of money turn

to their friendly banker, but the purpose of banks must be kept in mind: banks *rent* money, they do not give it away. Bankers are investing their depositors' money, and to avoid risking it unwisely they expect security for a loan. Without substantial "side collateral," banks can lend only a small amount based on the entrepreneur's personal creditworthiness.

SBICs. To cash in on the number of small companies with growth potential, many large banks and other entities have established Small Business Investment Corporations (SBICs). These act as venture capital sources that invest only in small businesses. SBICs receive priority funding or guarantees from the federal government, or both. But like other venture capital sources, they are profit-driven and quite selective when investing in a business. One big advantage of the SBIC, however, is that a company can expand its relationship with its bank to include the bank's SBIC. Financing arrangements that blend capital and debt from related sources can help to simplify financial matters.

Venture-capital Firms. What used to be a very small network of venture-capital firms in localized areas is now a much larger network with branch offices throughout the country. Again, though the available funds are large, the investors are very particular, and a quick return is mandatory to attract this financing. An entrepreneur should have the best possible verbal presentation and a plan for making the company grow rapidly. If the entrepreneur does not believe that the business can become a big company with super-quick growth, venture capital is not the route to take.

Limited and General Partnerships. One form, the research and development (R & D) limited partnership, involves specialized tax questions that demand professional help. Nevertheless, limited and general partnerships are a very good means of funding in the right situations. The word "partnership," however, is usually accompanied by the words "tax incentive." If the company cannot provide potential investors with tax write-offs through the use of its funds—either in R & D or depreciable assets that can give an investor some leverage—then the partnership may not be the way to go.

Asset-based Lending. Offered typically by larger banks, this type of financing requires strong collateral, such as receivables and inventory. This type of lending is not usually an initial source; it would come at a more advanced stage of the company's history. In a period of fast growth, asset-based lending can be used to turn inventory and receivables into cash. Asset-based lenders look for "clean" assets, an extremely strong earnings record, increasing sales, and top-flight management.

Public Offerings

Taking a company public is a long-range funding source that should be considered by the growing company. Planning to go public should start two or three years before the offering date, partly because most public offerings require audited financial statements for two or more previous years. If a company is inventory-intensive, the auditor must be present to observe the actual inventory count—otherwise, the auditor may be unable to complete an audit, thereby precluding the offering.

The process of making an initial public offering of securities is complex and time-consuming, and it requires the assistance of highly specialized investment bankers, legal counsel, and accountants. Becoming a public company entails making a significant, ongoing commitment. In most cases, public companies are required to file periodic reports with the Securities and Exchange Commission. The company and its management are responsible under federal securities law for the accuracy of these periodic reports.

Types of Offerings. The most common type of public offering is an *S-1.* While it can raise an unlimited amount of money, it requires three years' audited financial statements and substantial disclosure in the registration statement. An *S-18* offering, on the other hand, while requiring two years' audited financial statements, requires fewer disclosures than the S-1, but limits the offering amount to a maximum of $7.5 million.

The simplest public offering is a *Regulation A.* In most cases, it requires no audited financial statements, is limited to a total offering amount of $1.5 million, and requires less disclosure than does a "normal" S-1. But the limited offering amount may not be enough to justify the costs of making the offering.

Regulation D transactions are offerings that are exempt from the registration requirements of the Securities Act of 1933. The exemption is available depending on the amount of the offering and the number and types of investors; the disclosures required in the offering document also depend on the amount of the offering.

Other Sources

There are other funding opportunities available through the federal government and its agencies, such as the Small Business Administration and the Farmers Home Administration (if the company is in a rural area). Creative and comprehensive income tax planning should not be overlooked, either—it can put dollars in the entrepreneur's pocket. Regardless of the funding method used, quality of management is probably the most important ingredient for success.

Credit: Peat Marwick, *The Business Adviser,* June 1985, and Keith Voights

SBA Loans

Basic Small Business Loans

Uses. A small business unable to obtain financing in the private credit marketplace may be eligible, first, for a guaranteed/insured loan or, alternatively, for a direct loan if no bank will participate in a guaranteed loan. These loans may be used to construct, expand, or convert facilities; to purchase building equipment or materials; or to provide working capital. Direct loans have ranged from $1,000 to $350,000, and averaged $54,782, while guaranteed loans have ranged from $1,800 to $500,000, and averaged $113,589. Maximum terms are 7 years for working-capital loans and 25 years for regular loans.

Restrictions and eligibility. The borrower must meet the SBA's definition of a small business. At least one bank must previously have turned down the applicant. The applicant must agree not to discriminate in employment or service. He or she must be of good character; show an ability to operate a business successfully; have a significant stake in the business; and show that the business can operate on a sound financial basis. The applicant must be prepared to provide a statement of personal history, personal financial statements, company financial statements, and summary of collateral. The loan must be of such sound value or so secured as to provide reasonable assurance of repayment.

Application and selection. Applications are generally filed in the SBA field office serving the territory where the applicant's business is located. Approval takes 3 to 60 days from the date of application acceptance, depending on the type of loan. The applicant is notified by an authorization letter from the district SBA office or participating bank.

Additional requirements. Semiannual and annual financial statements must be provided during the life of the loan.

Literature, guidelines, regulations. A pamphlet, "Business Loans from the SBA," is available from the SBA.

Information contacts. Headquarters Office: Office of Business Loans, Small Business Administration, 1441 L Street, NW, Washington, DC 20416.

Regional or Local Office: Initial contact should be with a district SBA office:

Credit: Price Waterhouse, "Getting Government Help."

U.S. SMALL BUSINESS ADMINISTRATION

District Offices

Region I
302 High Street, 4th Floor
Holyoke, MA 01040
(413) 536-8770

Federal Building
40 Western Avenue, Room 512
Augusta, ME 04330
(207) 622-8378

55 Pleasant Street, Room 211
Concord, NH 03301
(603) 224-4041

Federal Building
One Hartford Square West
Hartford, CT 06106
(203) 244-3600

Federal Building
87 State Street, Room 205
Montpelier, VT 05602
(802) 229-0538

40 Fountain Street
Providence, RI 02903
(401) 528-4580

Region II
Carlos Chardon Avenue,
Room 691
Hato Rey, PR 00919
(809) 753-4002

970 Broad Street, Room 1635
Newark, NJ 07102
(201) 645-2434

100 South Clinton Street,
Room 1071
Syracuse, NY 07102
(315) 423-5383

100 State Street, Room 601
Rochester, NY 14614

Region III
109 North 3rd Street
Room 302, Lowndes Building
Clarksburg, WV 26301
(304) 623-5631

560 Penn Avenue, 5th Floor
Pittsburgh, PA 15222
(412) 644-2780

Federal Building
400 North 8th Street,
Room 3015
Richmond, VA 23240
(804) 771-2617

1111 18th Street, NW,
6th Floor
Washington, DC 20417
(202) 634-4950

Region IV
908 South 20th Street,
Room 202
Birmingham, AL 35256
(205) 254-1344

230 S. Tryon Street, Room 700
Charlotte, NC 28200
(704) 371-6563

1835 Assembly Street,
3rd Floor
Columbia, SC 29201
(803) 765-5376

100 West Capitol Street,
Suite 322
Jackson, MS 39269
(601) 960-4378

Federal Building
400 West Bay Street, Room 261
Jacksonville, FL 32202
(904) 791-3782

Federal Building
600 Federal Pl., Room 188
Louisville, KY 40202
(502) 582-5971

2222 Ponce De Leon Blvd.,
5th Floor
Miami, FL 33134
(305) 350-5521

404 James Robertson Parkway,
Room 1012
Nashville, TN 37219
(615) 251-5881

502 South Gay Street
Fidelity Bankers Building,
Room 307
Knoxville, TN 37902
(615) 524-8202

Region V
Four North, Old State Capital
Plaza
Springfield, IL 65806
(217) 492-4416

1240 East 9th Street, Room 317
Cleveland, OH 44199
(216) 522-4170

85 Marconi Blvd.
Columbus, OH 43215
(614) 469-6860

Federal Building
550 Main Street, Room 5028
Cincinnati, OH 45202
(513) 684-2814

477 Michigan Avenue,
Room 515
Detroit, MI 48226
(313) 226-7241

575 North Pennsylvania Street,
Room 578
Indianapolis, IN 46209
(317) 269-7272

212 East Washington Avenue,
Room 213
Madison, WI 53703
(608) 264-5261

100 North 6th Street
Minneapolis, MN 55403
(612) 349-3550

Region VI
5000 Marble Avenue, N.E.
Room 320
Albuquerque, NM 87110
(505) 262-6026

2525 Murworth, Room 112
Houston, TX 77054
(713) 660-4401

Post Office and Court House
Building
West Capital Avenue,
Room 601
Little Rock, AR 72201
(501) 378-5871

1611 Tenth Avenue, Suite 200
Lubbock, TX 79401
(806) 762-7466

222 East Van Buren Street,
Room 500
(Lower Rio Grande Valley)
Harlingen, TX 78550
(512) 423-8933

1661 Canal Street, 2nd Floor
New Orleans, LA 70112
(504) 589-6685

200 N.W. 5th Street, Room 670
Oklahoma City, OK 73102
(405) 231-4301

727 East Durango Street,
Room A-513
San Antonio, TX 78206
(512) 229-6250

Region VII
New Federal Building
210 Walnut Street, Room 749
Des Moines, IA 50309
(515) 284-4422

300 South 19th Street
Omaha, NE 68102
(402) 221-4691

815 Olive Street, Room 242
Saint Louis, MO 63101
(314) 425-6600

110 East Waterman Street
Wichita, KS 67202
(316) 269-6571

Region VIII
Federal Building
1000 East B Street, Room 4001
Casper, WY 82602
(307) 262-5761

Federal Building
657 2nd Avenue, North,
Room 218
Fargo, ND 58108
(701) 237-5771

301 South Park Avenue,
Room 528
Helena, MT 59601
(406) 449-5381

Federal Building
125 South State Street,
Room 2237
Salt Lake City, UT 84138
(801) 524-5800

101 South Main Avenue,
Suite 101
Sioux Falls, SD 57102
(605) 336-2980

Region IX
300 Ala Moana, Room 2213
Honolulu, HI 96813
(808) 546-8950

350 S. Figueroa Street,
6th Floor
Los Angeles, CA 90071
(213) 241-2200

3030 North Central Avenue,
Room 1201
Phoenix, AZ 85012
(602) 241-2200

880 Front Street, Room 4529
San Diego, CA 92188
(714) 293-5440

Region X
701 C Street
Anchorage, AK 99513
(907) 271-4022

101 12th Avenue
Fairbanks, AK 99701
(907) 456-0211

1005 Main Street, 2d Floor
Boise, ID 83702
(208) 334-1696

1220 S.W. Third Avenue,
Room 676
Portland, OR 97204
(503) 294-5221

W. 920 Riverside Avenue,
Room 651
Spokane, WA 99201
(509) 456-5310

Regional Offices

Region I
(Connecticut, Maine, Mass-
achusetts, New Hampshire,
Rhode Island, Vermont)
John F. Kennedy Federal
Building, Room 2113
Boston, MA 02203
(617) 223-2100

Region II
(New Jersey, New York, Puerto
Rico, Virgin Islands)
26 Federal Plaza, Room 3100
New York, NY 10278
(212) 264-4355

Region III
(Delaware, District of Columbia, Maryland, Pennsylvania,
Virginia, West Virginia)
231 St. Asaphs Road
Bala Cynwyd, PA 19004
(215) 596-5889

Region IV
(Alabama, Florida, Georgia,
Kentucky, Mississippi, North
Carolina, South Carolina,
Tennessee)
1720 Peachtree Street, NE
Atlanta, GA 30309
(404) 881-4749

Region V
(Illinois, Indiana, Michigan,
Minnesota, Ohio, Wisconsin)
Federal Building
219 South Dearborn Street,
Room 437
Chicago, IL 60604
(312) 353-452

Region VI
(Arkansas, Louisiana, New
Mexico, Oklahoma, Texas)
1100 Commerce Street,
Room 3C36
Dallas, TX 75242
(214) 767-0605

Region VII
(Kansas, Missouri, Nebraska)
911 Walnut Street, 23rd Floor
Kansas City, MO 64106
(816) 374-5288

Region VIII
(Colorado, Montana, North
Dakota, South Dakota,
Utah, Wyoming)
721 19th Street, Room 407
Denver, CO 80202
(303) 837-2607

Region IX
(Arizona, California, Hawaii,
Nevada, Pacific Islands)
Federal Building
450 Golden Gate Avenue
San Francisco, CA 94102
(415) 556-7487

Region X
(Alaska, Idaho, Oregon,
Washington)
710 2nd Avenue, 5th Floor
Dexter Horton Building
Seattle, WA 98104
(206) 442-5676

**SMALL BUSINESS INVESTMENT
COMPANIES (SBICs)**

Need High-Risk Capital?
Turn to SBICs

When entrepreneurs Steven Jobs and Ste-
phen Wozniak went searching for capital to
expand their fledgling Apple Computer Com-

pany, they turned to an oft-confused and
widely misunderstood source of high-risk
financing, Small Business Investment Companies. Impressed with Apple's ingenious
product—an easy-to-use and inexpensive
personal computer—the SBICs provided
sufficient funding to take the business from
humble beginnings to a major corporate enterprise.

That this turned out to be a stellar investment is an understatement; at the time, only a crystal ball could have determined that. To impartial observers—especially those asked to put up money—the risks appeared at least as great as the potential rewards. This was, after all, an unproven technology in a virgin market.

Why, then, did the SBICs (along with venture capitalists) back the company? Why were they willing to accept the risks?

"Because that's their business," says an executive with the National Association of Small Business Investment Companies, a trade group representing 300 SBICs across the nation. "Put simply, we make loans and investments in those business opportunities capable of generating substantial returns on our capital."

In a typical financing, an SBIC provides equity capital to launch or expand a small business. In return for its investment, the SBIC takes shares of the company's stock, claims a seat on the board, and plays an advisory role in the management function.

"The SBIC doesn't want to run the company," the SBIC executive says. "It just wants to see to it that the company is run well. That may mean adding to the entrepreneur's technical or marketing skills by recruiting administrators, financial executives, or others to round out the management team. Experienced executives know that for a company to perform well, it must have capable managers in each of the key business disciplines."

With the venture adequately financed and staffed, the SBIC monitors its progress, waiting (and hoping) for the day when it can go public. At this point, some or all of the common stock is sold, rewarding the investors with a tidy capital gain that can—in a successful deal—be ten times or more its initial investment. Thus the essential trade-off: the

SBIC accepts high risk in return for potentially high reward.

If this sounds like the modus operandi of venture capitalists, that's because the two financing sources function quite similarly. But there are critical differences. Most important, only the SBICs are licensed by the Small Business Administration, which requires that they operate under the following rules:

1. Financing must be limited to small companies (as defined by SBA size standards).
2. SBICs can take no more than 50 percent of a company's stock unless it files a plan indicating how it will reduce those holdings to less than 50 percent within seven years.
3. Loans must carry a minimum term of five years.

Although SBICs are best known for equity investment, lending—both straight loans and loans with equity components—accounts for more than half of their funding commitments.

"Typically, loans are made when the company seeking funds has an income flow and can afford to pay interest on its obligations," says the SBIC spokesman. "For example, when a new management team sought to modernize and turn around an old-line financial printing company, the executives turned to a group of three SBICs for loans to buy computers and sophisticated typesetting equipment. In addition to paying debt service on the loans, the borrower issued warrants allowing the SBICs to purchase shares of stock at a set price. Equity kickers of this kind give SBICs the incentive to make loans which, considering the degree of risk involved, could not be justified on an interest-only basis."

Because SBICs subordinate their debt to existing loans, financing can generally be arranged without objections from current lenders. Banks that would otherwise fight the extension of additional credit (for fear this will impair the borrower's ability to repay) are likely to approve subordinated debt (which they view as additional equity). Bottom line: the company can reach beyond the financing limits imposed on standard bank loans.

In some cases, SBICs function like banks, making interest-only loans often at below-market rates. This lending activity is enhanced by the SBIC's ability to borrow money—to a total of three times its own capital—from the Small Business Administration. This leveraging effect enables an SBIC with a $3 million capitalization to make loans and investments totaling $12 million ($3 million of capital plus $9 million borrowed from the SBA).

Under SBA guidelines, an SBIC's lending rate cannot exceed six percentage points more than its cost of money. Were the SBIC to borrow money from the SBA at 8.8 percent, deals closed in that month could carry a maximum interest rate of 14.8 percent. On average, however, the actual rate is only three to four percentage points above the cost of funds.

With its unique mix of debt and equity, its mandate to back only small companies, and its propensity for risk, SBIC financing is a boon to small business. The very companies deemed unacceptable by the banks (because they fall short on the classic lending ratios, such as debt to equity) can find a home here.

Not to say that SBICs are indiscriminate. Quite the contrary, SBICs are among the most sophisticated institutions. Their standards—though markedly different from the banks and finance companies—are exacting nevertheless.

Which leads to the million-dollar question: Who qualifies for SBIC financing? What kind of companies can attract start-up or expansion capital from them?

Although the criteria vary among the SBIC and by the type of financing sought, most look for the following:

1. A product or service with a strong market niche.

"A company seeking to start up in a crowded field isn't likely to attract SBIC capital unless it brings something unique to that field," the SBIC executive says. "Its product will have to be cheaper, faster, or more effective than the competition.

"Consider the SBIC financing for Cray Research. When Seymour Cray left Control Data to produce a new class of superfast computers, he enjoyed a reputation as a technical genius with good market sense. Rather than competing with IBM, he would cater to a small but growing niche in the computer market that would pay a premium for ultra-high-speed computers. With this concept carefully documented, and with Cray's abilities widely acknowledged throughout the industry, he raised the money to launch his company.

"Let me add, however that SBIC dollars are not limited to high-tech industries. All strive to maintain balanced portfolios, including companies in various markets and in various stages of the growth cycle. The same SBIC that backed Cray financed a traveling road show of "Sesame Street."

Adds the president of a Washington, D.C.-based SBIC: "Because we generally come in at a later stage than the venture capitalists, and because we look for companies with the ability to service debt, we find ourselves working more often with ongoing outfits in rather mundane fields than with high-tech start-ups. In recent years, we've financed everything from health spas to publishers of local telephone directories. These low-tech deals can be more attractive because they're easier to evaluate."

2. A strong and balanced management team. As noted, SBICs do not want to run companies. Having experienced hands on the helm gives the SBIC the confidence to lend or invest money.

3. Heart-pounding growth prospects. Forget all the standard measurements of solid corporate growth—say, 15 to 18 percent a year. From the SBIC's perspective, that's anemic. To attract these high rollers, you'll have to support growth projections of at least 40 percent a year. Not necessarily in gross sales or the number of employees but in net profits or the company's market value.

These are critical measurements because they determine, to a great extent, how much money the SBICs can take out above and be-yond what they have put in.

Companies interested in working with SBICs are advised to make contact without intermediaries.

"Ninety percent of an SBIC's decision is based on the company's management team," says an SBIC spokesman. "Having a slick CPA or financial adviser knock on the door for you won't mean a whit. In fact, it can be counterproductive. That's because the SBIC considers it vital to meet the entrepreneur—to get a feel for his capabilities. In the final analysis, that's going to have the greatest impact on its decision."

For a directory of NASBIC members (including contact names and investment criteria), send $1 to the National Association of Small Business Investment Companies, 1156 15th Street NW, Washington, DC 20005.

WHERE TO FIND IT

Directory of Small Business Investment Companies

ALABAMA
First SBIC of Alabama
16 Midtown Park East
Mobile, AL 36606
(205) 476-0700

Hickory Venture Capital Corp.
200 West Coast Sq., Ste. 624
Huntsville, AL 35801
(205) 539-1931

Tuskegee Capital Corp.
PO Drawer GG
Tuskegee Institute, AL 36088
(205) 727-2850

ALASKA
Alaska Business Investment
Corp.
PO Box 600
Anchorage, AK 99510
(907) 265-2816

Calista Business Investment
Corp.
516 Denali St.
Anchorage, AK 99501
(907) 277-0425

ARIZONA
FBS Venture Capital Co.
6900 E. Camelback Rd.,
Ste. 452
Scottsdale, AZ 85251
(602) 941-2160

Rocky Mountain Equity Corp.
4530 N. Central Ave., Ste. 3
Phoenix, AZ 85012
(602) 274-7558

Sun Belt Capital Corp.
14255 N. 76th Pl., Ste. A-1
Scottsdale, AZ 85260
(602) 998-4741

VNB Capital Corp.
15 E. Monroe, B-710
Phoenix, AZ 85001
(602) 261-1076

ARKANSAS
Capital Management Services,
Inc.
1910 N. Grant, Ste. 200
Little Rock, AR 72207
(501) 664-8613

First SBIC of Arkansas, Inc.
1400 Worthen Bank Bldg.
200 W. Capitol Ave.
Little Rock, AR 72201
(501) 378-1876

Independence Financial
Services, Inc.
PO Box 2297
Batesville, AR 72503
(501) 793-4533

Kar-Mal Venture Capital, Inc.
610 Plaza West Bldg.
Little Rock, AR 72205
(501) 661-0010

Power Ventures, Inc.
Hwy. 270 N., PO Box 518
Malvern, AR 72104
(501) 332-3695

Worthern Finance & Inv. Inc.
PO Box 1681—Fl. W10
Little Rock, AR 72207
(501) 378-1060

CALIFORNIA
Branch Office
Atlanta Investment Co., Inc.
141 El Camino Dr.
Los Angeles, CA 90212
(213) 273-1730

Bancorp Venture Capital
2633 Cherry Ave.
Signal Hill, CA 90806
(213) 595-1177

BankAmerica Ventures, Inc.
555 California St.
San Francisco, CA 94104
(415) 622-2230

Bay Venture Group
One Embarcadero Ctr.,
Ste. 3303
San Francisco, CA 94111
(415) 989-7680

Beverly Glen Venture Capital
214 S. Beverly Glen Blvd.
Los Angeles, CA 90024
(213) 272-7556

BNK Industry Inv. Co.
3932 Wilshire Blvd., Ste. 305
Los Angeles, CA 90010
(213) 388-1314

Brentwood Associates
11661 San Vicente Blvd.,
Ste. 707
Los Angeles, CA 90049
(213) 826-6581

Business Equity & Dev. Corp.
1411 W. Olympic Blvd.,
Ste. 200
Los Angeles, CA 90015
(213) 385-0351

California Capital Investors,
Ltd.
11812 San Vicente Blvd.
Los Angeles, CA 90049
(213) 820-7222

California Partners
3000 Sand Hill Rd.
Bldg. 2, Ste. 260
Menlo Park, CA 94025
(415) 854-1555

Camden Investments, Inc.
9560 Wilshire Blvd.
Beverly Hills, CA 90212
(213) 859-9738

CFB Venture Capital Corp.
530 B St., 2nd Fl.
San Diego, CA 92101
(619) 230-3304

Charterway Investment Corp.
222 S. Hill St., Ste. 800
Los Angeles, CA 90012
(213) 687-8534

Branch Office
Churchill International
444 Market St., 25th Fl.
San Francisco, CA 94111
(415) 398-7677

Churchill International
Oceanic Capital Corp.
Pan American Investment Co.
545 Middlefield Rd., Ste. 160
Menlo Park, CA 94025
(415) 328-4401

Branch Office
Citicorp Venture Capital, Ltd.
One Sansome St., Ste. 2410
San Francisco, CA 94104
(415) 627-6472
(Main Office in NY)

Branch Office
Citicorp Venture Capital, Ltd.
2200 Geng Rd., Ste. 203
Palo Alto, CA 94303
(415) 424-8000
(Main Office in NY)

Cogeneration Capital Fund
300 Tamal Plaza, Ste. 190
Corte Madera, CA 94925
(415) 924-3525

Continental Investors, Inc.
8781 Seaspray Dr.
Huntington Beach, CA 92646
(714) 964-5207

Branch Office
Cornell Capital Corp.
2049 Century Park E., 12th Fl.
Century City, CA 90067
(213) 277-7993
(Main Office in NY)

Crocker Ventures, Inc.
One Montgomery St.
San Francisco, CA 94104
(415) 983-3636

Crosspoint Investment Corp.
1015 Corporation Way
Palo Alto, CA 94025
(415) 968-0930

Developers Equity Cap. Corp.
9201 Wilshire Blvd., Ste. 204
Beverly Hills, CA 90210
(213) 278-3611

Dime Investment Corp.
2772 W. 8th St.
Los Angeles, CA 90005
(213) 739-1847

Enterprise Venture Cap. Corp.
1922 The Alameda, Ste. 306
San Jose, CA 95126
(408) 249-3507

Equitable Capital Corp.
855 Sansome St., Ste. 200
San Francisco, CA 94111
(415) 434-4114

First American Cap. Funding,
Inc.
18662 MacArthur Blvd.,
Ste. 400
Irvine, CA 92715
(714) 833-8100

First Interstate Capital, Inc.
515 S. Figueroa, Ste. 1900
Los Angeles, CA 90071
(213) 622-1922

First SBIC of California
4000 MacArthur Blvd., Ste. 950
Newport Beach, CA 92660
(714) 754-4780

Branch Office
First SBIC of California
333 S. Hope St., 25th Fl., H25-4
Los Angeles, CA 90071
(213) 613-5215

Hamco Capital Corp.
235 Montgomery St., #535
San Francisco, CA 94104
(415) 986-5500

HMS Capital
555 California St., Ste. 5070
San Francisco, CA 94104
(415) 221-1225

I.K. Capital Loans Co., Ltd.
8601 Wilshire Blvd., Ste. 600
Beverly Hills, CA 90211
(213) 657-0178

Imperial Ventures, Inc.
9920 S. LaCienega Blvd.,
14th Fl.
Inglewood, CA 90301
(213) 417-5888

Ivanhoe Venture Capital, Ltd.
737 Pearl St., Ste. 201
La Jolla, CA 92037
(619) 454-8882

Lasung Investment & Finance
Co.
3600 Wilshire Blvd., Ste. 1410
Los Angeles, CA 90010
(213) 384-7548

Latigo Capital Partners
23410 Civic Ctr. Way, Ste. E-2
Malibu, CA 90265
(213) 456-7024

Los Angeles Capital Corp.
606 N. Larchmont Blvd.,
Ste. 309
Los Angeles, CA 90004
(213) 460-4646

MCA New Ventures, Inc.
100 Universal City Pl.
Universal City, CA 91608
(818) 508-2937

Merrill, Pickard, Anderson &
Eyre I
Two Palo Alto Sq., Ste. 425
Palo Alto, CA 94306
(415) 856-8880

Metropolitan Venture Co., Inc.
5757 Wilshire Blvd., Ste. 670
Los Angeles, CA 90036
(213) 938-3488

Myriad Capital, Inc.
8820 S. Sepulveda Blvd.,
Ste. 204
Los Angeles, CA 90045
(213) 641-7936

Branch Office
Nelson Capital Corp.
1901 Ave. of the Stars, Ste. 584
Los Angeles, CA 90067
(213) 556-1944
(Main Office in NY)

New Kukje Investment Co.
958 S. Vermont Ave.
Los Angeles, CA 90006
(213) 389-8679

New West Ventures
4350 Executive Dr., #206
San Diego, CA 92121
(619) 457-0722

Branch Office
New West Ventures
4600 Campus Dr., #103
Newport Beach, CA 92660
(714) 756-8940

Opportunity Capital Corp.
50 California St., Ste. 2505
San Francisco, CA 94111
(415) 421-5935

Branch Office
Orange Nassau Capital Corp.
Westerly Place
1500 Quail St., Ste. 540
Newport Beach, CA 92660
(714) 752-7811
(Main Office in MA)

PBC Venture Capital, Inc.
PO Box 6008
Bakersville, CA 93386
(805) 395-3206

PCF Venture Capital Corp.
3420 E. Third Ave., Ste. 200
Foster City, CA 94404
(415) 571-5411

San Joaquin Capital Corp.
1675 Chester Ave., Ste. 330
PO Box 2538
Bakersfield, CA 93303
(805) 323-7581

San Jose SBIC, Inc.
100 Park Ctr. Pl., Ste. 427
San Jose, CA 95113
(408) 293-8052

Seaport Ventures, Inc.
770 B St., Ste. 420
San Diego, CA 92101
(619) 232-4069

Space Ventures, Inc.
3931 MacArthur Blvd., Ste. 212
Newport Beach, CA 92660
(714) 851-0855

Union Venture Corp.
445 S. Figueroa St.
Los Angeles, CA 90071
(213) 236-6292

Unity Capital Corp.
4343 Morena Blvd., Ste. 3A
San Diego, CA 92117
(619) 275-6030

Vista Capital Corp.
701 "B" St., Ste. 760
San Diego, CA 92101
(619) 236-1900

Wells Fargo Equity Corp.
One Embarcadero Ctr.,
Ste. 1814
San Francisco, CA 94111
(415) 396-4490

Westamco Investment Co.
8929 Wilshire Blvd., Ste. 400
Beverly Hills, CA 90211
(213) 652-8288

Branch Office
Wood River Capital Corp.
3000 Sand Hill Rd., Ste. 280
Menlo Park, CA 94025
(415) 854-7145
(Main Office in NY)

Branch Office
Worthen Finance & Inv. Inc.
3660 Wilshire Blvd.
Los Angeles, CA 90010
(213) 480-1908
(Main Office in AR)

Yosemite Capital Investment
448 Fresno St.
Fresno, CA 93706
(209) 485-2431

COLORADO
Colorado Growth Capital, Inc.
1600 Broadway, Ste. 2125
Denver, CO 80202
(303) 629-0205

Enterprise Fin. Cap. Dev. Corp.
PO Box 5840
Snowmass Village, CO 81615
(303) 923-4144

Mile Hi SBIC
1355 S. Colorado Blvd.,
Ste. 400
Denver, CO 80222
(303) 830-0087

CONNECTICUT
Asset Capital & Management
Corp.
608 Ferry Blvd.
Stratford, CT 06497
(203) 375-0299

Capital Impact
234 Church St.
New Haven, CT 06510
(203) 384-5670

Capital Resource Co. of
Connecticut L.P.
699 Bloomfield Ave.
Bloomfield, CT 06002
(203) 243-1114

The First Connecticut SBIC
177 State St.
Bridgeport, CT 06604
(203) 366-4726

Marcon Capital Corp.
49 Riverside Ave.
Westport, CT 06880
(203) 226-7751

Northeastern Capital Corp.
61 High St.
East Haven, CT 06512
(203) 469-7901

Regional Financial Enterprises
51 Pine St.
New Canaan, CT 06840
(203) 966-2800

SBIC of Connecticut
1115 Main St., #610
Bridgeport, CT 06604
(203) 367-3282

DISTRICT OF COLUMBIA
Allied Capital Corp.
1625 I St., NW, Ste. 603
Washington, DC 20006
(202) 331-1112

American Security Capital
Corp.
730 15th St., NW
Washington, DC 20013
(202) 624-4843

Broadcast Capital Fund, Inc.
1771 N St., NW, Ste. 420
Washington, DC 20036
(202) 429-5393

Columbia Ventures, Inc.
1828 L St., NW
Washington, DC 20036
(202) 659-0033

Branch Office
Continental Investors, Inc.
2020 K St., NW, Ste. 350
Washington, DC 20006
(202) 466-3709
(Main Office in CA)

Fulcrum Venture Capital Corp.
2021 K St., NW, Ste. 301
Washington, DC 20006-1085
(202) 833-9590

Syncom Capital Corp.
1030 15th St., NW, Ste. 203
Washington, DC 20005
(202) 293-9428

Washington Finance & Inv.
Corp.
2600 Virginia Ave., NW, #515
Washington, DC 20037
(202) 388-2900

Branch Office
Worthen Finance & Inv. Inc.
2121 K St., NW, Ste. 830
Washington, DC 20037
(202) 659-9427
(Main Office in AR)

FLORIDA
Caribank Capital Corp.
255 E. Dania Beach Blvd.
Dania, FL 33004
(305) 925-2211

First American Investment
Corp.
2701 S. Bayshore Dr., Ste. 402
Coconut Grove, FL 33133
(305) 854-6840

First Tampa Capital Corp.
501 E. Kennedy Blvd., Ste. 806
Tampa, FL 33602
(813) 221-2171

Ideal Financial Corp.
780 NW 42nd Ave., Ste. 304
Miami, FL 33126
(305) 442-4653

J & D Capital Corp.
12747 Biscayne Blvd.
North Miami, FL 33181
(305) 893-0303

Market Capital Corp.
PO Box 22667
Tampa, FL 33630
(813) 247-1357

Safeco Capital, Inc.
835 SW 37th Ave.
Miami, FL 33135
(305) 443-7953

Servico Business Inv. Corp.
1601 Belvedere Rd., Ste. 201
West Palm Beach, FL 33406
(305) 689-4906

Small Business Assistance
Corp.
2612 W. 15th St.
Panama City, FL 32401
(904) 785-9577

Southeast Venture Capital Ltd.
One Southeast Financial Ctr.
Miami, FL 33131
(305) 375-6470

Trans Florida Capital Corp.
1450 Avenida Madruga, #402
Coral Gables, FL 33146
(305) 665-5489

Universal Financial Services,
Inc.
2301 Collins Ave., Ste. M-109
Miami, FL 33139
(305) 538-5464

Venture Group, Inc.
5433 Buffalo Ave.
Jacksonville, FL 32208
(904) 355-6265

Venture Opportunities Corp.
444 Brickell Ave., Ste. 650
Miami, FL 33131
(305) 358-0359

Verde Capital Corp.
6701 Sunset Dr., Ste. 104
South Miami, FL 33143
(305) 666-8789

GEORGIA
Mighty Capital Corp.
50 Technology Park
Atlanta, Ste. 100
Norcross, GA 30092
(404) 448-2232

North Riverside Capital Corp.
5775-D Peachtree Dunwoody
Rd.
Atlanta, GA 30342
(404) 252-1076

Sunbelt Funding Corp.
PO Box 7006
Macon, GA 31298
(912) 474-5137

HAWAII
Bancorp Hawaii SBIC, Inc.
111 S. King St., Ste. 1060
Honolulu, HI 96813
(808) 521-6411

Pacific Venture Capital, Ltd.
1405 N. King St., Ste. 302
Honolulu, HI 96817
(808) 847-6502

IDAHO
First Idaho Venture Capital
Corp.
900 W. Washington
Boise, ID 83702
(208) 345-3460

ILLINOIS
Abbott Capital Corp.
9933 Lawler Ave., Ste. 125
Skokie, IL 60077
(312) 982-0404

Alpha Capital Venture Partners
3 First National Pl., Ste. 1400
Chicago, IL 60602
(312) 372-1556

AMOCO Venture Capital Co.
200 E. Randolph Dr.
Chicago, IL 60601
(312) 856-6523

Business Ventures, Inc.
20 N. Wacker Dr., Ste. 550
Chicago, IL 60606
(312) 346-1580

CEDCO Capital Corp.
180 N. Michigan Ave., Ste. 333
Chicago, IL 60601
(312) 984-5950

Chicago Community Ventures
Inc.
108 N. State St., Ste. 902
Chicago, IL 60602
(312) 726-6084

Continental Illinois Venture
Corp.
231 S. LaSalle St.
Chicago, IL 60697
(312) 828-8021

First Capital Corp. of Chicago
One First National Pl.,
Ste. 2628
Chicago, IL 60670
(312) 732-5400

Frontenac Capital Corp.
208 S. LaSalle St., #1900
Chicago, IL 60604
(312) 368-0044

Mesirow Capital Corp.
135 S. LaSalle St.
Chicago, IL 60603
(312) 443-5757

Branch Office
Nelson Capital Corp.
8550 W. Bryn Mawr Ave.,
Ste. 515
Chicago, IL 60631
(312) 693-5990
(Main Office in NY)

Northern Capital Corp.
50 S. LaSalle St.
Chicago, IL 60675
(312) 444-5399

Tower Ventures, Inc.
Sears Tower, BSC 43-50
Chicago, IL 60684
(312) 875-0571

The Urban Fund of Illinois,
Inc.
1525 E. 53rd St.
Chicago, IL 60615
(312) 753-9620

Walnut Capital Corp.
Three First National Plaza
Chicago, IL 60602
(312) 269-1732

INDIANA
Circle Ventures, Inc.
20 N. Meridian St.
Indianapolis, IN 46204
(317) 636-7242

Equity Resource Co., Inc.
202 S. Michigan St.
South Bend, IN 46601
(219) 237-5255

1st Source Capital Corp.
100 N. Michigan
South Bend, IN 46601
(219) 236-2180

Heritage Venture Group, Inc.
2400 One Indiana Sq.
Indianapolis, IN 46204
(317) 635-5696

Mount Vernon Venture Capital
Co.
9102 N. Meridian St.
PO Box 40177
Indianapolis, IN 46240
(317) 846-5106

White River Capital Corp.
500 Washington St., PO Box
929
Columbus, IN 47202
(812) 376-1759

IOWA
MorAmerica Capital Corp.
300 American Bldg.
Cedar Rapids, IA 52401
(319) 363-8249

KANSAS
Kansas Venture Capital, Inc.
One Townsite Plaza
First Nat'l Bank Towers,
Ste. 1030
Topeka, KS 66603
(913) 233-1368

KENTUCKY
Equal Opportunity Finance,
Inc.
420 Hurstbourne Ln., Ste. 201
Louisville, KY 40222
(502) 423-1943

Financial Opportunities, Inc.
981 S. Third St.
Louisville, KY 40203
(502) 584-1281

MidAmerica Venture Capital
Corp.
500 W. Broadway
Louisville, KY 40202
(502) 562-5448

Mountain Ventures, Inc.
PO Box 628
London, KY 40741
(606) 864-5175

LOUISIANA
Caddo Capital Corp.
3010 Knight St., Ste. 240
Shreveport, LA 71105
(318) 869-1689

Capital Equity Corp.
1885 Wooddale Blvd., #814
Baton Rouge, LA 70806
(504) 924-9205

Commercial Capital, Inc.
PO Box 1776—Holiday Office
Sq.
Covington, LA 70434-1776
(504) 893-5402

Branch Office
Commercial Capital, Inc.
PO Box 1299—1809 W. Thomas
St.
Hammond, LA 70404
(504) 345-8820

Commercial Venture Capital
Corp.
Commercial Nat'l Bnk Bldg.,
Ste. 200
Shreveport, LA 71101
(318) 226-4602

Dixie Business Inv. Co., Inc.
PO Box 588
Lake Providence, LA 71254
(318) 559-1558

First Southern Capital Corp.
PO Box 14205
Baton Rouge, LA 70898
(504) 769-3004

Louisiana Equity Capital Corp.
451 Florida St.
Baton Rouge, LA 70801
(504) 389-4421

Walnut Street Capital Co.
702 Cotton Exchange Bldg.
New Orleans, LA 70130
(504) 525-2112

MAINE
Maine Capital Corp.
70 Center St.
Portland, ME 04101
(207) 772-1001

MARYLAND
First Maryland Capital, Inc.
107 W. Jefferson St.
Rockville, MD 20850
(301) 251-6630

Greater Washington Investors,
Inc.
5454 Wisconsin Ave., Ste. 1315
Chevy Chase, MD 20815
(301) 656-0626

Suburban Capital Corp.
6610 Rockledge Dr.
Bethesda, MD 20817
(301) 493-7025

MASSACHUSETTS
Atlantic Energy Capital Corp.
One Post Office Sq.
Boston, MA 02109
(617) 451-6220

BancBoston Ventures, Inc.
100 Federal St.
Boston, MA 02110
(617) 434-5700

Branch Office
Boston Hambro Capital Co.
One Boston Pl., Ste. 723
Boston, MA 02106
(617) 722-7055
(Main Office in NY)

Branch Office
Churchill International
9 Riverside Rd.
Weston, MA 02193
(617) 893-6555
(Main Office in CA)

Branch Office
First SBIC of California
50 Milk St., 15th Fl.
Boston, MA 02109
(617) 542-7601
(Main Office in CA)

Massachusetts Venture Cap.
Corp.
59 Temple Pl.
Boston, MA 02111
(617) 426-0208

New England Capital Corp.
One Washington Mall, 7th Fl.
Boston, MA 02108
(617) 722-6400

New England MESBIC, Inc.
50 Kearney Rd., Ste. 3
Needham, MA 02194
(617) 449-2066

Orange Nassau Capital Corp.
One Post Office Sq., Ste. 1760
Boston, MA 02109
(617) 451-6220

TA Associates
  Advent III Capital Co.
  Advent IV Capital Co.
  Advent V Capital Co.
  Advent Atlantic Capital Co.
  Advent Industrial Capital Co.
  Chestnut Capital Corp.
  Devonshire Capital Corp.
45 Milk St.
Boston, MA 02109
(617) 338-0800

Transatlantic Capital Corp.
24 Federal St.
Boston, MA 02110
(617) 482-0015

UST Capital Corp.
30 Court St.
Boston, MA 02108
(617) 726-7138

Vadus Capital Corp.
One Post Office Sq.
Boston, MA 02109
(617) 451-6220

Worcester Capital Corp.
446 Main St.
Worcester, MA 01608
(617) 793-4508

MICHIGAN
Comerica Capital Corp.
30150 Telegraph Rd., Ste. 245
Birmingham, MI 48010
(313) 258-5800

Detroit Metropolitan SBIC
150 Michigan Ave.
Detroit, MI 48226
(313) 963-8190

Doan Resources L.P.
PO Box 1431
Midland, MI 48640
(517) 631-2471

Federated Capital Corp.
20000 W. Twelve Mile Rd.
Southfield, MI 48076
(313) 557-9100

Metro-Detroit Investment Co.
30777 Northwestern Hwy.,
Ste. 300
Farmington Hills, MI 48018
(313) 851-6300

Michigan Cap. & Service, Inc.
500 First Nat'l Bldg.
201 S. Main St.
Ann Arbor, MI 48104
(313) 663-0702

Michigan Tech Capital Corp.
Technology Park, 1700 Duncan Ave.
PO Box 529
Hubbell, MI 49934
(906) 487-2643

Motor Enterprises, Inc.
3044 W. Grand Blvd.,
Rm. 13-152
Detroit, MI 48202
(313) 556-4273

Mutual Investment Co., Inc.
21415 Civic Center Dr., Ste. 217
Southfield, MI 48076
(313) 559-5210

Branch Office
Regional Financial Enterprises
315 E. Eisenhower Pkwy.,
Ste. 300
Ann Arbor, MI 48104
(313) 769-0941

United Venture Capital, Inc.
17117 W. Nine Mile Rd.,
Ste. 910
Southfield, MI 48075
(313) 559-7822

MINNESOTA
Control Data Capital Corp.
3601 W. 77th St.
Minneapolis, MN 55435
(612) 921-4118

Control Data Community
Ventures Fund, Inc.
3601 W. 77th St.
Minneapolis, MN 55435
(612) 921-4352

DGC Capital Co.
603 Alworth Bldg.
Duluth, MN 55802
(218) 722-0058

First Midwest Capital Corp.
1010 Plymouth Bldg.,
12 S. 6th St.
Minneapolis, MN 55402
(612) 339-9391

Northland Capital Corp.
613 Missabe Bldg.,
277 W. 1st St.
Duluth, MN 55802
(218) 722-0545

North Star Ventures, Inc.
1501 First Bank Pl. W.
Minneapolis, MN 55402
(612) 333-1133

North Star Ventures II
1501 First Bank Pl. W.
Minneapolis, MN 55402
(612) 333-1133

Northwest Venture Partners
222 S. Ninth St., #2800
Minneapolis, MN 55402
(612) 372-8770

Retailers Growth Fund, Inc.
2318 Park Ave.
Minneapolis, MN 55404
(612) 872-4929

Shared Ventures, Inc.
6550 York Ave. S., Ste. 419
Minneapolis, MN 55435
(612) 925-3411

Threshold Ventures, Inc.
430 Oak Grove St., Ste. 303
Minneapolis, MN 55403
(612) 874-7199

MISSISSIPPI
Invesat Capital Corp.
PO Box 3288
Jackson, MS 39207
(601) 969-3242

Vicksburg SBIC
PO Box 852
Vicksburg, MS 39180
(601) 636-4762

MISSOURI
Bankers Capital Corp.
3100 Gillham Rd.
Kansas City, MO 64109
(816) 531-1600

Capital For Business, Inc.
911 Main St., Ste. 2300
Kansas City, MO 64105
(816) 234-2381

Branch Office
Capital For Business, Inc.
11 S. Meramec, Ste. 804
St. Louis, MO 63105
(314) 854-7421

Intercapco West, Inc.
7800 Bonhomme Ave.
Clayton, MO 63105
(314) 863-0600

Branch Office
MorAmerica Capital Corp.
Ste. 2724—Commerce Tower Bldg.
911 Main St.
Kansas City, MO 64105
(816) 842-0114
(Main Office in IA)

United Missouri Capital Corp.
10th & Grand
Kansas City, MO 64106
(816) 556-7103

MONTANA
Rocky Mountain Ventures, Ltd.
315 Securities Bldg.
Billings, MT 59101
(406) 256-1984

NEBRASKA
Community Equity Corp. of NE
6421 Ames Ave.
Omaha, NE 68104
(402) 455-7722

NEW HAMPSHIRE
Granite State Capital, Inc.
10 Fort Eddy Rd.
Concord, NH 03301
(603) 228-9090

Hampshire Capital Corp.
One Middle St., PO Box 468
Portsmouth, NH 03801
(603) 431-1415

Lotus Capital Corp.
875 Elm St.
Manchester, NH 03101
(603) 668-8617

NEW JERSEY
Capital Circulation Corp.
208 Main St.
Ft. Lee, NJ 07024
(201) 947-8637

ESLO Capital Corp.
2401 Morris Ave., Ste. 220EW
Union, NJ 07083
(201) 687-4920

First Princeton Capital Corp.
227 Hamburg Tpke.
Pompton Lakes, NJ 07442
(201) 831-0330

Monmouth Capital Corp.
125 Wyckoff Rd., PO Box 335
Eatontown, NJ 07724
(201) 542-4927

Raybar SBIC
PO Box 1038
Maywood, NJ 07607
(201) 368-2280

Rutgers Minority Investment
Co.
180 University Ave., 3rd Fl.
Newark, NJ 07102
(201) 648-5627

Tappan Zee Capital Corp.
201 Lower Notch Rd.
Little Falls, NJ 07424
(201) 256-8280

Unicorn Ventures, Ltd.
14 Commerce Dr.
Cranford, NJ 07016
(201) 276-7880

NEW MEXICO
Albuquerque SBIC
PO Box 487
Albuquerque, NM 87103
(505) 247-0145

Associated SW Investors, Inc.
124 Tenth St., NW
Albuquerque, NM 87102
(505) 842-5955

Equity Capital Corp.
231 Washington Ave., Ste. 2
Santa Fe, NM 87501
(505) 988-4273

Fluid Capital Corp.
8421 B Montgomery Blvd., NE
Albuquerque, NM 87111
(505) 292-4747

Southwest Capital Inv. Inc.
3500-E Commanche Rd., NE
Albuquerque, NM 87107
(505) 884-7161

NEW YORK
American Commercial Capital
Corp.
310 Madison Ave., Ste. 1304
New York, NY 10017
(212) 986-3305

AMEV Capital Corp.
Two World Trade Ctr.,
Ste. 5001
New York, NY 10048
(201) 775-9100

Amistad DOT Venture Capital
Inc.
801 Second Ave., Ste. 303
New York, NY 10017
(212) 697-9210

Atalanta Investment Co., Inc.
450 Park Ave., Ste. 1802
New York, NY 10022
(212) 832-1104

Beneficial Capital Corp.
645 Fifth Ave.
New York, NY 10022
(212) 752-1291

Boston Hambro Capital Co.
17 E. 71st St.
New York, NY 10021
(212) 288-7778

BT Capital Corp.
280 Park Ave.
New York, NY 10017
(212) 850-1916

The Central New York SBIC,
Inc.
351 S. Warren St., Ste. 204
Syracuse, NY 13202
(315) 478-5026

Chemical Venture Capital Corp.
277 Park Ave., 10th Fl.
New York, NY 10172
(212) 310-4949

Citicorp Venture Capital Ltd.
153 East 53rd St., 28th Fl.
New York, NY 10043
(212) 559-1117

Clinton Capital Corp.
419 Park Ave. S.
New York, NY 10016
(212) 696-4334

CMNY Capital Co., Inc.
77 Water St.
New York, NY 10005
(212) 437-7078

College Venture Equity Corp.
PO Box 135
Niagara Falls, NY 14303
(813) 248-3878

Cornell Capital Corp.
230 Park Ave., Ste. 3440
New York, NY 10169
(212) 490-9198

County Capital Corp.
25 Main St.
Southampton, NY 11968
(516) 283-2943

Croyden Capital Corp.
45 Rockefeller Pl., Ste. 2165
New York, NY 10111
(212) 974-0184

EAB Venture Corp.
90 Park Ave.
New York, NY 10016
(212) 687-6010

Edwards Capital Co.
215 Lexington Ave., #805
New York, NY 10016
(212) 686-2568

Elk Associates Funding Corp.
277 Park Ave., #4300
New York, NY 10172
(212) 888-7574

Equico Capital Corp.
1290 Ave. of the Americas,
Ste. 3400
New York, NY 10019
(212) 554-8413

Evergreen Venture Capital
Corp.
237 Glen St.
Glens Falls, NY 12801
(518) 793-1877

Everlast Capital Corp.
350 Fifth Ave., Ste. 2805
New York, NY 10118
(212) 695-3910

Fairfield Equity Corp.
200 E. 42nd St.
New York, NY 10017-5893
(212) 867-0150

Ferranti High Technology, Inc.
515 Madison Ave.
New York, NY 10022
(212) 688-9828

Fifty-Third Street Ventures,
L.P.
420 Madison Ave., 15th Fl.
New York, NY 10017
(212) 752-8010

J.H. Foster & Co., L.P.
437 Madison Ave.
New York, NY 10024
(212) 753-4810

The Franklin Corp.
1185 Ave. of the Americas,
27th Fl.
New York, NY 10036
(212) 719-4844

Fundex Capital Corp.
525 Northern Blvd.
Great Neck, NY 11021
(516) 466-8550

Genesee Funding, Inc.
183 E. Main St., Ste. 1450
Rochester, NY 14604
(716) 262-4716

The Hanover Capital Corp.
150 E. 58th St., Ste. 2710
New York, NY 10155
(212) 980-9670

Harvest Ventures
  Asea-Harvest Partners I
  Bohlen Capital Corp.
  European Dev. Cap. Ltd.
  Ptnrshp.
  Noro Capital Ltd.
  767 Ltd. Ptnrshp.
767 Third Ave.
New York, NY 10017
(212) 838-7776

Ibero-American Investors Corp.
Chamber of Commerce Bldg.
55 St. Paul St.
Rochester, NY 14604
(716) 262-3440

Intergroup Venture Capital
Corp.
230 Park Ave., Ste. 210
New York, NY 10169
(212) 661-5428

Irving Capital Corp.
1290 Ave. of the Americas,
3rd Fl.
New York, NY 10104
(212) 408-4800

Key Venture Capital Corp.
60 State St.
Albany, NY 12207
(518) 447-3227

Korean Capital Corp.
144-43 25th Rd.
Flushing, NY 11354
(212) 762-8866

Kwiat Capital Corp.
576 Fifth Ave.
New York, NY 10036
(212) 391-2461

Lincoln Capital Corp.
600 Community Dr.,
PO Box 3600
Manhasset, NY 11030-3600
(516) 365-5100

M & T Capital Corp.
One M & T Pl., 5th Fl.
Buffalo, NY 14240
(716) 842-5881

Medallion Funding Corp.
205 E. 42nd St., Ste. 2020
New York, NY 10017
(212) 682-3300

Midland Venture Capital, Ltd.
950 Third Ave., 11th Fl.
New York, NY 10022
(212) 753-7790

Minority Equity Capital Co.,
Inc.
275 Madison Ave., Ste. 1901
New York, NY 10016
(212) 686-9710

Multi-Purpose Capital Corp.
31 S. Broadway
Yonkers, NY 10701
(914) 963-2733

Nelson Capital Corp.
591 Stewart Ave.
Garden City, NY 11530
(516) 222-2555

North American Funding Corp.
177 Canal St.
New York, NY 10013
(212) 226-0080

North Street Capital Corp.
250 North St., RA-6S
White Plains, NY 10625
(914) 335-7901

NPD Capital, Inc.
375 Park Ave., Ste. 2201
New York, NY 10152
(212) 826-8500

NYBDC Capital Corp.
41 State St.
Albany, NY 12207
(518) 463-2268

Pan Pac Capital Corp.
121 E. Industry Ct.
Deer Park, NY 11729
(212) 344-6680

Questech Capital Corp.
600 Madison Ave.
New York, NY 10022
(212) 758-8522

R & R Financial Corp.
1451 Broadway
New York, NY 10036
(212) 790-1400

Rand Capital Corp.
1300 Rand Bldg.
Buffalo, NY 14203
(716) 853-0802

Realty Growth Capital Corp.
575 Lexington Ave.
New York, NY 10022
(212) 755-9044

Peter J. Schmitt Co., Inc.
PO Box 2
Buffalo, NY 14240
(716) 821-1400

Sherwood Capital Corp.
219 Westchester Ave.
Port Chester, NY 10573
(914) 939-9000

Small Business Electronics Inv.
Co.
60 Cutter Mill Rd.
Great Neck, NY 11021
(516) 466-6451

Southern Tier Capital Corp.
55 S. Main St.
Liberty, NY 12754
(914) 292-3030

Sprout Capital Corp.
140 Broadway, 48th Fl.
New York, NY 10005
(212) 902-2492

Sunnyside Funding Corp.
41-11 39th St.
Long Island, NY 11104
(718) 729-2707

Branch Office
Tappan Zee Capital Corp.
120 N. Main St.
New City, NY 10956
(914) 634-8890

Taroco Capital Corp.
19 Rector St., 35th Fl.
New York, NY 10006
(212) 344-6690

TLC Funding Corp.
141 S. Central Ave.
Hartsdale, NY 10530
(914) 683-1144

Transportation SBIC, Inc.
60 E. 42nd St.
New York, NY 10165
(212) 697-4885

Transworld Ventures, Ltd.
331 West End Ave., Ste. 1A
New York, NY 10023
(212) 496-1010

Triad Capital Corp. of NY
7 Hugh Grant St.
Bronx, NY 10462
(212) 597-4387

Vega Capital Corp.
720 White Plains Rd.
Scarsdale, NY 10583
(914) 472-8550

Venture SBIC, Inc.
249-12 Jericho Tpke.
Floral Park, NY 11001
(516) 352-0068

Watchung Capital Corp.
431 Fifth Ave., 5th Fl.
New York, NY 10016
(212) 889-3466

Winfield Capital Corp.
237 Mamaroneck Ave.
White Plains, NY 10605
(914) 949-2600

Wood River Capital Corp.
645 Madison Ave.
New York, NY 10022
(212) 750-9420

Branch Office
Worthen Finance & Invest. Inc.
535 Madison Ave., 17th Fl.
New York, NY 10022
(212) 750-9100
(Main Office in AR)

Yang Capital Corp.
41-40 Kissena Blvd.
Flushing, NY 11355
(718) 445-4585

NORTH CAROLINA
Delta Capital, Inc.
227 N. Tryon St., Ste 201
Charlotte, NC 28202
(704) 372-1410

Falcon Capital Corp.
311 S. Evans St.
Greenville, NC 27834
(919) 752-5918

Heritage Capital Corp.
2290 First Union Pl.
Charlotte, NC 28282
(704) 334-2867

Kitty Hawk Capital, Ltd.
2030 One Tryon Ctr.
Charlotte, NC 28284
(704) 333-3777

NCNB SBIC Corp.
One NCNB Plaza
Charlotte, NC 28255
(704) 374-5583

NCNB Venture Corp.
One NCNB Plaza, T19-3
Charlotte, NC 28255
(704) 374-5723

Vanguard Investment Co., Inc.
308-A S. Elm St.
Greensboro, NC 27401
(919) 378-0100

OHIO

A.T. Capital Corp.
900 Euclid Ave., T-18
Cleveland, OH 44101
(216) 687-4970

Capital Funds Corp.
127 Public Sq.
Cleveland, OH 44114
(216) 622-8628

Center City MESBIC, Inc.
40 S. Main St., Ste. 762
Dayton, OH 45402
(513) 461-6164

Clarion Capital Corp.
1801 E. 12th St., Ste. 201
Cleveland, OH 44114
(216) 687-1096

First Ohio Capital Corp.
606 Madison Ave.
Toledo, OH 43604
(419) 259-7146

Glenco Enterprises, Inc.
1464 E. 105th St., Ste. 101
Cleveland, OH 44106
(216) 721-1200

Gries Investment Co.
720 Statler Office Tower
Cleveland, OH 44115
(216) 861-1146

National City Capital Corp.
623 Euclid Ave.
Cleveland, OH 44114
(216) 575-2491

Branch Office
RIHT Capital Corp.
796 Huntington Bldg.
Cleveland, OH 44115
(216) 781-3655
(Main Office in RI)

Tamco Investors SBIC, Inc.
375 Victoria Rd., PO Box 1588
Youngstown, OH 44501
(216) 792-3811

Tomlinson Capital Corp.
3055 E. 63rd St.
Cleveland, OH 44127
(216) 271-2103

OKLAHOMA

Alliance Business Investment
Co.
One Williams Ctr., Ste. 2000
Tulsa, OK 74172
(918) 584-3581

Bartlesville Investment Corp.
PO Box 548
Bartlesville, OK 74003
(918) 333-3022

First OK Investment Capital
Corp.
120 N. Robinson, Ste. 880C
Oklahoma City, OK 73102
(405) 272-4500

Investment Capital, Inc.
300 N. Harrison
Cushing, OK 74023
(918) 225-5850

Southwest Venture Capital, Inc.
2700 E. 51st St., Ste. 340
Tulsa, OK 74105
(918) 742-3177

OREGON

Branch Office
First Interstate Capital, Inc.
1300 SW Fifth Ave., Ste. 2323
Portland, OR 97201
(503) 223-4334
(Main Office in CA)

Northern Pacific Capital Corp.
1201 SW 12th Ave.
Portland, OR 97205
(503) 241-1255

Branch Office
Norwest Growth Fund, Inc.
1300 SW Fifth Ave., Ste. 3018
Portland, OR 97201
(503) 223-6622
(Main Office in MN)

Trendwest Capital Corp.
PO Box 5106
Klamath Falls, OR 97601
(503) 882-8059

PENNSYLVANIA

Alliance Enterprise Corp.
1801 Market St., 3rd Fl.
Philadelphia, PA 19103
(215) 977-3925

Branch Office
First SBIC of California
PO Box 512
Washington, PA 15301
(412) 223-0707
(Main Office in CA)

First Valley Capital Corp.
One Center Sq., Ste. 201
Allentown, PA 18101
(215) 776-6760

Gtr. Phil. Ven. Cap. Corp., Inc.
225 S. 15th St., Ste. 920
Philadelphia, PA 19102
(215) 732-1666

Meridian Capital Corp.
Blue Bell West, Ste. 122
Blue Bell, PA 19422
(215) 278-8907

PNC Capital Corp.
5th Ave. & Wood St., 19th Fl.
Pittsburgh, PA 15222
(412) 355-2245

PUERTO RICO
First Puerto Rico Capital, Inc.
PO Box 816
Mayaguez, PR 00709
(809) 832-9171

North America Investment
Corp.
Banco Popular Ctr., Ste. 1710
Hato Rey, PR 00919
(809) 754-6177

Venture Capital P.R., Inc.
58 Caribe St.
Edificio Hideca Altos,
Condado Santurce, PR 00926
(809) 721-3550

RHODE ISLAND
Domestic Capital Corp.
815 Reservoir Ave.
Cranston, RI 02910
(401) 943-1600

Fleet Venture Resources, Inc.
111 Westminster St.
Providence, RI 02920
(401) 278-6770

Narragansett Venture Corp.
40 Westminster St.
Providence, RI 02903
(401) 751-1000

Old Stone Capital Corp.
10 Stone Sq., 11th Fl.
Providence, RI 02903
(401) 278-2536

RIHT Capital Corp.
One Hospital Trust Plaza
Providence, RI 02903
(401) 278-8819

SOUTH CAROLINA
Carolina Venture Capital Corp.
14 Archer Rd.
Hilton Head Island, SC 29928
(803) 842-3101

Reedy River Ventures, Ltd.
PO Box 17526
Greenville, SC 29606
(803) 297-9196

TENNESSEE
Chickasaw Capital Corp.
67 Madison Ave.
Memphis, TN 38103
(901) 523-6404

DeSoto Capital Corp.
60 N. Third St.
Memphis, TN 38116
(901) 523-6894

Financial Resources, Inc.
2800 Sterick Bldg.
Memphis, TN 38103
(901) 527-9411

Suwannee Capital Corp.
3030 Poplar Ave.
Memphis, TN 38111
(901) 325-4200

Tennessee Equity Capital Corp.
1102 Stonewall Jackson Ct.
Nashville, TN 37220
(615) 373-4502

Valley Capital Corp.
Krystal Bldg., Ste. 806
Chattanooga, TN 37402
(615) 265-1557

West Tennessee Venture Cap.
Corp.
152 Beale St., PO Box 300
Memphis, TN 38101
(901) 527-6091

TEXAS
Branch Office
Alliance Business Investment
Co.
3990 One Shell Pl.
Houston, TX 77002
(713) 224-8224
(Main Office in OK)

Allied Bancshares Capital Corp.
1000 Louisiana, Ste. 300
Houston, TX 77002
(713) 226-1625

Americap Corp.
6363 Woodway, Ste. 200
Houston, TX 77057
(713) 780-8084

BancTexas Capital, Inc.
PO Box 2249
Dallas, TX 75221
(214) 969-6145

Bow Lane Capital Corp.
2401 Fountainview, Ste. 950
Houston, TX 77057
(713) 977-7421

Branch Office
Bow Lane Capital Corp.
3305 Graybuck Rd.
Austin, TX 78748
(512) 282-9330

Brittany Capital Corp.
2424 LTV Tower, 1525 Elm St.
Dallas, TX 75201
(214) 742-5810

Business Cap. Corp. of
Arlington
1112 Copeland Rd., Ste. 420
Arlington, TX 76011
(817) 261-4936

Capital Marketing Corp.
PO Box 1000
Keller, TX 76248
(817) 656-7380

Capital Southwest Venture
Corp.
12900 Preston Rd., Ste. 700
Dallas, TX 75230
(214) 233-8242

Central Texas SBIC
415 Austin Ave.
Waco, TX 76701
(817) 753-6461

Charter Venture Group, Inc.
2600 Citadel Plaza Dr., 6th Fl.
Houston, TX 77008
(713) 699-3588

Chen's Financial Group, Inc.
1616 W. Loop South, Ste. 200
Houston, TX 77027
(713) 850-0922

Branch Office
Citicorp Venture Capital, Ltd.
Diamond Shamrock Twr.,
#2920-LB87
717 Harwood
Dallas, TX 75221
(214) 880-9670
(Main Office in NY)

Energy Assets, Inc.
1800 S. Tower, Pennzoil Pl.
Houston, TX 77002
(713) 236-9999

Energy Capital Corp.
953 Esperson Bldg.
Houston, TX 77002
(713) 236-0006

Enterprise Capital Corp.
3401 Allen Pkwy., Ste. 108
Houston, TX 77019
(713) 527-1613

Evergreen Capital Co., Inc.
8502 Tybor, Ste. 201
Houston, TX 77074
(713) 778-9889

First City Capital Corp.
One W. Loop South, Ste. 809
Houston, TX 77027
(713) 650-1029

FSA Capital, Ltd.
PO Box 1987
Austin, TX 78767
(512) 472-7171

Gill Capital Corp.
615 Soledad, PO Box 599
San Antonio, TX 78292
(512) 299-6514

The Grocers SBI Corp.
3131 E. Holcombe Blvd.
Houston, TX 77021
(713) 747-7913

Intercapco, Inc.
750 N. St. Paul, Ste. 500, LB#7
Dallas, TX 75201
(214) 969-0250

InterFirst Venture Corp.
PO Box 83644
Dallas, TX 75283
(214) 744-8050

Livingston Capital Ltd.
PO Box 2507
Houston, TX 77252
(713) 977-4040

Mapleleaf Capital Corp.
One W. Loop South, Ste. 603
Houston, TX 77027
(713) 627-0752

MESBIC Financial Corp. of
Dallas
7701 N. Stemmons Frwy.,
Ste. 386
Dallas, TX 75247
(214) 637-0445

MESBIC Financial Corp. of
Houston
1801 Main St., Ste. 320
Houston, TX 77002
(713) 228-8321

MESBIC of San Antonio, Inc.
2300 W. Commerce
San Antonio, TX 78207
(512) 224-0909

Mid-State Capital Corp.
PO Box 7554
Waco, TX 76714
(817) 772-9220

MVenture Corp.
PO Box 662090
Dallas, TX 75266-2090
(214) 741-1469

Omega Capital Corp.
755 S. 11th St., PO Box 2173
Beaumont, TX 77704
(409) 832-0221

Branch Office
Orange Nassau Capital Corp.
One Galleria Tower
13355 Noel Rd., Ste. 635
Dallas, TX 75240
(214) 385-9685
(Main Office in MA)

Red River Ventures, Inc.
777 E. 15th St.
Plano, TX 75074
(214) 422-4999

Republic Venture Group, Inc.
PO Box 225961
Dallas, TX 75265
(214) 922-5078

Retail Capital Corp.
7915 FM 1960 W., Ste. 300
Houston, TX 77070
(713) 890-4242

Retzloff Capital Corp.
15000 Northwest Frwy. #310A
Houston, TX 77040
(713) 466-4690

Rust Capital Ltd.
114 W. 7th St.,
1300 Norwood Twr.
Austin, TX 78701
(512) 479-0055

San Antonio Venture Group,
Inc.
2300 W. Commerce
San Antonio, TX 78207
(512) 224-0909

SBI Capital Corp.
PO Box 771668
Houston, TX 77215-1668
(713) 975-1188

Southern Orient Capital Corp.
2419 Fannin, Ste. 200
Houston, TX 77002
(713) 225-3369

Southwestern Ven. Cap. of TX, Inc.
PO Box 1719
Seguin, TX 78155
(512) 379-0380

Branch Office
Southwestern Ven. Cap. of TX, Inc.
N. Frost Ctr., Ste. 700
1250 NE Loop 410
San Antonio, TX 78209

Sunwestern Capital Corp.
6750 LBJ Frwy.
One Oaks Plaza, Ste. 1160
Dallas, TX 75240
(214) 239-5650

Texas Capital Corp.
333 Clay St., Ste. 2100
Houston, TX 77002
(713) 658-9961

Texas Commerce Investment Co.
PO Box 2558
Houston, TX 77252
(713) 236-4719

Trammell Crow Investment Corp.
2001 Bryan, Ste. 3900
Dallas, TX 75201
(214) 747-0643

United Mercantile Capital Corp.
444 Executive Ctr. Blvd.,
Ste. 222
El Paso, TX 79902
(915) 533-6375

United Oriental Cap. Co.
13432 Hempstead Hwy.
Houston, TX 77040
(713) 462-6264

VERMONT
Vermont Investment Capital, Inc.
Box 590
South Royalton, VT 05068
(802) 763-7716

VIRGINIA
Basic Investment Corp.
6723 Whittier Ave., #201
McLean, VA 22101
(703) 356-4300

East West United Investment Co.
6723 Whittier Ave., Ste. 206
McLean, VA 22101
(703) 821-6616

Enterprise Equity Corp.
7787 Leesburg Pike
Falls Church, VA 22043
(703) 734-1212

James River Capital Associates
9 S. 12th St.
Richmond, VA 23219
(804) 643-7358

Metropolitan Capital Corp.
2550 Huntington Ave.
Alexandria, VA 22303
(703) 960-4698

Norfolk Investment Co., Inc.
100 W. Plume St., Ste. 208
Norfolk, VA 23510
(804) 623-1042

Sovran Funding Corp.
Sovran Ctr., 6th Fl.
One Commercial Pl.
Norfolk, VA 23510
(804) 441-4041

Tidewater SBIC
1300 First Virginia Bank Tower
Norfolk, VA 23510
(804) 627-2315

UV Capital
PO Box 1776
Richmond, VA 23214
(804) 643-7358

WASHINGTON
Capital Resource Corp.
1001 Logan Bldg.
Seattle, WA 98101
(206) 623-6550

Clifton Capital Corp.
1408 Washington Bldg.
Tacoma, WA 98402
(206) 272-3654

Peoples Capital Corp.
2411 Fourth Ave., Ste. 990
Seattle, WA 98111-1788
(206) 344-8105

Seafirst Capital Corp.
Fourth & Blanchard Bldg.
Seattle, WA 98121
(206) 583-7051

Washington Trust Equity Corp.
PO Box 2127
Spokane, WA 99210
(509) 455-3821

WEST VIRGINIA
American Capital, Inc.
300 N. Kanawha St.
Beckley, WV 25801
(304) 255-1494

WISCONSIN
Bando-McGlocklin Inv. Co., Inc.
13555 Bishops Ct., Ste. 205
Brookfield, WI 53005
(414) 784-9010

CERTCO Capital Corp.
PO Box 7368
Madison, WI 53707
(608) 271-4500

Madison Capital Corp.
102 State St.
Madison, WI 53703
(608) 256-8185

Marine Venture Capital, Inc.
111 E. Wisconsin Ave.
Milwaukee, MI 53202
(414) 765-2151

Branch Office
MorAmerica Capital Corp.
600 E. Mason St.
Milwaukee, WI 53202
(414) 276-3839
(Main Office in IA)

SC Opportunities, Inc.
1112 7th Ave.
Monroe, WI 53566
(608) 328-8540

Super Market Investors, Inc.
PO Box 473
Milwaukee, WI 53201
(414) 547-7999

Twin Ports Capital Co.
1230 Poplar Ave.
Superior, WI 54880
(715) 392-5525

The Wisconsin MESBIC, Inc.
622 Water St., Ste. 500
Milwaukee, WI 53202
(414) 278-0377

WYOMING
Capital Corp. of Wyoming, Inc.
145 S. Durbin St., Ste. 201
Casper, WY 82601
(307) 234-5438

NON-SBIC MEMBERS
Accel Partners
One Palmer Sq.
Princeton, NJ 08542
(609) 683-4500

Alimansky Planning Group
790 Madison Ave., Ste. 705
New York, NY 10021
(212) 472-0502

R.W. Allsop & Associates
2750 First Ave., SE, Ste. 210
Cedar Rapids, IA 52402
(319) 363-8971

Allstate Insurance Co.—Venture
Capital Division
Allstate Plaza E-2
Northbrook, IL 60062
(312) 291-5681

Arthur Andersen & Co.
33 W. Monroe St.
Chicago, IL 60603
(312) 580-0033

Atlantic Venture Partners
PO Box 1493
Richmond, VA 23212
(804) 644-5496

Beacon Partners
71 Strawberry Hill Ave., #614
Stamford, CT 06902
(203) 348-8858

Berry Cash Southwest Ptnrshp.
1 Galleria Tower, Ste. 1375
13355 Noel Rd.
Dallas, TX 75240
(214) 392-7279

William Blair Venture Partners
135 S. LaSalle St.
Chicago, IL 60603
(312) 236-1600

Brownstein, Zeidman &
Schomer
1025 Conn. Ave., NW, Ste. 900
Washington, DC 20036
(202) 457-6560

Buchanan Ingersoll
1667 K St., NW, #900
Washington, DC 20006
(202) 955-5500

Capital Services & Resources,
Inc.
5459 Wheelis Dr., Ste. 104
Memphis, TN 38117
(901) 761-2156

Cardinal Development Cap.
Fund I
155 E. Broad St.
Columbus, OH 43215
(614) 464-5550

Carnegie Venture Capital Corp.
10889 Wilshire Blvd., Ste. 240
Los Angeles, CA 90024
(213) 208-1544

Chambers Financial Corp.
720 S. Colorado Blvd., Ste. 940
Denver, CO 80222
(303) 759-4869

Chappell & Co.
One Lombard St., 2nd Fl.
San Francisco, CA 94111-1128
(415) 397-5094

Cherry Tree Ventures
640 Northland Executive Ctr.
3600 W. 80th St.
Minneapolis, MN 55431
(612) 893-9012

Mr. Roger B. Collins
PO Box 700145
Tulsa, OK 74170
(918) 493-2571

Columbine Venture Mgmt., Inc.
5613 DTC Pkwy., #510
Englewood, CO 8011
(303) 694-3222

Corp. For Innovation
Development
One N. Capitol Ave., Ste. 520
Indianapolis, IN 46204
(317) 635-7325

Criterion Venture Partners
333 Clay St., Ste. 4300
Houston, TX 77002
(713) 751-2400

Deloitte, Haskins & Sells
1114 Ave. of the Americas
New York, NY 10036
(212) 790-0500

Development Credit Corp. of
MD
40 W. Chesapeake Ave.,
Ste. 211
PO Box 10629
Towson, MD 20204
(301) 828-4711

Development Corp. of Montana
555 Fuller Ave., NE
PO Box 916
Helena, MT 59624
(406) 442-3850

Development Finance Corp. of
New Zealand
100 Spear St., Ste. 1430
San Francisco, CA 94105
(415) 777-2847

Dineh Cooperatives, Inc.
PO Box 2060
Chinle, Arizona 86503
(602) 674-3411

The Early Stages Co.
244 California St., Ste. 300
San Francisco, CA 94111
(415) 986-5700

Ernst & Whinney
515 S. Flower St., Ste. 2700
Los Angeles, CA 90071
(213) 977-4232

Exchange Nat'l. Bank of
Chicago
120 S. LaSalle St.
Chicago, IL 60603
(312) 781-7026

FCA Investment Co.
3000 Post Oak Blvd., Ste. 1790
Houston, TX 77056
(713) 965-0077

Fine & Ambrogne
133 Federal St.
Boston, MA 02110
(617) 482-0100

First Chicago Investment
Advisors
Three First National Plaza,
Ste. 0140, 9th Fl.
Chicago, IL 60670
(312) 732-4171

Fluke Capital & Mgmt. Svcs.
Co.
11400 SE 6th St., #230
Bellevue, WA 98004
(206) 453-4590

Gamble Bellanca Enterprises
1515 SW Fifth Ave., Ste. 1001
Portland, OR 97201
(503) 222-3700

General Electric Ven. Cap.
Corp.
3135 Easton Tnpk.
Fairfield, CT 06431
(203) 373-3356

GM Management Co.
500 N. Broadway, Ste. 1575
St. Louis, MO 63102
(314) 342-2200

Golder, Thoma & Cressey
120 S. LaSalle St., Ste. 630
Chicago, IL 60603
(312) 853-3322

Great American Investment
Corp.
4209 San Mateo NE
Albuquerque, NM 87110
(505) 883-6273

Harrison Capital, Inc.
2000 Westchester Ave.
White Plains, NY 10650
(914) 253-7845

Hawley & Associates
999 Summer St.
Stamford, CT 06905
(203) 348-6669

Heizer Corp.
20 N. Wacker Dr., Ste. 4100
Chicago, IL 60606
(312) 641-2200

Walter E. Heller & Co.
101 Park Ave.
New York, NY 10178
(212) 880-7047

Helms, Mulliss & Johnston
227 N. Tryon St., PO Box 31247
Charlotte, NC 28231
(704) 372-9510

IEG Venture Mgmt., Inc.
401 N. Michigan Ave., #2020
Chicago, IL 60611
(312) 644-0890

Investors in Industry Corp.
99 High St., Ste. 1200
Boston, MA 02110
(617) 542-8560

Jones, Day, Reavis & Pogue
1700 Hunting Bldg.
Cleveland, OH 44115
(216) 238-7189

Jones, Day, Reavis & Pogue
327 Congress Ave.
Austin, TX 78701
(512) 442-3939

JVIG U.S. Management, Inc.
1008 N. Bowen Rd.
Arlington, TX 76012
(817) 860-5222

Kirkland & Ellis
200 E. Randolph Dr.
Chicago, IL 60601
(312) 861-2465

Knight & Irish Associates, Inc.
420 Lexington Ave., Ste. 2358
New York, NY 10170
(212) 490-0135

Lord, Bissell & Brook
115 S. LaSalle St., #3500
Chicago, IL 60603
(312) 443-0615

M&I Capital Corp.
770 N. Water St.
Milwaukee, WI 53202
(414) 765-7910

Mayer, Brown & Platt
520 Madison Ave.
New York, NY 10022
(212) 437-7132

Med-Wick Associates, Inc.
1902 Fleet National Bank Bldg.
Providence, RI 02903
(401) 751-5270

Menlo Ventures
3000 Sand Hill Rd.
Menlo Park, CA 94025
(415) 854-8540

Michigan Dept. of Treasury
Venture Capital Division
301 W. Allegan
Lansing, MI 48922
(517) 373-4330

Morgenthaler Ventures
700 National City Bank Bldg.
Cleveland, OH 44114
(216) 621-3070

New Enterprise Associates
300 Cathedral St., Ste. 110
Baltimore, MD 21201
(301) 244-0115

Nippon Investment & Finance
Co. Ltd.
39F, Nishi-Shinjuku 1-25-1,
Shinjuku-ku
Tokyo 160 JAPAN
(03) 349-0961

NBM Participatie B.V.
Postbus 1800
1000 BV AMSTERDAM
The Netherlands, NL
(020) 543-3346

North American Cap. Group,
Ltd.
7250 N. Cicero
Lincolnwood, IL 60646
(312) 982-1010

Oppenheimer & Co., Inc.
1 New York Plaza
New York, NY 10004
(212) 825-8225

Opportunity Capital, Inc.
7667 Cahill Rd.
Edina, MN 55435
(612) 829-0379

Oxford Partners
72 Cummings Point Rd.
Stamford, CT 06902
(203) 964-0592

Parker Hyde Corp.
2000 L St., NW, Ste. 200
Washington, DC 20036
(202) 466-3810

Pathfinder Venture Cap. Fund
7300 Metro Blvd., Ste. 585
Minneapolis, MN 55435
(612) 835-1121

Peat, Marwick, Mitchell & Co.
555 S. Flower St.
Los Angeles, CA 90071
(213) 972-4000

Peat, Marwick, Mitchell & Co.
Three Embarcadero Ctr.
San Francisco, CA 94111
(415) 335-5300

Peat, Marwick, Mitchell & Co.
1700 IDS Center
Minneapolis, MN 55402
(612) 341-2222

Peat, Marwick, Mitchell & Co.
1800 First Union Pl.
Charlotte, NC 28282
(704) 335-5300

Pepper, Hamilton & Scheetz
100 Renaissance Ctr., Ste. 3600
Detroit, MI 48243
(313) 259-7110

Peregrine Associates
606 Wilshire Blvd., Ste. 602
Santa Monica, CA 90401
(213) 458-1441

Pernovo, Inc.
1877 Broadway, Ste. 405
Boulder, CO 80302
(303) 442-1171

Piper, Jaffray & Hopwood, Inc.
733 Marquette Ave., Ste. 800
Minneapolis, MN 55402
(612) 371-3853

Quidnet Capital Corp.
909 State Rd.
Princeton, NJ 08540
(609) 924-7665

Richards, O'Neil & Allegaeret
660 Madison Ave.
New York, NY 10021
(212) 207-1200

Rodi, Pollock, Pettker,
Galbraith & Phillips
611 W. 6th St., Ste. 1600
Los Angeles, CA 90017
(213) 680-0823

Rothschild Ventures, Inc.
One Rockefeller Pl.
New York, NY 10020
(212) 757-6000

Santa Fe Private Equity Fund
524 Camino Del Monte Sol
Santa Fe, NM 87501
(505) 983-1769

SB Capital Corp., Ltd.
85 Bloor St. E.
Toronto, Ontario M4W 1A9
(416) 967-5439

Scientific Advances, Inc.
601 W. Fifth Ave.
Columbus, OH 43201
(614) 294-5541

Security Pacific Bus. Credit,
Inc.
228 E. 45th St.
New York, NY 10017
(212) 309-9302

The Small Business Advocacy,
Inc.
Towne Sq. Professional Ctr.
526 Nilles Rd., Ste. 5
Fairfield, OH 45014
(513) 829-0880

Stephenson Merchant Banking
899 Logan St.
Denver, CO 80203
(303) 837-1700

Tulsa Industrial Authority
616 S. Boston
Tulsa, OK 74119
(918) 585-1201

The Venture Capital Fund of
New England
100 Franklin St.
Boston, MA 02110
(617) 451-2575

Venture Economics, Inc.
Box 348, 16 Laurel Ave.
Wellesley Hills, MA 02181
(617) 431-8100

Venture Founders Corp.
100 Fifth Ave.
Waltham, MA 02154
(617) 890-1000

Vista Ventures
1600 Summer St.
Stamford, CT 06905
(203) 359-3500

The Wallner Co.
215 Coast Blvd.
La Jolla, CA 92037
(619) 454-3805

Whitehead Associates
15 Valley Dr.
Greenwich, CT 06830
(203) 629-4633

Branch Office
Xerox Venture Capital
2029 Century Park E., Ste. 740
Los Angeles, CA 90067
(213) 278-7940

Arthur Young & Co.
One Post St.
San Francisco, CA 94104
(415) 393-2733

Arthur Young & Co.
1111 Summer St.
Stamford, CT 06905
(203) 356-1800

Arthur Young & Co.
235 Peachtree St., NE
2100 Gas Light Tower
Atlanta, GA 30043
(404) 581-1300

Arthur Young & Co.
One Boston Pl.
Boston, MA 02102
(617) 725-1100

Arthur Young & Co.
200 Lomas Blvd., NW, Ste. 300
Albuquerque, NM 87102
(505) 842-9273

Arthur Young & Co.
277 Park Ave.
New York, NY 10172
(212) 407-1611

Arthur Young & Co.
800 Industrial Bank Bldg.
Providence, RI 02903
(401) 274-1800

Arthur Young & Co.
2121 San Jacinto, Ste. 700
Dallas, TX 75201
(214) 969-8666

Arthur Young & Co.
777 E. Wisconsin Ave., Ste.
2100
Milwaukee, WI 53202
(414) 273-3340

STANDBY LETTERS OF CREDIT

Bank Instruments Can Give Small Companies Financial Clout

A versatile banking instrument, the standby letter of credit, can give small companies the financial clout of giant corporations. By substituting the bank's credit standing for that of the firm, the letters enable management to close major transactions that might otherwise go to larger competitors.

Not to be confused with commercial letters of credit, which finance the movement of goods, standby letters of credit serve more as guarantees than financing tools. They can help companies bid on and obtain contracts, secure down payments on business deals, and arrange for additional credit from suppliers.

"Standby letters of credit are not really meant to be drawn down," says a vice-president of Manufacturers Hanover Trust. "Rather, they are designed to provide assurance that a company can meet its obligations.

"For example, assume ABC Company, a small business, is the low bidder on a contract to make custom machines for XYZ Company. But XYZ fears that ABC is too thinly capitalized to get the job done and threatens to award the contract to a larger firm.

"To prevent this, ABC can apply for a letter of credit naming XYZ as the beneficiary. Should ABC fail to perform according to the terms of the contract, XYZ will receive a percentage of the contract value, perhaps 10 to 15 percent. This assurance may allay XYZ's concerns about working with a small firm."

Standby letters of credit can prove valuable at the earliest stages of the bidding process. In many cases, companies must qualify as bidders by posting "bid bonds" for part of the contract's value.

"Small companies that don't have the cash on hand, or that prefer not to tie up their capital in this way, can use standby letters of credit to satisfy the bid-bond requirements," says a vice-president of New York's Citibank. "This can prevent the small firm from being shut out of the deal."

Standby letters of credit can also be used as advance payment bonds. It works this way: Assume ABC accepts a $10,000 order from XYZ and demands a 20-percent payment in advance. XYZ agrees, providing ABC obtains a standby letter of credit for $2,000. XYZ wants to recover its deposit should ABC fail to deliver the goods. The letter of credit provides that assurance.

"You can get quite creative with standby letters of credit," says the Manufacturers Hanover V.P. "For example, a company having trouble getting adequate credit from its suppliers can have its bank issue standbys naming the suppliers as beneficiaries. This will likely boost the firm's credit limit. A company limited to $15,000 of credit without bank backing might increase that limit to $30,000 or more with the standby letter."

But there is a caveat. Beneficiaries can often draw down standby letters of credit simply by claiming nonperformance. The bank, in turn, will look to its customer for reimbursement.

"If we get a written statement from the beneficiary to the effect that the contract terms have not been met, we are obligated to pay," the banker from Manufacturers Hanover warns. "That's why it is best to use standby letters of credit only with those parties you know are reputable and trustworthy."

Typically, applications for standby letters of credit are evaluated on the same basis as business loans. Fees, calculated on annual basis, generally range from 0.75 percent to 2 percent of the amount of the credit. As a rule, fees rise with the length of the period covered.

Companies shopping the market for the best terms and fees may also want to evaluate surety bonds. Similar in some respects to standby letters of credit, surety bonds may provide a greater level of protection against nonperformance claims. They are sold by major property and casualty insurance companies. Compare the two instruments to see which best meets your needs.

VENTURE CAPITAL

How to Attract Venture Capital

Sometimes a business has to be sold before it opens its doors. Entrepreneurs seeking start-up capital have to convince prospective investors that their product or service will succeed in the marketplace. Unless this initial sales effort succeeds, the venture may be doomed to the drawing board.

But convincing capital sources that a project merits cash investments is never easy. Hundreds of fledgling ventures compete for every dollar of risk capital. Who gets the money is a measure both of the project's promise and the founder's skill in packaging and promoting it.

"Many otherwise capable entrepreneurs fail to gain financing because they don't know how to sell their ventures to the investment community," says the president of a Connecticut-based venture management firm. "Typically, the person with a new business idea assumes that everyone else will share his excitement at the outset. But that can't be said of professional investors. Because they review ideas as businessmen not as gamblers, they become enthusiastic only if they are convinced that the project will succeed. So entrepreneurs seeking risk capital have to structure their ventures from a businessman's perspective."

The process involves four critical steps:

1. In stage one, venture assessment, the would-be entrepreneur subjects his idea to intensive scrutiny, looking for the strengths and weaknesses in current or projected products, markets, management, competition, and operations. An independent observer familiar with start-ups can bring objectivity to the process.

"When a group of entrepreneurs developed a product in the data communications field, one problem threatened to spoil their chances for venture-capital financing," the venture manager says. "The product had to compete with IBM in several key markets. To eliminate the problem, and to make the venture stronger in the process, the product was redesigned to make it compatible with IBM systems. This allayed investor fears and prompted financing from major telecommunications companies."

2. Venture development positions the company for ultimate success. In a typical case, two entrepreneurs—one strong in finance and the other in manufacturing—paired up to launch a company in the consumer products field. Proud of their capabilities and thrilled by the product's potential, they overlooked a major weakness. The management team lacked a strong marketing executive. Proven talent in all facets of the company's operations is vital for building investor confidence.

"Sometimes the people who dream up a commercially viable idea are not the best candidates to run the company because they have no management experience," the venture expert explains. "In one deal, I had to advise an entrepreneur to go out and hire a boss—someone to serve as the chief executive—before he approached capital sources."

3. In step three, preparation of the business plan, the entrepreneur creates a blueprint for the venture's development. The company and its products are fully described, along with management's strategy for growing from start-up to a stable and profitable enterprise.

4. With the puzzle pieces fit neatly together, the business proposal is now ready for the fourth and final stage: presentation to venture investors.

"The worst mistake is to blanket the investment community with hundreds of business plans," the venture manager warns. "Instead, limit submissions to those investors with a track record for investing in your field or industry. And never mail blind. Have an intermediary familiar with investors make the initial contact. This should ensure that the plan will get a fair reading."

Preparing a Venture-Capital Proposal

If you decide on venture-capital financing for your company, your next move will be to structure your proposal.

Your goal in preparing this proposal is twofold: to impress the venture-capital firm with your management team's planning ability and competence, and to help *you* think clearly about the strength and limitations of your enterprise.

Honesty is the most important byword in writing the proposal. All companies have flaws, and they should be discussed. Make your proposal brief, reliable, and consistent. Save heavy technical information for the appendices. The following organization is suggested but may, of course, be modified:

A. Proposition. Begin with a one-page statement of how much money you are seeking, how the money will be spent, the nature of your business, and when and if you will need subsequent financing. You may also wish to include terms for a suggested financing structure.

B. Summary. Use a page or two to highlight the most important information in the proposal.

C. History. Give relevant background on your company's history, including names of the founders, the original business purpose, and the state in which the company is incorporated. Also name predecessor companies and subsidiaries and the company's degree of ownership in each.

D. Capitalization. If your company is already in business, provide the most recent balance sheet. State the nature and terms of present financing (short- and long-term lenders, lessors, trade creditors) and include a chronology of the company's long-term financing.

E. Organization. Draw an organizational chart of the company and give detailed biographies of your directors and chief personnel. Discuss your work force, and tell what part might be unionized. Review your plans for the company's wage and salary structure and benefit plans. (Will you offer profit sharing and stock option plans?) Include a five-year forecast of how you expect the company's staffing needs and personnel to evolve.

F. Product. Describe the nature, applications, patent protections, and distinctive features of your product or service. Detail new product plans. Show photographs, engineering plans, or sales brochures in the appendices.

G. Manufacturing. Discuss your company's manufacturing facilities, including land, buildings, and equipment and its age. Outline your manufacturing method and quality control procedures. Name the raw materials and components you use, as well as your sources, costs, and any contracts you held. Analyze both your fixed manufacturing costs and your variable costs by product.

H. Market. State the nature, present size (dollar volume and units), and growth potential of your target market, and your market share. Draw on outside studies to support your assumptions. If you have already marketed the product, explain how it fared in the marketplace and why.

I. Marketing. Describe your pricing, marketing, sales, and distribution strategies for the next five years. Explain the rationale for these strategies and how you intend to put each of them into practice. If your company has a track record, list a few customers, sales agents, distributors, etc.

J. Competition. If you have competitors, list their names, market share, strengths, and weaknesses, and compare your recent performance with theirs. If you have no competitors, talk about where competition may come from in the future.

K. Use of Proceeds. Be specific about how you intend to use venture-capital financing ($250,000 to upgrade a plant, $100,000 to buy inventory, etc.).

L. Historical Financial Statements. Unless your company is a start-up, provide income statements, sources, and uses of funds statements and balance sheets from inception or for the last five years. Explain any unusual fluctuations in them as well as any accounting changes.

M. Forecast. Compile a five-year forecast of the company's financial statement incorporating the proposed financing. If your company is in the start-up or blueprint stage, you may provide a monthly forecast for the first year, a quarterly for the second year, and an annual for the next three years. If the company has a track record, provide a quarterly forecast for the first year, and then annual forecasts. Your CPA can help you prepare this forecast. Be sure to clearly state your assumptions.

Credit: KMG Main Hurdman, "Entrepreneur's Guide to Raising Capital"

AT A GLANCE

Types of Venture-Capital Firms

Traditional partnerships. Often established by wealthy families to aggressively manage a portion of their funds by investing in small companies.

Professionally managed pools. These are made up of institutional money and operate like traditional partnerships.

Investment banking firms. These usually trade in more established securities, but occasionally form investor syndicates for venture proposals.

Insurance companies. Often require a portion of equity as a condition of their loans to smaller companies as protection against inflation.

Manufacturing companies. These sometimes look upon investing in smaller companies as a means of supplementing their R & D programs (some "Fortune 500" corporations have venture-capital operations to help keep them abreast of technological innovations).

Small business investment corporations (SBICs). These are licensed by the Small Business Administration (SBA), and they may provide management assistance as well as venture capital. (When dealing with SBICs, the small business owner-manager should initially determine if the SBIC is primarily interested in an equity position, as venture capital, or merely in long-term lending on a fully secured basis.)

Credit: U.S. Small Business Administration and LaRue Tone Hosmer

Venture-Capitalist Pricing

Assume:

Your business has:

1. projected $2,000,000 annual net earnings by the end of the fifth year
2. outstanding 1,000,000 shares
3. requested $1,750,000 for expansion

The market is:

1. currently trading stocks in similar businesses at 12 times earnings (earnings multiple)
2. expected to be at the same level in five years

The venture capitalist:

1. requires a compounded annual return on investment of 40% (approximately five times investment over five years)
2. desires that your business go public in five years.

Then:

1. Earnings per share (EPS) are =
$$\frac{\$2,000,000 \text{ net earnings}}{1,000,000 \text{ shares}} = \$2.00 \text{ EPS}$$
2. Projected share price in year five is $24.00 = $2.00 EPS × 12 earnings multiple

3. The projected future market value of your business is $24,000,000 = $24/share × 1,000,000 shares
4. The present value of your business based on the venture capitalist's return objective is $4,460,000 where:

$$\text{Present Value (PV)} = \frac{FV}{(1 + i)^n}$$

FV = business's future value
i = stated return objective (rate of return)
n = number of years.

$$\$4,460,000 = \frac{\$24,000,000}{(1 + 40\%)^5}$$

5. The venture capitalist will require a 39% ownership interest in your business.

$$39\% = \frac{\$1,750,000 \text{ requested}}{\$4,460,000 \text{ present value}}$$
of your business

Credit: Price Waterhouse, *Business Review Newsletter*

WHERE TO FIND IT

National Venture Capital
Association
1655 N. Fort Meyer Drive,
Suite 700
Arlington, VA 22209
(703) 528-4370

III. The Better Mousetrap

Tips for Running Your Business Better than the Competition

◇ ══ ◇

Management Checklist for a Family Business

No small business is easy to manage, and this is especially true in a small family business. It is subject to all the problems that beset small companies plus those that can, and often do, arise when relatives try to work together.

The family member who is charged with managing the company has to work at initiating and maintaining sound management practices. By describing what is to be done and under what circumstances, such practices help prevent some of the confusion and conflicts that may be perpetuated by self-centered family members. Such relatives sometimes regard the company as existing primarily to satisfy their desires.

The questions in this checklist are designed to help chief executive officers review the management practices of their small family companies. The comments that follow each question are intended to stimulate thought rather than to include the many and various aspects suggested by the questions.

	Yes	No
Is executive time used on high-priority tasks?	☐	☐

The time of the owner-manager is one of the most valuable assets of a small business. It should not be dribbled away in routine tasks that can be done as well, if not better, by other employees. Never lose sight of the fact that you, as owner-manager, have to make the judgments that will determine the success of your business. You may want to run a check on how your time is used by keeping a log for the next several weeks. On a calendar memorandum pad jot down what you do in half-hour or hour blocks. Then review your notes against the questions: Was my time spent on management tasks, such as reviewing last week's sales figures and noting areas for improvement? Or did I let it dribble away on routine tasks,

187

What's Your Executive Style?

Are you a persuasive implementer? A cool-headed problem solver? A visionary pathfinder? Or a combination of all three?

Check the chart below to see which category most closely fits your managerial ways and means.

	Implementer	Problem Solver	Pathfinder
Key Word	Action	Analysis	Mission
Profile	Highly social, emotional, fast-talking, fast moving.	Logical, rational, casts an intellectually reserved shadow.	Impractical, stubborn, ignores the rules, acts impulsively.
Managerial Objective	To persuade, command, manipulate.	To determine the right answers.	To determine the right questions.
Archetypal Professions	Direct sales, lobbying, litigation law.	Engineering, accounting, systems analysis.	Architecture, the arts, theoretical science, entrepreneurship.
Archetypal Personalities	Dale Carnegie, Mary Kay Ash, George Patton.	Harold Geneen (ITT), Roy Ash (Litton), Cardinal Richelieu.	Steven Jobs, Golda Meir, Florence Nightingale, Napoleon.
Archetypal Quotes	"I'd rather have him inside the tent pissing out than outside pissing in." Lyndon Baines Johnson.	"Stop! Slide number 105 contradicts slide number 6." Robert McNamara.	"I have a dream." Martin Luther King, Jr.

Credit: *Working Woman*, March 1986, p. 25, and Harold Leavitt

such as opening the mail and sorting bills of lading? You may want to ask your key personnel to run the same sort of check on their time.

Do you set goals and objectives? Yes ☐ No ☐

Goals and objectives help a small company head toward profit. Goals and objectives should be specific and realistic. In addition they should be measurable, time-phased, and written. List your goals and objectives by writing them out for your present successful operations. Objectives that are written out in straightforward language provide a basis for actions by your key personnel. For example, state that you will sell a certain number of units this year rather than saying you will increase sales.

Do you have written policies? Yes ☐ No ☐

Flag this question and return to it later. Working through

this checklist should suggest changes that may be needed if you have written policies. By the same token, your business will provide input for writing out policies if there are none in writing.

Is planning done to achieve these goals and objectives?
In a sense, planning is forecasting. An objective, for example, for next year might be to increase your net profit after taxes. To plan for it you need to forecast sales volume, production of finished goods inventory, raw materials requirements, and all the other elements connected with producing your forecasts; you will want to make provision for watching costs, including selling expenses. If there are key employees who can provide input into the planning, ask them to become involved in it.

Yes No
□ □

Do you test or check the reality of your goals and plans with others?
Outside advisers may spot "bugs" that you and your people did not catch in the press of working through the details of goal setting and planning.

Yes No
□ □

Are operations reviewed on a regular basis with the objective of reducing costs?
Costs must be kept in line for a profitable operation. Review

Yes No
□ □

operations periodically (weekly or monthly) to ensure that overtime is not excessive, for example. What about quality product acceptance by customers? Costs may be excessive because of obsolete methods or machinery that has seen its best days. Can changes in plant layout or materials flow be made that will save time and materials? Determine the frequency of your reviews for the various types of operations and place a tickler on your calendar to remind you of these review dates.

Yes No

Are products reviewed regularly with the objective of improving them?
Products that your customers benefit from are the key to repeat sales. A regular review of your products helps to keep them up to the expectations of customers. Feedback from customers can be useful here. To reduce costs sometimes a product can be modified without sacrificing use and quality. If product obsolescence is a hazard, what plans are being made to substitute new products as existing ones become obsolete?

Yes No
□ □

Do you ask outside advisers for their opinions and suggestions on products and procedures?
Outside persons, such as friends in noncompeting lines

Yes No
□ □

of business and management personnel from local colleges and universities, can help you see the facts about your products and operating procedures. They can provide the fresh viewpoint of persons who are not so involved in the products and operations as you and your key personnel. The suggestions and counsel from a local management consultant may provide benefits far in excess of his or her cost. In this area some small companies set up a board of directors to satisfy the law concerning small corporations. But that is the end of it. Members of the board are not used for their knowledge and skill in business. They can make valuable contributions, and the owner-manager should use all possible opportunities for getting such concerned opinions about the various phases of the company.

Are marketing and distribution policies and procedures reviewed periodically?

Yes ☐ No ☐

The best-made product in the world can run into trouble if marketing and distribution policies and procedures are not right for it. Periodic checks can help you to be aware of changes that may be taking place in the channels through which you distribute. One approach is to check your competition; does it seem to be changing channels and policies? Can you still meet the requirements of your customers by using your traditional channels of distribution?

Are there periodic reviews of profit-and-loss statements and other financial reports?

Yes ☐ No ☐

In these reviews you can compare your operating ratios to those for your industry. It is also helpful to review your cash-flow projections to see what, if any, changes are needed in your financial planning.

Do you have an organization chart?

Yes ☐ No ☐

You may need only a simple organization chart to show accountability and to establish a chain of command. In a family business, accountability and chain of command should be spelled out so that the chief executive of the company has the "mandate" he or she needs for managing.

Do you use job descriptions for your key personnel?

Yes ☐ No ☐

When you and your key personnel write descriptions for their jobs, you and they have a clear understanding of what is to be done and by whom. Such an understanding is essential in any small business but especially critical when relatives are involved.

Spelling out duties may not prevent conflicts between you and an in-law, but such detail can help you resolve misunderstandings, if and when they occur. In addition, when and if a key person leaves, the job description is a helpful tool in recruiting and training a replacement.

Yes No

Do you periodically compare performance of key personnel with their job descriptions? □ □
Periodic comparison of performance helps your key personnel to be efficient. It also helps to pinpoint weak spots for you and them to work on for improvement.

Yes No

Do you provide opportunities for key personnel to grow? □ □
Your aim should be to help key personnel stay alert to new and more efficient ways to do things. Conferences, seminars, and workshops that trade associations and agencies, such as the Small Business Administration, sponsor can help key personnel grow in their management skills and outlook. Rotating job assignments is a way to make key personnel aware of the problems that their counterparts face. Include in your budget an amount to be spent during the year for personnel training and education.

Yes No

Do you face the issue when key personnel stop growing? □ □
Some owner-managers try to avoid the unpleasant task of facing the fact that a key person has stopped growing. It may be the result of not matching personnel and the job. Or in some family businesses, the cousin or brother-in-law never was interested in personal growth or any aspects of management. If there is little or nothing you can do about such a mismatch, face it and don't waste time trying to do the impossible. On the other hand, outside problems may be crowding in on the key person. Once you know why he or she stopped growing, you can determine what needs to be done. In some cases, additional training is the answer. In other cases, the motivation that results from broadened job responsibilities resolves the problem.

Yes No

Are there policies and plans for motivating employees? □ □
Working through others is by no means an easy task. First of all, people are not puppets that can be moved by strings. Life may be a stage, as the poet said, but most people in small business are reluctant to submit to directors. Look for ways—good communications, respect for their viewpoint, incentive pay, and so on—to

encourage people to *want* to do what you *need* them to do as employees in your company.

Do you have adequate employee benefit plans?

Yes ☐   No ☐

This includes life and health insurance, major medical, and pension. Benefit plans often are necessary to meet competition for skilled employees. Substantial plans can help to hold nonfamily key individuals in a family-owned business.

Do you have key personnel insurance on yourself, and is your family protected against your untimely passing?

Yes ☐   No ☐

If these precautions are not taken, your death could result in the rapid dissolution of the business.

Is there lack of communication among key personnel?

Yes ☐   No ☐

The routine passing of information among you and your key personnel may be all that you want it to be. But what about disagreement? Do key personnel refrain from expressing disagreement with you? Good communications should provide a forum for exchanging ideas and for airing differences of opinion. An early morning meeting once a week among you and your key personnel might provide a forum for exchanging ideas.

Does your record-keeping system present a realistic picture of your business? Is this the same type of record-keeping system that other companies in your industry commonly use?

Yes ☐   No ☐

Appropriate records should give the owner/manager answers to questions such as: Is there sufficient cash to operate the business? To pay back the bank? To pay taxes? Is too much capital tied up in inventory? Are accounts receivable being collected promptly? Bankers and other lenders need a realistic picture. Corporate records, if your company is a corporation, should be up to date including corporate minutes and record books. In checking out your record keeping, keep in mind that a poor system can result in excessive and meaningless information.

Do you seek legal and financial advice on major transactions?

Yes ☐   No ☐

The fine print in contracts causes trouble for some small business owners. They did not realize until it was too late what they had agreed to do. Legal and financial advice at the appropriate time can help the owner-manager to comprehend the full scope of your company's contractual obligations and allow you to make decisions based on facts rather than assumptions. Whenever possible use your standardized contract in making contractual obligations.

Yes   No

Do you document informal agreements with customers, suppliers, and others?   ☐   ☐
"He's as good as his word" is a fine attitude to have about customers, suppliers, and others with whom you work on a daily basis. But think for a moment; in being as "good as your word," how often do you forget? Memory slips. A note to yourself, or to a supplier to confirm a telephone conversation, for example, helps both of you to recall what you agreed or did not agree upon and prevents misunderstanding and hard feeling. Keep dated copies of all correspondence you send out. Later, these copies could be invaluable.

Yes   No

Do you plan your major financial decisions with the help of your accountant, lawyer, and other tax advisers?   ☐   ☐
An owner-manager cannot ignore the impact of federal and state income taxes, as well as other taxes, on your business. You should plan major financial decisions with the help of an accountant, lawyer, and other tax advisers.

Yes   No

Do your plans include self-development projects for yourself?   ☐   ☐
Sometimes an owner-manager sets up training for everyone in the company except himself or herself. Because conditions change so rapidly you should set aside some time for activities that will help you to keep abreast of your industry and the economic world in which your company operates. Your trade association should be a source of information about meetings, conferences, and seminars which you can use in such a program for yourself.

Yes   No

Are there plans for succession in the event of the untimely death of the family member who manages the company?   ☐   ☐
The successor may not be the same person who substitutes when the chief executive officer is sick or on vacation. Whether or not the successor is a family member, the transition will be smoother when the family agrees upon a successor ahead of time. Such agreement is necessary if the business is to bear the expense of grooming the successor.

Credit: U.S. Small Business Administration

Auditing the Auditors: How to Select and Rate Your CPA Firm

When ABC Apparel, a small manufacturer of women's sportswear, sought $1 million to modernize its outmoded factory, management confidently petitioned its bankers, believing approval to be a mere formality. With little existing debt and an excellent growth record, ABC appeared to be the model borrower.

But the family-owned fashion house was in for a rude surprise. A few days after the loan papers were delivered, the bankers turned thumbs down, blaming not the company, its financial performance, or its business prospects but—incredibly enough—its choice of accounting firms. Because ABC's income statement and balance sheet were prepared by a small, rather inconspicuous CPA firm, the bankers refused to open their coffers.

Bottom line: No loan.

"When I asked the bank for an explanation, the loan officer ushered me into his office," ABC's president recalls. "He whispered that they wanted to do business with us and would reconsider our application, providing we axed the two-person CPA firm we'd worked with since our founding and replaced them with one of the Big Eight.* At the time, I didn't even know what the Big Eight was, but I learned fast."

Others have learned that the Big Eight, though the largest accounting firms in the nation and for this reason favored by lending

*The Big Eight accounting firms are Price Waterhouse; Arthur Andersen; Arthur Young; Coopers & Lybrand; Deloitte, Haskins & Sells; Ernst & Whinney; Peat Marwick; and Touche Ross.

institutions, are not always the most attentive to small business. When a group of dentists banded together to form an investment club, they asked a Big Eight firm to structure an organization for joint purchases of real estate, stocks, and gems. The investors sought the clout and diversification that pooled funds would bring while still retaining individual ownership rights and personal tax advantages. They asked the CPAs to provide a framework for this.

Responsive at the outset, the accountants pledged to tailor their services to the group's needs and budget limitations. But when it came to delivering on this pledge, the accountants proved lackadaisical, uninterested, and preoccupied with more pressing matters. Partners failed to show up at client meetings, making eleventh-hour excuses about flat tires and the like. Worse yet, the firm played musical chairs with the client, shifting responsibility for the assignment to a revolving cast of partners. In this case, bigness may have worked against the client.

These incidents, all too familiar to thousands of small companies, underline the importance and the surprising complexity of hiring the right accountant. The critical choice—between a sole practitioner, a small to midsize firm (from 2 to 250 professionals), or a national behemoth (up to 25,000 professionals)—can have wide implications beyond the company's tax return or its method of accounting.

The choice is not an easy one. Just which size accounting firm will best service your business depends on a kaleidoscope of interrelated factors, including the company's industry, its stage in the corporate life cycle, and management's objectives.

Sometimes, a cost-benefit analysis comes into play. While most firms in the same size category charge similar fees, hourly rates generally rise along the size spectrum, increasing from sole practitioner to midsize firm and higher still for the giants. The differences can be staggering, with fees for partner services ranging from as low as $75 an hour to $200 or more. With this in mind, the smallest mom and pop companies may lean toward sole practitioners, most of whom charge at the bottom of the fee curve. Because these companies have relatively simple operations, the sophisticated services (strategic planning, computer consulting) available from the larger accounting firms may be overkill.

Fledgling ventures starting out on a shoestring may want to take this approach one step further, working at the outset with a bookkeeper rather than a CPA. Individuals, and in some cases bookkeeping divisions of accounting firms, can provide these rudimentary service at rates that are half as much as the lowest professional fees. The caveat here is that bookkeepers do not and cannot measure up to accountants in training or experience, drawbacks that may deprive the company of the widest range of tax advantages and that will surely weaken its position with lenders, most of whom insist that prospective borrowers be serviced by CPAs. One strategy is to work with a bookkeeper until the company's revenues are great enough (say, $100,000) to warrant ongoing tax planning or until it needs to raise money through financial institutions. At this point, it may be wise to shift to a CPA firm or to have accountants perform those services (such as tax planning and audits) that are beyond the scope of a bookkeeper.

Let's explore these other considerations:

Advantages of the Big Firms

1. Scope of Services
Today's big accounting practices are actually broad-based consulting firms offering a smorgasboard of services from standard accounting and auditing to microcomputer consulting, cash management, and feasibility studies. This unrivaled versatility is a strong selling point vis-à-vis small practitioners, most of whom are limited to traditional accounting functions such as filing tax returns and preparing financial statements.

As a venture grows from infancy to an established and profitable company, bigger firms can provide the full complement of services it needs along the way. Should management require assistance in computerizing its operations, in establishing a foreign subsidiary, or in creating employee pension plans, big firms can provide the necessary expertise in-house. The client is thus spared the confusion and the redundancy of dealing with a patchwork of outside consulting firms.

This is a major advantage. Increasingly, entrepreneurs starting out with small accounting firms find that they outgrow their CPAs in midstream and are forced, often at inopportune times, to shift to midsize or larger practitioners.

"When we launched our catering business from the basement of our home, we worked with a sole practitioner whose advice and counsel really made a difference in getting our fledgling venture off the ground," says the owner of a now prosperous food services firm with operations in 16 states. "But—and it was a big 'but' because we hated to sever our relationship with him—it became obvious to us at the end of the sixth year that we had to change accountants. Our one-man band just couldn't provide the depth of financial and consulting services we needed as a $30-million-a-year company.

"In hindsight, I'm pleased we made the transition—there's a marked difference in the scope of services available to us now—but for a while there it was touch and go.

Asking a professional firm to take over from another who had guided you from day one can be a tricky affair. At times I think we'd have been better off going with a big firm from the start, but maybe we couldn't have afforded them at the time.

2. Prestigious Reputation

What's in a name? In the byzantine world of accounting and finance, the answer is everything and nothing. While an obscure, modest-sized firm may be every bit as capable as the largest practitioners, the Big Eight's trump card is the influence it wields in the financial community. As the president of ABC Apparel learned, when it comes to raising capital (through loans or public offerings), commercial and investment bankers respond most favorably to financial statements stamped with a Big Eight imprimatur.

"When a lender or investor looks at financial statements, they want to know that they can rely on them," says ABC's former CPA. "Because they believe that the Big Eight have a higher standard of practice, they feel safe if a Big Eight name is on the documents. Conversely, they fret if the CPAs are unknown to them. Rather than inquiring as to the caliber of our practice, they simply demand that the prospective borrowers dump us in favor of the big boys. When they do, I can't blame them. Getting the money is more important than getting along with us."

Drawbacks of the Big Firms

1. The Sign-Em-Up and Sell-Em Syndrome

The wide sweep of expertise that enables a big firm to service a client's needs from cradle to grave is often matched by a high-powered sales drive designed to generate fees for the in-house practice units. To some, this blatant commercialism distorts the client-accountant relationship.

2. Small Fish, Big Pond

There's no disguising the fact that a small client in a Big Eight firm is a veritable lilliputian. Whoever doubts that hasn't tried competing for attention with IBM, GM, and GE (all Big Eight clients). For this reason, entrepreneurs who insist that their companies, no matter how small, dominate their outside relationships may be best advised to work with small practitioners.

While all the big firms now service small businesses through special units geared to this practice, it is still true that no single client can dominate. If that's what you're after, look to the sole practitioner (bearing in mind that you may pay a heavy price, in terms of limited services, for what some consider an ego trip).

Advantages and Drawbacks of Small Firms

Physicists like to remind us that every action has an equal and opposite reaction. Accounting's version of that rule may be that every advantage is a drawback in disguise. Consider the scope-of-practice issue.

Whereas the big firms peddle a massive inventory of services, smaller practitioners are content to handle the basic accounting functions, including audits and tax returns. Without the need to sell, sell, sell, relationships are relatively low-keyed. The trade-off, however, is that the client's systems and procedures may lag behind its evolution as a mature business venture—or worse yet, may thwart that development.

The "Big Pond, Small Fish" issue has two sides as well. While the small firms hold a clear advantage in granting accessibility to top partners, clients may find this to be a double-edged sword. True, the sole practitioner will be at his client's disposal round the clock, but with dozens of clients demanding the boss's time and attention, the professional may be harried, exhausted, and unable to provide the caliber of service clients expect. With more partners, staff, and assorted experts to share the burden, the larger firms may actually field a more responsive client service team.

Just which accounting firm to choose depends in large measure on your personal preference, your operating style, and your assessment of the relative strengths and weaknesses of big versus small practitioners. For those still sitting on the fence, the following guidelines may be useful:

Choose a Big Firm if Your Business

- Needs entree to the financial community for a major loan ($1 million or more) or public offering
- Is active overseas
- Can benefit from general consulting services

Favor a Small Firm if You

- Expect to spend less than $5,000 a year on accounting services
- Prefer to work with the managing partner rather than those without management responsibility

Let us assume you've tallied the pros and cons and have made your decision. Now that you've initiated your most critical outside relationship, you'll want to monitor the CPA's performance to confirm that you've made the right choice, that your needs are being met, and that you are paying appropriate fees for the services rendered. In short, it's your turn to audit the auditors. Consider the following:

1. Are bills itemized to indicate the type of work performed, the number of hours for each project, and most important, the rank of the professional performing the service? Because there is a great disparity between partner and associate hourly fees (from $50 to $200 or more in the Big Eight), you'll want to make certain you're being billed at the proper rate.

Also, confirm that partner time is reserved for sophisticated assignments, such as structuring an estate plan, and that associates do the "grunt work" of compiling information and filing routine forms.

2. Does your accountant show up at tax time only to disappear for the rest of the year? If that sounds all too familiar, chances are good that your business is not being properly serviced. Give serious thought to changing firms. The best CPAs keep abreast of client performance, anticipating and planning for operating changes rather than responding to them after the fact.

3. Is the client-accountant relationship static or dynamic? Has it matured along with the company? Contrary to popular opinion (one probably fostered by CPAs), you don't have to be an accountant to gauge this. Unless the accountants consistently bring fresh ideas to the table—unless there is evidence of creativity in tax, estate planning, and accounting procedures—odds are the firm is either incapable of inspired work or takes your account for granted—both clear signals to move on.

Although CPAs must function within professional standards, the best do everything legally and ethically possible to satisfy their clients' needs. There is the story of the business owner who sets out to hire an accountant, asking the managing partners of six leading firms "How much is two plus two?" At the first five firms, the answer is identical: "Two plus two equals four." Unimpressed, the entrepreneur visits the last firm, and after asking the now familiar question, knows immediately that he's found his firm. "How much is two plus two?" the accountant responds. "How much did you have in mind?"

Consider these additional criteria for selecting professional firms (including lawyers, and consultants as well as accountants):

1. Contact professionals in related disciplines because they often work together on business transactions; lawyers and accountants, for example, are in unique positions to recommend fellow professionals whose work they've observed at firsthand. This can lead to high-quality referrals and, ultimately, to productive relationships between the practitioners serving your business. Those used to functioning as a team are more likely to produce favorable results than those who are new to each other.

With a list of at least three candidates in hand, rate their strengths and weaknesses according to these guidelines:

2. Favor those practitioners with active small business practices. While all may feign interest in smaller companies, the client list (abridged versions are generally available from the firms) reveals their true orientation. Look for those firms, or practice divisions, where smaller companies account for at least 20 percent of the client base.

3. Check for signs of expertise in your field or industry. Look beyond promotional tactics (many firms claim expertise in fields they barely know), focusing again on the client base. Those practitioners with a substantial clientele in retailing, manufacturing, or software, for example, bring specialized knowledge and in many cases years of experience to these engagements. Because they have researched the issues repeatedly and have raised them before courts and government agencies, they are aware of obscure tax, audit, and legal issues others will have to learn on the job (often at the client's expense).

Credit: *Working Woman* magazine

Bad Checks

Types of Checks

Winning the battle of wits against bad-check passers is largely a matter of knowledge and vigilance. You have to know what you're up against, pass the information on to your employees, and be constantly on guard when accepting checks.

You are apt to get seven different kinds of checks: personal, two-party, payroll, government, blank, counter, and traveler's. And some customers may offer money orders.

A personal check is written and signed by the individual offering it. The individual makes it out to you or your firm.

A two-party check is issued by one person, the maker, to a second person who endorses it so that it may be cashed by a third person. This type of check is susceptible to fraud because, for one thing, the maker can stop payment at the bank.

A payroll check is issued to an employee for wages or salary earned. Usually the name of the employer is printed on it, and it has a number and is signed. In most instances "payroll" is also printed on the check. The employee's name is printed by a check-writing machine or typed. In metropolitan areas, you should not cash a payroll check that is handprinted, rubber-stamped, or typewritten as a payroll check, even if it appears to be issued by a local business and drawn on a local bank. It may be a different story in a small community, where you know the company officials and the employee personally.

A government check can be issued by the federal state, county, or local government. Such checks cover salaries, tax refunds, pensions, welfare allotments, and veterans benefits, to mention a few examples.

You should be particularly cautious with

government checks. Often they are stolen and the endorsement has been forged.

In some areas, such thievery is so great that some banks refuse to cash Social Security, welfare, relief, or income-tax checks unless the customer has an account with the bank. You should follow this procedure also. In short, know your endorser.

A blank check, sometimes known as a universal check, is no longer acceptable to most banks due to Federal Reserve Board regulations that prohibit standard processing without the encoded characters. This universal check may be used, but it requires a special collection process by the bank and incurs a special cost.

A counter check is still used by a few banks and is issued to depositors when they are withdrawing funds from their accounts. It is not good anywhere else. Sometimes a store has its own counter checks for the convenience of its customers. A counter check is not negotiable and is so marked.

A traveler's check is a check sold with a preprinted amount (usually in round figures) to travelers who do not want to carry large amounts of cash. The traveler signs the checks at the time of purchase and should countersign the check only in the presence of the person who cashes them.

In addition, a money order can be passed as a check. However, a money order is usually mailed. Most stores should not accept money orders in face-to-face transactions.

Some small stores sell money orders. If yours does, never accept a personal check in payment for money orders. If the purchaser has a valid checking account, why does he or she need a money order? The check is possibly no good.

Look for Key Items

A check carries several key items: name and location of bank, date, amount (in figures and spelled out), and signature. Close examination of such key items can sometimes tip you off to a worthless check. Before accepting a check, look for:

Nonlocal banks. Use extra care in examining a check that is drawn on a nonlocal bank and require positive identification. List the customer's local and out-of-town addresses and phone number on the back of the check.

Date. Examine the date for accuracy of day, month, and year. Do not accept the check if it's not dated, if it's postdated, or if it's more than 30 days old.

Location. Look first to be sure that the check shows the name, branch, town, and state where the bank is located.

Amount. Be sure that the numerical amount agrees with the written amount.

Legibility. Do not accept a check that is not written legibly. It should be written and signed in ink and must not have any erasures or written-over amounts.

Checks over your limit. Set a limit on the amount—depending on the amount of your average sale—you will accept on a check. When a customer wants to go beyond that limit, your salesclerk should refer the customer to you.

Low sequence numbers. Be more cautious with low sequence numbers. Experience indicates that there seems to be a higher number of these checks that are returned. Most banks that issue personalized checks begin the numbering sequence with 101 when a customer reorders new checks.

$$$ Amount of check. Most bad-check passers pass checks in the $25.00 to $35.00 range on the assumption that the retailer will be more cautious when accepting a larger check.

Types of merchandise purchased. Be watchful of the types of merchandise purchased. Random sizes and selections or lack of concern about prices by customers should indicate to you that caution should be exercised when a check is offered as payment.

Require Identification

Once you are satisfied that the check is okay, the question is, "Is the person holding the check the right person?" Requiring identification helps you to answer the question.

Keep in mind that no identification is foolproof. A crook is a crook no matter what type of identification you ask to see. If the person wants to forge identification, he or she can.

Some stores demand at least two pieces of identification. It is important to get enough identification so the person presenting the check can be identified and located if the check turns out to be worthless.

The following types of identification should be useful in determining the type to use in your store.

Current automobile operator's license. If licenses in your state do not carry a photograph of the customer, you may want a second identification.

Shopping plates. If they bear a signature or laminated photograph, shopping plates or other credit cards can be used as identification. The retail merchants' organization in some communities issues lists of stolen shopping plates, to which you should always refer when identifying the check passer.

Government passes. These can also be used for identification in cashing checks. Picture passes should carry the name of the employing department and a serial number. Building passes should also carry a signature.

Identification cards. Those issued by the armed services, police departments, and companies should carry a photo, a description, and a signature. Police cards should also carry a badge number.

Several types of cards and documents are not good identification. Some of them (for example, club cards) are easily forged, and others (for example, customer's duplicate saleschecks) were never intended for identification. Unless they are presented with a current automobile operator's license, do not accept the following:

Social Security Cards

Business Cards

Club or Organization Cards

Bankbooks

Work Permits

Insurance Cards

Learner's Permits

Letters

Birth Certificates

Library Cards

Initialed Jewelry

Unsigned Credit Cards

Voter's Registration Cards

Customer's Duplicate Cards

Some large stores photograph each person who cashes a check along with the identification. This procedure is a deterrent because bad-check passers don't want to be photographed.

Some stores, when in doubt about a check, will verify an address and telephone number in the local telephone directory or with the information operator. Someone intending to pass a bad check will not necessarily be at the address shown on the check. If the address and telephone number cannot be verified, the check should be considered potentially bad.

Compare Signatures

Regardless of the type of identification you require, it is essential that you and your employees compare the signature on the check with the one on the identification.

You should also compare the person standing before you with the photograph or description on the identification.

Set a Policy

You should set a policy for cashing checks, write it down, and instruct your employees in its use. Your policy might require your approval before a salesclerk can cash a check. When all checks are handled alike, customers have no cause to feel that they are being treated unfairly.

Your procedure might include the use of a rubber stamp. Many stores stamp the lower reverse side of a check and write in the appropriate information. Here is a sample of such a stamp.

Please Print	
Salesperson—Name and No.	
Auth. Signature	
Customer's Address	
Home Phone	Business Phone
Ident. No. 1	
Ident. No. 2	
Dept. No.	Amount of Sale
Take Send COD Will Call	

Your policy might also include verifying a check through the bank that issued it. Some banks will do this only if you are a depositor in the bank. It might be helpful to establish business accounts in several banks, particularly where many of your customers have accounts.

Credit: U.S. Small Business Administration and Leonard Kolodny, Manager, Retail Bureau

BAD DEBTS

How to Break the Bad-Debt Cycle

Making good on bad debts can make a big difference to a company's bottom line. By collecting on delinquent accounts, management bolsters cash flow, reduces high-interest borrowing, and generally improves profitability.

But getting cash from stubborn deadbeats can be about as easy as drawing blood from a stone. The problem—which has plagued business for years—is now compounded by the widespread practice of extending payment cycles beyond 30 days. To shore up their own cash flow, companies are making creditors wait 60 to 90 days or more for payment in full. Typically, small business is last in line.

"The late payment problem is exacerbated every time interest rates go up," says Jon Lunn, a credit executive with a national collection agency. "Customers prefer to keep their cash in money-market accounts rather than making payment to creditors. So we have a new breed of debtors: those who can pay their bills but prefer not to. They want to keep the float in their pockets."

But there are ways to prompt delinquent customers to pay up and to keep their accounts current. By getting aggressive about the collection process, small businesses can leapfrog more complacent creditors, advancing several places in the line of those waiting to be paid.

Consider these strategies:

1. Begin the collection effort within 10 days after the bill has passed its due date. "Too many firms wait until the bill is long overdue," the credit executive notes. "That's poor collection practice. The delay enables others to get paid before you. What's more, the longer an invoice remains unpaid, the less likely it will ever be collected."

Adds the credit manager for a marketer of security devices: "We call our customers as soon as an order is shipped, telling them that shipment has been made and that we will be looking for a check. We tie good payment performance to expansion of the customer's credit line. There's something in it for both of us."

2. Send bills to an individual rather than a company name. Poorly targeted invoices, caught in the mail-room shuffle, may take a week or more to get to the right party.

"Remember, companies owe you money," Lunn advises, "but people pay the bills. I recommend finding out the names of those people responsible for making your payments and addressing all calls and correspondence to them.

"If you visited all the customers who continuously promise to pay but never do, you'd see from their checkbooks that some of their other vendors get more than empty promises. Why were they paid and not you? Ten to one it's because they've been more aggressive. Most important, they've identified the person who could make the payment."

3. Keep collection correspondence short and to the point—a maximum of 80 words. Long letters do not get read.

4. Revise and update the wording of collection letters once every few years to keep the language fresh and effective. Established customers may know the content of your letters better than you do. Once that degree of familiarity sets in, the correspondence no longer has the desired impact. Keep the message strong and clear—just find different ways to say it.

5. Send a series of dunning letters, generally three or four, gradually stepping up the collection appeal with stronger language, including your intention to enforce payment if the debtor does not cooperate. Give each letter seven to ten days to win payment before following up with a more aggressive appeal.

6. Use the telephone to break collection deadlocks. Speak to the person in charge of your account, discussing the problem on a one-to-one basis.

"The key objective is to try and end the conversation with a firm commitment," the credit executive says, "not a vague promise of 'I'll attempt to send you something near the end of the month.' Better to get a commitment for a smaller amount at a specified time than a promise to pay more in a vague, indefinite period."

7. When payment plans are negotiated, have the debtor back up his pledge with a series of notes, postdated checks, or a letter confirming the arrangements. The objective is to get the debtor committed to retiring the obligation.

Although credit risks go hand in hand with business ownership, there are ways to reduce the possibility of heavy losses from insolvent accounts. One approach calls for an early-warning detection system to short-circuit emerging credit problems before they jeopardize the company's finances.

"The key is to identify those customers who, for one reason or another, may not be able to pay their bills," says Lunn. "By zeroing in on these high-risk accounts before they build up large balances, and by carefully con-trolling or cutting off the flow of credit to them, the small business can prevent horrendous problems from surfacing somewhere down the road.

"There's a simple way to do this. Those accounts likely to wind up in the bad debt column often drop telltale signs that this is imminent. The idea is to monitor these signs and to base credit decisions on them."

Look for the following early-warning signals from your customers:

1. Collection claims, suits, and judgments that are obtained by other suppliers. Subscribe to credit reporting services and trade associations that make this information available. Be certain the reports cover your major customers.

2. Reluctance to provide audited financial statements and bank references. Generally, this means the company has something to hide. "They may try to allay your fears by offering references from other suppliers," Lunn warns, "but this could be a setup. Those writing the references could be in cahoots with your customer or could be the only supplier they pay. As a rule, references are reliable only if you know and can vouch for the parties making them."

3. Partial or erratic payments on account. Customers consistently paying only part of their outstanding invoices may be seeking to appease the creditor while delaying the collection process.

4. Large purchases far exceeding the company's standard orders. This may be a veiled attempt to "stock up" before the credit crunch hits. Quite often, small firms fill only part of a company's orders for finished goods or raw materials, with bigger suppliers getting the lion's share of the contracts. But if the big boys have already shut off the flow of credit, the customer may suddenly be looking to the small company to fill the void. Because there's a definite problem with the account, the company should be wary of this kind of business. Euphoria over the big order has to be tempered by the fact that the account may not be paid. No business is good business if you don't get paid for it.

5. Abrupt or frequent changes of banks. This may indicate banking problems related to bad checks or other irregularities. Keep records of your customers' banks and monitor these relationships from time to time.

6. Pledging inventory to a local bank or finance company. If this is a new development, it may indicate emerging credit problems. It may also complicate legal matters should the creditor be forced to sue.

"Warning signs are not reason enough to curtail credit," says a partner with the accounting firm of Phillips, Gold, "but should be a cue to meet with the customer, to determine if there's a problem and to try and work out a satisfactory solution. Failing that, the company must protect its interests. That might mean shipping on a C.O.D. basis or not shipping at all."

Managing: Break-even Analysis

Break-even analysis can be an approach for dealing intelligently with uncertainty. There are always difficulties in estimating uncertain variables such as demand, but by specifying the levels of other variables such as costs or profit that affect the income of a firm, a required—or minimum—level can be found for the unknown quantity. Any problem requiring income estimation can be set up so that the most difficult variable to estimate is isolated for solution.

Break-even analysis is not a panacea. It's only one of the many tools available to the business decision maker. But it's a good tool with which to begin to approach decision problems.

Imagine a firm, the Acme Company. Acme has a vacant plant equipped sufficiently to produce a number of new products. Fixed costs for this facility are $250,000. Acme is looking at a potential new product for production in this plant. The product, an electric fork, will sell for $10 apiece and has variable costs for materials, labor, overhead, and other items of $7.50 per unit.

At present management feels certain that the market for this product is 2 million units per year. The physical capacity of the plant is 15,000 units per month, or 180,000 per year.

Simple Break-even Analysis

Should Acme make electric forks in its vacant plant? To begin to answer we need to find the contribution margin (CM) for the product. Contribution margin is simply what's left of revenue to cover fixed costs and profits after direct out-of-pocket (i.e., variable) costs have been subtracted; that is:

$$CM = Revenue - Variable\ Costs\ (VC)$$

When you subtract fixed costs (FC) from the contribution margin, you get earnings (before interest and taxes). You can then calculate the break-even level by dividing fixed costs by CM. If CM is expressed on a per-unit basis, the break-even (BE) volume will be expressed in units. If it's expressed as a percent of revenue, the break-even volume will be in dollars.

Let's look at Acme's electric fork project to see how this works.

Contribution on a Per-unit Basis

$$CM = Revenue\ (Price) - Variable\ Cost\ (VC)$$
$$= \$10 - \$7.50$$
$$= \$2.50$$

$$Break\text{-}even\ volume = \frac{Fixed\ Costs\ (FC)}{CM}$$
$$= \frac{\$250,000}{\$2.50}$$
$$= 100,000\ units$$

Contribution as a Percent of Revenue

$$CM\ \% = \frac{Price - VC}{Price}$$
$$= \frac{\$10 - \$7.50}{\$10}$$
$$= \frac{\$2.50}{\$10}$$
$$= 25\%$$

$$BE = \frac{FC}{CM\%}$$
$$= \frac{\$250,000}{25\%}$$
$$= \frac{\$250,000}{.25}$$
$$= \$1,000,000$$

Note that you can get the break-even dollar total by multiplying the break-even volume in units by the selling price or the number of units by dividing total revenue dollars at break-even by price.

What's the answer to Acme's question? Well, the simple answer is that it should go ahead. To break even they need to capture only 100,000 units' worth, or 5 percent, of the estimated market of 2 million units per year. Second, they'll be operating well under the plant's physical capacity of 180,000 units per year at break-even. Acme ought to be able to make a good profit using the vacant facility, if they can capture more than 5 percent of the market. With production and sales at capacity it looks as though they'd make a profit of $200,000 before taxes (80,000 units × $2.50 = $200,000), since all fixed costs will be covered at the 100,000-unit level.

Unfortunately, this is the *simple* answer. There are some difficulties with this easy-as-pie approach to Acme's product question.

Some Shortcomings of Break-even Analysis

The major problem is that no project really exists in isolation. There are alternative uses for the firm's funds in every case. For example, in Acme's case the vacant plant could be leased to another company or used for another product. We must, therefore, always consider not only the value of an individual project, but how it compares to other uses of the funds and facilities.

Nor does break-even analysis permit proper examination of cash flows. It's generally accepted in basic financial theory that the appropriate way to make investment or capital decisions is to consider the value of a proposed project's anticipated cash flows. If the discounted value of the cash flows exceeds the required investment outlay in cash, then the project is acceptable.

There are other objections. Break-even makes many restrictive assumptions about cost-revenue relationships. In normal use it's basically a negative technique, defining constraints rather than looking at benefits, and it's essentially a static tool for analyzing a single period. What all this theory boils down to is that break-even analysis is too simplistic a technique to be used to make *final investment decisions*.

You might well ask then: If that's true, what is break-even good for?

Some Basic Uses for Break-even

1. It's a cheap screening device. Discounted-cash-flow techniques require large amounts of expensive-to-get data. Break-even can tell you whether or not it's worthwhile to do more intensive (and costly) analysis.

2. It provides a handle for designing product specifications. Each design has implications for cost. Costs obviously affect price and marketing feasibility. Break-even permits comparison of possible designs before the specifications are frozen.

For example, in many small businesses a new product with an uncertain volume is often more feasible if it's made with temporary hand tools and jigs rather than with expensive production tooling. The first method typically has higher variable costs but lower fixed costs. This often results in a lower break-even for the project—and lower risks and potential profits. The more automated approach, on the other hand, raises the break-even but also raises the risks and profit potential for the company. Break-even lets you examine these trade-offs.

3. It serves as a substitute for estimating an unknown factor in making project decisions. In deciding whether to go ahead on a project, there are always variables to be considered: demand, costs, price, and miscellaneous factors. When most expenses can be determined, only two missing variables remain, profit (or cash flow) and demand. Demand is usually tougher to estimate. By deciding that profit must at least be zero (the break-even point), you can then fairly simply find the demand you must have to make the project a reasonable undertaking.

You still have to compare the demand

figure at break-even with the market share you think you can capture to judge the worthiness of the project, and you'll have to use your business sense here. But break-even gives you a way to attack uncertainty, to get onto the target if not into the bull's-eye. Let's look at some examples.

Break-even Applied to Uncertainty

Profit Margin
The typical break-even approach develops the volume needed for producing no profit. What if you think you're in business to make a profit?

Using the Acme example, let's say we'd like a 10-percent profit margin on the project. The original contribution margin for the electric fork was 25 percent, but that was at zero profit. In effect, our 10-percent profit acts like a variable cost, so we must adjust CM% accordingly: 25 percent − 10 percent = 15 percent. Now we can calculate break-even using the percent of revenue approach:

$$BE = \frac{FC}{CM\%}$$
$$= \frac{\$250,000}{15\%}$$
$$= \$1,666,667$$
$$\text{(or 166,667 units at \$10 each)}$$

This is still below plant capacity. Acme can now look at the market and make a judgment on the probability of selling that many electric forks.

Dollar Profit
What if Acme wants a fixed dollar profit of $150,000? Here we treat the profit as a fixed cost, so we've got to add it to the fixed cost

established for the plant: $150,000 + $250,000 = $400,000. We can now calculate the break-even volume using the per-unit approach:

$$BE = \frac{FC}{CM}$$
$$= \frac{\$400,000}{(\$10 - \$7.50)}$$
$$= \frac{\$400,000}{\$2.50}$$
$$= 160,000 \text{ units (or \$1,600,000)}$$

Again this is below capacity. And again somebody has to make a judgment on the likelihood of selling this many units.

Maximum Out-of-Pocket Cost
Suppose Acme's management can forecast sales with a degree of assurance. They judge that they can sell 150,000 of the new electric forks each year. What out-of-pocket expenses can they incur and still break even? First, we've got to change the break-even formula a little:

$$BE_{VOL} = \frac{FC}{CM}$$
$$BE_{VOL} \times CM = FC$$
$$CM = \frac{FC}{BE_{VOL}}$$

Now we can find the CM for these circumstances:

$$CM = \frac{\$250,000}{150,000 \text{ units}}$$
$$= \$1.67$$

Subtracting the CM of $1.67 from the selling price of $10, we get $8.33, the variable cost

Acme can incur on each unit and still break even. Similarly, if a $200,000 profit is desired at the proposed volume, we find that the contribution margin equals $450,000 divided by 150,000 units, or $3. At this level of desired profit, variable costs must be held to $7/unit.

This example shows how to use break-even analysis to help set product specifications. By isolating the *allowed* cost structure, the right product structure restrictions can be determined and the product engineered to the cost requirements or abandoned.

Selling Price

Assume again that variable costs for producing the fork are $7.50/unit and there are $250,000 in fixed costs. Add to those data the known sales volume of 150,000 forks and a desire to make a profit of $100,000 per year. What's the selling price?

$$CM = \frac{FC}{BE_{VOL}}$$

$$= \frac{\$250,000 + \$100,000}{150,000 \text{ units}}$$

$$= \frac{\$350,000}{150,000}$$

$$= \$2.33$$

The price must equal variable cost plus fixed cost: $7.50 + $2.33 = $9.83. This $9.83 selling price can now be compared to the existing market price to determine if the Acme fork has a good chance of selling or if the specifications must be altered to get the price down. This approach works well for bidding.

Advertising Decisions

Advertising is essentially a fixed cost. Any added fixed costs raise a firm's break-even point and thus require added revenue (or lowered variable costs) to pay for them. The money for fixed costs comes from the contribution margin.

In the Acme electric fork example CM% is 25 percent. Thus, four additional dollars of revenue are required to cover each additional dollar of fixed cost: $1 ÷ 25 percent = $4. (If the Acme project's CM% were 40%, it would take $2.50 to cover each additional fixed cost dollar, $10 if the CM percent were 10 percent.)

So, if Acme is considering a $2,500 expenditure for an ad, it knows it will need 4 × $2,500 or $10,000 in extra sales just to cover the cost of the ad. Here management isn't trying to guess how much in sales they'll get from the ad. Instead, they know how much they *must* get to be only as well off as they would be without any advertising. This approach provides a built-in standard for judging the results of advertising. If after an appropriate period added sales aren't enough to justify the cost of the ad, it can be abandoned as an approach.

Granting Credit

Suppose Acme is examining a prospective electric fork distributor as a potential credit customer. The distributor expects to buy 500 units per month from Acme. Terms will be net 30 days, and it's conservatively estimated the account will turn over eight times per year. What should Acme do?

First of all, when a new account is taken on, the potential loss for the supplier of credit is the variable cost of the balance carried. In addition, the creditor incurs the costs of carrying and administering the account.

Assume in this case that carrying costs amount to 10 percent of the average balance and administrative costs are fixed at $500 per year for the new account. The average expected balance is found by taking total sales and dividing by turnover.

Average expected balance

$$= \frac{500 \text{ units} \times \$10 \text{ per unit} \times 12 \text{ months}}{8 \text{ times}}$$

$$= \frac{\$60,000}{8}$$

$$= \$7,500$$

Fixed costs for taking on this account are, therefore, 10 percent of this average balance plus the administrative cost: $FC = (\$7,500 \times 10 \text{ percent}) + \$500 = \$1,250$.

To these fixed costs must be added the variable cost of the average balance, 75 percent of $7,500 in this instance. (That's the $7.50/unit variable cost divided by the $10 price—Acme incurs the $2.50/unit fixed cost up to break-even regardless of granting credit or, indeed, selling forks.) So the potential total cost, including possible loss of the outstanding balance, is:

$$\text{Total cost} = (\$7,500 \times 75\,\%) + \$1,250$$

$$= \$5,625 + \$1,250$$

$$= \$6,875$$

Taking into account that with the fork's CM% of 25 percent, $4 of revenue is needed to cover $1 of additional cost:

$$BE_{account} = \$6,875 \times 4$$

$$= \$27,500$$

Thus, Acme needs $27,500 in sales to the distributor to ensure that the account breaks even. Since expected yearly sales are $60,000, the account should hit that volume in under six months. Again, we've reached the point when managerial judgment must be brought into play.

This is not the most sophisticated approach to credit granting, but it does show the expected exposure to loss the account would add. The smaller the contribution margin and the slower the turnover, the higher the risks will be. Knowing the financial circumstances of the firm seeking credit, management can usually judge easily whether or not that firm can pay its bills for six months or whatever the break-even period turns out to be. This is the creative treatment of risk analysis.

Labor Costs

So far the examples have been simple and straightforward. Business life, alas, isn't. In the traditional version of break-even analysis variable costs generally include items such as material, labor, and overhead. In reality, however, some of these costs may not be variable over the operating range of the company.

Here are the figures from the original Acme example in more detailed form:

Product Price	$10.00/unit
Variable Costs	$ 7.50/unit
From: Material	$4.50/unit
Overhead & Other	$ .50/unit
Labor	$2.50/unit
Fixed Costs	$250,000/year

The labor cost is based on five crews of five people each at $10,000 per person per year, with each crew producing 20,000 forks annually.

For simplicity we assumed originally that at any level of production total variable costs were $7.50/unit. People, however, cannot in reality be shifted that smoothly. Thus, in a narrow range of production some labor costs become fixed in effect. This fact can change the break-even point of the firm. It also affects the contribution margin and pricing, promotion, and similar decisions.

Using the traditional approach it looked as though the break-even point was 100,000 units. It also appeared that, if another 10,000 units were made and sold, Acme would make a profit of $25,000 (10,000 units × $2.50 contribution margin per unit). In reality, however, the original break-even represents the effective capacity of the firm. An extra 10,000 units could be produced only if a new crew is put on, at a cost of $50,000. At the 110,000-unit level we actually find:

Sales: 110,000 units @ $10/unit $1,100,000
Less: Material @ $4.50/unit   495,000
       Overhead @ $.50/unit   55,000
       Labor: 6 crews   300,000
       Fixed Costs   250,000
       Profit   0

Credit: U.S. Small Business Administration and Peter Goulet

BOARD OF DIRECTORS

Outsiders Can Strengthen Small Companies

Outside directors—requisites in public corporations—can play a key role in privately held businesses as well. By serving as the owner's confidants, coaches, and alter egos, experienced directors bring a fresh perspective to a small company's managerial style and marketing approach.

Their role is to enhance rather than share business leadership. Typically, the CEO retains full control of the business but looks to the directors as trusted advisers with a wealth of experience in broad business management or specialized functions crucial to the firm's operations.

Candidates for directors include bankers, attorneys, management consultants, and business associates. Those willing to serve do so in order to maintain strong ties with the company or else because they enjoy the professional stimulation the work provides.

"Companies can gain by having a single director, but I recommend they go a step further and assemble a small board of outside advisers," says a partner with the small business practice of Deloitte, Haskins & Sells. "Management benefits enormously by having regular access to a group of people active in various business and professional disciplines.

"A company I know designs and manufactures high-quality custom fabrics. One board member, a patent attorney, provides invaluable advice on protecting the firm's designs, and another member, an executive with one of the company's major customers, offers helpful insights on market trends. Taken together they bring balance, depth, sophistication."

Consider these guidelines for working with outside directors:

1. Do not appoint close friends or family members. Most are reluctant to make the tough statements that may irritate or embarrass the company owner. "Yes men" may be polite, but they do little to improve operations.

2. Look for directors who complement management's strengths. "The business owner strong in sales and marketing is well advised to work with a director experienced in business finance," says a vice-president of Manufacturers Hanover Trust. "This kind of balance usually makes for a more successful company. In fact, we look more favorably on prospective borrowers when they have a good relationship with a sophisticated director."

3. Be prepared to pay directors modest fees, about $250 per meeting, plus expenses.

4. Hold regular meetings, monthly or quarterly, with the dates adjusted to the directors' schedules. Allow for at least two hours per session, giving each member the

opportunity to express himself freely on all business-related subjects.

5. Try to replace directors as they resign or retire from service.

WHERE TO FIND IT

Association of Management
Consulting Firms (ACME)
230 Park Avenue
New York, NY 10169
(212) 697-9693

BUDGETS

Planning and Control

Budgeting offers the best approach to planning and control for a small business.

A budget can take the place—only partly, not completely—of a business plan. Business plans consider "strategic" questions—critical success factors, competitor strengths, market trends, etc.—that cannot be addressed in a budget. However, the budget is a valuable planning tool because it requires explicit assumptions about such fundamentals as unit sales, sales revenue, output, material and labor inputs and costs, and overhead costs for the period. Putting all this down on paper makes it easier to assess whether or not your fundamental assumptions are realistic. Business planning does or could benefit almost all small firms. If it is not going to develop a real business plan, however, a firm should at least make a realistic budget. In addition, a budget is the starting point for a cash-flow forecast—a device that could save you from a cash-flow crisis.

A budget can also be a superb control device. By comparing a detailed set of financial statements to a budget for the period and analyzing variances between them, you can spot trouble. Investigation of "negative" variances may indicate sales shortfalls, uncontrolled costs, or both. If there are no apparent reasons for the variance, accounting errors or willful misappropriation may be revealed.

How to Proceed

Budgeting should normally take place during a firm's "slack" time and get started early enough to allow for appropriate review and revision, perhaps three to four months before the new year. The first step in the budget process is to define company goals for the next year in specific terms. For example, the company may wish to base its budget on a 9-percent growth rate for sales. Budget formulation would then become a matter of finding the most cost-effective way of reaching this goal. In practice, multiple goals (product growth, market penetration, profitability ratios, etc.) will better capture the varied and interconnected aspects of your business.

A budget, divided into increments that correspond to a firm's reporting cycle, is usually developed for one complete fiscal year at a time. Business results should be reported at least monthly and measured against the budget. Any deviations from the budget should be promptly investigated and resolved.

Actual preparation of the detailed budget will usually begin with those people responsible for profits or costs. Involving your people in the budgeting process should strengthen their commitment to achieving the budget's goals. In addition, to facilitate review and subsequent comparison, consult your firm's accountant or bookkeeper to ensure that the budget uses the same format and accounting principles as the internal financial statements. Budgets for sales, production, etc., should use assumptions that support company goals. One way of enforcing this is to insist that each functional budget list the assumptions behind it. These lists will indicate the level of thought that went into preparation and better enable you to review each budget. In addition, documentation of assumptions will facilitate later analysis of variances between the budget and actual results.

Once the proposed budgets for the company's various activities are complete, they should be integrated into a company-wide budget. The owner-manager should then review the full budget to ensure that it represents a realistic approach to company goals. After discussion, any questionable items must be approved or revised. You must also be alert to interrelationships among functions. For example, to what extent will a budgeted increase in sales activities increase demands on supporting services, such as accounting or personnel?

For most companies, the major budget items are those that add to the cost of sales figures. In wholesale or retail, this is typically based on estimates of the next year's product cost from major vendors or on a historical trend adjusted for known changes. In services, it is based on a collection of the direct costs to provide known levels of service, which may be adjusted for growth. In manufacturing, direct labor and material costs can readily be determined. Factory overhead, however, is difficult to budget because there are two kinds of overhead costs—fixed and variable.

Fixed overhead includes charges such as rent and salaries that must be paid regardless of production volume. Variable overhead includes costs that change with production volume, such as maintenance or electricity. A charge for both types of overhead must be absorbed by each unit manufactured, just as each unit absorbs a direct labor and a direct material charge. This is normally calculated by determining the total fixed overhead and adding to it the variable overhead based on anticipated production volume. This total overhead can then be allocated to units produced based on expected production.

Financial Reporting

From a control standpoint, a budget becomes valuable when you use it as a benchmark against which to assess actual results. Accordingly, your financial reporting system should provide you with meaningful and timely information. Many managers of smaller businesses, particularly those without a strong background in finance, leave report content and format to their accountant or bookkeeper. This individual, however, may not be aware of your reporting objectives and may base a format solely on ease of preparation.

Generally, monthly financial reports should include a detailed income statement, with an appropriate breakout of departmental or product line contribution margin, and a balance sheet. Such reports should also compare current year-to-date results with prior year-to-date and budgeted year-to-date results. Variances of current results from prior year results and from budgeted results should be expressed in dollars and as a percentage of the budgeted amount for analytical purposes. Copies of this comparison should be given to you, and appropriate portions to responsible managers for explanations of their department's variances. Together, determine what corrective steps should be taken.

The budget process normally extends over a year, during which budgets are submitted, reviewed, revised, adopted, compared to actual, and sometimes modified due to changing circumstances. But how should all this be implemented? Some argue that the budget should be "realistic," others that it be ambitious. Some feel that the budget should be held constant no matter what; others that budgets should be revised periodically to reflect major changes in circumstances.

These implementation choices tend to hinge on the principal emphasis of the owner-manager. If it is planning, the budget should probably be modified to meet changing circumstances. You may also want to adopt a *rolling budget,* budgeting for a "fifth" quarter as you finish the first quarter in any four-quarter period. If your emphasis is on control, it is probably best to keep the budget constant during the year. Chances are this will minimize the effort involved without sacrificing control. In either case, the budget for a small firm should be realistic.

Forecasting Cash Flow

A budget is the starting point for development of a cash-flow forecast. A business can show a profit yet have difficulty in paying bills and meeting payrolls. This is especially true if the business is growing; for the sake of growth, management may invest heavily in inventories and extend more credit. Such things tie up cash.

Budgets and cash-flow forecasts differ:

- Depreciation and amortization are not cash expenditures. If they are contained in the budget, as is proper, they should be eliminated from the cash-flow forecast.
- Credit sales generate cash only when the receivables are collected. If the average collection period is 30 days, sales of one

month will not be collected until the following month.
- Purchases and other expenses, such as interest on debt, are often recorded when incurred but paid at some subsequent date. The payment date may be contractual (payroll, interest payments, etc.) or discretionary (e.g., payables can be deferred until suppliers balk). Some assumptions must be made as to when claims on cash will be paid.
- Additional debt or equity in the business provides more cash.
- Cash is frequently used for capital investments. While budgets include periodic depreciation charges for plant and equipment, cash-flow forecasts show the entire initial outlay when a capital investment is made.
- Finally, dividends and taxes on income are cash drains. These payments can generally be scheduled.

The cash-flow forecast starts with an opening cash balance, usually the balance at the beginning of the year. The addition of cash-inflow items gives you total Cash Available. Deduction then of cash-outflow items indicates Net Cash Available or Required.

The partial worksheet below could be used to forecast cash flow for three months of a twelve-month period. It should suffice as a broad management tool. While cash flow may appear manageable over a twelve-month period, however, it may not be on a day-to-day basis. You should review the timing of cash inflows and outflows during each month to lessen the possibility of a missed payroll, unnecessary borrowing, or idle cash. Having developed a cash-flow forecast, you will have a preliminary idea of your needs and resources throughout the period. The next step is to compare, on a monthly basis,

CASH-FLOW FORECAST (PARTIAL)

Item	January	February	March
Cash at Period Beginning			
Add: Cash Sales			
Collection of Receivables			
Interest Income			
Miscellaneous Receipts			
Planned Borrowing			
Planned Equity Issue			
Capital Asset Sales			
Total Cash Available			
Deduct: Material Purchases			
Payroll			
Payments on			
—Manufacturing Expense			
—Sales Expense			
—G&A			
—Payroll Taxes			
—Interest			
—Debt Principal			
—Income Tax			
—Other Expenses			
Capital Expenditures			
Dividends or Withdrawals			
Total Cash Available (Required)			
Additional Borrowing			
Cash at Period End			

your forecast to actual cash inflow and outflow. This not only gives you an idea of where your original forecast went astray, to improve future forecasts, but allows you to pinpoint problem areas (e.g., slow collections).

While a budget will help you plan and control your business, a cash-flow forecast will help ensure that you effectively manage your most valuable resource—cash.

Credit: Price Waterhouse, *Business Review Newsletter*

AT A GLANCE

Business Records—How Long to Hold On

Accounting	Retention Period
Auditors' reports	Indefinitely
Bank reconciliations	1 year
Bank statements and deposit slips	3 years
Cash books	Indefinitely
Charts of accounts	Indefinitely
Checks—canceled—payroll and general	7 years
Depreciation schedules	Indefinitely
Dividend checks—canceled	6 years
Expense reports	5 years
Financial statements—end of year	Indefinitely
Fixed assets detail	Indefinitely
General ledgers and journals	Indefinitely
Inventory of products, materials, and supplies	7 years
Payroll—time cards	3 years
—individual time reports and earnings records	8 years
Subsidiary ledgers (including accounts receivable and accounts payable)	7 years
Trial balances—monthly	7 years
Vouchers—for payments to vendors, employees, etc.	8 years

Corporate Records	
Bylaws, charter, minute books	Indefinitely
Capital stock and bond records	Indefinitely
Checks—taxes, property, and settlement of important contracts	Indefinitely
Contracts and agreements still in effect	Indefinitely
Copyrights and trademark registrations	Indefinitely
Deeds and easements	Indefinitely
Labor contracts	Indefinitely
Mortgages, notes, and leases—expired	7 years
Patents	Indefinitely
Proxies	Indefinitely
Retirement and pension records	Indefinitely
Tax returns and working papers—revenue agents' reports	Indefinitely

Correspondence	
General	1 year
Legal and tax	Indefinitely
License, traffic, and purchase	6 years
Production	8 years
Routine—customers and vendors	1 year

Insurance	Retention Period
Accident reports	5 years
Claims—after settlement	7 years
Fire inspection reports	6 years

(Continued)

Accounting	Retention Period
Group disability records	8 years
Policies—all types—expired	4 years
Safety reports	8 years

Personnel	
Contracts—expired	6 years
Daily time reports	6 years
Disability and sick benefit records	6 years
Employment applications	3 years
Personnel files—terminated	6 years
Withholding tax statements	6 years

Purchasing and Sales	
Purchase orders	3 years
Requisitions	3 years
Sales contracts	3 years
Sales invoices	3 years

Traffic—Receiving and Shipping	
Export declarations	4 years
Freight bills	4 years
Manifests	4 years
Shipping and receiving reports	4 years
Waybills and bills of lading	4 years

Credit: Peat Marwick, "Tax Planning for the Owner-Managed Business"

CASH PARKING LOTS

How to Make Your Money Make Money

Your business is closed for the weekend. Lights off, doors locked, employees gone till Monday. No chance to make money until the new week rolls around. Or so you think. By investing in cash parking lots, your money can be working while you're not.

Here's how: If you're like most small businesses, you keep substantial balances in your checking account, allowing the cash to sit idle until it is needed to pay bills. But that only enriches the bankers at your expense. They have use of the money without compensating you. The solution is to invest idle balances in interest-paying accounts—called cash parking lots—that turn your money into more money.

Cash parking lots vary by term, yield, and level of safety. Which investment is right for your business depends on the amount of time the money will be available for investment and your appetite for risk. Consider the following options:

1. Sweep accounts function like standard

checking accounts except that all balances above a minimum level needed to compensate the bank for its services are automatically invested by the bank for your benefit. Instead of sitting idle, funds earn interest until they are released to cover checks written on the account. Because the sweep is made daily, after all checks have been processed against the account, the money is invested whenever it can earn money for your business—even overnight and on weekends.

The sweep feature, now offered as a cash-management service by many banks, is attractive because it shifts responsibility for investment from the business owner to the bank. You don't have to remember to invest the money: it's all done by the bank's computers. Yields, which fluctuate daily, vary from bank to bank but are generally competitive with money-market rates.

Safety also varies according to the bank's underlying insurance. If deposits are insured by the Federal Deposit Insurance Corporation (FDIC) or the Federal Savings & Loan Insurance Corporation (FSLIC), funds in the sweep accounts are also insured for up to $100,000 per account. Considering the recent failures of certain state-backed deposit insurance companies, it may be prudent to stick with those banks offering federal coverage.

2. Bank money-market accounts may be used when the sweep features are not available at your bank. Think of this option as a sweep without the automated feature. It works this way: You open two accounts at your bank, a standard checking account and a money-market account. Whenever balances in the former are large enough to invest—this may be as little as $1,000—you instruct the bank to transfer the funds to the latter and to return the money to the checking account when it will be needed again.

"Companies directing the movement of

their funds in and out of money-market accounts should get in the habit of making one last call before they go home on the weekends," a partner and cash-management specialist with Peat Marwick, CPAs. "That's to their banker, telling him to invest excess balances in their account until Monday morning. Because checks are never presented for payment on Saturday or Sunday, there's no reason to keep the money in a demand account when it can be put to work collecting interest."

One drawback is that some banks may limit the number of money-market transfers to between six and ten a month. Faced with this restriction, you may want to shift funds only when idle balances exceed a minimum level, say, $10,000. Another option is to invest idle cash in nonbank money-market funds, offered by mutual-fund families. These popular parking lots allow for unlimited deposits and withdrawals. The funds invest in a variety of money-market instruments, including T-bills and commercial paper, and are considered quite stable. Yields tend to be equivalent or slightly higher than bank money-market accounts but unlike the latter are generally uninsured. For those to whom safety is paramount, this risk, no matter how slight, must be weighed.

3. Cash-management accounts, offered by brokerage firms and insurance companies, provide a mix of services including a choice of money-market funds (standard, government instruments, and tax-exempt), check writing, and overdraft privileges. Most are uninsured and charge monthly or annual fees varying with the size and activity of the account.

This option is favored by those companies seeking to consolidate various financial functions, including securities holdings, in a single account. Because they offer a variety of investment options, cash-management accounts can serve as short- and long-term cash parking lots.

4. Certificates of deposit, generally issued in amounts over $500, can be used to park cash from a week to a year or more. Regardless of the term, investors are assured of a fixed rate of return. Unlike money-market funds, yields do not fluctuate with prevailing interest rates.

As a sweetener, companies with more than $100,000 to invest can often negotiate with their bank for a higher CD rate. Shopping around among various banks may also boost the yield. Depending on its need for money, a local competitor may offer a rate that is half a point or more above that of your regular bank.

CDs can go a long way in the peace-of-mind department. They are covered by the bank's underlying insurance, and because the rate is fixed, you know precisely how much money will be available to you at maturity.

Assume that the ABC Company collects $250,000 in January on the sale of a warehouse and must hold onto the money until June, when it will be used as the down payment on a new facility. Rather than dumping the cash in its checking account, management purchases a 7.6 percent (annual percentage rate), six-month CD that will pay $259,500 at maturity. By putting the money to work, ABC winds up with an extra $9,500 that can be applied to the cost of the property.

One caveat is that CDs are less liquid than sweep accounts or money-market funds. Should the cash be needed before the maturity date, you may have to pay a penalty for early withdrawal.

5. Qualified dividends funds—a quantum leap up the risk curve—are an interesting and little-known option for companies seeking to profit on longer term capital investments (six months or more). The funds have dual objectives: to earn a high level of current income through investments in a portfolio composed primarily of common and preferred stock and to gain capital appreciation on these securities.

The major attraction is in the funds' ability to act as a quasi-tax shelter. Because of the so-called dividend exclusion rule, corporations investing in qualified dividend funds can exclude from taxes 85 percent of that portion of the funds' dividends earned from common and preferred stock. In a typical example, Fidelity's Qualified Dividend Fund (QDF), about 90 percent of the dividends are eligible for this tax benefit.

Unlike money-market funds, which have a fixed net-asset value per share (generally $1), qualified dividend funds are subject to changes in value reflecting gains or losses in the underlying portfolio. On the upside, corporate shareholders can register capital gains as well as current income. But the opportunity to gain also carries the risk of loss. Should the net-asset value decline at the time the shares are redeemed, the corporation may find that it has less capital than it invested. One way to limit the risk—and with it the upside potential as well—is to invest in adjustable-rate preferred funds, which offer the dividend exclusion with less price volatility.

"Whatever approach you take, get in the habit of investing every penny of your idle balances," the CPA advises. "The results can be dramatic. When a small manufacturer of consumer goods started shifting its cash from demand accounts to various cash parking lots, management collected an extra $35,-000 a year in interest—enough to pay its utility bills—just by making the company's money work for a living too."

CONSUMER CREDIT

Categories of Consumer Credit

Consumer credit is divided into two categories, namely, purchase credit and loan credit. The consumer uses purchase credit to acquire merchandise from retail stores or to obtain services of various kinds. The consumer uses loan credit to borrow from banks, finance companies, credit unions, savings and loan associations, and other kinds of lenders.

Purchase credit. There are several types of purchase credit offered by retailers. The title affixed to each type may vary, but basically they are variations of the charge account, or ordinary open account, in which the customer arranges for credit service on a short-term basis of usually 30 days. This is generally thought of as a cash transaction where the credit privilege is offered as a convenience to the customer.

By the late 1920s, retail credit began to be recognized as a tool to increase sales volume. To meet the demands of customers for big ticket merchandise, i.e., furniture, refrigerators, etc., retailers started to use the installment credit purchase account more extensively. Under this plan, purchase arrangements were set forth in a contract, usually a conditional sales contract. Such contracts allow consumers to have use of some durable goods while paying for the items over a given number of months. A finance charge is added to cover the costs of extending this service privilege.

As the use of retail credit widened, credit managers developed further variations of the ordinary open account. The budget account, for instance, allows the consumer to purchase goods and pay for them over a specific number of months in regular installments. A charge is made for the credit service and a down payment is required.

In another variation, the revolving account, a fixed amount of credit is predetermined by the customer and the credit manager. The customer usually pays nothing down in advance, since no debt is incurred until a purchase is made.

The advantage of this type of account is that it allows the customer to purchase needs up to the ceiling. At the end of the month, the customer pays an agreed amount on the account, say one-sixth if the account is for six months' duration. The customer is then in an open-to-buy position and can purchase again until the ceiling is reached. A finance charge is made for this convenience.

The term option account, a third variation, has become common in retailing. This is a combination of the open account and the revolving account. Under this plan, the customer may pay in full when billed at the end of the month, or elect to make a partial payment and carry the balance over to the succeeding month. Thus, the customer pays a finance charge only if the revolving account plan is used. The charge is made only on the amount carried forward.

Loan credit. While loan credit is not granted by retailers, consumers use it to purchase merchandise from them. In the past, these loans were obtained mainly for the liquidation of indebtedness to retailers and others. By consolidating many obligations into one debt, the consumer can make smaller payments to one financial institution and eventually work his or her way toward solvency.

Credit cards. Credit cards have had a dramatic effect upon the various categories of consumer credit. There are several kinds of credit cards, notably those used for "travel and entertainment." Then there are the so-called TBA (tires, batteries, and accessories) cards issued by the large oil companies. These are most frequently used for the purchase of gasoline. The fastest growing cards are those issued by banks.

Credit Reporting Services

One reason that the extension of credit to the consumer has been so successful is the unique service of the credit bureau. This organization collects pertinent data on citizens living in the trading area who use credit. Businesses that need the service belong to the credit bureau and help to keep its files current by recording their customer experience in this depository. For the customer with a good credit record, and this constitutes 95 percent of the purchasers, credit extension is an almost routine matter.

Should a Retailer Offer Credit?

This is a question that retailers have to decide for themselves. A decision will depend largely upon what the competition is doing. Business survival is dependent upon meeting competition and making a profit.

In some lines of retail business, credit service is a must. This applies to durable as well as nondurable goods. Especially when a product carries a manufacturer's suggested sales price, the merchant who does not offer credit service is at a decided sales disadvantage.

Providing retail credit requires considerably more cash than is necessary in a cash-and-carry business. The cost of merchandise—not to mention the profit—is not returned to the credit retailer for at least one month and, in some instances, not for one to three years. As an example, under certain conditions it is estimated that a merchant will need $35,000 to $40,000 to carry install-ment sales credit amounting to $10,000 a month. However, the additional income produced through a finance charge will eventually warrant the extra cost of offering credit. Then, too, the offering of credit generates additional sales.

Of course, the extension of credit has its disadvantages, especially if the customer fails to repay in full. When collections begin to fall off on accounts receivable, capital reserves must be drawn upon in order to continue in business. Attempts to recover unpaid accounts through professional collectors may help, if placed in time. Unfortunately, as the accounts receivable age, chances for collection decline rapidly.

Should Retailers Have Their Own Credit Departments?

Most large retailers prefer to conduct their own credit departments. They believe there is a great deal of store loyalty generated through credit service. Whether customers come in to pay their accounts or simply mail their checks in payment, merchants know that customers shop more regularly where they have credit accounts.

Retailers tend to look upon credit customers as repeat business and cash customers as one-timers. This is not necessarily true, but it does have some merit. Credit customers also tend to spend more than cash customers. The credit department is no longer considered a nonproductive department because it generates sales and produces income from finance charges.

A great many retailers delegate the management of their credit departments to local banks, national credit card companies, and charge plans. These plans also give retailers access to a larger number of potential credit customers than they would if they ran their own credit departments. For a small percentage of the sales check, the specialized plan takes over the credit functions of the retailer, usually on a nonrecourse basis. It leaves retailers free to concentrate on increasing their sales volume. One must continue, however, to keep up with the changes taking place in the consumer credit industry. Should the retailer ever decide to leave the community plan, it may be necessary to organize one's own credit department.

The Federal Consumer Credit Law

On May 29, 1968, the President of the United States signed into law a federal regulatory statute known as the Consumer Credit Protection Act of 1968. Consumer credit transactions between sellers and lenders and the vast number of buyers and borrowers are regulated by the act, which became effective as of July 1, 1969. In addition to containing truth-in-lending features, the act applies to credit advertising, wage garnishments, and extortionate credit transactions. The law is administered through the Board of Governors of the Federal Reserve System and eight other federal agencies. The act has been amended to include consumer credit reporting and the regulation of unsolicited credit cards.

The Fair Credit Billing Act (FCBA) and the Equal Credit Opportunity Act (ECOA) were passed by the 93rd Congress, both effective October 28, 1977. The FCBA regulates methods and procedures creditors may use in billing credit card accounts and other revolving accounts upon which they impose a finance charge. The ECOA prohibits discrimination in the granting of any form of credit on the basis of sex or marital status.

Several states have also passed the Uniform Consumer Credit Code.

Data Processing in Credit

Recent developments in electronic data processing are being applied to the field of retailing and credit reporting. The retail credit and collection departments have welcomed this development because it speeds up the processing of vast amounts of paperwork, gives the credit manager a daily readout on the volume of credit sales and payments on account, and shows up delinquent accounts before they have a chance to age.

WHERE TO FIND IT

Small Business Administration
Washington, DC 20416

SBA issues several series of management and technical publications designed for owner-managers and prospective owners of small business.

Listings of these publications may be requested from SBA, P.O. Box 15434, Ft. Worth, TX 76119.

Ask for Free Management Assistance Publications (SBA 115A) and For-Sale Booklets (SBA 115B). The lists are free and may be used for ordering the free series from SBA or the for-sale series from Superintendent of Documents (GPO).

Small Business Bibliography, free. Each title deals with a specific kind of business or business function, giving reference sources in a manner similar to this bibliography. Reference listings are updated upon request to SBA as reprints are scheduled. Also, complete revision of each title is scheduled periodically.

> *Retailing* (**SBB 10**)
> *Basic Library Reference Sources* (**SBB 18**)
> *Data Processing in Small Business* (**SBB 80**)

Small Marketers Aids (four to eight-page leaflets), free. Each title gives guidance on a specific subject related to a small retail, wholesale, or service business.

Analyze Your Records to Reduce Cost (**SMA 130**)

Marketing Checklist for Small Retailers (**SMA 156**)

Small Business Management Series (for-sale booklets; prices vary, GPO).
The series covers a wide range of small business subjects; each booklet discusses one subject in depth.

Insurance and Risk Management for Small Business (**SBMS 30**) GPO.

Financial Recordkeeping for Small Stores (**SBMS 32**) GPO.

Credit: U.S. Small Business Administration

COSTING AND PRICING

Costing and Pricing Services

Many small businesses are not making a profit today because they do not know the basic concepts of costing and pricing. The situation is most serious in the service business because each service performed has a different cost. Frequently, the service business must bid for jobs by making a price quotation in competition with similar businesses. Can you calculate your costs for your service and quote a price that is competitive and returns a profit?

Without realizing what they are doing, some business owners set their selling price below their total cost. This may result in more business for the company, but a loss will be incurred on each sale. Occasionally, a small business owner who lacks a knowledge of costing will try to compensate by setting prices very high. The result is that the business is not price competitive and does not attract sufficient customers to survive. Frequently, a business earns a profit on some services and loses money on others without knowing which earn a profit and which incur a loss. The year-end income statement combines the profits and losses from the various services performed over the year. Therefore, it is impossible to determine the profitability of specific service jobs from a year-end income statement.

Use a simplified approach to cost accounting that reflects the needs of the small business and reports the cost with reasonable accuracy. The total cost of producing any service is composed of three parts: (1) the material cost, (2) the labor cost, and (3) the overhead cost. Direct materials and direct labor + overhead = total cost of service.

Cost Determination

Direct material cost. The direct material cost is made up of the cost to you for parts and supplies that are used on specific jobs. Once the list of parts and supplies to be used is developed, a check with the supplier will give an up-to-date material cost. The shipping and other handling (storage, etc.) costs for the parts should be included in the material cost.

Direct labor cost. The direct labor cost includes those labor costs identified with a specific service job. The labor cost involved in providing a service is determined by multiplying the number of direct labor hours required by the cost per direct labor hour. It is very important to determine accurately the number of direct labor hours involved to complete the service; therefore, you must use a time clock, worksheet, or a daily time card for each employee to determine the exact amount of labor time spent on each service job.

The hourly cost of direct labor can be figured (priced) two ways: (1) It can be the hourly wage only, with fringe benefits, Social Security, workers' compensation, etc. (all labor-related costs), allocated to overhead. (2) The hourly direct labor cost can include the hourly wages plus the employer's contribution to Social Security, unemployment compensation, disability, holidays and vacations, hospitalization, and other fringe benefits (payroll costs).

By this second method, the added payroll costs for vacations, holidays, and benefits are expressed as percentages of direct hourly wages. For instance, if two weeks of vacation and ten holidays are given annually, this amounts to four weeks per year, or 7.7 percent (i.e., four weeks off divided by fifty-two weeks $\frac{4}{52} = 7.7$ percent), of total labor cost was for time off. Thus, to determine the total direct labor cost per hour by this method, you must add the prorated cost of the payroll taxes, workers' compensation, holidays and vacation pay, hospitalization, etc., to the hourly wage paid. As a rule of thumb, the sum of the various payroll-benefit costs have generally been in the range of 20 to 30 percent of the hourly wages paid. It is more complicated to figure but more precise to use the higher labor cost (including labor-related payroll costs in addition to hourly wages in direct labor costs).

Overhead cost. Overhead includes all job-related costs other than direct materials and direct labor. Your overhead cost depends on which of the two ways you figured direct labor costs, with or without the labor-related payroll-benefits costs. If you did not include these expenses in direct labor, then you must include them in overhead. In our examples, however, these labor-related costs are included in direct labor and not in overhead. Either way the effect on the total job cost is the same, but your overhead cost varies accordingly.

Because they may not know how to allocate (or assign) overhead costs to the services performed, many small business owner-managers miscalculate or avoid considering overhead costs.

Overhead is the indirect cost of the service and is made up of indirect materials, indirect labor, and other indirect costs related to particular services. Indirect materials are too minor to include as direct material costs, e.g., incidental supplies and machine lubricants. Indirect labor is the wages, salaries, and other payroll-benefit costs incurred by workers who do *not* perform the service but who support the main service function, such as clerical, supply, and janitorial employees. Other costs, such as taxes, depreciation, insurance, and transportation, are also part of the overhead cost because the service cost includes a portion of all indirect costs (overhead).

· To figure the portion of overhead related to particular services or jobs, you allocate the various overhead costs by calculating the overhead rate.

The way you calculate the overhead rate should relate the overhead costs to the primary cause for the overhead cost being expended, reflecting a reasonable amount of total overhead to each service. The overhead rate can be expressed as a decimal, as a percentage, or as an hourly rate. The use of the overhead rate helps to assure that all the overhead costs expended throughout the year will be recovered as the business's services are sold throughout the year.

In a situation where employee wages vary a lot, as when higher-paid employees work with more expensive equipment, the overhead cost is allocated on the basis of direct labor cost. This occurs because a large proportion of the overhead cost will consist of equipment depreciation (other indirect cost), interest on the capital invested in equipment, and electrical costs. The overhead rate is determined as follows:

$$(1)\ \text{Overhead Rate} = \frac{\text{Total Overhead Cost}}{\text{Total Direct Labor Cost}}$$

This is the most common method for allocating overhead cost to the specific service performed. The above rate is suitable for machine shops and auto repair shops.

In some cases there is relatively little difference in the hourly wages paid to different employees. In other cases, no relationship exists between the level of the worker's skill and the amount of equipment used by the worker. Under such circumstances, total overhead cost may be allocated on the basis of direct labor hours as follows:

$$(2)\ \text{Overhead Rate} = \frac{\text{Total Overhead Cost}}{\text{Total Direct Labor Hours}}$$

The above rate is suitable for businesses such as secretarial services or janitorial services. The overhead costs result mainly from the work space, supervision, and electricity that the workers need in order to provide the service. Using formula (2), it is possible to determine the overhead cost per hour per employee.

Calculating the overhead cost. In determining the total overhead cost, a small business should not depend solely on last year's income statement. Due to inflation and business growth, last year's overhead cost does not accurately reflect today's overhead cost. The best approach is to project the overhead costs for the near future, that is, the anticipated overhead expenses for the next six months to one year. The projected overhead cost will reflect additional administrative salaries, the depreciation of new equipment that the business plans to purchase, rent increases, energy cost increases, etc.

To ensure that all overhead costs are included, it is best to project the overhead costs for a full fiscal year. This aids in the treatment of expenses that occur only once each year, such as business licenses.

Cost calculation example. Perhaps the most common type of service business is the repair business. The cost calculation procedure illustrated here for the repair business can be used for other types of service businesses. The only precaution that needs to be taken is that the appropriate overhead rate formula which reflects the business's operation, as discussed above, be used in the calculation.

It has been estimated, based upon previous experience, that a specific repair job will require $20 of parts and 2 hours of labor by an employee whose labor cost is $5.00 per hour (these estimates will be used throughout this example). As discussed earlier, the total cost of producing any service is composed of: (1) the material cost, (2) the labor cost, and (3) the overhead cost.

To determine the material cost (the cost of the parts), check the cost of the part in your inventory or get a price quote from your parts supplier. A parts wholesaler is the source of the $20 material cost in this example.

To determine the total direct labor cost, the number of hours of direct labor used is multiplied by the actual direct labor cost per hour. An employee whose actual direct labor cost is $5.00 per hour, including payroll taxes and fringe benefits (see Table 1), requires two hours to complete the repair job.

Labor Cost = Direct Labor Cost per Hour × Hours Required

Labor Cost = $5.00 per Hour × 2 Hours

Labor Cost = $10.00

The nature of the repair business is that overhead costs are more directly related to direct labor costs than to direct material costs. The total projected direct labor cost including payroll taxes and fringe benefits was determined to be $50,003.20. The formula selected to determine the overhead rate based upon the direct labor cost is:

$$\text{Overhead Rate} = \frac{\text{Total Overhead Cost}}{\text{Total Direct Labor Cost}}$$

$$= \frac{\$100,000}{\$50,003.20}$$

$$= \$2.00$$

In most small businesses, the overhead rate is between one and two (i.e., between 100 and 200 percent of the direct labor cost). Businesses that are very labor-intensive, such as a janitorial service, will have an overhead rate much less than 100 percent.

To determine the overhead cost allocated to a specific job, the labor cost is multiplied by the overhead rate as shown below.

$$\text{Overhead Cost} = \text{Direct Labor Cost} \times \text{Overhead Rate}$$

$$= \$10.00 \times 2.00$$

$$= \$20.00$$

To determine the total cost of the repair job, the material cost, the direct labor cost, and the overhead cost are added together:

Material Cost	$20.00
Direct Labor Cost	10.00
Overhead Cost	20.00
Total	$50.00

Pricing

Calculate the profit and add it to the total cost to get the price to charge for the service, in this case a repair job. Prices charged by competitors (similar service businesses), economic conditions of supply and demand, and legal, political, and consumer pressures all influence the profit you can expect for your service and hence the price you can charge

for your jobs. Inflation, the amount of business you have (i.e., number of jobs), and your productivity (the efficiency and quality of your business and service) also affect your profit and the way you figure your prices. You can choose from several pricing methods. Common business practice is to express profit as a percentage of the base used for pricing calculations no matter which pricing method you use.

Pricing alternatives. In considering the total cost of the repair job discussed above, the material cost can normally be predicted with a high degree of accuracy. Labor and overhead costs cannot be predicted with such a high degree of accuracy. An employee may not feel well on a given day or there may be an equipment breakdown; either will result in higher-than-expected labor costs. A provision to adjust for fluctuating labor and overhead costs can be established through your approach to profit. The profit can be applied to the three costs independently, allowing for variations in labor and overhead costs among jobs. For example, a 10 percent profit on material, a 30 percent profit on direct labor, and a 30 percent profit on overhead can be used to determine the price of the service.

Material Cost + Profit of Material
$20 + $20 × 10% = $22.00 $2
Direct Labor Cost + Profit on Direct Labor
$10 + $10 × 30% = $13.00 $3
Overhead Cost + Profit on Overhead
$20 + $20 × 30% = $26.00 $6
$50 Cost $61.00 Price $11 Profit

The concept of applying a different rate of profit on the three underlying costs (material, labor, and overhead) is one method of dealing with the large difference in predictability of costs that exists between labor and materials in most service businesses. To reflect the fluctuations in utilization and cost of labor and overhead from job to job, your profit on labor and overhead should normally be higher than profits on materials.

Direct cost pricing With this method you set your selling price based on direct cost, that is, on direct materials (DM) and direct labor (DL). DM of $20 plus DL of $10 equals Direct Costs of $30. Overhead (OH) costs are $20; so to earn the $11 profit you need, your selling price must be at least $31 above your direct costs. To find the percentage of profit on direct cost to charge, divide direct costs into overhead plus needed profit:

$$\$31\ (\$11 + \$20) \div \$30 = 103\tfrac{1}{3}\%$$

$$\text{Proof: } \$30 \times 103\tfrac{1}{3}\% = \$30 \times 1.033 = \$11$$

Profit margin pricing. This profit rate is expressed as a percentage of your full costs. Full cost is divided into the needed profit to get the percentage of profit margin:

$$\$11 \div \$50 = 22\%$$

$$\text{Proof: } \$50 \times 22\% = \$11$$

Profit can also be figured as percentages of assets used on the job. This method is called return-on-asset pricing. Thus, full cost per job plus the needed profit (rate of profit times the amount of assets used per job) equals the job price: $50 + ($80 × 14%) = $50 + $11 = $61. One of the most widely used pricing methods for service-oriented businesses is time and material pricing. Time is expressed as the labor cost per hour, calculated as (1) direct labor (DL) and payroll-benefits (see Direct Labor Cost explanation), including (2) overhead (OH) costs not related to materials and (3) needed profit. Material cost is the direct material (DM) cost and overhead (OH) plus 30 percent for needed profit. (Note that

overhead has been allocated to labor and materials.)

Time:
DL $5 per hr. × 2 hrs. = $10
OH $7 per hr. × 2 hrs. = $14
                          ____
                          24
                     7 needed profit
                          ____
                          $31

Material:
DM $20
OH   3
      ____
      $23 + ($23 × 30%) =
            $23 + $9 (profit) = $30
                                ____
                                $61

In most small repair businesses, there is not a large amount of overhead cost associated with obtaining parts besides a telephone call to order them. Charging a large amount of overhead to parts may result in pricing yourself out of the market.

By all these methods you are deriving a selling price for your service. Sometimes, however, you start with the selling price already established—by competition or economic conditions. Then you must figure out the most cost you can incur and still earn your needed profit.

Summary

The total cost of producing a service is composed of direct material, direct labor, and overhead costs. This cost information is used as a basis for setting prices and profit. From alternative pricing methods you select one that earns a satisfactory profit and is easy for you to use. Given regulations, competition, and the economy, you must have a pricing strategy that keeps your service competitive and profitable. The more exactly you figure your costs and set prices, the greater your chances for continued and profitable business.
Credit: U.S. Small Business Administration and James Salvate, Ph.D.

CREDIT AND COLLECTIONS

How to Put Cash in Your Hands

Small businesses strapped for cash may find the money they need is there for the asking. By being more aggressive with customers and suppliers—and by changing company policies accordingly—management can generate thousands of dollars in working capital. In many cases, it's a matter of challenging traditions and breaking bad habits.

A good example is the widespread practice of requesting customer payments in 30 days. All too often, this ties up cash a month or more beyond the time it could be working for the company. By changing payment terms to 15 days or less, management bolsters cash flow and reduces the need for costly borrowing.

"Many companies establish payment terms of net 30 days when they first start out in business—and stick with it over the years—because they feel they have to match their competitors," says an executive with Mid-Continent Adjustment Company, credit and collection consultants. "But that's not always the case. When a computer maintenance company changed its terms from 30 days to payment due upon receipt of invoice—in other words, to immediate payment—its customers didn't balk. Because the company's prices were 20 percent below major competitors, it could demand faster payment.

"Some companies that stay with traditional 30-day payment terms for fear of alienating customers may find that this fear is ill-founded."

Payment terms are only the tip of the iceberg. By taking a number of critical steps to accelerate collections and delay disbursements, small companies can shift the float in their favor, putting more cash at management's disposal—cash that can be used to pay the bills, to expand the company, or to produce investment income.

Consider these effective, but often overlooked, cash-management techniques:

1. Send invoices as soon as a sale is made. "Many companies have the bad habit of waiting days or weeks to send out their bills," the credit executive says. "That's a sure way to slow the payment cycle. Instead, they should send invoices the day the deal is made—in some cases, even before the product is shipped. Although customers won't pay until they get delivery, at least the billing cycle is underway when they do.

"For example, assume ABC Company gets an order June 1 and immediately bills the customer with a June 1 invoice for net due in 30 days. When the goods are delivered June 10, the customer has only 20 days to pay rather than the full 30. The company has cut 10 days off the float."

2. Begin the collection process the day after payments are due. Waiting for accounts to become seriously delinquent impedes cash flow and increases the risk of nonpayment.

"Small companies are often wary of asking customers for money because they think that will lead the account to buy elsewhere," says the executive with Mid-Continent Adjustment. "But that's generally untrue. In most cases, the people who are responsible for paying your account have nothing to do with ordering from you. What's more, by demonstrating that you are serious about collecting, you'll get paid ahead of others. Most small companies wait 60 to 90 days to begin collecting and then wonder why they have no cash."

3. Start the collection effort with a friendly reminder, leading up to sterner warnings and suspension of credit after 90

days. "Avoid the trap of trading dollars for dollars," says another credit executive with a commercial collection agency. "This happens when the customer sends a partial payment and the company ships more merchandise in return. That simply rolls over the debt and institutionalizes a policy of 90-day terms. There comes a point when additional business with that customer should be done on a C.O.D. or cash-in-advance basis."

4. On the disbursements side, negotiate for longer payment terms, asking certain vendors to permit payment within 60 days rather than the standard 30 days. Those suppliers in highly competitive industries may agree to the extension.

By asking for its money in 15 days and paying its bills in 60, the company gets 45 days float on the cash. That's money that used to be in other people's pockets.

Accountants and collection services can help to plan and implement cash-management programs.

COMPILATIONS AND REVIEWS

Low-Cost Options to Audited Financial Statements

When lenders and investors evaluate a business, they look first to the financial statements. Two key documents—the income statement and the balance sheet—are said to reveal a company's true financial position and the results of current operations.

But how much credibility the statements have depends in large part on the accountants' reports that accompany them. For big businesses, financial statements are typically prepared and signed by certified public accountants on the basis of full-scale audits. These audited statements assure third parties—including prospective lenders, partners, or purchasers of the business—that CPAs have performed comprehensive tests to determine that the company's financial position and current results are fairly and accurately presented.

But for small, privately held companies, audits can be a clear case of overkill: more accounting services, at more cost, than the business always needs. In many cases, management finds that it can replace audits with lesser-known accounting procedures—compilations and reviews—that can be used for similar purposes but at substantially less expense.

"Compilations and reviews—services performed by accountants—allow us to be associated with financial statements without auditing them," says a partner with a Garden City, New York–based accounting firm. "In these procedures, we perform less comprehensive tests than are required for audits. This is made clear in the reports that accompany the financial statements. Third parties have a good sense of what we've done and how much comfort they can take from this in their use of the statements."

Just what constitutes a compilation or review is determined by standards established by the American Institute of Certified Public Accountants. Put simply, the procedures involve the following:

Reviews. They may be described as independent perusal of financial statements based on tests more limited in scope than those used for audits. CPAs performing reviews make inquiries of management concerning accounting policies and transactions and apply analytical procedures to identify items or trends that appear unusual or in need of explanation. Based on these procedures, the accountant can give limited assurance about the financial statements providing they contain all appropriate disclosures required by generally accepted accounting principles.

Compilations. A less comprehensive procedure, they provide no assurance from the CPA. The accountant assembles data from the client's records and presents it in basic financial-statement format. Compilations are often used for internal purposes, giving management a clear look at its own financial condition and results of operations. They may also be used to supplement reviews.

"The company that is required by its bankers to provide annual reviews may be permitted to use compilations for interim quarterly reports," the CPA explains. "The motivation, from the small company's standpoint, is to save money."

In general, a review for any given company may cost 25 to 50 percent less than an audit, and compilations are even less expensive. Although there are no hard-and-fast rules, small companies may consider using the three types of financial statements to meet the following needs:

Audits: establishing new banking relationships, undertaking joint ventures, seeking substantial financing from new sources.

Reviews: applying for trade credit, applying for additional financing from established sources, establishing new vendor relationships.

Compilations: for personal financial statements (usually the business owner's) to guarantee bank loans, to satisfy supplier's requests for financial statements, for internal management use.

"The type of financial statement the company uses should be discussed between management and its accountant," says a New York-based CPA. "If third parties don't require audited statements, it may be wise to go with reviews or compilations for the economies they afford."

DECISION MAKING

Seven Steps to Better Decisions

A General Approach to Decision Making

Whether a scientist, an executive of a major corporation, or a small business owner, the general approach to systematically solving problems is the same. The following seven-step approach to better management decision making can be used to study nearly all problems faced by small business.

1. State the Problem. A problem first must exist and be recognized. What is the problem and why is it a problem? What is ideal and how do current operations vary from that ideal? Identify the symptoms (what is going wrong) and the causes (why it is going wrong). Try to define all terms, concepts, variables, and relationships. Quantify the problem to the extent possible. If the problem is not accurately and quickly filling customer orders, try to determine how many orders were incorrectly filled and how long it took to fill them.

2. Define the Objectives. What are the objectives of the study? Which objectives are the most critical? Objectives usually are stated by an action verb, such as to reduce, to increase, or to improve. Returning to the customer order problem, the major objectives would be: (1) to increase the percentage of orders filled correctly, and (2) to reduce the time it takes to process an order. A subobjective could include to simplify and streamline the order-filling process.

3. Develop a Diagnostic Framework. Next, establish a diagnostic framework, that is, decide what methods are going to be used, what kinds of information are needed, and how and where the information is to be found. Is there going to be a customer survey, a review of company documents, time and motion tests, or something else? What are the assumptions (facts assumed to be correct) of the study? What are the criteria used to judge the study? What time, budget, or other constraints are there? What kind of quantitative or other specific techniques are going to be used to analyze the data? (Some of these will be covered shortly.) In other words, the diagnostic framework establishes the scope and methods of the entire study.

4. Collect and Analyze the Data. Collect the data by following the methods established in Step 3. Raw data are then tabulated and organized to facilitate analysis. Tables, charts, graphs, indexes, and matrices are some of the standard ways to organize raw data. Analysis is the critical prerequisite of sound business decision making. What do the data reveal? What facts, patterns, and trends can be seen in the data? Of course, computers are now used extensively during this step.

5. Generate Alternative Solutions. After the analysis has been finished, some specific conclusions about the nature of the problem and its resolution should have been reached. The next step is to develop alternative solutions to the problem and rank them in order of their net benefits. But how are alternatives best generated? Again, there are several well-established techniques such as the nominal group method, the Delphi method, and brainstorming, among others. In all these a group is involved, all of whom have reviewed the

data and analysis. The approach is to have an informed group suggesting a variety of possible solutions.

6. Develop an Action Plan and Implement. Select the best solution to the problem but be certain to understand clearly why it is best, that is, how it achieves the objectives established in Step 2 better than its alternatives. Then develop an effective method (an action plan) to implement the solution. At this point an important organizational consideration arises—who is going to be responsible for seeing the implementation through and what authority does he have? The selected manager should be responsible for seeing that all tasks, deadlines, and reports are performed, met, and written. Details are important in this step: schedules, reports, tasks, and communication are the key elements of any action plan. There are several techniques available to decision makers implementing an action plan. The PERT method, to be covered shortly, is a way of laying out an entire project such as an action plan.

7. Evaluate, Obtain Feedback, and Monitor. After the action plan has been implemented to solve a problem, management must evaluate its effectiveness. Evaluation standards must be determined, feedback channels developed, and monitoring performed. This step should be done after three to five weeks and again at about six months. The goal is to answer the bottom-line question: Has the problem been solved?

Specific Decision-making Techniques

The following techniques are used frequently by business and government managers. Some are familiar (benefit-cost analysis), others more esoteric (linear programming). Some are used for planning projects, others for analyzing data. Most of these techniques are mathematical or have mathematical aspects to them. They all can be used during one or more of the steps of the general approach, as just outlined.

Systems analysis can be used by the small business owner to study the inputs, processes, and outputs of the entire company, a division, or an office, depending on the nature of the problem. Inputs are the resources (manpower, materials, facilities) used by the business to produce the output (goods or services). Processes are the methods and organization that manage the conversion of inputs to outputs. By using systems analysis, decision makers can evaluate the system's various components separately on the basis of established objectives (like cost or error rate). If a problem can be identified as belonging to a specific component of the system, it can be corrected without disrupting the other components.

Benefit-cost analysis is used to compare the pros and cons of various alternative solutions to a problem. To perform this type of analysis the manager must define the problem, determine objectives, develop alternatives, put a dollar value on all benefits and costs of each alternative, calculate the benefit cost ratio (B ÷ C) and/or the net benefit (B − C), and make the decision. This type of analysis establishes a clear relationship between expenditure (cost) and purchase (benefit). It can be used to study problems in which the costs and benefits of alternative ways to achieve an objective can be assigned dollar values.

Input-output analysis charts the flow of a product from one industrial sector, company, department, or facility to another. It shows what inputs produce what outputs. I/O analysis uses transaction tables, showing the purchasing and selling activities of buyers and sellers, and I/O coefficients, the product sold by A to B divided by the output of B. It is used most often by larger companies to help with longer-term planning, but smaller manufacturing firms also may find this useful.

Regression and correlation analysis is used to study the relationship between or among variables, for example, the relationship of household income to product sales. It can be used to determine how increases in household income affect sales volume. If management wants to study the relationship between sales and income, interest rates, and education, they would use multiple regression analysis. Correlation analysis refers to the study of how strong or accurate a relationship is, as well as such technical factors as measurement fit, deviation, and error. It often is used by companies to study demand, pricing, supply, and cost curves.

Modeling is used by management to simplify the complex world. A model is a (simplified) representation of a system, situation, or process. A model may be physical, symbolic, verbal, graphic, or mathematical. A good model strips away excess detail but leaves essential behavior. For example, a model could be a representation of a distribution system illustrated graphically with a flow chart. Models show relationships among the parts of a whole and assist with forecasting. Model building is used in the physical and social sciences, as well as in business management.

Linear programming is a widely used mathematical method of determining an optimum, single solution to a problem such as finding the minimum staff cost or the most nutritional mixture of ingredients. This technique can be done by hand, but today's computer software business management packages often contain linear programming instructions. The technique can only be used with problems that can be translated entirely into numbers and have a single, optimum objective or solution. For example, in an office situation (say, processing invoices), where there is a given total workload, an established workload per worker by skill (pay) level, and given staffing requirements, linear programming could be used to determine the least expensive mixture of worker skill levels to handle the given workload.

Econometric analysis is used by companies (and the government) for planning, forecasting, and model building. Through this type of analysis businesses can estimate demand cycles, cost and supply functions, income distribution changes, and so forth. Econometrics uses regression and correlation analysis. It is an attempt to quantify as many variables affecting a business as is possible. For example, using econometric analysis, household demand for Product X becomes the formula, $X = f(Px \div P, Pr \div P, y \div P) + e$, where Px is the price of product X, P is the general price level, Pr is the price of goods related to X, y is household income, and e is the estimated error. In simple English, household demand for a product is a function of its price relative to the price of goods in general, the price of related goods (either substitutes or complements), the real income of the household, and the error involved with random factors that might influence a shopper's decision to buy. Larger companies often develop econometric models to get a picture of the future economy and its impact on their operations.

Forecasting is making decisions based on predictions of future trends and events such as inflation and interest rates, employment levels, or supply costs—all of which can affect sales of small businesses. There are three types of forecasting techniques: (1) subjective or qualitative, where you rely on expert judgments, (2) time-series projections, where you use quantifiable observations over time, and (3) causal models, where you emphasize causal/correlational relationships. The principal emphasis in forecasting is looking for patterns and fluctuations over time.

Decision tree technique plots the sequence of alternative decisions needed to solve a larger problem. The actual decision tree looks like a flow chart. Each alternative decision has consequences that lead to other decisions. These are all drawn as branches of the tree. One also can add probability and payoff calculations for each decision. The major feature of the decision tree technique is that solutions to a complex problem can be sketched out on a single sheet of paper.

Program evaluation and review technique (PERT) sequentially charts the individual tasks and activities needed to complete a project. The result is a flow chart of the entire job. A time schedule and probabilities of meeting that schedule can be plugged in. The critical path (the longest time it will take to complete all the important tasks, which gives the completion date) also can be determined. PERT helps managers make decisions about scheduling and resource allocation and reduces uncertainty. PERT is often used on construction projects and was pioneered by Admiral Rickover when he ran the nation's nuclear submarine production program. However, PERT is a very flexible tool and also can be used, for example, to do market research.

EMBEZZLEMENT

Ounces of Prevention

There are many steps an owner-manager can take to cut down on the possibility of losses through embezzlement. Do you take the following precautions?

1. Check the background of prospective employees. Sometimes you can satisfy yourself by making a few telephone calls or writing a few letters. In other cases, you may want to turn the matter over to a credit bureau or similar agency to run a background check. (Keep in mind that the rights of individuals must be preserved in furnishing, receiving, and using background information.)
2. Know your employees to the extent that you may be able to detect signs of financial or other personal problems. Build up rapport so that they feel free to discuss such things with you in confidence.
3. See that no one is placed on the payroll without authorization from you or a responsible official of the company. If you have a personnel department, require that it approve additions to the payroll as a double check.
4. Have the company mail addressed to a post office box rather than your place of business. In smaller cities, the owner-manager may want to go to the post office to collect the mail. In any event, you or your designated key person should personally open the mail and make a record at that time of cash and checks received. Don't delude yourself that checks or money orders payable to your company can't be converted into cash by an enterprising embezzler.
5. Either prepare the daily cash deposits personally or compare the deposits made by employees with the record of cash and checks received. Make sure you get a copy of the duplicate deposit slip or other documentation from the bank. Make it a habit to go to the bank and make the daily deposit yourself as often as you can. If you delegate these jobs, make an occasional spot check to see that nothing is amiss.
6. Arrange for bank statements and other correspondence from banks to be sent to the same post office box, and personally reconcile all bank statements with your company's books and records. The owner-manager who has not reconciled the statements for some time may want to get oriented by the firm's outside accountant.
7. Personally examine all canceled checks and endorsements to see if there is anything unusual. This applies also to payroll checks.
8. Make sure that an employee in a position to mishandle funds is adequately bonded. Let employees know that fidelity coverage is a matter of company policy rather than any feeling of mistrust on your part. If would-be embezzlers know that a bonding company also has an interest in what they do, they may think twice before helping themselves to your funds.
9. Spot-check your accounting records and assets to satisfy yourself that all is well and that your plan of internal control is being carried out.
10. Personally approve unusual discounts and bad-debt write-offs. Approve or spot-check credit memos and other documentation for sales returns and allowances.
11. Don't delegate the signing of checks and approval of cash disbursements unless absolutely necessary and never approve any payment without sufficient documentation or prior knowledge of the transaction.

12. Examine all invoices and supporting data before signing checks. Make sure that all merchandise was actually received and that the price seems reasonable. In many false purchase schemes, the embezzler neglects to make up receiving forms or other records purporting to show receipt of merchandise.
13. Personally cancel all invoices at the time you sign the check to prevent double payment through error or otherwise.
14. Don't sign blank checks. Don't leave a supply of signed blank checks when you go on vacation.
15. Inspect all prenumbered checkbooks and other prenumbered forms from time to time to ensure that checks or forms from the backs of the books have not been removed and used in a fraudulent scheme.
16. Have the preparation of the payroll and the actual paying of employees handled by different persons, especially when cash is involved.

Credit: U.S. Small Business Administration

EMPLOYEE THEFT

Internal Controls Curb Employee Theft

Sometimes a company's profits go in the front door and out the rear. That's the case when dishonest employees divert cash or merchandise to their own accounts. The problem is widespread and difficult to detect.

"Virtually every transaction related to receiving of goods, invoicing, and accounts receivable is subject to fraudulent practices that can cost a small business thousands of dollars," says a vice-president of Stanton Cor-

poration, designers of employee honesty tests. "The losses are often camouflaged by false documentation and by collusion between several parties. The best defense is to understand how these schemes work and then to take decisive action against them."

Watch for these telltale signs of internal theft:

1. High Percentage of Refunds versus Sales. In one of the most common forms of internal theft, register clerks and sales personnel submit false refund slips, indicating a return of merchandise when none was made. The cash proceeds then go directly to the employees' pockets.

"Look for a pattern of refunds far exceeding the norm," says the Stanton vice-president. "For example, if one employee's refunds are double all others—say $100 for every $500 of sales—that warrants an investigation."

Consider these preventive measures:

- Require that department managers approve all refunds
- Route all returns through a central refund desk that is subject to management surveillance.
- Limit refunds to checks or store credit. Do not pay cash.

It is also a good idea to occasionally check the refund list, calling a random sample of customers to determine that the names are real and that the refunds were actually made.

2. Vendor Insists on Dealing with a Specific Buyer. This can signal collusion between the vendor and the buyer, with the latter accepting kickbacks for approving excessive or overpriced purchases.

"In one case, the buyer for a retail chain authorized orders for sunglasses in amounts substantially exceeding the stores' sales capacity," says the Stanton executive. "While the employee wound up with lavish gifts—including free trips to the Caribbean—his employer had to take deep markdowns on excess merchandise."

Short-circuit this scheme by requiring dual signatures for all merchandise orders.

3. Merchandise Shortages Detected after Delivery. Lax controls at the delivery platform prompt vendors to short-count merchandise, dropping off less than the invoice amount.

"Say a trucker delivers 100 cases of soup to a store once a week and notices that no one ever bothers to verify that the amount he's actually dropping off matches the invoice total," says an audit partner with Arthur Young, accountants. "That's inviting trouble. Sooner or later the trucker may start holding back a case or two—then five or ten—as he notices his scheme is not detected. At some point, he may enlist an insider to cover up the discrepancy in return for a share of the stolen goods."

Protect against this "shrinkage" by requiring that all goods be counted at the point of delivery and cross-checked by sales or stockroom personnel.

4. Refusal to Take Vacation Time. Employees engaged in fraudulent activities may be concealing complex schemes complete with fictitious names, phony invoices, and unauthorized checking accounts. Because they must be in the office to accept sensitive letters and telephone calls, many fear that absence from the job will prove their undoing. As a result, they refuse to take time off.

"Many schemes unravel when the employee becomes ill and simply cannot get to work," says the Arthur Young partner. "It's then that a customer calls to question a phony invoice, management is alerted, and the cat is out of the bag."

While the refusal to take vacations does not prove dishonesty—the employee may simply be a workaholic—experts view this as a red flag.

"You want to be alert to all potential problems and take offensive action against them," the CPA advises. "That's the best way to reduce or eliminate internal theft."

ESTATE PLANNING

"Tragedy Checklist" Helps Keep Business in the Family

When the owner of a retail clothing chain passed away unexpectedly, he left his family with a financial as well as personal loss. Minus his management skills, the company he founded faced imminent ruin. Years of hard work would go down the drain.

Because they knew little about the business, the heirs were helpless to save it. Their plight was all too common. As management generalists accustomed to performing all the critical duties singlehandedly, small business owners rarely prepare others to fill their shoes. Without a capable successor, the businesses struggle to survive. Many wind up being liquidated for a fraction of their former value.

But there is a way to prevent this. By compiling a "tragedy checklist," the entrepreneur can prepare in advance for his passing. In the process, he assures that the business will continue to support his heirs.

"The mark of a good entrepreneur is the ability to make himself dispensable, not indispensable," says an executive with April-Marcus, Inc., a consulting firm. "This means seeing to it that others—including, in a privately held business, close family members—are in position to run the company or intelligently dispose of it when the owner is no longer there. A tragedy checklist considers all the elements that should be put in place to assure little or no financial loss."

Consider these preventive measures:

1. Keep spouses fully informed of all aspects of the company's operations. Involve them in key business meetings, give them copies of critical documents, and make them privy to long-term plans.

"Keeping a spouse in the dark about your business only puts that person at the mercy of others in the event of your death," says a partner with the accounting firm of Philips, Gold. "They'll have to ask outsiders—some of whom may have conflicting interests—how best to run the business, when and if to sell it, and for how much."

Adds the April-Marcus executive, "The spouse should know those things that tend to stay locked up in the owner's head, like the existence of so-called invisible assets. Consider, for example, a retail shop holding a long-term lease for $10 a square foot in a market where rents for comparable properties have soared to more than $75 a foot. In some cases, subleasing the space may produce a greater profit than continuing to run the business in its current location. The heirs should be aware of this option. They should know just how valuable the lease is."

2. Designate an attorney or accountant to serve as a liaison between the company and the heirs. An experienced professional—who has been kept fully informed about the business—can help the survivors negotiate with bankers, employees, landlords, customers, suppliers, and prospective buyers.

3. Schedule annual estate-planning checkups to identify and correct problems that could block a smooth transition of the business interests.

"With advance planning, we can remove obstacles that would otherwise loom large were they still in place at the time of the owner's death," says a partner with a New York law firm. "For example, some commercial leases are written so they can be terminated, at the landlord's discretion, when the principal dies. That could cripple the company just when it is most vulnerable to a major change in operations. But by negotiating with the landlord, we can often get these negative provisions removed from the lease before they cause any damage."

4. Write a will, specifying who is to operate or dispose of the business and the terms under which they are to act.

"Be specific in your instructions," the lawyer advises. "Should you prefer that the company be sold, require that it be appraised to determine its market value and that it be placed on the market in a given period of time, say six months. Allowing the process to drag on may result in a lower sales price to the heirs."

All too many business owners operate under the theory that if they don't write out a will, they'll live forever. That's foolish and they know it. All it does is cause problems for the survivors. Everyone with substantial assets should have a will and should review it regularly to make certain it carries out their wishes.

INDUSTRIAL PURCHASING

An Effective Program

One of the most important aspects of managing a small plant is industrial purchasing, which is the process of securing the materials, supplies, and capital stock inputs required for production operations. An effective industrial purchasing program can have a vital impact on profit. For example, it has been shown that a 1½-percent savings in purchasing can translate into as much profit as a 10-percent increase in sales. The following introduction presents a broad outline of an effective purchasing program.

Specifications

Specifications writing provides a common basis for bidding. Well-written specifications should leave little room for error or misunderstanding and ensure your company of obtaining the materials needed. In writing specifications, the following elements should be considered:

1. Do not request features or quality that are not necessary for the items' intended use.
2. Include descriptions of the nature of any testing to be performed.
3. Include procedures for adding optional items.
4. Describe the quality of the items in clear terms.

How to Promote Purchasing Savings

The following types of action can help save money during purchase operations:

1. Substitution of less costly material without impairing required quality.
2. Improvement in quality or changes in specifications that would lead to savings in process time or other operating savings.
3. Developing new sources of supply.
4. Greater use of bulk shipments.
5. Quantity savings due to large volume, through consideration of economic order quantity.
6. A reduction in unit prices due to negotiations.
7. Initiating make-or-buy studies.

8. Application of new purchasing techniques.

Lease Versus Purchase

You may wish to consider leasing rather than purchasing capital equipment. It could save you money. Leasing permits a more effective timing of capital expenditures and a greater potential return. The value of conserved capital will vary from company to company and will be dependent on the particular company's ability to employ capital productively.

For example, a dollar in a microcomputer earns little for a retail store, but the same dollar, kept turning in merchandise by leasing the computer, generates a profit. Leasing also conserves capital by offering 100 percent financing since it often requires no down payment. Additionally, there are frequently included in the lease certain expenses such as installation and freight charges that allow such costs to be amortized over the life of the lease. There are also a variety of lease and related equipment financing methods that can be tailored to the terms, conditions, and services required by the user.

Leasing is a fast, easy way to acquire needed equipment, even when normal money lines are closed. This enables companies to obtain use of modern equipment and remain competitive.

Your Responsibility When Freight Arrives

What to Do at Time of Delivery
Verify Count—Make sure you are receiving as many cartons as are listed on the delivery receipt.

Carefully Examine Each Carton for Visible Damage—If damage is visible, note it on the delivery receipt and have the driver sign your copy.

Immediately After Delivery, Open All Cartons and Inspect for Merchandise Damage.

Steps to Take When Damage Is Discovered

Retain Damaged Items—All damaged materials must be held at the point received.

Call Carrier to Report Damage and Request Inspection.

Confirm Call in Writing—This is not mandatory but is for your own protection.

Steps to Take When Carrier Inspects Damaged Items

Have All Damaged Items in the Receiving Area—Make certain the damaged items have not been moved from the receiving area prior to inspection by carrier.

After Carrier-Inspector Prepares Damage Report—Carefully read it before signing.

Steps to Be Taken after Inspection Has Been Made

Retain Damaged Materials—Damaged materials should not be used or disposed of without permission by the carrier.

Do Not Return Damaged Items to Shipper—Without written authorization from shipper/supplier.

Cash Discounts

Cash discounts are often offered by the supplier to promote quick payment for merchandise. Therefore, give priority to invoices offering them, since cash discounts are an excellent source of savings. For example, many firms offering cash discounts give terms of 2% 10 days–net 30 days. This means that the seller is willing to let the buyer deduct 2% from the invoice if it is paid within 10 days. Since cash discounts offer important savings over a period of time, a company should promote the securing of them from the supplier through aggressive negotiations.

Inventory Control

A principal goal of inventory control is to determine the minimum possible annual cost of ordering and stocking each item. Most effective inventory management techniques emphasize the need to compute the amount of the following two major control values: (1) the order quantity, that is, the proper size and frequency of orders; and (2) the reorder point, that is, the minimum stock level at which additional quantities are ordered. The Economic Order Quantity (EOQ) formula is one widely used method of computing the minimum annual cost for ordering and stocking each item. The EOQ computation takes into account the cost of placing an order, the annual sales rate, the unit cost, and the cost of carrying the inventory.

Included in an EOQ-based inventory management system should be the two accepted methods of inventory control. The first relates to using a form of maximum/minimum standards. The second deals with methods applicable where materials are manufactured to order rather than for stock. The maximum/minimum method is of particular importance and is adaptable to materials that are comparatively standard in character, that is, their prices do not fluctuate widely and they are used in substantially regular quantities. A maximum/minimum system of inventory control assumes the use of a standard order—representing presumably the most economical quantity to purchase. Once this amount has been established it can be used more or less automatically for issuance of a purchase order at the proper time.

Remember, one of the most important goals in purchasing is to strike the most economic balance between cost of possession and cost of acquisition in determining order quantities.

Systems Contracting

Simply defined, systems contracting is a purchasing technique that enables a company to acquire repetitively used materials and services from suppliers so that the cost of these items is at the absolute minimum at their point of consumption. There should be a written contract with clear and precise descriptions to avoid misunderstanding.

Where properly implemented, systems contracting will greatly reduce the amount of paperwork. Additional benefits include the reduction of inventory shrinkage, reduction of obsolescence, improved expense control and reduction of inventory levels with a corresponding gain in usable floor space, and quite often a significant reduction in true costs of items covered. The main objectives of systems contracting are: (1) reduced costs, (2) improved service, and (3) increased profit.

WHERE TO FIND IT

U.S. Government Publications

Small Business Administration
    Washington, D.C. 20416

SBA issues a wide range of management and technical publications designed to help owner-managers and prospective owner-managers of small businesses.

Listings of currently available publications may be requested from **SBA**, P.O. Box 15434, Ft. Worth, TX 76119. Ask for list **115A** free publications and **115B** for for-sale publications.

Management Aids (4- to 8-page leaflets). Each title in the series discusses a specific management practice to help the owner-managers of small firms with their management problems. Free. Listed in **115A**.

The Equipment Replacement Decision (**MA 2.005**)
Business Plan for Small Manufacturers (**MA 2.007**)
Cash Flow for Small Plants (**MA 1.006**)
Should You Lease or Buy Equipment? (**MA 2.014**)
Stock Control for Small Stores (**MA 3.005**)
Profit by Your Wholesaler's Services (**MA 1.012**)

Credit: U.S. Small Business Administration

LEGAL TIME BOMBS

Threats to Small Business

When is a handshake more than a greeting, a phone call more than just talk, a letter more than correspondence? When they are legal time bombs waiting to explode. Millions of small companies face this exposure without knowing they are at risk.

The problem goes hand in hand with business management. While conducting what appear to be routine transactions, the self-employed create a web of contracts, commitments, and liabilities that can have dire legal consequences for their corporate and, in some cases, personal affairs.

"People do things in their day-to-day activities that have hidden legal implications," says a partner with the law firm of Ballon, Stoll & Itzler. "Because big businesses are generally aware of this, they have attorneys screen their dealings with the outside world. But small companies rarely consult with their lawyers unless they are getting involved in major commitments. What they don't recognize is that the little things are most likely to trip them up."

An attorney with the firm of Reisman, Peirez & Reisman cites this example:

"Consider the company writing to a major customer that 'if you can't live with the terms of our agreement, don't worry, we'll bend over backwards to meet your needs.' Well, that may be good business, but it's not good law. The company writing the letter may have voided the very contract on which its customer relationship is based. That's what a seemingly innocent letter can do."

Sometimes, the failure to write a letter can be equally damaging. "Let's say that Company A delivers merchandise to Company B that B later claims is defective and refuses to pay for," the Ballon, Stoll partner explains. "Should A simply send invoices without inquiring as to the cause of the problem, it may be in a weak position when the matter goes to court. A better approach is for A to write B to determine the nature of the complaint. A simple letter could be held as proof of A's intention to reasonably settle the matter and could shift the burden to B to respond in a reasonable period of time."

Lawyers warn of these other common time bombs:

1. Signing documents without carefully evaluating the implications. "Take the business owner negotiating for a corporate bank loan," says the Ballon, Stoll partner. "Typically, the bank will forward a batch of documents with instructions to 'sign by the check marks.' All too often, the applicant does so without reading the fine print. Unfortunately, if the business is ever in a financial bind and can't make the payments, the owner may be shocked to learn that he or she has personally guaranteed the loan. His or her personal assets may be used to satisfy the debt."

2. Personal loan agreements that violate state usury laws. "Typically, when a business owner lends money to another party, he draws up an agreement designed to assure himself a rate of return equal to or greater than that offered by banks," the lawyer explains. "But because state laws often put a lower limit on the interest rates allowed for loans made by individuals as opposed to those offered by lending institutions, what seems like a reasonable return may be illegal. The result? The debtor may be excused from repaying the loan. What was meant to be a loan may turn out to be an involuntary gift."

3. Property leases granting landlords arbitrary cause for evicting tenants. "When a lease becomes unprofitable to a landlord, he'll generally use any number of tactics to replace the current tenant with a new one," warns the Reisman, Peirez attorney. "One ploy is to strictly enforce the so-called use clause that defines the business activities allowed on the premises. For example, if a butcher starts selling grocery products, the landlord may insist that the groceries be removed. Well, the butcher may not have sufficient time to act or he may be unaware that if he doesn't act, his lease, or for that matter his business, will be in peril. Ignoring the landlord's communication may play right into his hands.

"The essential lesson for small business owners is to understand that the rules of business and the rules of law are seldom the same. Both aspects must be considered in every transaction."

What constitutes a legal time bomb varies from state to state. When in question, the safest approach is to consult an attorney.

MANAGEMENT PRINCIPLES

How to Be a Business Manager

The difference between a business owner and a business manager is the ability to lead.

While the former controls the stock, the latter guides the company. But the roles need not be separate and distinct. The ultimate goal of entrepreneurship is to make the owner a skilled manager as well.

Unlike their counterparts at major corporations, few business owners come to their posts with years of management experience. For them, leadership must be an acquired art.

"The weakness and the strength of small business owners is that they start off doing everything themselves," says a managing director of the consulting firm of Cresap, McCormick and Paget. "While this may be satisfactory during the company's infancy, to achieve sustained growth the business needs a manager rather than a chief cook and bottle washer. Entrepreneurs who fail to make this transition are rarely successful over the long term."

What does it take to be a successful manager? Consultants recommend the following practices:

1. Projecting the Future. This forces the owner to look beyond daily operations, asking "Where is my company now and where is it headed?" Projecting the future helps to identify problems and opportunities in the making, giving the company adequate lead time to adjust to changing market conditions.

"Owners surrounded by employees are only rarely forced to deal with the hard and potentially unpleasant issues that will confront them down the road," the consultant says. "So I suggest they forge relationships with professionals or business associates who can serve as devil's advocates. These should be independent and hard-headed people who can force the owner to deal with future issues he may prefer to avoid.

"Take the owner who has always kept his business open from nine to five and wants to stick to those hours. Well, changes in society,

namely the emergence of the two-paycheck family, may not allow that. With both husband and wife working, consumers are demanding more flexible shopping hours. But the owner who remains isolated from outside advice may stay put until the issue is forced. By that time, a crippling loss of business may have occurred."

2. Staying in Touch. Plush offices may do wonders for the owner's ego, but they may also insulate him or her from the front-line activities that determine the company's ultimate fate. Effective leaders break down the office walls by routinely meeting with customers and employees. Some hold staff lunches, other roll up their sleeves and pitch in on the shop floor.

A prominent retailer, who went on to become the president of a national department store chain, got a fix on customers by greeting them at a local subway station. He would ask if they shopped at his store and if not what he could do to gain their patronage. These so-called subway interviews kept him in touch with the marketplace and sent a clear message to employees and shoppers alike: the boss is committed to customer service.

3. Eyeing the Indicators. Even a small business can generate a blizzard of paperwork. The manager's job is to separate the wheat from the chaff, focusing on those key reports that give insight to the company's underlying performance.

"By identifying and monitoring critical indicators, the manager keeps his or her hand on the company's pulse," the consultant says. "For example, most entrepreneurs tend to focus on profit alone, while an equally important yardstick, return on equity, goes unnoticed. But the latter can be crucial because it puts profit in perspective. How much capital did it take to produce that profit? Is the return satisfactory? The owner may find that he or she would do better by investing the money in new or related ventures."

4. Emphasis on Simple Values. Effective managers transfer to employees their deep commitment to the company's driving principles. These are expressed in terms of simple values such as courtesy, quality, and attention to detail. The manager communicates ideals so that they are shared by those who work for him or her.

"Even those owners who know what it takes to become a manager will likely experience three crises as they make the transition," says an executive with the consulting firm of Arthur D. Little. "They have to let go of some of the reins, delegate authority, and groom successors. All can be painful but all are vital to the company's well-being."

MERGERS AND ACQUISITIONS

An Attractive Candidate

Corporate PacMan—the real-world game where one business swallows another—isn't limited to Wall Street giants. Even small business owners can play, selling out to cash-rich corporations and in the process turning company assets into liquid wealth. This makes money available for retirement, new investments, or a carefree life-style.

But the differences that distinguish big and small businesses can often stand in the way of successful sales or mergers. By clinging to the standards and practices of closely held companies and by failing to recognize the needs and concerns of corporate suitors, small business owners can block negotiations, thereby diminishing the likelihood of successful sales.

"The company interested in being purchased or acquired has to make itself an attractive candidate," says a partner with Winthrop, Stimson, Putnam & Roberts, a New York law firm active in corporate acquisitions. "In many cases, this means substituting some cherished small business practices for those more in line with major corporations.

"For example, a family-owned business is typically concerned with reducing reported income and in turn cutting taxes. So the company is saddled with expenses for cars, travel, and family employment. A prospective buyer looking at the bottom line sees earnings that are substantially lower than management has claimed them to be. This could thwart the deal or result in a lower offering price."

To prevent this, the lawyer suggests shifting from a tax to an earnings orientation, removing costly perks from the company's books and deadwood from the payroll. This will boost reported profits.

"It's also important to take a hard look at the balance sheet with the aim of cleaning up those matters prospective buyers may find objectionable," says an executive with the small business practice of Arthur Andersen, accountants. "For example, sell or dispose of obsolete inventory, settle delinquent accounts, and write off intangible assets of questionable value such as goodwill, patents, and trademarks. You want the balance sheet to look as strong as possible."

Consider these additional measures:

1. Plan in advance for a sale or merger by having annual statements audited for at least two years before a buyer is sought. "Investors must feel comfortable with the company's numbers—to know that sales, profits, and assets are accurately reflected in the financial statements," the lawyer says. "Audits conducted by prominent accounting firms can do a lot to build faith and confidence."

2. Be prepared to stay on as a senior executive through the postacquisition period. Buyers often want the former owner to guide

the business until a new management team is installed. This can take up to two years.

"The entrepreneur must also be prepared to relinquish some of the powers he or she enjoyed as owner," the lawyer says. "A proposed sale I was recently negotiating came apart at the seams because the small business owner refused to accept a managerial role during the transition. He wanted to remain a king—which was how he functioned as the company's owner—but there was no place for that in the corporate organization."

3. Be flexible and creative in structuring payment terms. "All too often, business owners decide how they want to be paid before a buyer is even found," says the Arthur Andersen executive. "But that leaves no room for negotiation. Typically, sellers want lump-sum cash payments and buyers want to pay off notes over five to seven years. By insisting on cash up front, the seller narrows the field of potential buyers and makes it less likely a deal will be concluded. It is much wiser to have the business valued and to negotiate for the best terms you can get."

Investment bankers, business brokers, and attorneys specializing in corporate acquisitions can help companies identify buyers and negotiate sales or merger agreements.

MISTAKES

The Entrepreneur's Survival Guide: Eight Common Business Mistakes and How to Avoid Them

So you're going into business for yourself. Or you have a company that, quite naturally, you want to make more profitable. What to do? Most likely, you'll work hard, cross your

fingers, and search tirelessly for the proverbial "secrets to success."

But hold it. Do these "secrets" really exist? For as long as entrepreneurs have been searching, no one has discovered the definitive rules guaranteed to assure success. What makes a successful business varies from market to market, company to company, entrepreneur to entrepreneur? While one industry thrives on service, another is geared to price; while one is focused on fashion, still another stresses quality.

But this much said, it is encouraging to know that you can learn from others—if not the secrets to success, then the most common causes of failure. Paradoxically, while the prerequisites for prosperity vary across the lot, the common mistakes of business ownership apply to a broad cross section of companies, industries, and entrepreneurs.

Postmortem examinations of failed companies—and studies of those stalled in the early stages of growth—reveal a pattern of oft-repeated blunders and oversights that consistently thwart management's objectives and in the process spoil their dreams of entrepreneurial success.

"We see similar threads running through many companies that wind up bankrupt," says a senior partner with the small business practice for accountants Touche Ross. "Most common are inadequate capital and inexperienced management. These two shortcomings can have a very damaging impact on all aspects of the company's operations. Enlightened entrepreneurs will try to anticipate these problems and will take steps to defend against them."

Consider the following list of common mistakes, along with the guidelines for avoiding them, a survival guide for entrepreneurs:

1. Mistaking a Hobby for a Business. The ranks of the self-employed are constantly depleted and replenished by would-be entrepreneurs who go into business for the wrong reason—namely, the dangerously mistaken belief that a lifelong hobby—such as cooking or interior decorating—can automatically be converted into a business.

The missing element is that a hobbyist—no matter how skilled or creative at her or his pursuit—lacks the critical business experience so essential to entrepreneurial success. The ability to whip up a glorious soufflé is not reason enough to open a restaurant. You must ask yourself, do I know how to buy food at wholesale? Can I plan menus? Figure minimum prices in relation to projected overhead? Precisely because they look easier to run than they are, restaurants, clothing shops, interior design services, and the like, attract more than their share of hobbyists who invest thousands of dollars only to find themselves out of business in a matter of months—or less.

This much said, hobbies can serve as promising springboards for business ventures, providing you complement your creative or technical skills with a strong grounding in the business aspects. This can be accomplished in one of two ways:

- Go to work for someone else before going into business for yourself. Consider this first step an apprenticeship. Soak up all you can about the problems, the opportunities, the angles in running a venture of the sort you want to start.
- Go directly into business with a partner strong in management experience. A hobbyist chef and an experienced restaurant manager may have the right combination of skills to get the venture off the ground.

2. Too Little, Too Late. No doubt every fledgling entrepreneur goes into business with an optimistic outlook. Why take the risk if the prognosis is poor?

This optimism can be both a blessing and a curse. Convinced that the venture will succeed, and that it will generate profits from day one, the founder fails to raise enough cash to carry the business through the early stages. The hard truth is that very few companies move immediately into the black; most sustain losses for months, even years, before turning profitable. Throughout this period, rent has to be paid, paychecks covered, inventory purchased. Unless there is enough cash on hand to meet the shortfall, the business will have to close its doors prematurely.

"I never anticipated the pressure I'd experience trying to make that payroll week after week," says a family practice attorney who went out on her own after three years with a major New York firm. "When I put $55,000 into a bank account to help defray initial operating costs, I thought it would last at least a year. As it happened, the funds were depleted in less than half that time. With no other cash to draw on, I had to perform a balancing act, holding money aside from this to pay that. By the time I was able to get more money, it was too little, too late. Eventually I gave up and went back to work for an established practice."

How to prevent this from happening to you:

- Create a "worse-case scenario," projecting, on a monthly basis, minimal revenue and maximum expenses for the first two years. Note the break-even point (the time at which income becomes sufficient to cover expenses) and calculate the amount of money necessary to cover the shortfall to that point. Add to this the amount of the initial investment required to launch the business and ongoing expenses for inventory and capital equipment. This is the *minimum* amount required to launch the business.

"It's also a good idea to do a cash-flow analysis, projecting the flow of cash in and out of the business, not just in the early years but throughout its life," the Touche Ross partner says. "The company may have $100,000 in receivables but if that money doesn't come in on the due date, interim cash may be required to fill the gap."

By arranging for a bank line of credit, you can draw cash to cover operating expenses as required. This creates a buffer between the entrepreneur and your creditors, allowing you to keep the business going even when income fails to cover expenses.

3. More Is More. In business, thinking big is a plus and a minus. Helpful in setting your ultimate objectives ("if you don't think big, you'll never be big," the saying goes) but detrimental in planning market strategy.

The classic error is to try to be all things to all people. Typically, the small business owner believes that appealing to the widest possible range of consumers is a sure-fire prescription for success. Instead, this broad-brush approach creates a company that is likely to be weak in several areas rather than strong in one.

A wiser approach is to narrow the company's focus, identifying a specific market segment and marshaling the necessary resources (merchandise, advertising, and personnel) to become a significant factor in it.

The fact is that less really is more. Consider McDonald's. From its earliest days as a lone burger outlet, founder Ray Kroc (a man certainly possessed of the big picture) kept the company focused on a narrow product line. Even as the menu was expanded to include breakfast and chicken entrees, McDon-

ald's never lost sight of its status, its preeminence, as a fast-food outlet.

Follow these "less is more" rules in your business:

- Appeal to a single age category (i.e., teenagers, middle-aged adults, or senior citizens)
- Focus on one socioeconomic group (i.e., white collar executives, blue collar workers)
- Stick to a single selling point (i.e., discount prices, high fashion, attentive customer service)

4. The Price Is Wrong. In a classic segment of the "Honeymooners" television show, Ralph Kramden goes broke running a popular restaurant jammed with hungry customers. The episode holds a lesson for real-life entrepreneurs. By setting giveaway prices, Ralph was losing money on every sandwich he sold.

All too often, small business owners are guilty of similar mistakes. By setting prices too high or too low, they effectively limit the company's profits, sales, or both. The right price tag can make the difference between a robust bottom line and one written in red ink. It strikes a delicate balance between the company's need to profit and the consumer's search for value.

Consider these pricing strategies:

- Start by establishing a price range within which you believe the product can be sold. The floor price is the minimum required to cover costs and maintain working capital. The ceiling—the maximum amount consumers will spend—varies with prevailing economic and competitive factors.
- Determine the ceiling price by conducting market research or by taking the "best-guess trial-and-error" approach. With the

latter, start at the highest possible figure and then scale back at the first sign of consumer resistance or competitive pressure.

- Build intangibles into the selling price. When the elements of prestige, status, and pride come into play, extravagant prices may be an advantage. Here, the ideal price defies both logic and the market mechanism.

The story is told of the merchant saddled with a large inventory of private-brand perfume that would not budge from the shelves. Priced at $15 a bottle, it experienced dismal sales. Acting on a hunch, the retailer tripled the price and advertised the item as a premium fragrance sold only in his shop. It worked like a charm: the entire inventory sold out within two weeks.

5. After-the-Fact Debt Defense. There's a widely held rule of thumb that the longer a debt goes unpaid, the harder it is to collect. Customers who refuse to pay long after the due date are unlikely to settle up unless they are faced with legal action. For small business, this makes for a costly and time-consuming remedy.

Surprisingly, most credit and collection systems—if they can be called "systems" at all—are based on this after-the-fact defense. Management virtually ignores customer payment patterns, freely extending additional credit until the account goes delinquent and the business is saddled with substantial debts that go right to the bottom line.

A better approach is to take the offense, implementing an early-warning detection plan to short-circuit emerging credit problems before they jeopardize the company's finances.

6. Bleeding the Business. Typically, entre-preneurs take all their company's earnings out of the business in cash or perks. Generous salaries, bonuses, and company cars are seen as the rewards of success. But they can also sow the seeds of catastrophe.

"Just as in one's personal finances, it's always a good idea to put away some corporate funds for a rainy day," says the Touche Ross partner. "Should the corporation be hit by an unexpected expense, management will want to have the cash on hand to cover it. But if the company has been bled, the cupboard may be bare. When capital is not available from other sources, the owner may have a crisis on her or his hands."

This crisis can be avoided by routinely saving some of the company's earnings. Just how much to put away depends on the firm's routine cash needs and management's projection of future requirements. The best approach is to establish a set amount, perhaps as a percentage of total earnings, and discipline yourself to leave this in the business.

"Accountants have to share some of the blame for owners taking too much out of their business," says one CPA. "Because there are tax disadvantages in withdrawing cash as salaries rather than dividends—the latter is taxed twice—we have generally advised clients to be aggressive in taking money out. But this doesn't mean to withdraw everything. The business should have some cash on hand for any and all eventualities."

7. The Fortress Complex. Unlike their counterparts in large corporations, small business owners tend to run their ventures single-handedly, making all key decisions without going through an elaborate approvals process. While there is strength here—the company can respond faster to emerging opportunities—the owner is insulated from other points of view.

Just how this can damage your business is

evident by the case of Smith's Steakhouse (a fictitious name not meant to represent an actual company), a regional restaurant chain run by the founder. Just as the nation's eating habits were undergoing dramatic change, moving away from red meat toward fish and salads, Smith's launched a major expansion, opening 15 new restaurants in three states—all with a heavy emphasis on a traditional steaks and chops menu. To date, all but one of the newer units is experiencing heavy losses, as are some of the older locations in the chain. Had the owner consulted with outside sources, the expansion might have been canceled or the new units planned as seafood houses.

"The best way to bring in outside opinions is to assemble an informal board of directors," says the Touche Ross partner. "Ask a banker, an accountant, and another local business owner to sit on the board, joining you once a month to discuss the company and to give their insights into its needs and requirements. This can be an excellent way to get free advice from knowledgeable sources and to expose the owner to other points of view."

8. Shooting in the Dark. Of the two components of business management—supervising daily events and plotting a course for the future—the latter often gets short shrift. The pressures of business leave little time for gazing into crystal balls.

But by focusing exclusively on the short term, the entrepreneur allows her or his company to veer from long-term objectives. Without a blueprint for growth—widely known as a marketing plan—the company is likely to founder in mid-course.

Take the case of Name Brand Apparel, a local retailer intent on becoming a regional chain. When will the first branch be built? What is the timetable for subsequent stores? How big should the chain become? Will it retain its current identity or adopt a different image?

"If you don't know where you are going, any road will take you there," says Joseph Mancuso, president of the Center for Entrepreneurial Management, a nonprofit organization active in small business affairs. "The theory behind a marketing plan is that it gives management a map with clear directions to where it should be going."

The following are major components of a typical marketing plan:

- Situation analysis takes a close look at the company's standing in the market including sales volume, competitive forces, and product strengths and weaknesses. A key step is to estimate the size of the total market and the firm's share of it. This serves as a yardstick for gauging the company's growth potential.

- Setting objectives and goals. Here, management establishes targets it will try to achieve in the coming months. Targets should be specific, quantitative, and measurable within a fixed period of time. An objective like "significant future growth" is too vague and should be replaced with something like "a 12-percent sales increase in nine months."

- Action programs assign the appropriate personnel and physical resources to accomplish the stated objectives. Management draws up a detailed work schedule, listing responsibilities, tasks, priorities, milestones, and deadlines for each program. This linkage of goals and strategies brings the market plan to life.

The rest is up to you. While these mistakes are by no means the only ones you can commit, anticipating and avoiding such common blunders can go a long way in the effort to build and maintain a profitable company.

Credit: *Working Woman* magazine

WHERE TO FIND IT

American Woman's Economic
Development Corporation
(AWED)
The Lincoln Building
60 East 42nd Street
New York, NY 10165
(212) 692-9100

PAYROLL

How to Cut the Payroll without Cutting the Staff

Cutting the payroll without cutting the staff—that's a magic act every small business would like to perform. And they can, with nothing more mysterious than creative compensation and tax planning. By exploring new ways to compensate employees and by capitalizing on cost-cutting opportunities, management can simultaneously trim expenses and boost productivity.

One approach is to replace part of the employees' base salary with variable compensation.

"The idea is to reduce the employees' fixed pay while at the same time offering them the opportunity to earn more in commissions, profit sharing, or bonuses," says an executive with Towers, Perrin, Forster & Crosby (TPF&C), compensation consultants. "This puts part of the employee's compensation 'at risk'—it is earned only if the company or the employee exceeds a certain quota. As a result, payroll costs decline when business is soft and rise only when the company is doing well.

"Take the employee earning $20,000 a year. By reducing his fixed pay to $18,000 but

offering him participation in a profit-sharing plan, management can cut the fixed payroll and increase motivation."

Another strategy calls for reducing salaries in exchange for nontaxable benefits.

"It's always hard to reduce salaries unless you give employees something attractive in return," says a manager with a national accounting firm. "Certain benefits, such as group medical or life insurance, can be just the thing. Because these benefits are not taxable to the employee, they will be worth more than an equivalent amount of salary."

Consider these additional compensation strategies:

1. To meet heightened work-load requirements, authorize increased overtime for existing personnel before hiring new employees. "Additions to the staff can add substantially to benefit costs," says the TPF&C executive. "Each new employee may be entitled to a complete benefits package. This coupled with additional expenses for training, space, and equipment can make it more cost-effective to pay overtime, even at time and a half, than to hire new people."

2. Before replacing retired or dismissed employees, determine if the function is really necessary or if it has been made obsolete by computer systems or changes in business operations. First determine if a job should be filled at all, then consider who, if anyone, should fill it.

3. Identify personnel who may qualify as independent contractors rather than employees. "The employer does not have to pay Social Security or federal unemployment taxes for independent contractors," says a tax partner with accountants Peat Marwick. "Nor does he have to pay for employee benefits. Taken together, all of this can mean substantial savings.

"Although the change to contractor status has to comply with certain tests—one of which is that the contractor is operating under his or her own control rather than the company's—it can be used to cut payroll costs in many situations."

4. Use temporary employment services to fill seasonal or other short-term personnel requirements. These employees are not entitled to qualified retirement plans or employee fringe benefits.

PERSONNEL RECRUITING

How to Hire a Key Employee

Much to his surprise, the person who conceives and founds a business often learns that he cannot singlehandedly guide its growth. A professional manager is needed to complement the owner's skills and, in some cases, to be groomed as his successor.

The position calls for a rare individual capable of bridging the gap between the entrepreneur's personal style and the company's need for disciplined management. Finding the ideal candidate can be a major challenge.

"The goal is to identify someone whose skills, background, and personal attributes make that individual ideally suited to run a small, closely held company," says a partner with Arthur Young Executive Resource Consultants. "That may mean overlooking executives with impressive experience in managing large organizations because their experience may not translate well to smaller ventures. You want every indication that the person's past performance can be successfully applied to the position at hand."

Search executives active in recruiting small business managers paint this portrait of the ideal candidate:

1. General management experience including profit-and-loss accountability for a company, division, or affiliate. The individual must be accustomed to the pressure of meeting specific bottom-line objectives.

2. Business skills that complement rather than duplicate the founder's. "In a typical case, we were asked to recruit a president for a young computer company founded by a technical wizard who was weak in the standard operating disciplines," explains the Arthur Young partner. "So we recommended an experienced manager strong in marketing and finance. Paired with the owner's manufacturing know-how, they made an excellent team capable of meeting the company's immediate and long-range challenges."

3. A track record in managing significant growth, taking a company from one stage of its life cycle to the next, higher level. "Anyone who has guided a company from $5 million in sales to $30 million, for example, is accustomed to juggling a lot of balls in the air, to making snap decisions, and to dealing with crises," the Arthur Young partner says. "All of which is par for the course in managing a growth company. The skills, the mental attitude, differ markedly from those involved in so-called maintenance management, where a firm experiences little or no growth."

4. The sensitivity to move onto the owner's turf, protecting his ego while at the same time having the self-confidence to take strong and independent action. Adding a 'yes man' to the payroll does little to shore up the founder's weaknesses.

"The smaller the company, the more essential that the chemistry be right," says the president of a New York-based executive placement firm. "That's something you can't possibly learn in the course of a two-hour interview. A better approach is to hire the candidate on a three-month trial basis, giving both parties, the entrepreneur and the manager, ample opportunity to see how they work with each other."

5. Willingness to shift gears regularly, serving one day as a strategic planner and the next as a hands-on sales rep demonstrating products to a key customer. The individual who has spent his career with a big corporation and is used to delegating much of his responsibilities to subordinates may not be flexible enough to run a small venture. He won't have that critical involvement in all facets of the company's operations.

6. Valid motivation for seeking the position. A corporate executive out of work and under financial pressure may accept the small company's offer as a last resort—only to leave once a more attractive opportunity comes along. To avoid this, favor those candidates who are currently employed or who appear genuinely interested in the greater challenge and involvement of an entrepreneurial environment.

Small business owners can launch a search of their own, using recruitment advertising and industry contacts to identify the ideal candidate. Or they can hire search consultants to find and recommend qualified managers. Professionals generally charge one-third of the first year's compensation. Ask business associates and trade groups for the names of reputable search firms.

PRICING

Savvy Pricing Can Boost Profits and Market Share

When a department store found itself saddled with an unsold inventory of "bargain" ties, the merchants took a deceptively simple action that changed the product's image and its ultimate fate in the marketplace: they raised the price from $5 to $25. Within weeks, the ties sold out.

Price, as the merchants proved, can say more about a product than name, packaging, or ingredients. And it can have a dramatic impact on sales, competition, and profit. But for many small businesses, pricing is little more than a knee-jerk response to costs.

"By routinely adding a fixed markup to costs, small companies may be artificially limiting profit potential and market share," says a vice-president of Arthur D. Little, a national consulting firm. "To structure prices properly, they must first consider the kind of goods they are selling. Ego-sensitive items, such as perfume and jewelry, can command at least twice their cost, while staples may be limited to cost plus 50 percent. Setting prices based on the products' appeal as well as the company's overall marketing objectives can maximize financial performance."

Sometimes, cutting prices can bolster the bottom line. Discounts and promotions, though they may reduce margins, can increase sales volume and aggregate profits.

"Loss-leader pricing is based on this strategy," says a small business partner for accountant Price Waterhouse. "Typically, items with wide appeal are sold near or below cost to draw customers into the store. Those who come for the bargains generally make additional purchases of profitable, full-priced merchandise.

"In a variation of this, called low balling, service firms pitching a new client intentionally price their work substantially below competitors' fees. The objective is to get a foot in the door—to prove to the client that the firm is capable of meeting its needs on an ongoing basis. Once a relationship is established, fees can be raised to more profitable levels."

Consider these additional pricing guidelines:

1. Unique or exclusive merchandise can escape the constraints of standard markups.

Because price comparisons are not possible, management is free to charge what the market will bear. Seeding product lines with these exclusive goods can help small companies raise total profits.

2. Anticipate consumer psychology: "People still believe that you get what you pay for," says the Arthur Little executive. "Too low a price can signify poor quality, or worse. When an auto parts chain that advertised recapped tires for $9.95 found few takers, they raised the price to $19.95 and sold out the first weekend. Clearly, the public believed that recaps for under $10 were too dangerous while the very same tires at a higher price were a good buy."

3. Maintain the integrity of list prices. Holding periodic sales, with prices discounted from list, gives consumers real bargains. "Rather than permanently reducing a $1 list item to 90 cents," the Arthur Little executive says, "management is usually better off promoting it for 80 to 90 cents from time to time and then returning to list. Even if the company ends up with the same gross income, it has given its customers a demonstrable savings and has held the line on regular prices."

4. Use "foul-weather" pricing to generate sales in recessionary periods. This calls for reducing prices below full product cost but keeping them high enough to cover out-of-pocket expenses and some part of fixed overhead. This can help small manufacturers maintain cash flow until business conditions improve. It is to be used only as a last resort.

Accountants and consultants can help structure pricing strategies.

Lease Financing Helps Close Sales

The age-old business formula—having the right product at the right price—may no longer be the secret to successful sales. Increasingly, attractive financing has to be part of the package. More than ever, manageable payment terms bridge the gap between "just looking" and completed transactions.

The type of financing that works best depends on the product and the amount of money involved. For mid- to big-ticket sales, leasing may be the right choice. By converting list prices into small monthly payments, it removes the cash obstacle that thwarts many sales.

"Tell a customer that a machine costs $25,000 and you're putting a formidable roadblock in his way," says an executive with a major leasing company. "He may not have the cash or may be reluctant to dilute his working capital. But with leasing, the $25,000 figure need not be quoted. Instead, the sales proposal is based on $600 per month for 60 months. This way, the buyer sees how to work the cost into his monthly budget. There's no need to shell out a lump sum."

Small companies can make the leasing option available to their customers. In a typical transaction, ABC Office Equipment arranges to sell a state-of-the-art word processing system to the law firm of Smith & Jones. Because the $50,000 price tag poses a cash obstacle, ABC sells the system to a leasing company, which in turn leases it to Smith & Jones for $1,200 per month.

"Not only is the sale closed but the vendor may wind up with a more profitable deal," the executive adds. "Because leasing customers focus primarily on the monthly payment rather than the total cost, the item can be sold at or near list price. That may be hard to do with cash sales. For the same reason, high-markup peripherals and accessories that might otherwise exceed the buyer's budget can be added to the sale."

Leasing companies range from local independents to bank subsidiaries operating on the national level.

"Vendors interested in offering their customers lease financing can work with us in one of two ways," says a vice-president of corporate marketing for Manufacturers Hanover Leasing. "With an informal arrangement, we stand ready to do a lease from time to time as the company's needs arise. They can count on us as a financing source. A step up from this, an ongoing relationship, is based on a formal contract that specifies a range of services we provide the vendor, including assistance in marketing and promoting leasing deals."

Small companies may promote lease financing as an attractive alternative to bank loans. Leases can be structured with little or no down payment, thus providing customers with 100 percent financing, as compared to 70 or 80 percent with term loans. And because leases can be negotiated independently of established credit lines, the company's borrowing power may not be diluted.

Credit terms for leasing deals vary with the leasing company and the size of the transaction. Generally, customers seeking lease financing must meet the following tests:

- Three to five years of satisfactory operations
- Sound credit history
- No liens or tax judgments
- The lease's dollar value must be in reasonable proportion to the corporation's net worth.

"We inform our customers that they can do a cash or lease deal," says the chairman of a company that installs energy conservation equipment, "and leave it to them to make the choice. Enough have chosen leasing to convince me that it's a potent marketing tool."

RATIOS

Key Ratios Can Reveal Business Trends

The familiar computer phrase "garbage in, garbage out" holds an important lesson for entrepreneurs. Business decisions, like computer programs, are only as good as the information on which they are based. To protect the company's interests, management must seek a steady flow of accurate and timely data.

One approach is to manage by the ratios. Put simply, this means assembling internal data into key formulas that provide revealing snapshots of the company's financial status. The results are then compared on a month-to-month and year-to-year basis, giving management insight into current conditions and a continuing record of its progress.

"By periodically reviewing critical ratios, small business owners can guide their companies toward higher profits, control their financial condition, and ensure that cash flow is adequate to meet the current volume of business," says a senior manager with the Houston office of accountants Peat Marwick. "Equally important, management can spot trends and changes early, and thereby can make effective operational changes where necessary."

The following ratios are computed from data in the company's financial statements:

1. Solvency ratios indicate the company's ability to meet short-term obligations. This test of liquidity projects the company's ability to match current assets and current liabilities

and therefore to pay its bills in a timely manner.

The most common measure of solvency, the current ratio, is computed by dividing current assets (including cash, inventory, and accounts receivable) by current liabilities (including property taxes, payroll, and certain loan payments). ABC Company, with current assets of $2 million and current liabilities of $1 million, has a current ratio of 2:1. If this is considered inadequate for its industry, ABC can shore up its current ratio by converting current liabilities to long-term liabilities. For example, management can try to change a revolving line of credit to a five-year term loan. In this way, only the first 12 months of payments would be counted with current liabilities.

"This makes good business sense," says a New York-based financial consultant. "Current liabilities should be financing current assets, and long-term liabilities should be financing long-term assets. Building an extension to your store or plant is for the long-term good of the business and should be financed with a term loan. On the other hand, inventory should be financed with a revolving line of credit that's paid down as the goods are sold."

2. Activity ratios serve as key barometers of the company's operations. "They indicate just how efficiently resources are being utilized," says the Peat Marwick manager. "For example, to keep the average investment in inventory low, inventory turnover—computed as the cost of goods sold over inventory—should be high. A decreasing rate of inventory turnover could mean too many slow-moving or obsolete items. This alerts management to identify these items and weed them out."

Keep in mind that inventory is a cash eater. When you buy inventory, you have to use cash, which you don't get back until the goods are sold. The goal then is to run the company with as little inventory as possible without limiting sales opportunities. Compare the ratio at given intervals to see how well you are performing.

Another major activity ratio, the average collection period, reveals how quickly receivables are being collected. It is figured by taking accounts receivable over average daily sales. For example, a company with an accounts-receivable balance of $100,000 and with average daily sales of $5,000 would have a ratio of 20:1, meaning it takes 20 days to collect on its accounts. Because 30 days is the target, the company is doing well. If the ratio were 50:1, the company could improve its performance by tightening up credit or being more aggressive in collections.

3. Profitability ratios put the bottom line in perspective, comparing this number to other benchmarks rather than viewing it as an isolated statistic. In a nutshell, profitability ratios indicate whether the assets and efforts invested in the business are earning a satisfactory return.

Key profitability ratios include:

- Net profit as a percentage of sales—figured by dividing income before taxes by net sales.
- Net profit to net worth—calculated by dividing income before taxes by tangible net worth.

Many trade associations publish lists of average ratios for their member companies. Small companies should obtain this data, comparing their performance to that of similar companies. This gives management an idea of how it stacks up against others and indicates where there is room for improvement.

ETCETERA

Comparing the Commonest Measurement Units

Approximate conversions from U.S. to metric and vice versa.

	When you know:	You can find:	If you multiply by:
Length	inches	millimeters	25
	feet	centimeters	30
	yards	meters	0.9
	miles	kilometers	1.6
	millimeters	inches	0.04
	centimeters	inches	0.4
	meters	yards	1.1
	kilometers	miles	0.6
Area	square inches	square centimeters	6.5
	square feet	square meters	0.09
	square yards	square meters	0.8
	square miles	square kilometers	2.6
	acres	square hectometers (hectares)	0.4
	square centimeters	square inches	0.16
	square meters	square yards	1.2
	square kilometers	square miles	0.4
	square hectometers (hectares)	acres	2.5
Mass	ounces	grams	28
	pounds	kilograms	0.45
	short tons	megagrams	0.9
	grams	ounces	0.035
	kilograms	pounds	2.2
	megagrams (metric tons)	short tons	1.1
Liquid volume	ounces	milliliters	30
	pints	liters	0.47
	quarts	liters	0.95
	gallons	liters	3.8
	milliliters	ounces	0.034
	liters	pints	2.1
	liters	quarts	1.06
	liters	gallons	0.26
Temperature	degrees Fahrenheit	degrees Celsius	5/9 (after subtracting 32)
	degrees Celsius	degrees Fahrenheit	9/5 (then add 32)

RELOCATIONS

Advance Planning Smooths the Way for Corporate Relocations

Small businesses are a transient lot. As leases expire, as companies outgrow their space, management packs up the computers, ships the inventory, and directs the staff to a new location. But all too often that's when the trouble begins.

"Because most companies fail to plan for a move, they find that although they're ready to do business at the new site, the new site isn't ready for them," says an executive with New York-based Relocation Management Systems, Inc. (RMS). "There's no phone service, no data lines, no room for the word processor, and no idea, on anyone's part, of what went wrong. But that's not hard to figure out. By viewing the move as a transaction that would somehow take care of itself, management sowed the seeds of its own predicament."

How to avoid the moving-day blues? How to make certain the new facility is right for the company and ready to do business the day the boss's desk is installed? Relocation consultants suggest a simple strategy: Begin planning long before the move is made.

"The idea is to build the company's space requirements into its business plan, projecting when current space will be inadequate to meet operating requirements and how much more space will be needed as the company trades up to a larger facility," the RMS executive explains. "For example, a distributorship with 50 employees, growing at about 10 percent a year, projects that it will have 67 employees in three years, five more people than its current offices can hold. Based on this projection, management draws a timetable for its next relocation, scheduling the search for new facilities in about 18 months with a planned move-in date a year later."

Once the need to move is established and a target date set, management must focus on the logistics of a smooth and timely relocation. Experts offer the following guidelines:

1. Reverse the standard action plan by arranging for telephone service first and a moving company last. "The movers only need about six weeks' lead time, but the telephone company may need six months to arrange for lines and equipment," says the RMS executive. "This is especially true in urban areas, where the phone companies are often swamped with back orders, causing long delays in new installations. To avoid a lapse in phone service, it's important to get your order into the pipeline as quickly as possible.

"Once the order is taken, ask for a confirmation number and hold onto it. Should the phone company lose its records, the number will get you back into the rotation without going to the end of the line."

2. Assign a single employee—office managers are prime candidates—to orchestrate the relocation. Authorize the individual to negotiate with vendors and to set deadlines for the move.

Relocation consultants can also fill this role, handling all aspects of the move from site selection to hiring the moving vans. Figure hourly fees of from $50 to $75, or roughly one-half percent of the total cost of the move.

3. Inform employees of the move as soon as the decision is final. "Be candid about which employees will be asked to move with the company and how management will help to defray their relocation costs," says a manager with Merrill Lynch Relocation Management. "The last thing you want is for the rumor mill to speculate on who is going along and who will be left behind. Fearing for their jobs, key people may seek employ-

ment elsewhere, depriving the company of valued talent."

4. Take competitive bids for all major services, comparing at least four vendors in each category. Savings of as little as 5 percent on telephones systems, interior construction, and movers can trim $10,000 or more from the relocation.

5. Make certain that vendors are experienced in serving small business. References are generally the best gauge of a vendor's capabilities. But don't accept the printed list of references the company routinely hands out. Instead, ask for the names of two clients the vendor has served within the past six months.

6. Compile a master checklist of everything likely to be affected by the move—from employee housing to the company's letterhead—and make certain that steps are being taken to ensure a smooth transition. The underlying objective of a planned relocation is to make sure the company functions efficiently until the last employee vacates the building and that the business starts up at the new location without interruption.

SELLING A BUSINESS

Watch for Hidden Costs

In the life of an entrepreneur, two events stand out: the day the business is launched and the day it is sold. While the former is widely recognized as a high-risk proposition, the latter is viewed as the pot of gold at the end of the rainbow. But this is misleading. Although the sale of a successful venture can be emotionally and financially rewarding, it is also fraught with as much risk as the initial decision to open the company's doors.

"When it comes to selling out, small business owners often focus on one factor only—how much they're going to get for the company," says a partner with the New York and Washington, D.C., law firm of Parker Chapin Flattau & Klimpl. "This shortsighted concern with the selling price blinds them to equally important considerations that can dramatically diminish their net proceeds from the sale. These 'hidden costs' are found in three major areas: continuing liabilities, tax implications, and agreements governing the owner's future activities.

"Let's take a look at the issue of continuing liabilities. Assume ABC Widgets sells out to competitor XYZ and in so doing retains responsibility for any claims against its products that were sold before the business changed hands. Because there were no apparent problems with its products, ABC felt comfortable with this stipulation, a common one in business sales.

"But note the word 'apparent.' Little did ABC know that soon after it accepted responsibility for the products it had sold that a customer would file, and win, a $1 million product liability suit for personal injury. Because ABC's product liability insurance was no longer effective due to the nature of the policy, the former owners were responsible for the full amount out of pocket—a sum nearly equaling the profit they'd earned on the sale of the business. A hidden cost nearly wiped out all the appreciation they'd built into the company through a decade of hard work."

What to do about hidden costs? Happily, every potential problem has a relatively effective safeguard. To protect against continuing liability, for example, management could maintain liability insurance covering transactions that took place during the time they owned the company or could insist on a sales contract that shifts liability to the new owners. Success in the latter—as in other contract provisions—depends on the seller's bargaining power.

Consider these additional "hidden cost" factors and ways to avoid them:

1. Sell Assets or Stock. A business can be sold as an ongoing entity—complete with goodwill, physical plant, customer relations, and the like—or its assets can be sold. In an increasing number of cases, buyers opt for the latter because it enables them to gain the company's most valuable components without taking on its liabilities—which, as in the product liability case, can lurk beneath the surface at the time of the sale.

"But from the seller's standpoint, the sale or exchange of the company's stock, rather than its assets alone, is usually the preferred type of transaction," the lawyer says. "If properly structured and negotiated, the seller winds up with cash or stock and triggers very few liabilities beyond possible tax on the profit received.

"But a buyer unwilling to take on all the skeletons in the seller's closet may want to acquire only those assets and obligations needed to continue business operations, leaving the rest in the seller's corporation. Negotiation of the purchase price must therefore be based on a firm understanding of which liabilities the buyer assumes and which are retained by the seller. Should the seller agree to an asset rather than a stock sale, he must act to limit his liabilities and in turn his potential for future losses."

2. Seller's Liabilities. At some point in the negotiations, the seller must inventory all of his other obligations. Some are straightforward, such as loans, supply contracts, leases, employment agreements; others are contingent liabilities, such as claims based on labor contracts, product warranties, and product liability.

"The seller's problem is to assess the likely cost of obligations not assumed by the buyer," the lawyer warns. "For example, let's say a seller has a union contract under which it has been contributing to the union's pension plan. Well, it turns out it's not really the union's pension plan because under the National Labor Relations Act it is a separate pension trust with an equal number of employee and employer trustees—in other words, a multiemployer pension plan.

"Let's further assume the seller has been contributing to the plan for many years and has not missed a single payment. Unfortunately, under the Multi-Employer Pension Plan Amendments Act, employers who withdraw may still be liable with respect to 'unfunded vested liabilities' of the fund, which can be triggered by a sale of assets. Sometimes liability can be avoided if it is small enough or if the fund receives a bond assuring it that the buyer will continue to make contributions at a similar rate for several years. But the bond can be expensive, and the parties had better agree who will bear the expense.

"This is a serious matter. We have heard of business owners who decided to sell out and retire only to be handed a bill by the pension fund, sometimes large enough to force them out of retirement."

3. Buyer's Failure to Perform. To complicate matters further, the buyer's agreement to assume certain liabilities in an asset sale may not take the seller off the hook. For example, should the buyer agree to honor a creditor's claim, only to refuse payment at a later date, the seller may be held "secondarily liable."

"A seller must review the buyer's financial condition to determine how safe the assumption of liability is," the lawyer advises. "If the buyer's financial condition appears weak, the seller should seek an increase in the purchase price, using the added funds to pay its creditors directly. It's also a good idea to ask a principal of the acquiring company to guarantee the payment of assumed obligations personally."

Sellers are also advised to seek covenants requiring the buyer to:

- indemnify and hold the seller harmless from the buyer's failure to perform.
- pay obligations to particular vendors in the order in which they mature so that the buyer pays obligations incurred by the seller prior to new obligations he may incur.

4. Representations and Warranties. Before a deal is signed, buyers will likely insist that the seller make certain warranties about the business, its assets and operations. Here too, hidden liabilities could expose the seller to substantial costs.

The lawyer offers sellers the following guidelines for negotiating warranties as part of the business sale:

- Accounts Receivable: Try to limit representations on the collectability of accounts receivable to assurances that the amounts due are bona fide. If this proves impossible, seek to obtain credit for doubtful accounts appearing on the books or insist on the right to participate in settlements.
- Inventory: The seller should resist guaranteeing the price at which inventory will be sold by the buyer. Instead, buyers should review the inventory in advance and should seek to reflect any risk of salability in the purchase price.
- Taxes: The buyer will seek to be indemnified by the seller against any taxes which may arise upon audit of tax years

preceding the sale. The least the seller should obtain is an agreement which allows him or her to participate in the audit and to contest IRS findings.

Let us assume that both parties are reasonable and the terms of the deal have been hammered out, with one notable exception: the owner's fate once he or she relinquishes control. Two major options are evident: to stay on in a management capacity or to start a new business. The terms of the sales agreement can have a major impact on both.

"Let's say you are 55 years old and do not want to retire or start again in a new venture," the lawyer says. "Should you stay on with the company in the capacity of a professional manager, it's best to seek an employment contract that will take you through to retirement. On the other hand, if you are 40 years old and selling your first business, you may have time to start two or three new businesses before you retire. So you'll want maximum freedom to pursue entrepreneurial interests the moment you leave the old company.

"The buyer, of course, will have a different objective. He'll want to keep you out of your old line with a strong noncompetition agreement. Your goal is to limit the terms of this agreement so as to provide you with the greatest flexibility in developing new business ventures.

"In sum, selling a business may not be as simple as it seems. The transaction can leave an unsuspecting seller with future liabilities that were never anticipated. The best defense is to weigh the nature, effect, and likelihood of all risks and reflect them in the selling price. Otherwise you may sell now and be forced to pay later."

Seek professional advice when buying and selling businesses. The tax rules and other costs are subject to change at any time.

SALESMANSHIP

Keep Small Business Growing

Salesmanship, some say, is a dying art. Up-staged by computer technology and mass promotions, the old-fashioned process of personal selling has lost its once-vaunted status as a vital component of business success.

But as every business discovers soon enough, technology cannot sell goods or services. By the same token, information systems are only as good as the people who use them. Unless salesmanship is made part of a company's culture—unless those responsible for generating new business learn the fundamentals of successful selling—the company will dry up like a pond deprived of rain.

"I recently received a business card from one of America's most successful entrepreneurs—a man who founded and presides over a major commercial enterprise," says Joseph Mancuso, president of the Center for Entrepreneurial Management. "His card could have carried the title of chairman, CEO, or any other executive rank. But instead it just had the man's name followed by the designation 'professional salesman.' That's his way of telling the world that no matter what talents a person brings to his business, none are more important than the ability to sell."

For small business owners, many of whom are strong in technical and financial disciplines but weak in sales, the goals are to sharpen their personal skills and to make salesmanship a key part of employee training. Consider these guidelines for successful selling:

1. When dealing with consumers, position yourself as an adviser rather than a salesman. Make it clear that you want to help the customer buy the product or service that meets his or her needs rather than the one that fulfills the company's marketing objectives. Trust is critical for enduring customer relationships.

2. In any consumer unit, key decision makers determine whether or not a purchase is made. Identify these individuals and direct your efforts to them.

"Every time I tried to sell to a major company that I knew was buying from the competition, I had the proverbial door slammed in my face," says a salesman for an office equipment distributor. "Only after a chance meeting with a purchasing assistant did I find that the office manager rather than the purchasing department had the authority to purchase photocopiers. For years I'd been wasting my time and energies on a prospect who couldn't buy from me no matter how persuasive I might be. That taught me a lesson: always sell to a name, not to a number or a department. Find out who makes the decisions and sell to them."

3. Know everything about your product there is to know. Be prepared to field consumer questions on technical specifications, performance standards, warranties, and equally important, on competitive products. Tell why your make or brand is superior.

4. Take the customer's perspective, explaining not why the product should be sold (to compensate the company and its sales reps) but why it should be bought (to fill a consumer need). Focus on the product's unique qualities: what it can do to improve the customer's career, life-style, appearance, or standard of living.

5. Never take "no" for an answer. Find a way to overcome consumer resistance to your product or service by offering other models (different colors, sizes, prices), extended payment terms, leasing plans, or special discounts. Even if a sale is not made,

leave the door open for a follow-up visit. Tell the prospect you will return with a proposal that will meet his or her needs.

6. Call on customers (in person or by telephone) within five days of the sale, asking if they are pleased with the product and if you can be of service in any way. Use this opportunity to correct budding problems that can interfere with customer satisfaction, thus reducing the likelihood of future sales.

7. Keep your name before the customer year-round. Remember birthdays, business anniversaries, holidays. Make it a practice to call on the customer now and then—or better yet take him or her to lunch—without selling a thing. Use these opportunities to build personal relationships, and business will surely follow.

Good salesmen, it is said, are masters of timing: they know when to sell and equally important, when not to sell.

Salesmanship means promoting your company as well as its products. Through the years, the legendary entrepreneurs have shared a common talent for self-promotion. Employing a mixed bag of marketing tools, they've turned obscure companies into household names and in the process have garnered invaluable exposure for their products and services.

These flamboyant business owners have recognized that a company's fate hinges on its ability to stand out from the crowd. Fortunately, this doesn't boil down to a spending contest. Even those companies with little or no money for standard promotions can outmaneuver cash-rich competitors, winning recognition while the others are struggling against anonymity. The difference, again, lies in the owner's flair for promotion.

"A super product or service isn't enough to guarantee success," Mancuso says. "The entrepreneur has to go out and sell it. That means taking every opportunity to address an audience, to do a newspaper interview, to call on prospective customers. The more creativity you bring to these opportunities, the more the company's name will be remembered and the more goods you will sell."

How can entrepreneurs capture public attention and make their companies better known in the marketplace? Consider these promotional tactics:

1. Attract Media Coverage. Publications are open to original stories about companies and their products. Identify that aspect of your business that makes it unique—be it a high-tech breakthrough or a creative credit plan—and bring it to the attention of newspapers and magazines. Although coverage is never guaranteed, persistence can pay off. Timely mention in a prominent publication can take the company from obscurity to instant recognition.

"When one of my clients first launched a consulting firm that helped troubled retailers revise and rejuvenate their operations, few merchants understood the concept," says a public relations executive. "But when an article explaining the firm's modus operandi appeared in *Business Week*, dozens of companies recognized a need for their services and hired them soon after. The article gave the firm momentum."

2. Create a Unique Calling Card. Convinced that first impressions are the most enduring, skilled promoters design calling cards that command attention, making the individual virtually unforgettable.

The president of a Houston bank foregoes the traditional business card in favor of silver dollars, with his name and phone number printed on gold labels affixed to the coins. "Customers tell me they keep business cards in two places," the banker says. "A stack of several hundred in a file drawer and mine alone sitting atop their desks. Because it is a conversation piece, it gets special treatment. That means more recognition for me and my bank. And don't forget, the cards are samples of what I'm selling: money."

3. Sponsor Seminars. Some of the most effective selling occurs in an educational format. Companies marketing state-of-the-art technology or sophisticated business services can use seminar programs to demonstrate their offerings and to establish themselves as sources of information.

"This strategy is particularly useful for professional firms," says a marketing consultant who conducts more than 50 seminars a year. "That's because they want to sell their services without appearing overly commercial. Take the lawyer creating a tax practice geared to corporate clients. By hosting seminars explaining the impact of the new tax reform act, he gains instant recognition as an expert in the field."

4. Star in Your Own Advertising. Featuring the entrepreneur in the company's ads does more than flatter the owner's ego. It gives the individual celebrity status, making him or her a more effective corporate salesperson.

"The owner's presence can add credibility to the advertising message," Mancuso says. "Consider Victor Kiam and his Remington razors. The man has turned what was once a troubled venture into a highly successful enterprise, much of it due to his personal magnetism. People see his face on television, they trust him, and they buy his products. A knack for promotion has helped this entrepreneur compete with the giants of his industry and beat them at their own game."

What makes for successful self-promotion varies from product to product and industry to industry. Consider your ultimate objectives and then design a personal sales program that can make your product and your company a household name.

RETAIL THEFT

The Hazards

In preventing theft, you should be aware of certain hazards.

Pricing

Loosely controlled pricing procedures constitute a major cause of inventory "shrinkage."

Case in point. Items in a thrift store were ticketed in pencil. Moreover, some tickets were unmarked. Since the store was inadequately staffed, many customers marked down prices, switched tickets, or wrote in their own prices.

Antitheft pointers. Price items by machine or stamp, not by handwriting.

Permit only authorized employees to set prices and mark merchandise.

Make unannounced spot checks to be sure that actual prices agree with authorized prices and price charge records.

Refunds

Refunds provide dishonest employees an easy means to ply their trade. There are more ways to lose money on returns or refunds than the average retailer dreams possible.

Case in point. In one store, many returned items were marked down to a fraction of cost because of damage. It was easy for clerks to get authorization to buy "as is" merchandise. When they were armed with an okay, they substituted first-grade items for "as is" stock.

Antitheft pointers. Insist on a merchandise inspection by someone other than the person who made the sale.

Match items to the return vouchers and then return the merchandise to stock as quickly as possible.

Keep a tight control on all credit documents. Spot-check customers by mail or telephone to make sure they got their refunds.

Popular Salespeople

The popular salesperson is a great asset—providing he or she is popular for the right reasons. However, many salespeople win "fans" because of the deals they swing and the favors they grant.

Case in point. Customers stood in line to wait for one veteran saleswoman. They refused to be served by anyone else. And no wonder! She switched tickets for many "special" customers, giving them substantial markdowns. Store losses amounted to about $300 a week, not including $25 a week in increased commissions for the crook.

Antitheft pointers. The popular salesperson may be your biggest asset. But don't take it for granted. Find out for yourself why he or she is so well liked.

Pay special attention to the salesperson who is visited by too many personal friends. To discourage such socializing, some retailers hire people who live outside the immediate store vicinity.

Cash Handling

The cashier's post is particularly vulnerable to theft. The experienced cash handler with larceny on his or her mind can rob a store blind in a hundred and one ways.

Case in point. A store owner's sales were high, but profits were dragging. The cause was traced to a cashier who rang up only some of the items bought by "customers." In most cases, the cashier didn't ring "put-downs" at all. (A "put-down" is the right amount of cash that a customer leaves on the counter, then leaves without waiting for a receipt.)

Antitheft pointers. Keep a sharp eye open for signals—nods, winks, and so on—between cashiers and customers.

Pay special attention to cashiers when they are surrounded by clusters of people.

Be alert to the use of over-ring slips to cover up shortages

Watch for items bypassed when ringing up sales.

Check personal checks to make sure they are not being used to cover up shortages.

Use a professional shopper to check for violations of cash register and related procedures.

Backdoor Thefts

Large-scale theft is carried on more often through the back than the front door. Hundreds, even thousands, of dollars' worth of merchandise can be stolen within a few seconds.

Case in point. A stock clerk parked his car at the receiving dock. He kept the trunk closed but unlocked. At 12:30 P.M., when the shipping-receiving manager was at lunch, the stock clerk threw full cartons of shoes into the trunk and then slammed it locked. Elapsed time: 18 seconds.

Antitheft pointers. Have a secondary check

by a worker or salesperson on all incoming shipments.

Insist on flattening all trash cartons and make spot checks of trash after hours.

Prohibit employees from parking near receiving door or dock.

Keep receiving door locked when not in use. Make sure locked door cannot be raised a few inches. A receiving door should be opened only by a supervisor, who remains in the area until it's locked.

Alarm on door should ring until turned off, with key held by store manager.

Distribute door keys carefully and change lock cylinders periodically.

Shoplifting

Shoplifting is greatest in the self-service store located in a metropolitan area. But regardless of location, no retailers can afford to leave themselves unprotected against shoplifters. The following actions can help to cut down on shoplifting losses.

Keep tight checks and controls on washrooms and fitting rooms.

Keep unused checkout aisles closed. Schedule working hours to assure adequate personal coverage during peak periods.

Keep doors that are used infrequently locked.

Post antishoplifting signs.

Display small inexpensive items behind the checkout counters.

Keep small expensive items in locked display cabinets.

Use plainclothes patrols in larger stores.

Make sure employees know what to do when they spot a shoplifter.

Turn over apprehended shoplifters to the police.

During busy periods, station a uniformed guard at your exit.

Credit: U.S. Small Business Administration and Saul D. Aster

Constitution of the American Small Business Population

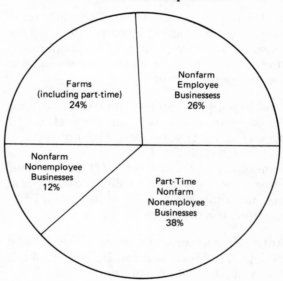

There are approximately 14 million small businesses in the United States, but a large proportion are part-time operations.

Source: National Federation of Independent Business Research and Education Foundation

IV. Today Your Market, Tomorrow the World

How to Make Your Small Business Bigger

◇══◇

Marketing Checklist for Small Retailers

If your retail firm is going to be successful over the long run, it must focus on serving customer needs and desires. The essence of marketing rests on your understanding the customer and delivering a unique product or service that he or she cannot find from your competition.

Your use of customer analysis and basic market research will enable you to predict which items will appeal to the tastes of customers. On the other hand, sound buying techniques and strong vendor ties are needed if you are to stock those items that effectively satisfy customer demand.

Pricing is a critical ingredient in your profit picture. Plan price policies that you will follow and be familiar with local, state, and federal regulations.

A wide variety of promotional methods is available to you. Choose the media mix that best advertises the uniqueness of your store to present and potential customers.

A serious commitment by management to planning both short and long-term goals is essential to future success. Operations and special services includes your firm's customer credit terms and insurance coverage. Of course, such services are taking on added importance for consumers and should be marketed with their needs in mind.

Your primary concern with financial analysis and control should focus on the flow of funds. To this end, the use and management of your financial records becomes the foundation of your business.

In answering the following questions, you will be reminded of what you might still need to do to round out all marketing aspects of your business. Each "no" answer reveals an opportunity to do more for your business.

Customer Analysis

Who Are Your Target Customers and What Are They Seeking from You?	Yes	No
Have you profiled your customers by age, income, education, occupation, etc.?	☐	☐
Should you try to appeal to the entire market rather than a segment(s)?	☐	☐

263

Are you familiar with your customers' life-styles? ☐ ☐

Are there new customer segments or special markets that deserve attention? ☐ ☐

Have you looked into possible changes taking place among your target customers that could significantly affect your business? ☐ ☐

Do you know where your customers live? ☐ ☐

Do you use census data from your city or state (e.g., neighborhood tracts, income, population)? ☐ ☐

Are you aware of the reasons why customers shop at your store (convenience, price, quality products, etc.)? ☐ ☐

Do you stress a special area of appeal, such as lower prices, better quality, wider selection, convenient location, or convenient hours? ☐ ☐

Do you ask your customers for suggestions on ways to improve your operation? ☐ ☐

Do you know what products or services your customers most prefer? ☐ ☐

Do you use "want slips"? ☐ ☐

Do you belong to a trade association or local chamber of commerce? ☐ ☐

Do you subscribe to important trade publications? ☐ ☐

Do you know what seasons and holidays most influence your customer buying behavior? ☐ ☐

Have you considered using a consumer questionnaire to aid you in determining customer needs? ☐ ☐

Do you know at what other types of stores your customers shop? ☐ ☐

Do you visit market shows and conventions to help anticipate customer wants? ☐ ☐

Buying

Have You a Merchandise Budget (Planned Purchases) for Each Season? **Yes** **No**

Does it take into consideration planned sales, planned stockturn, and planned markdowns? ☐ ☐

Have you broken it down by departments and merchandise classifications? ☐ ☐

Have you a formal plan for deciding what to buy and from whom? ☐ ☐

Have you identified areas of negotiation that allow you favorable terms for buying (e.g., payment terms, promotions assistance, transportation costs, special buys, etc.)? ☐ ☐

Have you identified all internal and external sources of market information available? ☐ ☐

Have you a system for reviewing and testing new items coming onto the market? ☐ ☐

Have you considered using a basic stock list or a model stock plan in your buying? ☐ ☐

Are you using either a unit or dollar merchandise control system? ☐ ☐

Do you keep track of the success of your buying decisions in previous years to aid you in next year's buying? ☐ ☐

Do you attempt to consolidate your purchases with several key suppliers? ☐ ☐

Does your buying reflect an improved return on investment? ☐ ☐

Have you established a planned gross margin for your firm's operations and are you buying so as to achieve it? ☐ ☐

Do you plan exclusive or private brand programs? ☐ ☐

Do you take advantage of cash discounts and allowances offered by your vendor/supplier? ☐ ☐

Do you have reasonable expectations from your vendor? ☐ ☐

Does he have reasonable expectations of you? ☐ ☐

Have you developed a trusting relationship with your vendor/supplier? ☐ ☐

Have you a useful vendor/supplier evaluation system for determining their performance? ☐ ☐

Pricing

Have You Established a Set of Pricing Policies and Goals?

	Yes	No
Have you determined whether to price below, at, or above the market?	☐	☐
Do you set specific markups for each product?	☐	☐
Do you set markups for product categories?	☐	☐
Do you use a one-price policy rather than bargain with customers?	☐	☐
Do you offer discounts for quantity purchases or to special groups?	☐	☐
Do you set prices to cover full costs on every sale?	☐	☐
Do the prices you have established earn the gross margin you planned?	☐	☐
Do you clearly understand the market forces affecting your pricing methods?	☐	☐
Do you know which products are slow movers and which are fast?	☐	☐
Do you take this into consideration when pricing?	☐	☐
Do you experiment with odd or even price endings to increase your sales?	☐	☐
Do you know which products are price-sensitive to your customers, that is, when a slight increase in price will lead to a big dropoff in demand?	☐	☐

Do you know which of your products draw people when put on sale? ☐ ☐

Do you know the maximum price customers will pay for certain products? ☐ ☐

If the prices on some products are dropped too low, do buyers hesitate? ☐ ☐

Is there a specific time of year when your competitors have sales? ☐ ☐

Do your customers expect sales at certain times? ☐ ☐

Have you determined whether or not a series of sales is better than one annual clearance sale? ☐ ☐

Have you developed a markdown policy? ☐ ☐

Do you take markdowns on a regular basis or as needed? ☐ ☐

Do you know what role you want price to play in your overall retailing strategy? ☐ ☐

Are you influenced by competitors' price changes? ☐ ☐

Are There Restrictions Regarding Prices You Can Charge?
Yes No

Are you sure you know all the regulations affecting your business, such as two-for-one sales and the like? ☐ ☐

Do you issue "rainchecks" to customers when sale items are sold out so they can purchase later at the sale price? ☐ ☐

Promotion

Are You Familiar with the Strengths and Weaknesses of Various Promotional Methods?
Yes No

Are the unique appeals of your business reflected in the store image (e.g., low prices, quality product, special services, etc.)? ☐ ☐

Are these appeals promoted on a consistent basis? ☐ ☐

Have you considered how various media and promotional methods might be used for your firm? ☐ ☐

Do you know which of your items can be successfully advertised? ☐ ☐

Do you know when it is profitable to use institutional advertising? ☐ ☐

Do you know when product advertising is better? ☐ ☐

Do you record sales of merchandise advertised on each ad? ☐ ☐

Do you check store traffic? ☐ ☐

Do you know which of the media (radio, television, newspapers, yellow pages, billboards) can most effectively reach your target group? ☐ ☐

Do you know what can and cannot be said in your ads (truth-in-advertising requirements)? ☐ ☐

Can you make use of direct mail? ☐ ☐

Do you have a mailing list? If so, has it been updated recently? ☐ ☐

Is a mailing list available through customer checks or credit card receipts? ☐ ☐

Do you use coupons in your print ads? ☐ ☐

Are your promotional efforts fairly regular? ☐ ☐

Do you concentrate them on certain seasons? ☐ ☐

Are certain periods of the week better than others? ☐ ☐

Do you use trade journals and out-of-town newspapers for promotional ideas? ☐ ☐

Have you considered specialty advertising? ☐ ☐

Do you participate in activities of your chamber of commerce, merchants' association, better business bureau, or other civic organizations? ☐ ☐

Is There Financial or Technical Assistance Available that You Can Use to Enhance Your Promotional Efforts?

Yes   No

Have you considered customer seminars and classes? ☐ ☐

Can you get help from local newspapers, radio, or television? ☐ ☐

Are cooperative advertising funds available from vendor/suppliers? ☐ ☐

Do you tie your local efforts to your supplier's national program? ☐ ☐

Do you join with other merchants in area-wide programs? ☐ ☐

Do you ask customers to refer your business to friends and relatives? ☐ ☐

Have you looked for ratios to estimate what comparable firms are spending on promotion? ☐ ☐

Do you make use of community projects or publicity? ☐ ☐

Would a newsletter be useful to contact customers or remind them of your store? ☐ ☐

Do you study the advertising of other successful retail firms as well as your competitors'? ☐ ☐

Are Your Products Displayed to Maximize Their Appeal within the Store?

Yes   No

Do you know which of your items have unusual eye appeal and can be effective in displays? ☐ ☐

Have you figured out the best locations in the store for displays? ☐ ☐

Are you making use of window displays to attract customers? ☐ ☐

Have you a schedule for changing various displays? ☐ ☐

Do you display attention-getting items where they will call attention to other products as well? ☐ ☐

Do you use signs to aid your customers' shopping? ☐ ☐

Do signs in your store provide useful price and product information? ☐ ☐

Do you know which items are bought on "impulse" and therefore should be placed in high-traffic areas? ☐ ☐

Do you have an attractive store-front? ☐ ☐

Do your vendor/suppliers offer financing of accounts receivable, floor displays, fixtures, and so forth? ☐ ☐

Management

Have You Developed a Set of Plans for the Year's Operations?

Yes No

Do your plans address changing consumer markets and life-styles? ☐ ☐

Do your plans provide methods to deal with competition? ☐ ☐

Do your plans address market potential? ☐ ☐

Do they contain creative approaches to solving problems? ☐ ☐

Do they include financial requirements? ☐ ☐

Are they realistic? ☐ ☐

Are they stated in such a way that you know when they have been achieved? ☐ ☐

Is there a system for auditing your objectives? ☐ ☐

Have you a formal plan for setting aside money to meet any quarterly tax payments? ☐ ☐

Are You Organized Effectively?

Yes No

Have you thought about the long-term direction of your business? ☐ ☐

Are job descriptions and authority for responsibilities clearly stated? ☐ ☐

Does your organizational structure minimize duplication of effort and maximize the use of each employee's skills? ☐ ☐

Do employees understand how they will be rated for promotion and salary increases? ☐ ☐

Does your wage schedule meet the local rate for similar work and retain competent employees? ☐ ☐

Would you or some of your employees profit by taking business education courses offered at local schools/colleges? ☐ ☐

Will training help your employees achieve better results? ☐ ☐

Do your experienced employees help train new and part-time employees? ☐ ☐

Have you good working conditions? ☐ ☐

Do you use positive personal leadership techniques like being impartial, giving words of encouragement and congratulations, and listening to complaints? ☐ ☐

Are you familiar with the Fair Labor Standards Act as it applies to minimum wages, overtime payments, and child labor? ☐ ☐

Do you avoid all forms of discrimination in your employment practices? ☐ ☐

Do you have a formal program for motivating employees? ☐ ☐

Have you taken steps to minimize shoplifting and internal theft? ☐ ☐

Have You an Effective System for Communicating with Employees?

Yes   No

Are they informed on those plans and results that affect their work? ☐ ☐

Do you hold regular meetings that include all personnel? ☐ ☐

Do your employees have their own bulletin board for both material you need to post and items of general interest? ☐ ☐

Have the "rules and regulations" been explained to each employee? ☐ ☐

Does each employee have a written copy? ☐ ☐

Is each employee familiar with other positions and departments? ☐ ☐

Do you have an "open door" policy in your office? ☐ ☐

Operations and Special Services

Do You Know What Type of Credit Program (if Any) You Should Offer?

Yes   No

Does the nature of your operation require some type of credit for your customers? ☐ ☐

Have you discussed credit operations with your local credit bureau? ☐ ☐

Would a credit program be a good sales tool? ☐ ☐

Is a credit program of your own desirable? ☐ ☐

Have you looked into other programs of credit cards? ☐ ☐

If you set up your own credit program, do you know what standards you should use in determining which customers can receive credit for what time periods and in what amounts? ☐ ☐

Do you know all the costs involved? ☐ ☐

Will the interest you charge pay for these costs? ☐ ☐

Do you know about the Fair Credit Reporting Act? ☐ ☐

Are you familiar with Truth-in-Lending legislation? ☐ ☐

Have you determined a safe percentage of your business to have on credit that won't jeopardize paying your own bills? ☐ ☐

Have you discussed your credit program with your accountant and attorney? ☐ ☐

Have You Adequate Insurance Coverage?

Yes   No

Do you have up-to-date fire coverage on both your building equipment and inventory? ☐ ☐

Does your liability insurance cover bodily injuries as well as such problems as libel and slander suits? □ □

Are you familiar with your obligations to employees under both common law and workers' compensation? □ □

Has your insurance agent shown you how you can cut premiums in areas such as fleet automobile coverage and proper classification of employees under workers' compensation, and by cutting back on seasonal inventory insurance? □ □

Have you looked into other insurance coverage, such as business interruption insurance or criminal insurance? □ □

Do you have some fringe benefit insurance for your employees (group life, group health, or retirement)? □ □

Do You Offer Any Special Customer Services? Yes No

Do you provide personal services for your customers? □ □

Do you provide time-saving services for greater customer convenience? □ □

Have you considered leasing services? □ □

Do you charge for delivery? □ □

Have you thought about using a commercial delivery service? □ □

If not, do you know how to work the delivery expenses into the selling price of your products? □ □

Have you selected competent and professional personnel to provide customer services? □ □

Have you a policy for handling merchandise returned by customers? □ □

Are your services purchased on a routine or contractual basis? □ □

Do you make use of gift services? □ □

Are your prices for services competitive? □ □

Do you measure the quality of your services through customer surveys or other methods? □ □

Financial Analysis and Control

Have You Established a Useful Accounting System? Yes No

Do you know the minimum amount of records you need for good control? □ □

Do you know all the records you should keep in order to meet your tax obligations on time? □ □

Do you use a cash or accrual accounting system? □ □

Do Your Sales Records Give You the Key Information You Need to Make Sound Decisions? Yes No

Do you have a cash-flow plan or budget? □ □

Can you separate cash sales from charge sales? □ □

Can sales be broken down by department? □ □

Can they be broken down by merchandise classification? ☐ ☐

Do they provide a way to assess each salesperson's performance? ☐ ☐

Do Your Inventory Records Give You the Key Information You Need to Make Sound Decisions?

Yes   No

Do they show how much you have invested in merchandise without the necessity of a physical inventory? ☐ ☐

Have you achieved the optimum balance between inventory and cash? ☐ ☐

If you hold too much inventory, are you aware of the additional costs? ☐ ☐

Do you know the difference between inventory valuation at cost and at market? ☐ ☐

Would a computer ease your inventory control procedures? ☐ ☐

Do you understand the pros and cons of the cost method of inventory accounting versus the retail method? ☐ ☐

Have you found an accounting method that shows the amount of inventory shortages in a year? ☐ ☐

Are you aware of inventory-related costs such as pilferage, obsolescence, and spoilage? ☐ ☐

Have you taken steps to minimize shoplifting and internal theft? ☐ ☐

Do Your Expense Records Give You the Key Information You Need to Make Sound Decisions?

Yes   No

Do you know which expense items you have the greatest control over? ☐ ☐

Are the records sufficiently detailed to identify where the money goes? ☐ ☐

Can you detect those expenses not necessary to the successful operation of your business? ☐ ☐

Do You Effectively Use the Information on Your Profit-and-Loss Statement and Balance Sheet?

Yes   No

Do you analyze monthly financial statements? ☐ ☐

Can you interpret your financial statements in terms of how you did last year and whether you met this year's goals? ☐ ☐

Do your financial statements compare favorably with other similar businesses in terms of sales, cost of sales, and expenses? ☐ ☐

Are you undercapitalized? ☐ ☐

Have you borrowed more than you can easily pay back out of profits? ☐ ☐

Can you see ways to improve your profit position by improving your gross margin? ☐ ☐

Have you forecasted financial statements for future growth? ☐ ☐

Credit: U.S. Small Business Administration

ADVERTISING STRATEGIES

Get More Mileage from Advertising Dollars

It's been said that the only good advertising is that which sells. Regardless of the medium or the message, the advertiser's objective is to attract attention and ultimately to land new business. But results don't always match expectations.

When the response is disappointing, advertisers generally blame their advertising rather than themselves. But that may be shortsighted. Unless management plays an active role in the advertising process, even the cleverest ads are likely to miss the mark.

"There's more to successful advertising than just words and pictures," says an executive with Dix & Eaton, a Cleveland-based advertising and public relations firm. "Decisions have to be made about how a firm's money will be spent—how to get the most mileage from its advertising dollars. Management must take a hands-on approach, becoming familiar with the fundamentals of effective advertising and using this as a framework for making key decisions about its own campaigns. Without this, the firm is likely to make costly errors.

"For example, small advertisers are often guilty of premature boredom. Rather than sticking with an ad and giving it time to build awareness, they replace it simply to go with a new look. In many cases that's precisely the time the ad is first getting widely noticed. Small advertisers have to learn that repetition is crucial to generating maximum response. A classic study on the subject found that the same ad run four times in the same publication continued to generate a high level of response each time it appeared."

Another crucial decision is how often advertisements should run in a given period of time. "Frequency is a key element of an advertising campaign," says an executive vice-president of Cargill, Wilson & Acree, an advertising agency. "Given the restrictions of a limited budget, there's always a trade-off between the size of an ad and the frequency with which it appears. Reduce the size from a full-page to a half and you can afford greater frequency; go the other way and you've got greater impact. Which option management chooses should be based on a hard-nosed evaluation of how best to reach its target market. Retailers, for example, will generally fare better favoring frequency over size. They have to keep their names in front of the public without letup."

Advertising executives offer these additional guidelines:

1. Avoid the temptation to create ads featuring the company president. Most consumers care more about the firm's products and services than who owns the stock. "Seeing your face in print may be an ego trip," the vice-president says, "but it's not necessarily the best way to sell—not unless you happen to be another Lee Iacocca."

2. Rethink "shotgun" strategies that allocate advertising expenditures to a wide range of media. Small firms that try to cover all their bases by spending money on billboards, trade magazines, radio, television, and newspapers spread themselves too thin. They don't have the dollars to make an impact all over the place. A wiser approach is to concentrate spending on one or two strong media, such as newspapers and magazines, and gain a real presence there.

This "less is more" concept applies to ad content as well. "Resist the urge to say everything about your company in a single ad," says the president of a New York marketing communications firm. "Car dealers, for example, often crowd their ads with information on new cars, used cars, and repair services. That kind of clutter only confuses the consumer. It's better to create separate ads for each product or service."

3. Complement media advertising with collateral sales literature. Many small advertisers fail simply because they don't prepare for success. They execute an effective ad campaign but have no mechanism for dealing with the response it generates. Unless pamphlets are on hand to service customer inquiries and unless brochures are available for sales calls, valuable leads will go to waste. You can't blame that on advertising. Being prepared is a management responsibility.

Advertising Budgets: How to Figure Them

If you want to build sales, it's almost certain you'll need to advertise. How much should you spend? How should you allocate your advertising dollars? How can you be sure your advertising outlays aren't out of line? The advertising budget helps you determine how much you have to spend and helps establish the guidelines for how you're going to spend it.

What you'd like to invest in advertising and what you can afford are seldom the same. Spending too much is obviously an extravagance, but spending too little can be just as bad in terms of lost sales and diminished visibility. Costs must be tied to results. You must be prepared to evaluate your goals and assess your capabilities—a budget will help you do precisely this.

Your budget will help you choose and assess the amount of advertising and its timing. It will also serve as the background for next year's plan.

Methods of Establishing a Budget

Each of the various ways in which to establish an advertising budget has its problems as well as its benefits. No method is perfect for all types of businesses, nor for that matter is any combination of methods.

Here, concepts from several traditional methods of budgeting have been combined into three basic methods: (1) percentage of sales or profits, (2) unit of sales, and (3) objective and task. You'll need to use judgment and caution in settling on any method or methods.

1. Percentage of Sales or Profits

The most widely used method of establishing an advertising budget is to base it on a percentage of sales. Advertising is as much a business expense as, say, the cost of labor and, thus, should be related to the quantity of goods sold.

The percentage-of-sales method avoids some of the problems that result from using profits as a base. For instance, if profits in a period are low, it might not be the fault of sales or advertising. But if you stick with the same percentage figure, you'll automatically reduce your advertising allotment. There's no way around it: 2 percent of $10,000 is less than 2 percent of $15,000.

Such a cut in the advertising budget, if profits are down for other reasons, may very well lead to further losses in sales *and* profits. This in turn will lead to further reductions in advertising investment, and so on.

In the short run a small business owner might make small additions to profit by cutting advertising expenses, but such a policy could lead to a long-term deterioration of the bottom line. By using the percentage-of-sales method, you keep your advertising in a consistent relation to your sales volume—which is what your advertising should be primarily affecting. Gross margin, especially over the long run, should also show an increase, of course, if your advertising outlays are being properly applied.

What percentage? You can guide your choice of a percentage-of-sales figure by finding out what other businesses in your line are doing. These percentages are fairly consistent within a given category of business.

It's fairly easy to find out this ratio of advertising expense to sales in your line. Check trade magazines and associations. You can also find these percentages in reports published by financial institutions such as Dun & Bradstreet.

Knowing what the ratio for your industry is will help to assure you that you will be spending proportionately as much or more than your competitors, but remember, these industry averages are not gospel. Your particular situation may dictate that you want to advertise more than or less than your competition. Average may not be good enough for you. You may want to out-advertise your competitors and be willing to cut into short-term profits to do so. Growth takes investment.

No business owner should let any method bind him or her. It's helpful to use the percentage-of-sales method because it's quick and easy. It ensures that your advertising budget isn't way out of proportion for your business. It's a sound method for stable markets. But if you want to expand your market share, you'll probably need to use a larger percentage of sales than the industry average.

Which sales? Your budget can be determined as a percentage of past sales, of estimated future sales, or as a combination of the two:

a. **Past sales.** Your base can be last year's sales or an average of a number of years in the immediate past. Consider, though, that changes in economic conditions can make your figure too high or too low.

b. **Estimated future sales.** You can calculate your advertising budget as a percentage of your anticipated sales for next year. The most common pitfall of this method is an optimistic assumption that your business will continue to grow. You must keep general business trends always in mind, especially if there's the chance of a slump, and hardheadedly assess the directions in your industry and your own operation.

c. **Past sales and estimated future sales.** The middle ground between an often conservative appraisal based on last year's sales and a usually too optimistic assessment of next year's is to combine both. It's a more realistic method during periods of changing economic conditions. It allows you to analyze trends and results thoughtfully and to predict with a little more assurance of accuracy.

2. Unit of Sales

In the unit-of-sale method you set aside a fixed sum for each unit of product to be sold, based on your experience and trade knowledge of how much advertising it takes to sell each unit. That is, if it takes two cents' worth of advertising to sell a case of canned vegetables and you want to move 100,000 cases, you'll probably plan to spend $2,000 on advertising them. Does it cost X dollars to sell a refrigerator? Then you'll probably have to budget 1,000 times X if you plan to sell a thousand refrigerators. You're simply basing your budget on unit of sale rather than dollar amounts of sales.

Some people consider this method just a variation of percentage of sales. Unit of sales, however, probably lets you make a closer estimate of what you should plan to spend for maximum effect, since it's based on what experience tells you it takes to sell an actual unit, rather than an overall percentage of your gross sales estimate.

The unit-of-sales method is particularly useful in fields where the amount of product available is limited by outside factors, such as the weather's effect on crops. If that's the situation for your business, you first estimate how many units or cases will be available to you. Then you advertise only as much as experience tells you it takes to sell them. Thus, if you have a pretty good idea ahead of time how many units will be available, you should have minimal waste in your advertising costs.

This method is also suited for specialty goods, such as washing machines and automobiles; however, it's difficult to apply when you have many different kinds of products to advertise and must divide your advertising among these products. The unit-of-sales method is not very useful in sporadic or irregular markets or for style merchandise.

3. Objective and Task

The most difficult (and least used) method for determining an advertising budget is the objective-and-task approach. Yet it's the most accurate and best accomplishes what all budgets should:

It relates the appropriation to the marketing task to be accomplished.

It relates the advertising appropriation

under usual conditions and in the long run to the volume of sales, so that profits and reserves will not be drained.

To establish your budget by this method, you need a coordinated marketing program with specific objectives based on a thorough survey of your markets and their potential.

While the percentage-of-sales or profits method first determines how much you'll spend without much consideration of what you want to accomplish, the task method establishes what you must do in order to meet your objectives. Only then do you calculate its cost.

You should set specific objectives: not just "Increase sales" but, for example, "Sell 25 percent more of product X or service Y by attracting the business of teen-agers." Then determine what media best reach your target market and estimate how much it will cost to run the number and types of advertisements you think it'll take to get that sales increase. You repeat this process for each of your objectives. When you total these costs, you have your projected budget.

Of course, you may find that you can't afford to advertise as you'd like to. It's a good idea, therefore, to rank your objectives. As with the other methods, be prepared to change your plan to reflect reality and to fit the resources you have available.

How to Allocate Your Budget

Once you have determined your advertising budget, you must decide how you'll allocate your advertising dollars. First you'll have to decide if you'll do any institutional advertising or only promotional advertising.

After you set aside an amount to build your image (if that's your plan for the year), you can then allocate your promotional advertising in a number of ways. Among the most common breakdowns are by: (1) departmental budgets, (2) total budget, (3) calendar periods, (4) media, and (5) sales areas.

1. Departmental Budgets. The most common method of allocating advertising dollars is percent of sales. Those departments or product categories with the greatest sales volume receive the biggest share of the budget.

In a small business or when the merchandise range is limited, the same percentage can be used throughout. Otherwise, a good rule is to use the average industry figure for each product.

By breaking down the budget by departments or products those goods that require more promotion to stimulate sales can get the required advertising dollars. Your budget can be further divided into individual merchandise lines.

2. Total Budget. Your total budget may be the result of integrated departmental or product budgets. If your business has set an upper limit for advertising expense percentage, then your departmental budgets, which are based on different percentages of sales in each area, might be pared down.

In smaller businesses the total budget may be the only one established. It, too, should be divided into merchandise classifications for scheduling.

3. Calendar Periods. Most executives of small businesses usually plan their advertising on a monthly, even a weekly, basis. Your budget, even if it's for a longer planning period, ought to be calculated for these shorter periods. It will give you better control.

The percentage-of-sales method is also useful here to determine how much money to allocate by time periods. The standard practice is to match sales with advertising dollars. Thus, if February accounts for 5 percent of

your sales, you might give it 5 percent of your budget.

Sometimes you might want to adjust advertising allocations downward in some of your heavier sales months, so you can boost the budget of some of your poorer periods. But this should be done only if you have reason to believe that a change in your advertising timing could improve slow sales (such as when your competition's sales trends differ markedly from yours).

4. Media. The amount of advertising that you place in each advertising medium—such as direct mail, newspapers, or radio—should be determined by past experience, industry practice, and ideas from media specialists. Normally it's wise to use the same sort of media your competitors use. That's where, most likely, your potential customers look and listen.

5. Sales Areas. You can spend your advertising dollars where your customers already come from, or you can use them to try to stimulate new sales areas. Just as in dividing your appropriation by time periods, it's wise to continue to do the bulk of your advertising in familiar areas. Usually it's more costly to develop new markets than to maintain established ones.

A Flexible Budget

Any combination of these methods may be employed in the formation and allocation of your advertising budget. All of them—or simply one—may be needed to meet your advertising objectives. However you decide to plan your budget, you must make it flexible, capable of being adjusted to changes in the marketplace.

The duration of your planning and budgeting period depends upon the nature of your business. If you can use short budgeting periods, you'll find that your advertising can be more flexible and that you can change tactics to meet immediate trends.

To ensure advertising flexibility, you should have a contingency fund to deal with special circumstances—such as the introduction of a new product, specials available in local media, or unexpected competitive situations.

Beware of your competitors' activities at all times. Don't blindly copy your competitors, but analyze how their actions may affect your business—and be prepared to act.

Credit: U.S. Small Business Administration and Stuart Henderson Britt

CUSTOMER SERVICE

Little Things Mean Big Business

Ask consumers why they patronize one business over another and time and again they'll point to the little things: friendly attitude, responsive service, informed and helpful personnel. This attention to detail—sorely lacking in many companies—can do more to build sales than sophisticated technology or high-powered marketing.

For small business, the point is crucial. Because few can match major competitors' aggressive pricing policies and costly promotional campaigns, they must counter with effective programs of their own. Here, size works to their advantage: the smaller the company, the easier it is to identify with consumers and to respond to their needs.

"We recently started spot-calling customers whose cars we've serviced to inquire if they are pleased with our work and if there are any problems we can rectify," says the president of an automobile repair shop located in Pleasantville, New York. "The program—which is supposed to demonstrate our commitment to customer service—is proving very successful. We're doing more work for existing customers and have developed new relationships through word of mouth."

Attention to detail communicates the company's respect for the consumer while simultaneously enhancing its appeal as an attractive and well-run operation. See if the following "little things" can add to your business:

1. Get to know regular customers by name. Greeting people on a first-name basis personalizes the business relationship, cementing bonds between the company and those most crucial to its success. With this in mind, one restaurateur requires his dining room staff to memorize five new customer names a week.

2. Encourage customers to fill out suggestion forms rating your company's services, products, and personnel. "This has a twofold effect," says the president of a family-owned health club. "It brings to my attention problems that I might not have seen and, equally important, it prompts employees to go that extra mile on the job. Knowing that I read all the forms makes them eager to avoid any negative comments from dissatisfied customers. If they're at fault, they'll be penalized; if the comments are favorable, they'll be rewarded."

3. Follow up on all substantial sales with hand-signed notes thanking customers for their patronage.

4. Offer regular customers the convenience of house charge accounts, authorizing purchases on the strength of signatures alone. Make the service dependent on good credit performance.

5. Establish company policies honoring

all reasonable requests for product returns and refunds. The willingness to take back defective or otherwise unsatisfactory goods generates invaluable goodwill.

6. Answer telephones promptly and courteously, making minimal use of recorded messages. Owners can monitor operator performance by occasionally dialing their companies, seeing how quickly the call is answered and how courteously the caller is treated.

7. Use the telephone as a marketing tool. Keep records of regular customers' birthdays and anniversaries, calling with gift suggestions on these occasions. "If we know that Mrs. Smith's birthday is September 1 and that she's fond of French designer dresses, we'll call Mr. Smith in mid-August to inform him of what we have in this line and to offer our help with a gift selection," says the owner of a Chicago women's shop. "While most of our competitors call customers only when their bills are past due, we call to show both our interest and our attention to their needs."

8. Offer convenience services, such as at-home shopping, free delivery, extended hours, and gift wrapping.

Like a chain that snaps at its weakest link, customer service is only as strong as the least committed employee. Unless the rank and file are enthusiastic and trained in the appropriate procedures, service will remain an empty promise.

"Owners and managers may be dedicated to customer service, but they rarely spend any time with customers," says John Tschohl, president of the Better Than Money Corporation, which offers training programs in customer service. "Instead, 90 percent of customer contact is with low-ranking employees, including sales clerks and telephone operators, whose performance can make or break a company's service program.

"The problem is, management puts these people in place without as much as an hour's training in customer service. The assumption is that they'll somehow learn by osmosis. But they won't. They've never been told precisely what good customer service entails or how they can contribute to it. That's the boss's job. Those owners and managers truly committed to customer service will go beyond lip service, drawing a straight line from corporate policies to the marketplace."

Follow these guidelines for making customer service part of your corporate culture:

1. Train employees in customer service policies, paying special attention to communication skills. Start with the basics, making certain that customers are addressed by name, are encouraged to ask for assistance, and are thanked for their purchases.

"The delicate balance here is to avoid the kind of plastic responses—like 'Have a nice day' or 'Thank you for shopping at Smith's'— that can turn people off," Tschohl cautions. "Instead, instruct employees to tailor their comments to the individual. Use a name if possible and refer specifically to the item purchased. Try something like 'That blue suit looks lovely on you, Mrs. Jones. Thanks for shopping with us on this cold winter's day.'"

2. Make employees experts in the company's products and services. Hold training sessions on product specifications, performance characteristics, warranties, and prices. Only with knowledge can the employee properly aid and service the customer.

3. Have employees focus on the customers' needs as well as on their own job responsibilities. "The critical prerequisite for good service, as well as for good salesmanship, is to learn as much as possible about your customers," says a management consultant with Peat Marwick. "Read annual reports, press clippings, and even the company's brochures before you go out to sell or service customers. Knowledge of their needs will impress

them and will help to cement business relationships."

4. Provide a mechanism for customer feedback. A suggestion box or special phone line to the president's office enables customers to voice complaints and requests, and alerts management to problems that might otherwise go unnoticed. "Studies show that for every person who complains, 26 others experience the same problem without reporting it," Tschohl says. "And most of those who remain silent—91 percent when a big-ticket purchase is involved—will just switch to a competitor. Feedback systems are critical because they can help correct deficiencies before they jeopardize customer relationships."

5. Base annual bonuses on customer service activity as well as on sales and administrative performance. This underlines the message that nothing is more important than serving the customer well. "Typically, small companies compete on the basis of costly promotions, expensive inventories, and elaborate facilities," Tschohl says, "while ignoring other competitive weapons—like a smile or a personalized greeting—that don't cost anything and can have the greatest impact of all."

DIRECT MARKETING

Expanding Your Business

For many companies, the shortest distance between two points is through direct marketing. This little-known process draws a straight line between a business and its customers, creating a medium for aggressive promotions and near-instant response.

An umbrella term for sales procedures geared to generate immediate results, direct marketing can be conducted by mail, telephone, broadcast, and space advertising. In each case, a message is conveyed, an offer is made, and a mechanism is provided for consumer response.

"That mechanism—be it a coupon, an 800 number, or an order card—is a critical element that distinguishes direct marketing from standard advertising," says the president of a New York direct marketing agency. "That's because direct marketing isn't out to build image or to lay the foundation for future business. Its purpose is to generate immediate and measurable sales. When a direct marketer advertises a kitchen utensil in a newspaper, he or she wants consumers to place orders, by mail or phone, as soon as the ad is seen."

Direct marketing can supplement a small company's traditional sales efforts. Merchants are now using catalogues and flyers, for example, to generate business beyond their local trading area.

"Companies can get started in direct marketing at any time," says an executive with a midsized advertising agency. "A small business can conduct a modest marketing test for under $10,000. Should that prove successful, management could gradually beef up the budget, perhaps with the profits from previous promotions."

Direct marketing involves three major steps:

1. Creating promotional tools—such as catalogues, advertisements, and direct mail letters—that stress the product's key benefits. "If you're marketing kitchen appliances, tell how they can make the buyer a better cook or how they can cut cleanup time in half," says the direct marketing executive. "In direct marketing, what the product is made of—plastic or stainless steel—is usually less important than what it does."

2. Selecting mailing lists and advertising media geared to the target market. Compa-

nies marketing software to attorneys, for example, may test lists of bar association members and subscribers to legal journals.

3. Monitoring results and revising tactics. "You know by the number of orders you get if the promotion has been successful, unsuccessful, or somewhere in between," the marketing executive says. "Generally, a response rate of 1 to 4 percent is considered satisfactory. But the monitoring and revising process can boost this performance. If one list produced an 8 percent response and another only brought 2 percent, the next mailing should focus on the more productive list or offer. The direct marketer continuously tests copy, price, and lists in order to get the optimum mix."

Direct marketing consultants offer these additional guidelines:

1. Give consumers an incentive to act. A gift with purchase and special sales prices are proven techniques.

2. Promote to existing customers as well as new prospects. Retailers testing catalogue sales will garner the highest response from customers who have shopped at their stores. Response rates to existing customers can be four to six times that of cold mailings.

3. Products sold by mail should be suitable for a markup of at least three times cost.

4. Advertising and direct marketing agencies can help small companies evaluate their sales potential. Most agencies charge on an hourly or project fee basis. Costs can be cut by hiring free-lancers to write copy and design sales materials.

5. Build on successful promotions by widening the product line. "We started out marketing a package of nuts and bolts organized in a 25-drawer cabinet," says the president of a direct marketing firm. "Our initial success cultivated a customer base and led to a full line of related products. Once you become known for a particular type of product, it's easier to sell to that market."

Direct Marketing Letters Link a Business and Its Sale Prospects

Of all the challenges of successful salesmanship, getting a foot in the door may be the most difficult. Convincing prospects that your business has something unique to offer—something not readily available from other sources—is half the battle in closing sales. Fortunately, a simple yet highly effective marketing device lets you get the message across.

Known as the "personalized direct marketing letter," this hybrid of written and oral communications paves the way for the critical sales call, giving small companies access to promising new markets.

"When used properly, the personalized direct marketing letter draws a straight line between a business and its target markets," says an executive with SIG Communications Group. "And it does so in a way that commands attention—that gives the company an opportunity to make its pitch to prospective customers."

Unlike mass mailing campaigns that blanket the market with computer-processed sales materials, personalized direct marketing letters take a more selective and intimate approach.

"Rather than mailing indiscriminately to thousands of 'dear sirs' or 'occupants,' personalized direct marketing letters are addressed to specific individuals by name and title," the SIG executive explains. "When a newsletter publisher active in the legal and accounting markets decided to sell his product to the banking community, marketing letters were addressed to a list of key bankers in position to buy the publication. Most important, each prospect was given the impression that the communication was addressed solely to him or her."

This personalized look is achieved by eschewing the trappings of bulk mailings.

"The difference is apparent in the envelope itself," says the president of a word-processing concern. "Rather than using cheap white stock, a mailing label, and a postage meter imprint—all of which connotes 'junk mail'—the envelope is of a good quality colored bond, is typed on a letter-quality printer, and carries a real stamp. These features indicate that there is something significant inside. This helps to assure that the letter will make it past the secretary's desk to the person it is addressed to and, most important, that it will be read."

Here the content comes into play. Personalized direct marketing letters open with a clear indication that the writer understands the prospect's business problems and has solutions for them.

"In his letter to the bankers, the newsletter publisher noted up front that banking had changed drastically in recent years and that executives needed a wide range of current information to stay competitive," the SIG executive says. "Because this addressed a real problem they were facing, the bankers recognized immediately that the writer had information that might benefit them.

"Similarly, when the proprietor of a foreign-car repair shop wrote a direct marketing letter to registered owners of exotic luxury cars, he mentioned in the first paragraph their two biggest concerns: high repair costs and poor customer service. He then promised to rectify both with lower hourly fees and such services as free pickup and delivery. The letter generated an enormous response."

At the conclusion of the letter—which should be limited to one page—the writer informs the prospect that he or she will be calling to discuss the proposal or to arrange an appointment for a face-to-face meeting.

This gives the small business the best opportunity to sell its products or services. Calls should be made a week to ten days after the letter is mailed. By then the prospect has had the opportunity to digest the contents and is ready to respond to the proposal.

Follow these additional guidelines for conducting effective personalized direct marketing campaigns:

1. Make follow-up calls during the midweek period, avoiding Mondays and Fridays, when prospects are apt to be less attentive.

2. Ask advertising, sales promotion, and direct marketing agencies for help in writing sales letters.

3. Figure costs of about $1.35 per letter, including creative work, production, and mailing.

4. Seek names of key prospects from industry associations, directories, and mailing houses.

"When all the proper steps are followed, personalized direct market letters can achieve a response rate many times that of bulk mailings," the SIG executive says. "It can be an effective tool for every company's marketing efforts."

EXPORTS

Export Management Companies Can Help You Tap Foreign Markets

Small companies seeking a partner in trade can turn to a little-known service that acts as your export department. Export management companies, specialists in overseas sales, serve as intermediaries between your products and foreign markets. Most handle everything from shipping documentation to credit approval.

"When working with export management companies, small businesses can sell their goods around the world without even knowing how to spell the word 'export,'" says the executive director of the National Association of Export Companies (NEXCO). "That's because EMCs assume responsibility for sales beyond domestic borders. Small companies timid about exporting because they know little about international markets or the procedures for selling to them can contract with export management companies to do all the work."

Typically, the relationship begins with an appraisal of the small company's export potential. Because EMCs are in business to profit from foreign sales, most will limit representation to those companies whose products are capable of cultivating substantial markets abroad.

"The days of American companies successfully selling pots and pans overseas are over," the NEXCO director says. "Low-value-added products are produced more economically by third-world countries. To compete overseas today, U.S. manufacturers need unique products that fill a market void or that have a technical advantage over competitive goods. Hot lines include computer equipment and software, security devices, and health-care products. While high-tech products are the most promising, the market is not limited to this. One successful exporter sells, of all things, sand to Saudi Arabia—a type of sand used for swimming pool filters that's not available in that country."

Once a product is deemed suitable for export, the export management company begins the marketing effort. Local agents and distributors are informed of the product's availability and armed with specifications and sample products to support their selling activities. The extent of the marketing effort varies with the size and sophistication of the EMC and the product's promise.

"When we agreed to market an American-made welding torch overseas, we promoted it in trade magazines and at welding industry trade shows," says a vice-president of Ferrex International, Inc., an EMC. "We also identified key markets—such as the sale of private-label torches to European welding companies—and guided our client in adapting its product for this market. In a decade, the product's sales went from zero to more than $1 million."

The client's relationship with an EMC can take one of two major forms:

1. The EMC purchases goods from the client—at a special trade allowance of 10 to 20 percent below the U.S. wholesale price—and resells the products at a profit overseas.

2. Less commonly, the EMC never takes title to the goods but simply sells and ships them for the client, taking a sales commission (generally about 15 percent) on the volume sold.

"We sell our products to the export management company at a discount from our standard distributor prices," says an executive vice-president for a manufacturer of personal safety equipment. "In return, we're assured of payment by the EMC as soon as our products reach them. They assume all responsibility for collecting from overseas customers."

In choosing an export management company, clients are advised to select those with a complementary product line. An EMC already active in the health care market is most likely to take on a new medical device and most likely to succeed with it.

AT A GLANCE

International Trade Information Matrix

A quick reference for matching International Trade Business needs with the assistance offered by public and private sector organizations.

Need \ Organization	U.S. Department of Commerce	U.S. Small Business Administration	Export-Import Bank of the United States	Overseas Private Investment Corporation	U.S. Department of Agriculture	U.S. Department of State	Department of the Treasury	General Agreement on Tariffs & Trade	United Nations	Embassies and Consulates	World Bank	Inter-American Development Bank	Asian Development Bank	State Departments of Commerce	Chambers of Commerce	Port Authorities	Commercial Banks	Export Management Companies (EMCs)	Trade Associations	Export Packers	Freight Forwarders	Custom House Brokers	Consulting Firms	Transportation Carriers	Credit Reporting Firms	Universities
Export/Import Training Programs	•	•	•	•	•								•	•			•		•				•			•
General Export Information	•	•		•		•	•						•	•	•		•		•		•		•	•	•	•
General Import Information					•		•						•	•	•		•					•	•			
Potential Foreign Markets	•	•		•	•	•	•	•					•	•	•		•	•					•			•
Trade Statistics	•					•	•									•	•						•			
Foreign Buyers and Representatives	•		•										•	•	•		•	•			•					
Foreign Sources of Supply	•							•					•	•	•		•			•		•	•			
Overseas Projects	•			•						•	•	•		•			•	•								
Overseas Investment Opportunities	•		•				•						•		•		•					•	•			
Foreign Firm Credit/Reliability	•	•					•								•		•								•	
Corresponding Overseas	•											•	•				•	•								
Translation Assistance										•			•				•						•			•
Overseas Travel				•						•			•				•	•								
Product Sales Promotion	•		•										•				•	•					•			
Export Financing	•	•	•	•	•					•	•	•					•	•					•			
Insurance of Overseas Shipments/ Investments			•	•													•				•					
Tax Incentives	•						•																			
Foreign Trade Zones	•						•																			
Collection Documents	•												•	•		•	•				•	•				
Shipping Documents	•																•				•	•	•			
Packaging and Shipping	•												•	•	•	•	•	•	•	•	•			•		

Credit: U.S. Small Business Administration

The search for the right EMC can be arranged through the National Association of Export Companies, which publishes details of prospective exporters in its member newsletter. Interested EMCs then contact the companies directly. To make use of this free service, send a brief description of your company, its product line, and the name of a responsible executive to NEXCO, 17 Battery Place, Suite 1425, New York, New York 10004.

Keep in mind that EMC relationships need not cover all overseas markets. Companies with experience in selling to European countries, for example, may want to limit EMC involvement to the Far East or Latin America.

When it comes to EMCs, everything is open to negotiation. Both parties have to work out a deal they can live with and, more important, that they can profit from.

WHERE TO FIND IT

EXPORTING

Listed below are the Washington, D.C., offices of federal government agencies offering export and foreign direct investment assistance:

U.S. Department of Commerce
International Trade Administration
14th Street and Constitution Avenue, NW
Washington, DC 20230

U.S. Department of Commerce
National Oceanic and Atmospheric Administration
National Marine Fisheries Service
Washington, DC 20235

U.S. Department of Commerce
Minority Business Development Agency
14th Street and Constitution Avenue, NW
Washington, DC 20230

U.S. Department of Agriculture
Foreign Agricultural Service
Washington, DC 20250

Export-Import Bank of the United States
811 Vermont Avenue, NW
Washington, DC 20571

Overseas Private Investment Corporation
1129 20th Street, NW
Washington, DC 20527

Office of the United States Trade Representative
600 17th Street, NW
Washington, DC 20501

Agency for International Development
Washington, DC 20523

U.S. Small Business Administration
Office of International Trade
1129 20th Street, NW, Suite 412
Washington, DC 20416

U.S. Government Agencies Assisting Overseas Investors and U.S. Exporters

Export-Import Bank

The Export-Import Bank (Eximbank) is an independent agency of the U.S. Government that supplements and encourages commercial bank financing of exports of U.S. goods and services through several programs.

Eximbank assists U.S. exporters to obtain pre-export financing through its Working Capital Guarantee program. This program provides repayment protection for U.S. commercial bank loans to U.S. exporters for such export-related activities as inventory buildup or export marketing operations.

Exporters who extend credit to their foreign customers may obtain payment protection through an Export Credit Insurance policy from the Foreign Credit Insurance Association (FCIA). FCIA sells and services several types of policies on behalf of Eximbank, including whole-turnover policies covering numerous short-term credit sales (up to 180 days) and policies covering individual medium-term credit sales (181 days to five years).

Exporters may arrange competitive medium-term commercial bank financing with the help of three Eximbank programs. Eximbank's Commercial Bank Guarantee provides payment protection for the lender. The Medium-term Credit program and the similar Small Business Credit program enable commercial banks to offer fixed-rate financing at the lowest interest rates permitted. The Medium-term Credit program is available to assist exporters, regardless of size, who are facing officially supported foreign competition. The Small Business Credit program is available to companies who meet the Small Business Administration's definition of a small business. There is no need to show competition for the Small Business Credit program.

Exporters competing for large export orders of heavy capital-equipment items or for contracts related to major project development may request a Preliminary Commitment outlining the long-term financing support available from Eximbank if the bidder wins the order. The Engineering Multiplier Program offers medium-term, fixed-interest-rate direct loans to support preconstruction services by U.S. architectural and engineering firms for a project with the potential to generate additional U.S. exports worth $10 million or twice the amount of the initial contract, whichever is greater. If the exporter is facing officially supported foreign competition, Eximbank may offer a long-term Direct Loan to the foreign purchaser, with interest fixed at the lowest level permitted. Eximbank may also offer a Financial Guarantee covering repayment of commercial financing denominated in U.S. dollars or other convertible currencies.

For more detailed information on Eximbank's programs, contact:

Export-Import Bank of the United States
811 Vermont Avenue, NW
Washington, DC 20571
(800) 424-5201 or (202) 566-8990
Telex: WU 89-461 or RCA 248460

For information on export credit insurance, contact:

Foreign Credit Insurance Association
40 Rector Street, 11th Floor
New York, NY 10006
(212) 306-5000
Telex: 5099

Overseas Private Investment Corporation (OPIC)

The Overseas Private Investment Corporation (OPIC) is the U.S. Government's principal catalyst for stimulating U.S. private capital investment in the developing nations. Organized in January 1971, OPIC has written some $24 billion in political risk insurance covering U.S. private investment in more than 100 developing nations and has provided more than $600 million in financing commitments.

OPIC offers investors insurance against currency inconvertibility, expropriation, and damage or interruption of operations from war, revolution, insurrection, and civil strife. In addition, OPIC makes direct loans and may participate in the financing of preinvestment surveys where investments are being made or contemplated by small U.S. firms. In selected cases, OPIC also provides U.S. lenders protection against both commercial and political risk by guaranteeing repayment of principal and interest on loans made to eligible investors.

These incentives are designed for investors making capital investments. The loan guarantees and U.S. dollar loans can provide eligible parties with the necessary financial support for the purchase of U.S. goods and services required for the implementation of an investment project in eligible developing countries. For example, OPIC has approved guarantees or insurance to local distributors of U.S. heavy equipment manufacturers for the expansion of existing facilities to support additional sales.

The guarantee assures U.S. private banks and institutional lenders repayment of principal and interest from loans made to eligible projects. These loans generally do not exceed 75 percent of total project financing from all sources, and the lending institution must be U.S.-owned. The project may be privately held by U.S. or by host country national or multinational entities where there is a significant U.S. interest in other respects.

Principal and interest for the term of the loan are guaranteed against default from any cause other than fraud or misrepresentation, for which the party seeking payment is responsible. The guarantee is backed by the full faith and credit of the United States, and the borrower pays a minimum guarantee fee of 1.5 percent annually on the outstanding principal. Interest rates are established through borrower-lender negotiations, with OPIC approval.

Dollar loans made from OPIC's Direct Investment Fund (DIF) cover projects too small to interest large institutional lenders or loans too short for institutional lending but too long for commercial banks. DIF loans are made only to projects that are sponsored by or significantly involve U.S. companies with annual gross sales of $120 million or less or U.S. cooperatives. DIF loans range from $50,000 to $4 million for periods of 5 to 12 years with varying interest rates, depending on OPIC's assessment of the financial risk and its opportunity to share in the project's financial success.

Both the guarantee and DIF loan must be applied to a new facility, modernization or expansion of an existing plant, or new input of technology or services. The project must be commercially viable and must make a significant contribution to the host country economy. Project sponsors are expected to remain at risk in the project through the life of the OPIC guarantee or loan. The project must have the approval of the host-country government, which must be one of about 100 countries and areas with which OPIC has signed a bilateral agreement permitting its programs.

Further information may be obtained from the:

Information Officer
Overseas Private Investment Corporation
1129 20th St., NW
Washington, DC 20527
(Toll free) 800-424-OPIC

Commodity Credit Corporation

The Export Credit Sales Program of the U.S. Department of Agriculture's Commodity Credit Corporation (CCC) is a commercial export financing program for U.S. agricultural commodities. Its basic objective is to extend credit to maintain, expand, or establish new commercial markets for eligible American companies. Moreover, the program is designed to meet competition from third-party suppliers and, as countries become able to purchase commercially, to replace long-term concessional sales.

The export financing is accomplished through CCC's purchase of the private U.S. exporter's accounts receivable. To qualify for the Export Credit Sales Program, a firm must sell to a purchaser whose request for agricultural credit has been approved by the Office of the General Sales Manager. Prices are negotiated between the exporter and importer on a regular commercial basis. Once made, the sale must be registered with the Office of the General Sales Manager by the exporter. All credit transactions require an irrevocable confirmed commercial letter of credit from an acceptable bank, authorizing CCC to draw when payment is due. The letter of credit is usually arranged by the importer, issued by a foreign bank, and advised through a U.S. bank. Once CCC receives the letter of credit and the necessary export documentation, the U.S. exporter is paid the value of the commodity FAS or FOB at U.S. ports (U.S. port value). CCC later obtains payment by drawing drafts on the letter of credit in accordance with the financing terms.

CCC credit terms are commercial, extending from 6 to 36 months with equal annual payments of principal, plus accrued interest comparable to commercial domestic rates.

The Export Credit Guarantee Program of CCC provides comprehensive risk protection to U.S. exporters or financial institutions when private credit is extended to finance export sales of U.S. agricultural commodities. The program protects the U.S. exporter or the exporter's assignee from nonpayments by foreign banks due to either commercial or noncommercial risks on export credit sales through the issuance of a payment guarantee by CCC. It is designed to stimulate private financing of U.S. agricultural exports and to expand and maintain export markets for those commodities.

Under the program, the foreign buyer contracts for the purchase of U.S. commodities on a deferred payment basis of three years or less. The purchaser then arranges for a letter of credit in favor of the U.S. exporter. This letter of credit covers the port value of the commodity to be exported and must be issued by a bank in the importing country. The exporter then registers the sale with CCC, pays a guarantee fee, and receives a payment guarantee. The accounts receivable and the CCC payment guarantee may be assigned to a bank in the United States that will pay the exporter for the accounts receivable and agree to receive deferred payments from the foreign bank. The payment obligation is then owed by the foreign bank to the U.S. bank. CCC's payment guarantee is operative only if the foreign bank fails to fulfill its obligation to pay the exporter or the assignee U.S. bank.

While coverage includes both commercial and noncommercial risks, CCC may require banks to take a small portion of risk on the principal and interest above the fixed amount stipulated by CCC in its press release announcing the availability of the guarantees. CCC has the authority to vary principal and interest coverage, including authorization of coverage up to 100 percent of the port value in some cases.

For more information on either of these programs, contact:

Assistant General Sales Manager,
Export Credits
Foreign Agricultural Service
Room 4079, South Building
U.S. Department of Agriculture
Washington, DC 20250

Small Business Administration (SBA)

The Small Business Administration (SBA) supports financial and management assistance programs to promote the development of small businesses. Administered through SBA field offices, these services generally include counseling, financial assistance, export workshops, and training.

Export counseling services are furnished at no charge to potential and current small business exporters by executives, advanced business students, and professional consultants. Members of the Service Corps of Retired Executives (SCORE) and the Active Corps of Executives (ACE), with years of practical experience in international trade, assist small firms in evaluating their export potential and strengthening their domestic operations by identifying financial, managerial, or technical problems. These advisers also can help small firms develop and implement basic "Export Marketing Plans," which show small firms where and how to sell goods abroad.

Through the Small Business Institute (SBI), advanced business students under faculty supervision from over 450 colleges and universities provide in-depth, long-term counseling to local small businesses. Additional export counseling and assistance are offered through Small Business Development Centers (SBDCs) that are located within some colleges and universities.

A third facet of the SBA counseling service is the Call Contract Program, which utilizes professional management and technical consultants. This program is employed where firms require highly sophisticated marketing information and production technology to identify and service overseas markets.

In addition, a free initial consultation with an attorney, to discuss international trade legal questions, can be arranged for small businesses by any local SBA office, under an agreement between the Federal Bar Association and the SBA.

Periodically, export training programs are conducted throughout the country under the joint auspices of SBA field offices, the U.S. Department of Commerce, and other agencies involved in international trade promotion. The range of topics and details varies from one-day introductory export overviews, to multisession "how-to" programs, to specialized one-subject seminars. These programs are conducted by experienced exporters and knowledgeable international traders. They discuss the procedures and techniques involved in exporting and encourage attendees to ask questions and share their experiences. Emphasis is placed on the practical application of successful exporting procedures to current and prospective small business exporters.

To help more small businesses export their products and services abroad, SBA has established the Export Revolving Line of Credit Loan (ERLC) program. ERLC loans are available only under SBA's guarantee plan. Prospective applicants should review the export financing needs of the business with their bank of account. If the bank is unable or unwilling to make a loan directly, the possibilities of a guarantee from the SBA should be explored. The participation of a private lender is necessary to obtain an ERLC.

Proceeds can be used only to finance labor and materials needed for manufacturing, wholesaling, or providing services for export, and to penetrate or develop foreign markets. Professional export marketing advice or services, foreign business travel, or participation in trade shows are examples of eligible expenses to develop foreign markets. Funds may not be used to pay existing obligations or to purchase fixed assets (other SBA programs may be used for these needs).

Through this program, SBA can guarantee up to 90 percent of a bank line of credit to a small business exporter. An applicant may have other SBA loans in addition to an ERLC, as long as the total outstanding balance of all such loans does not exceed $500,000 for SBA's share. Applicants must qualify as "small" under SBA's size standards and meet the other eligibility criteria applicable to all SBA loans. In addition, an applicant must have been in business (not necessarily in exporting) for at least 12 months prior to filing an application. The business must be current on all payroll taxes and have in operation a depository plan for the payment of future withholding taxes.

The EX-IM/SBA Cooperative Program allows the SBA, in cooperation with the Export-Import Bank, to participate in loans between $200,000 and $1 million. Eligibility requirements are the same as for the ERLC, and the maximum maturity is 18 months.

The SBA publishes Fact Sheets #42 and #51 as well as a brochure, entitled "Market Overseas with U.S. Government Help" (MA7.003), describing these and other services. Another free brochure, entitled "Is Exporting for You?", focuses on ten points to help small business firms decide to make the commitment to export.

For more specific information, contact your local SBA office and ask for the district office international trade designee; or contact your regional SBA office and ask for the Regional International Trade Officer; or:

Office of International Trade
U.S. Small Business Administration
1129 20th Street, NW, Suite 412
Washington, DC 20416

Trade and Development Program (TDP)

The Trade and Development Program (TDP) is one of three agencies of the International Development Cooperation Agency (IDCA), which also includes the Agency for International Development (AID) and the Overseas Private Investment Corporation (OPIC). TDP promotes both the economic growth of developing countries and the expansion of U.S. exports of technology, goods, and services in major projects in the developing world.

TDP's goals are to (1) promote U.S. exports, (2) contribute to the development efforts of friendly countries, and (3) facilitate open and fair access to natural resources of interest to U.S. business. By financing feasibility studies and other planning services for major projects in the third world, TDP seeks to increase the likelihood that U.S. goods and services will be used in implementation of the project, with an aim toward increasing new U.S. jobs. TDP is one of the few U.S. government agencies that can finance studies in strategically important middle-income countries such as China, Brazil, Korea, Turkey, and the major oil-producing countries.

TDP is active in areas such as energy development, telecommunications, transportation, minerals development, agribusiness, and industrial development throughout the developing world. Projects have included, among others, industrial facilities in China, telecommunications in the Philippines, cobalt mining in Peru, an electric load center in Guatemala, phosphate mining in Tunisia, a mineral port in Gabon, and a hydropower facility in Malawi.

For more information, contact:
Trade and Development Program
International Development Cooperation Agency
Room 309, SA-16
Washington, DC 20523

Credit: U.S. Department of Commerce, "A Guide to Financing Exports"

The Eximbank Political-Risks Policy

Companies exporting U.S. goods on credit terms can insure their foreign receivables against losses due to political reasons with the Short-term Political-Risks Policy offered by the Export-Import Bank of the U.S.

The Political-Risks Policy gives a company protection on its sales throughout the world against failure of a foreign buyer to pay an obligation because of specified political events.

What Is Covered

The Political-Risks Policy covers sales of U.S. products on a short-term credit basis. Short-term sales involve repayment terms ranging from payment upon delivery to payment at 180 days from the date of arrival of goods at the port of importation.

Types of Losses Covered

The Political-Risks Policy covers transfer risk as well as other political risks. Transfer risk is the inability to obtain United States dollars in a lawful market of the buyer's country. The buyer must deposit with the appropriate exchange authority the U.S. dollar equivalent of the total indebtedness in local currency on or before the due date, or within 90 days thereafter. Other political risks include, after a shipment has taken place, the cancellation or nonrenewal of an import or export license; the imposition of restrictions on the export of products not in place prior to the date of shipment; the cancellation (not due to the fault of the buyer) of valid authority to import the products; the imposition of any law, order, decree, or regulation that prevents the import of the products into the buyer's country. Other political risks also include the occurrence after shipment of war, hostilities, civil war, rebellion, revolution, insurrection, civil commotion, or other like disturbance occurring on or before the due date; requisition, expropriation, confiscation of or intervention in the business of the buyer by a governmental authority occurring on or before the due date. Eximbank indemnifies an exporter for 100 percent on a political loss.

The Political-Risks Policy does *not* apply to a loss due to exchange fluctuations or devaluations of the currency of the buyer's country occurring on or before the due date; to any loss resulting from a dispute between the exporter and the buyer (until such dispute is settled); to a loss due to the fault of the exporter or their agent; or to a loss due to the buyer's unwillingness to accept the products.

How the Policy Works

The Political-Risks Policy insures an exporter's sales to buyers in most countries throughout the world. Generally, a company is required to insure all eligible sales under the policy; however, confirmed letter-of-credit sales may be excluded if the exporter wishes. A Country Limitation Schedule, which is made a part of the policy, indicates the countries eligible for coverage and any special conditions or limitations on terms of sale.

Special Buyer Limits

The Political-Risks Policy establishes a $5,000,000 per country limitation of liability. This limit, however, may be superseded by a lesser amount specified in the Country Limitation Schedule and is subject to the aggregate limit specified in the policy declarations. A limit in excess of this amount may be authorized by endorsement upon application by the exporter.

Premium Rates and Payment Procedures

The premium rate for shipments made under the Political-Risks Policy is determined by the length of credit terms granted on those shipments. All Political-Risks Policies are endorsed with a composite rate or a rate schedule that states the appropriate premium rate applicable to each eligible shipment.

Shipment reports, accompanied by the premium payment, must be submitted to FCIA by the fifteenth of the month following the month of shipment. Premium must be paid on all shipments except those made to buyers in ineligible countries or those specifically excluded by policy endorsement.

At the beginning of each policy year, an advance premium is required.

Interest Coverage

Interest is covered on the gross invoice value set forth in the contract of sale between the exporter and the buyer. The interest rate insured is the six-month U.S. Treasury borrowing rates, plus 1 percent, or the contract interest rate if that is lower. Postmaturity interest must be stipulated by the seller in the contract of sale in order to be covered. Premium is due only on the gross invoice value of each shipment.

For Transfer Risk claims in countries with waiting periods in excess of 180 days, interest is covered to the earlier of the date of claim payment or the applicable waiting period plus 90 days. For all other political risk claims, interest is covered to the earlier of the date of claim payment or 270 days from the date of default.

Overdues and Claims

Exporters must report, on a monthly basis, all amounts that are 90 days past due. In all cases, these monthly reports of overdues should continue for as long as the overdue situation exists or until a proof of loss form is filed.

When claims are submitted, copies of all documents pertaining to the transaction, such as invoices, bills of lading, promissory notes, and guarantees, should be forwarded in conjunction with the proof-of-loss form to FCIA's Claims Department for review.

The general deadline for the submission of claims is 12 months after the due date.

FCIA is the agent of the Export-Import Bank in administering the Political-Risks Policy.

Your Competitive Edge in Selling Overseas

Foreign Credit Insurance Association: What It Is and What It Does

Foreign Credit Insurance Association is an association of leading insurance companies, operating in cooperation with and as agent of the Export-Import Bank of the United States (Eximbank), an independent U.S. government agency.

It offers insurance policies protecting U.S. exporters against the risk of nonpayment by foreign debtors.

And that reduces your risks in selling abroad.

Insures against Political and Commercial Default

The coverage protects against political risks and commercial risks.

Commercial risks may result, for instance, from economic deterioration in the buyer's market area, fluctuations in demand, unanticipated competition, shifts in tariffs, or technological changes.

Or one of the principals or key management members of the buyer's company may become inactive, causing the company to close. The buyer's major customer or government may alter purchasing patterns. The buyer may be subjected to an unexpectedly sharp increase in operating expenses. Natural disasters, such as floods and earthquakes, may also affect the buyer's ability to operate.

Political risks may befall the venture. War, revolution, and insurrection are all legitimate fears of exporters, who may find their licenses revoked, their assets expropriated, their shipments detained.

Foreign Credit Insurance Association policies insure you against these risks.

This Coverage Reduces Your Risk of Doing Business

Risk reduction is the primary benefit of Association insurance. Export credit insurance gives a company fundamental protection on the riskiest part of its asset portfolio: foreign receivables.

And that produces additional benefits.

One of the most widely used benefits reported by association customers is in connection with the discounting of receivables to obtain financing. Because the exporter is protected against nonpayment, he or she is often able to arrange for more attractive financing from banking sources. Consequently, he or she is also able to offer foreign prospects more attractive credit terms than would be possible without that protection.

In a world of high costs and fierce competition for export markets, the ability to offer attractive credit terms to an overseas cus-

tomer increasingly spells the difference between winning and losing a sale.

With the risk minimized, the exporter can undertake new business with existing capital. He can compete vigorously, entering markets he may otherwise find too risky. He can match foreign-supported selling terms. This leveraging of a firm's operating capital and productive facilities translates into enhanced profitability and additional job opportunities.

Cost is low. In fact, the cost of financing protected receivables may sometimes offset the cost of assuming the protection.

In summary, export credit coverage:

- reduces risk, protecting the exporter against the buyer's failure to pay his dollar (or other currency) obligation for commercial or political reasons.
- enhances the exporter's ability to obtain favorable financing.
- encourages the exporter to offer competitive credit terms to prospective buyers.
- supports prudent penetration of higher risk foreign markets.
- provides greater financial liquidity and flexibility in administering the foreign receivables portfolio.

Foreign Credit Insurance Offers a Broad Variety of Policies

Exporters are offered policies tailored to their needs. Multibuyer Export policies are written for a U.S. exporter to enable him to extend credit terms for products (including consumer durables such as hand tools, raw materials such as coal, and other similar products) on short-term sales, usually up to 180 days; but for certain products (such as bulk agricultural commodities and quasi-capital goods) terms of up to 360 days may be granted with FCIA approval.

Medium-term policies are issued on a case-by-case basis for credit terms usually ranging from 181 days to five years. Products eligible are of a capital or quasi-capital nature. A 15 percent cash down payment is required from the buyer.

Other policies are issued to cover services, operating leases, and finance leases. Two policies are also offered for use by commercial banks. The Bank Letter of Credit policy allows for the insured bank's confirmation of letters of credit by insuring the risk of nonpayment by the foreign bank. A Bank Deductible policy is also available to cover supplier and buyer credits. Below is a more detailed discussion of policy types.

A Policy for Companies Just Beginning to Export

Companies just beginning to export or with limited export volume may take advantage of the New-to-Export policy or Umbrella policy. The New-to-Export policy offers enhanced commercial risk protection for the first two years of a policy's life, which includes 95 percent commercial coverage, 100 percent political coverage, and no deductible.

To be eligible for the New-to-Export policy, companies must not have had direct Association coverage for two years preceding the date of application, and the following documentation must be submitted to FCIA:

- satisfactory references from a credit-reporting agency, two suppliers, and a commercial bank.
- signed financial statements or annual report for the latest fiscal year or start-up statements that reveal a positive net worth.
- a sales history showing average annual export credit sales during the preceding two fiscal years not exceeding $750,000

(together with affiliates and exclusive of sales made on terms of confirmed irrevocable letters of credit or cash in advance. In the case that the preceding fiscal year was the firm's first year of exporting, sales may not exceed $1,000,000).

For the company just beginning to export which feels that it needs some outside expertise in operating under a policy, the Umbrella policy is available. An Umbrella policy is issued to a qualified entity such as an insurance broker, bank, state, or municipal government agency, etc., as the policy *administrator;* the administrator then seeks to market the insurance policy to local exporters. In so doing, the administrator agrees to qualify the exporter and its buyers for the insurance and also agrees to report shipments and all overdues. The administrator acts as the insured's representative regarding communications with and reporting to FCIA and Eximbank.

To be eligible for the policy, exporters must present documentation as follows:

- signed financial statements or annual report for the latest fiscal year or start-up statements that reveal a positive net worth.
- average annual export sales history during the preceding two fiscal years not exceeding $2,000,000 (together with affiliates and exclusive of sales made on terms of confirmed irrevocable letters of credit or cash in advance).

The Multibuyer Export Policy Offers Full Financial Flexibility

The Multibuyer Export policy is generally written to cover shipments during a one-year period and insures a reasonable spread of an exporter's eligible sales. It enables premiums to be lowered, helps the exporter to make quicker credit decisions (providing faster service to overseas buyers), and reduces paperwork.

It helps the exporter to compete world-wide. The exporter can obtain financing and can offer competitive credit terms to attract and retain buyers around the globe, even in higher risk markets.

This policy insures short-term sales with repayment terms generally up to 180 days and, in an alternative version, covers medium-term sales, with repayment stretching out to five years (or longer under certain circumstances).

At policy inception and at each annual renewal, the exporter may choose to cover 90 percent of commercial risks and 100 percent of political risks, or choose equalized cover at 95 percent for both commercial and political risk. For short-term transactions, this coverage applies to the gross invoice amount and in many cases to interest at FCIA-specified rates. Medium-term sales require a minimum 15 percent cash payment by the buyer on or before due date of first installment, so the coverage here applies to the balance—the financed portion—of the transaction plus interest at FCIA-specified rates.

The policy is subject to limits. The aggregate limit represents the insurers' maximum liability under the policy. The exporter also makes his own credit decisions for shipments up to the amount of a discretionary credit limit (DCL), after checking the country limitation schedule (CLS) and documenting the creditworthiness of the buyer as specified in the DCL endorsement to the policy. For larger amounts, a special buyer credit limit (SBCL) is available upon application to Foreign Credit Insurance Association. The buyer's interest obligation is generally covered at a specified rate up to a limited time after the due date.

Certain agricultural commodities may be

insured under this policy, with terms extended to one year (if needed) and with commercial coverage increased to 98 percent.

The Multibuyer Export policy has a deductible feature similar to that of major medical and other forms of insurance.

The Medium-term Policy Covers Individual or Repetitive Shipments to Single Buyers

The Medium-term policy covers capital and quasi-capital goods of U.S. manufacture sold in international trade on terms from six months to five years (occasionally longer). Policies are written on a case-by-case basis. The exporter may insure either a single sale or repetitive sales to the same buyer and is not required to insure all of his medium-term transactions.

The foreign buyer must make a 15 percent cash payment on or before due date of first installment. The remaining financed portion is to be covered by a promissory note requiring payment in approximately equal installments on a monthly, quarterly, or semiannual basis.

The policy generally covers interest charges up to specified limits as well as principal due. Coverage is normally 90 percent of a commercial and 100 percent of a political loss.

A Combination Medium-term policy is utilized mainly to protect exporters in transactions with overseas dealers and distributors. It protects against risk in three areas:

- parts and accessories on terms up to 180 days.
- inventory financing, where the exporter may ship goods under a "floor plan" arrangement. Initial coverage is up to 270 days with no down payment required.
- receivables financing, with terms typi-

cally up to three years following the minimum cash payment upon resale by the dealer or at the end of the inventory period.

For medium-term transactions, the buyer must pay the normal 15 percent cash payment and coverage is on the remaining financed portion, plus interest, as described earlier.

Special Coverages Are Available

Exporters may want to avail themselves of preshipment coverage which dates from the execution of the sales contract rather than the date of shipment (useful for specially fabricated goods or those requiring up to 18 months factory lead time). Transactions requiring payment in the buyer's currency may be eligible for coverage, and political-only coverage for export sales may also be obtained.

Sales of Services and Leasing of Equipment Are Insurable, Too

Management consultants, engineering service firms, transportation companies, and similar businesses may obtain protection for payments to be made by foreign customers. The Association offers coverage to companies wishing to extend prudent terms to gain a greater share of the services market. Insurance coverage is also available on operating and finance leases to cover defaulted lease payments against commercial and political loss (up to the point when the lease requires the return of the asset due to protracted default). This coverage is available to any financially responsible leasing company, manufacturer, bank, trust, partnership, or other domestic or foreign entity that leases or participates in the financing of U.S. export

leases. Lease transactions may be either cross-border or international. Leased equipment can be either new or used but must be of U.S. manufacture. Payments may be in dollars or other hard currencies.

FCIA Branch Offices

Atlanta
Peachtree Center Tower
Suite 1416
230 Peachtree Street, NW
Atlanta, GA 30303

Chicago
20 North Clark Street
Suite 910
Chicago, IL 60602

Houston
Texas Commerce Tower
Suite 2860
600 Travis
Houston, TX 77002

Los Angeles
Crocker Center
Suite 2580
333 South Grand Avenue
Los Angeles, CA 90017

Headquarters
New York
40 Rector Street,
11th Floor
New York, NY 10006

FRANCHISING
═══════════════════════

Can You Franchise Your Business?

Spurred by dreams of instant wealth, everyone from pizza shop proprietors to tax preparers has jumped on the franchising bandwagon, setting up ventures to market their name, trademark, and business system to others. Some have succeeded, but many more have found it to be among the fastest and most agonizing routes to the bankruptcy courts. Like many get-rich-quick schemes, this one is not as easy as it looks.

How can you evaluate your prospects?

According to experts in the field, a business is franchisable if it meets the following tests:

1. The operation can be boiled down to a set of standardized procedures others can duplicate. Based on this prerequisite, a landscaping firm that succeeds on the strength of the owner's personal creativity is not a good candidate. There's no way to transfer the owner's talent to franchisees. A pizza shop, on the other hand, is ideal for franchising. Recipes, menus, and portion control can be documented in a franchise manual and thus passed on to others.

2. The company is in a growth market for franchised units. In saturated markets—such as the fast-food burger business—existing franchises have locked up the best locations, making it difficult for new ventures to succeed.

3. The business should be one that benefits from an established trademark. Franchisees, after all, will be buying a company's image and identification as well as its business system.

4. The company has substantial (and preferably increasing) sales and earnings for a period of at least three years. Financial performance must be revealed to prospective investors in the so-called disclosure document. Poor earnings, bankruptcy proceedings, or substantial lawsuits—all of which are reported—will discourage franchisees from buying into the venture.

5. The company yields high net profits as a percentage of gross sales. For a franchise operation to succeed, the franchisees must produce sufficient profits to compensate themselves adequately and to pay royalties to the franchisor. Without this dual payback, the system cannot work. For this reason, low-margin businesses are rarely franchisable.

6. The entrepreneur has sufficient capital to fund the development of a franchise operation and to carry it through to the break-even point. The amount of money needed to start a franchise system is usually underestimated. Up-front costs for market research, legal representation, preparation of franchise documents, and recruitment of a management team to operate and market the franchise can range from $200,000 to $500,000. To this add another 50 percent or more for working capital.

WHERE TO FIND IT

The International Franchise Association
1350 New York Avenue,
Suite 900
Washington, D.C. 20005

MARKETING

The Marketing Concept

The marketing concept rests on the importance of customers to a firm and states that: (1) all company policies and activities should be aimed at satisfying customer needs, and (2) profitable sales volume is a better company goal than maximum sales volume.

To use the marketing concept, a small business should (1) determine the needs of its customers (market research), (2) analyze its competitive advantages (market strategy), (3) select specific markets to serve (target marketing), and (4) determine how to satisfy those needs (market mix).

Percent Distribution of Employment and Establishments by Employment-size Class

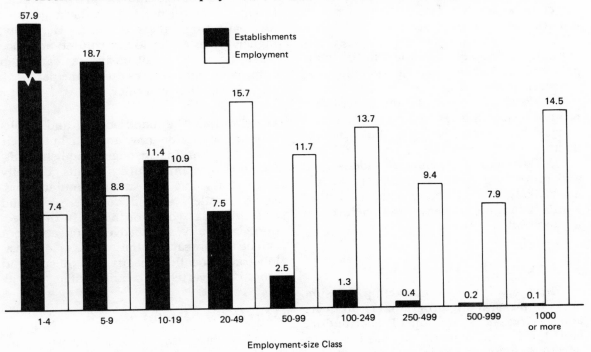

The vast majority of businesses in the United States are small. They also employ half of the private-sector work force.

Market Research

In order to manage the marketing functions successfully, good information about the market is necessary. Frequently, a small market research program, based on a questionnaire given to present customers and/or prospective customers, can disclose problems and areas of dissatisfaction that can be easily remedied, or new products or services that could be offered successfully.

Marketing Strategy

Marketing strategy encompasses identifying customer groups (target markets) that

a small business can serve better than its larger competitors and tailoring its product offerings, prices, distribution, promotional efforts, and services toward that particular market segment (managing the market mix). A good strategy implies that a small business cannot be all things to all people and must analyze its markets and its own capabilities so as to focus on a target market it can serve best.

Target Marketing

Owners of small businesses have limited resources to spend on marketing activities. Concentrating their marketing efforts on one or a few key market segments is the basis of target marketing. The major ways to segment a market are:

1. Geographical segmentation—developing a loyal group of consumers in the home geographical territory before expanding into new territories.

2. Product segmentation—extensively promoting existing best-selling products and services before introducing a lot of new products.

3. Customer segmentation—identifying and promoting to those groups of people most likely to buy the product. In other words, selling to the heavy users before trying to develop new users.

Managing the Market Mix

There are four key marketing decision areas in a marketing program: (1) products and services, (2) promotion, (3) distribution, and (4) pricing. The marketing mix is used to describe how owner-managers combine these four areas into an overall marketing program.

Products and services. Effective product strategies for a small business may include concentrating on a narrow product line, developing a highly specialized product or service, or providing a product-service package containing an unusual amount of service.

Promotion. This marketing decision area includes advertising, salesmanship, and other promotional activities. In general, high-quality salesmanship is a must for small businesses due to their limited ability to advertise heavily. Good Yellow-Pages advertising is a must for small retailers. Direct mail is an effective, low-cost medium of advertising available to small businesses.

Price. Price levels and/or pricing policies (including credit policy) are the major factors affecting total revenue. Generally, higher prices mean lower volume and vice versa; however, small businesses can often command higher prices due to the personalized service they can offer.

Distribution. The manufacturer and wholesaler must decide how to distribute their products. Working through established distributors or manufacturers' agents generally is most feasible for small manufacturers. Small retailers should consider cost and traffic flow as two major factors in site selection, especially since advertising and rent can be reciprocal. In other words, a low-cost, low-traffic location means you must spend more on advertising to build traffic.

Marketing Performance

After marketing program decisions are made, owner-managers need to evaluate how well decisions have turned out. Standards of performance need to be set up so results can be evaluated against them. Sound data on industry norms and past performance provide the basis for comparing against present performance.

Owner-managers should audit their company's performance at least quarterly. The key questions to ask are:

1. Is the company doing all it can to be customer-oriented?
2. Do the employees make sure the customers' needs are satisfied and leave them with the feeling that they would enjoy coming back?
3. Is it easy for the customer to find what he or she wants and at a competitive price?

Credit: U.S. Small Business Administration

WHERE TO FIND IT

Smaller Business Association of New England
(SBANE)
69 Hickory Drive
Waltham, MA 02154
(800) 368-6803

GROWTH STRATEGIES

Key Strategies Can Help Companies Grow

Why one business stalls in midcourse while another achieves sustained growth is not always clear. Certainly, there are no magic formulas, no secrets to success. But a number of principles and strategies common to the great entrepreneurs appear to link successful ventures in a wide range of businesses and industries.

"Call it vision, insight, or instinct, the legendary entrepreneurs are guided by principles that give their work an added dimension," says a vice-president with a national consulting firm. "Every action they consider has to mesh with these principles or it is rejected out of hand. This conceptual framework shapes the business building process—gives it strength, direction, consistency."

Surprisingly, profits are rarely the driving force behind the entrepreneurial success stories.

"If there's a lesson to be learned from the premier entrepreneurs, it's to put ideas ahead of money," says Joseph Mancuso, president of the Center for Entrepreneurial Management. "They believe that if you have a good concept and a sound strategy for implementing it, the money will follow. Those who focus primarily on how much money they can make turn their attention away from the factors that can really contribute to their company's success."

Bankers, venture capitalists, and consultants active with small business clients hold that the following principles and strategies have guided many companies from start-up to substantial enterprises:

1. Less Is More. This seeming contradiction can be vitally important in shaping a company's marketing strategy. The idea is to direct the firm's products or services to a limited market rather than aiming for the universe of potential buyers. This so-called segmentation marshals the firm's resources to achieve a manageable goal and in the process creates a clear image in the marketplace. Had McDonald's founder sought to satisfy gourmets as well as fast-food buffs, it is unlikely that the company would have pleased either.

2. Two Plus Two Equals Five. In planning business expansion—from opening new branches to taking on additional product lines—action should be taken only if the larger entity will be greater than the sum of its parts. Take the small retailer contemplating a merger with a local competitor. If the new business will simply be bigger than the separate firms, the deal may not be productive. With successful mergers, two plus two must equal five: the merged entity must provide additional strength or market presence that the parties to the merger did not have independently. For example, a local retailer strong in the downtown market merging with a suburban powerhouse may make both less vulnerable to competition from the national chains.

3. Spend Money to Make Money. The old adage that money goes to money is as true for corporations as it is for individuals. By investing in state-of-the-art technology, modern plants, and sufficient inventory, entrepreneurs can outmaneuver giant corporations and in the process compete more successfully for customers. Because big corporations are often slow to change, aggressive upstarts can often get a jump on emerging markets and maintain their share even after the giants invade. In recent years, small companies have scored with this strategy in computers, software, electronics, and retailing. The idea is to identify markets ripe for newer, faster, or more efficient products and services and to invest in facilities capable of providing this competitive edge. Lenders and investors are often sensitive to these opportunities.

4. Share the Pie. Giving employees a stake in the business creates a highly motivated work force that can have a positive impact on product quality, customer service, and cost control. By extending profit sharing or stock options beyond the executive suite to the rank and file, management makes allies of would-be adversaries and gains total worker commitment at a time when the company can benefit most from high productivity and aggressive salesmanship.

"Another rule of successful entrepreneurs is a play on the old saying, 'If at first you don't succeed; try, try again,'" Mancuso adds. "They're always trying different things on the theory that the more they attempt the more likely something will click. They never let the fear of failure stop them from taking risks. I guess that's what makes them entrepreneurs."

Marketing Professional Practices

When the small, century-old firm of Smith, Jones & Jones, attorneys at law, found its bread-and-butter banking practice losing ground to the newly aggressive national law firms, the managing partner took decisive steps to shift SJ&J's focus to the local real estate market. Property specialists were lured away from competitors, staff attorneys were given courses in real estate law, and a partner was assigned to manage the new practice.

Unfortunately, but all too predictably, that practice never developed. In launching its real estate unit, Smith, Jones & Jones committed a fatal error common to professional firms: It failed to inform the marketplace. SJ&J's new practice may have been the best-kept secret in town.

"The days when professional firms could sit around waiting for the phone to ring are over," says a consultant to the legal and accounting professions. "Today they have to market themselves and their services much as any other business. When New York accountants open a West Coast office, for example, they have to make their presence known in Los Angeles and they have to make it clear to prospective clients what they are offering above and beyond established competitors.

"We're talking about marketing, and the rub is that professional firms often view marketing as crass, commercial, and thoroughly undignified. So they do nothing, and in many cases their practice stagnates."

But this need not be the case. For many professionals, the aversion to marketing stems from an inaccurate assessment of what marketing really is. Leaving aside the razzle-dazzle tactics of mouthwash marketers, it is the process of identifying business opportunities and acting to take advantage of them.

"This can be done in a tasteful manner," says a New York public relations executive who counts law and accounting firms among his clients. "Take the process of creating demand. While many professionals shy away from advertising—fearing it will be perceived as too aggressive—they can accomplish similar results with public relations. The advantage here is that no one need know they are responsible for the effort."

Working behind the scenes with editors and reporters, publicists cultivate relationships between their clients (in this case, professional firms) and the press. It works this way: An architect is introduced to the appropriate editor at the *Wall Street Journal.* The publicist may propose a story—such as the architect's use of revolutionary building materials—or simply lay the groundwork for future contact by the journalist.

"It may be weeks, months, or more until the meeting produces concrete results, but it's usually well worth the wait," Wachs says. "When a professional firm is quoted in the press—when its opinion is sought on major issues—clients take notice. It's a proven way to generate business. Because the message is not paid for, and because it does not appear to be initiated by the client, it has extraordinary credibility with readers."

Public relations firms can be hired on a retainer or project basis. With the former, publicists maintain ongoing relations with the press, focusing primarily on media coverage of the client's professional activities. Fees generally start at $2,000 per month. While this arrangement is often productive for mid-size and larger firms, sole practitioners may find they get more for their dollars by limiting publicity expenses to a project basis.

"With this approach, the client establishes a goal—like getting an article placed in a given magazine—and agrees to compensate the publicists for their efforts in trying to accomplish that goal," the marketing consultant explains. "At our firm, the fee is based on the number of hours likely to be spent on the project. From my perspective, the smallest professional firms are usually best served by

working on a project basis. They're rarely newsworthy enough to warrant a retainer relationship."

Publicity has two major drawbacks. First, it is not a sure thing. Try as they may, publicists are often unable to get their client's name in print. Unless the professionals have a genuine news angle or can be established as legitimate authorities, behind-the-scenes maneuvers may come to naught.

Second, news coverage cannot be controlled. Inviting reporters to interview the firm's managing partner may result in a negative piece about his background, accomplishments, or reputation in the business community. Many a company has been stunned by the unpredictability of press encounters. Identify the risks at the outset.

Consider these additional strategies for marketing professional firms:

1. Host a series of seminars designed to update clients on technical developments, government actions, or trends in the profession. "Bringing in a prominent speaker, such as the head of a government agency, adds substance to these events and boosts the sponsor's prestige," the consultant says. "If clients are impressed with the speaker, they'll not only attend the function but will be indebted to the host firm for the insights they've gained. That could lead to new business—if not immediately following the seminar, then somewhere down the road."

2. Design a marketing brochure outlining the firm's history, key services, management biographies, and philosophy of practice. "Although many law firms still consider brochures to be unprofessional, we don't agree," says a partner with the nationally prominent Cleveland-based law firm of Jones, Day, Reavis & Pogue. "Our studies indicate that clients use brochures to identify the kinds of work various firms specialize in. While they won't select law firms solely on this basis,

we've learned that they use brochures to narrow the selection process. To my way of thinking, that makes brochures important to a firm's marketing program."

3. Encourage partners to join industry groups and trade associations active in the firm's key areas of practice. This facilitates client contact and enhances the firm's exposure in the field. "Our hypothetical law firm, Smith, Jones & Jones, could have paved the way for its real estate practice by combining high-visibility participation in industry organizations with an aggressive seminar program," the consultant says. "This dual approach would have informed the target market—developers, brokers, and mortgage lenders—of the firm's newly developed real estate expertise."

4. Test a series of tastefully produced advertisements in prominent business or professional publications. Despite the lingering bias against advertising, increasing numbers of professionals—including some of the most prestigious names in public accounting—are recognizing its usefulness in cultivating new markets and gaining immediate recognition for expanded services or practice specialties.

Professional advertising can be as discreet as a reproduction of the practitioner's business card:

Smith, Jones & Jones
Attorneys at Law

John Smith
Senior Partner: Real Estate
123 Rodeo Drive
Beverly Hills, California

5. Tap the underlying referral network that links the professions. "Lawyers, bankers, and CPAs often find themselves handling different aspects of the same transaction," says the managing partner of a midsize accounting firm. "Assume, for example, that an entrepreneur approaches his bank for a $5 million loan. Before coming up with the money, the banker will likely request an audited financial statement. If the businessman doesn't have an auditor, the bank may recommend two or three public accounting firms to do the work. We want to be included on that shopping list—and we usually are.

"How do we manage that? By cultivating relationships with all the major banks in our community. We invite them to seminars, send them our monthly newsletter, and take them to lunch at least twice a year. Because they're familiar with us and with the quality of our work, they recommend us over competitors."

The unwritten rule is always to return the favor, directing clients back through the established referral network. On the banker/ lawyer/accountant circuit, for example, this means referring CPA-firm clients in need to capital to bankers delivering audit engagements and to attorneys referring clients for tax and estate planning.

Just how professionals market their services depends on the firm's prevailing image and the partners' taste for promotional techniques. But a fundamental prerequisite for any and all marketing strategies is to recognize that a profession is a business as well as a scholarly pursuit.

"Professionals who don't admit that they're in business are at a disadvantage when it comes to running their firms," the Jones, Day partner says. "They don't recognize that doing high-quality work, though vitally important, isn't enough in today's complex and competitive markets. You have to evaluate client needs, gear up to service them, and communicate your capabilities. If we do something well, I want the world to know about it. Why be bashful about that?"

MERGERS

Mini-mergers Right for Small Companies

With Wall Street's mega-mergers dominating the business news, small companies may think that's a game only the giants can play. But the impression is misleading. By combining their assets and resources, privately held companies can conduct mini-mergers of their own, using the process to achieve rapid expansion or to bolster their competitive position.

"Mergers are most attractive when they produce a strategic alliance that benefits both parties," says an executive with the mergers and acquisition group for Arthur Young. "Assume, for example, that a software producer is successful in local markets but wants to reach a greater universe of potential customers. It has two choices: to expand its own distribution system or to merge with a company that has a national system in place. The latter approach will be faster and, because it relies on a proven operation, will likely be more effective. The small company experiences dramatic growth from the outset."

Similarly, companies in need of growth capital may seek mergers with cash-rich partners able to finance their growth internally. Blessed with virtually unlimited funds, and freed of burdensome debt service, management can achieve a level of growth that would be impossible on its own.

"The idea is to seek a merger where the combined entity is greater than the sum of its parts," the Arthur Young executive adds. "This happens when the strategic alliance gives the companies new capabilities—be they technical, financial, or marketing—that they lacked before the merger. Small business owners will want to determine when such alliances would help their companies grow and compete."

But there are other reasons to merge. For many, the opportunity to cash out after years of business ownership tops the list. By selling all or part of the stock to another company, the entrepreneur gains instant liquidity and may continue in a management capacity as well.

"Should the small company merge with a big, diversified business, there's a good chance the buyer will ask management to stay on and run the company," explains the Arthur Young merger expert. "In that case, the former owner has the best of both worlds: cash in pocket and a company to run.

"Considering the precarious position of small companies in many industries—where giant competitors can become dominant factors in the market overnight—many entrepreneurs take great comfort in this kind of deal. Having cashed out, they feel personally secure regardless of the company's fate."

In seeking a merger, small companies may find attractive candidates among suppliers and major customers. For the best results, compile a select list of the most likely merger partners, providing each with a formal proposal and a detailed description of your business, including financial statements and projections. All prospects may be approached directly or through intermediaries including attorneys, accountants, and business brokers.

Consider these additional guidelines:

1. Approach the market with a working knowledge of what the business is worth. Rely on professional appraisals or common pricing formulas, such as ten times earnings or two times book value. Indecisiveness on the seller's part can prompt buyers to submit low-ball bids.

2. Structure the merger to take advantage of favorable tax treatment.

Work with professionals in planning and implementing mergers. View the transactions as among the most important in your business career.

Mergers and Acquisitions

Advice of the National Law Firm of Jones, Day, Reavis & Pogue

Acquisitions generally involve five stages: (1) negotiations leading to a handshake or agreement in principle, or contingent agreement to buy and sell a business; (2) more detailed negotiations and study of the business leading to a binding agreement in which the purchaser is committed in writing to buy the business without any contingencies under his control; (3) completion of various governmental filings and agreements with other parties which must be done before the closing; (4) the closing day and moment at which there is a new owner of the business who has paid or signed a note for a price for that business; (5) a postclosing period in which some details of the transfer are completed and there may be a postclosing adjustment of price, and each side prepares its own closing volume containing the significant documents reflecting the transaction.

A fairly large number of transactions reach the handshake stage without ever reaching the closing stage. Often the buyer wants to maintain contingencies so as to be able to walk away from the transaction as long as possible, sometimes even until the day of closing. As closing approaches, each side has a greater and greater investment in legal and accounting fees and other costs, and therefore more commitment to close. The seller in particular, as the transaction becomes more widely known among employees, customers, and suppliers, may be seriously disadvantaged if the closing does not occur.

The process of negotiation continues from the beginning until after the closing, but often some very important parameters of the transaction are set in the initial discussions between the principals, leading to a handshake understanding. Is the seller selling assets or stock, or is the selling company to be merged into the buyer? Is the buyer paying with cash, notes, or stock? If stock, is the transaction to be tax-free or taxable to the seller? If there is a note involved, can the seller treat it as an installment sale for tax purposes? If there is a note, will the buyer personally guarantee it or otherwise secure it? Is part of the purchase price to be escrowed or held back by the buyer until some time after the closing when he or she knows more about what has been purchased? Is part of the purchase price to be contingent on results after the closing? Is there to be a postclosing price adjustment, depending on such factors as an audit of financial results up to the closing date? Are any disagreements concerning this to be arbitrated? Are any employees of the seller to remain under employment contracts, and if so for what length of time and at what compensation? Is the seller or any of its employees to sign a noncompetition agreement? If there are any finder's fees involved, who pays them? Will the parties try to agree on a tax allocation, or will each report the transaction in its own way? Who will pay the sales tax, if any, in an assets purchase? Are there conditions to closing such as the buyer's ability to obtain financing? Who pays the buyer's and seller's legal fees and other costs if closing does not occur? Must the buyer deposit any earnest money before closing and will this be escrowed? Will the buyer sign an early agreement that, if the transaction does not close, he or she will not disclose information about the seller's business learned in the investigation? Who bears product warranty costs and other claims relating to sales before closing? Who gets the benefit or cost if pension plans are underfunded or overfunded on the closing date, and how and when is this determined? Will the old pension plans be terminated and new ones established? Will union contracts be assumed or renegotiated?

All these matters may be discussed and some tentative agreements reached at early stages of the discussion. Often, the parties simply say to one another that they expect the usual conditions, representations, and warranties will be included in the agreements that the lawyers draw up. Of course, these "usual" items vary tremendously from deal to deal.

Throughout the discussions, there will be negotiations over how much the seller will represent or guarantee to the buyer about the business. Usually, this section of the agreement is many pages long, and there are many additional pages of disclosure schedules. The buyer often argues along these lines:

"I'm paying a lot of money for a business I can't possibly know as well as you, the seller. You've been running it for years; you know the employees, the customers, the suppliers, the equipment, and the whole experience of the business. You know where the problems and the risk are. Just tell me; disclose all of them to me in writing, and we will decide which you should bear and which I should bear. After all, you're getting the price I'm paying because of what I *think* the business is. If my thoughts are wrong, don't mislead me. Tell me now and tell me in writing how healthy the pig in the poke is. I have lenders (or partners or shareholders or family) who won't let me buy unless you put it in writing."

The seller may reply along the following lines:

"If you are buying the business, you must buy the whole business, and take the bad with the good. I (or any partners, shareholders, or family) can't let you take the assets and the earning stream, and leave me only with obligations of the business since I won't have the resources of the business to meet them. This is a good business, it's been here a long time, I've made a lot of money at it, and it's very valuable, but of course it has the usual risks of any business. If you own the business, you take on these risks. So I won't make any representations or warranties. Take the business as is and where is. You can go in and look at the business, the books, ask the employees questions, but I'm not representing or warranting anything about the business except that I own it, and after I sell it to you you'll own it."

The outcome of this discussion will be very important in assuring that the buyer learns what the seller knows and in resolving any disputes that arise after the business has been sold, or in deciding who pays any claims that come up after the business is sold. This general discussion will apply to many specific items covered under the agreements. In many cases, as to each item, it may be resolved by the seller limiting his representations and warranties to his best knowledge, although the buyer may refuse this and insist that if the seller doesn't know, he should find out. Sometimes exceptions are made for undisclosed items that are not "material" or that individually or in the aggregate fall below a certain amount. Sometimes there is a ceiling to the seller's liability for the representations and warranties, such as the total purchase price, and sometimes there is an expiration period so that if something about the business is discovered more than a certain period of months or years after the closing, the buyer of the business has no claim against the seller. Usually, the seller at least represents and warrants the financial statements of the business on which the buyer is relying, again sometimes with exceptions as to collectibility of accounts receivable and the like.

After an agreement in principle or contingent agreement is reached, which is typically nonbinding on either party or binding only on the seller, a great deal must be done to familiarize the buyer with the business, to prepare the necessary disclosure documents to the buyer and agreements concerning the transition of ownership of the business.

If there is a new corporation to be formed for the acquisition, it must be brought into existence. This should be done at an early stage, and if stock is to be purchased at lower rates by some than others, these purchases can take place early, before the value of the corporation grows as the acquisition grows nearer. This factor can be a very important part of the tax planning.

Tax planning should be completed during this stage, including an allocation of the purchase price among the assets being acquired in order to minimize the tax burden after the acquisition. If the parties can agree upon this, inclusion of this tax allocation in the purchase agreement will have a very persuasive effect upon the Internal Revenue Service. Financing arrangements with the banks or other lenders may also be negotiated during this period, and arrangements made as to security for the purchase price, including any mortgages, UCC filings, or personal guarantees by the buyer.

A detailed purchase agreement must be drafted, negotiated, and agreed upon. The buyer and to varying degrees his lawyers, accountants, other experts, and employees become thoroughly familiar with various aspects of the business being acquired through collection of documents, meetings with employees of the seller, plant visits, and the like. If the seller is a public company or otherwise subject to regulation, governmental filings may be examined. Disclosure schedules will be required of the seller, including copies of all material agreements of the business and information on any law suits or other claims made or threatened against the business. These disclosure schedules are ordinarily voluminous, and often the buyer provides that if he is not satisfied at his own discretion with their contents, he is not obliged to buy the business. Copies of leases, employment contracts, product warranties, distribution agreements, supplier agreements, patents, copyrights, trademarks, and a variety of other documents are included, and in each case the seller must agree to assign them, obtaining any necessary third-party consents or otherwise giving the buyer their benefit. This is ordinarily more complex in an assets acquisition, but an assets acquisition gives the buyer more opportunity to avoid assuming undisclosed liabilities that might later arise, and often more tax flexibility in allocating the purchase price, with or without agreement with the seller.

During this stage, any bulk-sales notices should be filed, to cut off claims of creditors against the buyer in an asset purchase. Title reports should be obtained on any real property to be included, and arrangements made for title insurance at the closing. Governmental filings may be necessary, such as Hart Scott Rodino antitrust notifications, securities law filings, and industrial-development-bond inducement agreements that must be obtained before there is a binding commitment to buy and sell the business.

The buyer may wish to have his accountants audit the financial statements during this period, or at least observe the physical inventory. The buyer may also station one or more of his employees at the principal places of business to become familiar with the accounting systems and methods of doing business. This will greatly aid in the buyer's understanding of the business and tend to avoid unpleasant surprises. The role of these people should be defined, preferably in writing.

An appraisal must be made of the pension-plan funding and of labor agreements, and plans must be made as to communication with employees on these subjects and with customers, suppliers, and other related parties.

Finally, the contingencies have been removed, any necessary approvals from governmental agencies, customers, suppliers, shareholders, or employees have been obtained, bulk-sales time periods have run out, title commitments are in place, security interests are ready for recording, escrows have been established, and all other preparations have been made for closing.

At the moment of closing, the legal ownership of the business changes. If an unforeseen material accident or change occurs in the business prior to that date, it is the seller's obligation in the first instance, and, depending upon the agreements, the buyer may or may not have an obligation to close with or without an adjustment in the purchase price. After that moment, in the first instance the problem is the buyer's but, depending upon the agreements, there may or may not be an obligation of the seller to reduce the purchase price or reimburse the buyer, and third parties may or may not have claims against the seller. The buyer must in any case be sure he has fire, business interruption, product liability, accident, any employee life or health, or other desired insurance in place from the closing on. The closing may occur "as of" a date before or after the actual date so that by agreement the profits and costs of operating the business from the

"as of" date will be the buyer's, and receivables or payables incurred after that date can be for the account of the buyer and those incurred before that date can be for the account of the seller. Even though such arrangements may be made and even required by binding contractual arrangements, the actual ownership of the business changes hands at the closing, when the bill of sale or stock is delivered or the merger becomes effective, and the buyer ordinarily does not pay the price until that moment.

After the closing, there are always bills or claims received or assets discovered that need to be adjusted between the parties in accordance with their agreements. Sometimes the purchase price is based on an audit that takes place on the closing date, the results of which are not available until later, or the price may have a variable depending upon the performance of the business after the closing. In either case, provisions must be made for a postclosing adjustment, and the payment of additional consideration by the buyer, or repayment of some consideration by the seller, or adjustment of the amount of promissory notes given by the buyer, or of an escrow account. These matters can often be the subject of dispute, which is usually worked out amicably but can be arbitrated or even litigated. The buyer and seller are often eager before closing to conclude the deal, and details considered insignificant before the closing suddenly seem quite important when bills are presented for them after the closing.

Within a short period of time after the closing, memories fade and the participants in the intense transaction have moved on to other pursuits, including the running of the business that has been acquired. The close working relationships that existed while the transaction was in progress are no longer present, and only the written documents remain. They can now be examined at leisure, although they were negotiated and signed under the pressure of time and concern over a multitude of issues. It is now these documents that define the relationship between the parties, and any specific issues that may arise might be governed by a very few words in a very long document. Accordingly, despite the pressures of time and negotiation, it is important for the parties themselves to be thoroughly familiar with the business and with all details of the documents they are signing *before* the closing occurs. There is no substitute for reading the documents and asking any questions before the closing rather than after.

NEW PRODUCTS

Hot New Products Find a Void and Fill It

Think of the hot products that have taken America by storm—hula hoops, designer jeans, personal computers. In case after case, the entrepreneurs behind these strokes of genius looked first to the marketplace for inspiration, then to the drawing board to create them. In classic marketing fashion, they found a void and filled it.

The lesson should not be lost on the next generation of entrepreneurs now tinkering with new product ideas. By first identifying consumer needs and behavior patterns, and by using this information to shape product ideas, they have a better shot at coming up with the next Cabbage Patch doll.

"When planning a new product—be it a simple gadget or a technical marvel—the inventor/entrepreneur must bear in mind that the product, no matter how exciting or innovative, will be successful only if it can be sold," says an executive with an advertising agency that has helped develop and introduce dozens of new products. "Although this rule appears obvious, many companies, caught up in the joy of creation, are blinded to it. They design a product, produce it, and only then see if there's a place for it in the market. That's a sure prescription for another Edsel.

"A wiser approach is to build market data into the product's design. Our experience indicates that the most successful new products begin with a profile of the target market and a detailed marketing plan."

Adds a vice-president of the Howard/Marlboro Group, a marketing and sales promotion firm: "I tell inventors that instead of marketing an invention they should find a market and invent for it. By this I mean that the market, not the product, should be the starting point. Unless you develop something for which there is an identifiable need or for which you can create impulse buying, your efforts will come to naught. The Patent Bureau is filled with millions of patents that never earned their inventors a dime. In most cases, that's because they failed to design a product with a particular consumer or market in mind."

With entrepreneurialism now sweeping the nation—and with new product ideas germinating at a record rate—the following guidelines for new product development may help to boost the success rate:

1. Conduct the search for "market voids" within your own sphere of interest. "Look at those products you use on the job, in a hobby, or in running your business, the marketing vice-president advises. "Chances are one of them doesn't do the job it's supposed to do. It's too slow, too clumsy, or too complicated. That's an open invitation to come up with a

superior design. Because you have firsthand experience in the field you know what the product must do to satisfy consumers. Go out and create it."

2. Don't invent the wheel, reinvent it. Modifying existing products rather than developing new ones from scratch assures the entrepreneur of an established market from the outset. People are already using a similar product. You're just making it faster, more efficient, or otherwise more attractive. You don't have to sell the basic concept. This provides a significant head start in the race to profitability.

3. Identify one of the major consumer groups likely to buy the product. "Until recently, marketers used to divide consumers into two groups, rich and poor," the advertising executive says. "But today, income is seen as only one of the factors determining buying habits. Another, perhaps more important factor is life-style. The entrepreneur must determine which of these four major life-style categories represents the target market: need-driven (practical or value-oriented consumers rarely given to impulse buying), belongers (brand-loyal shoppers generally resistant to change), personal achievers (trend setters willing to spend lavishly for fashion innovation and personal improvement), and socio-conscious (favoring products with strong health or environmental claims.)"

How these distinctions figure into new product planning is clear. Assume the ABC Company is introducing a frozen dessert for sale to local groceries and gourmet shops. To make inroads with "need-driven" consumers, the product will have to stress low price and speed of preparation—features that must be incorporated at the earliest stages of development. On the other hand, positioning the dessert for the "personal achievement" crowd calls for a markedly different appeal based

on taste and status. Same product, two markets, two prescriptions for success.

4. Determine the personality the product will bring to market. Successful products, from perfumes to wrist watches, base their sales appeal more on image than on intrinsic value. This helps the products stand out from similar items.

Advertising agencies and marketing consultants can help plan and promote new products.

PUBLIC RELATIONS

How Small Companies Can Make News

When small business makes news, once obscure companies become household names. Overnight, little-known products move to center stage, competing successfully with giant competitors for brand recognition, consumer attention, and sales. The business is on the map.

But how is this done? How can small companies make their way into the headlines? How can they compete for media attention with the GMs and GEs of the world?

"By being creative, innovative, and persistent—that's how," says Mark Wachs, president of a New York–based public relations firm that bears his name. "Precisely because they are not well known and because they don't generate spontaneous publicity, small companies have to work harder and smarter to make news. But with an innovative approach, they can make it happen.

"Take the case of a utility consulting firm that wanted press coverage of its energy conservation services. Rather than making a self-serving pitch—which is never effective—

management created an annual survey, providing rate information on each of the nation's top 24 utilities. The survey made *Business Week, Time* magazine, and dozens of local newspapers and magazines. With each story, word of the company's service reached a wider audience."

Another news-making tactic is to latch on to major stories, finding a way to associate your company with the news of the day.

"Tax season presents a golden opportunity for accounting firms, financial planners, and investment advisers who want to get their names in the news," says Stacey Winnick, president of the media relations firm of Ames Associates. "With the public keenly interested in any and all ways to cut their tax bills, the press welcomes story ideas from authoritative sources. By coming up with a unique tax-saving angle, and by communicating that to a newspaper or magazine, even the smallest companies can get their name in print."

Consider these additional news-making strategies:

1. Ask the publications most likely to report on your business for an "editorial calendar," listing the topics of special interest they will be covering throughout the year. "Knowing six months in advance that the local newspaper is planning a special section on real estate gives developers and leasing agents substantial lead time for proposing stories on their products or services," Winnick explains. "They get a head start on other companies seeking media attention."

2. Find the one aspect of your company that makes it unique, and use it as the focal point for attracting news coverage. "When a small investment bank decided to go up against the Morgan Stanleys and the First Bostons for publicity, the partners recognized they needed to stress something that

they did better than the giants," Wachs says. "So instead of talking about the standard investments in blue chip companies, they touted their specialty in researching junior growth stocks. Because the message was fresh and original, it appealed to business editors, who gave the company considerable ink."

3. Send your business card to editors and reporters specializing in your field. Note on the card your area of expertise, and follow up with an introductory phone call. With a little luck, your card will make it to a reporter's source file and you'll be called for comments on breaking stories.

4. Sponsor a local event that will draw attention to your company while simultaneously enhancing its image. When local authorities closed off part of a roadway to all but bicyclists and joggers, a gourmet food shop threw a party for the athletes, giving away free food and drink at the site. Coverage of the party, complete with pictures, made the local press. The store wound up with a positive image and a wider circle of prospective customers. It had the right story for the right media.

"In all media contacts, go through this simple exercise," Wachs says. "Ask yourself if, as a reader of the publication, you would be interested in reading the kind of story you're proposing. If you can say 'yes' to that objectively, you may have a good chance of getting your company in print."

TELEMARKETING

Sell Products and Services by Phone

When Alexander Graham Bell invented the

telephone, he never dreamed it would become a sophisticated marketing tool. But more than 100 years later, his invention has become the centerpiece of a modern business promotion. Telemarketing—the process of selling by phone—is now used in conjunction with advertising, public relations, and direct mail.

Telemarketing campaigns are designed to achieve any of three objectives: to sell products or services, to generate leads for sales representatives, or to extend customer relationships, such as subscription renewals.

"Telemarketing services are either inbound or outbound," explains the president of a telemarketing firm. "The former is a passive service, taking orders and dispensing customer information through an 800 number that is generally listed in a company's advertising. The latter actively seeks new business by identifying customers and providing the necessary information to close sales."

Outbound telemarketing is more complex than simply picking up a telephone and making random calls. Step one is to identify the key decision makers likely to order the client's products or services.

"Speaking to the first person who answers the phone, whoever that may be, is a sure way to undermine the marketing effort," says the telemarketing executive. "That person may have no interest in what you are selling or, equally bad, may not be in position to order it. So we are careful to identify the right party at the outset.

"Sometimes we can be surprised at our own findings. In doing a membership renewal drive for a medical association, we discovered that the doctors' assistants, rather than the physicians themselves, made the decision on whether or not to renew. The doctors had given them that authority."

In step two, a script is written outlining the product or service's key features and sales terms. This guides the telemarketing communicators in making phone presentations to prospective customers.

"There's more flexibility here than with direct mail campaigns," says a manager with a Connecticut-based telemarketing firm. "All our callers are aided by computers programmed to answer questions likely to arise during the sales presentation. Should someone want more information on a product's service program, the communicator need only push a button and the information comes up on the screen. We can anticipate customer concerns and respond to them."

Step three is the actual calling program, and step four is recording and monitoring the response.

Fees for telemarketing campaigns—based primarily on an hourly rate of about $35 per communicator—vary with the number of persons called. For a 10,000-name consumer list (of which, on average, 60 percent will be reached), figure $15,000 to $25,000. Business-to-business campaigns are about 30 percent more expensive than those aimed at consumers, primarily because all calls must be made during the prime rate hours of 9 A.M. to 5 P.M.

Although telemarketing is substantially more expensive than direct mail, proponents claim that it is more efficient in closing sales and therefore produces a greater yield on the promotional dollar.

"We use telemarketing to line up appointments for our sales representatives," says the president of a company that markets a computerized billing program for professional service firms. "It's all part of a three-stage selling process. First we mail brochures, then we generate leads through the phone calls, and finally our sales people visit these prospects to demonstrate the software. Telemarketing works well because it enables us to explain our product and effectively presell it before the sales rep arrives. The results have been ten times more effective than when we used direct mail alone."

But telemarketing may not be for everyone. Consider these drawbacks:

1. Costs may be prohibitive for low-margin products.

2. Customers may consider telephone sales, especially prerecorded messages, to be an invasion of privacy.

Interested parties should ask telemarketers for free consultations.

V. A Penny Saved

Cost-Cutting Strategies for Your Small Business

◇ ══ ◇

Look to Technology to Cut Energy Bills

Imagine spending thousands of dollars a year to light an empty office, to cool a vacant plant. Surprisingly, many companies do just that. Energy consultants claim that up to 30 percent of small business electric use is wasted on idle facilities and inefficient equipment. But technology can reverse this, slashing consumption and in turn trimming utility bills.

Waste in the small business setting is attributable to oversight and inefficiency. Office lighting, for example, rarely coincides with office use. Lights turned on in the morning stay on until the cleaning staff departs at night. Should employees leave their offices for lunch or business meetings, the lights stay on, illuminating vacant space.

"Small business owners try to combat this waste with the stick and the carrot—pleading with employees or berating them to be energy-conscious," says the president of a Hauppauge, New York-based manufacturer and installer of energy conservation systems.

"But that usually goes in one ear and out the other. Far more effective is to let technology do the work. Occupancy sensors can be installed to turn on the lights—as well as electric heating and cooling—when employees enter their offices and off again when they leave.

"The same can be done for other types of business facilities. Why light an entire warehouse all day when some of the aisles are vacant 99 percent of the time? By adjusting lights to the level of use, sensors can cut lighting bills by up to 40 percent."

Adds a vice-president of Johnson Controls, a Milwaukee-based company that installs energy systems nationwide:

"Microprocessors are at the heart of today's automated energy systems. They gather information on weather conditions, time of day, and internal temperatures and then make decisions on what and when to turn something on or off. This is clearly smart technology. For example, an optimum-start feature built into the microprocessor adjusts the morning start-up of heating and cooling systems to current temperature conditions. On a very hot day, the cooling system may go on an hour earlier than it would during average weather conditions."

Computers can also eliminate peak load charges levied by utilities for periods of heavy electric demand.

"A computer now controls the operation of our air conditioners, preventing them from drawing maximum power simultaneously," says the vice-president of a small manufacturer of thermometers. "This single change brought an instant reduction in our utility bills. Combined with technology that boosts lighting efficiency, we're saving 12 to 15 percent annually."

These other energy-saving devices are now available:

1. Motor correctors make production machinery and climate control equipment more efficient. "They realign the current and voltage in an electrical system whenever a motor is turned on," explains the president of the energy conservation system company. "Put simply, this enables motors to handle their standard workloads at lower energy levels."

2. Fluorescent light controllers restrict the flow of energy to fluorescent circuits, thus reducing waste. Savings can average 35 percent of fluorescent lighting costs.

Conservation devices can be purchased through electrical contractors, energy consultants, and direct from major manufacturers. But experts warn that piecemeal purchases are unlikely to yield maximum energy savings. A wiser approach is to install an integrated system based on an audit of the company's electrical use. System costs, including installation, start at about $5,000.

INSURANCE COST CUTTING

How to Counter Rising Insurance Rates

What do you do when your insurance premiums rise dramatically? You can throw up your hands and complain, but that does little to bring down high rates. A better solution is to take concrete steps to lower insurance costs.

Consider the following:

1. Compare quotes from competing carriers. Some may offer lower rates for your geographic area or type of business. Also, try contacting your trade association. Carriers that write the association's master policies or insure most of the members generally offer attractive rates.

2. Strip away layers of excess coverage. When rates were low, companies fell into the bad habit of acquiring more insurance than they really needed. Because coverage was cheap, they added layer after layer of unnecessary protection. The objective is to estimate your actual exposure to risk and figure coverage limits accordingly.

3. Increase deductibles from the standard $100 to the first $500 or $1,000 of loss. Because most companies can sustain modest losses, trading slighter greater risk for significantly lower premiums is usually favorable. In stepping up from a $100 to a $1,000 deductible, figure saving 15 percent on fire and theft policies and 30 percent on automobile coverage. Consider this a form of limited self-insurance.

4. Pay small settlements out of pocket. You can save money by paying those claims just above the deductibles from your own funds rather your insurer's. Take the case of ABC Company, which carries a $500 automobile deductible and is hit with a $600 accident claim. Asking its carrier to pay the insured portion, or $100, is counterproductive. A blemish on its record will likely push future rate increases far beyond the amount of the settlement.

5. Remove employees with poor driving records from the company's automobile policy. Even one driver with a history of accidents or traffic violations can increase the

company's premium by 25 percent. Experts advise shifting high-risk employees to non-driving duties and carefully screening new applicants by demanding copies of driving records along with résumés.

6. Limit insurance coverage to protect exclusively against catastrophic loss. A variation on the high-deductible theme, this strategy calls for voluntarily canceling policies written to protect against minor losses. Employee-benefit liability coverage, for example, protects companies from losses due to errors in employee benefit plans. Because such errors are rare, management may chose to forgo such policies in favor of tighter administrative controls.

Make risk management an integral part of your business operations. While it can't roll back the clock on insurance rates, it can help to control current costs and to moderate future increases.

LOGISTICS PLANNING

Business Logistics Tackles Hidden Costs

Think about it: what goes on before a sale is as critical to a company's profits as the sale itself. Inefficiencies in acquiring, handling, warehousing, and distributing goods can inflate overhead, taking a heavy toll on the bottom line. But a little-known management service known as business logistics reverses this, coordinating the flow of merchandise or raw materials into a company and out again to its customers.

Typically, merchandise handling is subdivided into separate and often autonomous decision units that rarely communicate with one another. The purchasing agent is independent of the warehouse superintendent, who stands apart from the transportation manager. Logistics planning breaks down

these walls, creating an integrated series of events.

"Decisions made in a vacuum lead to inefficiencies—and that costs the company money," says an executive with Drake Sheahan, logistics consultants. "For example, if the person responsible for picking and shipping an order isn't properly directed by the warehouse manager—if he doesn't have an up-to-date locator system—he may not know where the merchandise is stored at any given time. So it takes him two or three times as long to fill an order.

"This leads to a chain of inefficiencies. Aware of the delay in order fulfillment, the small business owner hires another employee or two to speed things up. But this only compounds the problem. More people are wandering around the warehouse looking for merchandise."

To correct this, logistics consultants change the perception of the warehouse from a simple merchandise holding bin to a key component of the distribution system. Storage patterns are redesigned so that every item can be seen and reached with minimal effort and that core merchandise—the 20 percent that typically accounts for 80 percent of the orders—is given the most accessible positions.

"When a food manufacturer found its operations bogged down by a crammed warehouse, management considered building another facility to handle the overflow," says a vice-president of logistics practice for A. T. Kearney, management consultants. "But a study of the company's needs revealed that adding to the current warehouse and improving the way merchandise was stored in it could triple capacity while only doubling the square footage. This saved $3 million over the cost of building an entirely new warehouse of equal capacity."

Adds the president of a small manufacturer of dolls and doll clothing: "When we asked a logistics consulting firm to study our operating efficiency, they found that we were producing bottlenecks by using the same loading dock for outgoing and incoming orders. Their solution was to do some of the shipping from a remote warehouse. This should relieve the congestion and get the goods moving faster."

Logistics consultants make these additional suggestions:

1. Print customer orders to conform to warehouse storage patterns. Employees fulfilling orders should be able to use the order slip as a guide to merchandise retrieval: goods at the top of the list near the warehouse entrance, mid-list merchandise down the aisles, and so on throughout the order. This speeds fulfillment by guiding employees along the most direct path.

2. Use freight consolidators to reduce shipping costs. These specialists give small companies clout by consolidating their shipments into bulk-rate loads, affording them the economies of scale generally reserved for the largest shippers.

3. Base inventory reorders on current demand factors. The goal is to strike a delicate balance between the need to preserve working capital and to have adequate stock on hand for customer orders.

"A simple analysis can help to maintain this balance most effectively," says the Drake Sheahan executive. "Assume the business has a $1 million inventory and typically reorders when it gets down to $500,000. That makes for an average inventory of $750,000. If management, in consultation with the sales people, recognizes that it doesn't need to reorder until inventory gets down to $100,000, the average inventory drops substantially. That money can be put to work for other business needs or can be placed in interest-bearing accounts."

Outside consultants are most effective when they prompt management to review and revise established practices that detract from the company's earnings. Major accounting firms and management consultants offer logistics services.

LONG DISTANCE

"Smart" Features Can Cut Long-Distance Costs

Substantial savings in long-distance telephone charges, widely advertised by discount carriers, may prove illusory for small companies still using traditional telephone hardware. Unless management invests in technical features designed to simplify access to long-distance lines, errors and inefficiencies can diminish the potential savings.

To pass the full measure of long-distance savings on to the small business, telecommunications consultants recommend upgrading telephone hardware to include these "smart" features:

Least-cost routing, a computerized feature designed into the phone system's "brain," directs phone calls to the least expensive long-distance carrier. "Assume the company uses several long-distance carriers. If an employee is calling a customer in the next state, there may be a number of different options on how the call can be placed. Because the employee does not have the time or the expertise to make this comparative analysis, least-cost routing does it for him. It removes the decision-making authority from an individual and gives it to a computer. The employee simply dials the number and the system takes it from there. Because telephone rates are changed quarterly, the system's internal program must be updated accordingly to ensure that the company benefits from the lowest possible call charges.

The president of a health care consulting service has watched her company's long-distance bills decline with the installation of smart features. "Our staff makes a lot of out-of-town calls. We used to pay a big price for the mistakes that go along with dialing what seemed like 502 digits every time they used the phone. So we added automatic dialing and call-memory devices. Since then there have been fewer errors and our bills reflect this."

Costs for smart devices vary with the specific features ordered and the number of telephone in use. For a small company with 10 telephones, speed dialing and private access codes can be installed for about $7,500. To add least-cost routing, which may require the installation of an entirely new telephone system, the cost rises to approximately $12,000.

One option is to switch from the "key" system used by most small companies to the more sophisticated PBX. "PBX becomes economical for the company with a minimum of 20 telephone lines," says a telecommunication consultant with Arthur Young, the national accounting firm. "The advantage of the PBX is that it often has more features built in and they can be applied separately to different phones in the same firm. PBX also provides more detailed billing information, and because it is expandable and programmable, it can probably meet the company's telecommunications needs for years."

Companies can look for a payback period on their investment of from one to five years, depending on hardware costs and the volume of telephone calls. This cost recovery is made possible by the reduction in errors and the more efficient use of long-distance services. "The bottom line is that every small business should take advantage of the lowest-cost carriers," the Arthur Young consultant adds. "But when this is done without the smart features, employees make mistakes, get frustrated, and eventually circumvent the company's system. They just call the number direct. That defeats management's objectives and costs the business more than it need pay for telephone services."

SURPLUS SALES

Want a Bargain in Business Equipment? Look to Uncle Sam

Some of the best bargains in business equipment are available from the federal government. A voracious buyer of goods and services, Uncle Sam is also an active seller, unloading enormous quantities of used merchandise to make room for new purchases. Everything from helicopters to typewriters goes for a fraction of original cost.

Most of the selling is done by the Defense Department, which carries an average surplus inventory of $5 billion. Typically, goods sell for 10 percent of their initial purchase price. Bargains are available—like a good-quality electric typewriter that recently sold for $100—because the military's performance standards exceed those of civilian organizations. A five-year-old pickup truck that is no longer acceptable to the army may be more than adequate for use as a local retailer's delivery van.

"Any of the 6 million items in the government's supply system can come up for disposal at any given time," says a spokesman for the Defense Property Disposal Service (DPDS). "We sell everything from dental equipment to heavy machinery, from boats to office furniture. Were it all listed together, it would fill the equivalent of 57 Sears catalogues."

Surplus goods are sold in three ways:

1. Auctions are conducted at any of the 134 Defense Property Disposal Offices located on military installations across the nation. Prospective bidders are notified by mail and are free to inspect the merchandise on or before the auction date.

2. Spot sales are conducted without the auction process. Prospective buyers are limited to a single bid, which is submitted in writing the day of the sale.

3. Sealed bidding is similar to spot sales except that the bids may be submitted at any time during the inspection period, which usually ranges from 20 to 30 days.

Surplus sales are conducted on a local and national basis, depending on the projected market for the goods. But bidders need not be located near the sales site. East Coast business owners interested in machinery being sold through a West Coast facility can bid by mail.

"All you have to do is get on our national bidders list," the DPDS spokesman says. "Applications are available by writing the Bidders Control Office, Box 1370, Battle Creek, Michigan 49016. You indicate the kinds of merchandise you want to bid on and we'll send you bid packages whenever goods of that sort are up for sale. You get brief descriptions of the property as well as the location, date, and terms of the sale. Those interested in local sales should contact their nearest military installation, asking for the Defense Property Disposal Office."

Surplus sales are governed by the following rules:

1. Payment must be made in cash, money order, or cashier's check. Business checks are accepted only if the company has established a bond with the Defense Department.

2. All purchased property must be removed from the site within 30 days. Buyers may claim goods themselves or make arrangements with private shippers.

3. Registered parties failing to bid on two consecutive sales will be purged from the bidders' list unless they file a written request to keep their names active.

4. Buyers can create a secondary market for government surplus.

"We buy large quantities of used clothing from the government and then resell it," says the general manager of an import/export firm. "We estimate what the goods are worth and place a bid on that basis. For our type of business, this can be an attractive way to acquire merchandise."

5. Surplus property is not guaranteed. All sales are final.

"Bidders should heed two caveats," the DPDS spokesman warns. "If they're not sure of what they're getting or if they're new to this type of buying, they should inspect the property before placing bids. What we call a 'heavy-duty transport vehicle' may be different from what they have in mind. Also, recognize that the most desirable items, such as trucks, command the highest prices. Property sells according to the market's assessment of its value. Ask yourself what it's worth to you and bid accordingly."

Used equipment, much of it high tech, is also available from private industry. As new generations of computers, laser devices, and data communications systems leave the drawing board, companies are forced to discard existing units, investing millions in state-of-the-art replacements. Though costly for those swept up in it, this cycle spells opportunity for small business.

The reason is clear: as new technology comes on stream, slightly used equipment goes up for sale, often at deep discount from original costs. Discarded by the former owners—primarily giant corporations forced by competition to remain at the cutting edge—this secondhand equipment can be more than adequate for smaller companies first computerizing or trading up to a second generation of technical capability.

Used equipment is available through brokers located in and around the high-tech centers. The Source, a brokerage firm based in Santa Clara, California, matches buyers and sellers through a nationwide data bank of available equipment.

"We're like a used-car lot for high-technology equipment," says a Source vice-president. "Our service functions on two levels. First, we help big corporations liquidate their high-tech equipment. This happens when they relocate to new facilities or graduate to a new generation of technology. Then we list the equipment in our catalogues, which are circulated to prospective buyers.

"Because change in the high-tech market comes fast and furious, much of the equipment up for sale is less than two years old. Companies willing to accept technology that is a notch down from the latest models—or that is current but slightly used—can save 40 to 50 percent or more over original costs. For example, an 18-month old Digital Equipment VAX 11/780 mainframe computer system, acquired new for $300,000, was available from us for $150,000. A three-year-old NEC 20-station telephone system with automatic dialing, originally retailing for $2,000, went for $700."

Brokerage listings, heavily weighted with manufacturing equipment, are also liberally sprinkled with computers, terminals, peripherals, electronic telephone systems, and copiers.

"We also accept special orders," says an executive with the Corporate Asset Exchange, another California-based broker. "If a customer wants something that's not currently listed in our catalogue, we'll search the market to try and locate it. Sometimes, this search yields previously owned but unused equipment that is still in the manufacturer's packing crates. For one reason or another, the company that bought it decided not to use it. Prices for this equipment are 30 percent or more off original cost."

Brokers will send product catalogues to prospective buyers across the nation. Those unable to personally inspect the equipment may seek conditional purchases. "When it's inconvenient for the buyer to see the equipment, we make the shipment on a trial basis," says the Source executive. "This gives him two to five days to inspect the equipment before the sale is final. During this time, the check is held in our escrow account."

Brokerage commissions, which generally range from 8 to 10 percent of the purchase price, are levied only if a sale is consummated. The cost is borne by the seller.

Though used equipment offers substantial bargains, there are drawbacks as well:

1. Selections are limited.
2. Used equipment may not be covered by warranty.
3. Custom equipment designed for the original buyer may not be ideal for a third party.
4. Small companies in highly competitive markets may not be able to sacrifice technical capabilities for lower price. Like their big competitors, they may need equipment that is at the cutting edge.

TELEPHONE AUDITORS

Reversing the Charges: Telephone Auditors Can Make the Phone Company Pay You

Are you paying more than you have to for telephone service? Are you enriching Ma Bell at your own expense? The answer is probably "yes." Telephone auditors—specialists in tracking down and returning telephone overcharges—claim that small companies routinely pay for nonexistent equipment, for calls never made, and for clerical errors in the phone company's favor.

"In any given year, we'll examine about 1,400 phone bills and find substantial errors in 40 percent of them," says the executive vice-president of a telephone auditing firm. "There's no intentional bill padding here, just a series of foul-ups including accounting mistakes, rating errors, and improper interpretation of tariff regulations. Add it all up and you have millions of dollars in extra charges going to the phone company that rightly belong to the telephone users. We specialize in getting that money back."

Overbilling can be traced, in part, to the current patchwork of telephone charges and the tendency of small business owners, confused by the complex bills, to pay the full amount without question. They act on faith, trusting that the bill is accurate. But all too often charges exceed actual usage by 5 to 25 percent.

Thus the need for audit services. Staffed by former telephone company insiders, auditors are skilled at detecting errors that escape the layman's eye. Companies interested in working with auditors may ask accountants to recommend a reputable firm, or they can check the Yellow Pages under "communications consultants." Some limit their services to companies with minimum monthly bills of $500; others accept clients of any size.

The service works like this:

1. You sign a letter of authorization allowing the auditor to retrieve past billing information from the long-distance carrier and the local operating companies. In effect, the auditor acts as your agent in negotiations with the phone companies.

2. Through written correspondence or an on-premises inspection, the auditor takes a physical inventory of your telephone equipment including telephone sets, lines, and extensions, as well as burglar alarm circuits, answering services, and dedicated data lines that hook into the phone system.

3. Results of the physical inventory are compared to phone bills, checking that charges reflect existing equipment and that the proper rates are applied.

The real sleuth work comes in when the billing accurately matches the physical inventory but does not provide for the least expensive rates. When an auditor examined a New York manufacturer of industrial equipment, for example, he discovered the five phone lines connecting the plant to the warehouse were being treated as individual extensions even though they qualified for lower rate billing under so-called cable carrying charges. Because the local operating company (in this case, New York Telephone) was mandated to provide the least expensive rate for any given service, the auditor was able to claim and win an $8,000 refund. The client's phone service remained exactly the same; all that changed was its billing classification and the amount it had to pay.

It usually takes four to six weeks from the date an audit begins until the claim is filed with the phone company and another month until the money is returned to its rightful owner.

Refunds are generally credited to current phone bills, with the remainder sent directly to the client company. Assume your current bill is $1,000 and you win a $2,200 refund. The monthly bill will be settled and you'll find an extra $1,200 in your mailbox. As added sweeteners, the phone company may pay interest in cases where the date of overcharging can be proven (negotiated settlements rarely provide for interest) and future phone bills will decrease as the erroneous charges are removed.

Reputable auditors work on a contingent-fee basis, charging only if their efforts result in refunds. Some limit their take to 50 percent of the refund; others take an additional 50 percent of the monthly savings multiplied by 60. Assuming a refund of $3,000 and monthly savings of $50, the auditor using this fee system will take $1,500 when the phone company pays up and another $1,500 (50 percent of $50 × 60) over five years.

One caveat: the telephone audit field has attracted more than its share of charlatans. Some use the lure of hefty refunds to gain substantial "retainers" and then fail to get money back from the phone company. Others use the audit as a foot in the door to gain consulting assignments or to sell telecommunications equipment. Reduce the risks by demanding proof of past refunds, by checking references, and by refusing to pay advance fees. Make all payments contingent on the auditor's performance. Ask accountants and attorneys for the names of reputable telephone auditors.

TELEPHONE SERVICES

How to Shop for Them

The breakup of Ma Bell—long heralded as a boon to telephone consumers—has left small businesses wondering just where the benefits are. Faced with a proliferation of bills, services, and competitive claims, companies are hopelessly confused, uncertain of how to proceed in a new era. Should they use A T & T or other common carriers? Should they buy equipment or lease? Many are groping for answers.

"The big change in the postdivestiture pe-riod can be summed up in a single word: choice," says an executive with Bridging the Gap Through Communications, a consulting firm based in Blauvelt, New York. "With the local operating companies now split from A T & T and with a multitude of carriers now competing for what was once Ma Bell's exclusive domain, companies find themselves having to choose between local carriers, long-distance carriers, and equipment vendors.

"While this competition can mean opportunity for telephone consumers, they must first do their homework, calculating current charges for each component of current service. Armed with this information, they can make intelligent comparisons of the various equipment and service vendors."

Adds a Philadelphia-based telecommunications coordinator for the accounting firm of Peat Marwick: "Companies are confused because they don't know how to compare one vendor to another. Assume a long-distance carrier tells ABC Company it can provide lower-cost service than the company's current carrier. How can ABC determine if this is true or just another sales pitch? The trick is to break down all usage costs into charges per minute. Say the company's 10 hours of monthly calls from New York to Los Angeles cost $216, or 36 cents a minute. By asking other carriers to quote their New York to Los Angeles rates per minute, management can easily shop for the lowest cost service."

Experts offer the following post divestiture checklist for telephone consumers:

1. Ask the local operating company and A T & T Information Systems for an itemized billing of all telephone equipment charged to your business. Because regular bills only summarize equipment charges, mistakes in the phone company's favor can easily escape detection. Compare the itemized bill to the equipment on your premises.

One telltale sign of overbilling is on-premises wire charges for companies that have converted from A T & T equipment to another supplier's. When private systems are installed, A T & T's wires are removed but the local operating company may continue to charge for them. In another common error, companies are charged for phones they don't have. Credit claims for all such discrepancies should be filed with the phone companies.

2. Companies first switching from rental to owned equipment will likely find immediate savings. "A firm that now rents for $1,000 per month," the Peat Marwick consultant says, "may be able to buy a similar system for $750 a month financed over seven years. Once the system is paid for, the only remaining costs are for maintenance. The drawback is that the company must then live with the system it has purchased. If the business expands or new technology comes on stream, management may find itself saddled with inadequate hardware. One safeguard is to buy a telephone system big and sophisticated enough to satisfy future as well as current needs."

3. Never base hardware purchase decisions on price alone. Make certain the vendor's service facilities are top-notch and that maintenance personnel are on call whenever your business is open. System down time can easily wipe out initial purchase savings and can seriously damage customer relations.

4. Companies seeking low-cost long-distance service should not rule out A T & T. The nation's biggest carrier has taken off the kid gloves and is now competing aggressively in many calling routes.

One approach is to use several different carriers, tapping those with the lowest rates for each of the company's major calling routes. A company with modest long-distance calling to most areas of the country but heavy usage between New York and Houston may use A T & T as its primary carrier and a supplemental carrier with the lowest rates between the two key cities.

"By trying to ignore the fact that change has occurred in the telephone market and by failing to compare alternative vendors," the Peat Marwick consultant says, "companies will pay more for telephone services and get less in return.

WATS Lines

In the relentless search for discount telephone services, small business may be overlooking the best buy of all. Wide area telephone service—best known by the acronym WATS—can save companies up to 15 percent over standard long-distance calls. Experts consider it the least known, most underutilized option in telecommunications.

WATS is recommended for companies making a minimum of 75 long-distance calls a month. Unlike standard long-distance billing, which treats each call separately, WATS charges are determined at the end of each month based on total usage. The more calls made, the lower the rate per call. All calls made within a wide geographic area, known as a WATS zone, are billed according to the same rate structure.

"Although the configurations vary by carrier, five separate WATS zones cover the continental U.S.," says a telecommunications consultant for the big accounting and consulting firm of Laventhol & Horwath. "Companies can subscribe to any one or all of the zones depending on where the bulk of their long-distance calls are made. Because the charge per minute of calling time increases with the number of zones covered, it's important to limit yourself to those zones that reflect your company's calling pattern."

With standard long distance, calls are made through a local telephone company and then relayed to a long-distance carrier. But WATS calls omits the middle connection. A dedicated line, installed when WATS service begins, links the calling party directly to the WATS service.

"Because there are fewer connections between the calling parties and because the dedicated line is reserved for a single user, voice quality on WATS lines tends to be superior to standard long distance," says a New York-based consultant. "There's less static, less interference, and fewer calls lost to technical failures. When your business relies on the telephone, this can be an important consideration.

"But there is a major drawback to WATS service. Each line can carry only one conversation at a time. Should many employees need access to the phones simultaneously, multiple line charges may make WATS less attractive than standard long distance."

Wide area telephone service—also referred to as "dedicated service" by some of the discount carriers—is available from A T & T Communications, MCI, Sprint, Allnet, and other long-distance companies. While rates vary from carrier to carrier, most offer a substantial savings over their own standard long distance. In one analysis of the calling patterns for a small, 20-person construction company that made about 500 long-distance calls a month, a consultant found that standard A T & T bills averaged about $980 a month. Computing the same calls with MCI's standard long-distance rates, the bill dropped to $849. But with WATS service, the savings were even more dramatic, with charges sliding to $779 for A T & T and $775 for MCI.

In figuring total WATS charges, companies must add initial connection fees and monthly service fees, which vary with the carriers.

Whether or not a company will save money with WATS depends on the frequency, duration, and location of its long-distance calls. Telephone consultants can perform a computer analysis, comparing the projected costs for WATS and standard long distance. Although this service is also available free of charge from telephone carriers, an independent analysis—because it is not subject to conflicts of interest—is recommended.

VI. Perks, Pensions, and Paychecks

Compensating the Owner and Your Employees

◇ ══ ◇

Plans Smooth the Transfer of Business Interests

It was a prescription for disaster. Smith and Jones, partners in an auto supply shop, insured each other for $100,000 and agreed to an informal estate plan. If one should die, the survivor would use his insurance to buy out the other's interests. Sound strategy, but with a fatal flaw: the plan was never put in writing.

When Smith died, greed triumphed. Claiming his partner's share was worth far less than $100,000, Jones offered to pay his estate $60,000, take it or leave it. Shocked by the turn of events and angered by the paltry offer, Smith's spouse took the case to court—where it has remained ever since. A sticky problem, but one that need not have occurred.

"By planning in advance for a principal's death or disability—and by framing that plan in a legal document—business owners can assure an orderly transfer of interests with little conflict and minimal taxation," says an executive with the Shulman Group, a financial services concern. "If properly drawn, the agreement gives control to the surviving owner and cash to the deceased's estate. Everyone gains."

But how is this accomplished? What kind of agreements work best? How can the principals avoid a potential disaster? Consider the following strategies:

1. Cross-purchase agreements provide for the surviving principal to purchase the deceased's business interests. Much like the Smith and Jones plan—except that it is put in writing—cross-purchase agreements contain the following provisions:

- A set price or pricing formula for the deceased's share of the company.
- An obligation by the deceased's estate to sell the business interests at the specified price, and for the survivor to buy it.

324

Scudder's Simplified Guide to SEPs and "KEOGHs"

	SEP	Money Purchase Pension/ Profit-Sharing Plan
Eligibility	Any sole proprietor, partnership, or incorporated business.	Any sole proprietor, partnership, or incorporated business.
Contributions	Up to 15% of earned income, but no more than $30,000 per participant.	Up to 25% of earned income, but no more than $30,000 per participant.
Deadlines	For establishment: April 15 For funding: April 15	For establishment: December 31 (or fiscal year end). For funding: Same as that for filing tax returns.
Distribution	May begin at age 59½, or earlier in the event of disability or death. Must begin by April 1 following the year age 70½ is attained.	*For 5% owners:* May begin at age 59½ or normal retirement age, whichever is later. May also begin at disability or death. Must begin by April 1 following the year age 70½ is attained. *For other participants:* May begin at age 59½ (or normal retirement age, if later) or job or plan termination, disability or death. Must begin by the *later* of April 1 following the year age 70½ is attained or retirement.
Tax Treatment	Contributions are tax-deductible. Earnings are tax-deferred. All distributions are treated as ordinary income.	Contributions are tax-deductible. Earnings are tax-deferred. Lump-sum distributions may be eligible for 10-year forward averaging. All other distributions are treated as ordinary income.
Reports and Filings	*Annually* Employees should be notified of the amount contributed for them.	*Annually* 5500 forms Summary annual reports *At the time of Adoption* Summary plan descriptions Notice to interested parties
Vesting	Full and immediate	Can be full and immediate or graduated.
Loans	Not available	May be available
Social Security Integration	Not available with IRS Model SEPs	May be available

Credit: The Scudder Funds

In most cases, life insurance is used to fund the cross-purchase agreement. The principals buy policies on each other's lives, naming themselves as beneficiaries. Each pays the premium with personal rather than corporate funds. In this way, they receive the death benefit tax-free and have the full amount to purchase the deceased's business interests.

"Cross-purchase agreements are not limited to transactions between partners or co-owners," the Shulman executive says. "They can also be effective in transferring business holdings to family members. Assume the principal wants to leave his company to his child and leave cash to his spouse. By entering into a cross-purchase agreement with a son or daughter, he can provide for the child to buy the company, paying the spouse for her stock. Here again, insurance is often used to make the purchase. The child holds a policy on the parent and uses the proceeds to buy the shares."

2. Stock-redemption plans function similarly to cross-purchase agreements except that the business rather than the principals buys the deceased's interests. With this approach, the company buys insurance policies on each of the principals, and uses the proceeds to purchase the stock from their estates.

In effect, stock-redemption plans create a market for the shares of small, privately held companies. With the plans in place, sellers are assured of ready buyers committed to paying fair prices for the stock. This liquidity is of enormous benefit to estate planning.

Many owners favor stock redemption plans because premiums are paid with the company's money rather than their own. But stock-redemption plans are limited to corporations—partnerships and proprietorships must use cross-purchase agreements.

A key benefit of both stock-redemption and cross-purchase plans comes in the form of potential tax savings.

"When business interests pass at death, the IRS can always say that they are actually worth more than the amount claimed by the estate and are thus subject to a greater tax," says a tax manager with accountants Grant Thornton. "But that's not likely when the value is built into a valid cross-purchase or stock-redemption plan. Providing the plan meets certain tests—including an arm's-length relationship between the principals and an obligation by both to honor the terms of the plan—the IRS will likely accept the stated value for tax purposes."

Work with an attorney in planning and writing cross-purchase agreements and stock-redemption plans.

The Two-Percent Difference

How well your firm's retirement plan assets are invested can make a big difference in the size of your retirement nest egg.

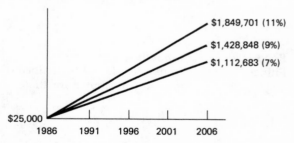

According to Merrill Lynch, if you invest $25,000 a year in your retirement plan for 20 years, the difference between settling for a 7 percent return and a 9 percent return is more than $300,000. And with an 11 percent return, the difference is a whopping $737,000.

LIFE INSURANCE

Buying Life Insurance through Retirement Plans—the Pros and Cons

When small business owner Bill Smith passed away, his family looked to the $500,000 in his pension plan as a financial cushion to cover education and living expenses. Smith had planned it that way. But he'd overlooked a key point: income taxes could reduce the family's net proceeds to roughly half the cash in the fund.

"This common oversight can have a damaging impact on a family's finances," says a vice-president of National Pension Service, Inc., a White Plains, New York consulting firm. "Because there is an unlimited marital deduction on estate taxes, many self-employed business owners and professionals assume that their pension assets will flow in full to their husbands and wives. But that's a misconception. Once the spouse receives the money from the pension plan, the proceeds are subject to income taxes. The deceased worked to fund his plan to a certain level without considering that part of the amount might go to Uncle Sam."

One solution is to purchase enough life insurance to cover the projected tax bite, thus enabling the heirs to retain the full amount of the pension plan assets. Whether this coverage should be included in the pension plan or purchased separately by the individual is a matter of debate. Two schools of thought clash on whether the tax advantages of purchasing coverage through qualified plans outweigh the diminished investment returns.

One side favors the tax angles.

"Buying insurance through a qualified plan—be it a Keogh or a corporate pension—is a way to gain coverage with pretax dollars. Assume a self-employed individual has a defined benefit plan to which he makes an annual deductible contribution of $30,000. If he allots $3,000 additional for insurance, making his total contribution $33,000, he still has $30,000 for pure investment and has purchased insurance with money that has not been taxed.

But the president of a Baltimore-based pension consulting firm claims that this view is myopic.

"Pension plan funds spent on insurance are not available for investment, which is the overriding goal of pension vehicles. Even with whole or universal life policies, which have investment components, the rate of return is not likely to be as good as the pension fund can obtain elsewhere. Why give the insurance company your money to invest when you can do it yourself?"

While the Baltimore-based consultant agrees that life insurance can play a critical role in estate planning—such as offsetting the heirs' income taxes—he recommends that coverage be purchased outside the pension plan.

"Even the apparent tax break in paying for premiums with pretax dollars is somewhat illusory. The savings are partially offset by the so-called PS-58 cost, which attributes a portion of the premium as current income to the individual. This is the cost of the pure term-insurance element of the whole life policy. Although this can be recovered if the policy is held until retirement, few hold the same policy that long."

Much as both sides of the insurance/pension plan debate disagree on the central issue, both say that the self-employed should arrive at a decision based on an overall view of their business and personal finances.

"You have to look at the positives and

negatives for each individual," says a New York-based small business consultant. "One of my clients, for example, wanted to gain the benefits of buying insurance with pretax dollars. But on close inspection I recognized that this was not the best approach. If purchased through the pension plan, the proceeds would flow to his estate, which already had a significant tax problem. So we set up a separate trust for the purchase of insurance coverage. He lost the cash-flow benefit of buying with pretax dollars but gained a sounder estate-planning position overall."

The insurance/pension plan issue is fraught with technical considerations. Contact your financial adviser before making a decision.

WHERE TO FIND IT

LIFE INSURANCE ORGANIZATIONS
Company Associations

American Council of Life Insurance
1850 K Street, NW
Washington, DC 20006
Telephone: 202-624-2000
Represents the life insurance business in legislative and regulatory areas at the federal, state, and local levels of government. Provides the public with information about the purpose and uses of life insurance, maintains research facilities to record the performance of the business, and measures attitudes of the public on issues relevant to the business.

Glossary of Life Insurance Terms

Accidental Death Benefit. A benefit in addition to the face amount of a life insurance policy, payable if the insured dies as the result of an accident. Sometimes referred to as "double indemnity."

Actuary. A person professionally trained in the technical aspects of insurance and related fields, particularly in the mathematics of insurance—such as the calculation of premiums, reserves, and other values.

Adjustable Life Insurance. A type of insurance that allows the policyholder to change the plan of insurance, raise or lower the face amount of the policy, increase or decrease the premium, and lengthen or shorten the protection period.

Agent. A sales and service representative of an insurance company. Life insurance agents may also be called life underwriters or field underwriters.

Annuitant. The person during whose life an annuity is payable, usually the person to receive the annuity.

Annuity. A contract that provides a periodic income at regular intervals for a specified period of time, such as for a number of years or for life.

Annuity Certain. A contract that provides an income for a specified number of years, regardless of life or death.

Annuity Consideration. The payment, or one of the regular periodic payments, an annuitant makes for an annuity.

Application. A statement of information made by a person applying for life insurance. It helps the life insurance company assess the acceptability of risk.

Assignment. The legal transfer of one person's interest in an insurance policy to another person.

Beneficiary. The person named in the policy to receive the insurance proceeds at the death of the insured.

Broker. A sales and service representative who handles insurance for clients, generally selling insurance of various kinds and for several companies.

Business Life Insurance. Life insurance purchased by a business enterprise on the life of a member of the firm. It is often bought by partnerships to protect the surviving partners against loss caused by the death of a partner, or by a corporation to reimburse it for loss caused by the death of a key employee.

Cash Surrender Value. The amount available in cash upon voluntary termination of a policy by its owner before it becomes payable by death or maturity.

Certificate. A statement issued to individuals insured under a group policy, setting forth the essential provisions relating to their coverage.

Claim. Notification to an insurance company that payment of an amount is due under the terms of a policy.

Convertible Term Insurance. Term insurance that can be exchanged, at the option of the policyholder and without evidence of insurability, for another plan of insurance.

Declination. The rejection by a life insurance company of an application for life insurance, usually for reasons of the health or occupation of the applicant.

Deferred Annuity. An annuity providing for the income payments to begin at some future date.

Deferred Group Annuity. A type of group annuity providing for the purchase each year of a paid-up deferred annuity for each member of the group, the total amount received by the member at retirement being the sum of these deferred annuities.

Deposit Administration Group Annuity. A type of group annuity providing for the accumulation of contributions in an undivided fund out of which annuities are purchased as the individual members of the group retire.

Deposit Term Insurance. A form of term insurance, not really involving a "deposit," in which the first-year premium is larger than subsequent premiums. Typically, a partial endowment is paid at the end of the term period. In many cases the partial endowment can be applied toward the purchase of a new term policy or, perhaps, a whole life policy.

Disability Benefit. A feature added to some life insurance policies providing for waiver of premium, and sometimes payment of monthly income, if the policyholder becomes totally and permanently disabled.

Dividend. A return of part of the premium on participating insurance to reflect the difference between the premium charged and the combination of actual mortality, expense, and investment experience. Such premiums are calculated to provide some margin over the anticipated cost of the insurance protection.

Dividend Addition. An amount of paid-up insurance purchased with a policy dividend and added to the face amount of the policy.

Endowment. Life insurance payable to the policyholder if living, on the maturity date stated in the policy, or to a beneficiary if the insured dies prior to that date.

Expectation of Life. The average number of years of life remaining for a group of persons of a given age according to a particular mortality table.

Extended Term Insurance. A form of insurance available as a nonforfeiture option. It provides the original amount of insurance for a limited period of time.

Face Amount. The amount stated on the face of the policy that will be paid in case of death or at the maturity of the policy. It does not include additional amounts payable under accidental death or other special provisions, or acquired through the application of policy dividends.

Family Income Policy. A life insurance policy, combining whole life and decreasing term insurance. The beneficiary receives income payments to the end of a specified period if the insured dies prior to the end of the period plus the face amount of the policy—either at the end of the period or at the death of the insured.

Family Policy. A life insurance policy providing insurance on all or several family members in one contract, generally whole life insurance on the principal breadwinner and smaller amounts of term insurance on the other spouse and children, including those born after the policy is issued.

Flexible Premium Policy or Annuity. A life insurance policy or annuity under which the policyholder or contractholder may vary the amounts or timing of premium payments.

Flexible Premium Variable Life Insurance. A life insurance policy that combines the premium flexibility feature of universal life insurance with the equity-based benefit feature of variable life insurance.

Fraternal Life Insurance. Life insurance provided by fraternal orders or societies to their members.

Grace Period. A period (usually 30 or 31 days) following the premium due date, during which an overdue premium may be paid without penalty. The policy remains in force throughout this period.

Group Annuity. A pension plan providing annuities at retirement to a group of people under a master contract. It is usually issued to an employer for the benefit of employees. The individual members of the group hold certificates as evidence of their annuities.

Group Life Insurance. Life insurance usually without medical examination, on a group of people under a master policy. It is typically issued to an employer for the benefit of employees, or to members of an association, for example a professional membership group. The individual members of the group hold certificates as evidence of their insurance.

Individual Policy Pension Trust. A type of pension plan, frequently used for small groups, administered by trustees who are authorized to purchase individual level premium policies or annuity contracts for each member of the plan. The policies usually provide both life insurance and retirement benefits.

Industrial Life Insurance. Life insurance issued in small amounts, usually less than $1,000, with premiums payable on a weekly or monthly basis. The premiums are generally collected at the home by an agent of the company. Sometimes referred to as debit insurance.

Insurability. Acceptability to the company of an applicant for insurance.

Insurance Examiner. The representative of a state insurance department assigned to participate in the official audit and examination of the affairs of an insurance company.

Insured or Insured Life. The person on whose life the policy is issued.

Lapsed Policy. A policy terminated for non-payment of premiums. The term is sometimes limited to a termination occurring before the policy has a cash or other surrender value.

Legal Reserve Life Insurance Company. A life insurance company operating under state insurance laws specifying the minimum basis for the reserves the company must maintain on its policies.

Level Premium Life Insurance. Life insurance for which the premium remains the same from year to year. The premium is more than the actual cost of protection during the earlier years of the policy and less than the actual cost in the later years. The building of a reserve is a natural result of level premiums. The overpayments in the early years, together with the interest that is to be earned, serve to balance out the underpayments of the later years.

Life Annuity. A contract that provides an income for life.

Life Expectancy. The average number of years of life remaining for a group of persons of a given age according to a particular mortality table.

Life Insurance in Force. The sum of the face amounts, plus dividend additions, of life insurance policies outstanding at a given time. Additional amounts payable under accidental death or other special provisions are not included.

Limited Payment Life Insurance. Whole life insurance on which premiums are payable for a specified number of years or until death if death occurs before the end of the specified period.

Master Policy. A policy that is issued to an employer or trustee establishing a group insurance plan for designated members of an eligible group.

Mortality Table. A statistical table showing the death rate at each age, usually expressed as so many per thousand.

Mutual Life Insurance Company. A life insurance company without stockholders whose management is directed by a board elected by the policyholders. Mutual companies, in general, issue participating insurance.

Nonforfeiture Option. One of the choices available if the policyholder discontinues premium payments on a policy with a cash value. This, if any, may be taken in cash, as extended term insurance or as reduced paid-up insurance.

Nonmedical Limit. The maximum face value of a policy that a given company will issue without the applicant taking a medical examination.

Nonparticipating Policy. A life insurance policy in which the company does not distribute to policyholders any part of its surplus. Note should be taken that premiums for nonparticipating policies are usually lower than for comparable participating policies. Note should also be taken that some nonparticipating policies have both a maximum premium and a current lower premium. The current premium reflects anticipated experience that is more favorable than the company is willing to guarantee, and it may be changed from time to time for the entire block of business to which the policy belongs. (See also: *Participating Policy*)

Ordinary Life Insurance. Life insurance usually issued in amounts of $1,000 or more with premiums payable on an annual, semi-annual, quarterly, or monthly basis.

Paid-up Insurance. Insurance on which all required premiums have been paid. The term is frequently used to mean the reduced paid-up insurance available as a nonforfeiture option.

Participating Policy. A life insurance policy under which the company agrees to distribute to policyholders the part of its surplus which its Board of Directors determines is not needed at the end of the business year. Such a distribution serves to reduce the premium the policyholder had paid. (See also: *Policy Dividend; Nonparticipating Policy*)

Permanent Life Insurance. A phrase used to cover any form of life insurance except term; generally insurance that accrues cash value, such as whole life or endowment.

Policy. The printed legal document stating the terms of the insurance contract that is issued to the policyholder by the company.

Policy Dividend. A refund of part of the premium on a participating life insurance policy reflecting the difference between the premium charged and actual experience.

Policy Loan. A loan made by a life insurance company from its general funds to a policyholder on the security of the cash value of a policy.

Policy Reserves. The measure of the funds that a life insurance company holds specifically for fulfillment of its policy obligations. Reserves are required by law to be so calculated that, together with future premium payments and anticipated interest earnings, they will enable the company to pay all future claims.

Policyholder. The person who owns a life insurance policy. This is usually the insured person, but it may also be a relative of the insured, a partnership or a corporation.

Premium. The payment, or one of the periodic payments, a policyholder agrees to make for an insurance policy.

Premium Loan. A policy loan made for the purpose of paying premiums.

Rated Policy. Sometimes called an "extra-risk" policy, an insurance policy issued at a higher-than-standard premium rate to cover the extra risk where, for example, an insured has impaired health or a hazardous occupation.

Reduced Paid-up Insurance. A form of insurance available as a nonforfeiture option. It provides for continuation of the original insurance plan, but for a reduced amount.

Renewable Term Insurance. Term insurance that can be renewed at the end of the term, at the option of the policyholder and without evidence of insurability, for a limited number of successive terms. The rates increase at each renewal as the age of the insured increases.

Reserve. The amount required to be carried as a liability in the financial statement of an insurer, to provide for future commitments under policies outstanding.

Rider. A special policy provision or group of provisions that may be added to a policy to expand or limit the benefits otherwise payable.

Risk Classification. The process by which a company decides how its premium rates for life insurance should differ according to the risk characteristics of individuals insured (e.g., age, occupation, sex, state of health) and then applies the resulting rules to individual applications. (See: *Underwriting*)

Separate Account. An asset account established by a life insurance company separate from other funds, used primarily for pension plans and variable life products. This arrangement permits wider latitude in the choice of investments, particularly in equities.

Settlement Options. The several ways, other than immediate payment in cash, that a policyholder or beneficiary may choose to have policy benefits paid. (See also: *Supplementary Contract*)

Stock Life Insurance Company. A life insurance company owned by stockholders who elect a board to direct the company's management. Stock companies, in general, issue nonparticipating insurance but may also issue participating insurance.

Straight Life Insurance. Whole life insurance on which premiums are payable for life.

Supplementary Contract. An agreement between a life insurance company and a policyholder or beneficiary by which the company retains the cash sum payable under an insurance policy and makes payments in accordance with the settlement option chosen.

Term Insurance. Life insurance payable to a beneficiary only when an insured dies within a specified period.

Underwriting. The process by which a life insurance company determines whether or not it can accept an application for life insurance, and if so, on what basis.

Universal Life Insurance. A flexible premium life insurance policy under which the policyholder may change the death benefit from time to time (with satisfactory evidence of insurability for increases) and vary the amount or timing of premium payments. Premiums (less expense charges) are credited to a policy account from which mortality charges are deducted and to which interest is credited at rates that may change from time to time.

Variable Annuity. An annuity contract in which the amount of each periodic income payment may fluctuate. The fluctuation may be related to securities market values, a cost of living index, or some other variable factor.

Variable Life Insurance. Life insurance under which the benefits relate to the value of assets behind the contract at the time the benefit is paid. The amount of death benefit payable would, under variable life policies that have been proposed, never be less than the initial death benefit payable under the policy.

Waiver of Premium. A provision that under certain conditions an insurance policy will be kept in full force by the company without further payment of premiums. It is used most often in the event of total and permanent disability.

Whole Life Insurance. Life insurance payable to a beneficiary at the death of the insured whenever that occurs. Premiums may be payable for a specified number of years (limited payment life) or for life (straight life).

Credit: American Council of Life Insurance, Washington, D.C.

MEDICAL INSURANCE

Putting a Lid on Health Care Costs

Faced with spiraling health care costs, small companies are rethinking their medical insurance plans, searching for new ways to contain premiums without cutting essential benefits. One solution, based on the old adage "half a loaf is better than none," has employees sharing more of the costs.

"The idea is for employer and employees to work together to achieve the ultimate objective—the continuance of some form of group medical insurance," says a partner with Hewitt Associates, a benefits consulting firm that practices nationwide. "With health care premiums far outstripping overall inflation, many companies are now viewing cost containment as a necessity. They cannot continue to absorb double-digit increases year after year.

"Employee sharing helps by shifting part of the benefit costs from employer to employees. This is done in two ways—by having employees pay a larger percentage of the insurance premium or by increasing front-end deductibles. Both options can help companies retain medical insurance plans without jeopardizing their finances."

Consultants recommend the following cost-sharing techniques:

1. Move away from "first dollar" medical benefits. Require that employees pay the first $100 to $200 of medical bills out of their own pockets before plan coverage becomes effective. Companies with existing deductibles can increase them by as much as 50 or 100 percent.

"This is highly effective because it immediately reduces medical insurance premiums while simultaneously discouraging employee abuse of the company's plan," the consultant adds. "When first dollar coverage is provided, employees tend to run to the doctor for every ache and pain. This inflates the plan's costs and in turn boosts premiums. But when policies are changed to provide for substantial deductibles, employees think twice about seeing the doctor for common colds and the like. Minor ailments are allowed to run their course."

2. Reduce reimbursement provisions from 100 percent to 80 percent of hospital costs, making employees responsible for the difference. This discourages extended hospital stays taken more for rest than for legitimate medical reasons.

3. Forbid weekend hospital admissions except in emergencies. "Many doctors are in the habit of admitting patients Friday night for Monday or Tuesday operations," the Hewitt partner notes. "In many cases, this is done simply to control the patient's diet. Well, considering today's hospital room costs, that's a heavy price to pay for proper eating. When employees are responsible for weekend expenses, they tell their doctors to admit them on Monday and that they'll watch their diets at home."

4. Call for mandatory second opinions on those types of elective surgery considered to be overprescribed. Ask insurance carriers or health care consultants to name these procedures and identify them in the plan. Require that employees undergoing such operations without a second opinion pay 50 percent rather than the standard 20 percent of costs.

Employee sharing is designed to redistribute benefit costs—and to cut down on waste and abuse—without subjecting the participants to financial disaster. To offset negative feeling brought on by stricter coverage provisions, companies can emphasize their "stop-loss" clauses that limit employees' annual medical expenses to a maximum figure, generally less than $1,500.

"While companies are asking employees to pay higher premiums and deductibles," the consultant says, "they are still giving them protection against catastrophes. Because that's everyone's major concern, plans calling for greater sharing of everyday expenses will still be valued by employees."

Benefits consultants and insurance carriers can help to restructure medical plans to control costs while retaining essential coverage. The ultimate goal, experts say, is to keep premiums in line with the Consumer Price Index.

MUTUAL FUNDS

Mutual Funds May Be a Wise Choice for Retirement Plans

Mutual funds—among the most popular investments for small business retirement plans—offer a wide range of stock selection strategies, risk levels, and rates of return. Which fund to choose depends primarily on the investor's temperament, but other factors, unique to retirement plans, must be considered.

As professionally managed portfolios of stocks and money market instruments, mutual funds free shareholders from the day-to-day responsibility for supervising their investments. This makes them ideal for long-term retirement accounts. But because individuals have different financial objectives, funds considered ideal for one plan may be wrong for others.

"The fundamental question of a conservative versus a speculative approach must be considered right off the top," says a mutual fund analyst and editor of *The No-Load Fund Investor,* a newsletter. "Regardless of one's tolerance for risks with ordinary invest-ments, when it comes to retirement accounts, age should be a determining factor. Younger investors—those with 20 years or more before retirement—should allot at least part of their retirement contributions to aggressive growth funds.

"Although this implies a greater risk than with conservative stock funds, the long lead time before the money is needed affords the investor a greater level of patience in waiting for opportunities to develop. Conversely, those investors near retirement age will not want to risk short-term dissolution of their capital with speculative funds.

"The key prerequisite is to determine the composition of the fund's portfolio and its investment strategy, both of which may be gleaned from the prospectus. Pay special attention to the types of stocks currently held in the portfolio, the cash position, and the statement of the fund's underlying objective. Taken together, these factors present a fairly accurate picture of how the fund's capital will be invested."

Consider these additional guidelines for selecting mutual funds:

1. Favor those fund groups featuring telephone switching privileges. This permits investors to shift capital from one type of fund to another to reflect changes in the economy or the stock market. At the first sign of a bear market, investors in growth stock funds may want to transfer holdings to money market funds—and then back to equities once the bulls regain control.

2. Avoid funds investing primarily in municipal bonds and other tax-exempt instruments. Because retirement plans are tax-sheltered, there is no reason to accept the lower yields generally associated with tax-free funds.

3. Compare the fund's performance to other funds in the same category. Check for yield and yield plus capital gain.

4. Postpone investments in funds operating for less than six months. The lack of meaningful performance data carries an additional risk that may be unacceptable for retirement plans.

5. Consider paying sales commissions, or "loads," only for those funds with a proven record of superior performance.

Insurance Against a Partner's Death

It's a common business arrangement. Smith and Jones, the co-owners of a booming restaurant chain, strike a deal: when either dies, the survivor will buy the other's shares, taking control of the company and giving liquidity to the deceased's estate. This "buy-sell agreement" is the perfect solution for both sides.

But one question looms. Where will the money come from? With the business valued at $2 million, the survivor will need $1 million to hold up his end of the deal, a sum far in excess of Smith's and Jones's personal assets. What to do?

One option that comes to mind is a line of credit. Providing the business is in good standing, bankers will be delighted to establish a million-dollar line, effectively reserving the cash until the money is needed. In most cases, interest payments will begin when the funds are drawn down.

Seems like the ideal solution, but there's a rub. Just when the company needs the money the bankers may balk, holding that the death of a principal changes the ground rules, making the risk unacceptable.

"In small business, the owners and the company they run are so closely intertwined that you can't really separate one from the other," says a vice-president with Manufac-

turers Hanover Trust. "So the passing of a principal can have a devastating effect on the company. He may have been the one who brought in the lion's share of the sales or who provided the technical genius that gave the company its marketing edge. With that gone, it's a different company. That's why we have to re-evaluate the credit at the time of death. There's a good chance the line would not be immediately available to the survivor."

But there's a way to secure the needed financing with a contract that's guaranteed to pay off at the time of death. It comes in the form of life insurance purchased by the partners on each other's lives.

"From the standpoint of estate planning, you can look at a whole life insurance policy as an insured line of credit," says an attorney and second vice-president with The Travelers. "In effect, the insurance contract says that the insurer will set aside $1 million for the beneficiary, will charge a premium (about 1 percent a year, depending on the insured's age) to keep the credit available, and will pay the $1 million at the time of death. At that time, there are no further premiums. With a bank line of credit, interest payments would first begin."

But what if the business is dissolved before either partner dies? Assuming the insured line of credit was in force for 20 years, the partners would have paid premiums of $200,000 each. What happens to this money? Is it lost in a black hole of unused insurance protection?

"Not at all," says an attorney with Forest Hills Financial Group, a pension consulting firm. "By that time, the cash value in the policies could be as high as a half million dollars each. So the partners would get back all of the premiums paid plus an additional return of $300,000. Providing the policies were held long enough for the cash values to build—in some cases as few as five years—there would be no penalty if they were canceled before either partner died. Sure, they may have done better with other investments, but only insurance would have guaranteed the cash in the event of death."

A partner with the accounting and consulting firm of Laventhol & Horwath agrees that "life insurance is a splendid way to fund buy-sell agreements," but points out that there are important differences between lines of credit and insurance policies.

"With the former, you have access to the money for use in the business at any time," the Laventhol & Horwath partner says, "and you don't pay anything until the money is borrowed. Insurance contracts, on the other hand, require payment throughout the years the money is not being used.

"The bottom line is that insurance, like other forms of financing, has its drawbacks too. But when it comes to achieving the objectives of a buy-sell agreement, there's no better way to provide for the needed cash."

The Lure of Phantom Stock

America, it is said, is a nation of entrepreneurs. While this may be an exaggeration, there's no doubt that fascination with business ownership is at a fever pitch. For the first time in a generation, the best and the brightest in business and industry—led by top-rated MBAs and corporate executives—are turning their backs on the Fortune 500 in favor of entrepreneurial opportunities. Suddenly the brain drain is flowing the other way.

Good news, bad news. As a small business owner you welcome—and rightly so—the opportunity to attract and retain talented and highly motivated people willing to forgo the perks and privileges of corporate life for the opportunity to build something from scratch—and in the process to share in the wealth.

The problem is, with most compensation plans, part of that wealth comes in the form of corporate stock. Those willing to accept the risks of entrepreneurial employment will demand no less a reward than an equity stake in their employer. And therein lies the rub. As the company's founder, chief executive, and sole owner you wince at the thought of sharing ownership, much less voting rights, with all but close family members.

A standoff? Not necessarily. A mysterious-sounding incentive plan, known as "phantom stock," lets you give employees a piece of the action without giving up a piece of the pie. Phantom stock is especially effective for small, closely held companies where management seeks to retain all the corporate stock while simultaneously giving key employees entrepreneurial incentive. To accomplish this, you simply vest employee accounts with fictional shares of stock that change in value in tandem with the real shares.

It works this way: Assume AAA Store's 250 shares of stock are worth $6,000 each. When executive Jane Smith joins the firm on June 1, 1987, a fictional stock account is created, granting her the equivalent of five shares of stock, or $30,000. On June 1, 1988, and each year thereafter, a new entry is made in Smith's account, reflecting the appreciation in the real shares plus dividends paid. Should AAA stock rise to $7,000 a share on the first anniversary of Smith's employment—and should each share earn $300 in dividends during the period—her phantom stock holding would be worth $36,500. If the company continued to prosper, this might be worth $150,000 in 10 years. Depending on the design of the plan, Smith may be entitled to deferred compensation equaling either the full amount or the $120,000 increase over the share value when the plan was launched—in either case, a substantial sum reflecting the company's long-term growth.

"The idea behind phantom stock is to simulate the rewards of business ownership," says a vice-president of Towers, Perrin, Forster & Crosby, compensation consultants. "It tells the key employees in a small, privately held company that they can gain almost as much as the owners."

Typically, the sum recorded in the employee's phantom stock account is distributed at death or retirement in a lump sum or on an installment basis. To meet this obligation, management may want to make contributions to a reserve account, putting aside some part of the stock increases and dividends annually. If properly managed, the account will have sufficient funds to satisfy the obligation on the due date.

Another option, which accomplishes dual objectives, calls for purchasing a key-man universal life insurance policy for the covered employee. With universal life, coverage amounts may be revised annually to correspond with changes in the employee's phantom stock account. In addition, a key-man policy feature can cover the company for the losses it sustains at the death of a valued employee.

"Say the employee's phantom stock is valued at $100,000 and the business estimates it will lose another $100,000 as a result of the key man's death," says a second vice-president of corporate financial planning for Travelers Insurance. "Management would purchase a $200,000 universal life policy, with the business as the beneficiary. When the proceeds are paid, half could be used to fund the phantom stock obligation and half to cover the company's expenses resulting from the loss of the key employee."

This approach offers several tax advantages. Universal life premiums are placed in an accumulation account similar to a money market fund. Because the earnings from this account remain in the policy (where they are used to pay for the insurance protection and to build the policy's cash value), the money is sheltered from tax when paid out as a death benefit.

Should the phantom stock proceeds be paid at retirement, the money can be withdrawn from the policy's cash value. In this case, the employer is taxed only on that portion which represents gain in excess of the premiums.

Assume your company has paid $80,000 in cumulative premiums for a policy that, with the investment earnings, is now worth $115,000. By drawing out $100,000 of this cash value to pay off the employee's phantom stock account at retirement, you'll be taxed only on $20,000—or the sum in excess of the policy's cost. But even this minimal tax can be avoided by taking the $20,000 over policy cost as a loan on the policy rather than a cash withdrawal.

Another approach calls for the purchase of annuity contracts to cover the estimated future value of the phantom stock. In this way, management backs into its funding requirement, first projecting the amount and date of the obligation and then structuring an annuity to cover it. For example, assume your general manager will retire in 15 years with a projected phantom stock account worth $100,000. To cover this, you buy a 15-year, 9.5-percent annuity calling for annual payments of about $3,000.

Like all incentive packages, phantom stock demands considerable planning and attention to detail. Consider the following potential problems:

1. While insurance products can serve as effective funding vehicles for phantom stock plans, higher yields may be available through other sources without insurance protection.

Explore certificates of deposit, T-Bills, mutual funds, and Ginnie Maes.

2. Phantom stock payments are deductible to the corporation as deferred compensation and are taxable to the employee or his beneficiary as ordinary income.

3. Phantom stock can lose its appeal as an employee benefit if the shares fluctuate sharply over the years. Should shares increase dramatically in one year, only to nosedive the next, key employees may be frustrated in their ability to lock in short-term gains. For this reason, you may want to use phantom stock to fund a bonus plan, paying out the stock appreciation and dividends annually. This provides for a more immediate link between the individual's efforts and his rewards.

4. Make certain that the formula for valuing the company stock adequately reflects its true value. Unless this link is established, employees will recognize that their efforts do not produce personal gain, thus defeating the very purpose of phantom stock—producing entrepreneurial incentive.

Review phantom stock plans with tax advisers and benefit consultants. Plans can be structured to satisfy both management and employee objectives.

"Strategic Compensation" Links Pay to Company Goals

When the family-owned ABC Apparel Company handed out its annual bonuses, management detected a disturbing pattern: executive compensation was at cross purposes with corporate objectives. While the company was committed to long-term expansion, the bonus system rewarded short-term efforts. In effect, those generating current

profits were favored over those laying the groundwork for future growth.

"Every business has two critical objectives," says a senior manager specializing in executive compensation with accountants Price Waterhouse. "To achieve high current profits and to provide for a prosperous future. Sounds reasonable enough, but there's a hitch. Providing for the future means investing in equipment that will keep the company efficient and competitive over the years. This conflicts with the countervailing goal of generating maximum profits year in, year out. Every dollar of earnings plowed back into the business means a dollar subtracted from the bottom line.

"This conflict is mirrored in compensation planning. While management wants to reward those employees whose efforts result in current profits, it also must encourage those engaged in projects with longer term payoffs, such as the development of employee training or quality control programs. Fortunately, both can be rewarded through so-called strategic compensation, an innovative payment system that combines the often disparate functions of strategic planning and executive compensation. With this approach, compensation extends beyond simple payment for services to a means of directing employee performance toward specific business objectives.

Consider ABC Apparel. As its bonus plan has evolved, 20 percent of the company's profits are simply placed into a pool and divided by participating executives according to rank and seniority. A Christmas present, pure and simple, that bears no relationship to ABC's operating goals.

"Strategic compensation can change this," the Price Waterhouse manager says. "Instead of promising vice-president Smith a bonus equal to 50 percent of salary in a good year and 25 percent in a downturn, why not link his compensation to the company's strategic plan?

"Say the plan calls for boosting ABC's market share by 3 percent annually over the next five years. Because Smith as general sales manager can have a substantial impact on the achievement of that goal, his compensation should be based, at least in part, on ABC's success in increasing its market share. With this in mind, a full 3 percent increase would mean a 50 percent bonus; 2 percent, 25 percent; and 1 percent or less—because it is so far off target—no bonus at all. Rather than basing Smith's bonus on a common profit pool achieved through collective effort, strategic compensation makes him personally accountable for his earnings and directs his efforts toward corporate objectives."

For small companies, strategic compensation presents a simple, inexpensive, and uncomplicated way to align executive performance with management objectives. Because the executive's paycheck is based on the achievement of company goals, he automatically adjusts his performance to reflect management's priorities. The net effect is like a built-in traffic controller, directing talent and energies to the most productive ends.

If strategic compensation sounds right for your company (and chances are it will be a vast improvement over your current system), consider these guidelines for designing and implementing an effective plan:

1. Start by determining who should qualify. Experts suggest limiting participation to senior employees whose on-the-job decisions can materially affect the company's performance. By controlling the number and the caliber of employees in the plan, management can allocate maximum rewards to those whose efforts make the difference between success and failure.

2. Define responsibilities: Establish for each executive in the plan a set of respon-

sibilities keyed to his position in the company. For example:

Executive Title	Executive Responsibilities
Store Manager	Store promotions
	Maintenance of proper inventory levels
	Personnel recruitment and training
	Branch store profit and loss
Production Manager	Meeting production quotas
	Maintenance of plant efficiency standards
	Development of cost-control programs
	Supervision of production personnel

Setting personal responsibilities is like drawing a straight line between the executive and his place in the strategic plan. Each key player knows what is expected of him.

3. Establish priorities. Create an action plan that lists the company's objectives (25 percent sales increase, five branch stores, 15 percent market share) in order of priority and communicate this to the executives. This ordering of goals helps to create a workable timetable for fulfilling the company's strategic plan and for guiding executive actions.

Consider the case of Jane Jones, branch manager for XYZ Stores. Assume management sets three primary goals for each of its retail shops: to increase inventory turnover, boost the average gross sale, and improve customer relations. By telling Jones which goals have top priority—and by making it clear that they will have the greatest impact on her compensation—management directs her efforts to the appropriate ends.

4. Identify the key leverage areas. Every business has certain activities or functions that, if they are really performed well, can have a significant impact on its growth and

profitability. These are the key leverage areas.

Let's look again at ABC Apparel. A minor player in the junior fashion market, the company finds that creative designs (those with strong appeal to the national retail chains) have an enormous impact on its year-to-year performance, often making the difference between red and black ink.

Clearly, design is a key leverage area. This must be reflected in ABC's compensation plan. Executive actions in the design function must be more carefully scrutinized—and must carry greater bonus credits—than those in nonleverage areas such as public relations and purchasing. (Again, this provides a built-in mechanism for distributing the greatest rewards to those whose efforts have the greatest impact on the company's bottom line.)

5. Set performance standards: Individual contributions to corporate goals lie at the heart of the strategic compensation system. But how are these contributions measured? Unless management establishes a fair and uniform policy for evaluating executive performance, employees find themselves operating in a vacuum. Incentive, motivation, morale decline. Consider these guidelines for setting performance standards:

a. Link standards to corporate objectives. Measure the executive's impact, positive or negative, on each defined goal.

b. Set realistic standards that are demanding without being overly ambitious. Asking executives to do the near impossible only snuffs out motivation: most will give up without trying.

"Use historical trends as a basis for setting performance standards," the Price Waterhouse manager says. "For example, if sales have increased 5 percent a year for the past decade, management seeking more robust growth may look for 6 to 7 percent increases—but not 15 percent. The latter would be unrealistic, a fact that would hardly escape sales executives."

c. Use qualitative as well as quantitative measurements. Relying solely on fiscal yardsticks may overlook the executive's leadership role, his ability to balance long and short-term objectives, or his value as a confidant to the owner or senior management.

d. Make certain performance standards are clearly outlined in the compensation plan. If not, executives are forced to aim at moving targets.

6. Adjust base and bonus compensation to an appropriate ratio. Executives must be certain of a minimum level of compensation regardless of performance. This base pay figure should be sufficient to attract and retain high-caliber executives. Here, competition is a critical consideration. Should the market rate for production managers range from $60,000 to $75,000, small companies seeking to compete for the best will have to set salaries at or near the high end of the spectrum. Some even go beyond this, actually topping market rates. This accomplishes three major objectives: the company earns a reputation as a generous payer, the best candidates automatically flock to its doors, and turnover (which can be more costly than high salaries) is substantially reduced.

"When you're paying the most," says the president of a Midwest office equipment dealer, "there's no other place for ambitious executives to go. Besides, when they know you're taking good care of them, key people have a more cooperative attitude. They have a vested interest in your success."

The incentive portion of pay (that amount over and above the base figure) generally ranges from 10 to 50 percent of compensation, with the most common split—60 percent base, 40 percent bonus—ideal for most small companies. Should you use this ratio, first set base pay and then add the bonus mechanism, providing for minimum and maximum compensation geared to individual performance.

7. Select the plan format. Any number of compensation plans—including cash bonus, profit sharing, stock, and deferred compensation—can be used to fund strategic compensation. However, the Price Waterhouse manager warns that "in practice, cash bonus and profit-sharing plans tend to have more of a short-term focus, whereas stock and deferred compensation plans suggest more of a long-term outlook."

Sometimes, what may be ideal from the company's standpoint may be unacceptable to its executives. Though management must adopt a long-term perspective—and employees must share it—executives will still crave immediate rewards for their efforts. Stock plans can address this apparent conflict by setting aside incentive stock awards on an annual basis (500 shares for Ms. Smith, 360 for Mr. Jones) but postponing actual granting of the stock until and if the strategic goals are met. This compromise offers the best of both worlds: immediate recognition plus long-term gains tied to corporate objective. Again, the very essence of strategic compensation.

Compensation consultants can help to structure the executive payment plan best suited for your business.

Sharing the Pie Attracts Talented Employees

It is often said that a company is only as good as the people who work for it. Talented employees, the thinking goes, can do more to build and maintain sales than hot products, savvy promotions, or state-of-the-art technol-ogy. With this in mind, how does small business compete for its share of the best and the brightest?

Try offering what giant corporations cannot: a share of the entrepreneurial pie. With millions of Americans now fascinated with entrepreneurialism—and eager to trade salaried positions for jobs with an equity stake—small companies can use their size as an advantage rather than a handicap, drawing a straight line between performance and compensation.

"Talented people will gravitate toward small business if they are offered an opportunity to share in its success," says an executive search and compensation consultant with Peat Marwick. "That means gaining a chunk of its equity, its profits, or both. Just how to share the wealth, and in the process to attract the most desirable employees, leaves the business owner with some critical choices. Most important is whether to give up part ownership of the business or just simulate ownership with creative compensation plans."

Consider these options:

1. Grant the employee a fixed share—say one to two percentage points—of the company's profits. This makes the individual a partner in the company's prosperity without diminishing the owner's equity or management control. Percentage compensation plans are easy to understand, simple to calculate, and provide strong incentive to perform at maximum levels.

2. Where a company is already highly profitable, management can limit a new employee's share of the take to that represented by customers or accounts he brings into the firm. Or a benchmark can be established, above which the employee's profit-sharing percentage kicks in.

"The idea is to base the employee's compensation on his contribution to the firm, rather than on its past performance," the

Peat Marwick consultant says. "This can be done by limiting profit sharing to so-called new profits. In a typical plan, you might offer the employee two percent of all profits in excess of the average for the three years before he joined the company."

3. With a "target incentive" plan, the employee is eligible to earn a bonus calculated as a percentage of base salary. This can range from 15 to 50 percent, depending on the employee's rank and level of responsibility in the company.

"Assume a manager's target bonus is 50 percent of salary," the consultant explains. "This is earned only if the company reaches certain performance goals—such as a 10 percent increase in sales or profits. Usually, nothing is paid unless the company comes reasonably close, say within 90 percent of its goal, and the bonus is increased to, say, twice the target if the company surpasses its goal by a wide margin."

4. Sharing stock in the company—easily the most attractive perk—can also be tied to employee performance. With so-called restricted awards, employees are granted stock but are denied the full benefits of the shares until they have served a minimum number of years, usually five. Until that time they may be entitled to dividends, but not to vote, sell, or transfer the shares.

Equity can also be distributed through stock options, which grant employees the right to purchase the company's shares at a fixed price over a specified number of years. In this way, employees can gain personally from increases in the value of the company's stock. The vice-president who is granted 5000 option at $10 a share and eventually buys the stock and sells it for $20 a share earns $50,-000.

Stock options come in two varieties: incentive options, which are taxed when the shares are sold; nonqualified options, which are taxed when the option is exercised, even if the stock is not sold at that time.

5. Where undiluted ownership is crucial to the entrepreneur, phantom stock can serve a useful role. With this equity alternative, employees are granted mock shares of stock that mirror the company's growth in value but do not carry ownership rights. Think of it as a way of sharing the benefits of equity without sharing the pie.

Lawyers, accountants, and benefits consultants can help to structure performance-based compensation plans.

Definitions of Short-term Incentives

To ensure consistent interpretation of results, we define the various short-term award payments as follows:

Current cash. Any award paid in cash, either immediately following the close of the year on which the award is based or in installments beginning in that year and continuing for a number of years during active employment.

Current stock. Any award paid in stock, either immediately following the close of the year on which the award is based or in installments beginning in that year and continuing for a number of years during active employment.

Deferred award. Any award paid in cash or stock, but not until termination of employment or retirement. The fact that the payment at termination or retirement might be in a lump sum or spread over several annual installments does not affect this classification.

Definitions of Long-Term Incentives

We define the various long-term awards as follows:

Stock options. A stock option grant is an opportunity to purchase shares of company stock at a stated price (typically, the current market value at date of grant) during a given period of time, frequently ten years.

Stock appreciation right. A right granted in connection with an option where the executive, in lieu of exercising the option, can receive a payment equal to the amount by which the fair market value of the stock exceeds the option grant price on the date the stock appreciation right is exercised. These payments can be made in cash, in shares of stock having an equivalent value, or in a combination of cash and shares.

Performance award. A contingent award earned in whole or in part according to the degree of achievement of predetermined performance goals over a specified period (usually three to five years).

- A Performance Unit Award is an award granted in the form of a contingent number of units or as a contingent cash award. Units may be granted with a fixed-dollar payment value with the number of units earned varying on the basis of performance achievements. Alternatively, a fixed number of units may be granted with the payment value of these units varying on the basis of performance achievements. Performance unit awards may be paid in cash, in shares, or in a combination of cash and shares.
- A Performance Share Award is a contingent grant of shares of company stock. The number of shares earned is based on performance achievements; the payment value of the shares earned reflects the market value of the shares at the time they are paid. Performance share awards may be paid in shares, in cash, or in a combination of shares and cash.

Phantom stock. Any award made in units analogous to an actual share of stock where the employee receives, after a specified period of time, a payment equal to the appreciation in the value of the underlying stock and frequently an amount equal to dividends paid during the period. These payments may be made in cash, in stock, or in a combination of cash and stock.

Stock grant. A grant of stock at no or nominal cost. The stock grant may be made in the form of restricted stock that is nontransferable and/or subject to substantial risk of forfeiture until some future conditions are met. The restrictions are frequently designed to lapse over a period of years, based on continuing service. Dividends declared on restricted shares may be paid currently or may be reinvested to "purchase" additional shares that are paid at the end of the restriction period.

Dividend unit. Any award made in units analogous to an actual share of stock where the employee receives cash payments equivalent to dividends paid on shares of the company's stock.

Credit: Towers, Perrin, Forster & Crosby

Is Your Pension Plan Still a Good Investment?

The business pension plan, long considered a key to carefree retirement, is no longer the panacea it used to be. Sweeping changes brought by the Tax Reform Act of 1986 have taken their toll, increasing plan costs and reducing some of the key tax benefits. In this context, some business owners may want to terminate their plans in favor of taxable investments.

"It's all in the numbers," says an executive with Seidman Financial Services, a New York-based financial planning firm. "When you factor in the negative provisions built into the new tax law, you find that some self-employed people—including those who had once derived great benefit from qualified retirement plans—may be better off shutting down these plans and investing for retirement on their own. Under current rules, corporate pensions and Keogh plans are not the great tax shelters they used to be."

Blame it on four key provisions of the Tax Reform Act:

1. A sharp decline in the top personal tax rate from 50 percent in 1986 to 28 percent (or in some cases 33 percent) by 1988 translates into a smaller tax break for every dollar contributed to a qualified plan.

"With a 50 percent tax rate," the Seidman executive explains, "each dollar of contribution saved 50 cents in taxes. But with the lower tax rates, the savings are limited to a maximum of 28 or 33 cents depending on the individual's bracket."

2. Required changes in the structure of pension plans makes it more expensive to fund employee participation. This is apparent in two critical areas: where employers could formerly rely on integration with Social Security to cover a substantial portion of the employees' contribution, a greater percentage will now have to be paid with the employer's own funds; and vesting requirements have been tightened requiring that employees be fully vested after fewer years of service to the company.

3. Annual retirement plan distributions in excess of $112,500 (or $150,000 for plans with assets of $562,500 as of August 1, 1986) will be subject to a 15 percent excise tax on that portion of income over these ceiling amounts.

"Many small business owners and professionals will find that the assets they already have in their plans are sufficient to give them annual retirement incomes of more than $150,000," the Seidman executive says. "So all future contributions will produce income subject to the 15 percent excise tax in addition to ordinary income tax, making for a combined rate of up to 48 percent. Faced with this heavy tax bite, it's a good idea to review the wisdom of retaining pension plans."

4. Traditionally, retirement plans were used to shift income from the taxpayer's most productive years to his retirement, when it was presumed his income and tax bracket would decline. But under the new law, the individual may find that his tax liability at retirement is equal to or greater (with the excise tax) than that of his working years. In this light, income shifting loses its appeal.

"Taken together, the negatives built into the Tax Reform Act have had a substantial impact on retirement plans," the Seidman executive says. "Take the case of a small business owner with $750,000 of assets in his pension plan. Were he to contribute $30,000 a year for the next 10 years he'd have an additional $434,597. Withdrawing that money over 20 years would produce annual payments of $25,231 (based on an eight percent investment yield).

"The entrepreneur's real cost to fund the pension plan is $38,500. That's $30,000 for his personal contribution, $8,000 for his employees (up from $6,000 under the old law), and $500 for administrative fees. Were he to terminate his plan, pay the tax on the $38,500, and invest the balance of $27,720 a year in a personal account for 10 years, he'd wind up with a 20-year retirement payout of $30,887 a year. This figure—which is based on a 5.76 percent return (the after-tax return on 8 percent)—would be about $5,600 more a year then if he invested in a qualified retirement plan. That's because the proceeds from the taxable plan are free of the excise tax and the contribution does not have to be shared with employees. Were the excise tax not a factor, the retirement plan would still yield only about $1,000 more income than the taxable investment."

So does it make sense to maintain your pension plan? Consider these other factors:

- Where contributions for employees are neglible (as in one-man corporations), pension plans still offer a much greater return than nonsheltered investments.

- Terminating pension plans can have a negative impact on employee morale. Small companies competing for top personnel must be willing to offer attractive salary and benefit packages.

"Whether to keep a pension plan or fold it is not an easy decision," the Seidman executive says. "You have to first crunch the numbers and then look beyond them, gauging the impact your action will have on the company and the people who make it work."

VII. Tax-Cutting Strategies for You and Your Small Business

◇ ═══ ◇

New Tax Law Ends the "Free Lunch"

Suddenly the three martini lunch is only a 2.4 martini tax deduction. Thank the Tax Reform Act of 1986 for that. Under the Act's rules, business meals are no longer the generous write-offs they used to be.

The law's major change wipes out that great American institution: the fully deductible business meal. Effective January 1, 1987, the write-off is limited to 80 percent of food, drink, and tips. So for a $100 meal, only $80 can be written off. The remaining $20 must be paid in full by the company.

"Add that up for a full year of business meals and you could be talking about thousands of dollars of nondeductible expenses," says a partner with the accounting firm of Seidman & Seidman. "Unless companies change their policies and practices regarding business entertainment—meaning they treat customers to fewer or less expensive meals— they'll find that the new law has increased their costs of doing business. It's a matter that deserves careful attention."

In a less visible provision, the new tax law changes the ground rules for deducting busi-ness meals, making it more difficult to claim a write-off, even at the new 80 percent level. In the past, meals were deductible providing the parties dined in an atmosphere condu-cive to business discussion. Whether busi-ness was actually discussed during the course of the meal was immaterial. But the new law imposes a stricter rule for deductibility, re-quiring that business be discussed sometime before, during, or after the meal.

"Let's say a manufacturer takes one of his suppliers out to dinner," the CPA explains. "Before the new law became effective, they could have enjoyed a night out together, said nothing about business, and still written off the full cost of a dinner in an expensive res-taurant. But that's a thing of the past. To qual-ify for the deduction now, they would have to discuss business in conjunction with the meal. Although there are no hard-and-fast rules as to what constitutes a business discus-sion, in this case it would likely pertain to the supply of parts, products, or raw materials to the manufacturer."

The new law brings changes not only in business meal deductions but also in the re-cordkeeping for them. In most cases, compa-nies will have to revise their accounting procedures to segregate meals from other business deductions. For example, assume a lawyer meets a client at his favorite restaurant for lunch. While the taxi ride to the luncheon is still fully deductible, the meal deduction is limited by the 80 percent rule. So both expenses must be treated differently.

"Add it to the list of paperwork headaches," the CPA says. "Where companies used to dump all their entertainment-related expenses into a single file, they'll now have to set up procedures for keeping separate records for meals and other expenses. Unless this is done on an ongoing basis, it will create an awful lot of extra work at tax time."

Documenting business meal deductions is also a more elaborate affair. To protect your write-off, you'll want to maintain a diary of all business meals listing the guest's name and business relationship, the date and location of the meeting, and the nature of the business discussion. As a general rule, the more elaborate the diary the more likely the deduction will stand.

Consider these other strategies for deducting business meals:

Shift the new tax cost to clients or employees. Assume your sales reps take their clients to business lunch. By reimbursing the employees for the cost of the meals and treating this as additional compensation, the company gets to deduct 100 percent of the meal and shifts the 80 percent limitation to the employees. The caveat here is that the plan may have a negative impact on employee morale.

Refrain from lavish or extravagant meals. The new law specifically disallows these excessive deductions.

"Since the term 'lavish and extravagant' is vague, just what will be allowed or disallowed will depend on the taxpayer's circumstances," the CPA says. "But when you host a customer to a $200 lunch and it is found to be excessive by $100, that incremental amount will not be deductible at all. The total write-off for the meal will be limited to 80 percent of the first $100, or $80."

Work with an accountant in setting up new business meal guidelines for your company.

Want a Tax Shelter? Try the S Corporation

Pity the poor tax shelter. With the passage of the Tax Reform Act of 1986, most exotic shelters have gone the way of the whooping crane. Only a few have survived. But one exception—the S corporation—has emerged from the legislative reform looking stronger than ever.

S corporations have always been attractive creatures. While standard corporations are taxed twice, first at the corporate level and then as dividends to the shareholders, S corporations avoid the corporate tax. All income flows directly to the shareholders.

"Profitable companies will find that this distinction is even more beneficial under the new law," says a tax manager with Touche Ross. "That's because for the first time personal tax rates are lower than corporate rates. So the S corporation not only escapes a layer of tax—that at the corporate level—but also qualifies for a lower tax rate than the standard corporation."

On the flip side, losses incurred by an S corporation also flow to the owners, meaning they can use the red ink to offset income from other sources. Assume, for example, that Smith—who earns $75,000 a year as a stockbroker—starts and manages an investment newsletter on the side. In the early years, the fledgling venture losses $30,000 annually. Because the business is an S corporation, Smith can claim those losses personally, thus reducing the taxable income from his brokerage commissions. Instead of paying tax on $75,-000 a year, his taxable base is reduced to $45,-000. While entrepreneurs have traditionally started businesses as S corporations and then switched to regular corporations once the ventures were in the black, many will find that it now makes sense (because of the lower personal tax rates) to remain S corporations even after the companies are profitable.

Consider these additional advantages of S corporation status:

- The sky's the limit on management salaries. With a standard corporation, the IRS can claim that high salaries exceed the value of services provided and must be taken, in part, as dividends (subject to the dual tax). But because all S corporation earnings flow to the shareholders, unreasonable compensation is never an issue.
- Long-term assets can be sold on a tax-advantaged basis. Gains on real estate, equipment, and other property held by the S corporation for at least 10 years are exempt from corporate taxes. This means owners liquidating their businesses after the 10-year holding period may avoid the dual tax levied on the sale of standard corporations. The bottom line: the owner gets to pocket more of the proceeds.
- S corporations are exempt from two bombshells of the 1986 tax law. A tightening up of the alternative minimum tax rules (requiring even those companies with more deductions than income to pay taxes) and the requirement that most corporations earning in excess of $5 million a year use the accrual basis of accounting (rather than the more flexible cash method).

Becoming an S corporation is as simple as filing form 2553 with the IRS. To be effective for current taxes, the election must be made before the 16th day of the third month of the company's fiscal year.

"Terminating the election is just as easy—you just inform the IRS that you want out," the Touche Ross manager says. "But once you voluntarily leave the S status, you can't return to it for another five years. So it's simple to get in and simple to get out—but once you're out, you're out for a while."

Should you rush to join the S corporation stampede? Not so fast. All tax strategies are fraught with a tangle of rules, drawbacks, and limitations. Review the pros and cons with an accountant or tax attorney.

How to Claim Home Office Deductions

The only tax shelter to put a roof over your head—the home office deduction—is no longer the generous write-off it used to be. A series of rules and limitations have made the deduction harder to claim and less valuable to those who qualify for it.

In the past, those performing occasional business functions in the home could write off the expenses associated with that activity, including a portion of the home's depreciation, utilities, and maintenance.

"Say an architect kept an office at his firm but also did occasional drawings in the den of his home," explains a tax partner with Israeloff, Trattner. "At one time, he could make a case for deducting expenses associated with the use of the den. Although that hasn't been true for years, many people still try to claim the deduction on that basis. But on audit, they get shot down. That's because occasional use of a room no longer qualifies for the home office deduction."

Under current rules, home offices must meet a series of tests to be eligible for tax write-offs:

- Must be used regularly and exclusively for business. Based on this rule, a room that doubles as a den and an office is generally disqualified. It fails to meet the exclusivity test.
- Must be maintained for the convenience of the employer.
- Must be the taxpayer's principal place of business. Because the architect performed the bulk of his duties at the firm's business offices, his at-home workplace could not be viewed as a "principal place of business."

Cut and dried? Well, not exactly. As with all provisions of the tax laws, there's as much gray here as black and white. First, there is an exception to the "principal place of business" test. Providing the taxpayer uses the home office for regular meetings with clients or customers, the home office deduction can be claimed even if he has a principal office outside of the residence.

Second, what qualifies as a "principal place of business" is a matter of interpretation.

"In most cases, the Internal Revenue Service takes a tough stand on this, arguing that the work space your company or employer provides is your principal office regardless of how much work you do at home," the CPA warns. "But the courts don't always agree. In one case, the IRS shot down a laundromat owner's attempt to write off a home office, holding that the laundromat was his principal place of business. But because the U.S. Court of Appeals found that it would be impossible to run the company from that type of facility, the owner's home office deduction was preserved."

Taking aim at home office deductions, the Tax Reform Act of 1986 has plugged up one of the loopholes in the law and restricted the amount of deductions available to legitimate users.

"For a while, people were getting around the standard home office tests by leasing part of their home to their employers, taking the rent as income which was sheltered by home office expenses," says a tax partner with the accounting firm of Oppenheim, Appel, Dixon. "But the new tax law put an end to that one by disallowing deductions in such leasing arrangements."

What's more, the new law holds that if business expenses other than those allocated to use of the home exceed gross income from the home office, then no home office expenses are currently deductible.

"Where a home office produces $25,000 of gross income," the Israeloff, Trattner partner explains, "and has wages, automobile, and supplies expenses of $26,000, home office expenses such as depreciation, maintenance, and insurance are not currently deductible. Meaning: it is now harder to use the losses from home offices to shelter income from other sources."

Consider these additional facts concerning the home office:

- Self-employed individuals with no other place of business are rarely challenged in claiming part of the home for office use.
- Those claiming the home office deduction on the basis of customer or client meetings are advised to keep diaries of these meetings.
- Keep the home office free of personal effects, such as beds or television sets. Take pictures of the room, showing that it is designed solely for business use. Make these pictures available to tax auditors.

"Remember, it's your job to prove that the deduction is valid," the Israeloff, Trattner partner warns. "Muster all the evidence at your disposal to do just that. You may need it in the event of an audit."

How to Write Off Bad Debts

Just when you thought bad debts couldn't weigh heavier on your business, the Tax Reform Act comes along and makes a bad thing worse. A popular way of writing off deadbeat accounts—the so-called reserve method—has been cut from the books, taking with it the flexibility in claiming bad debt deductions.

The reserve method was appealing because it allowed companies to write off bad debts on the basis of projected rather than actual losses. In some cases, this produced deductions that were greater than the losses they were meant to offset.

"Under the old law, a company that historically lost five percent of its receivables to bad debts could set up a reserve equal to that amount at the end of the tax year," explains a tax partner with Miller, Cooper & Co. "So if receivables totalled $500,000, the reserve write-off came to $25,000. This held even if the company's actual debt losses were less than $25,000. Although the shortfall was subtracted from the reserve the following year, the advance write-off amounted to an interest-free loan from Uncle Sam."

But that option is now closed. Bad debt deductions are generally limited to those that are proven uncollectible in the year they are claimed. Write-offs can no longer be based on projected losses. So the company with $10,000 in bad debts is limited to a $10,000 deduction in the year the debts go bad.

But what is a bad debt? How can you prove it is uncollectible? What qualifies for the write-off?

"Just saying you didn't think the account would pay up isn't good enough to take the deduction," the tax partner warns. "Nor is sending out a single dunning letter. To qualify for a bad debt deduction, you'll have to demonstrate that you exercised prudent business judgement in credit and collections. That means having a formal collections effort in-house or referring the account to outside professionals."

In determining deductibility, the length of time a debt is outstanding is not as important as the effort expended to collect on it. While the month-old debt of a now bankrupt company will likely be deductible, an account delinquent for six months or more may not qualify unless there was a prudent effort to recover the funds.

To preserve bad debt deductions, companies are advised to take a systematic approach toward credit and collections. Experts suggest the following approach:

- Bill accounts well in advance of the due date, clearly spelling out your payment terms and conditions.
- Send a follow-up invoice soon after the payment date, reminding the debtor of his obligation.
- If payment has not been received within 45 days, send a reminder notice. Follow up, on or about the 75th day, with a warning that the account will be turned over for collection.
- After 90 days, refer the account to a collection agency or an attorney specializing in debt collection.

"You'll want to favor those professionals that work on a contingent fee basis," the Miller, Cooper partner says. "That means you're not charged a fee unless they collect on the bad debt. The only commission you owe comes from debts that would likely have gone uncollected without their help. In a sense, you're paying for the service with found money."

Consider these other rules concerning bad debt deductions:

- Companies that had been using the reserve method will have to report the ending reserve balance as income. This can generally be spread over four years.

- A debt must be deducted in the year it becomes worthless. A delay in taking the write-off may result in a loss of the bad debt deduction.
- Carefully document all steps in the collection process, maintaining copies of correspondence and a log of telephone calls. You'll want to prove that you took every possible action to recover the debt.

How to Keep the Family Business in the Family

Suddenly it happens. The owner of a family business dies, leaving his heirs to run the show. As was his plan from the start, the next generation will take the helm. Or will it? All too often, the founder's death rewrites the script, forcing the family to sell out just to pay taxes.

It's a critical problem. With all of their equity tied up in the business, the heirs often find that there's no cash to settle the estate. The only course, it seems, is to sell the business the founder worked a lifetime to build.

"Assume Smith dies leaving a $5 million business to his daughters," says an attorney specializing in estate planning. "The estate tax on that inheritance will come to about $2 million. Although the women have the option of paying off the taxes in installments over a number of years, if this is still a burden they may have to sell the company just to pay Uncle Sam."

While little can be done once tragedy strikes, a bit of advance planning can help to keep the family business in the family. The simplest option is to purchase enough life insurance to cover the estate tax. But even here there is a little-known angle.

"Putting the coverage in a so-called irrevocable life insurance trust can shelter the proceeds from estate taxes," the lawyer advises. "The benefit is clear. Let's say the entrepreneur owns a $10 million business and a $5 million life insurance policy. His death leaves a $15 million estate which is fully taxable. But if the trust owns the policy, the estate, for tax purposes, is limited to the $10 million business.

"But there is a caveat. For this strategy to be effective, the entrepreneur must live for at least three years after the policy is put in the trust. Should he die before that period, the insurance proceeds will be taxable to the estate."

Consider these additional estate planning strategies:

- When partners run a company, a buy-sell agreement can be a versatile document, providing both the wherewithal to purchase the deceased's business interests and the liquidity needed by his heirs.

  It works this way: Smith and Jones are equal partners in Acme Products. Because neither wants to be in business with the other's relatives, they sign a buy-sell agreement stating that if one dies, the survivor can acquire the deceased's stock, thus gaining sole control of the company.

  Funds for the stock purchase come from life insurance policies Acme holds on the lives of Smith and Jones. Assuming Smith's stock is worth $2.5 million, the policy pays that amount, giving Jones the cash to buy out his former partner and, in turn, to pay off his heirs. Both sides achieve their objectives.

- Where an entrepreneur wants to begin shifting ownership in a business before his death—without simultaneously shifting control—an "estate freeze" may be the best approach. With this flexible estate planning technique, two classes of stock are issued, with the present owner taking preferred shares and his offspring getting common stock. In this way, current income and control stay with the founder, while future appreciation—as reflected in the common stock—goes to the next generation.

"Let's say the founder holds 1,000,000 shares of preferred stock and gives his two children 100 shares each of common," the attorney explains. "With his superior holdings, he out-votes them by a wide margin and collects the lion's share of current dividends.

"But if the company increases in value, going from $3 million to $5 million after the children get the common stock, all of that gain belongs to them. This may enable the entrepreneur to transfer wealth to the next generation without the payment of federal estate or gift taxes on the appreciation.

"Although the IRS often challenges estate freezes, holding that a gift tax is due on the distribution of common shares, careful planning can help to limit this. In this regard, it is wise to gift stock to your children when the company is in its infancy and is clearly of neglible value."

Review all estate planning options with attorneys and accountants specializing in this practice. And do it while there is still time. Waiting to act can put your business and your family's finances in jeopardy.

AUDITS

Facing a Tax Audit? Take the Offense

Nothing strikes fear in the heart of a small business owner like the notice of a tax audit. To most, the process conjures up visions of hostile examiners, back taxes, and penalties. But it needn't be that way. By taking an aggressive role in the audit, the entrepreneur can have a substantial impact on its outcome, leaving his finances intact when the agent leaves.

"While the Internal Revenue Service agent has the legal right to control the audit agenda, the taxpayer can take a number of critical actions to turn the process in his favor," says a former IRS revenue agent, now a manager with Arthur Young. "For example, he can try to determine in advance the scope of the audit examination. In so-called field audits—which are the common type of audit for small companies—the initial notice does not specify precisely which aspects of the company's taxes are slated for review.

"But a timely call to the agent may reveal this information, enabling management to prepare more effectively for the examination. Say the owner learns that the IRS will be focusing on travel and entertainment expenses for 1983. Ordinarily those records might be in storage. By having time to retrieve them and to make them ready for the examiner, the company demonstrates a level of cooperation that always impresses agents. It impressed me when I was an agent."

Adds a tax partner with Touche Ross: "Agents use a so-called smell test to determine if a company has full and complete records of its business transactions. If the first five or ten questions are met with documentation thoroughly supporting the company's deductions, the agent gets the impression that the taxpayer is in full compliance and is therefore less inclined to dig for evidence of underpayment. That's why it is imperative to bring every check, every bank statement, every depreciation schedule that might be needed by the examiner."

Consider these additional audit strategies:
1. Never volunteer information. Limit

your answers to those questions posed by the examiner, making certain to stay within the narrow framework of his inquiry.

"Beware of small talk as well," the former agent cautions. "In the audit environment, even the most innocuous comments can come back to haunt you. In one case, a casual conversation about vacations, initiated by the taxpayer, led to an examination and subsequent adjustment of his travel deductions. The agent found that personal travel was improperly attributed to the business."

2. Hire an accountant or lawyer experienced in the audit process. Armed with a power of attorney, these professionals can handle the entire audit often without the taxpayer's appearance before the examiner. By removing himself from the audit process, the taxpayer prevents his inexperience from negatively affecting the audit findings.

3. Bring documentation indicating how all significant tax deductions are calculated. These so-called summary work sheets are commonly used by professionals to support sensitive write-offs, including expenses for business cars and salaries to family members.

"Assume travel and entertainment expenses are broken down into four separate categories in the company's books," the Arthur Young manager explains, "one each for restaurants, airlines, hotels, and taxis, but they are consolidated on the tax return as a single figure. By demonstrating, through presentation of the summary work sheets, just how this number was arrived at, the taxpayer helps the examiner reconcile the deductions on the return and saves time for the parties involved."

4. At the beginning of the audit, try to direct the examiner's attention to those matters for which you have the most thorough and convincing documentation. Early evidence of honest and accurate returns sets the tone for a relatively low-keyed audit; conversely, encountering major problems at the start prompts the agent to distrust all facets of the return.

5. Never intimidate the agent. In the audit process, cooperation is always more productive than anger.

6. Take those findings you believe are unfair to the the IRS appellate division or the courts. Under the so-called hazards of litigation rule, appeals officers are authorized to settle those cases that are likely to go against the IRS in court. Professionals can help identify those issues best scheduled for the appeal process.

HOT TIPS

Checklist Reveals Overlooked Tax Deductions

Of all the high-write-off tax shelters, business ownership may be the most versatile. Unlike salaried employees, the self-employed are entitled to a long list of deductions from company cars to Keogh contributions. But for every deduction claimed, tax advisers warn, another may be overlooked.

"Many small business owners pay more tax than they have to," says a tax manager for Price Waterhouse. "That's because they're generally careless in reviewing business records and are uninformed as to the full scope of legitimate deductions.

"Take the business owner who makes frequent sales trips. Two costs associated with travel—telephone calls charged to home phones and passport fees—are often overlooked at tax time. By failing to write off these expenses, the individual winds up overpaying Uncle Sam."

Unclaimed deductions range from petty

cash transactions to substantial expenses of $1,000 or more. In many cases taxpayers play it safe, forgoing questionable write-offs for fear they will backfire in an audit, resulting in additional taxes, interest, and penalties. But a wiser approach is to maintain a separate file of "gray area" items, reviewing them with an accountant before filing tax returns.

Consider the following checklist of frequently overlooked business deductions:

- Annual membership fees for credit cards used for business purposes.
- Dues for business luncheon clubs.
- Golf and athletic club dues when membership is used for business.
- Parties, meetings, and other business entertaining at home. Deductible expenses include the cost of invitations, food, and drink.
- Business gifts up to $25 per person.
- Rental of tuxedos or dinner dresses used exclusively for business functions.
- Home or office alarm systems used primarily to protect business assets or personal investments.
- Salaries paid to family members for legitimate business services.

"Sometimes, a child home for vacation is put to work cleaning out an office or setting up a filing system," says a partner with Peat Marwick. "Because it is a one-time project, the owner may forget to deduct payments for the child's services. But he is entitled to do so."

- Tuition for college courses, seminars, and workshops taken to enhance the owner's knowledge of his business or profession.
- Fees and dues for business or professional organizations.
- Keogh plan custodian fees.
- Homeowner insurance riders for business property used at home.

- Safes and vaults used for protecting business or investment documents.

"Some self-employed people are too prudent in claiming deductions," the Peat Marwick partner says. "We see cases where Internal Revenue Service auditors actually find deductions taxpayers failed to claim themselves. That usually indicates that the taxpayers were being careless or overly cautious. Unless you hunt down every legitimate deduction before filing a return, you'll be cheating yourself."

PRIVATE RULINGS

Answers to Companies' Tax Questions

Anyone who runs a business knows the tax laws come in three shades: black, white, and gray. Exactly which transactions are subject to tax is not always clear. Faced with this ambiguity, entrepreneurs can petition the IRS for binding opinions on how business deals will be taxed.

The procedure—known as private rulings—gives business owners a reliable basis for projecting the tax implications of proposed transactions. It works like this: assume ABC and XYZ Companies want to merge but only if the merger will be viewed by the Internal Revenue Service as a nontaxable event. Because certain aspects of the deal make this unclear, the principals ask the IRS to rule on the matter before the corporate marriage is consummated.

With the aid of a tax professional, the companies prepare a full description of the proposed merger, including the current structure of the firms, the composition of the merged entity, and the terms of the deal. This is sent to IRS headquarters in Washington,

D.C. In most cases the government will take one of three actions: the request for a private ruling will be denied on technical grounds, additional information will be requested, or the tax implications of the proposed transaction will be spelled out.

"Should the IRS determine that the merger is not taxable, the companies can proceed on this basis without fear that the Service will change its mind at a later date," says a tax partner with accountants Arthur Young. "The ruling is an insurance policy that the course of action the companies intend to take will be accepted by the IRS.

"But this doesn't mean that a negative ruling should necessarily stop a company from moving ahead with its plans based on its own tax assumptions. If the parties involved, along with their professional advisers, believe that case law differs from the IRS interpretation of the tax code, they can do the transaction and be prepared to defend it in court."

Private rulings are governed by the following provisions:

1. The IRS will rule on interpretive rather than factual issues. "Assume a company wants to know if certain components of its physical plant are eligible for the investment tax credit," the Arthur Young partner explains. "Precisely what qualifies for the credit is an interpretive question and will likely be ruled on. But if management wants confirmation that the credit will yield a specific dollar figure, the IRS will refuse to rule on that."

2. Private rulings apply only to those taxpayers specifically cited in the ruling. Others contemplating similar transactions cannot rely on prior rulings to sanction their own actions. "Sometimes, we rule on an issue that has broad implications—well beyond the transaction at hand," says an IRS spokesman. "In such cases, we'll often publish the ruling in the *IRS Bulletin*, at which time it becomes an official revenue ruling. Taxpayers with similar fact patterns can then rely on this for guidance in their own affairs."

3. Rulings are generally issued within three to six months but complex issues requiring several levels of review can take nine months or more.

4. Taxpayers requesting private rulings are advised to support their positions with ample documentation, including rulings on similar cases and related court decisions.

5. Rulings cannot be used to sandbag ongoing tax examinations. "Companies currently being audited cannot try to outmaneuver the examiner by getting a private ruling on an issue he's contesting," the Arthur Young partner says. "The Service will shoot that down."

6. Rulings are generally limited to proposed rather than completed transactions.

Work with a tax adviser in requesting private rulings and in structuring transactions based on their outcome.

PROPERTY TAXES

How to Save on Them

When it comes to property taxes, how much is too much is often a matter of controversy: what the assessor deems equitable, the taxpayer considers excessive. For small business, the difference is more than semantics. Thousands of dollars can be at stake.

Because property taxes are generally based on a structure's market value, controversies can arise both on how the assessor arrives at market value and on the assets included in the assessment. But experts in property valuation say that business owners can help to settle disputes in their favor—and in the process achieve equitable assessments—by understanding the assessment process and by cooperating with assessors.

"Quite often, much of the assessment is made on the basis of a company's own records," says a vice-president of Marshall and Stevens, appraisers and valuation consultants. "If this does not provide an accurate reflection of the firm's assets, the assessment is likely to be wrong.

"Take the situation we call 'ghost assets.' Say a company modernizes its facilities and in the process removes part of its plant or office structure. In many cases, management fails to take this off the books. Of the assessments we review, 10 to 15 percent of the assets on the books no longer exist. By cleaning up its records and showing the assessor that these are ghost assets, the company can generally get them removed from the assessment rolls."

Consider these additional guidelines:

1. Construction costs that do not add value to a new building may in some cases be excluded from the assessment base. "As often happens with new construction, management of the company that will occupy the space may not like the way part of the interior looks once it is built," says a partner in the real estate practice with the accounting and consulting firm of Laventhol & Horwath. "So walls may be knocked down and replaced by others in different positions. In effect, the company has paid for these walls twice. If this construction overrun is included in the building's cost figures, the company's property tax may be unnecessarily high. Providing management can show that this did not add value to the building, it may be successful in getting it removed from the assessment."

2. Properties abandoned in place—those that are still standing but have little or no economic value—will likely qualify for reduced assessments. In some cases, the company finds it uneconomical to demolish the property even though it is not used. This should be brought to the assessor's attention.

3. Companies holding properties in various states should be familiar with the assessment formulas in each tax jurisdiction. "Some have unique assessing procedures," the Laventhol & Horwath partner says. "That's why it is important for the company to keep up with the tax procedures wherever it does business and to alert assessors to changes in property use. If this is not done, the firm may wind up paying more than it has to."

4. Tax disputes that cannot be solved with the local assessor may be appealed through administrative and court proceedings. Attorneys can advise on this process.

Property appraisers and consultants can help companies review their tax assessments, determine if reductions should be sought, and suggest the best way to achieve them.

SALARIES (UNREASONABLE COMPENSATION)

How to Set Salaries that Stick

In closely held corporations, how much money the boss earns is more than a business decision. The Internal Revenue Service has a say in the matter too. Salaries held to be "unreasonable" may be disallowed, subjecting income to double taxation.

It works this way: assume ABC Corporation president John Smith draws annual compensation of $300,000 for running his $600,000-a-year company. Providing this is deemed reasonable, the salary is deductible to the corporation. But if the IRS claims that Smith's compensation exceeds the value of his services by $150,000, half the corporate salary deduction will be disallowed.

"The tricky thing about the compensation issue is that there are no hard-and-fast rules regarding how much is too much," says a tax partner with accountants Alexander Grant & Co. "Compensation has to be commensurate with the services provided, but that's often a judgment call. Given the owners of similar businesses in different industries, one may get away with a $200,000 salary while the other is held to $100,000.

"But the lack of concrete rules can also work in the taxpayer's favor. Should the IRS hold a salary unreasonable, that determination can be reversed with the proper defense. Take the case of a principal whose salary doubles in response to a dramatic increase in corporate profits. If it can be proven that this compensation reflects not just current activities but also efforts in building the business over many years, the salary may stand."

Adds a tax partner with the national accounting firm of Seidman & Seidman: "A written employment contract providing the principal with an annual performance bonus—say 10 percent of earnings—also works well. As long as the percentage remains constant, the owner can profit handsomely in good years with little likelihood that the compensation will be challenged."

Another common defense against unreasonable compensation is a comparison of the disputed salary to that of executives in public corporations. "Some national business magazines publish surveys of CEO compensation," the Grant partner says. "These figures become benchmarks against which other salaries can be compared. If a public company pays its president $200,000 and the principal running a similar privately held company gets roughly the same, chances are good his salary will be deemed reasonable."

Switching from a regular corporation to the subchapter S form can neutralize the compensation issue. With S corporations, income flows directly to the shareholders. Because there is generally no tax at the corporate level, dual federal taxation is not a problem.

Tax advisers offer these additional guidelines:

- Establish a pattern of dividend payments. "It's generally a good idea to pay out some part of earnings as dividends, perhaps a fixed dollar amount per year," says a tax principal with accountants Arthur Young. "Examiners often see this as a sign that the company is being reasonable."
- Include a provision in the corporation's minutes requiring that the principal reimburse the corporation for any part of his compensation deemed to be unreasonable.
- Income taken in the form of profit-sharing plans, pension contributions, and other perks will be included with aggregate compensation.

Review all compensation strategies with a tax professional.

TRAVEL

How to Claim Tax Deductions for Business Travel

Tax-deductible travel, one of the perks of business ownership, is also a red flag to Internal Revenue Service auditors. Exactly who can travel where for how long is not always clear. But the general rule is that the more exotic the travel—including Caribbean seminars, ocean cruises, and weekends abroad—the more vulnerable the tax deductions.

Typically, the issue boils down to whether the travel is predominantly for business or pleasure. The answer can mean the differ-

Small Business by State

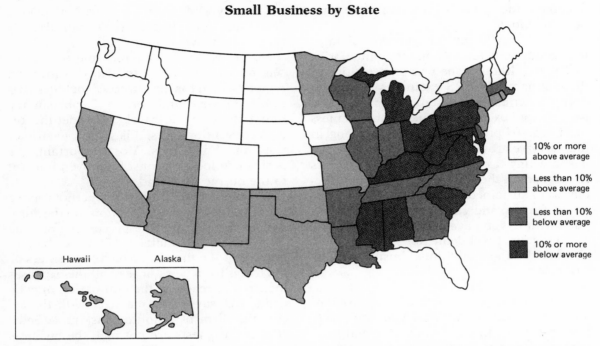

10% or more
above average

Less than 10%
above average

Less than 10%
below average

10% or more
below average

The number of small businesses per capita varies from state to state. Some of the reasons for this variance include: differences in per capita income, farm population, and the number of big businesses.

Source: National Federation of Independent Business Research and Education Foundation

ence between generous write-offs and no write-offs at all.

"Take the rules on air travel," says a Long Island-based CPA. "In general, business owners can deduct domestic airline fares providing the travel is primarily for business. This means a small businessman traveling from New York to California for five days of work and two days of vacation could deduct the full fare providing he could prove the trip was taken for business purposes.

"While this 'mostly business' rule may not be an issue for routine trips to out-of-state customers, attending seminars on tropical is-

lands is another matter. Here it may be harder to convince the IRS that the trip was primarily business-related."

Claiming deductions for spouses further complicates the issue. Unless the spouse plays a legitimate role in the business and performs business-related functions on the trip, that person's travel expenses will not be deductible.

"The old argument that 'I took my spouse along because everyone else took theirs and it wouldn't look good if I was the only exception' doesn't stand up in an examination," the CPA adds. "To get the deduction, you have to document the spouse's involvement in business functions.

"One of my clients, an importer of Japanese goods, took his wife on semiannual trips to Tokyo. Although she was an executive of the company, the IRS examiner wanted to disallow her expenses on the basis that Japanese custom excludes women from business meetings. To prove the examiner wrong in this case, we provided a full diary of her business meetings as well as copies of documents she signed on the trip. As a result, the write-offs were sustained. The point is that if you know the law and can prove that you complied with it, you have a good chance of preserving your travel deductions."

Consider these additional business travel strategies:

1. Exchange letters with clients, distributors, and other contacts on your itinerary, first informing them of your visit and then summarizing the outcome on your return. This creates a body of evidence as to the business nature of the travel and the approximate time devoted to business or professional pursuits.

2. When a spouse's expenses are not deductible, business travelers can still claim a substantial portion of joint bills. Should the couple pay $100 per night for a hotel room, $80 of that, providing it is the standard single rate, may be written off.

3. Be wary of attending conventions or seminars held outside the North American region (which for tax purposes includes Bermuda, Mexico, and certain Caribbean nations). Because this travel falls under the foreign convention rules, it is subject to stricter tests and limitations. Most important, the designated location must be proven integral to the business at hand.

4. For ordinary foreign travel (not related to conventions), base deductions on the duration of the trip and the percentage of time spent on business affairs. "If more than 75 percent of the time is devoted to business or the trip is for a week or less, all the expenses incurred in reaching the destination may be deducted," says a tax manager with the accounting firm of Deloitte, Haskins & Sells. "But if these tests are not met, the business owner may have to allocate expenses as business- and non-business-related. This means that if on a 10-day trip to England only two days are spent on business, roughly 20 percent of all expenses, including air fare, could be deducted."

Plan all travel deductions with the advice of a tax professional.

VIII. Going On-Line

How to Put Computers to Work for Your Business

◇ ══ ◇

Selecting the Right Computer System for Your Business

Two options for your own in-house computer system are the *minicomputer* and the *microcomputer*.

A *minicomputer* is a general purpose computer that can be programmed to do a variety of tasks and is generally designed so input can be entered directly into the system. For example, data such as a sales order is put into the computer at the same time the order is written. A minicomputer can be operated by users who don't have special computer knowledge. The costs for minicomputer equipment begin around $25,000 and range to above $200,000.

The *micro* or *personal computer* is a household word if not quite yet a universal household system. It is inexpensive, small, lightweight, and can be set on a desk. Such computers run programs that do an astonishing variety of tasks and can be operated easily by personnel who do not have special computer knowledge. They can satisfy the needs of many small business owners. The micro or PC usually handles one task at a time. Some have modest capabilities for multi-tasking and multi-user applications

(more than one program and terminal at one time).

Choosing the Right Computer

To computerize your business you will have to choose the right programs, select the right equipment, and implement the various applications. This involves training personnel, keeping up security, maintaining equipment, supplies, and day-to-day operation. If you follow a well-laid-out plan and make well-informed choices, your computer system should provide the information and control intended.

Computer Components

Hardware

Component	Function
Central Processing Unit (CPU)	The CPU performs logic calculations, manages the flow of data within the computer, and executes the program instructions.
Main Memory	Memory is measured in the "K" you'll often hear mentioned—for example 32K (32,000 positions). It is simply a storage area readily accessible to the CPU.

Mass Storage	This storage is simply "nonmain." There are a number of devices available, such as disk, diskette, and magnetic tape.
Input Device(s)	These units are used to enter data into the system for processing. An input device commonly used with computers is a combination keyboard and televisionlike display screen called a CRT (cathode ray tube).
Output Device(s)	These display the data. The most common output device is a printer.

Software

Component	Function
Operating System Software	Software that tells the hardware how to run.
Applications Programs	Software written to perform a particular function, such as word processing, accounts receivable, payroll, or inventory control "applications."
Compilers and Interpreters	Special software that translates programs into machine language that the CPU can execute.

Choosing the Right Programs (Software)

A program is a set of instructions that tells the computer to do a particular task. Programs are written in a language (such as FORTRAN, COBOL, BASIC) that is easy for people to work with. These programs are usually referred to as *software*.

The software determines what data or information is to be entered into the computer and what output or report is to be returned by the computer after it has performed as instructed by the program. The act of entering information into a computer is called inputing the data.

Generally, there are three types of software:

Compilers and interpreters. Special software that translates programs written in people language (such as FORTRAN, COBOL, BASIC) into machine language that the CPU can execute.

Operating system software. The programs that control all the separate component parts of the computer, such as the printer and disk drives, and how they work together. Systems software generally comes with the computer and must be present before the application software can work.

Applications software. Software composed of programs that make the computer perform particular functions such as payroll check writing, accounts receivable posting, or inventory reporting. Application software programs, particularly the more specialized ones, are normally purchased separately from the computer hardware.

Because the application software provides the features that will assist you and your business, it should always be evaluated and decided upon before you look at computer equipment. Before beginning your search for application software that is right for you, identify *what the software will have to accomplish*. Your time will be well spent if you research and write down your requirements.

To help you determine your requirements, prepare a list of all functions in your business in which speed and accuracy are needed for handling volumes of information. These are called applications. For each of these applications make a list of all reports that are currently (or will need to be) produced. You should also include any preprinted forms such as checks, billing statements, or vouchers. If they don't exist, develop a good idea of what you want—a hand-drawn version will help. For each report list the frequency with which it is to be generated and the number of copies needed.

In addition to printed matter, make a list of information you would like to see displayed on the computer video screen (CRT). Again, design a hand-drawn version. List the circumstances under which you would like to see this information displayed.

For each application make a list of all materials that are used as input into your manual system. These may include items such as time cards, work orders, receipts, etc. Describe the time period in which these items are created, who creates them, and how they get into the system. Also, describe the maximum and average expected number of these items generated in the appropriate time period. As with the reports, include copies of the input items or drawn drafts.

For all files you are keeping manually or expect to computerize (customer files, employee files), list the maximum and average expected number of entries in an appropriate time period, such as 10 employees per year, 680 customers per year. Normally a file, manual or otherwise, is cleaned out after a specified time and the inactive entries are removed. The maximum number should reflect the number expected to be in the file just before the cleaning out process is begun.

Identify how you retrieve a particular entry. Do you use account numbers or are they organized alphabetically by name? What other methods would you like to use to retrieve a particular entry? ZIP code? Product purchased?

Note which of your requirements are a "must" and those on which you will compromise. The more detailed you are, the better your chance of finding application software that will be compatible with your business. It is also true that the more detailed you are, the more time it will take to research and evaluate each alternative application software package.

If after compiling all your information you find your needs are fairly complex, you may wish to engage the services of a small business consultant to assist you in evaluating your software requirements. Or you can submit the list to software retailers, custom software vendors, or mail-order software houses. They, in turn, should provide you with software that meets as many of your requirements as possible.

At this point you will have to review the software and verify for yourself the extent to which it actually meets your needs. Ask yourself these questions: Does it cover all of my "musts"? How many of my other requirements does it fulfill? Does it provide me with additional features I had not thought of earlier but now believe to be important?

After you have found one or more software packages that fit your needs, there are other general features you should check out before you make your final decision to buy a computer.

- Does it come with effective documentation? Is the operating manual written for the novice? Is the information organized so you can utilize it effectively after you become an experienced user?
- How easy is the software to use (user-friendly)? Does the information that is displayed on the computer screen make sense? Is there a "help" facility?
- How easy is it to change? Can you change data that has already been processed? Can you yourself change the "program" in-

structions such as payroll withholding rates, or will you have to pay the vendor to change these for you? If yes, what will it cost?

- Will you be required to change any of your business practices? If so, are these changes that you should make anyway? Will it provide the accounting and management information you need?
- How well is the software documented? You should be able to understand the general flow of information: which program does what and when.
- Does it have security features such as passwords or user identification codes? Can it prevent unauthorized access to private information?
- Is it easy to increase the size of files?
- Will the software vendor support the software? Does the vendor have a good track record? Will the vendor make changes, and if so, how much will the changes cost?
- How long has the vendor been in business? What are the vendor's prospects for staying in business?

If you find a ready-made software package that fits your system needs and price range, take it. You may still have to do a lot of work adapting your procedure, but generally you will be better off than if you design your own software system.

Although some different manufacturers' software and hardware can be adapted to work together compatibly, such standardization is not yet prevalent. That is why it is so important that first you find the right software and then select the hardware that can handle it.

Preparing a Request for Proposal

If you can't find software packages that fit your needs, prepare a request for proposal (RFP) to send to selected hardware vendors

and turnkey systems houses. (Turnkey systems houses are companies that put together complete hardware and software systems.)

The form of your RFP depends upon the kind of proposals you are soliciting—turnkey system with custom software, a turnkey system with packaged software, or hardware and/or software in separate packages.

Because most first-time users get turnkey systems, the following guidelines apply to RFP's for this method:

1. Give a brief description of your company.
2. Describe the business operation to be computerized.
3. Submit the materials you designed and accumulated earlier.
4. Describe the criterion that will be used to evaluate proposals and request a response for each criteria (i.e., maintenance, technical support, training).
5. Specify which of your requirements must be met exactly and which must be met only in substance. Distinguishing between discretionary and nondiscretionary requirements is important when dealing with software packages.
6. Request a detailed price quotation that includes all charges to meet your needs, including one-time charges for equipment, setup, training, application and systems software, and ongoing charges such as maintenance and technical support. Request financing alternatives such as lease-purchase and direct or third-party lease.

Selecting the Right Equipment (Hardware)

Choosing the software is by far the most difficult job in deciding upon the computer system that is right for you. Because most software is written for one or several specific computers, you will probably have narrowed your equipment choices down considerably by the time you have selected your software.

You should review the choices and ask the same questions about potential computer hardware vendors that you asked when evaluating software vendors. Don't forget to check the cost of shipping, installation, and equipment maintenance.

The computer and associated equipment known as hardware consists of a number of components, each doing a different job. They include:

Processor. The *"thinking"* part of the computer is known as the processor or Central Processing Unit (CPU) and is designed to execute software instructions, perform calculations, control the flow of data to and from the memory, and control other hardware components.

Computer memory. Computer memory usually is measured in bytes (which is a grouping of binary digits or bits). Roughly speaking, each byte of memory holds one character of data, either a letter or a number. A 2K (2,000 bytes) memory in practical terms holds about one double-spaced typed page. There are two kinds of memory, ROM (Read-Only Memory) and RAM (Random Access Memory).

ROM is a program stored in the computer memory; it cannot be changed by the user or an externally entered program.

RAM. Random Access Memory is located in the Central Processing Unit (CPU) and is normally measured in "K's" or 1,000's (64K = approximately 64,000 characters or about 32 pages of information). RAM is used to store all the information necessary for the CPU to do its job: the program running the portion of data that is currently being processed and some portion of the system software. Infor-

mation stored in RAM lasts only as long as the power is on. Once the power is turned off, all RAM information is erased.

DOS is software that controls the interactions among the CPU, disk drive, keyboard, video monitor, and printer. These two, the DOS and application program, may need about 55K.

Storage. Just as a company retains its relatively permanent records in a file cabinet, so a computer must rely on a relatively permanent method of maintaining its information. Disks are the most common form of storage for small business computers. They resemble a small phonograph record. They may be "floppy" or "hard." A floppy disk is made of soft, thin plastic encased in a stiff paper envelope; it comes in 3½-, 5¼-, and 8-inch diameters. Hard disks are made of metal, have faster access, and have more storage capacity. Hard disks are also much more expensive than "floppies," but their greater storage capacity and speed usually make up for the difference in cost. Information on the disk is recorded, retrieved, and erased through a disk drive that is controlled by the system and application software.

Terminal. In order for a computer to perform useful work, you must be able to communicate with it. Most often this two-way communication is carried out with the help of a terminal consisting of a typewriter-like keyboard used to enter data into the computer and a CRT display screen (cathode ray tube). The video display should be able to display 24 lines of 80 characters on the screen at one time. For some users, 16 lines of 64 characters may be adequate. Some monitors (video screens) can handle color and graphics more readily than character display. Color graphics quality is determined somewhat by "pixels" or picture elements. If a display is "280 by 192 pixels," the screen is divided into 280 rows and 192 columns. The larger the number of pixels, the finer or more precise the picture display will be.

Printer and drives. The main output of a computer system is usually printed material—reports, checks, invoices, etc. As with all other hardware choices you make, you must choose a printer that can do the job for you. The print quality of various printers ranges from dot matrix to typewriter quality. Disk drives are single- or double-sided, and disks come in 8-inch standard, 3½-inch, or 5¼-inch diskettes.

Warmware. Warmware is the critical after-the-sale service and support you will require, particularly for the software. If you choose wisely, the combined software and hardware packages can become an invaluable tool to enable you to better manage your business. However, without the qualified people to train your staff, install the system, and be available to answer future questions, your system may never get off the ground, Once up, running, and relied upon, a computer system failure without the necessary vendor warmware support can make it very hard for you to carry on your business.

Evaluate the Computer System

If you can, try to find companies using the system that you've selected and that have configurations and applications as close to yours as possible. Use the following criteria to evaluate your computer system:

1. Hardware Capacity	Does the hardware have adequate processing capability to meet your requirements within the acceptable time frames?
2. Quality of Systems Software	The quality of the system software (operating systems and utilities) dramatically affects how difficult the system is to program and use.
3. Systems Documentation	What kind of systems documentation does the vendor provide and how is it updated? Can it be understood at some basic level by the user? Is it designed so other experts can understand how things were done and change them when necessary?
4. Service and Maintenance Support	When your system breaks down, how long will it take to get it fixed? Who will do it? Will it be subcontracted? Are there any provisions for backup during down time?
5. Expandability and Compatibilities	What are the technical limits of your system and how close to those limits is your current configuration? Is there software compatibility among the vendor's product lines?
6. Security	What security features will your system have to

	prevent unauthorized use of the system or unauthorized program modifications?
7. Financial Stability of Vendors	Satisfy yourself about the financial stability of your vendor.
8. Environmental Requirements	Mini- and microcomputers generally do not require special environments such as raised floors, special wiring, or special air conditioning. Some may, however, and it pays to find out in advance.
9. Price	With computers you generally get what you pay for. Low price should not be a prime evaluation criterion.

Credit: U.S. Small Business Administration and Michael Stewart and Alan Shulman

WHERE TO FIND IT

A SELECTION OF
ELECTRONIC NETWORKS
(DATA BASES)

DIALOG Information Services
Palo Alto, CA
(800) 334-2564
Bibliographic/abstracts of
general reference in data bases

I. P. Sharp Associates
Infoservices
Rochester, NY
(800) 387-1588

Mead Data Central
Dayton, OH
(800) 227-4908
Lexis: Full-text legal data bases
Nexis: Full text of 150 news
and business data bases

SDC Information Services
Orbit Search Service
Santa Monica, CA
(800) 421-7229

Implementing Computer Systems: Myths

Myth No. 1: There Is No Need for a Detailed Implementation Plan

The implementation of an application package requires most of the same steps as a custom system. While there is no need to design, code, and test the newly developed programs, all the other steps are still required. These include:

- Identifying and planning hardware site, appropriate air conditioning, line conditioning, uninterrupted power supply, lighting, soundproofing, security, etc.
- Changing firm procedures to integrate and support the new system.
- Training affected individuals.
- Designing, ordering, and implementing new forms.
- Testing the application package in your environment.
- Loading all your data onto the new system.
- Changing over to the new system.

These steps and relevant substeps should be identified in a detailed project implementation plan. Starting with the vendor's plan, challenge it and prepare a plan that makes sense for your firm in terms of timing and content. Revise it as necessary as the project progresses. Remember, this is your project—not the vendor's! Define major tasks to be completed, assign responsibility and completion dates, and identify hours to complete each task.

Myth No. 2: Your Staff Will Love It (or a Project Team that Includes Users Is Not Necessary)

Nothing dooms a project to failure like a system "forced" upon those who must use it. Avoid this problem by assembling a project team consisting of users, the vendors, and members of data processing where applicable. Select a project manager. The project manager need not be a data-processing technician. Rather, he or she should have the following characteristics to keep morale up and the project on target:

- Enthusiasm, high energy level.
- Leadership capability, communications and project management skills.
- Problem-solving ability.
- Knowledge of the firm as a whole and how departmental functions interrelate.
- More enthusiasm (a cheerleader, a "yea-sayer").
- A builder of esprit de corps.

There is a new word, "cyberphobia." It means fear of computers. The existence of a computer system in your office can cause all kinds of concern, fear, resistance, and confusion. Why? Computerization results in change. Even if the old ways are not working, they are familiar and comfortable. Further, there is a common fear of the computer itself. Here is where the project team and the project manager can help. By soliciting user concerns and ideas, and communicating through open discussions about project plans, progress, and the impact of the system on employees, many of these fear barriers can be broken down. The project team must meet regularly to perform the tasks on the time-phased implementation plan. At project team meetings, the project manager should lead the review of progress made, assist in identifying and resolving problems, and identify tasks to be accomplished in the following period.

The project manager should have access to a steering committee of top executives to resolve higher level problems, policy issues, and organizational conflicts, and to report overall progress.

Myth No. 3: The Vendor Will Implement the System for You

Most vendors are in business to develop and sell a product. Few are organized structurally or financially to attract and maintain appropriate support staff for all their installations. Those that have larger staffs charge from $60 to $120 per hour for implementation services above a typically small number of "free" hours.

The implementation process can be an outstanding forum for users to learn and become comfortable with the system, experiment with it, and identify improvements and simplifications during the less threatening period before the system becomes "live." Involving users early in the implementation process typically permits staff to develop a positive attitude and success mentality regarding the change. Because a company usually can control the time of its staff better than it can control the vendor's staff, the user/vendor implementation team approach ensures more successful implementations within the required time frame.

Myth No. 4: If the Package Does Not Fit, Modify It

Nothing in life is perfect, especially application software, which is typically much less expensive than custom-developed software and almost always can be implemented in a much shorter time frame than a custom system. The 20 to 40 percent concession you must make on certain "nice-to-have" features that would be available in a custom system is more than offset by the cost, convenience, ongoing vendor support, and reliability advantages of the application package.

I usually tell clients, "If you feel the urge to modify a package, lie down . . . until that feeling goes away!" Most vendors will not warrant or support their package if you modify it. In addition, all future vendor enhancements and releases must be further modified and tested by you to keep your system current.

If you must modify, use an approach that will not compromise or corrupt the integrity of the application package. Either develop programs that process files after the application package is through processing them, or work with preprocessors, i.e., programs that process data before the data is entered into the application package.

Myth No. 5: Since the Package Is Already Written Nothing Can Go Wrong . . . Go Wrong . . . Go Wrong . . .

Application packages are traditionally designed to meet requirements of many companies within a particular industry or application area. Accordingly, they are developed using a series of parameters, codes, switches, and tables that are initialized at the beginning of an installation for your particular

firm. This initialization process represents a tailoring or "customizing" of the system for your specific client environment. Such parameters can include:

- Report formats
- Audit trails
- Validation rules
- Reporting responsibilities and other relationships
- Classification schemes
- Module integration requirements
- Processing sequences
- Security
- Backup procedures

In addition, every computer system is part of a larger firm system that includes policies, procedures, people, and company objectives. An application package that works in one company's environment may not work properly or well in another. Furthermore, putting up your new files is a major effort that can introduce many errors into the new system. It may be necessary to write new procedures manuals, which integrate the new applications with existing office functions. This should be done *before* data is entered into the system so that the computer will be able to generate reports according to the users' information requirements.

Myth No. 6: Because the System Is Used at Dozens of Other Locations, a Systems Test Is Not Required

This is one of the most frightening myths because it appears very sound on the surface. Often a user will select a system on the basis of a vendor demonstration and a view of the application at a live reference site. However, as noted above, once all the system's codes, tables, and parameters have been set, and once we consider the other system elements (people, policies, procedures, and objectives), the application is unique. An appropriate systems test is needed to check and ensure that the system is operating as the users expect *and* the users are operating as the system expects.

Vendors and users frequently misunderstand each other when discussing systems functions and capabilities. It is only during a rigorous test, with carefully planned test data and results that "flex the system," that users will appreciate the nuances and functionality of the system, e.g., how a negative number in inventory quantity affects a turnover ratio.

Myth No. 7: Putting Your Files on the New System Is a Snap

All firms have a significant amount of data to be entered into the new system before it is ready for use. Such things include client, inventory, and vendor records; charts of accounts and account balances; and other items unique to your firm.

Putting up your new files (called "converting") is a time-consuming task that must be planned and executed very carefully and quickly. Appropriate cut-offs, reconciliations, and balancing routines are necessary to ensure all data is entered accurately, completely, and in synchronization with other related data.

This is the time to analyze your inventory, client, and account coding/numbering system to ensure that it provides the computer with the ability to give you the reports and analyses you need. Correcting a bad numbering system later will take great effort at best or may never be corrected at worst—and limit the value of your system.

Schedule overtime and part-time help, if necessary, to get the data in quickly. If you don't, it may take months to learn whether the system can do what you want. Every weekly delay reduces your chances of getting a no-charge resolution.

Myth No. 8: An Acceptance Test Is Not Needed Once a Systems Test Has Been Performed with Vendor Data

Vendor data typically is developed to show a system in its best light, including how quickly a system responds to inquiries. Once all the parameters are set up, it is critical for users to develop their own acceptance test to ensure that all key features of the system are operating as anticipated. The purpose of this test is not to say that the system is fine, but to find any problems or bugs in the system before going live with production and before fully paying the vendor.

Myth No. 9: Vendor Training Is of Limited Benefit

Many firms wrongfully assume that people who have experience with accounts receivable or general ledger systems on a manual basis, or on a previously automated system, can automatically bring those talents into using, controlling, and managing a new system without additional or specialized training. Others believe that the documentation provided by the vendor will supply all the necessary training.

Credit: Laventhol & Horwath *Perspective* magazine, 1985, and Warren S. Reid

Computerized Accounting

On the surface, the situation seemed ideal. A small importer of specialty chemicals had soared in three and a half years from a start-up selling a half dozen items to a $2.5 million-a-year-business with an inventory of more than 70 products. With a growing customer list and markets in 50 states, the company's marketing team seemed to have little on its mind but how to keep up with demand.

But to the astute sales manager, this was just the calm before the storm. "I recognized that because our business was so good—because it was growing so rapidly—our accounting and administrative procedures, all of which were performed manually, would soon be inadequate for our needs and would have a negative impact on our sales, effectively stunting our business," the executive says. "For example, when an order was filled, a clerk would physically record this in the inventory records, reducing the quantity in stock by the appropriate amount.

"Or at least that's what they were supposed to do. But with so many transactions to record, the clerk would occasionally forget to reduce the inventory figure. So subsequently, when a customer ordered 15 bags of sodium sulfite and we found, contrary to the inventory log, that there were only 10 actually in stock, it was panic time. We couldn't completely fill an order we'd written.

"The point is that when we were a smaller company, with fewer items in inventory, we could keep a mental balance. But those days are long gone. And every mistake in the inventory accounting costs us money and goodwill. For this and other reasons, we recognized the need to transfer our manual accounting procedures to a computerized system."

This decision, an increasingly common one at thousands of small companies, stems from the realization that computerized accounting can offer the business three critical benefits: speed, accuracy, and a rich lode of management information. For an executive with the chemical company, the need for data processing capabilities made itself abundantly clear in two areas beyond inventory management.

1. Commission Payments. "I had to spend three or four hours a week just figuring commission checks for my sales representatives. For each sale I'd have to subtract the various costs including freight, interest, and the cost of goods, then check the appropriate commission rate to come up with gross profit. I'd multiply this figure by the correct percentage to come up with the actual commission. Going through that process meant I was wasting management time on clerical duties. When we decided to buy a computer system, I made certain that it could perform this function automatically."

2. Sales Data. While computer systems are widely touted as time savers—and no doubt they are—their ability to provide executives with information not readily available in manual systems may be their single greatest contribution to the management function.

"Over time, customers develop an order pattern—say the purchase of a metric ton of hydroquinone every six weeks. With a manual accounting system, it's difficult to ascertain these patterns. You'd have to go back through the invoices, checking when each customer bought what and compiling this data into a useful format. Who has the time for that? But with computerized accounting, the system does this for you, generating monthly reports from the actual shipments.

"The benefit is clear. When I detect a change in the order pattern, especially a reduction in the normal quantities, I can have the appropriate sales rep determine the cause and act to rectify any problem that may be resulting in a loss of business. These are problems we wouldn't know about without the computer reports."

Is computerized accounting right for your business? Is the appearance of smooth and prosperous operations misleading (the calm before the storm)? Or are you already struggling with an antiquated accounting system that is negatively affecting your company's growth, profitability, and competitiveness?

The president of a Cincinnati-based computer consulting firm offers these telltale signs indicating that the time is right to computerize the accounting function:

1. Accounts Receivable: A multiplicity of prices charged to customers makes invoicing slow, cumbersome, and subject to frequent error. The calculation of sales taxes and the posting of sales information to the general ledger absorb an unacceptable amount of clerical time. Lack of up-to-date information on outstanding customer balances: who owes how much for how long and, equally important, who is entitled to additional credit.

2. Inventory: Inability to determine the number of "turns" for each inventory product. Without this data, slow-moving items may weigh down the inventory mix, prompting the company to tie up cash in products that should be removed or severely limited in inventory.

3. Lack of knowledge as to "what's in stock" without physically counting the goods. Inaccurate information in inventory count.

4. Accounts Payable: Bills processed too late to benefit from vendor discounts. Vendor bills frequently overpaid or paid more than once.

5. General Ledger: Excessive time required to produce monthly trial balances and financial statements. Difficulty in comparing budgeted to actual results and current to prior year results.

Once the decision to go computer is made, the search for the ideal system must begin with the appropriate software.

"Only a fool chooses the hardware first and then force-feeds the software into it," the consultant warns. "Because it's the software that can make or break a business, it has to be the first consideration. Once you find the right accounting package to fill your company's needs, you'll be able to find any number of boxes to make it run."

Not that software selection is simple. With hundreds of competing programs now blanketing the market—each claiming to be the ultimate in speed, efficiency, and ease of operation—confusion is the order of the day. But what seems at first blush like an impossible challenge can be simplified by basing the evaluation on a handful of critical features.

"Rule number one is to ignore the hype and fluff associated with software marketing," says a manager of systems planning for a major financial services company and a former senior consultant with accountants Peat Marwick. "Reading through all the pamphlets and advertisements may do more to confuse than inform you about the key elements of each program. The best approach is for the small business person to educate himself on the art and science of software selection."

Start by evaluating programs according to the four basic elements of general ledger software:

1. Account coding structure, which is at the heart of the system, determines the type and quality of reports available to the user. Look for flexible systems that allow you sufficient options in setting up the chart of accounts to reflect the realities of your business.

"If the user wants to generate cost information on each product line, he'll need sufficient digits in the coding structure to break down the information to the desired level of detail," the systems manager explains. "The greater the variety of data you want to retain on each product—such as costs associated with sales, manufacturing, and administration—the more digits you will probably need."

2. Journal entry recording is the mechanism for recording accounting transactions. Programs vary in the amount of information needed to complete bookkeeping entries and in how errors are handled.

Assume the user tries to enter a transaction to an invalid account number. Most systems will display a message indicating an error has been made. But more helpful systems will go a step further, providing on-line help screens that spell out the nature of the error and offer suggestions for correcting it.

Evaluate these additional aspects of journal entry recording:

a. How the system handles recurring journal entries, such as depreciation and rent. For companies with many such entries, the ease with which the system performs these functions will be a major consideration.

b. The number of accounting periods the system can handle. If the company needs 13 accounting periods and the system handles only 12, the software is inappropriate.

3. The budgeting mechanism compares actual and projected financial information including costs, sales, margins, and profits. Determine if the system tracks this information month to month or year to date. The former will allow for trend analysis, indicating whether the business is meeting or exceeding its budgeted goals. Some of the more powerful systems allow the user to create multiple budgets, providing for adjustments in mid-course. Consider whether this is important to you.

4. Reporting capabilities should produce a full complement of financial statements, including the balance sheet, income statement, and statement of changes in financial position. Beyond these fundamentals—offered by most general ledger systems—more sophisticated programs can create reports on cash flow, operating results, and statistical analysis.

"Software selections must be made with one eye on the program and the other on the company's operating needs," the systems manager says. "This determines how much flexibility, sophistication, and detail will be required. A business that takes its orders over the phone, for example, will need to check customer credit and inventory status on line. Without this feature, the program will be inappropriate even if it is a state-of-the-art marvel in every other aspect. In the final analysis, the software has to do the job— that's what you're buying it for."

Consider the following additional factors:

1. Software packages are composed of various "modules," including those for account receivables, inventory, accounts payable, and general ledger. Typically, each costs about $800 to $1,000. The idea is to purchase the right number and combination of modules to meet the company's accounting needs.

"The objective is to come up with an integrated system," says a manager with the Big Eight accounting and consulting firm of Arthur Young. "Say you receive an invoice from a supplier. With a manual system, you would have to post it to a specific expense category, to the appropriate vendor account, and to the general ledger—three different documents. But an integrated computer system will allow you to make one entry and will automatically send that data to all of the appropriate files."

2. Buy packaged "off-the-shelf" software rather than custom programs written especially for your business. The latter are far more expensive—$25,000 or more compared to $3,000 to $8,000 for commercial packages

(depending on the number of modules purchased).

"It's generally uneconomical and unnecessary to buy custom accounting programs for microcomputers," the Arthur Young manager says. "Accounting packages have become more sophisticated in recent years, performing most of the functions companies demand of a computerized system. But anyone looking for perfection is bound to be disappointed. Expect a good program to do a maximum of 80 percent of the things you'd like from computerized accounting and learn to live without the rest or find other ways to accomplish it.

"For one of our clients, a company that had to reduce customer billing by the rolling average of its co-op advertising subsidies, we found a way to off-load this data from one packaged program to another rather than going through the expense of creating a custom program. A little creativity can go a long way in fulfilling the company's needs."

The bottom line: go the custom route only when packaged software does not perform functions critical to your business. In such cases, trade associations may make custom programs with these features available at costs far less than programs developed from scratch.

3. When choosing the right hardware to run your accounting software, don't base your decision on price alone. Compare several vendors, selecting the one with the best combination of service, training, and warranties.

4. Allow two months for the selection and installation of a computerized accounting system and then another six months for adequate training and full implementation.

5. Run parallel systems (manual and computer) for at least one to two months or until you feel that you can rely on the information produced by the computer system. Running the manual system longer than necessary defeats the purpose of computerizing.

6. Unless the company has more than 40 employees, farm out the payroll to data-processing services such as ADP rather than preparing it in house.

7. Consider working with a computer consultant from the analysis of the company's needs through the system selection and installation. These trained professionals can help to prevent costly mistakes. Fees range from $50 to $150 per hour. For the name of a consultant in your area, call the Independent Computer Consultants Association at 800-GET-ICCA. Accounting firms can also be helpful.

"The small company has to overcome two fears," says a vice-president of Open Systems, a software company. "The fear of buying a computer and the fear of using it. If there's trouble in overcoming the latter, a CPA or computer consultant may be able to bridge the gap."

The Right Software Puts Computers to Work

When computer power turns into computer problems, chances are the software is at fault. All too often, programs touted as "user friendly" turn out to be anything but. They are clumsy, complex, and a killer to learn. In the end, they do more harm than good.

What to do? Kick the computer? Curse the software? Neither is very productive. A wiser approach is to bite the bullet, writing off the system and returning to the marketplace for programs that match your company's needs and your employees' computer skills. This time the choice must be based on a thorough review of the options.

"When you go into a computer store and

look at the small business accounting programs sitting there on the shelves, one package looks much the same as another," says a microcomputer services consultant for Arthur Young. "But that's not true. Some are strong in inventory management, others in order entry, and still others in receivables processing. To strike a good match—one that results in an efficient computer system—you'll need to select a program with a mix of strengths in sync with your company's operating needs.

"For example, a small manufacturer usually needs a software system capable of performing job cost accounting, which is a means of analyzing costs from raw materials to finished products. But many of the programs on the retail store shelf don't have this feature. So the manufacturer will want to identify which of the programs can perform job cost accounting and then narrow his choice to that group.

"The idea is to make a checklist of your most critical computer needs and match them—feature by feature—to the available software. In the final analysis, you buy the program that comes closest to covering all the bases. That's the best way to assure yourself of an effective computer system."

- Equate the complexity of the system to the skill of your in-house staff. Generally speaking, the more sophisticated the software, the harder it is to learn and use. While you may want the power and flexibility of a state-of-the-art program, it will do little but collect dust if the staff is confused or intimidated by it.

"The more advanced programs give you choices in the kinds of financial reports you want the system to produce and how you want those reports to look," the consultant says. "But to achieve this customized effect, someone on staff has to know how to design balance sheets and income statements. If the user lacks these skills, it may be better to buy a so-called cookbook program that has all the standard reports built in. There's less flexibility but also a much smaller margin for mistakes."

While the simpler software may seem to be the natural choice whenever employee skills are weak, that's not always the case. As always, the system must satisfy the company's key operating requirements. Should management need sophisticated order-entry systems that validate customers' ID numbers, cookbook programs may not fill the bill. Here, the company may opt for the more sophisticated program, hiring microcomputer consultants to do the custom work and to teach the staff to take over from there.

- Project the company's growth curve—especially in the number of transactions it will have to process—and buy a system capable of expanding along with it.

"Time and again, small companies outgrow their systems soon after they are set up," the Arthur Young consultant says. "When that happens, it's usually because a program is suitable for a single-user system only—meaning only one person can use it at a time. As the volume of transactions rises, this limited setup leads to a logjam as different people in the company wait in line to access the system. That's why you'll want to select software that has the ability to expand into a multiuser or networking format.

- Buy only from those software producers with an established mechanism for user support. This can be a toll-free number manned by trained technicians or a local service representative available for on-site assistance. Because the start-up phase of software installation inevitably leads to stubborn glitches, you'll need a skilled hand to unravel the knots and get the system humming.

"Most of the vendors allow you to attend classes on the use of their software," says another computer consultant, "but don't believe it if they say that's all you'll need to get up and running on your own. That's because the classes teach generic use of the program; applying it to your business is another matter. For that you'll need continuing support."

CONSULTANTS

Computer Consultants Can Help You Bridge the Technology Gap

If your idea of "user friendly" is a computer that turns itself on, does its work, and then goes dark until it is needed again, you may have to wait a few years for technology to catch up to your dreams. But if you're willing to settle for someone who'll take the mystery out of computer operations, a trained consultant may be just the person you're looking for.

Consultants serve as human links between computers and the companies that must harness their technology for commercial applications.

"No one buys his first car without learning how to drive it," says a spokesperson for the Independent Computer Consultants Association (ICCA), a nonprofit organization representing 4,000 consultants. "But many small business owners think they can buy their first computer without learning how to use one. That leads, invariably, to disaster. Because the owner cannot make the system perform the functions it was purchased for,

the computer becomes a source of frustration rather than a management tool."

Qualified consultants can help bridge the technology gap, making computers indispensible even to those who have resisted its powers. Consultants' services fall into these major categories:

1. System Selection. Ideally, consultants should be hired before the computer is purchased. This way, the buyer benefits from independent guidance in the selection process, including recommendations on the right combination of hardware and software for the company's business needs. This can help to prevent costly mistakes.

In a typical case, a retailer contracted to purchase a $50,000 computer based on a salesman's claim that 10 employees, functioning at separate terminals, could access the system simultaneously. But when a consultant—brought in before the purchase was consummated—analyzed the system, he knew from experience that it could handle no more than four terminals. The order was canceled and a more versatile system purchased in its place.

In a similar problem, small companies often enter the computer age through the purchase of microcomputers but then fail to trade up to the more powerful minicomputers once they outgrow the starter units.

"A telltale sign of inadequate computer power is the extensive addition of peripherals to the system," says an information services consultant for the accounting firm of Touche Ross. "Typically, management hopes to make up for the system's limitations by adding on all sorts of extra equipment. But there comes a point when the system bogs down.

"Take the company that grows from 1,000 to 2,000 accounts in five years. If there are many transactions associated with those accounts, there's a good chance that a more powerful computer will be needed. The consultant's job is to help management time the move from one class of computer to another."

2. Systems Applications. In putting computers to work, small companies make two common and interrelated mistakes: computerizing what should remain a manual function and leaving as manual what will benefit most from computerization. Consultants can help on both ends, advising management on those functions most amenable to computer applications.

"Just how things get crossed up is illustrated by the case of an architectural firm that wanted to computerize a series of charts it had prepared, listing the square footage figures for each of its buildings," the ICCA spokesperson explains. "But because the charts were not subject to change and the numbers would not be used for mathematical calculations, the consultants advised that it would be cheaper and more efficient to do the work on a typewriter rather than a computer.

"On the other hand, the same firm prepared complicated customer reports manually. One report listed on separate sheets of paper all the furniture and accessories scheduled to be installed in a building. Working with this manual format, clients were unable to judge the impact a change in a type of desk or chair would have on the overall budget. But now that the reports are computerized, designers and clients alike can learn instantly the financial implications of projected changes."

3. Training. Contrary to advertising claims, few computer buyers can simply plug in their units and get down to business. In corporate settings, the staff will need training whenever new hardware or software is acquired or when existing systems are applied to novel functions.

Unlike computer stores, which hold classes on general computer operations, consultants often prefer a narrower approach, limiting the training to specific tasks. This shrinks the learning process, making it easier for those with little computer aptitude to get the job done.

The explosive growth in microcomputers—now as much a part of the American workplace as telephones and typewriters—has been matched by a staggering increase in the ranks of computer consultants. Behind every micro, some say, lurks an expert trained to make it work.

Good news, bad news. With thousands of first-time owners now wrestling with computer technology, the abundance of skilled consultants can only help small business tap the computer's potential as a management tool. The problem is, the lure of hefty fees has brought marginal practitioners into the field. Without uniform standards for consultants' education or expertise, companies in the market for their services have little to rely on but *caveat emptor*.

"Just as there are incompetent lawyers and doctors, there are incompetent computer consultants," says the ICCA spokesperson. "Some have too little training, others are light on experience, and still others accept highly technical assignments that are beyond their scope of expertise. But this doesn't change the fact that the great majority of computer consultants are capable and conscientious individuals who bring a legitimate service to the business community. It's the client's job to separate the wheat from the chaff—to search for those professionals who can help them make the most of computer technology."

Start the search with referrals from trusted sources, including accountants, attorneys, and business associates. Professional organizations representing computer consultants can also be helpful. Through its toll-free referral service (call 800-GET-ICCA), the Independent Computer Consultants Association provides the names of members active in various specialties (such as computing for warehouses or medical offices) and links callers to state chapters offering local referrals.

Another professional group, the Institute of Management Consultants, maintains a data base of computer consultants who focus on the broader practice of computer technology and its place in the management function. Most shy away from purely technical problems or those assignments confined to isolated computer applications. When requesting referrals, describe your company and a brief summary of its consulting requirements. Write the IMC at 19 West 44th Street, New York, New York 10036.

With referrals in hand, work your way down the list, subjecting each candidate to an extensive review of fees, track record, and business practices. Consider the following guidelines:

1. Beware of consultants charging too little or too much. The former may be uncertain of their skills, and the latter may be getting rich at the client's expense. Be concerned if the consultant charges less than $40 an hour or more than $150. Anything between $50 and $150 an hour is within reason. Expect to pay more for the gurus who focus on the cutting-edge technologies and less for the grunts whose practices are limited to routine functions such as small business accounting systems.

2. Make certain that consultants are free of conflicting vendor relationships. Those earning commissions on the purchase of hardware or software may base their recommendations on personal gain.

3. Involve close advisers in the selection process, asking those with related expertise to meet with the consultant. Third parties familiar with the issues may be better equipped to gauge the consultants' professional skills. Certified public accountants, for example, can help to evaluate consultants specializing in accounting systems.

4. Call at least two of the consultant's current or former clients, asking specific questions about his accomplishments, shortcomings, and billing practices. The more probing your inquiry, the more candid the response is likely to be.

5. As with all professional relationships, never consider the choice of a computer consultant irreversible. Retain the individual only as long as he or she performs for your company.

WHERE TO FIND IT

Where to Call When Your Computer Goes on the Blink

Apple
(800) 538-9696 for the address of your local repair center
or write
Main office:
20525 Mariana Avenue
Cupertino, CA 95014

IBM
(800) 426-3333 for general information
(800) IBM-2468 for service contracts and supplies (ask for Systems Product Division)
or write
Main office:
Old Orchard Road
Armonk, NY 10504

Tandy/Radio Shack
(800) 433-5502 for contract service
(817) 338-2392 for technical information
or write
Main office:
1800 One Tandy Center
Fort Worth, TX 76102

COMPUTING

What Portable Computers Have to Offer

Portable computers are the current darling of the information processing marketplace. While each manufacturer has its own idea of what is "portable," the systems generally can be classified into three size groups:

- Transportable or suitcase size (28–35 pounds)
- Portable or briefcase size (9–16 pounds)
- Laptop or book size (4–6 pounds).

The transportable systems are usually full-function personal computers with built-in 9-inch cathode ray tube (CRT) displays. The machines can do anything a desktop system can do but they need less desk space. They can be moved easily but are too heavy to carry around on a daily basis.

As the computers get smaller, they become more portable and also more unique. Portable and laptop computer displays vary in size and technology. Liquid crystal displays (LCD), similar to most pocket calculators, are the most common but the least readable. LCD screens have significant glare and are sensitive to viewing angle. Back-lit LCD and gas plasma technologies, employed by only a few systems, are more readable and less sensitive to viewing angle.

Some portables use 3½-inch diskettes instead of the 5¼-inch size found on desktop computers. This new size may well be a future standard, but for the present it limits the exchange of data and programs between portables and desktops. A significant benefit of certain portables is their ability to run spreadsheet programs and to transfer such programs to or from a desktop computer via cable.

Most laptops do not offer diskette drives but data can be moved between systems via communications services. These systems are not truly full-function PCs; they are more likely to be used as convenience word processors and low-volume terminals.

The smaller overall size of portables and laptops makes them more personal and able to fit the work habits of the user. The unique features appeal to personal preferences for keyboard layout, screen size, viewing angle, etc. This uniqueness, however, creates problems in developing standards for information interchange.

When evaluating various portable computers, it is easy to become enamored of the "exclusives" offered by the manufacturers. If you are a single-unit purchaser, that is acceptable. It's your system and you can buy what you like and need. For the multiple-unit business purchaser, however, more care must be given to certain system characteristics. The most significant criteria for a firm-wide standard are:

- *Viewability*—Can the screen be easily read in a business environment, particularly with overhead lighting? Most systems fail to meet this criteria.
- *Compatibility*—Can the popular commercial software and your firm's software run without modification and without maintaining separate versions? Can files be easily exchanged between systems (i.e., are diskettes the same size and format)? Many systems fail to meet these criteria.
- *Portability*—Can the system be carried from place to place on public transportation?
- *Expandability*—Can the system be expanded to include the same features and external devices as a desktop system? Business users tend to favor function and ease of use over price.
- *Price*—Is the cost per system equal to or less than a comparable desktop system?

Options such as built-in modems, built-in software, battery packs, and external monitor adapters are of added value but their worth is highly dependent upon the application.

Vendor stability is a further consideration. The portable market is more attractive to entrepreneurs than is the desktop market. You should select a vendor that is likely to be in business for the next three to five years so you can obtain parts and service. Portables take more abuse than desktops, so serviceability cannot be ignored.

These are just some thoughts to consider when evaluating the characteristics and usefulness of a portable computer.

Credit: Deloitte, Haskins & Sells, *DH&S Review*, February 17, 1986

PROGRAMS

How to Put Your Computer to Work

For thousands of small companies, the microcomputer boom has turned out to be a high-tech bust. Costly hardware, acquired to automate everything from bookkeeping to inventory control, has instead sat idle like giant paperweights atop the boss's desk—machines in search of a job.

The problem, for many, is in harnessing the computer's power for useful business functions. Without the proper training and the appropriate software, the technology remains awesome but impractical.

"A great many of the micros purchased in recent years are now sitting in closets collecting dust," says a partner with the national accounting firm of Seidman & Seidman. "One of my clients, for example, bought a computer only to realize that he'd never given any thought to its business applications. Nine months later it has yet to be plugged in.

"Companies that focus solely on hardware, ignoring the software and the training that bring the technology to life, find themselves saddled with 'closet computers.' But there's no need to write off the investment. By learning the best uses for microcomputers and by acquiring the right programs to perform these functions, even the smallest companies can benefit fully from this powerful technology."

But what are the best uses for microcomputers? How can they improve on manual functions? How can they make your company more successful?

Experts in microcomputer applications suggest applying the computer's capabilities to those functions for which easy-to-operate, packaged programs are now widely available. This can turn closet computers into management tools. Consider the following:

1. Word Processing. Simplest of all computer applications, word processing brings added speed and efficiency to clerical and paperwork functions. In one time-saving procedure, drafts of commonly used documents—including contracts, form letters, and dunning notices—are stored in the computer, ready for instant retrieval when the need arises.

"Take the contractor who has to compete with a dozen similar firms," says an information systems consultant for the accounting and consulting firm of Laventhol & Horwath. "Producing accurate and timely proposals is a major part of his marketing effort. Rather than reinventing the wheel every time his firm bids, he will fare better by storing a model proposal in the computer and simply customizing it, in the word processor, for prospective jobs. Because this speeds the process, it can give the company an edge on its competitors."

2. General Accounting. Automates the standard accounting functions, including payroll, general ledger, and accounts payable and receivable that small companies have traditionally performed manually. Computerizing the process reduces errors and puts timely information at management's disposal. An aged-receivable report, for example, indicates which accounts are overdue, thus allowing for more effective collections and improved cash flow.

3. Spreadsheet. This highly flexible software—which allows for the manipulation of numeric data, including financial projections and budgeting—adds a vital dimension to the management function by enabling entrepreneurs to conduct "what-if" exercises.

"Change any number in a spreadsheet format and the system automatically recalculates all the others," the consultant explains. "This is what makes the programs so useful. Assume a small business owner wants to increase his net profits by 10 percent. What will produce the desired objective? Increasing sales by 20 percent? Cutting costs by 15 percent? By plugging these projected changes—also known as 'what-if scenarios'—into the spreadsheet, he can learn, in an instant, their impact on the bottom line. In effect, the computer indicates how he can achieve his objectives."

4. Data Base. Serves as an electronic filing cabinet for a wide range of business data including customer names, sales leads, and employee information. It enables management to create, sort, and extract lists from the base for marketing or administrative functions.

"One useful application is to combine the data base and word processing capabilities,"
the consultant says. "The data base can extract from the customer list those individuals likely to purchase a specific product, and the word processor can write them sales letters offering this merchandise. In this way, the company directs its marketing efforts to the most promising prospects."

While most small business programs are easy to use, those wary of computers may want to seek professional assistance at the outset. "The small company has to overcome two fears," says a vice-president of Open Systems, a software company. "The fear of buying a computer and then the fear of using it. If there's trouble in overcoming the latter, a CPA or computer consultant may be able to bridge the gap."

TELEPHONE SOFTWARE

Computer Programs Can Help Cut Telephone Bills

Personal computers are joining the battle against rising telephone bills. A new generation of software, designed especially for PCs, can help small companies monitor calls, identify employee abuse, and implement cost-saving strategies.

The idea is to maintain constant surveillance of the telephone system's internal traffic mechanism, known as the station message detail recording port (SMDR). Through this unit comes a flow of information on a company's telephone activity, including numbers dialed, extensions from which they were dialed, length of calls, and time of day they were placed.

The president of an independent telephone consulting firm says that the new programs rank as a significant development in the telecommunications field. "They provide a link between two technologies the small company already has: a modern telephone system and a personal computer. The programs make these technologies perform to their fullest potential and give management a tool for controlling telephone costs."

Fed with data from the SMDR, the computer programs generate a wide range of cost control information including:

1. A list of exceptionally long or expensive calls. Because the callers and destinations are identified, management can determine if the calls were placed for legitimate business purposes. Unauthorized or excessive calls can be controlled in this way.

2. Telephone cost trends broken down by local service and long distance. A heavy volume of calls made to a specific geographic region may indicate the need to switch from regular lines to WATS service.

3. A comparison of common carrier tariffs. "Companies making long-distance calls today have many options on how the calls can be placed," says a vice-president of a software concern active in the telecommunications market. "Call-accounting software can take some of the confusion out of this by providing a basis for evaluating the tariffs of competing common carriers. Armed with this information, management can see to it that all calls are placed through the most economical routes."

4. Allocation of client calls for billing purposes. Professional firms that bill clients for calls made on their behalf can generate printouts itemizing the appropriate charges. Client codes are dialed with the phone numbers at the time the calls are placed and the computer program keeps track of the charges.

"We're implementing our call-accounting system in several stages," says a law firm office manager. "Right now, it's providing detailed information on all telephone calls. In stage two, we plan to use it to automate client billing. The system can allocate client charges including the cost of the call and the lawyer's time spent on the phone. This should be a major improvement over the manual procedures now in use."

For the systems to be effective, computers must be operated throughout the business day. But they need not be limited to call-accounting functions. With the addition of related hardware, known as a micro buffer, personal computers using call-accounting software can perform other tasks, including word processing and spreadsheet analysis, while the system continues to monitor telephone calls. This can be a major advantage over so-called dedicated systems, which require the purchase of hardware and software reserved exclusively for call-accounting functions.

Still, the new programs do have drawbacks:

1. They are expensive, ranging from $2,500 to $10,000 or more depending on the number of telephones in the company's system.

2. Personnel must be trained to use the software.

3. Common carrier charges, built into the software, must be updated regularly to reflect changing tariffs.

Work with a telephone consultant in reviewing call-accounting software.

IX. The Bottom Line

How to Create Personal Wealth

◇ ══ ◇

Money Managers Put Your Money to Work

Ever think you're too busy managing your business to manage your money? You're not alone. Preoccupied with building a venture, even the most successful entrepreneurs often shortchange their personal and pension assets, allowing them to go unattended for years. The bottom line: they work hard to make money but fail to make that money work for them.

It's a matter of time and expertise. With business ownership a round-the-clock job, the hours available for personal finance are precious and few. When push comes to shove—when both business and personal affairs call for attention—it's the personal side that usually suffers.

"Even when the entrepreneur can devote adequate time to personal finance, he's rarely capable of achieving maximum results," says a principal with Dubin & Swieca, a New York firm that helps individuals select and monitor money managers. "That's because there's more to shrewd investing than simply picking a stock and letting it sit there until the urge comes over you to sell. In today's sophisticated financial markets—made more complex than ever by a host of securities options

and program trading—the novice is at a distinct disadvantage. He needs a professional investor—one who devotes himself exclusively to the money markets—to manage his personal finances.

"Take the function of asset allocation. That means deciding what percentage of a portfolio should be invested in such assets as stocks, corporate bonds, Treasury bills, or money market funds. The mix should constantly change to reflect prevailing economic conditions. In most cases, a professional money manager is going to do this much more effectively than a part-time investor."

But how do you find a money manager? How do you rate and track his performance? When do you trust him with your money and when do you call it quits? Consider the following guidelines:

1. Relative Performance. Check money manager rankings available from rating services or through financial magazines. Look beyond current returns for evidence of superior performance over at least five years.

"You'll want a manager who consistently outperforms the market," says the Dubin & Swieca spokesman. "Gauge this by comparing his performance to a market barometer, such as the Standard & Poor's Index. Providing your account is weighted toward equities, it should perform at least as well, certainly no more than a few percentage points below the index. Portfolios skewed toward bonds should compare equally well to a major bond index."

2. Preservation of Capital. While it is relatively easy to profit in a soaring bull market, the best managers earn their stripes by limiting losses in a downturn. Here again, comparison to an index is important. In the third quarter of 1986, a flat period for the stock market, the S & P index declined 7 percent. The better managers would have limited their losses in equity accounts to this figure or even scored modest gains.

3. Inflation Hedge. Weigh the manager's performance against the prevailing rate of inflation. Earning 15 percent annually on an investment portfolio—widely considered a satisfactory yield—is really inadequate in a period of 12 percent inflation. The real rate of return is only 3 percent. Because a cornerstone of sound investing is to provide a hedge against inflation, you'll want to favor a money manager whose portfolio exceeds increases in the Consumer Price Index by 7 to 10 percent.

4. Tailor-made. Inform the manager of your financial goals, including how long you want to invest and the limits of risk you are prepared to accept. Put this in writing and check that your portfolio conforms with these instructions. Evidence of speculative growth stocks in a conservative pension portfolio may indicate that the manager is taking unacceptable risk in order to beef up a sagging return. Keep abreast of this by checking monthly statements of stock holdings.

5. Bite the Bullet. Give the money manager a long enough rope to prove himself, but not so long as to hang you with it. Consider an inadequate performance over 12 to 18 months as reason to terminate the money manager and seek another to take his place.

Expect to pay a professional manager an annual fee of 1 percent of the assets under his control. Brokerage fees may add an additional 1 to 2 percent to this figure.

Money Managers

"For pension plans with a minimum of $100,000 in assets, we identify a financial professional to manage the money and then evaluate and report on his performance four times a year," says the Dubin & Swieca spokesman. "If the account is not faring well under his management, we'll terminate his contract and find a replacement. This frees the business owner from having to administer and track his pension plan and provides built-in protection against chronic mismanagement."

Working from a list of approved money managers, investment management consultants select a professional whose investment style best matches the client's financial status and long-term objectives.

"Most business owners pick money managers on the basis of a sales pitch or social contacts," says the Dubin & Swieca spokesman. "Both are poor criteria for choosing someone who'll control your financial destiny. To qualify for our list, money managers must have a five-year track record showing a minimum 18 percent compounded annual rate of return on pension plans."

Once selected, the money manager assumes responsibility for all investment decisions, including portfolio composition, when to buy and sell, and cash positions. Stock trades may be routed through the investment consultants or a brokerage firm, which executes transactions at the money manager's direction and provides records of account activity. This data forms the basis of the account monitoring and evaluation.

Consultants compare each plan's return to that achieved by other money managers, the stock market averages, and the inflation rate. All of this is included in the quarterly reports. Armed with this information, the entrepreneur knows if the money manager is scoring as well as his peers and if asset growth is outpacing inflation.

The underlying strategy of investment management consulting is to juggle money managers to achieve the highest possible return. Modest increases in annual yield can produce enormous increases in long-term capital accumulation. The entrepreneur earning 10 percent on $100,000 for 15 years winds up with about $400,000; by raising the yield to 15 percent, the lump sum soars to approximately $800,000.

"For years I had my accounts with standard brokerage firms only to find that no one took interest in them—no one accepted responsibility for their performance," says one small businessman. "The results were just fair. But with consultants now selecting and evaluating my money managers, I've been averaging a 15 to 20 percent return."

Fees for investment management consulting range from annual retainers to formulas based on asset values. At Dubin and Swieca, the annual fee of 3 percent of plan assets covers money management services, brokerage commissions, and reporting.

Ask accountants and attorneys for the names of investment management consultants.

Tracking the Market

The S&P 500: A Useful Market Indicator

The Standard & Poor's 500 Composite Stock Price Index, known as the S&P 500, is designed to provide investors with a truly representative measure of stock market performance. The S&P was introduced in 1957 and is one of the U.S. Commerce Department's 12 leading business indicators.

The S&P tracks 500 companies traded on the New York Stock Exchange, the American Stock Exchange, and the Over-the-Counter market. The Index is weighted by market value, so that each company's stock influences the index in proportion to its market importance.

As of June 30, 1986, the 6 largest companies in the index, based upon market value of shares, were as follows:

THE S&P's 500 TOP SIX

Ticker	Company	Shares (Millions)	Price Per Share	Market Value (Millions of $)	% of S&P 500
IBM	International Business Machines	616	$147	$90,185	5.1
XON	Exxon Corporation	724	61	44,069	2.5
GE	General Electric	456	81	36,820	2.1
T	American Telephone & Telegraph	1,069	25	27,134	1.5
GM	General Motors	318	78	24,667	1.4
RD	Royal Dutch Petroleum	268	81	21,577	1.2

The S&P 500 is comprised of four major groups: 400 industrials; 40 public utilities; 20 transportation; and 40 financials. Stocks making up the Index represent about 80 percent of the market value of issues traded on the NYSE.

When a stock is removed from the Index, it is usually because a company was acquired by or merged with another company. Occasionally, a stock will be removed because a company has financial problems or it is no longer representative of its industry.

Stocks are added to the Index for three reasons: (1) replacement of a dropped stock, adding the new one to the same industry group if possible; (2) the result of periodic review that keeps industry groups up-to-date and refines the coverage of the Index; and (3) establishment of a new industry group to reflect what appears to be the development of a broad and more than transitory investor interest in the group.

Monitoring the Market

Standard & Poor's uses computers linked directly with the market to measure the 500 every 2 minutes. These frequent readings are available on desk top terminals but are not otherwise published. Hourly readings of the 500 and its major components are disseminated on financial news tickers and the American Stock Exchange ticker. The daily high, low, and closing values are carried in the media nationally.

How It Differs from the Dow
The Dow Jones Industrial Average is an arithmetic average of 30 stocks, rather than a market-value weighted index like the S&P 500. Higher priced stocks therefore tend to carry more weight in the index than do less expensive ones. Over the short run, the S&P 500 and the Dow tend to track each other fairly

closely. However, over a longer period, their performance diverges as a result of the differing make-up of the two averages.

In a broad market move, the S&P 500 should move 1 point for every 7 points gained or lost by the Dow. If the 500 does not move in this fashion, the Dow's movement is probably not reflective of broader market activity. A random view of activity for these market indicators is shown below:

MOVEMENT OF DOW VERSUS S&P 500

| | Closing Value | | Dow/S&P |
	Dow	S&P 500	Ratio
September 3	1,881.33	250.08	
September 2	1,870.36	248.52	
Increase	10.97	1.56	7.03
September 10	1,879.50	247.06	
September 11	1,792.89	235.18	
Decrease	86.61	11.88	7.29

Uses of the S&P
Individual investors can rely upon the S&P 500 index for a representative picture of stock market performance. The *Wall Street Journal, New York Times,* other publications, and most TV and radio business programming, provide investors with daily high, low, and closing figures for the Index. Many of these sources also report this Index's best and worst performing groups—data which S&P supplies to news organizations on a monthly basis.

You can use this measure as a gauge to see how your portfolio is performing. In addition, the performance of a stock that you own can be compared against the performance of the S&P 500's representative industry group. For example, Coleco's performance could be measured against that of the Toy Industry group index, while the performance of Kellogg Co. could be compared with that of the Food Industry group index.

It is always good to keep informed about how your investments are doing—the Dow, S&P 500, and other tools can certainly be helpful to you in this regard.

Credit: Deloitte, Haskins & Sells

Mutual Fund Glossary

"Asked" or "Offering" Price. The price at which a mutual fund's shares can be purchased. The asked or offering price means the current net asset value per share plus sales charge, if any.

"Bid" or "Sell" Price. The price at which a mutual fund's share are redeemed (bought back) by the fund. The bid or redemption price usually means the current net asset value per share.

Capital Gains Distributions. Payments to mutual fund shareholders of long-term gains realized on the sale of the fund's portfolio securities. These amounts usually are paid once a year.

Capital Growth. An increase in market value of a mutual fund's securities which is reflected in the net asset value of fund shares. This is a specific long-term objective of many mutual funds.

Diversification. The mutual fund policy of spreading its investments among a number of different securities to reduce the risks inherent in investing.

Income Dividends. Payments to mutual fund shareholders of dividends, interest, and short-term capital gains earned on the fund's portfolio securities after deduction of operating expenses.

Investment Objective. The goal—e.g., long-term capital growth, current income, etc.—that an investor or a mutual fund pursues.

Management Fee. The amount paid by a mutual fund to the investment adviser for its services. The average fee industrywide is about one-half of one percent a year of the fund's assets.

Mutual Fund. An investment company that stands ready to buy back (redeem) its shares at their current net asset value; the value of the shares depends on the market value of the fund's portfolio securities at the time. Also, most mutual funds continuously offer new shares to investors.

Net Asset Value Per Share. The worth of a share of a mutual fund. This is derived by taking a fund's total assets—securities, cash, and any accrued earnings—after deduction of liabilities and dividing by the number of shares outstanding.

No Load Fund. A mutual fund selling its shares at net asset value without the addition of sales charges.

Portfolio. A collection of securities owned by an individual or an institution (such as a mutual fund). A fund's portfolio may include a combination of stocks, bonds, and money market securities.

Redemption or Redemption Price. The amount per share (shown as the "bid" in newspaper tables) the mutual fund shareholder receives when he or she cashes in shares. The value of the shares depends on the market value of the fund's portfolio securities at the time and is the same as "net asset value per share" as shown above.

Sales Charge. An amount charged to purchase shares in many mutual funds. The maximum charge is 8.5 percent of the initial investment. The charge is added to the net asset value per share in the determination of the offering price.

Credit: Investment Company Institute, Washington, D.C.

AT A GLANCE

Investment Data Bases

Citicorp Information Services
399 Park Avenue, 2nd Floor
New York, NY 10043
(800) 241-2476

Compuserve
Information Services Division
5000 Arlington Centre Blvd.
Columbus, OH 43220
(800) 848-8199

Dow Jones News/Retrieval
P.O. Box 300
Princeton, NJ 08540
(800) 257-5114

E.F. Hutton & Co., Inc.
1 Whitehall, 5th Floor
New York, NY 10004
(800) 334-2477

Newsnet
945 Haverford Road
Bryn Mawr, PA 19010
(800) 345-1301

The Source
1616 Anderson Road
McLean, VA 22102
(800) 336-3366 (outside VA)
(800) 572-2070 (in VA)

Telescan
11011 Richmond Avenue, #600
Houston, TX 77042
(713) 952-1060

Trade Plus
480 California Avenue
Palo Alto, CA 94306
(800) 952-9900 (outside CA)
(800) 972-9900 (in CA)

Warner Computer Systems, Inc.
1 University Plaza, #300
Hackensack, NJ 07601
(800) 626-4634 (outside NJ)
(201) 489-1580 (in NJ)

INVESTMENT GROUPS

Small Companies Can Be Investment Groups Too

Sometimes a small business owner may want to go into partnership with his employees. Not in the business he owns, but in personal investments. By acting collectively, the boss and his executives may wind up with greater gains than if they pursue investments independently.

This is most evident in the purchase of tax shelters. Rather than buying units in a widely marketed deal, entrepreneurs can have shelters designed exclusively for their management team. Keeping the deal in house means more equity for the investors' dollars.

"A substantial portion of the money raised for most tax shelter deals goes to cover the syndicator's costs and fees," says an executive with Astor Securities, Inc., an investment advisory firm that structures tax shelters for small businesses. "This includes fees for legal and accounting work, printing of the offering memorandum, sales commissions, and most important, compensation to the syndicator for his risks in marketing the shelter. But all of this can be cut by as much as 20 percent if the syndicator knows he has a ready buyer in hand to take the entire deal.

"In a typical case, a syndicator marketing a real estate shelter plans to sell limited partnership shares totaling $1.6 million. Of this amount, $556,000 would cover his costs, including a general partnership fee of $275,000. But by negotiating the purchase of the entire deal on behalf of a small business investment group, we were able to cut the costs by $359,000, or about 20 percent of the equity raised. As a result, the investors bought the same property for $1.24 million that was originally slated for $1.6 million. That's like getting it wholesale."

Just how an investment is split between the owner and his top employees is up to the parties involved. In one shelter, involving the purchase of a garden apartment development for $1.3 million, the deal was divided into 26 shares at $50,000 each with the payments due over a five-year period. The boss took 10 shares, leaving his four top employees with four shares each. Terms called for annual tax-deductible contributions of $10,000 per share, income stream to the investors beginning in the second year, and sale of the property in the tenth year for a projected annual rate of return in excess of 25 percent. Here again, the return was enhanced because fees were kept to a minimum.

Cost savings are not the only advantage of keeping a deal in house. Consider the following:

1. Selection. Working with an investment adviser, the group can gain a customized shelter rather than one sold to investors off the rack.

"When one of my clients expressed an interest in buying real estate in a small college town in Vermont, we searched the market for a suitable investment," the Astor executive explains. "Because his group was willing to absorb the entire deal, they had more clout with the syndicators and a wider range of options. The deal they found—the purchase of a factory building being converted into condominiums—was just what the entrepreneur had in mind. This kind of selectivity is impossible with big brokerage firm deals."

2. Control. By functioning as a cohesive unit, the group can exert tighter control over the general partner's performance. A move to terminate the general partner's contract, for example—should that be necessary due to fraud or negligence—is more likely to succeed if the investors are working together. On the positive side, just knowing that the investors are united makes the general partner more responsive to their needs.

Group investments need not be limited to tax shelters. Many traditional investments, such as real estate and venture capital, can also be structured this way. Leading professional firms have long pooled capital for joint investments, often buying the buildings in which they work.

But not everyone endorses the group approach. "I worry about the lack of diversification," says an executive with Asset Management Group. "Given the opportunity to put my clients in one $500,000 deal or five $100,000 deals, I favor the latter. I'm always wary of putting all an investor's eggs in one basket."

Investment advisers and small brokerage firms can structure group investments.

LEVERAGED BUYOUTS

Can Help You Buy and Sell Companies

Sometimes, the greatest rewards of entrepreneurship come with the sale of a business. Instantly, years of sweat equity are turned into personal wealth. That's why small business owners should be familiar with an innovative sales option, leveraged buyouts.

Put simply, LBOs (as the procedures are widely known) use a company's assets and cash flow to finance its sale. The assets collateralize the loan and the cash flow repays it. This built-in resource widens the ranks of prospective buyers, enabling those without sufficient capital of their own to bid for the company.

"Assume the entrepreneur who created a business from scratch finally wants to get liquid," says a corporate finance executive for Ladenburg, Thalmann, investment bankers. "He recognizes from the outset that his own general manager is the ideal candidate to buy the business. The man knows the company well and is eager to take an ownership position. But one problem looms: the manager lacks the financial resources to make the purchase."

In many cases, LBOs can help fill the gap. By using the company's assets (such as real estate, receivables, and equipment) for collateral—and by attracting lenders and investors who will take equity in the company in return for current income and appreciation—the buyer with little or no money of his own can claim 15 to 25 percent of the company.

"In a typical deal, the president of an apparel company agreed to buy the business from the chairman for $10 million," the investment banker explains. "Because he had only $500,000 to invest, he had to assemble an investment group with whom he would share equity in the business. Using this approach, he landed a $5.5 million bank loan collateralized by the company's assets, and attracted $4 million from investors who provided debt convertible into equity. All financing was made to the company, which would repay it with its own funds."

LBOs can also be used by entrepreneurs to buy out their co-owners.

"Take the case of two brothers who owned a company," says a senior vice-president of Fleet National Bank. "When the older man decided to sell out, his younger brother—seeing a chance in a lifetime to control the business—was eager to buy the shares. But with a purchase price of $4 million (for his brother's stock), the deal seemed to be beyond his means. All of his equity was tied up in the business. He had no cash to invest."

The bankers solved the problem by finding an investor willing to put up $1 million of his own funds and by making a $3 million loan to the company. In a classic leveraged buyout, the proceeds were paid to the former owner and the bank debt was paid with the company's earnings.

"The bottom line," the banker says, "is that the investor wound up with 30 percent of the company—this for only $1 million of his own cash—and the younger brother increased his equity from 50 to 70 percent without investing a dollar of personal funds."

LBOs need not involve sales to insiders. When the owners of a valve manufacturing concern decided to sell their company for $8 million, they turned to an outside investor who put up $1 million of his own and who arranged for a bank loan of $4 million to the company.

"In a leveraged buyout, a number of transactions occur more or less simultaneously," the banker adds. "In this case, the bank lent $4 million to the company and the investor provided his $1 million—all of which was immediately turned over to the former owners, along with $3 million in long-term notes, for their equity. Because the loans and notes were to be repaid by the company, the buyer was able to leverage his purchase of an $8 million company with a relatively small personal investment."

Who qualifies for leveraged buyouts? What kinds of companies are eligible for this financing? Successful candidates will have the following:

- Products or services in a clearly defined market niche.
- Sufficient operating margins to carry additional debt.
- The strength and flexibility to weather adverse economic conditions, such as rising interest rates.

As specialists in corporate finance, investment bankers can structure leveraged buyouts, doing everything from valuing the company to finding investors. Fees for this turnkey service range from 3 to 8 percent of the purchase price, with the larger deals qualifying for the lower rates. Look for bankers active in the small business market.

PERSONAL WEALTH

How to Turn Business Income into Personal Wealth

When it comes to creating wealth, small business owners have two chances to strike it rich: by boosting the value of company stock and by converting business income into a portfolio of personal investments. Although entrepreneurs often view these activities as separate and distinct, financial advisers suggest a synergistic approach, using the proceeds of the business to acquire outside holdings.

"Typically, entrepreneurs are so consumed by their businesses that their personal finances get little or no attention," says a New York-based investment adviser. "As a result, they short-change themselves. Their personal wealth fails to reflect the success they've achieved in building profitable companies. To gain the full benefit of business ownership, a substantial part of salaries, bonuses, and dividends should be applied to a formal program of personal investments. This brings balance and diversity to the individual's finances and increases the opportunities for creating substantial wealth."

Financial advisers offer the following checklist of investment options suitable for wealth building programs:

1. Real Estate. Entrepreneurs investing for Keogh, corporate pension, or profit-sharing plans—which have built-in tax shelters—may want to play the real estate market through the purchase of participating mortages. With this option, the investor lends money for real estate developments. The return is twofold: an income stream and participation in the gain when the property is sold.

2. Single-premium Deferred Annuities. High-tax-bracket investors seeking to accumulate capital on a tax-deferred basis may find that annuities provide an ideal mix of safety, yield, and tax advantages. With a single-premium deferred annuity—generally available from insurance companies—the individual invests money that grows on a tax-sheltered basis until maturity or when the investor chooses to terminate the contract.

A $100,000 investment in a 20-year annuity will produce (at an 11 percent yield) about $800,000. This can be taken in a lump sum or in income of approximately $88,000 a year for life. Although the proceeds are subject to taxation, it is anticipated that the investor will be in a lower tax bracket at the time the income is received.

3. Zero-coupon Tax-free Bonds. These go a step further than annuities, providing for tax-free compounding and no tax obligation when the bond matures. The instruments—issued by states and municipalities—assure a guaranteed sum at maturity.

"Let's say an entrepreneur wants $500,000 in 1998 to buy out one of his partners," explains one investment adviser. "One sure way to have the cash on hand is to purchase a 9 percent single-premium deferred annuity in 1988 for $217,000. Because interest on the investment accumulates tax-free, there is greater compounded growth than if a portion were removed every year to pay Uncle Sam. The bond will be worth the needed half million dollars at maturity."

Financial advisers offer these best bets for personal investments:

1. Investors disillusioned with the stock market's performance may find more promising opportunities in foreign corporations, especially those in emerging markets.

"International mutual funds offer small investors the opportunity to own shares in hot companies in Japan, Korea, Germany, Italy, and other regions that may experience greater economic growth than the U.S.," says the president of a financial services firm. "The funds can also gain from changes in currency values. Although there are risks—foreign countries are not immune to recessions—with investments of as little as $1,000 and with diversified, professionally managed portfolios, the risks are commensurate with the potential rewards."

2. For intermediate-term investments with high payback potential, real estate development deals are often hard to top. Unlike real estate tax shelters that call for the purchase and resale of existing properties, development partnerships build and sell commercial facilities and garden apartments.

"Historically, this has been the most lucrative type of real estate investment," the investment adviser says. "That's because the developers turn vacant land into substantial assets. In a typical development program, investors purchase partnership shares for $5,000 each. Minor tax advantages based on loan interest and depreciation are gained in the first two years, but the bulk of the return, earned on the sale of the property, comes in the third year. One syndicator active in this type of investment has averaged a 26 percent annual compounded return on investors' capital, with full payoff made within 28 months of the initial investment."

3. For hedging investment portfolios against the risk of double-digit inflation, financial advisers suggest that precious metals account for at least 5 percent of total assets. Those reluctant to match their wits against the precious metals markets may prefer to invest in gold and silver mutual funds.

Funds that limit their investments to the stocks of metals-related companies—such as gold mining and exploration outfits—are viable alternatives to investments in pure bullion. Because they invest in businesses rather than idle assets, the funds can pass along some of the traditional benefits associated with metals but with somewhat greater stability.

Just when to invest in the funds, or any other metals play, depends on interest rates and inflation. You'll want to start buying as soon as it appears that inflation will exceed the yield on interest-paying investments.

4. Ginnie Maes, the highest-yielding instruments backed by the full faith and credit of the U.S. Government, offer an attractive combination of safety, yield, and liquidity. Used to fund portfolios of residential mortgages, Ginnie Maes carry 25- to 30-year terms but are generally paid off in half that time.

"Because the principal is generally returned to the investors in bits and pieces as the various mortgages are paid off, there's always a reinvestment problem," the investment professional says. "For this reason, I suggest investing in Ginnie Maes through unit trusts or mutual funds. Both manage the investments and provide for continuous reinvestment."

Most investments can be made through brokers and financial advisers. Make certain to base all selections on an integrated plan that links business and personal finances.

Six Ways to Take Money Out of a Closely Held Business

Business is booming. Your company is headed for another year of record profits. So why did you just find yourself at your local bank borrowing the money for the down payment on a vacation home at high interest rates? Why does it seem so hard to translate your company's success into tangible personal wealth?

Like most owner-shareholders, you probably have much of your capital sunk into the company. In fact, you may find that the more your company is worth, the harder it is to get at the cash it represents without jeopardizing the lower corporate tax rate you enjoy. Well, there are ways, short of liquidation, that allow you to get your hands on the money without serious tax consequences. Most of these strategies require careful planning and the aid of a tax professional.

Pay yourself a decent salary. Your most obvious source of cash is your salary. But the IRS takes a dim view of "excessive" pay. The tax code permits deductions only for "reason-able" compensation. But what is reasonable? Judges have found $1 million reasonable compensation for one owner but $65,000 too much for another. It depends on the facts of each case.

There are some guidelines, however, that you can follow to minimize the likelihood of an IRS inquiry. The reasonableness of an owner's compensation, which includes salary, retirement, and other benefits and perquisites, depends on his or her duties and qualifications, the size and complexity of the business, the compensation of executives in similar jobs in similar companies, and even how hard the owner works in the performance of his duties.

Taking profits out of a closely held corporation through salaries, rather than dividends, is smart because salaries are deductible while dividends come out of after-tax earnings and are much more costly. Some business owners pay themselves a year-end bonus, but this can provoke an IRS inquiry because it looks like a dividend. To avoid being challenged on this point, you should set salaries early in the year and tie the year-end bonus into some performance measurement. For example, the bonus might depend upon surpassing prior-year results or outperforming some previously established average industry growth rates.

Hire some family members. One common method for drawing more cash out of your company is to put family members on the payroll. Be certain, however, that the services for which the family members were hired are actually provided by them. Indeed, you should be prepared to prove that the services are necessary and that you would have to pay someone who is not related to you an equivalent amount to perform them. Common sense is the key here. Obviously, if you hire your eight-year-old to be company treasurer, you're going to be in trouble with the IRS.

Take advantage of your fringe benefits. One of the most obvious, though frequently overlooked, strategies is to take advantage of the tax-deductible benefits available to corporate employees. Health care and group life insurance are benefits you would have to pay for out of after-tax income if you weren't incorporated. Payments for retirement plans, annual professional conventions, legitimate business expenses—including travel and entertainment costs—are other fringe benefits to be considered. Make sure you're taking advantage of all the benefits to which you are entitled.

These are only a handful of strategies that are available to the business owner to help him more fully reap the rewards of success. In today's difficult tax environment, however, you need professional assistance to make certain you're taking advantage of all of the planning opportunities available to you.

Credit: Peat Marwick *World,* September-October 1985

PUBLIC OFFERINGS

IPOs, Fastest Route to Raising Millions, Have Drawbacks Too

Of all the routes to business wealth, initial public offerings (IPO) may be the fastest track to overnight success. By selling stock on the open market, small companies can raise millions in a matter of months. But for some, the price of success may be greater than the rewards.

Often overlooked is that the initial public offering, or IPO, transforms a closely held company to one that is publicly owned. Instantly, the prerogatives of private entrepreneurship give way to a host of legal responsibilities both to the government and the corporate shareholders.

"Behind the glamour of going public—of raising capital in the public markets for the first time—there is a new set of rules in which the business must operate," says a partner with accountants Price Waterhouse. "The net effect is that the business owner, once answerable only to himself, is now obligated to keep shareholders abreast of his performance. While this does not necessarily offset the benefits of an IPO, the entrepreneur should consider the pros and cons of an offering before taking this major step."

Financial advisers offer this summary of IPO benefits and drawbacks:

1. Cash may be obtained for major expansion, new product development, additional facilities, or to retire debt. Because this is equity capital, it does not carry interest charges or a repayment schedule. "For a promising young company, the initial public offering is probably the easiest and the fastest way to raise millions of dollars," says an executive with Ladenburg, Thalmann, investment bankers. "Management gets a check for the proceeds as early as a week after the shares go on sale."

2. The company's principal owners gain substantial liquidity. Because their stock is now publicly traded, share values may be easier to determine and buyers more readily found. Stock may be sold to buy personal property, to make investments, or to set aside cash for retirement.

3. IPOs may help small firms attract and

retain high-caliber employees. "Today, the most skilled and talented people often want an entrepreneurial stake in the companies they work for," the investment banker explains. "To accommodate them, management can issue stock for incentive plans, including stock options and bonuses. Shares of public companies are best suited for this because of their liquidity and ascertainable market value."

4. IPOs may pave the way for future financing. "If the stock price rises after the initial public offering, additional stock can be offered at a higher price per share," says the Price Waterhouse partner. "In addition, an IPO can increase a company's net worth and improve its debt-to-equity ratio. This may permit borrowing on more favorable terms."

5. On the minus side, public offerings lift the veil of privacy from closely held firms. Says the investment banker, "Suddenly, due to the financial reporting requirements, the small business owner finds that his salary, bonuses, and other perks are public information. Even worse, he may be subject to class-action suits launched by disgruntled shareholders who are displeased with the firm's performance. The entrepreneur may find it difficult to adjust to this fishbowl existence."

6. Stock prices may decline after an initial public offering, thus lowering the company's net worth. "This can be mitigated by selecting an investment banker that will work with the stock after the offering," the CPA says. "By making a market for the shares, the banker can have a positive effect on liquidity and in turn on stock prices."

7. Costs associated with an IPO can be high. Price Waterhouse notes that for a $5–10 million offering, the underwriter's commission claims 7 to 10 percent of the proceeds and the company incurs $200,000 to $300,000 in miscellaneous expenses, including legal and accounting fees.

Review the opportunities and obligations of public offerings with professionals familiar with securities laws.

REAL ESTATE

The Hidden Asset

Of all a company's assets, real estate may be the most deceptive. Commonly overlooked, undervalued, and poorly utilized, it is dismissed as a number on the balance sheet or a place to do business. But that's short-sighted. Land, office buildings, retail stores, and warehouses are among a company's most precious assets, both for their intrinsic value and as vehicles for tax, financing, and growth strategies. By recognizing real estate's versatility, small business owners can bring greater sophistication to their corporate, and in some cases, personal finances.

"In company after company, real estate is a hidden asset," says a tax partner specializing in real estate for the accounting and consulting firm of Laventhol & Horwath. "Management fails to perceive its true value and in turn fails to capitalize on its real worth to the firm.

"Consider this: a company carries property on the books for its purchase price—what it paid for the real estate, say, ten years ago—even though this represents a fraction of its current value. Because the appreciation is 'hidden,' the company never thinks of cashing in on it. But there are several ways to draw on this value, all of which should be explored.

"For example, a law firm practiced for years out of a small building it owned on Wilshire Boulevard in Los Angeles. As huge office towers were built all around it, the firm's land and air rights soared in value. After much deliberation, the partners made a wise decision. They sold the property to a developer, earned millions on the deal, and relocated the practice to another facility."

The story illustrates a key real estate maxim: that property should be put to the "highest and best use." For a lilliputian building to occupy a space suitable for an office tower is to accept less for the property than its fullest potential. To realize the property's maximum value, management, like the law partners, may have to sell out and move to alternate facilities—its bank account all the richer for having done so.

"The fundamental strategy," says the Laventhol & Horwath partner, "is to identify the company's real estate holdings, determine if they are being put to their highest and best use or if they would be more valuable for other purposes, and act accordingly. Real estate consultants can perform this analysis, giving management a clear view of the options. If the location is not integral to the company's operations, and if the analysis indicates that a profitable sale can be concluded, it may be best to relocate."

For those companies committed to their current facilities, another option, the sale-leaseback, enables management to extract the cash value of appreciated property without abandoning the site. The property is sold but is immediately leased back from the buyer on a long-term basis, generally 25 years with extension options. To some, this offers the best of both worlds: up-front cash and continued use of the property.

"Companies in need of growth or working capital can use the sale-leaseback as a means of low-cost financing," says a partner with accountants Oppenheim, Appel, Dixon. "The cost of money through this approach, as reflected in the lease payments, is likely to be at least 200 basis points less than general debt rates.

"In many cases, the seller in a sale-leaseback deal can gain the right to repurchase the property at the end of the lease. We suggest that companies negotiate to have this repurchase option based on a fixed price rather than a 'market price' formula."

Another option for selling business property calls for marketing part of a company's real estate and retaining the balance for its own use. "Sometimes, companies have more space than they need," says the president of a Long Island, New York, development firm. "If so, they should consider partitioning off the excess and selling it, perhaps as office condominiums. The condo approach works well because it allows for small sales to modest buyers rather than having to engineer a major transaction and because it gives the seller an ongoing profit opportunity as the condominium manager."

Commercial condominiums, slow to catch on but now growing in popularity, may be equally attractive to small companies and professional practices in the market for acquiring modest-sized office space. Rather than leasing facilities—which is essentially paying for use of another party's real estate—management may prefer to purchase space. The advantages are twofold: the company gains an equity position that is likely to appreciate over the years, and it is entitled to tax benefits including depreciation and mortgage-interest deductions. If the condominium—for that matter, any real estate—is held by the company owner rather than his corporation, the write-offs can be claimed by the individual, thus offsetting income from other sources.

"But there are drawbacks to the condo approach," says a principal with the New York-based real estate consulting firm of Jones Lang Wootton. "Growth companies can find themselves restricted by the limited space they've acquired. Should the need arise for larger facilities, it would be easier to relocate if the company is leasing. Ownership of any kind is a less flexible means of acquiring and using space."

A real estate specialist with the San Diego, California, office of accountants Arthur Young agrees, warning that ownership is generally best only for those small firms that can meet three tests: little or no growth, good cash flow, and considerable knowledge of local real estate.

"Buying property is a complicated affair, fraught with all kinds of risks. Unless a small business has a handle on the area's real estate market—including prices and the desirability of various locations—it can wind up making a poor investment. Leasing reduces the risks."

To the untutored, real estate can truly be an arcane and bizarre business, rife with invisible pitfalls and hidden opportunities. Consider these additional guidelines for conducting more profitable and sophisticated real estate transactions.

1. Cash in on Below-market Leases. "You don't have to own space to profit from it," says the Jones Lang Wootton consultant. "Suppose a corporate tenant is renting space, under an old lease, for $10 a square foot while the market rate for equivalent space has soared to $40. If the tenant has a considerable amount of time left in the lease, he can earn a substantial profit on that $30 spread by subleasing the space (providing the lease allows for this) to a third party.

"In many cases, the owner of the building or a party looking to buy the property may be interested in purchasing the lease rights. This affords them the opportunity to get out from under a low-rate lease and to boost the property's income stream. The tenant, for its part, gets a cash payment based on the discounted value of its lease."

Although the sublease strategy has a glaring weakness, in that the tenant engineers his own eviction, the rewards may well be worth the inconvenience. The cash proceeds can be put to use in the company's principal business activities, thus helping to fuel expansion at a lower cost than if the money were borrowed.

2. Sell Off Excess Land. "Quite often, companies building manufacturing facilities acquire substantially more property than they need," says another New York-based real estate consultant, "but they never dispose of the excess once the construction is complete. The feeling is that whatever was originally part of the acquired site must remain part of it. Not true. Land that is not needed for the company's current or future operations should be converted into capital. One of our clients had an outmoded facility situated on a piece of property adjacent to New York's East River. A valuable piece of real estate was being tied up simply because no one thought to sell it. When the property was finally identified as excess and put up for sale, it brought the company $25 million."

3. Refinance Appreciated Property. "Assume a company built its headquarters 10 years ago for $5 million," says the Oppenheim Appel Dixon partner. "It put up $1 million and took out a $4 million mortgage. Now the property's worth $8 million. Well, there's value in that real estate that can be drawn out through refinancing. Based on the current market value, the company could get a new mortgage for about $7 million, thus freeing up $3 million or more in capital. This could

be used in lieu of other lines of credit at lower rates than would be generally available.

"The underlying rule is to monitor property values, to know how much equity you have and how that can be put to the most effective use."

Real estate attorneys, accountants, and consultants can help to structure the most profitable and cost-effective sales, purchases, and leases. Ask business associates or trade associations for the names of experienced professionals.

Index

399